CONFORMED *to* HIS IMAGE

CONFORMED *to* HIS IMAGE

Biblical and Practical Approaches to Spiritual Formation

KENNETH BOA

ZONDERVAN®

ZONDERVAN.com/
AUTHORTRACKER
follow your favorite authors

We want to hear from you. Please send your comments about this book to us in care of zreview@zondervan.com. Thank you.

ZONDERVAN

Conformed to His Image
Copyright © 2001 by Kenneth Boa

Requests for information should be addressed to:

Zondervan, *Grand Rapids, Michigan 49530*

Library of Congress Cataloging-in-Publication Data

Boa, Kenneth.
    Conformed to His image : biblical and practical approaches to spiritual formation / Kenneth Boa.
        p. cm.
    Includes bibliographical references.
    ISBN 978-0-310-23848-5 (hardcover)
    1. Spiritual life—Christianity. I. Title.
BV4501.2 .B592 2001
248.4—dc21   2001026319

Published in association with the literary agency of Wolgemuth & Associates, Inc.

Interior design by Todd Sprague

Printed in the United States of America

10 11 12 13 14 • 42 41 40 39 38 37 36 35 34 33 32 31 30 29 28 27 26 25 24 23 22 21 20 19 18

In memory of my maternal grandmother,
Lottie Mae Bacle Kelley
(Granny Mable, as I called her),
who more profoundly shaped me
through her love, encouragement, time, and mentoring
than did any other person

CONTENTS

FACET 1
Relational Spirituality: Loving God Completely, Ourselves Correctly, and Others Compassionately

FACET 2
Paradigm Spirituality: Cultivating an Eternal versus a Temporal Perspective

FACET 3
Disciplined Spirituality: Engaging in the Historical Disciplines

FACET 4
Exchanged Life Spirituality: Grasping Our True Identity in Christ

FACET 5
Motivated Spirituality: A Set of Biblical Incentives

FACET 6

Devotional Spirituality: Falling in Love with God

FACET 7

Holistic Spirituality: Every Component of Life under the Lordship of Christ

FACET 8

Process Spirituality: Process versus Product, Being versus Doing

FACET 9

Spirit-Filled Spirituality: Walking in the Power of the Spirit

FACET 10

Warfare Spirituality: The World, the Flesh, and the Devil

FACET 11
Nurturing Spirituality: A Lifestyle of Evangelism and Discipleship

FACET 12
Corporate Spirituality: Encouragement, Accountability, and Worship

ANNOTATED CONTENTS

FACET 1
Relational Spirituality: Loving God Completely, Ourselves Correctly, and Others Compassionately

As a communion of three persons, God is a relational being. He originates a personal relationship with us, and our high and holy calling is to respond to his loving initiatives. By loving God completely, we discover who and whose we are as we come to see ourselves as God sees us. In this way, we become secure enough to become others-centered rather than self-centered, and this enables us to become givers rather than grabbers.

FACET 2
Paradigm Spirituality: Cultivating an Eternal versus a Temporal Perspective

This section contrasts the temporal and eternal value systems and emphasizes the need for a paradigm shift from a cultural to a biblical way of seeing life. The experience of our mortality can help us transfer our hope from the seen to the unseen and realize the preciousness of present opportunities. Our presuppositions shape our perspective, our perspective shapes our priorities, and our priorities shape our practice.

FACET 3
Disciplined Spirituality: Engaging in the Historical Disciplines

There has been a resurgence of interest in the classical disciplines of the spiritual life, and this section looks at the reasons for this trend and the benefits of the various disciplines. It also focuses on the needed balance between radical dependence on God and personal discipline and discusses the dynamics of obedience and application.

FACET 4
Exchanged Life Spirituality: Grasping Our True Identity in Christ

The nineteenth and twentieth centuries saw the growth of an experiential approach to the spiritual life that is based on the believer's new identity in Christ. Identification with Christ in his crucifixion and resurrection (Romans 6; Galatians 2:20) means that our old life has been exchanged for the life of Christ. This approach to spirituality moves from a works to a grace orientation and from legalism to liberty because it centers on our acknowledgment that Christ's life is our life.

F A C E T   5
Motivated Spirituality: A Set of Biblical Incentives

People are motivated to satisfy their needs for security, significance, and fulfillment, but they turn to the wrong places to have their needs met. This section presents the option of looking to Christ rather than the world to meet our needs. A study of Scripture reveals a number of biblical motivators: these include fear, love and gratitude, rewards, identity, purpose and hope, and longing for God. Our task is to be more motivated by the things God declares to be important than by the things the world says are important.

F A C E T   6
Devotional Spirituality: Falling in Love with God

What are the keys to loving God, and how can we cultivate a growing intimacy with him? This section explores what it means to enjoy God and to trust in him. Henry Scougal observed that "the worth and excellency of a soul is to be measured by the object of its love." We are most satisfied when we seek God's pleasure above our own, and we gradually become conformed to what we most love and admire.

F A C E T   7
Holistic Spirituality: Every Component of Life under the Lordship of Christ

There is a general tendency to treat Christianity as a component of life along with other components such as family, work, and finances. This compartmentalization fosters a dichotomy between the secular and the spiritual. The biblical alternative is to understand the implications of Christ's lordship over every aspect of life in such a way that even the most mundane components of life can become expressions of the life of Christ in us.

F A C E T   8
Process Spirituality: Process versus Product, Being versus Doing

In our culture, we increasingly tend to be human doings rather than human beings. The world tells us that what we achieve and accomplish determines who we are, but the Scriptures teach that who we are in Christ should be the basis for what we do. The dynamics of growth are inside out rather than outside in. This section talks about becoming faithful to the process of life rather than living from one product to the next. It also focuses on what it means to abide in Christ and to practice his presence.

FACET 9
Spirit-Filled Spirituality: Walking in the Power of the Spirit

Although there are divergent views of spiritual gifts, Spirit-centered believers and Word-centered believers agree that until recently, the role of the Holy Spirit has been somewhat neglected as a central dynamic of the spiritual life. This section considers how to appropriate the love, wisdom, and power of the Spirit and stresses the biblical implications of the Holy Spirit as a personal presence rather than a mere force.

FACET 10
Warfare Spirituality: The World, the Flesh, and the Devil

Spiritual warfare is not optional for believers in Christ. Scripture teaches and illustrates the dynamics of this warfare on the three fronts of the world, the flesh, and the devil. The worldly and demonic systems are external to the believer, but they entice and provide opportunities for the flesh, which is the capacity for sin within the believer. This section outlines a biblical strategy for dealing with each of these barriers to spiritual growth.

FACET 11
Nurturing Spirituality: A Lifestyle of Evangelism and Discipleship

The believer's highest call in ministry is to reproduce the life of Christ in others. Reproduction takes the form of evangelism for those who do not know Christ and edification for those who do. This section develops a philosophy of discipleship and evangelism and looks at edification and evangelism as a way of life; lifestyle discipleship and evangelism are the most effective and realistic approaches to unbelievers and believers within our sphere of influence.

FACET 12
Corporate Spirituality: Encouragement, Accountability, and Worship

We come to faith as individuals, but we grow in community. This section discusses the need for community, challenges and creators of community, the nature and purpose of the church, soul care, servant leadership, accountability, and renewal.

CONCLUSION
Continuing on the Journey

What does it take to stay in the race? This concluding chapter considers a variety of issues related to finishing well, including intimacy with Christ, fidelity in the spiritual disciplines, a biblical perspective on the circumstances of life, teachability, personal purpose, healthy relationships, and ongoing ministry.

APPENDIX A :
The Need for Diversity

This appendix portrays the current hunger for spirituality and the reasons for this hunger. There are a variety of approaches to the spiritual life, but these are facets of a larger gem that is greater than the sum of its parts. *Conformed to His Image* takes a broader, more synthetic approach by looking at all of these facets and seeing how each can contribute to the whole. Some people are attracted to different facets, and this relates in part to our personality profile (the Myers-Briggs Type Indicator is a valuable tool for this purpose). Readers are asked to identify the ones they are most and least attracted to and are encouraged to stretch themselves by trying one they would normally not pursue.

APPENDIX B :
The Richness of Our Heritage

This appendix outlines a brief history of spirituality by tracing prominent approaches to the spiritual life through the ancient, medieval, and modern churches. This provides a broader perspective and a sense of continuity with others who have pursued intimacy with God before us. Twelve recurring issues and extremes emerge from this overview, and this appendix concludes with a word about the variety of approaches that can illuminate our journey.

Glossary
Works Cited
Subject Index
Scripture Index

PREFACE

Although I was exposed to a number of strong Christian influences as I was growing up, it was only about a month after graduating from Case Institute of Technology that I had a personal encounter with Jesus Christ. That summer of 1967 was a strange one indeed as I moved to Berkeley, California, as a new Christian still immersed in the fleeting flower-child culture. During the next six months, I had virtually no contact with other believers and was moving through a painful transitional process from an evolutionary mindset that was influenced by occultism and Eastern thought to a gradually emerging Christian world view. Six months after my conversion, I found myself at Dallas Theological Seminary, which was a culture shock for me at that point in my journey! It took two semesters at Dallas before the things I had previously learned in various disciplines began to converge in a coherent framework based on a growing understanding of Scripture.

In the years that followed, I have enjoyed the privilege of being exposed to a wide variety of approaches to spiritual formation and discipleship. Particularly fascinating is how each approach was presented with a certain finality by its proponents, who claimed that their style of spirituality is the best available. Each time I discovered another set of useful tools, but the toolbox never seemed to be complete.

I have been involved with people ranging through the spectrum from liberalism to fundamentalism, with charismatics and anticharismatics, and with people from strongly Reformed to strongly Arminian traditions. I have had the privilege of becoming close to Orthodox Christians, Catholic Christians, and all stripes of Protestant Christians. I have participated with the monks at a Cistercian (Trappist) monastery, and I have spent time with evangelists who have boldly shared their faith in extraordinary circumstances. I have enjoyed relationships with Anglo-Catholics, with

Pentecostals, with scholars in philosophy of religion societies at Oxford University, with missionaries who minister throughout the world, with people in cult awareness ministries, deliverance ministries, apologetics ministries, evangelism ministries, discipleship ministries, campus ministries, youth ministries, business ministries, and ministries to lawyers and doctors.

At one point in my journey, I discovered the spiritual disciplines and immersed myself in them. At another point, I found myself captivated by writings that centered on the exchanged life—Christ's life for our life. During yet another period I focused on the spiritual life as a product of being filled and empowered by the Spirit. I also went through a time when spiritual warfare became particularly real for me. The same thing happened with each of the other facets of spirituality, and I began to see a pattern. As important as each of these approaches has been to me, no one of them is sufficient; there is always more.

This has been a source of both frustration and excitement. Frustration, because my quests for a quick fix, a one-size-fits-all, or a controllable technique have all failed. Excitement, because I am beginning to see that we can hardly scratch the surface of all that God has for us and that there are always new surprises. Seen this way, the pursuit of God becomes the greatest adventure of all.

The body of Christ is extraordinarily diverse, and through my experiences with so many facets of the spiritual life in my own journey of faith, I have discovered an appreciation for the unique merits of each.

In *Conformed to His Image*, I want to present a synthetic and comprehensive approach to the spiritual life that will expose you to a number of beneficial facets. Each of these has value as part of a greater whole, and it is my hope that this book will stretch your thinking and encourage you to "press on toward the goal for the prize of the upward call of God in Christ Jesus" (Philippians 3:14).

I pray that as a result of reading this book you will

- develop a greater appreciation for the unique way God has made you
- become aware of a wider array of options for your spiritual journey
- get out of a possible spiritual rut
- desire to experiment with other facets of the faith
- appreciate the manifold legacy that has been bequeathed to us by those who have gone before
- expand your horizons and be encouraged to move out of your comfort zone
- have instilled in you a greater passion for Christ and a greater desire to participate in his loving purposes for your life

PREFACE

Romans 8:29 gives us the most concise revelation of God's ultimate intention for those whom he foreknew, predestined, called, justified, and glorified. His purpose is nothing less than that we become "conformed to the image of His Son." This process of growing conformity to Christ was conceived before the foundation of the world, it is being realized as a divine-human process in the present, and it will be fulfilled when we stand in the presence of his glory, "blameless with great joy" (Jude 24).

INTRODUCTION
A Gem with Many Facets

CHAPTER OVERVIEW

The introduction describes the current hunger for spirituality in our time and offers several reasons for this growing interest. The spiritual life is portrayed as a journey in which pilgrims can use a variety of approaches. This book develops twelve facets of Christian spirituality that relate to practical experience on a personal and corporate level, and these facets are briefly summarized. It is natural to be attracted to some of these approaches more than others, but it is also beneficial to be exposed to all of them.

THE CURRENT HUNGER FOR SPIRITUALITY

These days, religion is out but **spirituality** is in. There has been a remarkable hunger and quest for spiritual answers to the big questions of life in the last three decades. In the past, there was a general moral consensus in the Western world that was loosely based on a Judeo-Christian **world view**, but this was accompanied by a growing tendency to secularize culture by marginalizing religion and replacing it with a popular faith in scientific progress and humanistic inquiry. But pure **naturalism** corrodes by the acids of its own assumptions. As the Enlightenment project of arriving at final answers and solutions to the human condition by means of unaided human reason began to totter and crumble, the quest for transcendent solutions became more appealing.

In an increasingly **postmodern** world, there is a new skepticism about the quest for objective truth, a new relativism concerning moral standards, and a new multiculturalism that encourages us to pick and choose ideological options. This smorgasbord mentality has led to a frightening lack of discernment and an uncritical openness to pantheistic spiritualities and New Age philosophies and techniques. In our time, one can freely promote Native American spirituality, Eastern mysticism, Western European paganism, shamanic medicine, techniques for achieving cosmic consciousness, or any form of yoga without fear of public criticism.

Taking their cue from education and the media, people are becoming more antagonistic to any authority that appears to be external or traditionally based. Thus religion is on the way out, while spiritualities that appeal to inner subjective and experiential authentication are on the way in. As the former Soviet Union shows, humans cannot live in an ideological vacuum; when one ideology is abandoned, people quickly embrace another, whether for weal or for woe.

Paralleling this growing popular interest in spirituality has been a pronounced increase in the church's appetite for spiritual renewal. The problem is that many people, especially certain leaders in mainline denominations, have failed to discern "the spirit of truth and the spirit of error" (1 John 4:6). Reimaging of God in radical feminist categories (e.g., the worship of Sophia and Gaia), Buddhist tantrism, Hinduistic meditative techniques, and pagan symbolism has been surfacing more frequently in churches that have moved away from the authority of Scripture to espouse liberal theologies. Nevertheless there are authentic, biblically orthodox, and time-tested approaches to the spiritual life that have been taking hold in many communities of believers, and this is what this book means when it uses the term *spirituality*.

From a human standpoint, there are a number of reasons for the growing awareness of spirituality among followers of Christ:

- the influence of the ambient cultural interest in spirituality
- growing dissatisfaction with the shallowness and sterility of the Christian subculture
- a quest for meaning, purpose, and significance among followers of Christ
- greater availability of and exposure to the classics of spirituality
- a more intense movement toward accountability and discipleship
- influential writers and teachers who have become committed to communicating these truths

A JOURNEY AND A PILGRIMAGE

The concepts in this book describe a journey into spirituality. The spiritual life is an all-encompassing, lifelong response to God's gracious initiatives in the lives of those whose trust is centered in the person and work of Jesus Christ. Biblical spirituality is a Christ-centered orientation to every component of life through the mediating power of the indwelling Holy Spirit. It is a journey of the spirit that begins with the gift of forgiveness and life in Christ and progresses through faith and obedience. Since it is based on a present relationship, it is a journey with Christ rather than a journey to Christ. As long as we are on this earth we never arrive; the journey is not complete until the day of our resurrection, when the Lord brings us into complete conformity with himself.

This journey with Jesus is a spiritual pilgrimage in that we have confessed that we are "strangers and exiles on the earth" (Hebrews 11:13). Once we are in Christ, we become sojourners and aliens on this planet; our citizenship has been changed from earth to heaven (Philippians 3:20), and we must grow in the realization that no earth-bound felicity can fully satisfy the deepest God-given longings of our hearts. During this brief pilgrimage, the terrain we encounter varies from grassy meadows to arid deserts and treacherous mountains. This pilgrim-life is filled with joy and travail, with pleasures and afflictions, with clarity and confusion, with assurance and doubt, with comfort and pain, with relationships and alienation, with hope and despair, with obedience and disbelief, with confidence and uncertainty. But there are two critical truths to bear in mind when our surroundings become precarious: others have preceded us in this journey, and some have left maps along the way to guide us through the territory ahead; and God has equipped us with the spiritual resources he knows we will need throughout the journey.

TWELVE FACETS OF SPIRITUALITY

There are a variety of approaches to the spiritual life, but these are facets of a larger gem that is greater than the sum of its parts. The diversity and complexity of the spiritual paths that have been taken by godly pilgrims of previous centuries is rich and impressive. Some of these paths were blazed through courage and suffering and through reciprocity with complex historical, social, and cultural rhythms, but most followers of the Way have ignored the topographical maps that have been left behind or have torn off all the parts that are unfamiliar to them. The most common stumbling stone is to mistake a part for the whole. Like the blind men who feel different parts of an elephant, one assumes that the spiritual life is a trunk, another takes it to be a tail, and a third concludes that it is a leg.

Anyone who studies the four Gospels should be suspicious of an approach that reduces the nuances of the spiritual life into a single formula or method. The Gospels are not biographies but highly selective thematic portraits that reveal different aspects of Christ's life that should stand in dynamic tension with one another. The synergism of this tensioned interplay resists neat categorization, and so it is with the dynamics of a Spirit-led journey with Christ. In contrast to the conceit of those who seek to quantify and control, the humility of **wisdom** always whispers that there is more, much more. When we approach the spiritual journey with an open and teachable spirit, we will continue to gain fresh insights from the Word of God, the people we meet, and the books we digest.

In these postmodern times, there is a growing desire for an authentic spirituality that will touch our lives in a meaningful and practical way. The biblical vision of the spiritual life as a redemptive relationship with the living and personal Creator of all things can satisfy this deep desire, but most accounts of this vision are fragmentary or one-sided. The purpose of *Conformed to His Image* is to offer a more comprehensive, balanced, and applicable approach to what it means to know Christ. This book will address this need by presenting not one or two but a variety of pathways in the spiritual life and showing how each of these pathways can contribute to the dynamic process of spiritual growth. We will look at several facets of the gem of the spiritual life and see how each can contribute to the larger whole.

I do not claim that the twelve facets that are presented here are exhaustive, but they do cover a substantial part of the terrain. I created these categories in an attempt to reflect the various dimensions of biblical truth as they relate to practical experience on a personal and corporate level. Because of this, some of them are rooted in historical traditions (e.g., disciplined and devotional spirituality), some are linked to more recent movements (e.g., exchanged life and Spirit-filled spirituality), and others portray hands-on applications of Christian principles (e.g., paradigm, holistic, and process spirituality). This book is not a history of Christian spirituality (appendix B, "The Richness of Our Heritage" briefly outlines this history) but a practical handbook to **spiritual formation**.

These twelve facets will be developed in *Conformed to His Image*.

Relational spirituality. As a communion of three persons, God is a relational being. He is the originator of a personal relationship with us, and our high and holy calling is to respond to his loving initiatives. By loving God completely, we discover who and whose we are as we come to see ourselves as God sees us. In this way, we become secure enough to become others-centered rather than self-centered, and this enables us to become givers rather than grabbers.

Paradigm spirituality. This approach to spirituality centers on the radical contrasts between the temporal and eternal value systems and emphasizes the need for a paradigm shift from a cultural to a biblical way of seeing life. Experiencing our mortality can help us transfer our hope from the seen to the unseen and realize the preciousness of present opportunities. Our presuppositions shape our perspective, our perspective shapes our priorities, and our priorities shape our practice.

Disciplined spirituality. There has been a resurgence of interest in the classical disciplines of the spiritual life, and this approach stresses the benefits of these varied disciplines. At the same time, it recognizes the needed balance between radical dependence on God and personal discipline as an expression of obedience and application.

Exchanged life spirituality. The twentieth century saw the growth of an experiential approach to the spiritual life that is based on the believer's new identity in Christ. Identification with Christ in his crucifixion and resurrection (Romans 6; Galatians 2:20) means that our old life has been exchanged for the life of Christ. This approach to spirituality moves from a works to a grace orientation and from legalism to liberty because it centers on our acknowledgment that Christ's life is our life.

Motivated spirituality. People are motivated to satisfy their needs for security, significance, and fulfillment, but they turn to the wrong places to have their needs met. This approach emphasizes looking to Christ rather than **the world** to meet our needs. A study of Scripture reveals a number of biblical motivators: fear, love and gratitude, rewards, identity, purpose and hope, and longing for God. Our task is to be more motivated by the things God declares to be important than by the things the world says are important.

Devotional spirituality. What are the keys to loving God, and how can we cultivate a growing intimacy with him? This approach explores what it means to enjoy God and to trust in him. We gradually become conformed to what we most love and admire, and we are most satisfied when we seek God's pleasure above our own.

Holistic spirituality. There is a general tendency to treat Christianity as a component of life along with other components such as family, work, and finances. This compartmentalization fosters a dichotomy between the secular and the spiritual. The biblical alternative is to understand the implications of Christ's lordship in such a way that even the most mundane components of life can become expressions of the life of Christ in us.

Process spirituality. In our culture, we increasingly tend to be human doings rather than human beings. The world tells us that what we achieve and accomplish determines who we are, but the Scriptures teach that who we are in Christ should be the basis for what we do. The dynamics of growth are inside out rather than outside in. This approach considers what it means to be faithful to the process of life rather than living from one product to the next. It also focuses on abiding in Christ and practicing his presence.

Spirit-filled spirituality. Although there are divergent views of spiritual gifts, charismatics and noncharismatics agree that until recently, the role of the Holy Spirit has been somewhat neglected as a central dynamic of the spiritual life. This approach considers how to appropriate the love, wisdom, and power of the Spirit and stresses the biblical implications of the Holy Spirit as a personal presence rather than a mere force.

Warfare spirituality. Spiritual warfare is not optional for believers in Christ. Scripture teaches and illustrates the realities of this warfare on the three fronts of the world, **the flesh**, and the devil. The worldly and demonic systems are external to the believer, but they entice and provide opportunities for the flesh, which is the capacity for sin within the believer. This approach develops a biblical strategy for dealing with each of these barriers to spiritual growth.

Nurturing spirituality. The believer's highest call in ministry is to reproduce the life of Christ in others. Reproduction takes the form of evangelism for those who do not know Christ and edification for those who do. It is important to develop a philosophy of discipleship and evangelism and view edification and evangelism as a way of life; lifestyle discipleship and evangelism are the most effective and realistic approaches to unbelievers and believers within our sphere of influence.

Corporate spirituality. We come to faith as individuals, but we grow in community. A meaningful context of encouragement, accountability, and worship is essential to spiritual maturity, since this involves the others-centered use of spiritual gifts for mutual edification. This approach stresses the need for community, challenges and creators of community, the nature and purpose of the church, soul care, servant leadership, accountability, and renewal.

Although the discussion of each of these facets in this book is limited, I have tried to distill the essence of each of these diverse but beneficial approaches. There are many other ways to explore the vast territory of spiritual formation, including these books from the wide range of helpful resources:

Simon Chan, *Spiritual Theology*

Bruce Demarest, *Satisfy Your Soul*

Michael Downey, *Understanding Christian Spirituality*

Richard J. Foster, *Streams of Living Water*

Benedict J. Groeschel, *Spiritual Passages*

James Houston, *The Transforming Power of Prayer*

Kenneth Leech, *Experiencing God*

M. Robert Mulholland Jr., *Invitation to a Journey*

Alister E. McGrath, *Christian Spirituality*

Allan H. Sager, *Gospel-Centered Spirituality*

Gary Thomas, *Sacred Pathways*

Rowan Williams, *Christian Spirituality*

UNITY IN DIVERSITY

A quick look at these twelve approaches underscores how truly different we are from one another. As you read them, you were undoubtedly more attracted to some of these approaches than to others. You probably thought that some of them would be hard for you but easier for some of your friends to pursue. Some of them may be unfamiliar, and you may not have encountered people who have taught or practiced them.

As Paul puts it so beautifully in 1 Corinthians 12–14, the body of Christ is a diverse and composite unity in which the members exhibit different gifts and different ministries.

It is good that we are different and that we need each other to grow into fully functioning maturity, because no component in the body can be complete without the others.

It can be liberating to discover that because of our unique temperaments and circumstances, we are free not to be drawn to some approaches to spirituality. This is the purpose of appendix A, "The Need for Diversity," where these differences are discussed in detail. As this appendix shows, some of us are extraverts and can never be alone, while others are consistently drawn to solitude. Some of us base our decisions on detailed investigation, and others can move quickly, almost instinctively, through life. Some of our friends say we place too much of an emphasis on thinking and not enough on feeling or vice versa. Our many temperamental differences are reflected in the way we practice the different facets of spirituality.

We shouldn't be ashamed of our differences. We can see how God has used dissimilar people throughout the history of the ancient, medieval, and modern church, and this is the focus of appendix B, "The Richness of Our Heritage." C. S. Lewis said that he preferred theological reading to devotional books, and great intellectuals from John Calvin to Thomas Aquinas have always been numbered among God's people. Martin Luther's approach was balanced by his friend and co-worker Philipp Melanchthon. Francis of Assisi called the church to change in very different ways than did John Chrysostom.

The appendix about the history of spirituality provides perspective and a sense of proportion concerning the ways in which God has used a great diversity of people through the centuries. Because of this we inherit a great legacy of different models and approaches.

QUESTIONS FOR PERSONAL APPLICATION

- What is your understanding of spiritual formation?
- As you reflect on your spiritual journey, what have been the most significant experiences you have had with God? Can you discern any pattern in these experiences?
- Where would you like to go from here? Are you willing in advance to pay what it may cost?
- As you read the brief description of the twelve facets, which three were the most attractive to you? Which three were the least attractive? What does this tell you about yourself?

F A C E T   1

R E L A T I O N A L
S P I R I T U A L I T Y

Loving God Completely, Ourselves Correctly, and Others Compassionately

As a communion of three persons, God is a relational being. He originates a personal relationship with us, and our high and holy calling is to respond to his loving initiatives. By loving God completely, we discover who and whose we are as we come to see ourselves as God sees us. In this way, we become secure enough to become others-centered rather than self-centered, and this enables us to become givers rather than grabbers.

1

RELATIONAL SPIRITUALITY
Loving God Completely

CHAPTER OVERVIEW

Since God is a relational being, we who are created in his image are also called to right relationships, first with him and then with each other. This chapter considers the causeless, measureless, and ceaseless love of God and the fitting response of loving God completely. We move in this direction by knowing him more clearly, loving him more dearly, and following him more nearly.

CHAPTER OBJECTIVES

- An enhanced appreciation for the greatness and glory of God
- A greater sense of the dilemma of our dignity and depravity
- A better grasp of God's causeless, measureless, and ceaseless love
- An understanding of what it means to love God with our minds, wills, and emotions

WHAT IS MAN, THAT YOU TAKE THOUGHT OF HIM?

The God of the Bible is infinite, personal, and triune. Because God is a communion of three persons, one of his purposes in creating us is to display the glory of his being and attributes to intelligent moral creatures who are capable of responding to his relational initiatives. In spite of human rebellion and sin against the person and character of the Lord, Christ bore the awesome price of our guilt and inaugurated "a new and living way" (Hebrews 10:20) by which the barrier to personal relationship with God has been overcome. Because the infinite and personal God loves us, he wants us to grow in an intimate relationship with him; this is the purpose for which we were created—to know, love, enjoy, and honor the triune Lord of all creation.

Because God is a relational being, the two great commandments of loving him and expressing this love for him by loving others are also intensely relational. We were created for fellowship and intimacy not only with God but also with each other. The relational implications of the Christian doctrine of the Trinity are profound. Since we were created in God's image and likeness, we too are relational beings. The better we know God, the better we know ourselves. Augustine's prayer for this double knowledge ("May we know thee, may we know ourselves") reflects the truth that our union with Christ is overcoming the alienation with God, with ourselves, and with others that occurred at the Fall.

Our Greatness and Smallness

Human nature is a web of contradictions. We are at once the grandeur and degradation of the created order; we bear the image of God, but we are ensnared in trespasses and sins. We are capable of harnessing the forces of nature but unable to rule our tongue; we are the most wonderful and creative beings on this planet but the most violent, cruel, and contemptible of earth's inhabitants.

In his *Pensées*, Blaise Pascal described the dignity and puniness of humanity: "Man is but a reed, the most feeble thing in nature; but he is a thinking reed. The entire universe need not arm itself to crush him. A vapour, a drop of water, suffices to kill him. But, if the universe were to crush him, man would still be more noble than that which killed him, because he knows that he dies and the advantage which the universe has over him; the universe knows nothing of this."

The Glory of God

Psalm 8 explores these twin themes, sandwiching them between expressions of the majesty of the Creator of all biological and spiritual life: "O LORD, our Lord, how majestic is Your name in all the earth" (vv. 1a, 9). The living God has displayed his splendor above the heavens, and he has ordained praise from the heavenly host to the mouth of infants and nursing babes (vv. 1b–2). When, after our Lord's triumphal entry into Jerusalem, the children cried out in the temple, "Hosanna to the Son of David," the chief priests and the scribes became indignant, and Jesus quoted this passage to them (Matthew 21:15–16). The children's simple confession of trusting love was enough to silence the scorn of his adversaries and "make the enemy and the revengeful cease" (Psalm 8:2b).

In Psalm 8:3–4, David's meditation passes from the testimony of children to the eloquence of the cosmos: "When I consider Your heavens, the work of Your fingers, the moon and the stars, which You have ordained; what is man that You take thought of him? And the son of man that You care for him?" From the time David wrote those words until the invention of the telescope in the early seventeenth century, only a few thousand stars were visible to the unaided eye, and the universe appeared far less impressive than we now know it to be. Even until the second decade of the twentieth century, it was thought that the Milky Way galaxy was synonymous with the universe. This alone would be awesome in its scope, since our spiral galaxy contains more than 200,000,000,000 stars and extends to a diameter of 100,000 light years (remember that a light second is more than 186,000 miles; the 93,000,000 miles between the sun and the earth is 8 light minutes). But more recent developments in astronomy have revealed that our galaxy is a member of a local cluster of about 20 galaxies and that this local cluster is but one member of a massive supercluster of thousands of galaxies. So many of these superclusters are known to exist that the number of galaxies is estimated at more than 100,000,000,000.

What is humanity, indeed! The God who created these stars and calls them all by name (Isaiah 40:26) is unimaginably awesome; his wisdom, beauty, power, and dominion are beyond human comprehension. And yet he has deigned to seek intimacy with the people on this puny planet and has given them great dignity and destiny: "Yet You have made him a little lower than God, and You crown him with glory and majesty!" (Psalm 8:5). These words are applicable to all people, but they find their ultimate fulfillment in Jesus Christ, as the quotation of this passage in Hebrews 2:6–8 makes clear.

We were made to rule over the works of God's hands (Psalm 8:6–8), but we forfeited this dominion in the devastation of the Fall ("but now we do not yet see all things subjected to him" [Hebrews 2:8b]). However, all things will be subjected under the feet of Christ when he returns (1 Corinthians 15:24–28), and we will live and reign with him (Romans 5:17; 2 Timothy 2:12; Revelation 5:10; 20:6).

As wonderful as our dominion over nature will be, our true cause of rejoicing should be in the fact that if we have placed our trust in Jesus Christ, our names are recorded in heaven (Luke 10:20). "What is man that You take thought of him? And the son of man that You care for him?" The infinite Ruler of all creation takes thought of us and cares for us, and he has proved it by the indescribable gift of his Son (2 Corinthians 9:15; 1 John 4:9–10). In the words of C. S. Lewis, glory means "good report with God, acceptance by God, response, acknowledgment, and welcome into the heart of things. The door on which we have been knocking all our lives will open at last." Let us exult in hope of the glory of God!

GOD'S LOVE FOR US

We have seen that the love of God is the wellspring of biblical faith and hope. Consider these truths about the love of God from Paul's epistle to the Romans. In the book of nature, God reveals his eternal power and divine nature (1:20), and in the book of human conscience, he reveals our imperfection and guilt (2:14–16). But only in the book of Scripture does God reveal his limitless love that can overcome our guilt and transform us into new creatures in Christ. God's loyal love for us is causeless (5:6), measureless (5:7–8), and ceaseless (5:9–11). Nothing in us merited or evoked his love; indeed, Christ died for us when we were his ungodly enemies. God's love is spontaneous and unending—he loved us because he chose to love us, and if we have responded to Christ's offer of forgiveness and relationship with him, nothing can separate us from that love or diminish it (8:35–39). This means that we are secure in the Lord's unconditional love; since we belong to Christ, nothing we do can cause God to love us more, and nothing we do can cause God to love us less.

For people who have experienced pain and rejection caused by performance-based acceptance and conditional love, this description seems too good to be true. Isn't there something we must do to merit God's favor or earn his acceptance? If we are afraid others would reject us if they knew what we are like inside, what of the holy and perfect Lord of all creation? The Elizabethan poet George Herbert (1593–1633) captured this stinging sense of unworthiness in his superb personification of the love of God:

> Love bade me welcome; yet my soul drew back,
> Conscious of dust and sin.
> But quick-eyed Love, observing me grow slack
> From my first entrance in,
> Drew nearer to me, sweetly questioning,
> If I lacked anything.
> "A guest," I answered, "worthy to be here."
> Love said, "You shall be he."
> "I, the unkind, ungrateful? Ah, my dear,
> I cannot look on thee."
> Love took my hand, and smiling did reply,
> "Who made the eyes but I?"
> "Truth, Lord, but I have marred them; let my shame
> Go where it doth deserve."
> "And know you not," says Love, "who bore the blame?"
> "My dear, then I will serve."
> "You must sit down," says Love, "and taste my meat."
> So I did sit and eat.

Beyond all human faith, beyond all earthbound hope, the eternal God of love has reached down to us and, in the ultimate act of sacrifice, purchased us and made us his own.

How do we respond to such love? All too often, these revealed truths seem so remote and unreal that they do not grip our minds, emotions, and wills. We may sing about the love of God in worship services and learn about it in Bible classes but miss its radical implications for our lives. Spiritual truth eludes us when we limit it to the conceptual realm and fail to internalize it. We dilute it through cultural, emotional, and theological filters and reduce it to a mental construct that we affirm more out of orthodoxy than out of profound personal conviction. How do we move in the direction of loving God completely?

LOVING GOD COMPLETELY

In the last few years, I have adapted and used this prayer by St. Richard of Chichester (1197–1253) in my own quiet times before the Lord: "Thanks be to thee, O Lord Jesus Christ, for all the benefits which thou hast given us; for all the pains and insults which thou hast borne for us. O most merciful Redeemer, Friend, and Brother, may we know thee more clearly, love thee more dearly, and follow thee more nearly; for thine own sake."

Loving God completely involves our whole personality—our intellect, emotion, and will. "And you shall love the Lord your God with all your heart, and with all your soul, and with all your mind, and with all your strength" (Mark 12:30). The better we come to know God ("may we know thee more clearly"), the more we will love him ("love thee more dearly"). And the more we love him, the greater our willingness to trust and obey him in the things he calls us to do ("follow thee more nearly").

May We Know Thee More Clearly

The great prayers in Ephesians 1 and 3, Philippians 1, and Colossians 1 reveal that Paul's deepest desire for his readers was that they grow in the knowledge of Jesus Christ. The knowledge the apostle had in mind was not merely propositional but personal. He prayed that the Lord would give them a spirit of wisdom and of revelation in the knowledge of him, that the eyes of their hearts would be enlightened, and that they would know the love of Christ that surpasses knowledge (Ephesians 1:17–18; 3:19).

The occupational hazard of theologians is to become so engrossed in the development of systematic models of understanding that God becomes an abstract intellectual formulation they discuss and write about instead of a living person they love on bended knees. In the deepest sense, Christianity is not a religion but a relationship that is born out of the trinitarian love of the Father, Son, and Holy Spirit.

When Thomas Aquinas was pressed by his secretary, Reginald of Piperno, to explain why he stopped working on his uncompleted *Summa Theologica*, he said, "All that I have written seems like straw compared to what has now been revealed to me."

According to tradition, in his vision he heard the Lord say, "Thomas, you have written well of me: what shall be your reward?" and his reply was, "No reward but yourself, Lord." Our greatest mental, physical, and social achievements are as straw compared with one glimpse of the living God (Philippians 3:7–10). Our Lord invites us to the highest calling of all—intimacy with him—and day after day, we decline the offer, preferring instead to fill our stomachs with the pods of short-lived pleasures and prospects.

What does it take to know God more clearly? The two essential ingredients are time and obedience. It takes time to cultivate a relationship, and unless we set aside consistent time for disciplines such as solitude, silence, prayer, and the reading of Scripture, we will never become intimate with our Lord. Obedience is the proper response to this communication, since it is our personal expression of trust in the promises of the Person we are coming to know. The more we are impressed by him, the less we will be impressed by people, power, and things.

Love Thee More Dearly

To know God is to love him, because the more we grasp—not merely in our minds but also in our experience—who he is and what he has done for us, the more our hearts will respond in love and gratitude. "We love, because He first loved us" (1 John 4:19). When we discover that the personal Author of time, space, matter, and energy has, for some incomprehensible reason, chosen to love us to the point of infinite sacrifice, we begin to embrace the unconditional security we longed for all our lives. God's love for us is spontaneous, free, uncaused, and undeserved; he did not set his love on us because we were lovable, beautiful, or clever, because in our sin we were unlovable, ugly, and foolish. He loved us because he chose to love us. As we expand our vision of our acceptance and security in Christ who loved us and gave himself for us, we begin to realize that God is not the enemy of our joy but the source of our joy. When we respond to this love, we become the people he has called us to be. By God's grace we need to grow in love with him in our thoughts, in our emotions, and in our actions. The theme of loving him more dearly is developed later in the section on devotional spirituality.

Follow Thee More Nearly

As we grow to know and love God, we learn that we can trust his character, promises, and precepts. Whenever he asks us to avoid something, it is because he knows that it is not in our best interests. And whenever he asks us to do something, it is always because it will lead to a greater good. If we are committed to following hard after God, we must do the things he tells us to do. But the risk of obedience is that it will often make no sense to us at the time. It is countercultural to obey the things the

Holy Spirit reveals to us in the Scriptures. Radical obedience sometimes flies in the face of human logic, but in these times our loving Father tests and reveals the quality of our trust and dependence on him. If we love Jesus, we will keep his commandments (John 14:15); he taught us that obedience to his commands is the way we test and express our abiding relationship with him (John 15:10). Our great task in the spiritual life is to will to do his will, to love the things he loves, and to choose the things he sets before us for our good. The theme of following him more nearly is developed in the sections on holistic and process spirituality.

QUESTIONS FOR PERSONAL APPLICATION

- What is your view of our greatness and smallness? How do you deal with the tension between these images?
- How does nature speak to you about the glory of God? How often do you reflect on God's attributes through the created order?
- What are the implications of the love of God in your heart and mind?
- How do you practice the triple prayer "may I know thee more clearly, love thee more dearly, and follow thee more nearly"?

2

RELATIONAL SPIRITUALITY
Loving Ourselves Correctly

CHAPTER OVERVIEW

We can be defined either by our world or by our God. To love ourselves correctly is to see ourselves as God sees us. This involves a process of exposure to the truths of Scripture with a view to understanding our new identity in Christ Jesus. This chapter contains an inventory of these truths in the form of a series of affirmations from Scripture.

CHAPTER OBJECTIVES

- Gaining perspective on the role of identity in defining our approach to life
- Learning to see ourselves in the way God sees us
- A clearer understanding of who God says his children are

THE ISSUE OF IDENTITY

A story is told about the American playwright Arthur Miller that illustrates the issue of personal identity. Sitting alone in a bar, Miller was approached by a well-tailored, slightly tipsy fellow who addressed him thus:

"Aren't you Arthur Miller?"

"Why, yes, I am."

"Don't you remember me?"

"Well . . . your face seems familiar."

"Why, Art, I'm your old buddy Sam! We went to high school together! We went out on double dates!"

"I'm afraid I—"

"I guess you can see I've done all right. Department stores. What do *you* do, Art?"

"Well, I . . . write."

"Whaddya write?"

"Plays, mostly."

"Ever get any produced?"

"Yes, some."

"Would I know any?"

"Well . . . perhaps you've heard of *Death of a Salesman?*"

Sam's jaw dropped; his face went white. For a moment he was speechless. Then he cried out, "Why, you're ARTHUR MILLER!"

Sam recognized his high school friend Arthur Miller, and he was familiar with the dramatist Arthur Miller, but he didn't realize the two were one and the same. There is a sense in which this happens in our experience as believers in Christ—we know ourselves and each other in a superficial way, but we do not grasp who we are at the core of our being. Like a man who has forgotten his name, we can wander about the streets of life without knowing our true identity.

WHO DEFINES YOU?

We are constantly in danger of letting the world instead of God define us, because that is so easy to do. It is only natural to shape our self-image by the attitudes and opinions of our parents, our peer groups, and our society. None of us are immune to the distorting effects of performance-based acceptance, and we can falsely conclude that we are worthless or that we must try to earn God's acceptance. Only when we define ourselves by the truths of the Word rather than the thinking and experiences of the world can we discover our deepest identity.

All of us have encountered psychobabble about self-love, including the call to look within ourselves to discover the answers to our problems. But the Scriptures exhort us to look to Christ, not to self, for the solutions we so greatly need. I have come to define the biblical view of self-love in this way: *loving ourselves correctly means seeing ourselves as God sees us.* This will never happen automatically, because the scriptural vision of human depravity and dignity is countercultural. To genuinely believe and embrace the reality of who we have become as a result of our faith in Christ requires consistent discipline and exposure to the Word of God. It also requires a context of fellowship and encouragement in a community of like-minded believers. Without these, the visible will overcome the invisible, and our understanding of this truth will gradually slip through our fingers.

SEEING OURSELVES AS GOD SEES US

What does it mean to see ourselves as God sees us? Contrary to our culture, the biblical doctrine of grace humbles us without degrading us and elevates us without inflating us. It tells us that apart from Christ, we have nothing and can do nothing of eternal value. We are spiritually impotent and inadequate without him, and we must not put our confidence in the flesh (Philippians 3:3). Grace also tells us that we have become new creatures in Christ, having been transferred from the kingdom of darkness to the kingdom of his light, life, and love. In him, we now enjoy complete forgiveness from sins and limitless privileges as unconditionally accepted members of God's family. Our past has been changed because of our new heredity in Christ, and our future is secure because of our new destiny as members of his body.

Thus a biblical understanding of grace addresses both human depravity and human dignity. It avoids the extreme of worm theology (I'm worthless, I'm no good, I'll never amount to anything, I'm nothing but a rotten sinner) and the opposite extreme of pride and autonomy ("What do you have that you did not receive? And if you did receive it, why do you boast as if you had not received it?" [1 Corinthians 4:7]). Grace teaches us that the most important thing about us is not what we do but who and whose we are in Christ. In Scripture, doing (our actions) should flow out of being (our identity); the better we grasp our identity in Christ, the more our actions should reflect Christlike character.

WHO DOES GOD SAY I AM?

The following biblical affirmations about our identity in Jesus Christ are derived from a few selected passages in the New Testament. These passages teach a portion of the many truths about who we have become through faith in God's Son.

- I am a child of God.
  But as many as received Him, to them He gave the right to become children of God, even to those who believe in His name.

  John 1:12

- I am a branch of the true vine, and a conduit of Christ's life.
  "I am the true vine, and My Father is the vinedresser. . . . I am the vine, you are the branches; he who abides in Me and I in him, he bears much fruit, for apart from Me you can do nothing."

  John 15:1, 5

- I am a friend of Jesus.
  "No longer do I call you slaves, for the slave does not know what his master is doing; but I have called you friends, for all things that I have heard from My Father I have made known to you."

  John 15:15

- I have been justified and redeemed.
  Being justified as a gift by His grace through the redemption which is in Christ Jesus.

  Romans 3:24

- My old self was crucified with Christ, and I am no longer a slave to sin.
  Knowing this, that our old self was crucified with Him, in order that our body of sin might be done away with, so that we would no longer be slaves to sin.
  Romans 6:6

- I will not be condemned by God.
  Therefore there is now no condemnation for those who are in Christ Jesus.
  Romans 8:1

- I have been set free from the law of sin and death.
  For the law of the Spirit of life in Christ Jesus has set you free from the law of sin and of death.
  Romans 8:2

- As a child of God, I am a fellow heir with Christ.
  And if children, heirs also, heirs of God and fellow heirs with Christ, if indeed we suffer with Him so that we may also be glorified with Him.
  Romans 8:17

- I have been accepted by Christ.
  Therefore, accept one another, just as Christ also accepted us to the glory of God.
  Romans 15:7

- I have been called to be a saint.
  To the church of God which is at Corinth, to those who have been sanctified in Christ Jesus, saints by calling, with all who in every place call upon the name of our Lord Jesus Christ, their Lord and ours.
  1 Corinthians 1:2; Ephesians 1:1; Philippians 1:1; Colossians 1:2

- In Christ Jesus, I have wisdom, righteousness, sanctification, and redemption.
  But by His doing you are in Christ Jesus, who became to us wisdom from God, and righteousness and sanctification, and redemption.
  1 Corinthians 1:30

- My body is a temple of the Holy Spirit, who dwells in me.
  Do you not know that you are a temple of God and that the Spirit of God dwells in you?
  1 Corinthians 3:16

Or do you not know that your body is a temple of the Holy Spirit who is in you, whom you have from God, and that you are not your own?
  1 Corinthians 6:19

- I am joined to the Lord and am one spirit with him.
  But the one who joins himself to the Lord is one spirit with Him.

  1 Corinthians 6:17

- God leads me in the triumph and knowledge of Christ.
  But thanks be to God, who always leads us in triumph in Christ, and manifests through us the sweet aroma of the knowledge of Him in every place.

  2 Corinthians 2:14

- The hardening of my mind has been removed in Christ.
  But their minds were hardened; for until this very day at the reading of the old covenant the same veil remains unlifted, because it is removed in Christ.

  2 Corinthians 3:14

- I am a new creature in Christ.
  Therefore if anyone is in Christ, he is a new creature; the old things passed away; behold, new things have come.

  2 Corinthians 5:17

- I have become the righteousness of God in Christ.
  He made Him who knew no sin to be sin on our behalf, so that we might become the righteousness of God in Him.

  2 Corinthians 5:21

- I have been made one with all who are in Christ Jesus.
  There is neither Jew nor Greek, there is neither slave nor free man, there is neither male nor female; for you are all one in Christ Jesus.

  Galatians 3:28

- I am no longer a slave but a child and an heir.
  Therefore you are no longer a slave, but a son; and if a son, then an heir through God.

  Galatians 4:7

- I have been set free in Christ.
  It was for freedom that Christ set us free; therefore keep standing firm and do not be subject again to a yoke of slavery.

  Galatians 5:1

- I have been blessed with every spiritual blessing in the heavenly places.
  Blessed be the God and Father of our Lord Jesus Christ, who has blessed us with every spiritual blessing in the heavenly places in Christ.

  Ephesians 1:3

- I am chosen, holy, and blameless before God.
  Just as He chose us in Him before the foundation of the world, that we should be holy and blameless before Him.

  Ephesians 1:4

- I am redeemed and forgiven by the grace of Christ.
  In Him we have redemption through His blood, the forgiveness of our trespasses, according to the riches of His grace.

  Ephesians 1:7

- I have been predestined by God to obtain an inheritance.
  In Him also we have obtained an inheritance, having been predestined according to His purpose who works all things after the counsel of His will.

  Ephesians 1:10–11

- I have been sealed with the Holy Spirit of promise.
  In Him, you also, after listening to the message of truth, the gospel of your salvation—having also believed, you were sealed in Him with the Holy Spirit of promise.

  Ephesians 1:13

- Because of God's mercy and love, I have been made alive with Christ.
  But God, being rich in mercy, because of His great love with which He loved us, even when we were dead in our transgressions, made us alive together with Christ (by grace you have been saved).

  Ephesians 2:4–5

- I am seated in the heavenly places with Christ.
  And raised us up with Him, and seated us with Him in the heavenly places in Christ Jesus.

  Ephesians 2:6

- I am God's workmanship created to produce good works.
  For we are His workmanship, created in Christ Jesus for good works, which God prepared beforehand so that we would walk in them.

  Ephesians 2:10

- I have been brought near to God by the blood of Christ.
  But now in Christ Jesus you who formerly were far off have been brought near by the blood of Christ.

  Ephesians 2:13

- I am a member of Christ's body and a partaker of his promise.
  The Gentiles are fellow heirs and fellow members of the body, and fellow partakers of the promise in Christ Jesus through the gospel.

  Ephesians 3:6; 5:30

- I have boldness and confident access to God through faith in Christ.
  In whom we have boldness and confident access through faith in Him.

  Ephesians 3:12

- My new self is righteous and holy.
  Put on the new self, which in the likeness of God has been created in righteousness and holiness of the truth.

  Ephesians 4:24

- I was formerly darkness, but now I am light in the Lord.
  You were formerly darkness, but now you are Light in the Lord; walk as children of Light.

  Ephesians 5:8

- I am a citizen of heaven.
  For our citizenship is in heaven, from which also we eagerly wait for a Savior, the Lord Jesus Christ.

  Philippians 3:20

- The peace of God guards my heart and mind.
  And the peace of God, which surpasses all comprehension, will guard your hearts and your minds in Christ Jesus.

  Philippians 4:7

- God supplies all my needs.
  And my God will supply all your needs according to His riches in glory in Christ Jesus.

  Philippians 4:19

- I have been made complete in Christ.
  In Him you have been made complete, and He is the head over all rule and authority.

  Colossians 2:10

- I have been raised up with Christ.
  Therefore if you have been raised up with Christ, keep seeking the things above, where Christ is, seated at the right hand of God.

  Colossians 3:1

- My life is hidden with Christ in God.
  For you have died and your life is hidden with Christ in God.

  Colossians 3:3

- Christ is my life, and I will be revealed with him in glory.
  When Christ, who is our life, is revealed, then you also will be revealed with Him in glory.

  Colossians 3:4

- I have been chosen of God, and I am holy and beloved.
  So, as those who have been chosen of God, holy and beloved, put on a heart of compassion, kindness, humility, gentleness and patience.

  Colossians 3:12

- God loves me and has chosen me.
  Knowing, brethren beloved by God, His choice of you.

  1 Thessalonians 1:4

I recommend reviewing frequently this powerful inventory, since it reminds us of truths we quickly forget amid the worries and cares of this world. The more we embrace these affirmations from Scripture, the more stable, grateful, and fully assured we will be in the course of our lives.

QUESTIONS FOR PERSONAL APPLICATION

- To what degree are you defined by the world? By the Word? How can you develop your identity more fully in the latter?
- What does it require to see yourself as God sees you?
- Which five from the list of biblical affirmations resonate the most with you? Which five seem the most remote to your experience? How can you make these more real in your thinking and practice?

3

RELATIONAL SPIRITUALITY
Loving Others Compassionately

CHAPTER OVERVIEW

The closer our walk with God, the more we are empowered to manifest our love for him through acts of love and service to others. When we understand that Christ's resources are our resources, we can become secure enough to serve other people without expecting reciprocity. Loving Christ more than people increases our capacity to love, serve, forgive, and give ourselves away for people.

CHAPTER OBJECTIVES

- An ability to see the implications of our vertical relationship with God on our horizontal relationships with people
- A vision of greatness as God defines it
- A realization that Christ's resources have been given to us now that we are in him
- An enhanced appreciation for the relationships we have been given
- An understanding of the importance of forgiveness in our relationships

FROM THE VERTICAL TO THE HORIZONTAL

We have seen that we were created for an intimate relationship with the infinite and personal God who loves us. He initiates this relationship, and we love him because he first loved us. Loving God completely is the key to loving self correctly (seeing ourselves as God sees us), and this in turn is the key to loving others compassionately. As we grow in our understanding of God's unconditional love and acceptance of us in Christ, we are increasingly liberated from using people to meet our needs.

EXPRESSING GOD'S LOVE ON THE HORIZONTAL

This developing vertical relationship of loving the Father, Son, and Holy Spirit will find its manifestations on the horizontal, since there is no act that begins with the love of God that does not end with the love of neighbor. The great and foremost commandment ("You shall love the Lord your God with all your heart, and with all your soul, and with all your mind" [Matthew 22:37]) is the foundation for the second great commandment ("You shall love your neighbor as yourself" [Matthew 22:39]). After washing the feet of his disciples, Jesus elevated the *standard* by which we are called to love others: "A new commandment I give to you, that you love one another, even as I have loved you, that you also love one another" (John 13:34). "This is My commandment, that you love one another, just as I have loved you" (John 15:12; cf. 1 John 3:23). The *sphere* of this new commandment is universal. It extends first to our brothers and sisters in the body of Christ and beyond this to our neighbors in this world who do not know Jesus.

Our faith in the work Christ accomplished for us in the past and our hope of the future completion of this work when we see him are demonstrated in the present through the choices and works of love. The more we love God, the more we will express his transcendent love in others-centered deeds of kindness and goodness. "Beloved, let us love one another, for love is from God; and everyone who loves is born of God and knows God. The one who does not love does not know God, for God is love. By this the love of God was manifested in us, that God has sent His only begotten Son into the world so that we might live through Him. In this is love, not that we loved God, but that He loved us and sent His Son to be the propitiation for our sins. Beloved, if God so loved us, we also ought to love one another" (1 John 4:7–11).

The section on corporate spirituality discusses the necessity of community in our spiritual formation. While we come to faith in Christ as individuals, we do not grow in isolation but through the interdependence of the body of Christ. Our modern world view is highly individualistic, autonomous, and self-serving, but as we will see, the biblical world view is covenantal, interdependent, communal, relational, and self-transcending.

THE QUEST FOR GREATNESS IN THE SIGHT OF OTHERS

Near the end of our Lord's earthly ministry, his disciples were arguing about who would occupy the best positions in his kingdom. They refused to listen to his increasingly frequent words about his coming crucifixion and focused instead on the part they wanted to hear. When James and John approached Jesus and said, "Grant that we may sit, one on Your right and one on Your left, in Your glory" (Mark 10:37), the other disciples became indignant because they wanted the same places. Jesus told them that the one who wished to be great among them will be their servant and whoever wished to be first among them will be slave of all. "For even the Son of Man did not come to be served, but to serve, and to give His life a ransom for many" (Mark 10:43–45).

Weeks later, when Jesus celebrated the Passover with his disciples on the night before his own sacrifice, the dispute surfaced again. Christ's rebuttal to their quest for recognition was that true greatness is found in those who are willing to serve. "For who is greater, the one who reclines at the table or the one who serves? Is it not the one who reclines at the table? But I am among you as the one who serves" (Luke 22:27).

THE ESSENCE OF TRUE GREATNESS

John 13 records a visual parable that communicated this precise issue to the disciples with poignancy and clarity. It is evident that there was no servant to wash the feet of the Lord and his men before they reclined at the table. This must have been an embarrassing situation; foot washing was a customary part of hospitality in the ancient Near East, but it was obvious that if the disciples were fighting for a prominent place, none of them would volunteer to be the servant of all. Their embarrassment became acute when Jesus rose from supper, laid aside his garments, tied a towel around himself, and began to wash the disciples' feet and wipe them with the towel. His lesson was evident: if their Teacher and Lord became their servant, they should also serve one another (vv. 13–15).

The key to Christ's willingness to serve others in place of being served by them is found in the crucial truth that Jesus knew that "the Father had given all things into His hands, and that He had come forth from God and was going back to God" (John 13:3). He knew his dignity and power ("the Father had given all things into His hands"), he knew his significance and identity ("and that He had come forth from God"), and he knew his security and destiny ("and was going back to God").

Jesus derived his identity from his relationship with his Father and not from the opinions of his family and peers. Consider these passages:

- "Can any good thing come out of Nazareth?" (John 1:46).
- "Why is He eating and drinking with tax collectors and sinners?" (Mark 2:16).
- "Is not this the carpenter, the son of Mary, and brother of James and Joses and Judas and Simon? Are not His sisters here with us?" And they took offense at Him (Mark 6:3).
- "The Son of Man came eating and drinking, and they say, 'Behold, a gluttonous man and a drunkard, a friend of tax collectors and sinners!'" (Matthew 11:19).
- "If You do these things, show Yourself to the world." For not even His brothers were believing in Him (John 7:4–5).
- They said to Him, "We were not born of fornication" (John 8:41).
- The Jews answered and said to Him, "Do we not say rightly that You are a Samaritan and have a demon?" (John 8:48).
- When He left there, the scribes and the Pharisees began to be very hostile and to question Him closely on many subjects, plotting against Him to catch Him in something He might say (Luke 11:53–54).

Jesus was criticized, rejected, slandered, misunderstood, plotted against, betrayed, denied, and abused by his family and friends, his disciples, the Jewish religious leaders, and the Romans. As his ministry progressed, our Lord faced increasing levels of hostility and opposition. In spite of all this, he knew who and whose he was, and his relationship with the Father gave him the power and security to love and serve others. It would have been impossible for Jesus to have done this if he had allowed himself to be defined and bound by the opinions of the people around him.

CHRIST'S RESOURCES ARE OUR RESOURCES

Just as Jesus knew who he was, where he came from, and where he was going, so all who have put their trust and hope in him should know the same. But few do. Only as we frequently renew our minds with the spiritual truth of the Scriptures will we move our thinking into alignment with the reality of who we are in Christ. Like Christ, we have dignity and power; every spiritual blessing has been given into our hands (Ephesians 1:3, 19; 3:16, 20–21). We also have significance and identity; we have become the children of God (Romans 8:16; 1 John 3:1–2). And we have been given the security and destiny of knowing that nothing can separate us from the love of God in Christ (Romans 8:18, 35–39). These limitless resources meet our deepest needs and overcome the human dilemma of loneliness, insignificance, and meaninglessness.

When these truths begin to define our self-image, they make us *secure enough to love and serve others* without seeking our interests first. Because of our security and significance in Christ, we do not need to be controlled by the opinions and responses of others. We have nothing to prove because we know who and whose we are. Rather than trying to impress and manipulate people, we can do our work with excellence as unto the Lord (Colossians 3:23). The more we are concerned with what God thinks of us, the less we will be worried about what others think of us. And when we are no longer enslaved to people's opinions of us, we are free to love and serve them as Christ loves us—with no strings attached.

THE RISKS AND REWARDS OF RELATIONSHIPS

As these truths about what God has already accomplished for us become clearer in our thinking, we grow in awareness of our true freedom in Christ and desire to express this freedom and security in the way we approach relationships. Instead of one-upmanship, we can take pleasure in putting others first. Our *identification* with Christ leads to and is the basis for our *imitation* of Christ. Paul invited the Philippians to do this when he told them to "do nothing from selfishness or empty conceit, but with humility of mind regard one another as more important than yourselves; do not merely look out for your own personal interests, but also for the interests of others" (Philippians 2:3–4). The apostle then used the servanthood of Jesus as the model for the mindset that we as his servants should embrace in our service to others (see 2:5–8).

But it is one thing to exalt the virtues of being a servant and another to be treated as one. It requires the sufficiency and security of a growing realization of our identification with Jesus Christ to minister with others-centered concern to people who misunderstand us and may never respect us. We will need to review frequently the truth that our performance and our acceptance by other people has nothing to do with our dignity and value, since this is determined by God and not by the world. When we suffer rejection and indifference, the pain will be real, but it need not destroy us, since we have made the radical decision to look to God and his resources alone for our true and unchanging identity and worth.

If I had to choose one word to summarize the theme of the Bible from Genesis to Revelation, that word would be *relationships*. We have seen that God is a community of being—in the mystery of the divine Trinity, the three persons of the Godhead enjoy perfect mutual love. We have also seen that God created us in his image as relational beings whose ultimate source of fullness and enjoyment should have been found in fellowship and intimacy with God. Through his loving initiative, God has overcome the alienation and separation caused by human sin by sending his Son into the world to pay for our guilt and to give us his life. The restoration of our vertical relationship with God that was made possible through Christ's atonement becomes the basis for the restoration of righteous horizontal relationships with others. In Scripture, righteousness is a relational concept, since it refers to good, just, and loving associations with God and others.

As children of God through faith in Christ, we are called to a lifestyle of growing others-centeredness and diminishing self-centeredness as Christ increases and we decrease. While we are aware that in a sinful world such a lifestyle makes us more vulnerable to the pains of rejection, indifference, demands, misunderstanding, and betrayal, we also realize that a wise person finds more joy in serving others than in pursuing possessions, power, performance, or prestige. Both the Old and the New Testaments resonate with this theme and repeatedly tell us that a vital vertical relationship with the Lord is the key to quality horizontal relationships with others. The apostle Paul exemplified this wisdom when he described his Philippian readers as "my joy and crown" (4:1) and encouraged them to "rejoice in the Lord always; again I will say, rejoice!" (4:4). The Lord should be the ultimate source of our joy and the continual source of our joy, whether our circumstances and dealings with people are positive or negative.

The more we take pleasure in loving and serving God, the greater our capacity to take pleasure in loving and serving people. Thus Paul could write to the Thessalonians, "For who is our hope or joy or crown of exultation? Is it not even you, in the presence of our Lord Jesus at His coming? For you are our glory and joy" (1 Thessalonians 2:19–20; cf. 3:9). When we are secure in Christ, the rewards of investing our lives in people exceed the pains that people can cause. Paul saw people not only as a source of joy but also as a reward, both in the present and in the future. When we love and serve people with eternal values in mind, there is great reward in being part of the process of people coming to Christ and growing in their character and relationships with their mates, children, and associates. There is joy in being used of God in encouraging, comforting, and building up others in our arenas of influence.

Jonathan Edwards observed that the ultimate good in life is to treat things according to their true value. The converse is also true, and we face the ever-present danger of treating the eternal as though it were temporal and the temporal as though it were eternal. The world system switches the price tags and encourages us to pursue things that will not last. "That which is highly esteemed among men is detestable in the sight of God" (Luke 16:15b). If we want to be rich toward God (Luke 12:21), we must give our lives in exchange for the things God declares to be important.

The heart always provides for what it values (Matthew 6:19–34), and if we value God first, our capacity to love him and others will expand. If we value the world first, we will miss out on not only the joys of knowing God but also the joys of this life. Relationships will degenerate into contacts, and we will seek to manipulate people to get what we think we want. We will be driven to accomplish and impress, and this will detract from quality time with those we love. Activities will take precedence over intimacy, both with God and with people. The idol of accomplishment will erode the aesthetics of the spirit and leave us busy and weary. We will work harder to influence people, and by seeking our security in their responses, we will become disconnected from our true security in Christ. The only way off this treadmill is repentance and return to the pursuit of Christ in place of the pursuit of the world.

It has been said that "everyone ought to fear to die until he has done something that will last forever." These are strong words, but they deserve serious consideration, as does this statement that has been attributed to Joan of Arc: "It is not a tragedy to die for something you believe in, but it is a tragedy to find at the end of your life that what you believed in betrayed you." This thought captures the essence of our ongoing struggle between the claims of the temporal and those of the eternal. Scripture repeatedly reminds us that "the world is passing away, and also its lusts; but the one who does the will of God lives forever" (1 John 2:17). This planet is transitory; when the day of the Lord comes like a thief, "the earth and its works will be burned up" (2 Peter 3:10). Yet something in us longs for the eternal, for that which will not pass away. We cannot satisfy this longing through earthly accomplishments, naming buildings and land after ourselves, building corporate empires, collecting valued possessions, or pursuing other forms of human endeavor, because all of these things are destined to disappear. What, then, can we do on this planet that will always live? What can give permanence to the work of our hands (Psalm 90:17)? The answer lies in the biblical truth that after their fleeting years on earth, people go on into eternity. When we invite Christ to manifest his life in and through us, when we represent the Lord Jesus in our spheres of influence and encourage others to know him better, we are investing in something that transcends this planet.

This should be our prayer for ourselves and for those who enter into our sphere of influence. All of us want to do something that will endure. It is frightening to think that we could run life's course in vain, ending up without a single work that will live on beyond the grave. But the Lord Jesus has promised that when we allow him to accomplish his work in and through us, the results will last forever. We cannot take our earthly possessions with us, but according to the gospel, we can take people with us. We bring nothing into this world, and we can take nothing material out of it. But if we are investing in the lives of people, our investments will accrue dividends forever, since people were made in the image of God to inhabit eternity.

FIVE KINDS OF PEOPLE

In *Restoring Your Spiritual Passion*, Gordon MacDonald observes that we encounter five kinds of people. First, there are the very resourceful people (VRPs) who add to our lives and ignite our passion. These are mentors, and they are often older men or women who are willing to build their experience and wisdom into our lives. It is wise to search for such people prayerfully, since they are less likely to search for us. Second, there are the very important people (VIPs) who share our passion. These people love us enough to ask us tough questions and keep us honest as they work together with us and share our vision. Third, there are the very trainable people (VTPs) who catch our passion, and these are people newer to the faith in whose lives we have been called to make an investment. These three groups correspond to Paul, Barnabas, and Timothy, and we need exposure to all three for spiritual growth and reproduction.

Fourth, there are what MacDonald calls the very nice people (VNPs) who enjoy our passion but do not contribute to it. These people make up the large majority of congregations in the relatively unpersecuted Western churches, and most church programs focus on accommodating them and their needs. Finally, there are the very draining people (VDPs) who sap our passion by causing conflicts and constantly looking for comfort and recognition. If we are not careful, the VNPs and VDPs we encounter will absorb the majority of our available time. This does not mean that we should not treat them with dignity and compassion, especially since it is possible for such people to change when they become open to the ministry of the Holy Spirit in their lives. Jesus ministered to those who were sick, suffering, curious, and critical, but he spent the majority of his time with his Father and with his disciples. In the same way, we can protect ourselves from difficult people without writing them off. We have all encountered people who seem to be one taco short of a combination plate, but by the grace of God, it is possible for a VDP to become a VRP.

THE GRACE OF FORGIVENESS

One of the most important dynamics in relational spirituality is the grace of forgiveness.

Forgiven by God

It has been observed that there is no sin so great that God will not forgive, but there is no sin so small that it does not need to be forgiven. The Old and New Testaments center on the theme of redemption and forgiveness, stressing the human condition as one of alienation and moral guilt before the holiness of the Creator. Through God's mighty and loving act of redemption in the cross of Christ, he can offer the gracious gift of forgiveness without compromising the perfection of his justice and character. And through the grace of divine forgiveness, our alienation can be overcome and a loving, secure relationship as true members of God's family can be inaugurated.

The dynamic of forgiveness involves the response of repentance and confession. We must humble ourselves before God and admit the reality of our sinfulness, asking him for the gift of forgiveness and new life in Christ. And having put our trust in Christ alone for our salvation, we stay in fellowship with him by asking the Spirit to search our hearts and reveal any areas of unconfessed sin, by acknowledging these to the Lord, and by thanking him for his forgiveness (Psalm 139:23–24; 1 John 1:9).

God's forgiveness erases the sin from existence. In imagery from the Old Testament, he removes it "as far as the east is from the west" (Psalm 103:12). He casts our sins behind his back (Isaiah 38:17), he wipes out our transgressions for his own sake (Isaiah 43:25), he remembers our sin no more (Jeremiah 31:34), and he casts all our sins into the depths of the sea (Micah 7:19). In imagery from the New Testament, we are assured that "when you were dead in your transgressions and the uncircumcision of your flesh, He made you alive together with Him, having forgiven us all our transgressions, having canceled out the certificate of debt consisting of decrees against us, which was hostile to us; and He has taken it out of the way, having nailed it to the cross" (Colossians 2:13–14).

Even after coming to Christ, many people find it difficult to accept God's unconditional forgiveness. There is still a lingering natural disposition to think we must work off the debt and earn divine forgiveness. Guilt feelings can cause people to revisit the sin instead of laying hold of God's forgiveness. The idea that we have outsinned the grace of God is a failure to grasp the height and depth of God's grace and love.

Forgiving Others

> *I was angry with my foe:*
> *I told it not, my wrath did grow.*
> WILLIAM BLAKE

Having been forgiven by the grace of God on the basis of Christ's finished work on the cross, we are exhorted to manifest forgiveness in our relationships with others (see Matthew 18:21–35). Thus Paul exhorts us to "be kind to one another, tender-hearted, forgiving each other, just as God in Christ also has forgiven you" (Ephesians 4:32; cf. Matthew 5:12). Elsewhere he writes: "So, as those who have been chosen of God, holy and beloved, put on a heart of compassion, kindness, humility, gentleness and patience; bearing with one another, and forgiving each other, whoever has a complaint against anyone; just as the Lord forgave you, so also should you. Beyond all these things put on love, which is the perfect bond of unity. Let the peace of Christ rule in your hearts, to which indeed you were called in one body; and be thankful" (Colossians 3:12–15).

The Cost of Forgiveness

When we forgive those who have hurt us, we acknowledge that we too have needed forgiveness and that we are not as different from the offender as we might like to think. There is a natural tendency in all of us to excuse our own faults and to blame others for their faults, an inclination to reach for grace and understanding in our own situation and to reach for justice and possibly revenge when the same wrong is committed by others. Instead, Scripture calls us, as people who have experienced God's forgiveness, to take the place of the other person.

In Christ, we are to offer grace rather than justice to the wrongdoer (*charizomai*, one of the words used in the New Testament for forgiveness, means "to deal graciously with"; notice how it is used in 2 Corinthians 2:6–8). This is often a difficult and unnatural act, because it does not seem fair to those who have been wronged. To forgive others is to release them from any obligation to make up to you what they have taken from you. But as Lewis B. Smedes argues in *Forgive and Forget*, "When you release the wrongdoer from the wrong, you cut a malignant tumor out of your inner life. You set a prisoner free, but you discover that the real prisoner was yourself."

Thus to forgive as we have been forgiven by God is an act of faith, since it means that we are releasing the right to resentment and that we entrust justice to God rather than seek it ourselves (see Romans 12:19). To forgive is to act on the truth that it is only God and not we who can change another person.

It has been quipped that "there's no point in burying a hatchet if you're going to put a marker on the site." But when we have been seriously injured by another, we want to put a marker on the site so that we can dig up our resentments from time to time. Because forgiveness can feel like outrageous injustice, it can be a lengthy process rather than a once-for-all event. This is evident in the painful process Joseph went through in forgiving his treacherous brothers (Genesis 42–45).

Long after you have forgiven, the wound can linger in your memory. As Smedes observes, forgiving is not the same as forgetting or excusing or smoothing things over. True forgiveness is costly, especially when there is no repentance on the part of the wrongdoer. But it is the only way to release us and others from the bondage of guilt (see Christ's gracious restoration of Peter in John 21:15–19) and to break the vicious cycle of blame. Part of the cost is letting loose of the pride that can allow trivial things to corrode a relationship for years or decades.

As an exercise before God, take a piece of paper and write down the names of those who have hurt you over the years through disloyalty and betrayal. Offer this list to God along with all the pain it rekindles, and make a choice through faith in Christ to forgive each person on the list. Then crumple the paper and burn it before the Lord who forgave you from the cross.

HOW LONG WILL IT LAST?

I have attended a number of funerals in the past few years, and the difference between funerals for believers and unbelievers is the difference between day and night, between heaven and earth, and between hope and despair. The homecoming ceremony for a person who knew Jesus Christ is a time when our hope in Christ has a true payoff. We discover that our faith is more real and powerful during these pivotal times when we are forced to acknowledge our lack of control. For a follower of Christ, death is not the end but the doorway to a new and greater domain. The body is left behind, but the spirit is in the presence of the Lord until the day when it is joined to a new and glorified resurrection body. Scripture assures us that when we are absent from the body, we will be at home with the Lord (2 Corinthians 5:6–8), and it comforts us with the truth that "God will bring with Him those who have fallen asleep in Jesus" and that "the dead in Christ shall rise first. Then we who are alive and remain will be caught up together with them in the clouds to meet the Lord in the air, and so we shall always be with the Lord" (1 Thessalonians 4:13–18).

When a loved one departs this life, the far-reaching implications extend into the three dimensions of time.

Past

Whenever I hear of the passing of someone I knew and loved, a flood of memories surges into my consciousness. Images of the person's life multiply, flashing across the screen of my mind in such a way that I can see all the years of my relationship with the person simultaneously. In times like this, the mind seems to search for and collect all the treasures and troubles and display them in a vivid array that forces one to realize the impact of the other's life as though for the first time. And I discover not only how much I was shaped by that impact but also the truth that this person took a part of me away with him or her, for there were certain responses and facets of my personality that only this person could elicit.

Present

The influence of significant others creates ripple effects that continue to touch our lives long after these people are gone. We cannot measure the repercussions because they keep compounding and reverberating in subtle ways through the years and generations. The fullness of this process will not be evident until the day of Christ, but it reminds us once again that each of us is called to the present process of fulfilling God's unique purpose for us during the few years of our earthly sojourn.

Another implication for the present is the importance of treating each relationship as though it could be our last contact. This kind of closure would produce a lifestyle of few regrets, because it would mean that we do not leave behind any unfinished business such as speaking our love, forgiving and asking forgiveness, or expressing our gratitude for all the other person has done and meant.

Future

The passing of one who is beloved is a reminder of our own mortality and of the brevity of our pilgrimage in the world. Ecclesiastes 7:2 tells us that "it is better to go to a house of mourning than to go to a house of feasting, because that is the end of every man, and the living takes it to heart." Funerals are memoranda of reality, and for a time they open a window of vulnerability to the truth of the temporal versus the eternal. While our defenses and diversions are down, they invite us to answer the questions Where is my hope? Am I hoping in the promises and rewards of the world, or am I laying hold of a hope that will never fade or disappoint? Scripture tells us that those who put their hope in Christ will not be disappointed (Romans 9:33). This hope is an anchor of the soul (Hebrews 6:19), and it strengthens the believer to remain steadfast during the tempests of life.

QUESTIONS FOR PERSONAL APPLICATION

- How relevant are the two great commandments in your daily experience?
- Why are we more concerned with impressing others than with pleasing Jesus?

- How do you define greatness in people?
- What are the keys to true humility and servanthood?
- To what extent do you believe that Christ's resources are your resources? What prevents you from fully embracing this concept?
- How do you view relationships? Do you lean more toward the side of self-protection or toward the side of transparency?
- How do you treat the difficult people in your life?
- To what extent do you think you may be harboring resentment and unforgiveness because of what others have done? How will you address this issue?

F A C E T   2

P A R A D I G M
S P I R I T U A L I T Y

Cultivating an Eternal
versus a Temporal Perspective

This section contrasts the temporal and eternal value systems and emphasizes the need for a paradigm shift from a cultural to a biblical way of seeing life. The experience of our mortality can help us transfer our hope from the seen to the unseen and realize the preciousness of present opportunities. Our presuppositions shape our perspective, our perspective shapes our priorities, and our priorities shape our practice.

4

PARADIGM
SPIRITUALITY
Life Is a Journey,
but Where Are We Going?

CHAPTER OVERVIEW

Biblical realism requires a grasp of the brevity of our sojourn on earth so that our hope is fixed not on the prospects of this passing world but on the promises of the everlasting God. A growing realization of our mortality should cause us to treasure the opportunities of the present.

CHAPTER OBJECTIVES

- A better grasp of the brevity of our earthly sojourn
- Developing a balance of biblical realism about the present and hope for the future
- A greater appreciation for the preciousness of present opportunities

ONE YEAR TO LIVE

Suppose your doctor tells you, after a routine physical examination, that you have a terminal illness. You seek a second and third opinion, and all agree that at best you have one year to live. There will be no discernible effects of the disease until it has reached its course.

How would this scenario affect your vision of life, your roles on this earth, and the ways you invest your remaining time? The degree to which it would alter your present perspective and practice is the distance between your current view of life and the biblical view of life. The latter emphasizes the brevity of our earthly sojourn and stresses the urgency of investing our most precious asset, time, in a way that will have lasting consequences. The former view typically denies the imminence of death and treats the temporal as though it were eternal.

A GRASP OF LIFE'S BREVITY

Time, like an ever-rolling stream,
Bears all its sons away;
They fly forgotten as a dream
Dies at the op'ning day.
The busy tribes of flesh and blood
With all their cares and fears,
Are carried downward like a flood
And lost in following years.

These verses from Isaac Watts's hymn *O God, Our Help in Ages Past* are based on the profound contrast in Psalm 90 between the eternality of God and the brevity of our earthly sojourn. This psalm, written by Moses near the end of his journey, counsels us to number our days in order to present to God a heart of wisdom (v. 12). David's meditation in Psalm 39:4–7 develops the same theme:

LORD, make me to know my end,
And what is the extent of my days;
Let me know how transient I am.
Behold, You have made my days as handbreadths,
And my lifetime as nothing in Your sight;
Surely every man at his best is a mere breath.
Surely every man walks about as a phantom;
Surely they make an uproar for nothing;
He amasses riches and does not know who will gather them.
And now, Lord, for what do I wait?
My hope is in You.

Isaiah 40:6b–8 uses a different metaphor to develop the radical contrast between the temporal and the eternal (see also Psalm 103:15–18 and 1 Peter 1:24–25):

All flesh is grass, and all its loveliness is like the flower of the field.
The grass withers, the flower fades,
When the breath of the LORD blows upon it;
Surely the people are grass.
The grass withers, the flower fades,
But the word of our God stands forever.

James adds this sobering thought: "You do not know what your life will be like tomorrow. You are just a vapor that appears for a little while and then vanishes away" (4:14; cf. 1:11).

BIBLICAL REALISM AND HOPE

The Scriptures drive home these images to remind us that our stay on this planet is briefer than most of us are inclined to think. This may seem to be a pessimistic and morbid way of viewing human life, but upon further analysis, it turns out to be a realistic and hopeful approach. It is realistic because it is better to know things as they are than to believe things as they seem. It does not require divine revelation to realize that, as George Bernard Shaw put it, "The statistics on death are impressive. One out of one dies." Our few decades of life on earth last no longer than the flower of a field in relation to the many generations that come and go.

It comes as no surprise to see this perspective as realistic, but it is surprising to discover that it is also hopeful. It is hopeful because it informs us that there is more to life than what we presently see, and it assures us that our longing for more than this world can offer is not merely a dream. The biblical vision of God's invitation to us is not only forgiveness but also newness of life in Christ, a new quality of relational life that will never fade or tarnish.

Three dominant world views are vying for our allegiance. The first of these claims that ultimate reality is material and that everything in the universe is the impersonal product of time and chance. There are variations of this view, but it is best known as naturalism, atheism, and humanism.

The second world view claims that ultimate reality is not material but spiritual. However, this spiritual agent is not a personal being but the all-that-is. Variations of this view include monism, pantheism, transcendentalism, and the New Age movement.

Theism, the third world view, distinguishes between the creation and the Creator and declares that ultimate reality is an infinite, intelligent, and personal Being. Christian theism affirms that this personal God has decisively revealed himself in the person and work of Jesus Christ.

Only the third world view offers genuine hope beyond the grave, since the first predicts annihilation, and the second, reincarnation. Contrary to the pop version of reincarnation in the West, the religions of the East teach that reincarnation is undesirable, since it brings us around and around on the painful wheel of life. The Eastern vision of salvation is absorption into the ocean of being. But this is not a vision of personal consciousness or relationships; it is a spiritual version of annihilation.

Instead of annihilation or reincarnation, the Scriptures teach resurrection into an eternally new existence of light, life, and love characterized by intimacy with our Lord and with one another. Everything we go through now will be more than worth it in the end, because the divine Architect of the universe, the God and Father of our Lord Jesus Christ, never builds a staircase that leads to nowhere.

TWO COMPETING PARADIGMS

A **paradigm** is a way of seeing based on implicit or explicit rules that shape one's perspective. A paradigm shift takes place when the rules or boundaries change, so that we no longer see things from the same perspective; when the rules change, our way of seeing is altered. The most celebrated example of a paradigm shift is the Copernican revolution in astronomy. Until the time of Copernicus, the reigning paradigm was Ptolemy's geocentric system; the sun and planets were thought to orbit the earth. For centuries, astronomers held to this Ptolemaic way of viewing the solar system in spite of the fact that a number of observations did not fit this model. But instead of questioning the paradigm, astronomers invented complicated theories of epicycles to explain why some planets appeared to stop, go backward for a while, and then resume their original direction. Copernicus's breakthrough was the realization that all of these observations make perfect sense by switching from a geocentric to a heliocentric (sun-centered) view of the sun and planets—in other words, we do not live in a terrestrial system but in a solar system. Copernicus published his views posthumously because he realized that this radical shift would meet with a hostile response, especially by those in the religious establishment.

In a similar way, the temporal and eternal perspectives are competing paradigms of life. We can live as if this world is all there is, or we can view our earthly existence as a brief pilgrimage designed to prepare us for eternity. The men and women in Hebrews 11 embraced the latter perspective: "All these died in faith, without receiving the promises, but having seen them and having welcomed them from a distance, and having confessed that they were strangers and exiles on the earth" (Hebrews 11:13). By contrast, those who adopt a temporal paradigm treat the temporal as though it were eternal and the eternal as though it were temporal.

Suppose someone plans to move from Dallas to Atlanta, where he knows he will spend the remaining fifty years of his life. He carefully prepares for the two-day drive by poring over every detail of the journey, including what clothing he will wear, what rest stops he will use, where he will refuel his car, what motel he will stay at, all meals he will eat, and where he will eat them. Nothing on the journey is left to chance, but he doesn't know what he will do when he arrives in Atlanta. The absurdity of this scenario is easy to see, and yet the bulk of people we encounter are living their lives in this way. In this analogy, the two-day trip is our earthly sojourn, and the fifty-year stay is our eternal destiny. But what is obviously ludicrous on a temporal scale seems acceptable when we speak of eternity, perhaps because our eternal destiny seems so vague and wispy to many of us.

Marcel Proust observed that "the real act of discovery consists not in finding new lands but in seeing with new eyes." The problem is that we have been captured by a temporal paradigm because we live in a temporal arena. It takes great risk to shift to a biblical paradigm, because the biblical paradigm challenges everything that our culture reinforces. The more we have invested in the cultural paradigm and the better we are at functioning within it, the more we think we may lose by changing to the biblical paradigm. Only when we renew our minds with biblical truth and reinforce this truth through relationships with other children of the kingdom do we begin to see that we are on a brief pilgrimage. When we see this, we discover that we must pursue the things that will last rather than the things that are passing away. The problem is that this temporal/eternal shift, unlike the Copernican revolution in astronomy, is reversible; we can flip-flop between these opposing perspectives. This is an ongoing struggle that we can expect to encounter for the remainder of our worldly sojourn.

"A SHORT AND FEVERED REHEARSAL"

Prospero, a magician who rules an enchanted island, is the protagonist of Shakespeare's last play, *The Tempest*. When Prospero addresses his guest Ferdinand in the fourth act, it is as though Shakespeare himself, nearing the end of his life, reflects directly through his character:

> *Our revels now are ended. These our actors,*
> *As I foretold you, were all spirits and*
> *Are melted into air, into thin air;*
> *And, like the baseless fabric of this vision,*
> *The cloud-capped towers, the gorgeous palaces,*
> *The solemn temples, the great globe itself,*
> *Yea, all which it inherit, shall dissolve,*
> *And, like this insubstantial pageant faded,*
> *Leave not a rack behind. We are such stuff*
> *As dreams are made on, and our little life*
> *Is rounded with a sleep.*

At the end of the play, Prospero gives up his magic and turns his thoughts to the grave. Just so, the playwright would create no more works on the stage of life; reflecting on the brevity of earthly existence, he understood that the temporal achievements of humanity as a whole would come to an end. This is consistent with the biblical vision of the fiery consumption of all human attainments on the day of God. "But the day of the Lord will come like a thief, in which the heavens will pass away with a roar and the elements will be destroyed with intense heat, and the earth and its works will be burned up" (2 Peter 3:10).

If we examine the heart's deepest longings, it becomes evident that these aspirations cannot be satisfied by any of the offerings of this transitory world. There is insufficient time, opportunity, and energy even to scratch the surface of our deep-seated hopes and dreams. A. W. Tozer put it well in his devotional classic *The Knowledge of the Holy*: "The days of the years of our lives are few, and swifter than a weaver's shuttle. Life is a short and fevered rehearsal for a concert we cannot stay to give. Just when we appear to have attained some proficiency we are forced to lay our instruments down. There is simply not time enough to think, to become, to perform what the constitution of our natures indicates we are capable of."

EXPERIENCING OUR MORTALITY

Few people attain this wisdom in the first three decades of life. In *Dead Poets Society*, Robin Williams plays an English teacher in a private school who makes a dramatic attempt to communicate this truth to a group of adolescents. He gathers the students before an old trophy case and invites them to look closely at the faces of a class that graduated seventy or eighty years before. As the camera slowly pans in to a close-up of the faces in the photograph, we see all the hope and ambition of youth in their eyes and smiles. In the voice-over, Williams tells his students that the people in the photo were just like them, but now they are pushing up daisies. He exhorts them to seize the moment—carpe diem!

But it usually requires the sobering struggle of the midlife crisis (or midlife process, depending on the way we go through it) before we experientially grasp our mortality. As we discover the decline of our capacities and the increase of our responsibilities, we realize with clarity and force that we will not be able to fulfill many of our earthly hopes and dreams. This can be traumatic for those whose expectations are limited to this planet, but for believers whose hope is in the character and promises of God, it can be a powerful reminder to transfer their affections and ambitions to their only true home, the kingdom of heaven.

Tozer adds: "How completely satisfying to turn from our limitations to a God who has none. Eternal years lie in His heart. For Him time does not pass, it remains; and those who are in Christ share with Him all the riches of limitless time and endless years."

The responsibilities and pressures of this world clamor for our attention and tend to squeeze our inner lives and starve our souls. When this happens, we lose sight of the things that matter and focus on the things that are passing away. Our value systems become confused when we invest more of our thought and concern in things that are doomed to disappear than in that which will endure forever.

The apostle John warns us of this when he writes, "Do not love the world nor the things in the world. If anyone loves the world, the love of the Father is not in him. For all that is in the world, the lust of the flesh and the lust of the eyes and the boastful pride of life, is not from the Father, but is from the world. The world is passing away, and also its lusts; but the one who does the will of God lives forever" (1 John 2:15–17).

James adds, "Whoever wishes to be a friend of the world makes himself an enemy of God" (James 4:4). And Jesus admonishes those who are more concerned with the opinions of people than the approval of God, saying, "That which is highly esteemed among men is detestable in the sight of God" (Luke 16:15). These are strong words, but we would be foolish to disregard them. As Augustine wrote, we must care for our bodies as though we were going to live forever, but we must care for our souls as if we were going to die tomorrow.

THE PRECIOUS PRESENT

Does this mean that we should be so heavenly minded that we are of no earthly good? In fact, it is the opposite—when people become heavenly minded, they treasure the passing opportunities of this life and become more alive to the present moment. Rather than being overwhelmed with the problems of life, they understand that these too will pass and that "the sufferings of this present time are not worthy to be compared with the glory that is to be revealed to us" (Romans 8:18). Instead of taking things for granted, they learn to savor blessings and joys that are otherwise overlooked.

Thornton Wilder portrays this so well in *Our Town*, a play depicting a young woman who dies in childbirth. In the third act, the Stage Manager allows Emily to go back and observe a single day of her brief life, but the dead advise her to "choose the least important day in your life. It will be important enough." Emily selects her twelfth birthday and is soon overwhelmed by the experience.

"I can't. I can't go on. It goes so fast. We don't have time to look at one another. . . .

"I didn't realize. So all that was going on and we never noticed. Take me back—up the hill—to my grave. But first: Wait! One more look.

"Good-by, Good-by, world. Good-by, Grover's Corners . . . Mama and Papa. Good-by to clocks ticking . . . and Mama's sunflowers. And food and coffee. And new-ironed dresses and hot baths . . . and sleeping and waking up. Oh, earth, you're too wonderful for anybody to realize you."

She looks toward the Stage Manager and asks abruptly, through her tears: "Do any human beings ever realize life while they live it?—every, every minute?"

The Stage Manager answers, "No. . . . The saints and poets, maybe—they do some."

Instead of wasting time as though we had a million years to live on earth, we would do well to remember the apostle Paul's exhortation: "Be most careful then how you conduct yourselves: like sensible men, not like simpletons. Use the present opportunity to the full, for these are evil days. So do not be fools, but try to understand what the will of the Lord is" (Ephesians 5:15–17 NEB).

Eubie Blake, who smoked since he was six and refused to drink water, was reported to say after his hundredth birthday, "If I'd known I was going to live this long, I'd have taken better care of myself." When elderly people are asked what they would change if they had another opportunity to go through life, their answers are generally more illuminating than this. Many say that they would reflect more, risk more, and do more things that would last.

Most of us have squandered more money and time on toys and diversions than we would like to admit. We are allotted only a few years to labor in this vineyard. Are we squandering or investing the precious resources of time, talent, and treasure that have been entrusted to us by our heavenly Master?

QUESTIONS FOR PERSONAL APPLICATION

- If you knew you had only one more year to live, how would you spend your time, and how would this differ from the way you are presently spending your time?
- To what degree are you aware of your mortality in your feelings and experience? Why is it helpful to cultivate this awareness?
- What are the implications in your life and thinking of a temporal versus an eternal perspective? Do you sense yourself being pulled in both directions? How does this affect your value system?
- If you were granted two hundred years of healthy life on this planet, how would you invest them? What would you seek to achieve with this additional time and opportunity? How does this relate to your view of activity in heaven?

5

PARADIGM SPIRITUALITY
Can We Trust God?

CHAPTER OVERVIEW

The temporal and the eternal are two competing paradigms that promote radically divergent value systems, and it is not natural or easy to pursue the invisible above the visible. Only when our perspective is shaped and reinforced by biblical **presuppositions** will we be able to live in accordance with godly priorities.

CHAPTER OBJECTIVES

- Understand the radical differences between a temporal value system and an eternal value system
- Think through the implications of our presuppositions and how these shape our perspective
- Gain an enhanced understanding of the relationship of perspective, priorities, and practice

THE RISK OF LETTING LOOSE

Any attempt to pursue the claims of both the temporal and the eternal is like holding onto two horses that are galloping in opposite directions. The simultaneous pursuit of the kingdom of the world and the kingdom of Christ is impossible—at any point, one or the other will prevail. Many people have tried to have it both ways, but this can never be more than a matter of adding a spiritual veneer over the same furniture that is manufactured and promoted by the world system.

It takes great risk to let loose of everything we have been taught to clamor after and control. It is never comfortable or natural to treasure the invisible over the visible, the promises of God over the promises of the world, the things that will not be fulfilled until the return of Christ over the things the world says we can have here and now. We want control and security on our terms, yet the Scriptures tell us that the only true security comes from abandoning the illusion of control and surrendering ourselves unreservedly to the person and purposes of God.

TWO RIVAL VALUE SYSTEMS

The **temporal value system** demands no trust and dependence upon God because it is based on what is seen; the **eternal value system**, by contrast, is unseen and therefore requires a walk of faith (2 Corinthians 5:7). "For in hope we have been saved, but hope that is seen is not hope; for who hopes for what he already sees? But if we hope for what we do not see, with perseverance we wait eagerly for it" (Romans 8:24–25).

Our culture bombards us with the message that this world is all there is and tells us that the goal of life is maximize your pleasure and minimize your pain. Build a name for yourself if you can, and establish progeny. There are many variations, but the enticing wisdom of this world, as observed by the Preacher in Ecclesiastes, always derives from what is "under the sun." The wisdom that comes from above, from beyond the sun, tells us that we are immortal creatures and that this brief moment on this planet is as nothing compared with the eternal existence that awaits us.

James tells us that there is warfare between an earthly and demonic wisdom and a heavenly and divine wisdom (James 3:13–17). Each of us is required to make a choice. Which will we believe? How consistent is our behavior with our belief?

In this warfare, the world promotes pleasure as an end in itself. It implies that people who are willing to forgo earthly pleasures in their pursuit of the ways of God are missing out on the good life. The Word says that knowing God is the greatest pleasure of all. God is the Source of true pleasure; by comparison, everything else is a shadow.

The world exalts recognition and approval of people. The Word exhorts us to desire the approval of God. "For am I now seeking the favor of men, or of God? Or am I striving to please men? If I were still trying to please men, I would not be a bond-servant of Christ" (Galatians 1:10).

The world tells us to pursue fame and popularity. Using the arena of history, Paul Johnson illustrates the futility of the quest for popular relevance: "the study of history moves on, remorselessly, like time itself. Today's sensation becomes tomorrow's irrelevance. The best-seller of one decade becomes the embarrassment of another. The revolutionary theory which convulses the academic world gets cut down in the next age to an ironic footnote." In contrast, the Word calls us to emulate the servanthood of Christ. It has been well said that everyone ought to fear to die until we have done something that will always live. Since people will go into eternity, our others-centered acts of kindness and sacrificial service that are born out of the love of Christ will endure forever.

The world raises wealth and status as a standard of success, security, and identity. But as C. S. Lewis noted in *The Screwtape Letters*, "Prosperity knits a man to the World.

He feels that he is 'finding his place in it,' while really it is finding its place in him. His increasing reputation, his widening circle of acquaintances, his sense of importance, the growing pressure of absorbing and agreeable work, build up in him a sense of being really at home in earth." The Word elevates the standard of integrity and character. ("But you, are you seeking great things for yourself? Do not seek them" [Jeremiah 45:5].) God sometimes grants the severe mercy of taking his children's toys away for a time so that they will transfer their hope from the creation to the Creator.

The world drives us to amass power over people and circumstances; the Word tells us to walk humbly before our God. "Humble yourselves, therefore, under the mighty hand of God, that He may exalt you at the proper time, casting all your anxiety upon Him, because He cares for you" (1 Peter 5:6–7).

But the crucial contrast lies in where these opposing value systems ultimately lead (table 5.1).

TEMPORAL	ETERNAL
Pleasure	Knowing God
Recognition of people	Approval of God
Popularity	Servanthood
Wealth and status	Integrity and character
Power	Humility
↓	↓
Emptiness	Fulfillment
Delusion	Reality
Foolishness	Wisdom

TABLE 5.1

People *think* they want pleasure, recognition, popularity, status, and power, but the pursuit of these things leads to emptiness, delusion, and foolishness. God has set eternity in our hearts (Ecclesiastes 3:11), and our deepest desires are fulfillment (love, joy, peace), reality (that which does not fade away), and wisdom (skill in living). The only path to this true fulfillment lies in consciously choosing God's value system over that which this world offers. This choice is based on trusting a Person we have not yet seen. "And though you have not seen Him, you love Him, and though you do not see Him now, but believe in Him, you greatly rejoice with joy inexpressible and full of glory, obtaining as the outcome of your faith the salvation of your souls" (1 Peter 1:8–9).

As the story of the wedding at Cana illustrates, the world pours out its best wine first and switches to the cheap wine after people's discernment has been dulled. But our Lord's miracle of turning the water into wine teaches us that for those who follow him, the best is reserved for last.

OUR PRESUPPOSITIONS SHAPE OUR PERSPECTIVE

Part of the problem is that we often fail to review the nonnegotiables to which we claim to be committed. For me, the fundamental presuppositions that form the bedrock of my world view are, as Francis Schaeffer put it, God is there, and he is not silent. That is, the Author of all creation is a person who has revealed himself to humanity in "many portions and in many ways" (Hebrews 1:1), including the general revelation of creation and conscience and the special revelation of dreams, visions, prophets, apostles, and clearest of all, his personal revelation in the person and work of Jesus Christ. I see the Bible as God's declaration of his character and ways, his love letter to the people he sent his Son to redeem, and his blueprint for how to live life with wisdom, purpose, faith, love, and hope.

Since this is my fundamental presupposition about life, everything should flow out of it. It shapes my perspective on who God is, who we are, where we came from, why we are here, where we are going, and how we should relate to others.

THE IMPLICATIONS OF OUR ASSUMPTIONS

I have discovered that while everyone has a world view, a philosophy, a set of presuppositions about life that they hold by faith, few people are aware of it. Of the few who can express their fundamental assumptions about human existence, only a fraction have thought through the logical implications of these assumptions. And of this small fraction, only a handful have contrasted these logical implications with the way they live. This is one reason why the majority of people can move through life with such a discrepancy between belief and practice.

What are the logical implications of the view that the infinite and personal God exists and has decisively revealed himself in Christ and the Scriptures? There are several, but the most important is that life is about God and not about us; all things have been created by him and for him (Colossians 1:16), and we exist to serve God and not to persuade God to serve us. In essence, the Lord's repeated message to us in Scripture is "I am God, and you are not."

Another implication is that since we were created for relationship with the Author of every good thing, we can have no higher purpose than to grow in the knowledge of God and, by his grace and power, to become increasingly like him.

A third implication is that since the Bible was inspired by the living God, we would be wise to learn, understand, experience, and apply its precepts and principles. The Scriptures reveal that our brief earthly sojourn is designed to prepare us for eternal citizenship in heaven. Thus it would be the heart of folly to become entangled and enmeshed in that which is "highly esteemed among men" but is "detestable in the sight of God" (Luke 16:15). In our careers, for example, we should execute our tasks with quality and care as servants of Christ rather than pleasers of men (Colossians 3:22–24). Our ambition must be different from that of others; instead of pursuing position, power, prestige, or wealth, we should seek the approval of our God (2 Corinthians 5:9).

A fourth implication is that we can expect to be pulled again and again toward the temporal and away from the eternal, because the truths of Scripture are countercultural. Whenever we are lured away from obedience and service into disobedience and selfishness, it is because we have been deceived into thinking that we know better than God what is best for us or that God is not in control. Obedience flows out of trust, and we will obey either the devices and desires of our own hearts or the word of him who made us, loves us, and redeemed us.

Our presuppositions shape our perspective. Our perspective in turn shapes our priorities, and our priorities shape our practice.

OUR PERSPECTIVE SHAPES OUR PRIORITIES

Years ago, a minister waited in line to have his car filled with gas just before a long holiday weekend. The attendant worked quickly, but there were many cars ahead of the minister. Finally the attendant motioned him toward a vacant pump.

"Reverend," said the young man, "sorry about the delay. It seems as if everyone waits until the last minute to get ready for a long trip." The minister chuckled, "I know what you mean. It's the same in my business."

If ours is an eternal perspective, we will be gripped by the biblical truth that our brief earthly sojourn is designed to prepare us for an eternal heavenly citizenship. The more we align ourselves with this perspective, the more it will have an impact on our short-term and long-term priorities.

My friend Gordon Adams uses the analogy of life as a brief stay in a hotel. In some cases the hotel is a fleabag; in others, there may be mints on the pillows and flowers on the table. But whatever the hotel's rating, we are living out of suitcases while we are there. And since we know it is not our home, we don't concern ourselves with changing the decor, even if we dislike the curtains and wallpaper. God never intended room service to replace good home-cooked meals; it is a mistake to confuse hotel life with the glorious dwelling place he is preparing for those who know and love his Son.

Part of our problem is that God's promises seem vague and distant—we have no memories of heaven. But he has given us his word that he will more than make it worth our while. "For here we do not have a lasting city, but we are seeking the city which is to come" (Hebrews 13:14). If we remember that here we are sojourners, strangers, and aliens in exile, our priorities will begin to reflect those of Abraham, who "was looking for the city which has foundations, whose architect and builder is God" (Hebrews 11:8–10).

Another friend of mine, Max Anders, wrote *The Good Life*, a practical exposition of Paul's epistle to the Ephesians. In it, he draws a sharp contrast between the offerings of the world and those of the Word. While the former touts money, ambition, sex, and clout, the latter promises wealth (Ephesians 1–3), purpose (4:1–5:17), love (5:18–6:9), and true power (6:10–20). Too often, however, our priorities reveal that we are chasing shadows when God offers us real substance.

What will endure in the end? Is there anything we can take with us, or do we leave everything behind? When we travel to another country, we must exchange our currency. The currencies of this world will do us no good in the next unless we previously invested them for Christ's sake in the lives of other people. Others-centered relationships that express the love of Christ are the currency of heaven.

OUR PRIORITIES SHAPE OUR PRACTICE

Listen to the words of someone I had the privilege of meeting on two memorable occasions:

> We have a clear sense of birth, but a theoretical sense of death. Understand that you have a certain number of days. There is no good time to die. You don't retire from life and get ready for death. When you leave this planet you will never again have the privilege of sharing the Gospel, serving the lost, feeding the poor. This is not a guilt trip but a reminder to enjoy the opportunity and privilege of representing Christ to the world. This proceeds out of love. The love you give back to him drives the opportunities you have. We must not just wait to get to heaven but relish the only opportunities we will have. (June 1986)

> I am trying to come to grips on a daily basis with what it means to seek first his kingdom. Part of this means not pursuing what our system rewards. There is a problem of drifting back into complacency. God has not promised me tomorrow. There are things to accomplish on this side, and it takes a measure of faith to believe there is something on the other side. (March 1987)

Mark Pett was suffering from terminal cancer when I took these notes during our conversations. We were the same age, and like me, he was engaged in vocational ministry. Mark gained an extraordinary measure of wisdom through the pain he experienced until he went to be with the Lord in February 1988. He stressed the privilege of practice and the window of opportunity to make a difference during our earthly sojourn.

If our priorities shape our practice, then our practice will reveal our priorities. If our practice does not include such elements as an ongoing renewal of the mind through consistent time in Scripture, a commitment to cultivating growing intimacy with God through prayer, and a sensitivity to the opportunities the Lord gives us to love and serve believers and seekers in our arena of influence, then our priorities are not in alignment with those of Scripture.

Two one-liners that I picked up from my friend Bill Garrison always challenge me. The first is, "Write your obituary now and see if it will play well in heaven." The second is, "What are you taking under your arm to the ultimate show and tell?"

"We must work the works of Him who sent Me as long as it is day; night is coming when no one can work. . . . So then, while we have opportunity, let us do good to all people. . . . Conduct yourselves with wisdom toward outsiders, making the most of the opportunity. . . . Therefore be careful how you walk, not as unwise men but as wise, making the most of your time, because the days are evil" (John 9:4; Galatians 6:10a; Colossians 4:5; Ephesians 5:15–16).

Your presuppositions will shape your perspective, your perspective will shape your priorities, and your priorities will shape your practice.

QUESTIONS FOR PERSONAL APPLICATION

- What can you do to move further in the direction of treasuring the unseen and eternal above the visible and temporal?
- How did you identify with the elements in the chart that contrasts the temporal and the eternal? Why do people find it difficult to believe the truth about their respective outcomes?
- What are your fundamental presuppositions about life, and how do these shape your perspective and priorities?
- To what extent does your practice reveal your true priorities versus your professed priorities?

FACET 3

DISCIPLINED SPIRITUALITY

Engaging in the Historical Disciplines

There has been a resurgence of interest in the classical disciplines of the spiritual life, and this section looks at the reasons for this recent trend and the benefits of the various disciplines. It also focuses on the needed balance between radical dependence on God and personal discipline and discusses the dynamics of obedience and application.

6

DISCIPLINED SPIRITUALITY
Dependence and Discipline

CHAPTER OVERVIEW

Discipline should work in concert with dependence, since grace is not opposed to effort but to earning. The multiple benefits of the time-tested disciplines of the faith contribute to spiritual formation in the same way that training prepares us for skillful endeavor.

CHAPTER OBJECTIVES

- A balanced view of both dependence and discipline
- An appreciation for the multiple benefits of the spiritual disciplines

TWO EXTREMES

It is easy to slip into one of two extremes regarding the Christian life. The first extreme overemphasizes our role and minimizes God's role. This position is characterized by the mentality of striving for and living for Jesus. It emphasizes knowledge, rules, rededication efforts, and human activities and virtually ignores the ministry of the Holy Spirit. The second extreme overemphasizes God's role and minimizes our role. This position is characterized by a let-go-and-let-God passivity. It stresses experience, the supernatural, and the person of the Holy Spirit and downplays the human element.

The biblical balance is that the spiritual life is both human and divine. Paul places these elements back to back in Philippians 2:12–13: "So then, my beloved, just as you have always obeyed, not as in my presence only, but now much more in my absence, work out your salvation with fear and trembling; for it is God who is at work in you, both to will and to work for His good pleasure." On the human side, we are responsible to work out, not work for, our salvation. On the divine side, God gives us the desire and empowerment to accomplish his purposes.

As an exercise, read the following passages to see the interrelationship of the human and the divine in the outworking of the Christian life: John 14:15–17; 15:4–11, 26–27; Romans 12:1–8, 17–21; 15:30–32; 1 Corinthians 15:10; 2 Corinthians 2:14; 3:1–6; 6:16–7:1; Galatians 2:20; Ephesians 6:10–20; Philippians 4:13; Colossians 1:9–12, 28–29; 1 Thessalonians 5:22–24; 2 Thessalonians 2:13–17; Hebrews 4:14–16; 10:19–25; James 4:7–10; 1 Peter 1:22–25; 4:11; 5:6–10; 2 Peter 1:1–11; 1 John 2:3–6.

Dependence

The life of Christ can be reproduced in us only by the power of the Holy Spirit. As an inner work of God, it is achieved not by human effort but by divine enabling. Apart from Christ and the power of his Spirit, we can accomplish nothing in the sight of God (John 15:4–5; Acts 1:8). Therefore it is crucial that we develop a conscious sense of dependence upon the Spirit's power in all that we do (see Ephesians 1:19; 3:16; 5:18). "But I say, walk by the Spirit, and you will not carry out the desire of the flesh" (Galatians 5:16). "If we live by the Spirit, let us also walk by the Spirit" (Galatians 5:25). The word for "walk" in the first verse is general and refers to life in its totality. The word for "walk" in the second verse is specific and refers to the step-by-step process of daily life. Just as Jesus walked in total dependence upon the life of his Father (John 6:57; 14:10), so we must rest in the same source of power. We were never meant to create life but to receive and display Christ's life in us.

Discipline

Dependence is critical, but there is no growth in the Christian life apart from discipline and self-control ("discipline yourself for the purpose of godliness" [1 Timothy 4:7]). Spirituality is not instantaneous or haphazard; it is developed and refined. The Epistles are full of commands to believe, obey, walk, present, fight, reckon, hold fast, pursue, draw near, and love. The spiritual life is progressively cultivated in the disciplines of the faith; you and I will not wake up one morning to find ourselves suddenly spiritual. This is why Paul uses the metaphors of an athlete, a soldier, and a farmer to illustrate the discipline of the Christian life (see 1 Corinthians 9:24–27; Ephesians 6:10–18; 2 Timothy 2:3–6). We grow in godliness as we hear and obediently respond to the Word. Spiritual maturity is characterized by the ability to recognize and apply the principles of Scripture to daily experience (Hebrews 5:11–14). The Bible comes alive when its precepts are put into practice, but this does not happen apart from human choice. We must choose to have our minds and emotions guided and strengthened by the Holy Spirit.

THE BENEFITS OF THE DISCIPLINES

There has been a resurgence of interest in the classical disciplines of the spiritual life, and in this chapter we will look at the reasons for this trend and the benefits of the various disciplines. Although we will focus on discipline, or human responsibility, we must be careful never to lose sight of dependence, or divine sovereignty, since both are equally important.

A number of recent authors have called believers to savor the wealth of the spiritual disciplines that have informed Catholic and Orthodox spirituality for centuries but that have been largely overlooked by Protestants. These authors include Richard J. Foster (*Celebration of Discipline, Freedom of Simplicity, Prayer: Finding the Heart's True Home*), Dallas Willard (*The Spirit of the Disciplines*), Henri J. M. Nouwen (*The Way of the Heart*), Bob Benson Sr. and Michael W. Benson (*Disciplines for the Inner Life*), Donald S. Whitney (*Spiritual Disciplines for the Christian Life*), James Earl Massey (*Spiritual Disciplines*), Siang-Yang Tan and Douglas H. Gregg (*Disciplines of the Holy Spirit*), R. Kent Hughes (*Disciplines of a Godly Man*), and John Ortberg (*The Life You've Always Wanted: Spiritual Disciplines for Ordinary People*). All of these writers are united in their view of the spiritual disciplines as crucial means to the pursuit of God. They argue that the classical disciplines of the Christian faith are not optional but essential practices for those who not only love Jesus but also want to become like him.

The bulk of Christian churches and denominations pitch their message so low that even if their members practiced the spiritual regimens they propose, it is unlikely that they would be distinguishably different from their neighbors. In our Christian subculture, mental assent to doctrine is not directly linked to rigorous pursuit of discipleship. The radical and countercultural biblical message of personal transformation by following Christ has often been reduced to a culture-bound spiritual veneer. Appalled by this, a growing number of leaders in the body of Christ have realized that something more is required of believers than being spectators. They have come to see the need for engaging in the means of transformation that have been modeled for centuries by Christlike men and women. Without a personal commitment to inward change, believers will be dominated, motivated, and manipulated by the cultural network of their society. This is where the historical disciplines of the faith come in.

For many people, the word *discipline* reeks with negative connotations. We often associate it with tyranny, external restraint, legalism, and bondage. But a closer look at Scripture and the lives of the great saints in the history of the faith reveals the opposite. The book of Proverbs, for instance, argues that far from limiting our freedom, personal disciplines enhance it and give us options we could never have had otherwise. Wisdom is a skill that is developed through instruction and discipline, and this skill in the art of living under the Lord's dominion frees us to become the people God intended us to be. The pursuit of wisdom, discernment, understanding, and the knowledge of God (see Proverbs 2) requires not only an appetite but also a willingness to pay the necessary price. For years, I have desired the ability to sit before the keyboard of a piano and make glorious music. But my craving to do so has never been matched by a willingness to invest the time, energy, and discipline to make it happen. Only those who pay this price have the freedom to make the instrument sing. Thus discipline is the pathway to freedom rather than bondage. Like the children's story about the impulsive train that wanted to break loose from the rails and go in its own direction, we may not discover the true freedom of the rails until we bog down in the earth of our own pursuits in disregard of God's design.

In the New Testament, a quick survey of the Gospels through the lens of discipline reveals that the Lord Jesus engaged in all the classic disciplines, such as solitude, silence, simplicity, study, prayer, sacrificial service, and fasting. Jesus understood that these practices were not optional for those who have a passion for the Father's pleasure and honor. Our Lord did not engage in these disciplines as ends in themselves but as means to know and obey his Father. They moved him in the direction of the foremost commandment (Deuteronomy 6:5; Mark 12:30): "You shall love the Lord your God with all your heart, and with all your soul, and with all your mind, and with all your strength."

Yet we have bought the illusion that we can be like Christ without imitating his spirituality. If we wish to be like our Master, we must imitate his practice; if we believe he knew how to live, we must seek the grace to live like him. To ask the question What would Jesus do? without practicing the habits we know he practiced is to attempt to run a marathon without prior training. What is evident to us on the physical plane is often obscure to us on the spiritual level. It is absurd to think that we could excel at any sport such as golf or tennis without investing the needed time, training, and practice. But when it comes to living the Christian life, we suppose that we are doing well if we attend church and open a Bible once or twice a week. If believers expended the same time and energy in cultivating their spiritual lives as they are willing to invest in becoming reasonably skillful at any sport or hobby, the world would look with wonder at the power of the body of Christ.

We desire to know Christ more deeply, but we shun the lifestyle that would make it happen. By relegating the spiritual to certain times and activities, we are ill prepared to face the temptations and challenges of daily living in a Christlike way. It is easy to deceive ourselves into thinking that without the active and painful formation of godly character, we will have the capacity to make the right choices whenever we need to. But if we have not been exercising and training and practicing behind the scenes, we will not have the skill (wisdom) to perform well when it counts. The disciplines off the stage prepare an actor to perform well when the curtain rises, and the hours of training off the field give an athlete the freedom to play well when the game begins. Similarly, the daily regimen of the spiritual disciplines equips us to live well during the uncertainties and vicissitudes of life. This is what Dallas Willard called the law of indirect preparedness; the disciplines in the background of our lives prepare us for the unexpected times when we will need to respond in appropriate ways. Willpower alone will not be enough, unless our wills have been trained and strengthened through ongoing practice. When it comes to running a race, meaning well and trying hard will do us little good if we are out of shape through lack of training.

There is no shortcut to spiritual formation. After the initial burst of enthusiasm, we soon discover that launching the process is much easier than following through. As anyone who attempts to learn a new skill quickly realizes, the early learning stages can be particularly challenging, because everything seems so unnatural. Only those who are willing to persevere reach the point where they begin to get the hang of it. But in the spiritual arena, we never arrive. Scripture encourages us to continually press on toward the goal and to reach forward to what lies ahead so that we may lay hold of that for which Christ Jesus laid hold of us (Philippians 3:12–14). This requires a lifelong commitment to the disciplines that Jesus, the apostles, and godly followers of the Way have practiced through the centuries. None of the people whose spiritual vitality we have admired regarded these disciplines as optional, and it would be naïve to suppose that we are history's first exceptions.

The disciplines of the faith are never ends in themselves but means to the end of knowing, loving, and trusting God. As we implement them in a consistent way, we cultivate holy *habits*. As these habits grow, they guide our behavior and character in such a way that it becomes more natural for us to live out our new identities in Christ. Our daily choices shape our habits, and our habits shape our character. Our character in turn guides the decisions we make in times of stress, temptation, and adversity. In this way, the godly actions of maturing believers are outward displays of increasing inner beauty.

The spiritual disciplines are the product of a synergy between divine and human initiative, and they serve us as means of grace insofar as they bring our personalities under the lordship of Christ and the control of the Spirit. By practicing them, we place our minds, temperaments, and bodies before God and seek the grace of his transformation. In this way, we learn to appropriate the power of kingdom living. These disciplines are both active and passive, both initiatory and receptive; they connect us to the power of the indwelling Holy Spirit, who manifests the life of Christ in us and through us. Thus we should work hard but receive everything we are and have by God's grace. It takes the touch of God on our lives for us to form habits that are alive and pleasing to him.

If we fail to see these disciplines and habits as responses to divine grace, we will slip into the trap of thinking that they have value in themselves. Those who think this way suppose that when they meditate or fast, they are spiritually superior to those who do not. Their disciplines become external, self-energized, and law-driven. They are tempted to quantify spirituality by reducing it to a set of external practices rather than an internal, grace-drawn process of transformation. Instead, we must see the disciplines as external practices that reflect and reinforce internal aspirations. Spiritual growth is inside out, not outside in; our focus should be more on the process of inner transformation than on outward routines. This understanding will free us from thinking that the disciplines we practice are magical in themselves or that others should be engaging in the same activities that we practice. Spiritual disciplines are good servants but poor masters; they are useful means but inadequate ends.

To summarize, here are a few of the many benefits of practicing the spiritual disciplines:

1. They encourage imitation of Christ and allow us to act in ways that are centered in God's will.
2. They connect us with an ongoing tradition of time-tested ways of incarnating the spiritual life.
3. They give us a rule of conduct that directs us in the path of growing skill in living before God.
4. They equip us with resources on the three warfare fronts of the world, the flesh, and the demonic.
5. They confer perspective and power, and they encourage us to embrace God's purpose for our lives.
6. They bestow a controlled freedom to respond to changing circumstances in a more biblical manner; they allow our lives to be dominated more by the things above than the things below.
7. They remind us daily that the spiritual life is a balance between radical dependence and responsible action; both grace and self-discipline are required for spiritual maturity.
8. They are vehicles for internal transformation. Given enough time, an average person who consistently practices spiritual disciplines will achieve spiritual productivity and proficiency.
9. They replace habits of sin by cultivating habits that lead to character (e.g., integrity, faithfulness, and compassion).
10. They increase our willingness to acknowledge the daily cost of discipleship and remind us that whatever comes quickly and cheaply is superficial, while the insights that we learn from pain will endure.

We will look at a number of these disciplines in the next chapter and focus on the disciplines of solitude, silence, study, meditation, and prayer.

QUESTIONS FOR PERSONAL APPLICATION

- How do you balance the issues of dependence and discipline?
- Which benefits of the spiritual disciplines speak most clearly to you?
- Is there a discrepancy between how your mind and your emotions respond to the idea of spiritual disciplines?
- How do the disciplines relate to training and skill?
- What is the law of indirect preparedness?
- How can you sustain the disciplines without falling into the trap of externalism?

7

DISCIPLINED SPIRITUALITY

What Are the Spiritual Disciplines?

CHAPTER OVERVIEW

This chapter outlines twenty disciplines of the faith and focuses on two disciplines of abstinence (solitude and silence) and three disciplines of engagement (study, **meditation**, and prayer). A number of suggestions are offered for practicing these five strategic disciplines.

CHAPTER OBJECTIVES

- An ability to think through the various spiritual disciplines
- An understanding of the disciplines of solitude, silence, study, meditation, and prayer

---

There is no standardized list of spiritual disciplines, but some are more prominent in the literature than are others. Richard J. Foster develops a threefold typology of inward disciplines (meditation, prayer, fasting, and study), outward disciplines (simplicity, solitude, submission, and service), and corporate disciplines (confession, worship, guidance, and celebration). Dallas Willard divides the disciplines into two classes: disciplines of abstinence (solitude, silence, fasting, frugality, chastity, secrecy, and sacrifice) and disciplines of engagement (study, worship, celebration, service, prayer, fellowship, confession, and submission). Other writers categorize other activities, including journaling, dialogue, witness, stewardship, and listening, as disciplines.

We will begin with a concise description of twenty disciplines. Then, using Willard's typology, we will look more closely at two disciplines of abstinence (solitude and silence) and three disciplines of engagement (study, meditation, and prayer). Remember, however, that these disciplines are merely tools to help us grow. It would be a mistake to claim that every follower of Christ should practice all of these disciplines in a consistent or rigorous way. Some will be more essential for you at one time, and some will serve you better at other times. You will find that some of the disciplines are nonnegotiable while others can be pursued intermittently. Depending on your temperament and circumstances, you will be drawn to some and indifferent to others. Still, it is wise to engage occasionally in the ones you would normally dismiss, so that you can experience their unique benefits.

THE DISCIPLINES

Solitude and Silence

Solitude is the most fundamental of the disciplines in that it moves us away, for a time, from the lures and aspirations of the world into the presence of the Father. In solitude, we remove ourselves from the influence of our peers and society and find the solace of anonymity. In this cloister we discover a place of strength, dependence, reflection, and renewal, and we confront inner patterns and forces that are alien to the life of Christ within us.

Silence is a catalyst of solitude; it prepares the way for inner seclusion and enables us to listen to the quiet voice of the Spirit. Few of us have experienced silence, and most people find it to be uncomfortable at first. Silence is at odds with the din of our culture and the popular addiction to noise and hubbub. This discipline relates not only to finding places of silence in our surroundings but also to times of restricted speech in the presence of others.

Prayer

Prayer is personal communion and dialogue with the living God. Seen from a biblical perspective, prayer is an opportunity and a privilege rather than a burden or a duty. It is the meeting place where we draw near to God to receive his grace, to release our burdens and fears, and to be honest with the Lord. Prayer should not be limited to structured times but should also become an ongoing dialogue with God as we practice his presence in the context of our daily activities.

Journaling

Many people have found that keeping a spiritual diary heightens their understanding of the unique process of spiritual formation through which God has been taking them. By recording our insights, feelings, and the stream of our experiences, we clarify the progress of our spiritual journey. This discipline relates closely to those of prayer, meditation, and study; journaling enhances personal reflection, encourages us to record perspectives we have received from Scripture, and serves as another form of prayer.

Study and Meditation

The discipline of study is central to the process of renewing the mind in such a way that we can respond appropriately to the truths of God's Word. Study of Scripture involves not only reading but also active involvement in observation, interpretation, and application of its contents. This discipline also includes devotional reflection on the beauties and intricacies of nature as well as exposure to gifted writers and teachers in the past and in the present.

Meditation is a close relative of the disciplines of prayer and study, and it also depends on the disciplines of solitude and silence. Meditation has become such a lost art in the West that we typically associate it with Eastern religions. Far from emptying the mind, however, biblical meditation focuses the mind on the nuances of revealed truth. To meditate on the Word is to take the time to ponder a verse or a passage from Scripture so that its truth can sink deeply into our being.

Fasting and Chastity

The spiritual discipline of fasting is abstention from physical nourishment for the purpose of spiritual sustenance. This difficult discipline requires practice before it can be effective, since it is not natural for us to pursue self-denial. There are different methods and degrees of fasting, but all of them promote self-control and reveal the degree to which we are ruled by our bodily appetites. Fasting can also consist of abstention from other things that can control us, such as television and other forms of entertainment.

The discipline of chastity is relevant to all believers, whether they are single or married. This discipline recognizes that the sexual appetite is a legitimate part of our natures, but it encourages us to resist the painful consequences of improper feelings, fantasies, obsessions, and relations that are so frequently reinforced in our culture. Chastity elevates loving concern for the good of others above personal gratification.

Secrecy

The practice of secrecy is dependence on God alone for what should and should not be noticed by others. Secrecy is the opposite of grasping and self-promotion, since it teaches us to love anonymity and frees us from the bondage of the opinions of others. Secrecy is not a false humility but a heartfelt desire to seek the praise and approval of God regardless of what people may think.

Confession

This discipline sets us free from the burden of hidden sin, but it requires transparency and vulnerability in the presence of one or more people whom we implicitly trust. When we uncover and name our secrets, failures, and weaknesses, they lose their dominion by virtue of being exposed. We are generally more concerned about the disapproval of people whom we can see than we are about the disapproval of God whom we cannot see, and this makes repentance and confession before others difficult.

Fellowship

For some people, enjoying community is not a discipline but a delight. But in our individualistic culture many people are more inclined toward autonomy and independence than to body life. For them, a willingness to seek mutual encouragement and edification is a discipline that will eventually pay dividends through regular exposure to a diversity of natural and spiritual gifts. We will discuss and develop the discipline of community in the section on corporate spirituality. There we will see that our experience with God is mediated through the body of Christ and that *koinonia* (communion, fellowship, close relationship, association) with other believers plays an essential role in our spiritual formation. This dynamic of fellowship should not be trivialized by reducing it to punch and cookies or potluck suppers.

Submission and Guidance

The discipline of voluntary submission to others as an expression of our submission to Christ is based upon the biblical mandate for us to seek the good of others rather than our rights. Mutual subordination and servanthood free us from having to be in control and to have things go our way. By imitating Christ in this discipline of self-denial, we become increasingly concerned with the needs of others.

The discipline of guidance involves the recovery of spiritual direction. In recent years, the evangelical community has become aware of the need for seeking spiritual guidance; this comes through accountability to mentors whose credibility is established by experience and maturity. Guidance is also a corporate discipline in which a body of believers seeks a Spirit-directed unity.

Simplicity, Stewardship, and Sacrifice

These disciplines reinforce each other, since they relate to our attitude and use of the resources that have been placed at our disposal. The discipline of simplicity or frugality refers to a willingness to abstain from using these resources for our own gratification and aggrandizement. A mindset of simplicity helps us resist the cultural endorsement of extravagance and consumption that entices us away from gratitude, trust, and dependence upon the Lord. This discipline frees us from the multiplicity of fleshly desires and anxiety over trivial things, and it helps to deliver us from the bondage of financial debt.

The related discipline of stewardship encourages us to reflect on our lives as managers of the assets of Another. In addition to the usual trilogy of time, talent, and treasure, I include the stewardship of the truth we have received as well as the relationships with which we have been entrusted. In this discipline, we periodically review the ways we have been investing these assets.

Sacrifice is a more radical discipline than simplicity in that it involves the occasional risk of giving up something we would use to meet our needs rather than our wants. This is a faith-building exercise that commits us to entrust ourselves to God's care.

Worship and Celebration

To worship is to be fully occupied with the attributes of God—the majesty, beauty, and goodness of his person, powers, and perfections. For the individual, worship often involves devotional reflection on the person and work of Jesus Christ as our mediator to the Father. In a corporate setting, believers are united in heart and mind to honor and extol the infinite and personal God. The discipline of worship expands our concept of who God is and what he has done.

Celebration focuses on all that God has done on our behalf. It is the discipline of choosing gratitude rather than grumbling and remembrance rather than indifference. When we celebrate, we review and relive the history of God's blessings, and this stimulates a renewed sense of devotion. Celebration, whether individual or corporate, is taking pleasure, amazement, and joy in how good God has been to us in specific ways and times. To revel in God's goodness is to gain a new sense of perspective.

Service

The discipline of service does not call attention to itself but concentrates instead on the needs and concerns of others. True service does not look for recognition but is born out of love for Jesus and a desire to follow him in washing the feet of the saints. In this discipline, we take on roles that are passed over and that do not call attention to ourselves; we steadfastly refuse to live for appearance and recognition, choosing instead to show kindness, courtesy, sensitivity, and concern for people who are often overlooked.

Witness

The reason many believers are not involved in evangelism is that they do not see it as a discipline that requires a corresponding lifestyle. To witness is to choose to go beyond our circle of believing friends and to walk dependently in the power of the Spirit as we invest in relationships with those who have not yet met Christ. The discipline of witness takes seriously the biblical mandate of bearing witness to Jesus by building nonmanipulative relationships with eternity in view.

TWO DISCIPLINES OF ABSTINENCE

The Discipline of Solitude

Although many believers, especially extraverts, avoid this primary discipline of the faith, the spiritual cost in doing so is great. Even a casual look at the Gospels reveals that solitude was an indispensable practice in the life of the Lord Jesus (see Matthew 14:23; Mark 1:35; Luke 5:16; John 6:15), as it was in the lives of all the great saints who have preceded us. In the solitude of the wilderness Jesus prepared to inaugurate his public ministry (Matthew 4:1–11); in the solitude of the mountain he prepared to select his disciples (Luke 6:12–13); and in the solitude of the garden he prepared to sacrifice his life for the sins of the world (Matthew 26:36–46). Solitude transcends loneliness; whenever Jesus sought solitude, it was to be in the presence of his Father. Solitude also transcends place, since Jesus practiced an inner solitude of heart and mind even when he was in the midst of people.

In solitude we remove ourselves from the siren calls and illusions of our society and wrestle with the need for ongoing transformation as we meet with the Lord. Dietrich Bonhoeffer in *Life Together* warned: "Let him who cannot be alone beware of community. . . . Let him who is not in community beware of being alone." Times deliberately spent away from interaction with other people nurture depth, perspective, purpose, and resolve. They deliver us from the tyranny and distractions of daily routine and prepare us for the next stage of the journey through an inner call rather than an external compulsion. By periodically distancing ourselves from schedules, noises, and crowds, we become less captivated by the demands and expectations of others and more captivated by the purposes of God. In this way, we measure and define ourselves in terms of what God thinks rather than what people think. This in turn empowers us to serve and show compassion to others, since we are less manipulated by human expectations and more alive to divine intentions.

Extended times spent in solitude can be frightening, since they remove our external props and force us to confront sinful and selfish attitudes and behaviors. Such times can make us uncomfortably vulnerable before God, but this is as it should be, since this process drives us to the grace, forgiveness, and love of Christ. The purgation of solitude diminishes arrogance and autonomy and fosters humility and trust. As this discipline moves us in the direction of greater Christlikeness, ministry to others becomes an extension of our being.

It is good to have a place for daily meeting alone with the Lord. But we can also carry an inner spirit of solitude with us. Each day is clustered with opportunities for little moments of solitude (e.g., driving alone) if we come to see them in this way.

More extended seasons of solitude can be pivotal in our growth, but they require planning and resolve. I periodically plan a one-day personal retreat for solitude, silence, prayer, and reflection in the country or in a monastery. I have always profited from these retreats, but they never happen unless I put them in my calendar far enough in advance. Even then, I am tempted to find a dozen excuses for not going when the time arrives. This is where the discipline of choice over feelings comes in.

The Discipline of Silence

Solitude and silence are companion disciplines; silence gives depth to solitude, and solitude creates a place for silence. Similarly, both of these disciplines can be practiced inwardly (whether we are with people or not) as well as outwardly.

"Where shall the word be found, where will the word resound? Not here, there is not enough silence." When T. S. Eliot wrote these words, he succinctly captured the essence of our *Zeitgeist*, the spirit of our time and culture. The contemporary epidemic of drivenness to crowds, words, music, entertainment, and noise is inimical to the life of the spirit and points to an inner emptiness. I am convinced that many people would begin to experience withdrawal symptoms if they were deprived of these sounds for more than an hour. Only a minority of us know what total silence is like.

"In repentance and rest you will be saved, in quietness and trust is your strength" (Isaiah 30:15). The transformational discipline of silence encourages us to grow "in quietness and trust" by being hushed before God so that we can listen with our spirit to him and enjoy his presence. This discipline also extends to our relationships with people. Silence in the presence of others can be practiced by deliberately speaking less than we otherwise would. James encourages us to turn this practice into a lifestyle: "Everyone must be quick to hear, slow to speak and slow to anger" (James 1:19; also see 1:26; 3:2–12). Solomon added, "When there are many words, transgression is unavoidable, but he who restrains his lips is wise" (Proverbs 10:19). Consider how much less people would say if they eliminated boasting (Proverbs 25:14; 27:1–2), gossip and slander (Proverbs 11:13; 18:8; 20:19), flattery (Proverbs 26:28; 29:5), nagging (Proverbs 19:13; 21:9, 19; 27:15–16), and quarreling (Proverbs 20:3; 26:21; 2 Timothy 2:23–24) from their speech! Although words can have healing and life-giving power, there are far more occasions when I have regretted opening my mouth than I have regretted remaining silent. Words are like toothpaste in a tube; once the words are out, we cannot unsay them. The discipline of silence increases our psychic margin by giving us the time and composure to weigh our words carefully and use them in more appropriate ways. Silence not only increases our poise and credibility but also enables us to be better observers and more effective, others-centered listeners. In addition, this discipline makes us less inclined to use words to control people or manipulate them into approving and affirming us.

Although many people have observed that it is easier to be silent than to speak in moderation, it would be well worth spending a day in unbroken silence. (If you try this, it goes without saying that you should previously inform others of your intention.) Such a verbal fast would be a real source of illumination about our social strategies and devices.

Henri Nouwen observed that silence "can be seen as a portable cell taken with us from the solitary place into the midst of our ministry." The discipline of silence before

God and people relates to the practice of self-control; the more we develop inner control and composure, the less we will feel compelled to gain outward control over people and circumstances.

THREE DISCIPLINES OF ENGAGEMENT

The Discipline of Study

Since the study of Scripture is the primary vehicle for laying hold of a divine perspective on the world and our purpose in it, this discipline is pivotal to our spiritual nourishment and growth (2 Timothy 3:16–17). Consistent study of the Word cultivates eternal values and priorities, provides guidance for decision making, assists us in overcoming temptation, and enhances our knowledge of God and of ourselves.

The problem is that most people are daunted by the prospect of personal Bible study, since they have little idea of what to do. A hit-and-miss approach provides little spiritual nourishment. Without an ability to understand and apply the truths of Scripture in a practical and meaningful way, believers miss the benefits of exploring and discovering biblical truths for themselves. This is why so many Christians have only a secondhand knowledge of the Bible and rely almost exclusively on the input of teachers and preachers.

Many helpful resources offer useful methods and can guide you through the process of effective Bible study. But a brief list of principles and suggestions may help.

- Maintain a posture of openness and honesty before the Word so that you will be disposed to gain new insights and change your thinking. Be responsive to what you read and study and be willing to apply and obey what you learn. Remember that you are engaging in this discipline to meet God and know him better.
- Avail yourself of the whole counsel of Scripture (the historical, poetical, and prophetical books as well as the Gospels and Epistles).
- Try to be consistent in your exposure to Scripture; this will often require the choice to study whether you feel like it or not.
- Do not regard the Bible as a textbook; it is not merely an object to be observed but an oracle to be obeyed. Approach it with a proper attitude of reverence, care, and receptivity.
- Try to be systematic in your choice of topics, chapters, and books that you study so that your input will come from all parts of Scripture and touch upon every aspect of your life.
- Ask, answer, accumulate, and apply. *Ask* key questions that when answered will provide insight into the meaning of the passage. Use the text (immediate and broad context) as well as standard tools (a concordance, Bible dictionary or encyclopedia, or a Bible commentary) to *answer* your questions.

Accumulate practical principles such as promises to claim, commands to obey, or sins to confess. *Apply* these principles to your life and relationships.

- Have a plan for daily Bible readings so that you will get a comprehensive exposure to Scripture. Reflect on your readings and respond to them in a personal way.

- Use a card to write down key passages that speak to you, and carry one or more of these cards with you. By reviewing these cards from time to time, you can memorize a significant number of verses. The verses you memorize will be of great benefit to you, especially in times of temptation and trials.

- Try studying a whole book of Scripture either synthetically or analytically. In the *synthetic method,* you seek a comprehensive picture that will help you see how the pieces of the puzzle fit together. Start with a short book and read it several times. Record the principles you find and create a title for each paragraph in the book. Finally, write a paragraph to summarize the main theme of the book. Show how each of the book's paragraphs contributes to the development of this theme. In the *inductive* or *analytical method,* you focus on the details and particulars of a passage and employ a more in-depth analysis of the Word. Start with a single paragraph and read it several times. As you read and reflect on your paragraph, engage in observation, interpretation, correlation, and application. In *observation,* you ask basic questions of the text, look for key words, phrases, and verses, find connecting words and progressions of thought, and discover contrasts and comparisons. In *interpretation,* you seek to understand the things you have observed to discern the meaning and purpose that the author had in mind. In *correlation,* you relate the passage you are studying to the overall context and coordinate it with other sections of Scripture. In *application,* you derive specific principles from what you have learned and seek to implement them in your life.

- The *topical method* of Bible study helps you discover the development of a theme through the pages of Scripture. Choose a specific topic and decide whether you wish to trace it from Genesis to Revelation or limit yourself to its use in a section or book of the Bible or in a series of selected verses. You may want to choose a theme such as sin, redemption, forgiveness, love, or wisdom. Or you may study a concept such as speech, the family, stewardship, or work. Use a concordance (*Nave's Topical Bible* is also helpful) to find the passages you will work with. Make your observations, ask questions, look for answers, and then formulate an outline of the topic to organize your key thoughts. Check and supplement your results by using a Bible encyclopedia. Summarize your findings, and be sure to end with a set of specific applications.

- The *biographical method* involves a study of the failures and successes of Bible personalities. This is an excellent way to uncover spiritual principles and discover insights into the way God works in people's lives. If the person you want to study is a major figure in Scripture, you may want to confine your study to a particular book or a portion of his or her life. Use a concordance to find the relevant passages. As you work with these verses, create a list of the events in the person's life and then arrange them in a chronological sequence. Use this list to develop a biographical outline with the associated verses. With this outline, move through the character's life and make a set of observations, interpretations, and applications.

The discipline of study is not limited to the Bible but extends to the classics of the faith (St. Augustine, *Confessions*; Bernard of Clairvaux, *On the Love of God*; Thomas à Kempis, *The Imitation of Christ*; John Calvin, *Institutes of the Christian Religion*; St. Francis de Sales, *Introduction to the Devout Life*; Blaise Pascal, *Pensées*; John Bunyan, *Pilgrim's Progress*; François Fénelon, *Christian Perfection*; William Law, *A Serious Call to a Devout and Holy Life*, to name just a few) as well as contemporary writers and teachers. Study can also relate to a growing knowledge and appreciation of the wonders of creation as well as an awareness of the benefits and dangers of our culture.

It is well to sustain an attitude of humility and teachability so that you will always have the mindset of a learner. In this way, you will remain fresh and alive to new perspectives and insights and resist the encroaching disease of hardening of the categories.

The Discipline of Meditation

It is impossible to think about nothing. Try it, and you will be aware of yourself trying to be aware of nothing—a zoo of images and thoughts will run through your mind in spite of your efforts to squelch them. When you ask someone what she is thinking about and she responds, "Oh, nothing," you know this cannot be so. Since the mind does not shut off, the issue is not whether we will think or even meditate; it is what we will think about and where we will direct our thoughts.

Listen to this old proverb:

Sow a thought, reap an act;
Sow an act, reap a habit;
Sow a habit, reap a character;
Sow a character, reap a destiny.

Whether we like it or not, we are always sowing thoughts, since our minds are constantly dwelling on something. The experience of discursive meditation is universal, but the practice of directed meditation is rare. The discipline comes in the effort to deliberately choose that upon which we will set our minds and in the skill of gently returning to it when we find that we have wandered.

As the saints in previous centuries have attested, meditation is an integral component of Christian spirituality, and yet it has fallen into disuse in our time. Many believers have become suspicious of the idea; they think it refers only to the consciousness-voiding techniques of Buddhism, Hinduism, or the New Age movement. However, as the psalms make clear, a biblical approach to meditation does not empty one's consciousness but fills it with the truths of God's revealed Word. To meditate on Scripture and on the person and works of God is to take nourishment for our souls by extending our roots more deeply into holy ground. The more we take root downward, the more we will bear fruit upward (Isaiah 37:31). As we focus our minds, affections, and wills on the Lord and on his words (Joshua 1:8; Psalm 1:2–3; John 6:63), we commune with him and manifest the fruit of his abundant life (John 15:4–8).

The apostle Paul underscored the importance of the believer's thought life when he instructed the Colossians to set their minds on the things above, not on the things that are on earth (Colossians 3:1–2). "For those who are according to the flesh set their minds on the things of the flesh, but those who are according to the Spirit, the things of the Spirit" (Romans 8:5). Similarly, the apostle exhorted the Philippians to engage in a biblical form of positive thinking: "Finally, brethren, whatever is true, whatever is honorable, whatever is right, whatever is pure, whatever is lovely, whatever is of good repute, if there is any excellence and if anything worthy of praise, dwell on these things" (Philippians 4:8). This is not an easy practice; it is far easier to dwell on thoughts that are untrue, dishonorable, wrong, impure, and ugly, and on things that are of bad repute, shoddy, and worthy of blame. Gossip and criticism are often more appealing in conversation about others than commendation and praise. In addition, we are more likely to view our circumstances in terms of the benefits we lack rather than the blessings we have received, and this is why our prayers are high on petition and low on thanksgiving. (If you don't believe this, try offering nothing but prayers of thanksgiving for twenty minutes, and see how often you have the impulse to slip in prayers of request.) Remember that the heart will make room for that upon which it dwells.

Some suggestions will assist you in this life-giving discipline.

- Choose brief passages from Scripture that are meaningful to you. One or two verses can become the theme of one day's meditation.
- Select specific times for brief interludes of meditation on the text you have chosen for the day. These times could be before meals and coffee breaks, or you could use a watch with an alarm to remind you at regular intervals through the day (when the alarm sounds, immediately set it for the next brief meditation break).

- Use your imagination and begin to visualize the concepts in the text in as many ways as you can. Put yourself into the words and into the historical context of the verse.
- Ponder each word and phrase of the text and try to gain as many insights as you can. Creatively approach it from different angles, and ask the Spirit of God to minister to you through this process.
- Personalize the passage by putting it in the first person and praying it back to God. Commit yourself to pursue and apply the truths you have found in it.
- Offer praise and worship to God on the basis of your day's meditation.
- Jim Downing in *Meditation* suggests a plan that involves the daily reading of every thirtieth psalm, the first corresponding to the day of the month. Five minutes before going to bed, read through the next day's psalms until you find a verse that particularly speaks to you. Then close your Bible, and be sure to make that your last waking thought. If you wake up during the night, think about the verse. In the morning, read through the five psalms with your verse in mind and let it be the theme of your meditation that day.
- Meditation directs the conscious mind during the day and is an excellent way to practice the presence of God. The H.W.L.W. habit—His Word the Last Word before retiring—programs the subconscious mind during the night (Psalm 63:6; Proverbs 6:22).
- The only way you will develop skill in meditation is by doing it, even when it does not seem to be effective.

The Discipline of Prayer

The concept of communicating with God, of talking directly and openly with him just as we would talk with an intimate friend, is one of the great truths of Scripture. As John Piper observed in *The Pleasures of God*, "Prayer is God's delight because it shows the reaches of our poverty and the riches of His grace." When prayer is overlooked or appended as an afterthought to service, the power of God is often absent. It is dangerously easy to move away from dependence upon God and to slip into the trap of self-reliance. But prayer and action are complementary, not contradictory, and it is wise to overlap them as much as possible. Christian service is most effective when prayer not only precedes it but also flows together with it.

Why Should We Pray?

There are many reasons for making this discipline the centerpiece of your spiritual journey. Here are ten:

1. Prayer enhances our fellowship and intimacy with God (Psalm 116:1–2; Jeremiah 33:2–3).
2. The Scriptures command us to pray (Luke 18:1; Ephesians 6:18; 1 Thessalonians 5:16–18; 1 Timothy 2:1).
3. When we pray, we follow the example of Christ and other great people in Scripture like Moses and Elijah (Mark 1:35; Numbers 11:2; 1 Kings 18:36–37).
4. Prayer appropriates God's power for our lives (John 15:5; Acts 4:31; Ephesians 3:16; Colossians 4:2–4).
5. We receive special help from God when we pray (Hebrews 4:16).
6. Prayer makes a genuine difference (Luke 11:9–10; James 5:16–18). As William Temple observed, "When I pray, coincidences happen; when I don't, they don't."
7. Prayer develops our understanding and knowledge of God (Psalm 37:3–6; 63:1–8; Ephesians 1:16–19).
8. Our prayers and God's answers give us joy and peace in our hearts (John 16:23–24; Philippians 4:6–7). Our problems may not disappear, but in prayer we gain a new perspective on our problems along with the peace and patience to stand firm.
9. Prayer helps us understand and accomplish God's purposes for our lives (Colossians 1:9–11).
10. Prayer changes our attitudes and desires (2 Corinthians 12:7–9).

Suggestions for Enhancing Your Practice of Prayer

Choose the best time. Select a particular time of the day, and dedicate it only to personal prayer. For most of us, the morning is best, because we have been refreshed by the previous night's rest and we are not yet absorbed in the demands of the day. This is often the time we can most consistently keep, and during morning prayer we can dedicate the day to the Lord. It is extremely wise to bring him into our decision-making process by thinking through and planning the day's activities in prayer. "If God is not first in our thoughts and efforts in the morning, he will be in the last place the remainder of the day" (E. M. Bounds).

Choose the best place. Select a place where there will be a minimum of interruptions and distractions. If possible, pray away from your phone and your desk. When the weather and your schedule permit, you may want to try praying during a walk.

Set a minimum time for daily prayer. Try to be realistic—don't attempt too much at first, or your prayer life will become mechanical and discouraging. Start with a few minutes and gradually build from there. Faithfulness on this level will lead to an increased appetite, and you will look forward to the times you spend with God. "In prayer, quality is always better than quantity" (Robert Coleman). Nevertheless, quality should not become a substitute for quantity. "Surely the experience of all good men confirms the proposition that without a due measure of private devotions the soul will grow lean" (William Wilberforce).

Be consistent. Regard your prayer time as a daily appointment you have made with God and respect it as such. If the discipline of regular time with God is not a matter of the highest priority, your spiritual life will suffer, and this will ultimately affect every other aspect of your life. Set your heart to pursue the person, knowledge, and ways of God by spending regular time with him.

Focus on the person of God. Prepare your heart and mind for prayer by releasing all stresses and concerns and giving them to the Lord. It is a good practice to read or meditate upon a passage of Scripture and then to concentrate your attention on the presence of Christ in your life. Rest in his presence, "casting all your anxiety on Him, because He cares for you" (1 Peter 5:7).

Come before him in humility. You are in the unmediated presence of the holy God who is like a blazing light and a consuming fire, before whom all things are manifest. Judge yourself to be sure that you are approaching him in honesty and openness, with no barriers of unconfessed sin, because he hates sin and cover-ups. Sometimes we get too casual before the One who spoke the hundreds of billions of galaxies into existence.

Come expectantly to the throne. The significance of prayer is not what we are asking but the Person we are addressing. Come in simplicity and trust like a child to a father. Expect the supernatural—ask him for something only he can do ("Is anything too difficult for the LORD?" [Genesis 18:14]) and watch what happens.

Pray at all times in the Spirit. "We do not know how to pray as we should, but the Spirit Himself intercedes for us with groanings too deep for words" (Romans 8:26). Our prayers should be initiated and energized by the Holy Spirit, who "intercedes for the saints according to the will of God" (Romans 8:27).

Strive for a balanced diet. Our prayers should incorporate all the elements of confession, adoration, supplication (intercession and petition), and thanksgiving. We are usually short on adoration and thanksgiving.

Pray Scripture back to God. By personalizing passages of Scripture and offering them back to the Lord, you integrate them in your life and experience and think God's thoughts after him. (My *Handbook to Prayer* and *Handbook to Renewal* are designed to guide you through this process.)

Do not do all the talking. Practice times of silence before the Lord so that you can be sensitive to the promptings of his Spirit. Be responsive to him by confessing any areas of exposed sin, interceding for others, praying for wisdom, and submitting to his desires.

Make prayer a part of your relationships with people. Personal prayer is crucial, but it must not crowd out corporate prayer. Prayer should be a part of the home and part of Christian friendships. Great benefit can be derived from setting up a prayer partnership with another person, a prayer cell with a few people, a prayer fellowship with several people, or a prayer group in the church.

Plan special times of prayer during the year. You may want to consider setting aside one or more special times (a morning or an evening or a whole day) for a personal or small-group prayer retreat. This can be especially meaningful when it is done in the context of planning for the next several months or when a critical decision must be made.

Practice the presence of God. Helmut Thielicke noted that "prayer is no longer the active soil of our life, our home, the air we breathe." We should desire not only to have one or more times that are formally dedicated to prayer during the day but also to be conscious of the presence of God throughout the day. In this way, each task is rendered in his name and done in conscious dependence upon him. When ministry becomes a substitute for prayer, it becomes self-dependent and ineffective.

Another desirable habit we should seek to cultivate is to pray for others as we see them and talk with them. This can radically affect our attitudes and behavior. A third beneficial habit is to begin to associate our work with prayer. "It is not prayer in addition to work, but prayer simultaneous with work. We precede, enfold, and follow all our work with prayer. Prayer and action become wedded" (Richard Foster).

Lectio Divina

The ancient art of **lectio divina**, or sacred reading, was introduced to the West by the Eastern desert father John Cassian early in the fifth century. It has been practiced for centuries by Cistercian monks (e.g., Michael Casey, *Sacred Reading* and *Toward God*) and is being rediscovered in wider parts of the Christian community. This extraordinarily beneficial approach combines the disciplines of study, prayer, and meditation into a powerful method that, when it is consistently applied, can revolutionize one's spiritual life. Sacred reading consists of four elements.

1. *Lectio (reading).* Select a very short text and ingest it by reading it several times. I normally choose a verse or a brief passage from the chapters I read from the Old and New Testaments in my morning Bible reading.
2. *Meditatio (meditation).* Take a few minutes to reflect on the words and phrases in the text you have read. Ponder the passage by asking questions and using your imagination.
3. *Oratio (prayer).* Having internalized the passage, offer it back to God in the form of personalized prayer.

4. *Contemplatio (contemplation).* For most of us, this will be the most difficult part, since it consists of silence and yieldedness in the presence of God. **Contemplation** is the fruit of the dialogue of the first three elements; it is the communion that is born out of our reception of divine truth in our minds and hearts.

In spite of a multitude of inner distractions and times when God seems silent, practice and perseverance in *lectio divina* is profoundly rewarding. We will discuss this method at greater length in the section on devotional spirituality.

Any of the disciplines mentioned in this section can contribute to our spiritual training, especially as they become habits in the way we order our lives.

QUESTIONS FOR PERSONAL APPLICATION

- Are you more drawn to the disciplines of abstinence or to the disciplines of engagement? What does this tell you about your temperament? (Also see appendix A.)
- As you read the brief descriptions of twenty spiritual disciplines, which ones were the most attractive to you, and which were the least attractive? Rank them from 1 to 20, with 1 being the most attractive. Now look at your list of disciplines 16–20. What would it take to pursue one of them for the next month, and how could you benefit from such a pursuit?
- As we focused on the disciplines of solitude, silence, study, meditation, and prayer, which of these seem the most remote to you? How can you combine some of these disciplines in your times with God?

EXCHANGED LIFE SPIRITUALITY

Grasping Our True Identity in Christ

The nineteenth and twentieth centuries saw the growth of an experiential approach to the spiritual life that is based on the believer's new identity in Christ. Identification with Christ in his crucifixion and resurrection (Romans 6; Galatians 2:20) means that our old life has been exchanged for the life of Christ. This approach to spirituality moves from a works to a grace orientation and from legalism to liberty because it centers on our acknowledgment that Christ's life is our life.

8

EXCHANGED
LIFE
SPIRITUALITY
Grasping Our True Identity in Christ

CHAPTER OVERVIEW

Exchanged life spirituality concentrates on the reality of a new identity through the in-Christ relationship that can dramatically transform us as we progressively grasp it in our experience. It stresses that the spiritual life is not a matter of trying to do things for Jesus but of claiming and resting in what he has already done for us. This chapter sets the stage for this issue of identity by considering our God-given needs for love and acceptance, significance and identity, and competence and fulfillment.

CHAPTER OBJECTIVES

- A clearer sense of the principles involved in exchanged life spirituality
- An appreciation for God's character and his loving plan that flows out of his character
- An understanding of our God-created needs for love and acceptance, significance and identity, and competence and fulfillment

The nineteenth and twentieth centuries saw the growth of an experiential approach to the spiritual life that is based on the believer's new identity in Christ. Identification with Christ in his crucifixion and resurrection (Romans 6; Galatians 2:20) means that our old life has been exchanged for the life of Christ. This approach to spirituality moves from a works to a grace orientation and from legalism to liberty because it centers on our acknowledgment that Christ's life is our life.

When I was in seminary, I took a memorable course taught by Howard Hendricks on the spiritual life. In the first half of the course, he constructed a series of contrasts and emphasized that the spiritual life is not:

a crisis but a continual process
based on knowledge but on obedience
external but internal
automatic but cultivated
the product of energy but of divine enablement
a dream but a discipline
an unusual experience but a normal experience
a list of rules but a life relationship
to be endured but enjoyed
theoretical but intensely practical

In the second half of the course, Hendricks defined and developed the spiritual life as "the life of Christ reproduced in the believer by the power of the Holy Spirit in obedient response to the Word of God." The personal and experiential apprehension of "the life of Christ reproduced in the believer by the power of the Holy Spirit" is central to what writers like Hudson Taylor, F. B. Meyer, and Charles Solomon have called the exchanged life. Others have called it the abiding life (Andrew Murray), the victorious life (Charles Trumbell and Bill Gillham), the highest life (Oswald Chambers), life on the highest plane (Ruth Paxon), the normal Christian life (Watchman Nee), the fullness of Christ (Stuart Briscoe), the saving life of Christ (Ian Thomas), the overflowing life (F. R. Havergal), the Christian's secret to a happy life (Hannah Whitall Smith), the larger life (A. B. Simpson), and victory over the darkness (Neil T. Anderson).

Exchanged life spirituality concentrates on the reality of a new identity through the in-Christ relationship that can dramatically transform us as we progressively grasp it in our experience. This approach to the spiritual life commonly stresses a number of principles:

- The substitution of Christ's life for the self-life. Those who are in Christ have "laid aside the old self with its evil practices" (Colossians 3:9; Ephesians 4:22) and "have put on the new self who is being renewed to a true knowledge according to the image of the One who created him" (Colossians 3:10). This new self "has been created in righteousness and holiness of the truth" (Ephesians 4:24).
- Our identification with Christ in his crucifixion, burial, resurrection, and ascension (Romans 6:2–11; Galatians 2:20; Ephesians 2:5–6; Philippians 1:21; Colossians 3:1–4). The list of affirmations in chapter 2 illustrates the multifaceted nature of our new identity in Christ. Exchanged life spirituality stresses the in-Christ relationship and the importance of experiencing and expressing his life in us.
- Our freedom from the law of sin and of death through the Spirit of life in Christ Jesus (Romans 8:2). The key to our freedom from the power of sin is

our co-crucifixion with Christ and the indwelling power of the Spirit. We are no longer under law but under grace (Romans 6:14).

- We must know these truths, acknowledge them by faith to be true regardless of feelings to the contrary, and present ourselves to God as people who are alive from the dead (Romans 6:6–13). Although we may not feel this way, Scripture declares that in Christ, we have already become saints, children of light, and citizens of heaven (1 Corinthians 1:2; Ephesians 5:8; Philippians 3:20).

- The basis of our salvation is also the basis of our sanctification (Galatians 3:2–3; 5:5; Colossians 2:6). Just as we were justified by grace through faith, so we are sanctified by grace through faith. Good works are not attained by dependence on our own fleshly efforts, achievements, or merits; instead, they flow from the power of the Spirit of Christ who indwells us (Galatians 5:16–25).

- Brokenness, or realizing the bankruptcy of our own resources and efforts, and unconditional surrender are part of the process of appropriating Christ as life (Romans 7:14–25; 12:1–2; 2 Corinthians 12:9–10; Galatians 5:24).

- Only Christ himself can live the Christian life, and he does this in us and through us (John 15:1–8; cf. 2 Corinthians 2:14). As branches of the true vine, we do not create life, but we receive it through our connection with the vine. The new life that flows in and through us is displayed in the fruit we bear, and this fruit not only nourishes others but also contains the seeds of its own reproduction. This life is sustained by receiving and abiding as branches in Christ the vine.

- It requires "a spirit of wisdom and of revelation in the knowledge of Him" for us to move from a cognitive to a personal and experiential knowledge of these spiritual truths (Ephesians 1:17–19; Colossians 1:9). The eyes of our hearts must be enlightened in order for us to grasp the nature of our new calling, inheritance, and power (Ephesians 1:18–19).

- The spiritual life is an inside-out rather than an outside-in process (Ephesians 3:16–19). The Father strengthens us "with power through His Spirit in the inner man" (Ephesians 3:16). In this way, sanctification is a divine-human dynamic in which our outworking ("work out your salvation with fear and trembling" [Philippians 2:12]) is an expression of God's inworking ("for it is God who is at work in you, both to will and to work for His good pleasure" [Philippians 2:13]).

- The exchanged life is not a matter of trying to do things for Jesus but of claiming and resting in what he has already done for us (Galatians 2:20). The new nature we possess in him is now our deepest identity, and the practice of sin is incompatible with the new creations we have become as children of God (2 Corinthians 5:17; 1 John 2:1–2; 3:1–10). While we are in this body, we will experience the pull of the old beliefs, attitudes, and dispositions, but we must see ourselves as new people, adopted into God's family, who need not yield to the lures of the flesh (Romans 8:12–17).

The insights and benefits of exchanged life spirituality are sometimes obscured by erroneous theology. Proponents of this approach have been known to slip into the errors of perfectionism (we no longer sin, or repentance for sin is unnecessary) and passivity (the Christian life is all of Jesus and none of me, so I should let go and let God). Some exchanged life teachers have also slipped into a form of experiential gnosticism, teaching that when people come to apprehend the Cross and their identity in Christ, everything is suddenly different and permanent victory is theirs. Some people may experience a dramatic realization of their union with Christ and get off the treadmill of performance-based acceptance, but others may come to understand these identity truths in more gradual ways. The spiritual life should not be reduced to a sudden experience or series of experiences, as meaningful as these may be. Spirituality also involves a process of transformation in which we are progressively conformed to the image of Christ in our character and conduct.

This section will glean the strengths of exchanged life teaching and seek to offer a balanced perspective that sees these truths as valuable contributions to a wider approach to the spiritual life.

Before doing this, however, we will look at God's character and plan, the needs he has built into us, and our response to his plan to satisfy our needs through our new position as members of a spiritual family, a spiritual body, and a spiritual temple.

GOD'S CHARACTER AND PLAN

People without a relationship with their personal Creator are hungering for love, happiness, meaning, and fulfillment, but nothing that this planet offers can fully satisfy these longings. In theory, Christians acknowledge that God alone can meet these needs, but in practice many believers hardly differ from unbelievers in the ways they try to have their needs met. This is because they have missed one of the most important principles of Scripture: love, joy, and peace cannot be obtained by pursuing these things as ends in themselves; they are the overflow and the by-product of the pursuit of God.

Moses prayed in the wilderness, "Let me know Your ways that I may know You, so that I may find favor in Your sight," and God responded, "My presence shall go with you, and I will give you rest" (Exodus 33:13–14). Like Moses, we should pray to know God and his ways. By putting him first, everything else falls into place.

In our quest for greater knowledge and spiritual growth, we sometimes overlook or forget the foundational truths of the faith. Unless we remember to return and build upon the basic biblical doctrines, our spiritual progress will be stifled. The most basic of all these truths is the character of God, and in this holy ground the Christian life is rooted.

God's character is fundamental to everything else. In Scripture he has revealed his person, powers, and perfections. In his person, he is the self-existent, infinite, eternal, and unchanging Creator of all things. In his powers, he alone is omnipresent, omnipotent, and omniscient. In his perfections, his attributes include holiness, justice, truthfulness, love, and goodness. We cannot hope to understand the spiritual life unless we lay hold of and cling to the truth of God's character, especially his love and goodness.

God's *love* is manifested in the fact that he is a giver. From the beginning, he has given in spite of the fact that people have rejected his gifts more than received them. The essence of love is to give and to seek the highest good of the recipient.

> For God so *loved* the world, that He *gave* His only begotten Son, that whoever believes in Him should not perish, but have eternal life.
>
> *John 3:16 (emphasis added)*

> Husbands, *love* your wives, just as Christ also loved the church and *gave* Himself up for her.
>
> *Ephesians 5:25 (emphasis added)*

If we want to understand what God has done for us, we must believe that all his actions are born out of love. When God loves, he is simply being himself (1 John 4:8).

God's *goodness* is manifested in his plan of bringing salvation upon the earth and in his ultimate intention for humanity. In the ages to come, his desire is to "show the surpassing riches of His grace in kindness toward us in Christ Jesus" (Ephesians 2:7). He wants to be kind to us forever, and he is committed to our joy. God always acts for our benefit—he initiates redemption, blessings, beauty, and purpose in life. Scripture portrays the relationship he wants with us in terms of a shepherd and his sheep, a father and his children, and a husband and his wife.

However, sheep can go astray, children can rebel, and a wife can be unfaithful. This rebellion and rejection of God's love and goodness have led to the problem of evil and suffering. All of us live in a world of pain, injustice, disease, and death, and in the midst of this it is easy to blame God for our problems. But our environment has been distorted by sin, and sin is that which is contrary to the character of God. Christ entered into our environment of natural and moral evil in order to overcome sin and death. "For God did not send the Son into the world to judge the world, but that the world might be saved through Him" (John 3:17). If we want to understand God and his goodness, we must cling to his character in the face of life's pain:

> The LORD is gracious and merciful;
> Slow to anger and great in *lovingkindness*.
> The LORD is *good* to all,
> And His mercies are over all His works.
>
> *Psalm 145:8–9 (emphasis added)*

The better we grasp the love and goodness of God's character, the less we will be tempted to think that he is carrying out his plans at our expense. It is always to our advantage to conform to his will, because it leads to our highest good. Obedience to God produces joy and fulfillment; disobedience produces sorrow and frustration. There is greater pain in disobedience than in faithfulness. Everything God asks of us is for our good; everything he asks us to avoid is harmful. This is what Evelyn Underhill calls "the sanity of holiness."

Because of who he is, God can be trusted. His plan reflects his character. This plan involved innocent creatures created in his image who would continue to develop physically, intellectually, emotionally, and spiritually in such a way that they would glorify God by becoming more like him and displaying to the entire universe the beauty of his handiwork. The physical and the spiritual were perfectly integrated, and God's people were to enjoy unimpeded fellowship with him and each other.

But love always involves a choice, and God's loving and good purpose was distorted by human rebellion. Faced with the decision of whether to abide in God's life or try to create life of their own, the man and the woman sought to establish themselves as the base for their own meaning. Thus they became sinners by nature and antithetical to the character of God. Beauty was replaced by ugliness, holiness with evil, kindness with cruelty, generosity with greed, love with hate, peace with violence, security with fear, and joy with anger. The Adamic inheritance of physical and spiritual death has been passed from generation to generation, and no one is untainted by sin.

Left to ourselves, we are unable to fulfill the purpose for which we have been created. But God has not left us to ourselves—with the Fall he immediately began to put into effect a plan that would restore humanity to his ultimate intention. God is not only our Creator but also our Redeemer; in Christ he has made it possible for us to be given a new heredity. By removing us from the line of Adam and placing us in the line of Christ, he has once again placed us in a position where we will ultimately show forth his glory in our spirits, souls, and bodies. In this way, he will demonstrate through us to all creation that he is who he says he is.

OUR OLD AND NEW NATURES

Prior to the Fall, people were in harmony with God and their environment. In their innocence, they were alive to God in their spirits and enjoyed daily and direct communion with him. This fellowship was reflected in their growing and expanding minds, emotions, and wills. Their bodies were flawlessly adapted to the perfect world in which they lived; they were fully suited to the exquisite creation around them.

But because of their rebellion against God, humans and their world were radically changed. They suffered spiritual death in that their spirits were cut off from God. When their spirits died, their sin nature was born, and their minds, emotions, and wills came under the dominion of sin with all its distorting effects. Their bodies also began to deteriorate; physical maladies and death became harsh realities. Pain and evil spread, and the creation itself was corrupted (Romans 8:20–22).

Fallen people sin because they are sinful by nature. It is not that they are sinners because they commit certain sins. Without the redemptive work of Christ, we would be cut off from God without hope of restoration, because "those who are in the flesh cannot please God" (Romans 8:8). But in his love and goodness, God has provided a way to deliver us from this slavery to sin and death. When people place their trust in Christ, they become new creatures (2 Corinthians 5:17) with spirits that are fully in tune with God. "And if Christ is in you, though the body is dead because of sin, yet the spirit is alive because of righteousness" (Romans 8:10). The believer's new self is in the likeness of God and has been "created in righteousness and holiness of the truth" (Ephesians 4:24).

Unlike those who are fallen, those who are redeemed are able not to sin. As they walk in the Spirit, they please God and exhibit Christlikeness. But there is a warfare in the Christian's life between the inner self and the outer self. The inner self joyfully concurs with the law of God (Romans 7:22), but there is still a law or power of sin in the outer self (Romans 7:23). Our deepest identity as spiritual beings has been transformed, but our redemption is not yet complete. We still await the "the redemption of our body" (Romans 8:23) when we will be brought into conformity with the glory of Christ's resurrected body (Philippians 3:21). Then the inner and the outer will be perfectly integrated; we will be free from the power of sin, and our minds, emotions, and wills will be continually under the dominion of the Spirit of God. Until that time comes, we have been called to the task of allowing God to gradually conform our outer selves to the righteousness and holiness that was created in our inner selves at the moment of salvation. We cannot consistently behave in ways that are different from what we believe about ourselves. A battle rages, but we must realize that the warfare is between the new creatures we have become in Christ (2 Corinthians 5:17) and the mortal remnants of the old people we were in Adam (Romans 5:12–21).

OUR GOD-CREATED NEEDS

This conflict in the believer's life between the inner self and the outer self, this warfare between the spirit and the flesh, is most evident in the territory of our physical and psychological needs and the course we take to fulfill them. These needs are legitimate and God-implanted, and it is his intention to satisfy them and thus draw us to himself. We are inherently motivated to have our needs met, but it is extremely easy for us to be deceived into the world's thinking that they can be met in some place other than the hand of God. This can lead only to frustration, because no person, possession, or position can take the place of what God alone can do.

In addition to physical needs like food, clothing, shelter, rest, and protection from danger, we have a set of psychological needs that are related to our sense of personal worth. These have been listed in various ways, but for our purposes it will be helpful to divide them into three major categories.

Love and Acceptance

Everyone needs the security that comes from feeling unconditionally loved and accepted by at least one other individual. A person is incomplete without a sense of belonging and a belief that someone genuinely cares that he or she exists. The problem is that in our experiences, this need is at best only imperfectly met, and in many cases, almost completely unmet. Direct and indirect *appearance rejection* by parents, peers, and society leads to a sense of *insecurity* and a feeling that we must earn acceptance and love. Some people go to great lengths to pursue other people's approval (often based on physical appearance), while others try to overlook this area by compensating in one of the others.

Significance and Identity

People need a sense of personal significance and identification with someone or something greater than themselves. They need to feel that they are worthwhile and that life is meaningful. But experiences of *personhood rejection,* whether direct or indirect, threaten one's sense of personal worth and purpose for living. This can lead to feelings of *inferiority* and various attempts to earn significance, often based on status. By finding the right partner, living in the right neighborhood, driving the right car, wearing the right clothes, or having the right friends, many people try to find identity and worth. Those who do not do well in this area may try to excel in one of the others in order to minimize failure.

Competence and Fulfillment

Another universal human need is the sense of competence and fulfillment that comes from the belief that one's life has made a difference and that he or she has accomplished something that will last. This is thwarted by direct and indirect experiences of *performance rejection* that can lead to feelings of personal *inadequacy.* Many people seek to validate their worth and find fulfillment through achievement and performance. This may take the form of academic, musical, and athletic accomplishments, but it is especially prominent as the motivating factor in pursuing career success. Once again, those who do not do well in this area may seek to compensate by stressing one of the others.

Thus people generally seek to validate their personal worth through appearance, status, and talent. Carried far enough, efforts to find love and acceptance lead to sensuality and immorality; efforts to find significance and identity lead to materialism and greed; and efforts to find competence and fulfillment lead to excessive competition and aggression. In extreme cases, these can lead in turn to perversion, theft, and violence.

It is deceptive to turn to people, things, and circumstances to meet our needs, because none of these can fully satisfy them. Yet many believers frequently fall into this trap, sometimes applying a Christian veneer over the same futile process used by non-Christians. God has set eternity in our heart (Ecclesiastes 3:11), and he alone can fill the void. This is not to say that it is wrong to be concerned about our appearance, our possessions, or our accomplishments. Whatever we do as "ambassadors for Christ" (2 Corinthians 5:20) should be characterized by excellence, because it is done to the glory of God (1 Corinthians 10:31; Colossians 3:23). But if our joy and peace depend upon how we look, what we own, or how well we perform, we are looking not to the Creator but rather to the creation to meet our God-given needs.

In the next chapter we will look at God's plan to meet our needs and our response to God's plan.

QUESTIONS FOR PERSONAL APPLICATION

- Which of the ten principles that summarize the exchanged life make the most sense to you? Which ones seem remote or unclear? What are your initial impressions of the strengths and weaknesses of this approach to spiritual formation?
- In your own words, what is the essence of the exchanged life?
- How does God's plan flow out of and reflect his character?
- What is your understanding of the old and new natures?
- Which one of the three categories of psychological needs is the most important to you? Where do you usually turn to have this need met?

9

EXCHANGED LIFE SPIRITUALITY
God's Plan to Meet Our Needs

CHAPTER OVERVIEW

In Christ we have become members of a spiritual family, a spiritual body, and a spiritual temple, and through this new identity God can satisfy our deepest needs. The process of knowing, reckoning, and yielding ourselves to God as new people who have received the life of Christ enriches our understanding of grace-based living (Romans 6).

CHAPTER OBJECTIVES

- An appreciation of God's plan to meet our deepest needs through our participation in a spiritual family, a spiritual body, and a spiritual temple
- Encouragement to respond to God's gracious plan by knowing, reckoning, and yielding
- A better sense of what it means to have Christ's life in us
- A greater desire to avoid the sometimes subtle pulls of legalism and license by growing in liberty

---

By trusting in Christ, we are placed in a position where we will be restored to God's ultimate intention for his people. Christ *redeemed* us by paying the penalty for our sins and delivering us from the bondage of sin.

In Him we have redemption through His blood, the forgiveness of our trespasses, according to the riches of His grace.

Ephesians 1:7

For He delivered us from the domain of darkness, and transferred us to the kingdom of His beloved Son, in whom we have redemption, the forgiveness of sins.

Colossians 1:13–14

And when you were dead in your transgressions and the uncircumcision of your flesh, He made you alive together with Him, having forgiven us all our transgressions, having canceled out the certificate of debt consisting of decrees against us, which was hostile to us; and He has taken it out of the way, having nailed it to the cross.

Colossians 2:13–14

As a result of our redemption, God's holy demands have been *propitiated,* or satisfied, and we have been *justified,* or declared righteous, by the living God (Romans 3:24; Titus 3:7); Christ's righteousness has been *imputed,* or placed on our account (Romans 5:18–19; 2 Corinthians 5:21). Because the barrier of sin has been removed, we are now *reconciled* to God and have full access to him; as his adopted children we can call him "Abba! Father!" (Romans 8:15). Moreover, our old selves have been crucified with Christ, so that we have become identified with him in his death, burial, resurrection, and ascension to the right hand of the Father (Romans 6:3–11; Galatians 2:20; Ephesians 2:5–6; Colossians 3:1–4). Our former identity in Adam was put to death; our new and eternal identity in Christ became a living reality when we placed our faith in him.

Without Christ, we were out of harmony with God; life was all about self, and we were driven to use people, things, and circumstances to meet our needs. In Christ, we are in harmony with God; for us as believers, life should be all about the One who has already fully met our needs.

A SPIRITUAL FAMILY

God the Father desires to create a community of spiritual beings to whom he can reveal himself, from whom he can receive the glory, praise, and honor due his name, and with whom he can give and receive love (Ephesians 1:4–6). This desire is being realized in his plan to create a spiritual family that he can love and accept in eternal fellowship (Galatians 4:4–7; Ephesians 2:19). We are that family, and Christ is the firstborn (Colossians 1:18).

As members of God's family, our need for unconditional love and acceptance is fully met. We are secure in God's limitless love. Even when we were in rebellion against him as his enemies, he demonstrated his love toward us "in that while we were yet sinners, Christ died for us" (Romans 5:8).

For I am convinced that neither death, nor life, nor angels, nor principalities, nor things present, nor things to come, nor powers, nor height, nor depth, nor any other created thing, shall be able to separate us from the love of God, which is in Christ Jesus our Lord.

Romans 8:38–39

See how great a love the Father has bestowed upon us, that we should be called children of God; and such we are.

1 John 3:1

A SPIRITUAL BODY

God the Son desires to create a community of spiritual beings of whom he can be the head and with whom and through whom he can rule all creation (Ephesians 1:9–10, 22–23). This desire is being realized in his plan to create a spiritual body that has significance and identity as an extension of the incarnation of Christ (Ephesians 1:9–12). We are that body, and Christ is the head (Ephesians 1:22–23; Colossians 1:18).

As individual parts of Christ's body, our need for true significance and identity is fully met. We have meaning and purpose because of who we are in Christ. God did not save us according to our works "but according to His own purpose and grace which was granted us in Christ Jesus from all eternity" (2 Timothy 1:9).

But just as it is written, "Things which eye has not seen and ear has not heard, and which have not entered the heart of man, all that God has prepared for those who love Him."

1 Corinthians 2:9

Blessed be the God and Father of our Lord Jesus Christ, who according to His great mercy has caused us to be born again to a living hope through the resurrection of Jesus Christ from the dead, to obtain an inheritance which is imperishable and undefiled and will not fade away, reserved in heaven for you.

1 Peter 1:3–4

A SPIRITUAL TEMPLE

God the Holy Spirit desires to create a community of spiritual beings who will receive and reflect the likeness of God and glorify him forever (Ephesians 2:21–22). This desire is being realized in his plan to create a spiritual temple of living stones into whom he can invest his likeness and power, competent to serve and glorify him in eternal fulfillment (1 Peter 2:4–5). We are that temple, and Christ is the cornerstone (Ephesians 2:20).

As living stones in God's temple, our need for lasting competence and fulfillment is fully met. The Holy Spirit has blessed every believer with spiritual gifts, and we have been given the time, opportunities, and abilities to accomplish his purposes for us. The things we do in his power will last forever.

And for this purpose also I labor, striving according to His power, which mightily works within me.

Colossians 1:29

That He would grant you, according to the riches of His glory, to be strengthened with power through His Spirit in the inner man.

Ephesians 3:16

As an exercise, read the following verses to see how they relate to our three personal-worth needs: 1 Corinthians 1:5–9; 2 Corinthians 1:21–22; 2:14; 3:4–6; Galatians 4:4–7; Ephesians 1:6, 9–12, 18; 2:10; 3:11–12, 16–20; 5:2; 6:10–18; Philippians 2:13; Colossians 1:11, 21–22, 27; 3:3; 2 Timothy 1:7; 1 Peter 1:5.

As followers of Jesus, we must look beyond people, things, and circumstances to meet our needs. All of these are unstable and inadequate, and if we depend on them, we will fail. Moving in the direction of the flesh will not meet our needs; at best it can only provide a deceptive façade of security and significance. Instead, we must dare to believe that if everything else is taken away, our God is enough. This does not minimize the fact that there will be pain when relationships break down and when failure and rejection occur. These things are painful, but they will not destroy us when we derive our self-image from God rather than people. From an ultimate standpoint, we are loved, we are significant, and we are competent, but only in him and only in the plan to which he calls us.

Why then do so many believers continue to act as nonbelievers when it comes to the quest for security, meaning, and fulfillment in life? The answer lies in the fact that three powerful forces oppose our walking in the Spirit: the flesh, the world, and the devil (Ephesians 2:2–3).

The *flesh* is the power or "law of sin" which is in our members (Romans 7:14–25). It is not the same as the "old self," which was put to death at the cross (Romans 6:6). Although we received a new spirit when we came to Christ, we are encased in the same body with its physical needs and cravings. Nor was our soul or personality (mind, emotions, and will) instantly transformed. Old attitudes, values, habits, and actions were not eradicated but continue to surface. Our mental, emotional, and volitional processes must gradually be brought into conformity with the new person we became in Christ, but this takes time, willingness, and the work of the Holy Spirit. We have been programmed into thinking that our identity is based on what others think or what we think about ourselves rather than what God thinks about us.

This programming is largely a product of the second of the three forces, the *world*. We live in a culture that promotes values and perspectives that are totally opposed to those of the Bible. Our circumstances are so overwhelmingly real that we lose sight of who we are in Christ. Even though Scripture tells us that we are pilgrims and strangers on earth and that our citizenship is in heaven, we are prone to live as though this physical existence is the supreme reality. Unless we habitually reprogram our minds with the truths of Scripture, we will be profoundly influenced by a culture that tells us to find meaning in hedonism and materialism.

The third force that works against our spiritual life is the *devil*. Satan and his minions utilize the world and the flesh to accomplish their purpose of defeating the lives of Christians and rendering them ineffective. But Satan can oppress us only while we are controlled by the flesh. He cannot defeat the life of Christ in us.

All three of these forces wage war against the spiritual vitality of the believer, and it is essential in this warfare that we cultivate an eternal rather than a temporal perspective. Everything hinges on how we respond to God's plan to satisfy our needs for personal worth.

OUR RESPONSE TO GOD'S PLAN

In Romans 6, Paul describes a threefold process that moves from the inner to the outer person and aligns the believer with spiritual truth. It begins with *knowing* one's identity in Christ (6:3–10), progresses to *reckoning* or considering these truths to be so (6:11), and climaxes with *yielding* or presenting oneself to God (6:12–14).

Knowing

Christians often suffer from spiritual ignorance and amnesia; many believers either do not know or have forgotten who they are in Christ. As a result, their self-image is derived from the wrong source. Using a variation of Luke 9:18–20, we can ask of ourselves three fundamental questions:

> Who do you say that you are?
> Who do people say that you are?
> Who does God say that you are?

All too often, our sense of identity is based on our answers to the first two questions rather than the third. When this happens, we will unavoidably arrive at unbiblical conclusions and base our sense of personal worth on the wrong things. As believers in Christ, our identity must not be based on what people say but on what God says of us. He says that he unconditionally loves and accepts us regardless of how we feel or perform (Romans 5:8). He tells us that we have become "united with Him [Christ] in the likeness of His death" and that we will also be united with him "in the likeness of His resurrection" (Romans 6:5).

Believers know that Christ died for them, but many do not know that they also died in and with him. We must realize that "our old self was crucified with Him, in order that our body of sin might be done away with, that we would no longer be slaves to sin; for he who has died is freed from sin" (Romans 6:6–7). Through our co-crucifixion with Christ, we have died to the bondage of sin, and God has already accomplished this. We may not *feel* this is true, but we must never reason from our performance to our position; our security and significance in Christ are not threatened by earthly failure or rejection. Instead, we must base our behavior on our belief. Who we are should determine what we do, and not vice versa. Ideally, our behavior will reflect who we are, but it does not make us who we are. Our identity is based on our new birth in Christ. We have his righteousness (Philippians 3:9; 2 Corinthians 5:21), and his life is our life.

A firm understanding of our salvation (Romans 1–5) is essential to our growth in sanctification (Romans 6–8).

Reckoning

After Paul describes our identification with Christ in his death, burial, and resurrection life (Romans 6:3–10), he moves from knowing the truth to believing the truth. "Even so consider yourselves to be dead to sin, but alive to God in Christ Jesus" (Romans 6:11). We must not only learn the truth but also count it to be so. When the truth is "united by faith" in those who hear (Hebrews 4:2), believers can enjoy God's rest (Hebrews 4:3–10). But this does not happen automatically. We are told to "be diligent to enter that rest" (Hebrews 4:11) by taking hold of truths that we have not fully experienced and believing them in spite of appearances to the contrary. "Sin need have no more power over the believer than he grants it through unbelief. If he is alive unto sin it will be due largely to the fact that he has failed to reckon himself dead unto sin (Ruth Paxon)."

Reckoning is a process that is neither natural nor easy. Most writers who advocate the exchanged life agree that believers often have to come to the end of their resources before they are able to have a genuine realization of their co-crucifixion with Christ. In most cases, only when people reach the point of brokenness and surrender are they ready to turn from the self-life to the Christ-life. James McConkey observed that "faith is dependence upon God. And this God-dependence only begins when self-dependence ends. And self-dependence only comes to its end, with some of us, when sorrow, suffering, affliction, broken plans and hopes bring us to that place of self-helplessness and defeat." In the university of life, these are not courses anyone would elect to take, since they involve pain and the frightening prospect of the loss of control. (From a biblical point of view, we are abandoning the *illusion* of control, since we were never in control of our lives—we just thought we were.) But as F. B. Meyer put it, "If you are not willing, confess that you are willing to be made willing" (cf. John 7:17). When we surrender full control of our life and plans to Christ, we discover his peace. When we lose our lives for his sake, we find his life instead.

As we "fight the good fight of faith" (1 Timothy 6:12) by reckoning what God has said about our position in Christ to be true, the Holy Spirit will add assurance and make these truths more real in our experience. Thus Paul prayed in Ephesians that God would give his readers "a spirit of wisdom and of revelation in the knowledge of Him" (Ephesians 1:17).

I pray that the eyes of your heart may be enlightened, so that you may know what is the hope of His calling, what are the riches of the glory of His inheritance in the saints, and what is the surpassing greatness of His power toward us who believe.

Ephesians 1:18–19a

We should not approach the spiritual life in an academic and theoretical way. God's truth is designed not merely to inform us but also to transform us. We actually have become new creatures; we are part of a new species with a new heredity and inheritance as children of God and citizens of heaven. We have been removed from death in Adam to life in Christ. Eternal life is Christ's life, and we received his life at the time of our spiritual birth (Romans 6:4–6; 8:9; 2 Corinthians 5:14–17; Galatians 2:20; Ephesians 1:4; 2:6, 10; Colossians 1:12–14; 3:1–3; 1 John 3:1–2). Christ is not merely alongside us or in front of us; he is *in* us, and he wants to express his life *through* us. Moreover, the New Testament is even more emphatic that we are *in* him. We are in a position of victory in Christ, who is at the right hand of God (Ephesians 1:20). The Epistles do not tell us to *feel* this truth but to trust and honor God by accepting that it is so. In this way, we start with the character and promises of God and not with ourselves. This is not a matter of passivity (the let-go-and-let-God idea can be overdone) but of active choice that is energized by divine grace. Nor is this a matter of sinless perfection but of gradual growth in a context of spiritual warfare against the flesh, the world, and the devil. The flesh, which is the capacity to live life in our own power rather than in the power of the Spirit, is neither removed nor improved; we will not be rid of this propensity until we are resurrected.

Yielding

As we come to know the truth about our identification with Christ and couple it with faith by reckoning it to be true, it is important that we act upon it by presenting or yielding ourselves to God as new creatures in Christ.

Therefore do not let sin reign in your mortal body so that you obey its lusts, and do not go on presenting the members of your body to sin as instruments of unrighteousness; but present yourselves to God as those alive from the dead, and your members as instruments of righteousness to God.

Romans 6:12–13

When we are progressively transformed by the renewing of our minds (Romans 12:2) in the truths of Scripture, our thinking is brought into greater conformity with what God, not the world, says about us. We can present ourselves to God as "those alive from the dead" because we have come to know and believe that this is who we are. In the same way, our bodies can become living and holy sacrifices that are acceptable to God (Romans 12:1) as we present our members to him as "instruments of righteousness" (Romans 6:13).

If we want our spiritual lives to flourish, this threefold process of knowing, reckoning, and yielding should become a daily habit (Luke 9:23). It is easier to unlearn spiritual truth than it is to learn it. If we do not regularly reinforce this process, it will gradually slip away from us.

As we take God at his word by believing him in spite of circumstances and appearances to the contrary, we gain a divine perspective on our problems and walk more in his power and less in our own resources. The daily reckoning that we are "dead to sin but alive to God in Christ Jesus" brings us into a deeper understanding that Christ's life is now our life and his destiny is now our destiny. We have exchanged the old for the new, and in him we have love, meaning, and fulfillment.

Thus we have seen that our true identity is not in our "outer man" but in our "inner man" (2 Corinthians 4:16). We are spiritual beings who are temporarily clothed with the perishable and mortal, but the time is coming when "this perishable must put on the imperishable, and this mortal must put on immortality" (1 Corinthians 15:53). When the Lord returns, what we are outwardly will be perfectly conformed to the righteousness of Christ that has been imputed to us inwardly. Until then, we must set our minds "on the things above, not on the things that are on earth" (Colossians 3:2) and put to death the deeds of the body by walking in conscious dependence on the power of the Spirit (Romans 8:13). We are inherently motivated to have our needs met, but we must continually remind ourselves that they have already been fully met in Christ. This truth can liberate us from the bondage of selfishness and pride. It can free us from being grabbers and allow us to become givers who expect and need nothing in return. As C. S. Lewis observed at the end of *Mere Christianity*, "Your real, new self (which is Christ's and also yours, and yours just because it is His) will not come as long as you are looking for it. It will come when you are looking for Him. . . . Give up yourself, and you will find your real self. Lose your life and you will save it. . . . Keep back nothing. Nothing that you have not given away will ever be really yours. Nothing in you that has not died will ever be raised from the dead. Look for yourself, and you will find in the long run only hatred, loneliness, despair, rage, ruin, and decay. But look for Christ and you will find Him, and with Him everything else thrown in."

If we try to gratify our needs, we will experience frustration and failure. If we pursue God and hunger and thirst for him and his righteousness, we will be satisfied (Matthew 5:6) and our needs will be fulfilled. It all reduces to trust: can we trust God as a person and believe that truth is what God says it is, regardless of how we feel? This leads us back to where we began—the character of God. As we affirm the goodness and love of God, we will realize that he is not carrying out his program at our expense but for our highest good. Disobedience to him is self-destructive, while obedience to his desires is self-fulfilling. Armed with this attitude, we can say no to the pull of the flesh, the world, and Satan, and yes to Christ in what he calls us to do. When we respond to the truth in obedient action, a reciprocal process is set in motion. Just as attitude leads to action, so action creates or reinforces attitude. This is not an either-or but a both-and. Faith grows as we put it into action. When we begin to act as though Christ is manifesting his life in and through us, we are acting in accordance with biblical reality. This in turn makes these truths more real to us, which then makes them easier to act upon. At any given time, we are reinforcing either a positive or a negative cycle of attitudes and actions. This is why it is so important to renew our minds with the truths of Scripture on a regular basis and respond to them by putting them into action.

THE LIFE OF CHRIST IN US

The spiritual life is the *life of Jesus Christ* that has been reproduced in the believer. Christ's life is "resident in, reigning over, and released through the human life" (Jack R. Taylor). "I have been crucified with Christ; and it is no longer I who live, but Christ lives in me; and the life which I now live in the flesh I live by faith in the Son of God, who loved me and gave Himself up for me" (Galatians 2:20). Our hearts have become Christ's dwelling place, and this truth grows more real in our awareness and experience as we lay hold of it by faith (Ephesians 3:17). Paul reached the point where he so identified his life with Christ's life that he was able to say from a prison cell in Rome, "For to me, to live is Christ and to die is gain" (Philippians 1:21). This is the goal of the Christian life—a growing understanding of our union with Christ both in our thinking and in our practice.

Jesus summed it up in these simple but profound words in John 14:20: "you in Me, and I in you." The "you in me" refers to our relationship with Christ by virtue of our life in him. The "I in you" speaks of our fellowship with Christ by virtue of his life in us. The former relates to our position or standing; the latter relates to our practice or state. Our relationship with God is actual—it was determined by our spiritual *birth* in Christ. Our fellowship with God is potential—it is developed by our spiritual *growth* in Christ.

These spiritual truths have been well summarized:

Jesus Christ gave his life for you [salvation]
so that he could give his life to you [sanctification]
so that he could live his life through you [service]

We cannot produce biological or spiritual life; we were created to *receive* spiritual life and to display it (John 15:1–8). Nevertheless, Scripture exhorts us to "grow in the grace and knowledge of our Lord and Savior Jesus Christ" (2 Peter 3:18). This involves an ongoing process of walking in fellowship with God in obedient response to the light of his Word. Growth in our apprehension and application of our identity in Christ is not uniform. As in nature, so also in the spiritual life—there are spurts of growth followed by periods of relative dormancy. There are no experiential shortcuts on the path to maturity in Christlikeness.

> If we say that we have fellowship with Him and yet walk in the darkness, we lie and do not practice the truth; but if we walk in the Light as He Himself is in the Light, we have fellowship with one another, and the blood of Jesus His Son cleanses us from all sin.
>
> *1 John 1:6–7*

When we succumb to temptation in thought, word, or deed, we are living beneath the dignity of the new identity we have received in Christ Jesus. When the light of Scripture reveals areas of sin, we must respond to the light by confessing our sins so that we can continue to enjoy fellowship with the God of light and holiness. "If we confess our sins, He is faithful and righteous to forgive us our sins and to cleanse us from all unrighteousness" (1 John 1:9). From a biblical point of view, it is not normal for Christians to live in defeat, especially when cleansing and fellowship are so readily available. As we abide in Christ, his life in us can qualitatively affect every aspect of our earthly existence, including our family, work, thoughts, attitudes, and speech.

LEGALISM, LICENSE, AND LIBERTY

Authentic spirituality avoids the twin extremes of **legalism** and **license**. Legalism is striving in the effort of the flesh to achieve a human standard of righteousness. It is easy to be victimized by the pharasaic attitude that equates spirituality with conformity to an artificial code of behavior. Confusing the standards of Christians with Christian standards, many believers think that following a set of do's and don'ts leads to personal holiness.

Legalism emphasizes an external set of rules and prohibitions rather than the inner life in the Spirit. Because of the influence of a number of Judaizers, the Galatians were in danger of exchanging their freedom in Christ for the yoke of the law (Galatians 5:1–8). In his corrective epistle to the Galatians, Paul stressed the crucial truth that the same principle that *saves* a believer (grace through faith) also *sanctifies* a believer (see table 9.1).

> This is the only thing I want to find out from you: did you receive the Spirit by the works of the Law, or by hearing with faith? Are you so foolish? Having begun by the Spirit, are you now being perfected by the flesh?
>
> *Galatians 3:2–3*

For sin shall not be master over you, for you are not under law but under grace.

Romans 6:14

But now we have been released from the Law, having died to that by which we were bound, so that we serve in newness of the Spirit and not in oldness of the letter.

Romans 7:6

	LAW	GRACE
Says	Do	Done
Emphasizes	What we do	What God does
Lives out of	The flesh (self-life)	The Spirit (Christ-life)
Draws on	Our resources	God's resources
Deals with	External rules, regulations, standards	Inner heart attitude
Primary focus	Ought to, should, must	Want to
Creates	Bondage, duty, obligation	Freedom
Lives life from the	Outside in	Inside out
Declares	Do in order to be	You are; therefore do
Produces	Guilt and condemnation	Acceptance and security
Leads to	Defeat	Victory

TABLE 9.1

Christian growth is not achieved by outer rules or ritual but by an inner relationship. Christlikeness is developed "through the Spirit, by faith" (Galatians 5:5).

While legalism promotes a do-what-you-have-to-do mentality, license, the opposite extreme, is characterized by a do-what-you-want-to-do mentality. This stems from an attitude that takes the grace of God for granted and minimizes the consequences of sin (Romans 6:1, 15). Christians can easily get locked into the quest for pleasure, prosperity, popularity, or power. But the cost of success in these areas often entails a compromise in personal integrity and morality.

The biblical balance between the excesses of legalism and license is **liberty**. Instead of doing what we have to do or doing as we please, we have the true freedom in Christ to do as he pleases. Liberty in Christ stresses inner transformation as the key to outer manifestation. Growth in grace is accomplished by knowing and depending upon the person of God. Lack of divine blessing comes from unbelief, not from failure of devotion. "To preach devotion first, and blessing second, is to reverse God's order, and preach law, not grace. The Law made man's blessing depend on devotion; Grace confers undeserved, unconditional blessing: our devotion may follow, but does not always do so,—in proper measure" (William Newell).

OUR POSITION AND OUR PRACTICE

Only as bondslaves of Christ do we have real liberty. But freedom always entails responsibilities and consequences (Galatians 6:7–8). We must not only know the truth but also put it into practice (table 9.2).

OUR POSITION	OUR PRACTICE
Romans 1–11	Romans 12–16
Ephesians 1–3	Ephesians 4–6
Colossians 1–2	Colossians 3–4
Belief	Behavior
Who we are	What we do
Attitudes	Actions
Standing	State
Being	Becoming
Determined	Developing
Spiritual wealth	Spiritual walk
Birth in Christ	Growth in Christ
Based on Christ's death	Based on Christ's life
Our relationship with God	Our fellowship with God
By grace through faith	By grace through faith

TABLE 9.2

By position, we mean who we actually are in Christ Jesus at this moment; we do not need to wait until we see him for it to be true of us. Having entered by faith into the new life that is available in Christ, we are called as members of God's family to grow in such a way that our practice conforms more and more to our position in the heavenly places in Christ. This is the process of the spiritual life, and the basis of this process is our new identity in Christ.

Some advocates of the exchanged life have reacted so strongly to legalism and do-it-yourself spirituality that they have promoted the opposite extreme. This form of teaching overlooks the process, growth, obedience, and discipline aspects of progressive transformation, character development, and corporate nurture. Scripture often refers to these progressive dynamics of spiritual formation, and if we ignore this dimension, we are in danger of reducing the spiritual life to a form of instantaneous perfectionism that requires no change on our part.

Indeed, there is a significant difference between human efforts to do things for Jesus and inviting him to live and manifest his life through us. But when we abide in him and walk in the Spirit, is it only Christ in us—and not us at all—who is loving and serving others? Is the spiritual fruit of love, joy, peace, patience, kindness, goodness, faithfulness, gentleness, and self-control instantly created by dependence and surrender, or do these Christlike qualities also progressively develop as part of the believer's character? How do we relate the exchanged life truths to exhortations like the following in 2 Peter 1:5–8?

> Now for this very reason also, applying all diligence, in your faith supply moral excellence, and in your moral excellence, knowledge, and in your knowledge, self-control, and in your self-control, perseverance, and in your perseverance, godliness, and in your godliness, brotherly kindness, and in your brotherly kindness, love. For if these qualities are yours and are increasing, they render you neither useless nor unfruitful in the true knowledge of our Lord Jesus Christ.

We must affirm and rejoice in the truth of Christ living in and through us, but we should also avoid the passive and inert notion that we are left unchanged. Exchanged life spirituality emphasizes the powerful dynamic of abiding in Christ's life rather than creating our own, but this does not mean that we are not being gradually transformed into his image as we move through the developmental stages of spiritual infancy, childhood, adolescence, and maturity. Christ transforms us in the very process of living in and through us.

Sanctification is a divine-human process that involves both dwelling in the power of his Spirit in our inner being and the gradual formation of Christlike character and behavior. Thus we must retain the balance of dependence and discipline, of divine sovereignty and human responsibility. This is why we use the metaphor of a journey to show that while abiding and obedience keep us on the path, they do not instantly bring us to the journey's end. While exchanged life spirituality stresses the idea that abiding leads to obedience, disciplined spirituality stresses the idea that obedience leads to abiding. Both are true, but they come at the spiritual life from different angles.

Thus no single model of the spiritual life fully captures the mysterious process that mutually incorporates both the divine and the human. Exchanged life spirituality focuses on the Christ-in-us relationship ("I in you"), while some of the other facets of spirituality focus on the us-in-Christ relationship ("you in Me"). The both-and of Christ living in us and of us becoming conformed to his image needs to be sustained by affirming and living in both truths.

Christian spirituality is a mysterious divine-human synergy. When we eliminate one side or the other, we resolve the tension at the cost of biblical fidelity. The balance between the two extremes of willfullness (performance) and willessness (passivity) is willingness (participation).

If we define the concept of Christ "living through us" as the process of receiving and displaying his indwelling life, this fits well with a number of texts, including the allegory of the vine and the branches in John 15. As we abide in him and he abides in us, we are receiving his life rather than creating our own independent life. We draw our biological and spiritual life from him, but this by no means eliminates our personalities or character development. (For a biblically articulate treatment of our identification with Christ, I recommend *Birthright* by David C. Needham.)

The movement from position to practice is the most difficult aspect of the spiritual life. Other facets of spirituality (e.g., holistic and process spirituality) address the central question of how we can get our faith to work in the nitty-gritty details of everyday living, and we will consider this in the sections that follow.

QUESTIONS FOR PERSONAL APPLICATION

- What is the meaning of a spiritual family, body, and temple to you? Prayerfully meditate on the texts that are related to each so that these biblical images will resonate more deeply in your inner being.
- To what extent do you identify with Paul's struggle with the flesh in Romans 7:14–25? How do you relate this conflict to the truths in Romans 6 and 8?
- What has been your experience with the dynamic of knowing, reckoning, and yielding (Romans 6)?
- What is your understanding of "you in Me, and I in you" (John 14:20)?
- In your practice, do you sometimes find yourself drawn to law-based living more than grace-based living? What effect does this have on your relationships with God and others?

F A C E T   5

M O T I V A T E D
S P I R I T U A L I T Y

A Set of Biblical Incentives

People are motivated to satisfy their needs for security, significance, and satisfaction, but they turn to the wrong places to have their needs met. This section presents the option of looking to Christ rather than the world to meet our needs. A study of Scripture reveals a number of biblical motivators: these include fear, love and gratitude, rewards, identity, purpose and hope, and longing for God. Our task is to be more motivated by the things God declares to be important than by the things the world says are important.

10

MOTIVATED SPIRITUALITY
Why Do We Do What We Do?

CHAPTER OVERVIEW

Just as a variety of temporal things can motivate our actions, there are also several biblical incentives that can encourage us to persevere in the quest to be conformed to the image of Christ. In difficult times, the realization that there are no other options can cause us to cling to the Lord. A second **motivator** is the **fear of the Lord**, which involves a holy fear of his displeasure.

CHAPTER OBJECTIVES

- An awareness that as followers of Christ, we can be drawn to both temporal and biblical incentives
- The realization that there are difficult times when a lack of other options may be the only thing that keeps us anchored to obedience
- An appreciation of the critical import of the fear of the Lord in our thinking and practice

What motivates people to behave the way they do? Why do we sometimes avoid evil and at other times choose it? Or from another perspective, why do we do the right thing on some occasions and fail to do it on others?

People are motivated to satisfy their needs for security, significance, and fulfillment, but they turn to the wrong places to have their needs met. This chapter will present the option of looking to Christ rather than the world to meet our needs. Our task is to be more motivated by the things God declares to be important than by the things the world says are important.

Because believers have a new nature and are indwelled by the Spirit of God, they have more options than do unbelievers. They can choose to walk by the Spirit and do things that are pleasing to God, whereas those who do not know Christ cannot please

God, since even their good deeds are tainted by the fallen nature. "The heart is more deceitful than all else and is desperately sick; who can understand it?" (Jeremiah 17:9). "For all of us have become like one who is unclean, and all our righteous deeds are like a filthy garment" (Isaiah 64:6). "They turn, but not upward, they are like a deceitful bow" (Hosea 7:16). "For from within, out of the heart of men, proceed the evil thoughts, fornications, thefts, murders, adulteries, deeds of coveting and wickedness, as well as deceit, sensuality, envy, slander, pride and foolishness. All these evil things proceed from within and defile the man" (Mark 7:21–23).

VERTICAL AND HORIZONTAL MOTIVATORS

The Bible tells us that the problem with the human condition is internal and that the only solution is a changed heart. The transformation available through the new birth in Christ is wrought from the inside out, so that in Christ we become new creatures. Nevertheless, while we are in this body and in this world, believers are susceptible to the same influences that exert a pull on unbelievers. Worldly or temporal motivators include fear of loss, guilt, pride, hope of personal gain, reputation, prestige, and pleasure. These are "horizontal" motivators, since they are related to the short-term dynamics of the visible and the now. Biblical motivators, however, are more "vertical," since they relate to the long-term dynamics of the invisible and the not yet. It is not surprising, then, that believers find it easier to be prompted by the former than by the latter. Even when our actions are based upon thinking rather than emotions, it is natural for our thinking to be shaped by a temporal and human perspective. It is only as we yield ourselves to the lordship of Christ and renew our minds with spiritual truth that our thought life will be shaped by an eternal and godly perspective.

At first the biblical motivators seem remote and external, but as we press on in the process of spiritual maturity and growth in Christ, they become more real and internal. But this is a gradual process, and it is never completed in this brief earthly sojourn. While we are in this world we will never arrive at a perfect motivational structure; instead, we will find ourselves pulled by the natural and the spiritual. This is why it is important to avoid the paralysis of analysis—if we waited until we had perfect and unalloyed motives before we acted, we would be unable to do anything.

At this point, I have distinguished seven motivators in Scripture, but it would be easy to argue that some should be combined or that others should be added. Nonetheless, we will discuss these motivators in view of their implications for our lives:

No other options. When we come to Christ, we effectively admit the inadequacy of every other approach to life. Although this is a negative motivator, it can have real power in times of doubt and pain.

Fear. This can be both negative (fear of consequences) and positive (fear of God).

Love and gratitude. This is a frequently cited positive motivator.

Rewards. Scripture talks much more about rewards as incentives for faithfulness and obedience than we might have supposed.

Our identity in Christ. This should have profound implications for our behavior.

Purpose and hope. It is important for us to cultivate a biblical purpose for living and a hope that is founded on the character of God.

Longing for God. The vision of God has been a recurring theme in devotional literature, although it is not as common in the Christian literature of our time.

These seven biblical realities can keep us walking with Christ in the context of life's ambiguities and uncertainties. Some of these realities may be relevant at certain times and uncompelling at others. In some situations, we may be prompted by more than one of them, and in other situations we may act without being consciously aware of any of them. Our actions, even when they are related to areas of ministry, are often based on an alloy of temporal and biblical motivations.

By looking at the list, you can see that these motivators relate to different stages and aspects of the spiritual journey and that some may seem to be more accessible than others. For instance, we may be able to identify more with love and gratitude than with longing for God. But remember that they are all facets of the same gem, since they are integrated in the character and promises of the living God. In a sense, they are components of a single passion—a concern for one thing above all else, the one thing most needed (Luke 10:41–42). When we are not propelled and impelled by one ultimate attraction, we are pulled by multiple desires. The worries of the world, the deceitfulness of riches, and the desires for other things (Mark 4:19) can choke the word in our lives and prevent us from bearing lasting fruit. When we turn from the lures of the world to the person of Christ, we discover "the magnet that draws, the anchor that steadies, the fortress that defends, the light that illumines, the treasure that enriches, the law that commands and the power that enables" (Alexander Maclaren).

In this chapter we will look at the first two of these seven motivators—no other options and the fear of the Lord.

NO OTHER OPTIONS

The first of these biblical motivators is actually negative, but there are times when it can become the only thing that keeps us anchored to the process of obedience. This reality is best illustrated in the aftermath of Jesus' controversial discourse on the bread of life in the sixth chapter of the gospel of John. When the Lord said, "I am the living bread that came down out of heaven; if anyone eats of this bread, he shall live forever; and the bread also which I shall give for the life of the world is My flesh" (v. 51), his audience was repulsed by the thought of cannibalism. Their sense of revulsion increased when

Jesus added, "He who eats My flesh and drinks My blood has eternal life, and I will raise him up on the last day. For My flesh is true food, and My blood is true drink. He who eats My flesh and drinks My blood abides in Me, and I in him" (vv. 54–56).

These mysterious words caused many of Jesus' disciples to stumble, and they began to argue with one another. John goes on to say that "as a result of this many of His disciples withdrew and were not walking with Him anymore. So Jesus said to the twelve, 'You do not want to go away also, do you?' Simon Peter answered Him, 'Lord, to whom shall we go? You have words of eternal life. We have believed and have come to know that You are the Holy One of God'" (John 6:66–69).

I doubt that Peter had a clearer understanding of Jesus' difficult statements than did the many disciples who withdrew from him. The difference is that while the disciples who left were simply curious or even convinced, Peter and the other disciples who continued to walk with Jesus were committed. Their commitment to the Lord extended beyond their mental grasp, because they had learned to trust him even when they could not understand him. But Peter and the others who stayed with Jesus understood this much: when they committed their lives to him, there was no turning back. They realized that nothing else in this world would do and that there was nowhere else they could go.

In the same way, when we give our lives to Christ, we acknowledge the same thing. To come to him means to abandon every alternative and to admit the bankruptcy of all other approaches to meaning, value, and purpose in life.

In a universe without God, there is no source of ultimate *meaning*. As I discuss in *I'm Glad You Asked*, the universe is expanding, and left to itself, the galaxies will grow farther apart and the stars will eventually burn out. All will be cold, dark, and lifeless. On the scale of cosmic time, the human race (let alone the life of an individual) flashes into existence for the briefest moment before passing into nothingness. From an ultimate standpoint, all that we do is meaningless, since no one will be left to remember in the endless cosmic night. Without God and immortality, our life and indeed that of the whole human race is futile. In the words of Ernest Nagel, "Human destiny is an episode between two oblivions." We may have the illusion of meaning because others are still around, but in the long run, all of us will disappear, and our work and sacrifice will make no difference to an impersonal and indifferent cosmos.

Similarly, without a personal God, there is no basis for *morality*, since values such as right and wrong are relative and have no absolute mooring. If we are the product of an accidental combination of molecules in an ultimately impersonal universe, human values such as honesty, brotherhood, love, and equality have no more cosmic significance than do treachery, selfishness, hatred, and prejudice.

In a godless reality we are also stripped of *purpose*. An impersonal universe is bereft of purpose and plan; it moves only toward decay, disorder, and death. It is

Macbeth's "tale told by an idiot, full of sound and fury, signifying nothing." We may try to embrace short-term purposes, but when they are seen from the larger perspective, they are pointless, because the universe itself is pointless.

Few people have thought through these logical implications of a world without God, and no one can live consistently with them. All of us act as though human existence has meaning, as though moral values are real, and as though human life has purpose and dignity. That is, we act as though God exists, since all these things presuppose an infinite personal Creator.

In spite of this, even as believers we may be tempted in difficult times to question the validity of following Christ and obeying Scripture. We may wonder if it is worth it all. In times like these, this negative motivator may be the only thread that holds us in contact with reality—where else can we go? Either Christ is the way, the truth, and the life, or he is not; there is nothing in between. And if he is who he claims to be, there is no genuine way, no absolute truth, and no eternal life apart from him. The honesty of admitting this during times of trial and loss can help us cling to God even when there appears to be no positive reason for doing so. To paraphrase a line in C. S. Lewis's *Screwtape Letters*, Satan's cause is never more in danger than when a human, no longer desiring but still intending to do God's will, looks round upon a universe from which every trace of him seems to have vanished, and asks why he has been forsaken, and still obeys.

THE FEAR OF THE LORD

For we must all appear before the judgment seat of Christ, that each one may be recompensed for his deeds in the body, according to what he has done, whether good or bad. Therefore, knowing the fear of the Lord, we persuade men.
2 CORINTHIANS 5:10–11A

We hear little about the fear of the Lord in our time, and it is hardly in evidence in the community of believers as a source of behavioral motivation. But even a superficial study of a concordance will reveal that the fear of God is highly prized not only in the Old Testament but also in the New. Paul's statement quoted above makes it clear that the fear of the Lord is a solid component in his motivational structure. It is part of the reason that he suffered so much in the process of persuading people about the Good News of forgiveness and newness of life in Christ Jesus (compare his statement 1 Corinthians 9:16: "woe is me if I do not preach the gospel").

What does it mean to fear God? Consider Jesus' words to the multitude that gathered to hear him: "I say to you, My friends, do not be afraid of those who kill the body and after that have no more that they can do. But I will warn you whom to fear: fear the One who, after He has killed, has authority to cast into hell; yes, I tell you, fear

Him!" (Luke 12:4–5). Although the living and omnipotent God is worthy of far more reverence than we accord to people, Jesus knows that our natural tendency is to be more concerned about the opinions and responses of people whom we can see than about the favor of God whom we cannot see. Jesus' words remind us that succumbing to this tendency to play to the visible over the invisible is a serious mistake, because the consequences of disobedience to God are so much greater than the consequences of disobedience to people. God's authority is absolute, and our ultimate disposition is in his hands alone. Therefore anything short of absolute surrender to his claims on our lives is a misguided attempt at autonomy, and this is a game we can never win.

But what are we to make of the apostle John's familiar words in 1 John 4:18? "There is no fear in love; but perfect love casts out fear, because fear involves punishment, and the one who fears is not perfected in love." John has been describing the confidence we as believers in Christ have in the day of judgment, knowing that we are recipients of the love of God. This love dispels the terror of condemnation and assures us that we abide in Christ because he has given us of his Spirit (4:13). But John is not dispelling the need for a holy awe and reverence of God. Indeed, when he saw the glorified Christ (Revelation 1), he fell at the Lord's feet as a dead man. At that point, the Lord laid his right hand upon John and said, "Do not be afraid: I am the first and the last, and the living One; and I was dead, and behold, I am alive forevermore, and I have the keys of death and of Hades" (Revelation 1:17–18).

The Old and New Testaments relate the fear of God to knowing him, loving him, obeying him, and honoring him: "Moses said to the people, 'Do not be afraid; for God has come in order to test you, and in order that the fear of Him may remain with you, so that you may not sin'" (Exodus 20:20). "Oh that they had such a heart in them, that they would fear Me and keep all My commandments always, that it may be well with them and with their sons forever!" (Deuteronomy 5:29). "You shall fear only the LORD your God; and you shall worship Him, and swear by His name" (Deuteronomy 6:13). "And now, Israel, what does the LORD your God require from you, but to fear the LORD your God, to walk in all His ways and love Him, and to serve the LORD your God with all your heart and with all your soul" (Deuteronomy 10:12). "Behold, the fear of the Lord, that is wisdom; and to depart from evil is understanding" (Job 28:28). "The secret of the LORD is for those who fear Him, and He will make them know His covenant" (Psalm 25:14). "For great is the LORD, and greatly to be praised; He is to be feared above all gods" (Psalm 96:4). "If You, LORD, should mark iniquities, O Lord, who could stand? But there is forgiveness with You, that You may be feared" (Psalm 130:3–4). "Do not be wise in your own eyes; fear the LORD and turn away from evil" (Proverbs 3:7). "But for you who fear My name, the sun of righteousness will rise with healing in its wings" (Malachi 4:2). "Then those who feared the LORD spoke to one another, and the LORD gave attention and heard it, and a book of remembrance was written before

Him for those who fear the LORD and who esteem His name" (Malachi 3:16). "So the church . . . enjoyed peace, being built up; and going on in the fear of the Lord and in the comfort of the Holy Spirit, it continued to increase" (Acts 9:31). "Therefore, having these promises, beloved, let us cleanse ourselves from all defilement of flesh and spirit, perfecting holiness in the fear of God" (2 Corinthians 7:1). "Be subject to one another in the fear of Christ" (Ephesians 5:21). "Work out your salvation with fear and trembling" (Philippians 2:12). "Therefore, let us fear if, while a promise remains of entering His rest, any one of you may seem to have come short of it" (Hebrews 4:1). "And if you address as Father the One who impartially judges according to each man's work, conduct yourselves in fear during the time of your stay upon earth" (1 Peter 1:17). "Fear God, and give Him glory, because the hour of His judgment has come; worship Him who made the heaven and the earth and sea and springs of waters" (Revelation 14:7). "Who will not fear, O Lord, and glorify Your name? For You alone are holy" (Revelation 15:4). "Give praise to our God, all you His bond-servants, you who fear Him, the small and the great" (Revelation 19:5).

The fear of the Lord not only means cultivating a reverential awe of God but also relates to the mindset of a subject in a great kingdom. It is the recognition that the King has all power and authority in his hand and that the subject's life, occupation, and future are dependent on the good pleasure of the King. It is the ongoing acknowledgment of his sovereignty and the truth that our lives are in his hands. It is the foundation for wisdom because it leads to a sense of profound dependency, submission, and trust.

A deepening understanding that we are Christ's bondservants should be part of our motivational structure (see Luke 17:7–10). It can draw us away from the folly of trusting in people more than trusting in God. "Cursed is the man who trusts in mankind and makes flesh his strength, and whose heart turns away from the LORD. . . . Blessed is the man who trusts in the LORD" (Jeremiah 17:5, 7). It is a fundamental spiritual blunder to be more concerned about pleasing people than about pleasing God and to be more afraid of human disapproval than divine disapproval.

We would be wise to cultivate a holy fear, awe, and wonder before the magnificence, might, glory, and greatness of the Creator and Ruler of heaven and earth. Like John, when we see the glorified Christ, what we now dimly perceive about his powers and perfections will become much more clear. Perhaps we will react as did two of the animals in *The Wind in the Willows* when they saw "the Piper at the Gate of Dawn":

> "Rat!" he found breath to whisper, shaking. "Are you afraid?"
>
> "Afraid?" murmured the Rat, his eyes shining with unutterable love. "Afraid! Of *Him*? O, never, never! And yet—and yet—O Mole, I am afraid!"
>
> Then the two animals, crouching to the earth, bowed their heads and did worship.

"The fear of the LORD is the beginning of wisdom, and the knowledge of the Holy One is understanding" (Proverbs 9:10).

In the next chapter we will consider the third and fourth motivators: love and gratitude, and rewards.

QUESTIONS FOR PERSONAL APPLICATION

- Which of the seven horizontal motivators have been most operative in your thinking and behavior?
- Rank the list of seven vertical motivators in the order of practical appeal to you. What does this tell you about the nature of your spiritual walk?
- Have you had experiences in which the reality of no other options was the one thing that tethered you to the Lord? Why might such experiences be necessary?
- What does the fear of the Lord mean to you? Is this concept real or remote? How can it more richly inform your belief and behavior?

11

MOTIVATED SPIRITUALITY
Love, Gratitude, and Rewards

CHAPTER OVERVIEW

The third biblical motivator is a growing response of love and gratitude as we come to see God's gracious actions and provisions in new ways. Scripture also encourages us to pursue the rewards that our Lord will give to those who have been faithful to the opportunities they have been given.

CHAPTER OBJECTIVES

- A growing sense of love and gratitude for the Lord in light of what he has done for us
- A better grasp of rewards as biblical incentives to fidelity to God
- A clearer understanding of what Scripture says about rewards in the kingdom of heaven

LOVE AND GRATITUDE

The third biblical motivator is positive in nature: it is the response of love and gratitude for who God is and all the wonderful things he has done for us. The Bible is clear that God's love for us is always previous to our love for him. "The one who does not love does not know God, for God is love. By this the love of God was manifested in us, that God has sent His only begotten Son into the world so that we might live through Him. In this is love, not that we loved God, but that He loved us and sent His Son to be the propitiation for our sins" (1 John 4:8–10). The infinite and unchanging Source of love reached down to us even when we were his enemies in foolish rebellion against his person and purposes. "But God demonstrates His own love toward us, in that while we were yet sinners, Christ died for us" (Romans 5:8). Someone once put it this way: "I asked Jesus how much he loved me. He stretched out his arms and said, 'This

135

much'—and died." Jesus loved us when we were unlovable and unworthy of his attention and care. Because of his agonizing work as our sinbearer, the way has been opened for those who were "formerly alienated and hostile in mind, engaged in evil deeds" (Colossians 1:21) to become God's beloved children, members of his royal family forever. This love humbles us because it is undeserved, but it elevates us because it means that when we come to God by entrusting ourselves to his Son, nothing we do can separate us from his love (Romans 8:38–39).

The more we come to grasp and enter into this divine love, the more we will want to reciprocate by loving and honoring the eternal Lover of our souls. As John writes, "We love, because He first loved us" (1 John 4:19). The security and significance of God's unquenchable love gives us a basis for responding with love for God and expressing that love through acts of loving service to others. In his Upper Room Discourse Jesus said, "Just as the Father has loved Me, I have also loved you; abide in My love. If you keep My commandments, you will abide in My love; just as I have kept My Father's commandments and abide in His love" (John 15:9–10). There is a mutual relationship between abiding in the love of Christ and keeping his commandments. When we dwell in his unmerited love, we begin to see that his commandments are not burdensome but liberating. Abiding in his love, we become more inclined to obey him not only because it is in our best interests but also because it is pleasing to him. Thus the apostle Paul wrote, "We have as our ambition, whether at home or absent, to be pleasing to Him" (2 Corinthians 5:9). The ambitions of this world are directly or indirectly tied to self-aggrandizement; the ambition of a true disciple is not exaltation of the self but exaltation of Christ. As we grow in discipleship, our motivational structure is shaped more and more by Christ's love for us and our developing love for him ("For the love of Christ controls us" [2 Corinthians 5:14]). This relationship is reciprocal: the more we love him, the more we will desire to obey him; the more we obey him, the more we will grow in our personal knowledge of and love for him.

Let me offer two questions that can help you assess where you are in this spiritual journey. Do you love God more for himself than for his gifts and benefits? Are you more motivated to seek his glory and honor than you are to seek your own? These questions are pivotal, not trivial, and I encourage you to make them a matter of prayerful reflection rather than casual notice. If you cannot honestly answer yes to either of them, do not be disheartened, but ask yourself a third question: Do you want your answer to be yes? If so, offer this intention to the Lord as the desire of your heart, for with such offerings he is pleased. But a fourth question follows hard on the heels of the third: Since this level of commitment always costs, are you willing to pay the price? "If you love Me, you will keep My commandments. . . . He who has My commandments and keeps them is the one who loves Me; and he who loves Me will be loved by My Father, and I will love him and will disclose Myself to him. . . . If anyone loves Me, he will keep My word; and My Father will love him, and We will come to him and make Our abode with him. He who does not love Me does not keep My words" (John 14:15, 21, 23–24). The cost of obedience will take many forms, but if we commit ourselves to loving Jesus, he will give us the needed grace.

Gratitude is closely related to love, since both are based on God's gracious character and the expression of his character in the many benefits he has showered upon us. If we consider the depth and breadth of God's care and blessings in our lives, we will realize that it is only right that we should give thanks in everything (1 Thessalonians 5:18). However, we are typically more inclined to view our lives in terms of what we lack than in view of what we have already received. Instead of seeing the fullness of what we have received in Christ, we tend to approach our experiences from a deficiency perspective. Our gratitude ages quickly when we overlook God's gifts, take them for granted, or regard them as our due.

We would be wise to keep a grateful memory alive by periodically reviewing what once was, what might have been, and what could well be again apart from the grace of God. We should be amazed by and thankful for the multitude of good things in our lives, including the ones we often overlook, such as food and covering, health, freedom, friends, open access to the Scriptures, and most of all, the riches available to us in a relationship with Christ Jesus. As our gratitude for who God is and what he has done begins to grow, it becomes a meaningful source of motivation for service to our Lord and to others.

Gratitude for what God has done for us in the past can also motivate us to trust him in the present for what he is going to do in the future. John of Avila observed that "one act of thanksgiving when things go wrong is worth a thousand thanks when things go right." When we develop the habit of recounting the blessings we have received as God's beloved children, we become more inclined to view the hardships and disappointments we face from a long-term stance (Romans 8:18, 28). Love and gratitude are healthy biblical motivators that can help us stay in the process of growth in Christlikeness.

In *Loving Christ*, Joe Stowell retells the story of the woman and Simon and how the woman loved much because she was forgiven much. Then he writes:

> Mark it down: Loving Christ is a response—a response to His enduring, unwarranted love for us. His amazing grace motivates us like nothing else to live out our lives in unique and, when necessary, courageous ways that express our deep affection and honor for Him before a watching and often critical world. Why would you or I forgive a parent who had abused us? Why would anyone endure a difficult marriage out of conviction that it is the right and best thing to do? Why do Sudanese Christians permit themselves to be sold into slavery rather than deny the name of Christ? Why do people leave lucrative and highly applauded positions to take some paltry task in the kingdom work of Christ?

Why have martyrs gladly died and others lived in terrible situations with a good and uncompromised spirit? Believe me, this selflessness does not arise out of a sense of obligation and duty. These qualities do not provide sufficient resolve. When the chips are down or the stakes are high, mere commitment is rarely enough to lead us through to victory.

These selfless actions are motivated by a desire to express love and gratitude to Jesus for the wonderful things he has done for us.

REWARDS

Scripture teaches universal accountability before God. All people will be required to give an account to their Creator, but there will be a significant difference between God's judgment of believers and unbelievers. Entrance into heaven is solely a matter of the grace of God and not of works, since "all have sinned and fall short of the glory of God" (Romans 3:23). God's justice would mean that all would be eternally separated from the holiness of God, but God's grace offers us far more than justice requires.

Scripture also affirms that the experience of heaven and hell will not be uniform, since there appear to be degrees of punishment (e.g., Luke 12:47–48; Matthew 11:21–24; Revelation 20:12) and, as we will see, degrees of reward. While salvation is by grace, rewards in the kingdom of heaven are based on works. This means that the quality of our life on this planet has eternal consequences and that how we live in this temporal realm will have a direct bearing on the quality of eternity.

Whether we like it or not, each one of us is accountable to God, and no one will escape his righteous judgment. Unbelievers will face judgment at the great white throne (Revelation 20:11–15) and will be judged on the basis of their works. Believers will stand before the judgment seat of Christ (2 Corinthians 5:10), where their works will also be judged (1 Corinthians 3:10–15). The difference is that there is "no condemnation for those who are in Christ Jesus" (Romans 8:1; see John 5:24), because Christ bore their judgment and gave them his life. Nevertheless, the judgment seat of Christ is not a trivial matter, since it can involve loss as well as reward in the kingdom of heaven. I sometimes put it this way: It's easy to lip-synch in the chorus of life, but each of us will have to sing solo before God.

When we come to Christ, he becomes the foundation of our life and the basis of our entrance into heaven. The superstructure we build upon the foundation is made of our works, which consist of "gold, silver, precious stones, wood, hay, straw" (1 Corinthians 3:12). At the judgment seat, the superstructure is set on fire to test the quality of each one's work. We will be rewarded for that which endures the test of purgation by fire (gold, silver, precious stones) and suffer loss for that which is burned up (wood, hay, straw). In view of the fact that believers can be disqualified from rewards through lack of faithfulness or receive the approval of God because of faithfulness (see 1 Corinthians 9:25–27; Philippians 3:10–14; 2 Timothy 2:12; 4:7–8; James 3:1), it is perilous to live complacently, as though we will avoid a day of reckoning.

Thus fear of loss and hope of reward are two legitimate biblical motivators, and our Lord stressed their importance on multiple occasions (e.g., Matthew 6:19–20; 19:27–30; Luke 12:42–44; John 12:25–26; Revelation 22:12). In three of his parables, Jesus illuminated the condition for rewards and revealed that it is quite different from the criteria the world uses to determine compensation. According to the parable of the vineyard (Matthew 20:1–16), rewards are not based on the amount of time one labors in God's vineyard. The providence of God determines the amount of this world's goods and the length of time with which we are entrusted. Our responsibility relates to the way we invest the time we have been granted, whether we are given one or seventy years after our conversion to Christ.

The parable of the talents (Matthew 25:14–30) and the parable of the minas (Luke 19:11–27) teach us that rewards are based neither on the gifts and abilities we have received nor on the level of our productivity. Instead, they are determined by the degree of our faithfulness to the opportunities we have been given. If rewards were based on time, talent, or treasure, those who are relatively rich in these assets would be rewarded for possessing things that come from the providential hand of God. The fact that rewards are based on faithfulness to the assets and opportunities we have been given is the divine equalizer that gives every believer, regardless of economic, social, intellectual, or vocational status, the possibility of being approved by God.

Faithfulness relates to the issue of stewardship of the assets and resources of another. I see several facets of stewardship that include not only time, talent, and treasure but also truth and relationships. Here again, the question is not how much truth we have been exposed to or the size of our relational influence but what we are doing with the truth and the people God has given us. In the New Testament, faithfulness also relates to the degree of our obedience to God's precepts and principles as revealed in Scripture, including our participation in the Great Commission, as well as the way we respond to the circumstances in which we have been placed. God's approval relates more to the focus of our heart than to the measurable achievements that are usually associated with what our world calls success.

Although Scripture frequently encourages us to pursue reward with God, it tells us little about the nature and content of that reward. I believe the principal reason for this is that in our present state, we are limited in our capacity to grasp the real nature of heavenly rewards (1 Corinthians 2:9). But we can be well assured that they will be worth any temporal sacrifice to gain. In my theological reflection, I currently think of four areas that appear to be related to rewards. The first of these is greater responsibility in the kingdom of heaven (Luke 16:10–12; 19:17–19). Believers will be granted different spheres of authority based on their faithfulness on earth. The second area has to do with reflecting and displaying the glory and character of God. "Those who have insight will shine brightly like the brightness of the expanse of heaven, and those who lead the many to righteousness, like the stars forever and ever" (Daniel 12:2–3; cf. 1 Corinthians 15:40–41; 2 Corinthians 3:13–18). We are not called to glorify ourselves but to receive and display the glory of the majestic perfections of the infinite and wondrous God of all creation.

The third area of rewards relates to the nature and depth of our relationships with people in heaven. I believe there must be some continuity between the relationships we develop with people on earth and the corresponding relationships we will experience in heaven. There are always consequences to relational intimacy and distance; those who have developed rich relationships with people through others-centered love and sacrifice will be enriched by those relationships forever. As Paul wrote to the believers in Thessalonica: "For who is our hope or joy or crown of exultation? Is it not even you, in the presence of our Lord Jesus at His coming? For you are our glory and joy" (1 Thessalonians 2:19–20). Similarly, in the parable of the unrighteous steward, Jesus exhorts his followers to "make friends for yourselves by means of the wealth of unrighteousness, so that when it fails, they will receive you into the eternal dwellings" (Luke 16:9). That is, when we nurture relationships by leveraging our temporal assets of time, talent, and treasure into the spiritual good of others, there will be people who will welcome us into heaven. In addition, Paul comforted his readers by affirming that in the resurrection, they would once again be with the people they loved who have died in Christ (1 Thessalonians 4:13–18). The more we love and serve others in Christ, the richer our relational rewards.

The fourth area relates to our capacity to know and experience God. Just as there is a continuity between earthly and heavenly relationships with the people of God, so those who cultivate a growing appetite for the experiential knowledge of God in this life will presumably know him better in the next life than those who kept God in the periphery of their earthly interests. As A. W. Tozer put it, "Every Christian will become at last what his desires have made him. We are the sum total of our hungers. The great saints have all had thirsting hearts. Their cry has been, 'My soul thirsteth for God, for the living God: when shall I come and appear before God?' Their longing after God all but consumed them; it propelled them onward and upward to heights toward which less ardent Christians look with languid eye and entertain no hope of reaching." I can conceive of nothing more significant and compelling than the **beatific vision** of the living God, and if our capacity for this vision relates to faithfulness in this life, every other concern should pale in comparison.

Since there will be a day of reckoning, we would be wise to order our lives with this truth in mind. The Bible calls us away from complacency to the pursuit of discipleship and fruit bearing. It cautions us not to be seduced by the things our culture declares to be important, because "that which is highly esteemed among men is detestable in the sight of God" (Luke 16:15). The bulk of what the world tells us to pursue is directly related to the opinions of others. But in the end, people's opinions will be irrelevant; when we stand before God, only his opinion will matter.

It has been observed that the apostle Paul had only two days on his calendar: today and *that* day (the day he would stand before Christ), and he lived every today in light of that day. He reveled in God's great gift of justification and encouraged believers to grow in sanctification, but his great hope was in God's promise of glorification. "I consider that the sufferings of this present time are not worthy to be compared with the glory that is to be revealed to us" (Romans 8:18). "Therefore we do not lose heart, but though our outer man is decaying, yet our inner man is being renewed day by day. For momentary, light affliction is producing for us an eternal weight of glory far beyond all comparison, while we look not at the things which are seen, but at the things which are not seen; for the things which are seen are temporal, but the things which are not seen are eternal" (2 Corinthians 4:16–18). "For our citizenship is in heaven, from which also we eagerly wait for a Savior, the Lord Jesus Christ; who will transform the body of our humble state into conformity with the body of His glory, by the exertion of the power that He has even to subject all things to Himself" (Philippians 3:20–21). "I have fought the good fight, I have finished the course, I have kept the faith; in the future there is laid up for me the crown of righteousness, which the Lord, the righteous Judge, will award to me on that day; and not only to me, but also to all who have loved His appearing" (2 Timothy 4:7–8).

The Scriptures teach that it is not mercenary to be motivated by reward; instead, Jesus encouraged us to long to hear "Well done, good and faithful servant; enter into the joy of your Lord." The New Testament is replete with exhortations to pursue God's rewards, affirming that they are more than worth the cost. "Blessed is a man who perseveres under trial; for once he has been approved, he will receive the crown of life which the Lord has promised to those who love Him" (James 1:12). "And without faith it is impossible to please Him, for he who comes to God must believe that He is and that He is a rewarder of those who seek Him. . . . [Moses considered] the reproach of Christ greater riches than the treasures of Egypt; for he was looking to the reward" (Hebrews 11:6, 26). "Beloved, now we are children of God, and it has not appeared as yet what we will be. We know that when He appears, we will be like Him, because we will see Him just as He is. And everyone who has this hope fixed on Him purifies himself, just as He is pure" (1 John 3:2–3).

C. S. Lewis argued in *The Weight of Glory* that our problem is not that our desires are too strong but that they are too weak. "We are half-hearted creatures, fooling about with drink and sex and ambition when infinite joy is offered us, like an ignorant child who wants to go on making mud pies in a slum because he cannot imagine what is meant by the offer of a holiday at the sea. We are far too easily pleased." In comparison with what God wants to give us, the best this world can offer is toys, trinkets, and tinsel.

We should be motivated by the fact that we are in the process of becoming what we will be in eternity. We should give it everything we have, because eternal gain will be worth anything we sacrificed in our brief earthly sojourn. Meanwhile, God uses the pulley of restlessness to draw us to himself. Meanwhile, God uses the pulley of restlessness to draw us to himself, knowing that our hearts can find true rest in him alone (Matthew 11:28–30).

The Pulley
When God at first made man,
Having a glass of blessings standing by,
Let us (said he) pour on him all we can;
Let the world's riches, which dispersèd lie,
Contract into a span.

So strength first made a way;
Then beauty flow'd, then wisdom, honour, pleasure.
When almost all was out, God made a stay,
Perceiving that alone of all his treasure
Rest in the bottom lay.

For if I should (said he)
Bestow this jewel also on my creature,
He would adore my gifts instead of me,
And rest in Nature, not the God of Nature:
So both should losers be.

Yet let him keep the rest,
But keep them with repining restlessness:
Let him be rich and weary, that at least,
If goodness lead him not, yet weariness
May toss him to my breast.

George Herbert

QUESTIONS FOR PERSONAL APPLICATION

- To what extent have love and gratitude prompted your actions toward God and people? What can you do to make them more real in your mind and heart?
- What is your own understanding of rewards? Why do you think Jesus spoke so much about rewards in heaven?
- As you reflect on your daily practice, does the biblical promise of rewards in the kingdom of heaven impinge upon the way you relate to people and circumstances? How could these incentives be more compelling in your belief and behavior?

12

MOTIVATED SPIRITUALITY

Identity, Purpose and Hope, and Longing for God

CHAPTER OVERVIEW

As we grow in our understanding of our security and significance in Christ, we come to view sin as beneath the dignity we have in him. A biblical sense of purpose and hope can also contribute to our spiritual fidelity. Finally, the psalmists and great saints were also motivated by a longing for God above any of his gifts.

CHAPTER OBJECTIVES

- Realization that in light of our new identity in Christ, we have nothing we need to prove and that sin is incompatible with who we have become in him
- Encouragement to examine our purpose for living and what we are hoping in
- An increased longing for God and the realization that he is the only Being who can truly satisfy our souls

The last three of the seven biblical motivators are our identity in Christ, purpose and hope, and longing for God.

OUR IDENTITY IN CHRIST

Joe Louis was the world heavyweight boxing champion from 1937 until he retired in 1948. During his time of service in the army, Louis was driving with a fellow GI when he was involved in a minor collision with a large truck. The truck driver got out, yelling and swearing at Louis, who just sat in the driver's seat, smiling. "Why didn't you get out and knock him flat?" asked his buddy after the truck driver had moved on. "Why should I?" replied Joe. "When somebody insulted Caruso, did he sing an aria for him?"

This is one of my favorite illustrations because it is so relevant to the theme of identity. The truck driver didn't know the identity of the person he was cursing, for if he had, he would have treated him in a dramatically different way! But Joe Louis knew who he was—the best boxer in the world—and therefore he had nothing to prove. Many other men in his position would have been tempted to fight back or at least return insult for insult. But Louis was secure enough in his identity to understand that such a response would only be degrading. The truck driver's opinion of him was irrelevant to Joe's self-understanding.

I have come to view this issue of identity as a powerful potential source of motivation for believers, particularly during times of temptation and spiritual warfare.

So far in this section on seven biblical motivators, we have looked at rewards, love, gratitude, fear, and the lack of other options as factors that can keep us in the race and move us away from disobedience and toward Christlikeness. Understanding our true identity in Christ can also be a significant component of godly motivation, but this rarely seems to be the case. The problem is that most people who have received God's gift of forgiveness and life in Christ have either forgotten or have never grasped what it means to be a child of God.

Charlie Chaplin entered a Charlie Chaplin look-alike competition in Monte Carlo—and came in third! We too get mixed signals about our identity. Our parents, friends, associates, and society give us one set of impressions, and to the extent that we expose ourselves to Scripture, we discover a different picture. The usual way of resolving these conflicting inputs is to filter out the biblical passages that do not fit the self-perception we have picked up from the world. For instance, many of us have experienced significant amounts of performance-based acceptance. Because of this, we may conclude that love is conditional and must be merited. When Scripture tells us that as believers in Christ we are unconditionally loved and accepted by the Father, we find it difficult to internalize because that acceptance is radically opposed to everything the world has told us. When we read in Ephesians 1–2 that we are not only members of God's family but also already seated with Christ in the heavenly places, we are inclined to think Scripture must be talking about someone else. When Romans 6 tells us that we have died with Christ and no longer need be dominated by the power of sin, we say that our experience suggests otherwise.

Our culture tells us that our worth is determined by our accomplishments and encourages us to pursue significance and meaning through the things we do. Scripture tells us that our worth is determined by what Christ was willing to do for us and that in him we have an unlimited and unchanging source of meaning and purpose. Who we are in Christ is not shaped by what we do but by what he did on the cross and continues to do in our lives. Our performance does not determine our identity; instead, our new identity in Jesus becomes the basis for what we do. If we perceive ourselves to be worthless or inadequate, this will be manifested in our behavior. But if we choose to acknowledge the truth of Scripture, we will begin to see God and ourselves in a new light. In spite of what our culture and experiences have taught us to feel, the New Testament tells us that we became new creatures when we trusted in Christ. In him, we have been granted great dignity, security, forgiveness, unconditional love and acceptance, hope, purpose, righteousness, wholeness, and peace with God. We may not *feel* that these things are so, yet Scripture does not command us to feel the truth but to believe it. This is a matter of acknowledging its authority by taking God at his word in spite of how we feel or who we think we are.

As we study Scripture and make the faith decision to regard its proclamations as true, we are inviting the Holy Spirit to make these truths more real not only in our thinking but gradually in our feelings as well. This internalization process requires the discipline of mental renewal through time in the Word, equipping through good teaching, and fellowship with like-minded people in the spiritual journey.

We honor God when we allow him to define us and tell us who we are regardless of our feelings or experiences to the contrary. In Christ, we are overcomers who have been adopted into God's family. We are set free from bondage to Satan, sin, and death; we are called and equipped to accomplish an eternal purpose that will have enduring results. Further, we are raised up with Christ and are partakers of his life; we are sealed, anointed, indwelled, and empowered by the Holy Spirit. We are recipients of an imperishable inheritance that is reserved in heaven for us; we are members of the body of Christ and joint heirs with him. We have been chosen, redeemed, forgiven, and set apart; we are destined to be raised in a glorified body in which we will behold God and live in communion with him forever. Since these things are so, and since nothing can separate us from the love of God that is in Christ Jesus our Lord (Romans 8:38–39), we are spiritual champions who are called to live as such. Like Joe Louis, when we know who we are, we have nothing to prove. Furthermore, the degradation of sin is beneath the dignity of the people we have become in Christ. When we are tempted to covet, lust, lie, become envious, or succumb to any other work of the flesh, we should say, "That is no longer who I am." While we are on this earth, the lust of the flesh, the lust of the eyes, and the boastful pride of life will be constant snares, but we are more than conquerors when we remember that our deepest identity is in Christ and invite him to rule and live through us.

PURPOSE AND HOPE

In 1902 Meyer Kubelski, a Jewish immigrant from Russia, gave his son a violin for his eighth birthday. It cost Meyer fifty dollars, a small fortune in those days.

The son loved music and soon was playing well enough to give concerts at the Barrison Theater in Waukeegan, the town where the Kubelskis lived. By the age of eighteen he had teamed up with a woman pianist in vaudeville.

One night as Benjamin Kubelski was playing, he felt impelled, between numbers, to tell the audience about a funny incident that had happened to him during the day.

"The audience laughed," he recalled later, "and the sound intoxicated me. That laughter ended my days as a musician." Jack Benny, as the young Kubelski later called himself, had found his rightful career.

Most people never stumble, as Benny did, into a career path that so happily meshes ability and passion. But even if the fit is perfect, a career is not the same as a biblical purpose for one's life. Vocational setbacks and retirement do not derail God's purpose for us, because his intentions transcend the circumstances and seasons of our lives. Even marriage and children cannot be equated with God's unchanging reason for our being.

Laying hold of a sense of purpose can be a significant source of motivation, but the problem is that even as believers, we are more inclined to pursue temporal rather than biblical purposes. In fact, most people fail to wrestle with the issue of purpose; without reasoned purposes to guide them, they base their decisions instead on activities and objectives that have become ends in themselves.

This is the antithesis of the way the Lord Jesus ordered his earthly life. Jesus had a clear understanding of the purpose of his life, and he derived his purpose from his Father and not his own ambitions or aspirations. The hallmark of his life was to learn his Father's will and walk in the power of the Spirit to bring it to fruition. The Gospels record three particularly clear purpose statements that related to our Lord's life mission: "For even the Son of Man did not come to be served, but to serve, and to give His life a ransom for many. . . . For the Son of Man has come to seek and to save that which was lost. . . . I glorified You on the earth, having accomplished the work which You have given Me to do" (Mark 10:45; Luke 19:10; John 17:4). Jesus' purpose was to glorify his Father by seeking, serving, and saving the lost.

The apostle Paul also had a well-defined sense of purpose that involved a passion for knowing and pleasing Christ and for remaining faithful to his personal calling to evangelism and edification (see Philippians 3:10, 13–14; 2 Corinthians 5:9; 1 Corinthians 9:24–27; 2 Timothy 4:7–8).

We cannot lay hold of God's unique purpose for our lives without spending time with him and inviting him to clarify his purpose for us in his timing and way. It is never too late to begin wrestling with the reason for our earthly existence, since God in his sovereignty can use all our previous experiences to prepare us for our true mission. Ask the Lord to give you a personal purpose statement and a passion to fulfill it. (My personal purpose statement is "to be a lover and servant of God and others.") In this way your activities and objectives will take on a depth of meaning.

Hope is related to purpose, for both of these biblical motivators move us toward long-term gain. Some people have no hope, most have a misplaced or an ill-defined hope, and a few have a proper hope. It is not uncommon for those who know Christ to succumb to the error of putting their hope in him for their eternal destiny and putting their hope in the world for everything else. When this happens, the pursuit of security, significance, and satisfaction takes precedence over the pursuit of Christ. Ironically, the more we pursue these things for themselves, the more elusive they become. They are given to us in their fullness only as the overflow of seeking first the Lord's kingdom and righteousness.

Hebrews 6:11–20 instructs us to fix our hope solely on the character and promises of the God of Abraham, Isaac, and Jacob. There is but one safe refuge for hope in this world, and that is the unchanging character of the triune God and the certain promises of Scripture that flow out of his character. "This hope we have as an anchor of the soul, a hope both sure and steadfast and one which enters within the veil, where Jesus has entered as a forerunner for us" (Hebrews 6:19–20). In the Bible, hope is assured by God's character.

A godly hope is also achieved through adversity. We are more likely to come into contact with our hope during times of trial and affliction than during times of success and prosperity, since the latter has a way of knitting our hearts to the promises of this world rather than the promises of the Word. As Paul told the Romans, "We exult in hope of the glory of God. And not only this, but we also exult in our tribulations, knowing that tribulation brings about perseverance; and perseverance, proven character; and proven character, hope; and hope does not disappoint, because the love of God has been poured out within our hearts through the Holy Spirit who was given to us" (5:2–5). In the same epistle he added, "I consider that the sufferings of this present time are not worthy to be compared with the glory that is to be revealed to us. . . . For in hope we have been saved, but hope that is seen is not hope; for why does one also hope for what he already sees? But if we hope for what we do not see, with perseverance we wait eagerly for it" (8:18, 24–25). Morris Inch notes in *Psychology in the Psalms* that biblical hope "does not reduce the ingredients of living, but adds God to the equation. Hope shouts, not because there is no enemy, but because God gives the triumph. Hope sings, not because there is no night, but because God gives songs in the night. The pulse of hope is praise."

We lay hold of biblical hope by faith (Ephesians 1:18), and the more it motivates us, the more it becomes evident to others (1 Peter 1:3; 3:15). It also assures us that whatever God calls us to do will be more than worth it all. "Therefore, my beloved brethren, be steadfast, immovable, always abounding in the work of the Lord, knowing that your toil is not in vain in the Lord" (1 Corinthians 15:58).

LONGING FOR GOD

As the deer pants for the water brooks, so my soul pants for You, O God. My soul thirsts for God, for the living God; when shall I come and appear before God?
PSALM 42:1–2

As we conclude this portrait of biblical motivators, we approach the one motivator I believe to be the highest but the least commonly experienced spiritual source of motivation: the longing for God.

Moses' great prayer in the wilderness was "I pray You, show me Your glory!" (Exodus 33:18). The psalmists cultivated a passion for God's presence and understood that anything of true value comes from his hand. The sages who wrote the wisdom literature stressed that nothing can compare with knowing God. The prophets were overwhelmed by the splendor and majesty of God and endured ridicule and rejection in order to be pleasing to him. Jesus taught his followers to hunger and thirst more for God's kingdom and righteousness than for anything else; the apostles' deepest longing was to behold the infinite lover of their souls.

Longing to see God and to enter his consummate presence is an oft-repeated theme in the writings of the great saints, but that longing is rarely expressed in the Christian literature of our time. I find myself longing to long for God in the way some of these men and women did. Six hundred years ago, for instance, Julian of Norwich in her *Revelations of Divine Love* asked God for the three faithful wounds of contrition for her sins, compassion for others, and an intense longing for God. She wrote,

> At the same moment the Trinity filled me full of heartfelt joy, and I knew that all eternity was like this for those who attain heaven. For the Trinity is God, and God the Trinity; the Trinity is our Maker and keeper, our eternal lover, joy and bliss—all through our Lord Jesus Christ. . . . We have got to realize the littleness of creation and to see it for the nothing that it is before we can love and possess God who is uncreated. This is the reason why we have no ease of heart or soul, for we are seeking our rest in trivial things which cannot satisfy, and not seeking to know God, almighty, all-wise, all-good. He is true rest. It is His will that we should know Him, and His pleasure that we should rest in Him. Nothing less will satisfy us. . . . We shall never cease wanting and longing until we possess Him in fullness and joy. Then we shall have no further wants. Meanwhile His will is that we go on knowing and loving until we are perfected in heaven. . . . The more clearly the soul sees the blessed face by grace and love, the more it longs to see it in its fullness.

In his autobiography, *Surprised by Joy*, C. S. Lewis related true joy to what he called *Sehnsucht* or longing. He spoke of the stab and pang of acute longing as homesickness for a place and a time we have not yet visited that is beyond the edge of the imagination. Lewis also spoke of this longing in *The Weight of Glory:*

> The sense that in this universe we are treated as strangers, the longing to be acknowledged, to meet with some response, to bridge some chasm that yawns

between us and reality, is part of our inconsolable secret. And surely, from this point of view, the promise of glory, in the sense described, becomes highly relevant to our deep desire. For glory meant good report with God, acceptance by God, response, acknowledgment, and welcome into the heart of things. The door on which we have been knocking all our lives will open at last. . . . Apparently, then, our lifelong nostalgia, our longing to be reunited with something in the universe from which we now feel cut off, to be on the inside of some door which we have always seen from the outside, is no mere neurotic fancy, but the truest index of our real situation. And to be at last summoned inside would be both glory and honour beyond all our merits and also the healing of that old ache.

Things which eye has not seen and ear has not heard, and which have not entered the heart of man, all that God has prepared for those who love Him.

1 Corinthians 2:9

There have been times when a walk in the woods, a painting, a photograph, or a piece of music created a sudden and profound sense of longing within me. When I thought about it, I realized that in each case, the vehicle that caused the longing pointed not to itself but to that which is beyond the created order, to God. These are fleeting moments, but they are enough to remind me of the reality of my pilgrim status and to awaken desire for something more than anything this world can offer.

Along similar lines, Henri Nouwen in *The Return of the Prodigal Son* describes his encounter with Rembrandt's painting of this parable and the remarkable effect this painting had on his self-understanding. "It had brought me into touch with something within me that lies far beyond the ups and downs of a busy life, something that represents the ongoing yearning of the human spirit, the yearning for a final return, an unambiguous sense of safety, a lasting home." It is an aspiration to turn to our Father's house and to find the deep satisfaction of his embrace and of being treasured by him. "In My Father's house are many dwelling places; if it were not so, I would have told you; for I go and prepare a place for you. If I go and prepare a place for you, I will come again and receive you to Myself, that where I am, there you may be also" (John 14:2–3).

Laying hold of our true desire is the theme of *The Sacred Romance* by Brent Curtis and John Eldredge and of *The Journey of Desire* written by John Eldredge after the loss of his beloved co-laborer and friend. These books portray heaven as the great restoration of the beauty we long to see on a cosmic scale, the grand affair of complete intimacy among the people of God; and the great adventure of fruitful, creative, activity without frustration and disappointments.

Coming to Christ is "not an end but an inception, for now begins the glorious pursuit, the heart's happy exploration of the infinite riches of the Godhead. That is where we begin, I say, but where we stop no man has yet discovered, for there is in the awful and mysterious depths of the Triune God neither limit nor end. . . . To have found God and still to pursue Him is the soul's paradox of love, scorned indeed by the too-easily-satisfied religionist, but justified in happy experience by the children of the burning heart," wrote A. W. Tozer in *The Pursuit of God*. This holy desire, this transcendent ambition, is captured in Jesus' penetrating words, "seek first His kingdom and His righteousness; and all these things will be added to you" (Matthew 6:32–33). "Jesus took it for granted that all human beings are 'seekers.' It is not natural for people to drift aimlessly through life like plankton," John Stott observes in *Christian Counter-Culture*. "We need something to live for, something to give meaning to our existence, something to 'seek,' something on which to set our hearts and our minds."

God waits to be wanted, but he must be wanted for himself and not for some lesser good he may provide. May we ask for the grace to long for the beatific vision, for the vision of God himself. "There will no longer be any curse; and the throne of God and of the Lamb will be in it, and His bond-servants will serve Him; *they will see His face*, and His name will be on their foreheads" (Revelation 22:3–4, emphasis added).

QUESTIONS FOR PERSONAL APPLICATION

- How often do you reflect upon and reinforce your understanding of your identity in Christ? Have your emotions and experiences filtered out the reality of some of these truths?
- As you review your spiritual journey, what impact has a biblically based sense of identity had in your experience? Do you find yourself trying to prove something by impressing others or defending yourself?
- To what degree do you embrace a biblically derived purpose and hope as opposed to a temporally derived sense of purpose and hope?
- How do you relate to the idea of longing for God? Has this played any role in your motivational structure? How can you nurture such a holy longing?

D E V O T I O N A L
S P I R I T U A L I T Y

Falling in Love with God

What are the keys to loving God, and how can we cultivate a growing intimacy with him? This section explores what it means to enjoy God and to trust in him. Henry Scougal observed that "the worth and excellency of a soul is to be measured by the object of its love." We are most satisfied when we seek God's pleasure above our own, and we gradually become conformed to what we most love and admire.

13

DEVOTIONAL SPIRITUALITY
Our Image of God

CHAPTER OVERVIEW

Devotional spirituality revels in the glorious attributes of God and aspires to lay hold of God's desires for us. God's world, his Word, his works, and his ways reveal his attributes to those who wish to know him. This is illustrated in three psalms on the beautiful attributes of God.

CHAPTER OBJECTIVES

- An understanding that we steadily become conformed to what we most love and admire
- An appreciation for the way God reveals himself in his world, his Word, his works, and his ways, and a desire to love him through all four
- A renewed vision of the glorious attributes of God

"There is but one God, the Father, from whom are all things and we exist for Him; and one Lord, Jesus Christ, by whom are all things, and we exist through Him" (1 Corinthians 8:6).

We do not exist for ourselves—we exist *for* the Father and *through* the Son. The world tells us that we derive our existence from it and that we should live for ourselves, but the Word teaches us that all we are and have comes from the Father who formed us for his pleasure and purposes.

Ultimate reality is not the cosmos or a mysterious force but an infinite and loving Person. The implications of this, if we think about it, are astounding and pervasive. The infinite personal Lord of all is an unbounded loving community of three timeless and perfect persons. In the superabundance of his joy and life, he is at once solitude and society, the one and the many, supernal being as communion. The magnificent God who abounds in personal plenitude has no needs, yet he invites us to participate in the intense and interpenetrating life of the three eternally subsistent selves. Jesus prayed on our behalf "that they may all be one; even as You, Father, are in Me and I in You, that they also may be in Us . . . . I in them and You in Me, that they may be perfected in unity, so that the world may know that You sent Me, and loved them, even as You have loved Me" (John 17:21, 23). The impenetrable mystery of us being in the divine Us and the divine Us being in us transcends our imagination, but if it is true, all else pales in comparison.

Devotional spirituality revels in the glorious attributes of God and aspires to lay hold of God's aspiration for us. It prepares our souls for the "mystic sweet communion" of living entirely in God and in one another as the three persons of God eternally live and rejoice in one another. It instills in us a passion for Christ's indwelling life and inspires us to swim in the river of torrential love that flows from his throne of grace.

In 1677, Henry Scougal observed in *The Life of God in the Soul of Man* that "the worth and excellency of a soul is to be measured by the object of its love." Our souls become emaciated when their pleasure is affixed to position, possessions, and power, because these things are destined to corrupt and perish. But as we gradually and often painfully transfer our affections from the created and finite world to the uncreated and infinite Maker of the world, our souls become great and glorious. As we take the risk of seeking God's pleasure above our own, we discover a greater satisfaction and contentment than if we sought these things as ends in themselves. As we learn to fix our eyes on Jesus, not for his benefits but for himself, we find that we have all things in him.

Scripture teaches us that we steadily become conformed to what we most love and admire. Hosea declared that the people of Israel "became as detestable as that which they loved" (Hosea 9:10). But when we turn the focus of our love from the idols of this world system to the beauty of Christ, we discover the liberty of the Spirit of the Lord. *We become like our focus;* in the process of beholding the glory of the Lord, we are being "transformed into the same image from glory to glory, just as from the Lord, the Spirit" (2 Corinthians 3:18). We gradually come to resemble what we worship. If our heart's desire is fixed on something in this world, it becomes idolatrous and soul-corrupting. But if we draw our life from loving communion with the caring, radiant, majestic, and unfathomable being who formed us for himself, our souls become noble as they grow in conformity to his character.

GOD'S WORLD, HIS WORD, HIS WORKS, AND HIS WAYS

God in his inner essence is a mystery beyond our comprehension; we will never know him as he knows himself. The great pilgrims along the way have discovered that progress from superficial to substantive apprehension of God is not so much a movement from darkness to light as it is a plummeting into the ever-increasing profundity of the cloud of unknowing. Kallistos Ware in *The Orthodox Way* distinguishes the *essence* of God and the *energies* of God. In his essence, God is radically transcendent, but in his energies, he is immanent and omnipresent. As Ware notes, "The Godhead is simple and indivisible, and has no parts. The essence signifies the whole God as he is in himself; the energies signify the whole God as he is in action. God in his entirety is completely present in each of his divine energies." As we reflect on God's revelatory actions, we come to know him more clearly, and this enables us to love him more dearly, and to follow him more nearly. God makes himself known to us through his world, his Word, his works, and his ways.

Loving God through His World

"The heavens are telling of the glory of God; and their expanse is declaring the work of His hands" (Psalm 19:1). "O LORD, how many are Your works! In wisdom You have made them all; the earth is full of Your possessions" (Psalm 104:24). Read Psalm 19:1–6 and Psalms 104 and 148 carefully and prayerfully, and you will be struck by the manifold ways in which God designed the heavens and earth to display his glory, wisdom, and greatness.

Meditation on the created order is too often neglected as a meaningful component of devotional spirituality. This is unfortunate, because creation abounds with resplendent wonders on every order of magnitude from the microcosm to the macrocosm that point beyond themselves to the beauty and unimaginable brilliance of the Creator of the cosmos. Consider these marvels of order and design: particles and atoms, light and colors, microbes and diatoms, snowflakes, insects, seeds, flowers, leaves, shells, rocks and minerals, fruits, vegetables, plants, small and large birds, small and large fish, whales, small and large animals, trees, mountains, clouds, weather, the seasons, our earth, the planets, stars, nebulae, our galaxy, clusters and superclusters of galaxies.

"You formed my inward parts; You wove me in my mother's womb. I will give thanks to You, for I am fearfully and wonderfully made; wonderful are Your works, and my soul knows it very well" (Psalm 139:13–14). Of all God's created works, the human body best displays God's creative skill and design. I recommend three books that will help you worship God by reflecting on the marvels of the human and spiritual body: *Fearfully and Wonderfully Made* and *In His Image* by Dr. Paul Brand and Philip Yancey, and *More Than Meets the Eye* by Richard A. Swenson. These books portray the way physical systems like cells, bone, skin, motion, blood, the head, and the sensation of pain teach spiritual truth.

Two things have helped me love God through his world. The first is an occasional trip to special places where I am encompassed in the natural order. In such places I sometimes sit back and stare at the stars until I realize that I am no longer looking up but also down and that I am enveloped by the splendor and grandeur of the heavens. An experience like this is humbling because it dramatically shifts my perspective and reminds me that apart from God and his grace, I am nothing. I gain a similar sense of awe by looking at recent photographs of star clouds and distant galaxies. The explosion in scientific knowledge in our time gives us access to avenues of appreciating God that were never before available.

The second thing I use to stimulate wonder is a set of field lenses and a miniature high-intensity flashlight. I use this "nature kit" from time to time to observe otherwise invisible colors and patterns in flowers, insects, rocks, and so forth. The very act of slowing down enough to observe and appreciate the rich intricacy and diversity of the created order is a healthy exercise in recollection and renewal.

There is no limit to the images and insights that can be gleaned from nature if we take the time and have the eyes to see. We would do well to cultivate a childlike sense of amazement and awe at the things we tend to overlook every day. Our artificial environments and busy schedules make us forget that we are surrounded by mystery and majesty. I encourage you to make the effort to enjoy more frequent and deliberate contact with God's creation and to develop a deeper appreciation for the complexity, beauty, and resplendence of the heavens and earth. As you do this, you will sense that the God who designed all this and spoke it into being is utterly competent, trustworthy, and lovable.

Loving God through His Word

"Open my eyes, that I may behold wonderful things from Your law" (Psalm 119:18). The Word of God restores the soul, imparts wisdom, rejoices the heart, enlightens the eyes, reveals God's righteousness, and endures forever (Psalm 19:7–9). Scripture was revealed not merely to inform us but also to transform us. In *Shaped by the Word*, M. Robert Mulholland Jr. contrasts two approaches to Scripture, **informational reading** and **formational reading** (table 13.1).

INFORMATIONAL READING	FORMATIONAL READING
Seeks to cover as much as possible	Focuses on small portions
A linear process	An in-depth process
Seeks to master the text	Allows the text to master us
The text as an object to use	The text as a subject that shapes us
Analytical, critical, and judgmental approach	Humble, submissive, willing, loving approach
Problem-solving mentality	Openness to mystery

TABLE 13.1

There is an important place for informational reading of Scripture and for exegetical and topical methods of Bible study. But those who approach Scripture in this way often overlook the formational approach that centers on speaking to the heart more than informing the mind. The Bible is not merely an object but a divinely inspired oracle that is "living and active" (Hebrews 4:12) and has the power to transform those who receive it in humility and obedience (James 1:21–22). Devotional spirituality stresses the formative power of revealed truth and encourages us to love God through his Word. We will look at a time-tested method of doing this in the next chapter.

Loving God through His Works

> *Say to God, "How awesome are Your works!"*
> *Come and see the works of God,*
> *Who is awesome in His deeds toward the sons of men.*
> *I shall remember the deeds of the LORD;*
> *Surely I will remember Your wonders of old.*
> *I will meditate on all Your work*
> *And muse on Your deeds.*
> *You are the God who works wonders;*
> *You have made known Your strength among the peoples.*
> *You have by Your power redeemed Your people.*
> *Psalm 66:3, 5; 77:11–12, 14–15*

The psalmists frequently reviewed and reflected upon God's historical acts of redemption, protection, and provision. Both Testaments abound with accounts of how God has worked in specific and dramatic ways in the lives of people and in the destiny of nations. He has demonstrated his just and loving purposes in the arena of human history, and prayerful consideration of his mighty works of creation, redemption, and consummation is another way of enhancing our worship and devotion for the triune Godhead.

"Worthy are You, our Lord and our God, to receive glory and honor and power; for You created all things, and because of Your will they existed, and were created.... Worthy are You to take the book and to break its seals; for You were slain, and purchased for God with Your blood men from every tribe and tongue and people and nation. You have made them to be a kingdom and priests to our God; and they will reign upon the earth.... Worthy is the Lamb that was slain to receive power and riches and wisdom and might and honor and glory and blessing.... To Him who sits on the throne, and to the Lamb, be blessing and honor and glory and dominion forever and ever" (Revelation 4:11; 5:9–10, 12–13).

Loving God through His Ways

"He made known His ways to Moses, His acts to the sons of Israel" (Psalm 103:7). Moses knew the Lord not only through his works but also through his ways. God's ways concern his personal involvement in our lives and our experiences of his peace, power, provision, protection, compassion, and care. It is good to build a personal history of God's providential care by reviewing and remembering the things he has done at various points along your spiritual journey. Remember his surprising answers to prayer, the way he drew you to himself, the way he carried you through turbulent waters, the way he provided for your needs when circumstances looked hopeless, the way he encouraged and comforted you in your distress, the way he exhorted you through others and disciplined you for your good, and the way he seeks to strip you of your hope in the things of this world so that you will learn to hope only in him.

> *Come and hear, all who fear God,*
> *And I will tell of what He has done for my soul.*
> *Certainly God has heard;*
> *He has given heed to the voice of my prayer.*
> *Blessed be God,*
> *Who has not turned away my prayer*
> *Nor His lovingkindness from me.*
> *Your way, O God, is holy;*
> *What god is great like our God?*
>
> *Psalm 66:16, 19–20; 77:13*

"I will tell of what He has done for my soul." Grateful reflection on what God has done for your soul is a vital component of devotional spirituality.

God's ways also relate to the multifaceted attributes of his person, powers, and perfections. Our capacity to love God is related to our image of God, so we do well to pray for the grace of growing apprehension of the glories of his attributes: his unlimited power, presence, and knowledge; his holiness, justice, goodness, truthfulness, and righteousness; his goodness, grace, compassion, mercy, and love; his beauty, glory, greatness, transcendent majesty, and dominion; and his self-existence, eternity, infinity, and immutability. As Dallas Willard puts it in *The Divine Conspiracy*, God is "an interlocking community of magnificent persons, completely self-sufficing and with no meaningful limits on goodness and power." He is the absolute answer to the perennial quest for the true, the good, and the beautiful.

THREE PSALMS ON THE BEAUTIFUL ATTRIBUTES OF GOD

Psalm 139

There is no higher calling than to love and worship the infinite and personal God of creation and redemption. A. W. Tozer observed that what comes into our minds when we think about God is the most important thing about us. Our image of God shapes our spiritual direction and future and is forged in the times we spend in communion with him. In contrast to the world, God's economy measures greatness not in terms of ability or accomplishments but in the vitality and integrity of a person's walk with the Lord. King David was a gifted man who was rich in achievements, yet his greatness lay in his choice to give his heart wholly to God. In the midst of his struggles, David took time to meditate and stretch his vision of the living God, and this provided him with a renewed perspective about the things that really matter.

If we unthinkingly take life for granted and lose our sense of wonder at God and his creation, our capacity to worship will atrophy. David's ongoing amazement and wonder is captured in Psalm 139, a beautiful meditation on the knowledge, presence, power, and holiness of the Ruler of all creation.

The All-Knowing God (vv. 1–6)

"O Lᴏʀᴅ, You have searched me and known me." As he reflects on the omniscience of God, David is overwhelmed by the truth that God has exposed him and intimately knows him. The same is true of us: God has mined us to the depths of our being, and his knowledge besieges us all around ("You have enclosed me behind and before, and laid Your hand upon me"). He knows our actions, our words, our thoughts, and our motives. Such knowledge is overwhelming, not only because it is beyond our comprehension but also because it exposes all our pretenses. Yet it is comforting to know that there is no need of pretense before God; he knows us through and through, including our darkest thoughts and deeds, and still loves us unconditionally.

The All-Present God (vv. 7–12)

"Where can I go from Your Spirit? Or where can I flee from Your presence?" Not only does God know us, but also he is with us all the time; he "sees the invisible and penetrates the inaccessible" (Derek Kidner). There is no escape—height or depth, day or night, past or future—nothing can conceal us from the Hound of Heaven. This can be a disturbing thought, especially in times of disobedience and rebellion; the impulse to hide from God's presence dates back to the first sin (Genesis 3:8). But this truth can also be a source of great comfort and assurance, because we know that as believers in Christ, we are never alone. He gave us his promise that he is with us always (Matthew 28:20), and we can find our security in his enfolding presence.

The All-Powerful God (vv. 13–18)

"I will give thanks to You, for I am fearfully and wonderfully made; wonderful are Your works, and my soul knows it very well." The third stanza of this psalm portrays the omnipotence of the Creator by a poetic description of the wonder of human birth. What artist would create his magnum opus in darkness? Yet God wove us together with all our variegated colors in the hiddenness of the womb ("the depths of the earth"). He formed us to be a unity of body, soul, and spirit with all our capacities for thought, communication, morality, and aspiration. His eyes saw our embryos, and he appointed all the days that were ordained for us on this planet. The all-powerful Lord of creation is worthy of all worship and trust, since nothing is too difficult for him (Jeremiah 32:17; Luke 1:37).

The All-Holy God (vv. 19–24)

As David concludes his meditation, the reality of his plight with his opponents ("men of bloodshed") confronts him again. He responds by aligning himself with the God of holiness and justice and declares that God's enemies are his enemies and God's cause is his cause. In the last two verses he takes us full circle ("O LORD, You have searched me and known me"): "Search me, O God, and know my heart; try me and know my anxious thoughts; and see if there be any hurtful way in me, and lead me in the everlasting way." As he faces opposition, the psalmist wants to remove any doubt about his walk with God. Does he know my situation? Does he care? Am I committed to his purposes? The answer is a resounding yes—he knows us intimately and is present with us in any adversity we face. The Lord also knows what is in our hearts, and we would be wise to follow David's practice of inviting him to illuminate areas of disobedience and rebellion in our lives so that he can lead us in the everlasting way.

Psalm 145

Imagine someone from a preliterate culture who stumbles upon a New Testament left inadvertently by a traveling missionary. The native picks up the strange object and brings it to the elders of his village, but because they have never heard of reading or writing, they are unable to discern the meaning of the mysterious black markings on the pages. They may come to revere the alien object, but unless an outsider comes and explains it to them, the living words it contains will never be more than dark squiggles on a gossamer white substance.

Our world is like that book; unless an Outsider explains it to us, we will reduce its glory to the impersonal forces of time plus chance, or we will worship the creature rather than the Creator. But this is a failure to grasp the higher levels of meaning—the markings are letters, the letters combine into words, the words conform to grammatical principles and form sentences, the sentences convey ideas, the ideas lead to aesthetic, ethical, and spiritual truth, and all truth comes from the infinite personal God.

The Word of God calls us to view the world and all of life from a divine rather than a human perspective. Our final integration point and source of meaning is upward, not downward, heavenly, not earthly, the Creator, not the cosmos. The world would define us by default; do nothing, and it will fill your eyes and ears with its system of values. The Word will define us only by discipline; we must choose to sit under its daily tutelage, or our minds will never be renewed and transformed by eternal values.

The last of the Davidic psalms exhorts us to fly with the wings of the Spirit to the pinnacle from which we can see everything from a biblical viewpoint. The more the eyes of our heart become accustomed to that vision, the more we will be amazed by the greatness, goodness, and grace of the living God. Psalm 145, a skillfully constructed acrostic poem, invites the people of God to let their spirits resonate with his Spirit as it alternates calls to praise and reasons for praise.

The Greatness of God (vv. 1–6)

"I will extol You, my God, O King, and I will bless Your name forever and ever. Every day I will bless You, and I will praise Your name forever and ever" (vv. 1–2). This paean of praise is prompted by the psalmist's meditation on "the glorious splendor" of God's majesty and on his wonderful works (v. 5). "Great is the LORD, and highly to be praised; and His greatness is unsearchable. One generation shall praise Your works to another, and shall declare Your mighty acts" (vv. 3–4). David understood that the human mind cannot begin to fathom God's greatness, and he would have agreed with these affirmations from Isaiah and Romans: "'For My thoughts are not your thoughts, neither are your ways My ways,' declares the LORD. 'For as the heavens are higher than the earth, so are My ways higher than your ways, and My thoughts than your thoughts.' ... Oh, the depth of the riches both of the wisdom and knowledge of God! How unsearchable are His judgments and unfathomable His ways!" (Isaiah 55:8–9; Romans 11:33). We will never be bored in heaven, because God's greatness and knowledge are boundless; the surprises will never end, and the joy will ever increase.

The Goodness of God (vv. 7–13)

"They shall eagerly utter the memory of Your abundant goodness and will shout joyfully of Your righteousness. The LORD is gracious and merciful; slow to anger and great in lovingkindness. The LORD is good to all, and His mercies are over all His works" (vv. 7–9). Because of his greatness, God is in control and will accomplish his purposes in spite of the malevolent forces of the world, the flesh, and the devil. Because of his goodness, God loves us unconditionally and without limit. Those who trust in him are therefore secure in the One who "loved them to the end" (John 13:1), knowing that he is always committed to their best interests. The more we embrace these biblical truths by faith, the more stable our lives will become, because our hope will be founded on the unchanging character of God rather than the ebb and flow of outward circumstances and inward feelings.

The Grace of God (vv. 14–21)

"The LORD sustains all who fall and raises up all who are bowed down. The LORD is righteous in all His ways, and kind in all His deeds. The LORD is near to all who call upon Him, to all who call upon Him in truth. He will fulfill the desire of those who fear Him; He will also hear their cry and will save them" (vv. 14, 17–19). The greatest human need is for that which we do not deserve and can never earn—the grace of

God. When we acknowledge our desperate need for God's grace, this itself is an evidence of his grace in our lives, since the natural pull of the flesh is toward the arrogance of autonomy. Begin each day by asking to grow in the grace of our Lord Jesus Christ and choosing to walk in the power of his Spirit.

Psalm 117

God's Worthship

Worship is the submission of all our nature to God. It is the quickening of conscience by his holiness; the nourishment of mind with his truth; the purifying of the imagination by his beauty; the opening of the heart to his love; the surrender of will to his purpose—and all of this gathered up in adoration, the most selfless emotion of which our nature is capable and therefore the chief remedy of that self-centeredness which is our original sin and the source of all actual sin.

WILLIAM TEMPLE

When we contemplate the gracefulness of a flower or the grandeur of a tree, we properly respond with aesthetic admiration. Similarly, we respond to our pets with affection and at times to other people with self-giving love. If nature is worthy of admiration, animals of affection, and human beings of sacrificial love, how then should we respond to the infinite and personal Author of all biological and spiritual life? The biblical answer is clear—God alone is worthy of worship. Blessing and honor and glory and dominion forever belong to the Creator and Redeemer (Revelation 5:13), and every tongue in heaven, on earth, and under the earth, including all who have rebelled against him, will confess this to be so (Philippians 2:10–11).

The worthship of God is the theme of Psalm 117, the shortest in the Psalter. In spite of its brevity, this two-verse psalm captures the essence of God's character and purpose for humanity. "Praise the LORD, all nations; laud Him, all peoples! For His lovingkindness is great toward us, and the truth of the LORD is everlasting. Praise the LORD!"

We were born to worship God. In *Desiring God*, John Piper modifies the Shorter Catechism's answer to the question "What is the chief end of man?" For him, the chief end of man is to glorify God by enjoying him forever. We honor God most when his glory becomes our greatest pleasure; we worship God best when we pursue our joy in him above all.

The psalmist begins with an invitation to praise that reaches beyond Israel to all the nations. Paul quotes this verse in Romans 15:11 to support his argument that in fulfilling God's covenant promises to Israel, Christ also extended grace and mercy to the Gentiles.

The Loyal Love of God

The second verse furnishes two wonderful reasons for worshiping God. The first is that "His lovingkindness is great toward us," or more literally, "His loyal love prevails over us." According to the Scriptures, God's love is causeless, measureless, and ceaseless (see Romans 5:5–11). The more we think about these truths, the more astounding the implications become. As A. W. Tozer prayed in *The Knowledge of the Holy*, "We are sure that there is in us nothing that could attract the love of One as holy and as just as Thou art. Yet Thou hast declared Thine unchanging love for us in Christ Jesus. If nothing in us can win Thy love, nothing in the universe can prevent Thee from loving us. Thy love is uncaused and undeserved. Thou art Thyself the reason for the love wherewith we are loved. Help us to believe the intensity, the eternity of the love that has found us. Then love will cast out fear; and our troubled hearts will be at peace, trusting not in what we are but in what Thou hast declared Thyself to be."

All of us need the security of unconditional love and acceptance, and this we discover in Christ. We can do nothing to make him love us more, and nothing we can do will make him love us less (see Romans 8:35, 38–39). Our prayer as believers in Christ should not be that we have more of him but that he has more of us.

The Faithfulness of God

The second reason given in Psalm 117 for worshiping God is that his faithfulness is everlasting. He has revealed his plans for his children, and his promises transcend anything we could have imagined. His purpose for us is our transformation—body, soul, and spirit—into the image and character of Jesus Christ. Because this is so, we must "hold fast the confession of our hope without wavering, for He who promised is faithful" (Hebrews 10:23; cf. Romans 4:21; 1 Thessalonians 5:24). Because he is faithful, God's plans and promises for us will never waver. There is no real security in people, possessions, or position; sooner or later, all of these will let us down. Our only true security is in the unchanging character and promises of the Lord.

God's loyal love and faithfulness should be the cause of childlike wonder and awe, but for most believers, these have become religious platitudes, mere words that no longer grip their hearts or imaginations. It is easy to lose our first love and forget what we were before we knew Christ and what we would be without him. Ask God for the grace to make you a worshiper, one who is amazed by his steadfast love and astonished by his faithfulness. Nourish your heart on high thoughts of God through devotional reading of the Scriptures, and worship him in Spirit and truth.

QUESTIONS FOR PERSONAL APPLICATION

- How rich is your image of God? How can you enhance this image and thereby enrich your soul?
- In what ways have you been able to love God through his world? His Word? His works? His ways?

- Which of God's attributes listed in "Loving God Through His Ways" are the most meaningful to you? Which seem the most remote? What does this tell you about your image of God?
- Read the three psalms (139, 145, 117) that were used in this chapter to extol the attributes of God. Which of these psalms means the most to you, and why?

14

DEVOTIONAL SPIRITUALITY

The Contemplative Way

CHAPTER OVERVIEW

Followers of the contemplative approach make the love of God their supreme and unrivaled object in life. This hunger and thirst for righteousness is the soul's love affair with its *summum bonum*, the highest good for which it was created. There will be seasons of dryness and darkness, but when our desire is for God's manifest presence, the way of the heart will seek his embrace.

CHAPTER OBJECTIVES

- An increased respect for the experiential way of the heart as a response to God
- A greater desire to seek and know the God who knows and loves us
- Recognition of the role of seasons of dryness and darkness in the spiritual life

In *The Little Prince* by Antoine de Saint-Exupéry, there is an enchanting story in which a fox asks the little prince to tame him. The fox says, "To me, you are still nothing more than a little boy who is just like a hundred thousand other little boys. And I have no need of you. And you, on your part, have no need of me. To you, I am nothing more than a fox like a hundred thousand other foxes. But if you tame me, then we shall need each other. To me, you will be unique in all the world. To you, I shall be unique in all the world . . ."

After a brief dialogue the fox goes on to say, "My life is very monotonous. I hunt chickens; men hunt me. All the chickens are just alike, and all the men are just alike. And, in consequence, I am a little bored. But if you tame me, it will be as if the sun came to shine on my life. I shall know the sound of a step that will be different from all the others. Other steps send me hurrying back underneath the ground. Yours will call me, like music, out of my burrow."

The little prince went on to tame the fox by observing the proper rites, and when the hour of the little prince's departure drew near, the fox gave him the present of a threefold secret. The first part of this secret is that "it is only with the heart that one can see rightly; what is essential is invisible to the eye."

This secret is the essence of the **contemplative** way. We must invite God to "tame" us so that we will learn the freedom of obedience to Christ and find our identity in his pleasure.

Because some people have negative associations with the idea of contemplation, let me make three points that should help reduce confusion.

First, contemplative spirituality is not the beginning point for those who are new to the faith. Spiritual infants need to grow in their knowledge of Scripture and "the elementary principles of the oracles of God" (Hebrews 5:12). "For everyone who partakes only of milk is not accustomed to the word of righteousness, for he is an infant. But solid food is for the mature, who because of practice have their senses trained to discern good and evil" (Hebrews 5:13–14). The disciplines of extensive Bible study and grounding in good theology should be regarded as prerequisites to the practices that will be discussed in this and the next chapter.

Second, meditation and contemplation must always be tethered to the truth of the Word. Contemplation is not an introspective New Age practice of altered consciousness or voiding the mind of content. Engagement in bogus **mysticism** and introspection leads at best to sloppy sentimentality and self-delusion and at worst to demonic influences. We circumvent this dangerous territory by commitment to sound doctrine, by being comfortable with a high view of Scripture, and by approaching the Word with a willingness to study it and put it in practice. The contemplative way should never be regarded as an end in itself or a substitute for obedience and faithful living in this world.

Third, meditation and contemplation are not limited to people with certain personalities, temperaments, and abilities. Some will naturally find this approach to be more attractive and accessible than others. But regardless of natural attraction, this way of developing spiritual passion and longing for God is beneficial for all mature believers.

The monastics described the way of contemplation as holy simplicity (*sancta simplicitas*)—the steady focus of the heart in the pursuit of a changeless good. Followers of the contemplative approach make the love of God their supreme and unrivaled object in life. This hunger and thirst for righteousness is the soul's love affair with its *summum bonum*, the highest good for which it was created. This involves both contrition (broken-heartedness) and cherishing (worshipful attention). It shifts the center of focus so that the gaze of the heart is turned away from ourselves to the triune God. It is the gradual development of a spiritual reflex so that we experience the liberty of the single, clear eye that is steadily fixed on Jesus (Luke 11:34; Hebrews 12:2).

To You I lift up my eyes,
O You who are enthroned in the heavens!
Behold, as the eyes of servants look to the hand of their master,

As the eyes of a maid to the hand of her mistress,
So our eyes look to the LORD our God,
Until He is gracious to us.

Psalm 123:1–2

Although the contemplative approach to Christian spirituality involves disciplines of renewing the mind and engaging the will, it is primarily an experiential way of the heart. It travels the mysterious path of realized fellowship with God through experiences of personal, loving, and intimate perception. Since "prayer is to religion what original research is to science" (P. T. Forsythe), contemplatives explore the spiritual milieu of apprehending God not by hearsay but by personal encounter. They have learned to "taste and see that the LORD is good" and to take refuge in him (Psalm 34:8). They have acquired a growing thirst for the river of living water that springs from the throne of God (see Ezekiel 47:1–12; Revelation 22:1–2). "If anyone is thirsty, let him come to Me and drink. He who believes in Me, as the Scripture said, 'From his innermost being will flow rivers of living water'" (John 7:37–38). Because Christ indwells us, his life is an artesian well that would flow out of us. Contemplative prayer draws from this well by turning inward toward the God who is closer to us than we can conceive. This form of prayer invites the mind to descend into the heart and to bow in silence before the living God. This concept of the heart refers to "the deepest psychological ground of one's personality, the inner sanctuary where self-awareness goes beyond analytical reflection and opens out into metaphysical and theological confrontation with the Abyss of the unknown yet present—one who is 'more intimate to us than we are to ourselves,'" as Thomas Merton wrote in *Contemplative Prayer*. Contemplative prayer nourishes the interior life and begets a luminous serenity that can permeate the various components of exterior life. It is a spiritual homing device that attunes us to the Presence that alone can satisfy our deepest longings.

"Cease striving, and know that I am God. . . . In repentance and rest you will be saved, in quietness and trust is your strength" (Psalm 46:10; Isaiah 30:15). Many of us suffer from the delusion that activity, accomplishments, size, and hubbub endear us to God and confirm his blessing. Although it runs against the grain of our surrounding culture, we must learn to practice the art of stillness, of quietness, of listening, and of receiving if we desire to be intimate with God. Because it takes time and loving attention to sustain a quality relationship, the Lord is more interested in our presence with him than in our performance for him. While we come to love God by knowing him, it is just as true that we come to know God by loving him. Contemplative prayer seeks to apprehend God through love and faith in such a way that theology is not merely speculative but lived. When the will is driven by affective intention, we desire to know God for himself, even when this knowledge leads us beyond the level of human ideas into the darkness of faith.

In *The Love of God*, Bernard of Clairvaux distinguishes four degrees of love. In the first, we love ourselves for our own sake, and in the second, we love God for our own blessing. In the third degree of love, we love God for God's own sake. Few sustain this blessed degree of love that is unsullied by self-interest in which we love those things that belong to Jesus Christ "even as Christ sought our interests, or rather sought us, and never looked after His own." But Bernard goes on to say, "Blessed is the man who can attain the fourth degree of love. Then he will love himself only in God!" To be possessed by this degree of divine love can only be a gift that is marked by the fragrance of heaven, not of earth.

The contemplative way is enriched by a venerable tradition that reaches back to the desert spirituality of Antony, Evagrius, and John Cassian and is perpetuated in the *Rule* of St. Benedict. It is expounded in the works of John Climacus, Simeon the New Theologian, Aelred of Rievaulx, Bernard of Clairvaux, Jan van Ruysbroeck, Richard Rolle, the anonymous author of *The Cloud of Unknowing*, Teresa of Avila, John of the Cross, François Fénelon, and many others. In more recent years, it has found a diversity of expression in the writings of Evelyn Underhill, Frank Laubach, Thomas Kelly, A. W. Tozer, Thomas Merton, and Henri Nouwen. The hearts of these remarkable followers of Christ were unified and wholly attuned to God. They were consumed by what Rolle called *The Fire of Love*, an experiential encounter with God that is marked by holy desire. This excerpt from Blaise Pascal's testimony of his conversion in 1654 well illustrates this consuming passion:

Year of Grace 1654
Monday 23 November, feast of St. Clement, Pope and Martyr, and of others in the Martyrology.
Eve of St. Crysogonus, martyr and others.
From about half past ten at night to about half an hour after midnight,

FIRE

"God of Abraham, God of Isaac, God of Jacob" (Exodus 3:6), not of philosophers and scholars.
Certitude, heartfelt joy, peace.
God of Jesus Christ.
God of Jesus Christ.
"My God and Your God" (John 20:17).
"Your God shall be my God" (Ruth 1:16).
The world forgotten, everything except God.
He can only be found in by the ways that have been taught in the Gospels.
Greatness of the human soul.

"O righteous Father, the world has not known You, but I have known You"
   (John 17:25).
Joy, Joy, Joy, tears of joy.

After his death Pascal's *Memorial* was found sewn into his clothing; evidently he carried it with him at all times.

DETACHMENT AND DESIRE

As the deer pants for the water brooks,
So my soul pants for You, O God.
My soul thirsts for God, for the living God;
When shall I come and appear before God?

Psalm 42:1–2

O God, You are my God; I shall seek You earnestly;
My soul thirsts for You, my flesh yearns for You,
In a dry and weary land where there is no water.

Psalm 63:1

God's grace is always previous to our desire to know him. His love initiates our relationship with him, and when we love God, this is our response to his interior invitation to personal intimacy. "We love, because He first loved us" (1 John 4:19). He has lavished the riches of his grace upon us by calling us into the eternal life that our Lord defined as knowing the only true God and Jesus Christ whom he sent into the world (John 17:3). The nature of our response to God's initiatives shapes the quality of our earthly sojourn and heavenly existence. Positive reciprocation and a developing habit of sensitivity to the loving overtures of the living God makes us increasingly attentive and receptive to the subtle activity of the Spirit within us. This answering love of the created personality inspires a holy quest for God and a spiritual receptivity that is sustained by humility, trust, and obedience. "When You said, 'Seek My face,' my heart said to You, 'Your face, O LORD, I shall seek'" (Psalm 27:8). In this quest, we learn to approach God less as an object or intellectual construct and more as a personality with whom we have an ongoing encounter in affective union. To rest in God who loves us, draws us near to him, and lets us find him is to lay hold of the power of obedient submission to grace.

The fire of divine love purges as well as enflames. It creates in us a growing realization of our spiritual poverty, of our desperate need, and of our cold indifference. As the theologian Karl Rahner expressed it, the human person is the mystery of infinite emptiness, and God is the mystery of infinite fullness. As we become aware of our spiritual indigence, our deluded complacency is shattered and we discover our abject nothingness before God. In the contemplative tradition, this is called **compunction** of heart *(compunctio cordis)*. Compunction involves the sorrowful realization of our preoccupation with selfish interests; in this state we are pierced and stung by the truth of our sinful condition and distance from God. But the tears of compunction also relate to desire for God, the One whom we seek. It is this desire for God that sets us on the difficult path of self-emptying and self-denial, of losing our lives so that we may lay hold of Christ's life (Matthew 10:38–39). Desire for God requires a fundamental reorientation—away from narcissistic enslavement to earthly desires, acquisitions, and ambitions and toward an others-centered pursuit of God and love for people. This transformational shifting of our center from the I to the Thou involves a painful and gradual purgation of the desire for perishing things that desensitize us to heavenly desire.

Thus **detachment** from the temporal and desire for the eternal work together; detachment from the world is caused by and enhances attachment to Christ. The pursuit of God *(quaerere Deum)* heightens our awareness of being exiles, pilgrims, and sojourners who increasingly long to be "at home" with him (2 Corinthians 5:2–9; Philippians 1:23; 3:20). Because we are gradually conformed to what we desire, we should pray for the grace of holy desire. Even if we do not desire God above all else, do we desire to desire him above all else? "It is not what you are nor what you have been that God sees with his all-merciful eyes, but what you desire to be." These encouraging words from *The Cloud of Unknowing* underscore the importance of intention of heart *(intentio cordis)*, the movement of our being toward God. The focus of our intention is sharpened by love for Christ and dulled by earthly attachment. This is why the author of the epistle to the Hebrews exhorts us to "lay aside every encumbrance and the sin which so easily entangles us, and let us run with endurance the race that is set before us, fixing our eyes on Jesus, the author and perfecter of faith" (Hebrews 12:1–2). Even though we stumble in practice, holy intention and sincerity of desire are pleasing to our heavenly Father.

As we respond to the promptings of grace, we move in the direction of purity of heart *(puritas cordis)*. As Søren Kierkegaard put it, purity of heart is to will one thing; an undivided heart is integrated, harmonized, and simplified. Simplicity in this sense is the opposite of the duplicity that is caused by a heart that is sundered by inordinate attachment to a multiplicity of finite things. A life lived in accordance with the gospel becomes more centered on the one thing necessary, the good part that will not be taken away (Luke 10:42). The undivided heart loves in all things God's will rather than the things themselves. This purity of communion with God is never attained quickly or fully; it is the fruit of the grace of God and decades of stumbling pursuit. In the mystery of divine love, the more we find God, the harder we pursue him. May we echo the great prayer of Moses, "I pray You, show me Your glory!" (Exodus 33:18).

SEASONS OF DRYNESS AND DARKNESS

Entanglement, double-mindedness, compromise, and complacency are enemies of spiritual progress. Unless we have an acute sense of need, we will not grow in grace. In his goodness, God sometimes dislodges us from our illusions and complacency by allowing us to experience trials and brokenness in our outer world or by leading us through the desert of dryness and darkness in our inner world. Thus devotional and contemplative spirituality involves alternating patterns and combinations of sorrow and joy, of delight and emptiness, of warm experience and feelings of abandonment. These patterns are evident in the Psalter, and this is one of the reasons why psalmody is central to the contemplative tradition.

Growth in prayer is similar to growth in marriage; just as romantic love alone cannot sustain a marriage for very long, so a relationship with God that is driven solely by feelings becomes shallow and unstable. The quest for fervent experiences and tangible results is the mark of a psychocentric approach to prayer. If we are to mature into theocentric prayer, we must be weaned of our dependence on feelings and press on to purity of intention and will even when positive sensations are absent. We must stop measuring the quality of our times of prayer and meditation by how well we feel during them, since difficult and apparently fruitless times of prayer may contribute more to our development than times of consolation and enthusiasm. As in other areas of life, we often learn more from experiences of weakness and dryness in prayer than we do from gratifying successes. This is why fidelity to the process of showing up before God on a daily basis is critical. We may experience alternating darkness and light as the Lord draws us through ever-deepening rhythms of death to self and life in Christ. These rhythms confront us with new realizations of the veil of self that separates us from the manifest presence of the holy God. They reveal our desperate condition and our need to renounce our exaggerated estimates, our deluded images, and our attachment to reputation and accomplishment. Outward trials and inward dryness become means of grace when they drive us to a more profound realization of our helplessness and emptiness before God. They cause us to see that the false self is far worse than we ever imagined and that Christ is far greater than we ever dreamed. In this condition in which God exposes our absurd hiding places, we become more spiritually supple and willing to surrender to his loving purposes. When Augustine cried out, "May I know you, may I know myself!" *(Noverim te, noverim me)*, he knew that the better we know God, the better we will know ourselves. The joy of growing attachment to Christ leads inevitably to the pain of growing detachment from the false self. Humility of heart *(humilitas cordis)* involves a progressive awareness of God's grace, acceptance, and presence and a consequent willingness to affirm that his will for us is "good and acceptable and perfect" (Romans 12:2). The more we forget ourselves, the more we come to see that all things are "from Him and through Him and to Him" (Romans 11:36).

A rich tradition relates to what St. John of the Cross called "the dark night of sense" and "the dark night of the spirit." Followers of Christ since the time of the Eastern and Western patristics and monastics have attempted to describe the spiritual journey of those who have seriously sought union with God. The movement toward Christian proficiency generally leads to a point in which the senses are stripped of all pleasure and joy in prayer. This experience of aridity and apparent destruction is a gracious purifying process that leads the soul to direct its attention toward God and to know itself only in him. Those who submit to these painful purifications learn to persevere in the pursuit of God even in the absence of spiritual consolations. This night of the soul leads through dread to eventual joy, not despair; it refines the intentions of the heart and creates greater simplicity and sincerity.

Even so, Thomas Dubay in *Fire Within* observes that "comparatively few of those who reach the first night grow beyond it." This is largely due to an unwillingness to endure the pain of entire abandonment to worldly values and minor disobediences. The second night, the dark night of the spirit, is an even deeper darkness that may begin years after the first. In it, the more subtle roots of pride and impurity are withered by a divine purification that denudes the soul of human approaches to affections, feelings, memories, intellect, and will. The soul feels wretched, abandoned by God, and undone but learns to cling to him alone until the blessing of God's infused love becomes more real than ever.

These seasons of dryness and darkness are not punishments but purifications and graces that deal with the deep spiritual fissure of the sinful self. They teach the soul to listen to and embrace God's will in its impenetrable mystery. They are signs of progress in prayer when they are accompanied by the surrender of control and by personal abandonment to God, not for his gifts but for himself. Some diligent followers of Christ experience these nights as decisive events, while others experience them more than once in increasingly intense ways as they draw closer to God. The passionate knight of faith longs to break through the barriers that separate him from the divine Presence and realizes with growing poignancy that no earthly grail will ever satisfy his longing, since it is directed toward the infinite and the unbounded.

Relationships must grow in mutual freedom, so no technique or set of steps will assure an encounter with God. "The wind blows where it wishes" (John 3:8), but we impatiently assume that God should show up on the relatively rare occasions when we do. If the truth be told, God knocks on our doors a great deal more than we do on his. Along these lines, there has been a tendency of late for people to read about the "dark nights" and to dignify their ordinary trials, disciplines, and difficult outward circumstances by diagnosing them as dark nights of sense or the spirit. But on most cases, dryness and aridity in prayer are not related to spiritual endeavor but to a lack of serious pursuit.

LIMITS OF HUMAN REASON

The contemplative way affirms that the highest love of God is spiritual, not intellectual. John Chrysostom and Gregory of Nyssa wrote of the incomprehensibility of God and of the "mystical night" in which God is hidden in darkness that is beyond our understanding. God cannot be captured and possessed in the way we seek to grasp and investigate an object. We can know him only as a transcendent subject, a person who chooses to reveal aspects of himself to us.

Knowing God involves the mind but moves beyond reason and formulation to faith and trust. If we were to use an analogy from physics, we would say that the rainbow of colors we see represents only a tiny fraction of the whole spectrum of electromagnetic radiation. This spectrum begins with high-energy and high-frequency particle gamma rays, nuclear gamma rays, and x-rays; it moves through the middle range of ultraviolet to infrared wavelengths of light; and it ends with the lower-energy and lower-frequency range of microwaves, radio and television communications, and sound waves. Just as the electromagnetic radiation that is visible to human eyesight is but a speck on a much larger spectrum, so human reason can perceive only a minute trace of the awesome mystery we call God. Acknowledging both the value and the limits of reason, we come to see that growth in the experiential and personal knowledge of God is produced by faith, hope, and love. Faith brings us to an awareness of ourselves not only as known by God but also as invited to participate in union and communion with him. Hope inspires us to dare to long for the infinite and to transfer our aspirations from the earthly to the eternal as we "rest in the LORD and wait patiently for Him" (Psalm 37:7). And love seeks to possess the Beloved as it increasingly realizes the degree to which we have already been possessed by him.

QUESTIONS FOR PERSONAL APPLICATION

- Did you have a difficult time relating your experience to the content of this chapter? If so, why?
- What is the longest time you have ever spent alone with God? Was this a positive experience? What keeps you from spending more extended times with him?
- How can you move from the mind to the heart in your encounters with the Word? Do you desire to do this, or does this sound too mystical to you?
- What do you learn about yourself when you are alone with God?
- What do compunction of heart, intention of heart, purity of heart, and humility of heart mean to you?
- What experiences have you had with seasons of dryness and darkness? What did you learn from these experiences?

15

DEVOTIONAL SPIRITUALITY
The Practice of Sacred Reading

CHAPTER OVERVIEW

The ancient practice of sacred reading involves a process of moving from the mind to the heart through reading, meditation, prayer, and contemplation. This chapter offers several suggestions for each of these elements and for sacred reading as a whole.

CHAPTER OBJECTIVES

- Learning to treasure the revealed Word through formational reading
- Better appreciation for the nature and benefits of meditation
- Desire to adapt the Scriptures into personal prayers
- Willingness to experiment with contemplation, the prayer of silence

At the end of the section on disciplined spirituality, I mentioned the ancient art of sacred reading *(lectio divina)* that was introduced to the West by the Eastern desert father John Cassian early in the fifth century. The sixth-century *Rule* of St. Benedict that has guided Benedictine and Cistercian monastic practice ever since prescribed daily periods for sacred reading. In spite of the simplicity and power of this method of praying through sacred Scripture, it gradually fell into disuse and obscurity. By the end of the Middle Ages it came to be seen as a method that should be restricted to the spiritually elite. As time passed, even monastics lost the simplicity of sacred reading as it was replaced by more complicated systems and forms of mental prayer. In recent decades, however, this ancient practice has been revitalized, especially by those in the Cistercian tradition. Writers like Thomas Merton *(Contemplative Prayer, New Seeds of Contemplation, Spiritual Direction and Meditation)*, Thomas Keating *(Intimacy with God, Open Mind, Open Heart)*, Michael Casey *(Sacred Reading, Toward God, The Undivided Heart)*, and Thelma Hall *(Too Deep for Words)* have been promoting sacred reading in Catholic circles, and Protestants are now being exposed to this approach as well. *Lectio divina* involves a progression through the four movements of reading, meditation, prayer, and contemplation. (I have created a series of four sacred reading journals that guide people through this process. These are: *Sacred Readings, Historic Creeds, The Trinity,* and *The Psalms.*)

READING (*LECTIO*)

In his study of monastic culture, *The Love of Learning and the Desire for God,* Jean Leclercq distinguished two distinct approaches to Scripture that were used in the Middle Ages. While medieval universities were urban schools that prepared clerics for the active life, rural monasteries focused on spiritual formation within a liturgical framework to equip monks for the contemplative life. The scholastics approached Scripture by focusing on the page of sacred text *(sacra pagina)* as an object to be studied and investigated by putting questions to the text *(quaestio)* and by questioning oneself with the subject matter *(disputatio)*. By contrast, the monastics approached Scripture through a personal orientation of meditation *(meditatio)* and prayer *(oratio)*. While the scholastics sought science and knowledge in the text, the monastics sought wisdom and appreciation. Those in the schools were more oriented to the objective, the theological, and the cognitive; those in the cloisters were more oriented to the subjective, the devotional, and the affective.

Most contemporary approaches to Bible study have more in common with the scholastics than with the monastics. In terms of a distinction that was made in the first chapter in this section, they are more concerned with informational reading than with formational reading. There is a legitimate need for both approaches, because an overemphasis on one or the other can lead to the extremes of cold intellectualism or mindless enthusiasm. But when evangelicals study Scripture, they typically look more for precepts and principles than for an encounter with God in the depths of their being. The practice of *lectio divina* can correct this lack of balance, because it stresses reading Scripture for spiritual formation through receptive openness to God's loving call of grace. *Lectio* is not an intellectual exercise that seeks to control and to gather information but a voluntary immersion in the Word of God that seeks to receive and to respond. Spiritual reading melds revelation with experience. It is done in the spirit of the collect for the second Sunday in Advent in the 1928 *Book of Common Prayer:*

> Blessed Lord, who hast caused all holy Scriptures to be written for our learning; Grant that we may in such wise hear them, read, mark, learn, and inwardly digest them, that by patience and comfort of thy holy Word, we may embrace, and ever hold fast, the blessed hope of everlasting life, which thou hast given us in our Saviour Jesus Christ.

May we learn to hear the holy Scriptures and to "read, mark, learn, and inwardly digest" them.

Suggestions for Reading

- Choose a special place, preferably away from your desk and other areas of activity, that is suitable for this purpose. Sanctify this space by reserving it as a regular meeting place with the Lord.
- Choose a special time in which you can be alert and consistent. Invite God to lead you to rearrange your life to allow more time with him. This will be more a matter of *making* time rather than finding time. Making time for this purpose is a response to God's calling in a world of constant external demands. Although this will not work for everyone, I recommend exchanging the last hour of the night for an extra hour in the morning. (Most of us could redeem a significant amount of time by reducing and being more selective in our intake of television.) Whenever it is, give God your best time, when you are least sluggish, and when you can be quiet, still, and unpressured by outward hindrances.
- Consistency is critical, since there will be many temptations to postpone and neglect sacred reading. The benefits of *lectio* are attained gradually over a long term.
- Since *lectio divina* engages the whole person, your bodily posture is important. A seated position in which your body is erect but not tense or slouched is best for the four movements of *lectio*. It is good to be attentive and alert without sitting in a way that will eventually impede your circulation or breathing.
- Try to be systematic in the way you select your Scripture texts. They can emerge from a daily Bible reading program or from a lectionary that gives you daily Old Testament, gospel, and epistle readings. Or your passages can come out of a devotional guide (I often use my *Handbook to Prayer* and *Handbook to Renewal* for this purpose).
- To avoid distraction, it is better to use a Bible without study notes. Use an accurate translation rather than a paraphrase (I use the updated edition of the NASB) for *lectio divina*.
- If Bible teachers and ministers did both *sacra pagina* (exegetical study) and *lectio divina* on the texts they select, this practice would greatly enhance their teaching and preaching.
- Keep the passage brief—do not confuse quantity with quality.
- It is also helpful to apply this method of slow, deliberate, and prayerful reading to other resources such as the creeds, traditional and patristic texts, and classic spiritual books. Samples of some of these resources are available in *Devotional Classics*, edited by Richard J. Foster and James Bryan Smith. Older literature has a way of challenging the biases of our modern presuppositions, if we will let it penetrate us.

- Begin with a prayer of preparation: for example, "Open my eyes, that I may behold wonderful things from Your law" (Psalm 119:18) or "Let the words of my mouth and the meditation of my heart be acceptable in Your sight, O LORD, my rock and my Redeemer" (Psalm 19:14). Start with a clear intention to know God's will for your life with a resolution in advance to do it.

- Slowly read the text again and again until it is in your short-term memory. Try making your first readings audible, since this will make them slower and more deliberate. Bear in mind that in antiquity, reading always meant reading aloud.

- Seek the meaning of the text; ask questions. But come more as a disciple than as a collector of information. See Scripture as iconographic; that is, a verbal window into the reality of life that turns your perspective around.

- Listen to the words in humility accompanied by a willingness to obey. Hearing the Word must be united by faith (Hebrews 4:2) with an intention to apply it in practice (James 1:22). Open yourself to be addressed by the Word in your attitudes, habits, choices, and emotions. There will be times when you resist a penetrating living encounter with God, and these generally have to do with areas of disobedience. Thus it is wise to examine your being and doing in the light of the text by asking, "Lord, what are you saying to me in this passage?"

- Remember that unlike ordinary reading, in *lectio* you are seeking to be more shaped by the Word than informed by the Word. This first step of reading prepares you for the remaining three movements of meditation, prayer, and contemplation. But the whole process should be infused with a prayerful attitude.

- Seek to avoid the usual pragmatic reflex that seeks to net out some immediate nugget or benefit. Approach sacred reading with no conditions, demands, or expectations. The Word may not meet your perceived needs, but it will touch your real needs, even when you don't discern them.

MEDITATION (*MEDITATIO*)

As you move from reading to meditation, you are seeking to saturate and immerse yourself in the Word, to luxuriate in its living waters, and to receive the words as an intimate and personal message from God. The purpose of meditation is to penetrate the Scriptures and to let them penetrate us through the loving gaze of the heart. The term "mental prayer" is often associated with meditation, but this could be misleading, since *lectio*, *meditatio*, and *oratio* involve not only the mind but also the heart. Meditation attunes the inward self to the Holy Spirit so that our hearts harmonize and resonate with his voice. Meditation is a spiritual work of holy desire and an interior invitation for the Spirit to pray and speak within us (Romans 8:26–27) in such a way that our whole being is transformed into greater conformity with Jesus Christ. It is an intentional process of building our passion for Christ by meeting with him and spending time with him to know him more clearly, to love him more dearly, and to follow him more nearly. By meditating on God's truth, we are inviting Christ to be formed in us (Galatians 4:19) by a deliberate dwelling on his words. Thus mental prayer should not be seen as an abstract exercise but as a vital vehicle for the metamorphosis of the soul.

"This book of the law shall not depart from your mouth, but you shall meditate on it day and night, so that you may be careful to do according to all that is written in it; for then you will make your way prosperous, and then you will have success" (Joshua 1:8). This familiar verse tells us that the path to success as God defines it is the habit of making space in our lives to meet with God in his holy Word with a heart intention to apply what he reveals through obedient action. Only those who delight in God's Word and habitually meditate on it (Psalm 1:2) will experience the fullness and stability of God's purpose and calling. May you be one of them.

Suggestions for Meditation

- God's love for us teaches us to love him; thus we should not regard meditation as an objective method or technique but as a person-specific process. It is good to experiment with different approaches until you find a pattern of meditation that resonates best with your soul.
- Acknowledge the holiness of the God you are approaching and the richness of the gift of faith that makes it possible for you to enjoy an encounter with him through his Spirit.
- Meditation is a long-term process that builds upon itself. The more we absorb Scripture, the greater our mental storehouse becomes. As this process continues for months and years, we experience the phenomenon of *reminiscence*, in which a word or phrase spontaneously evokes a wealth of imagery from other parts of Scripture. This can be an exciting and creative experience in which we see connections and rhythms we never perceived before. These chain reactions, the fruit of habitual meditation, develop "the mind of Christ" (1 Corinthians 2:16) in us.
- Allow enough time to enjoy the text; to rush this process is like running through a great art gallery.
- Meditation on Scripture involves chewing or ruminating (*ruminatio*) on a word, phrase, passage, or story. To carry this analogy further, when we masticate the text in our minds, we release the full flavor as we assimilate its content.
- Don't force meditation or make impatient demands of immediate gratification and results. Meditation will do you little good if you try to control the outcome.

- When you encounter something that speaks particularly to you, you should note it so that you can reflect on it later. You may find it helpful to make written reminders that you can carry with you.
- It may also be beneficial to keep a journal of your reflections on the text. If you do this, you will need to be open and honest in the things you record. A journal is a private record that can be reviewed from time to time.
- Personalize the words of the text and *realize* them; receive them as God speaking to you in the present moment. Try to hear the passage as though for the first time, personally addressed to you.
- When a passage speaks to you, consider meditating on the same text for several days before moving on to another.
- The millions of images we have been exposed to through television, movies, magazines, and newspapers have not sharpened but dulled our creative imagination. More than ever, we need to develop and sanctify our imagination, because the truth of Scripture and spiritual experience is "impregnated with a mysterious light impossible to analyze" (Jean Leclercq). A sanctified imagination will enable us to grasp more than we can see, but we need the lifeline of Scripture to tether us to the truth.
- Many people have found it helpful to engage the five senses when meditating on biblical stories, especially the stories in the Gospels. This process makes the scene more present and real to us and it helps us transition from the cognitive, analytical level to the affective, feeling level of our being.
- It can also be illuminating to put yourself in the story. How would you have reacted, and what would you have thought and said if you were there?
- The *Spiritual Exercises* of Ignatius of Loyola incorporates these and other meditative techniques and has useful insights on contemplating the incarnation, life, death, resurrection, and ascension of Christ. The various meditations and prayers prescribed in *Introduction to the Devout Life* by Francis de Sales (e.g., on our creation, the end for which we were created, sin, death, humility, God's love for us) are also valuable resources. But because of differing temperaments, not everyone will find such methodical meditation schemes to be of help. Most people are sensory, but some are more analytical, and others are more intuitive. Intuitives will benefit more from savoring the truths of a passage than from its imagery. "Pray as you can, not as you can't!" (Dom Chapman).
- Meditation on the psalms *(meditatio psalmorum)* has edified the saints for thousands of years and should be a regular part of our spiritual diet. It is enormously beneficial in all seasons and conditions of life to savor and absorb the meaning of the psalms in the depths of one's heart.

- Ideally, meditation should address the mind, the emotions, and the will. Ruminating on Scripture stimulates our thinking and understanding and it also elevates the affections of the heart. It reaches the will when we resolve to let the passage shape our actions. Intellect, imagination, and volition should not be divorced from one another.

- Accept the fact that you will often encounter problems with distraction and inattention. Do not be disturbed when your mind wanders, but gently and calmly return to the text before you. "It is much better to desire God without being able to think clearly of Him, than to have marvelous thoughts about Him without desiring to enter into union with His will," Thomas Merton advises in *New Seeds of Contemplation*. Normally it is best to resist the temptation to be distracted by practical concerns, but sometimes it can be helpful to turn these concerns into subjects of meditation in light of the truth of the text.

- Remember that meditation does not need to produce evident affection or consolation in order to be beneficial. The quest for moving experiences can lead to the self-deception of emotional melodrama and counterfeit mysticism.

PRAYER (*ORATIO*)

The discipline of prayer is usually associated with a personal dialogue (colloquy) with God, though the majority of the prayers people offer appear to be petitionary monologues. In *lectio divina*, prayer is specifically related to the two prior movements of sacred reading and meditation on the text. *Oratio* is the fruit of *meditatio*, and it is the way in which we interiorize what God has spoken to us through the passage. The transition from meditation to prayer may be subtle or unnoticed, but it is a response of the heart to what has been largely occupying the mind. It is a movement from truth to implication, from hearing to acknowledgment, from understanding to obedience.

Depending on how the "living and active" word is shaping us (Hebrews 4:12), this period of prayer can be sweet and consoling, or it can be painful and revealing. The two-edged sword of the Spirit has a way of exposing the thoughts and intentions of the heart, and when our selfish, distorted, and manipulative strategies are "open and laid bare to the eyes of Him with whom we have to do" (Hebrews 4:13), *oratio* becomes a time for compunction, confession, and repentance. When the soul is exposed and we see our interior and exterior lives more as God sees them, this experience can be both devastating (in light of God's holiness) and exhilarating (in light of God's forgiveness and compassion). At other times, we may be gripped by the power of spiritual truth (e.g., the kindness and love of the Father, the grace and faithfulness of the Son, the fellowship and presence of the Spirit) and respond in adoration or thanksgiving. *Oratio* is a time for participation in the interpenetrating subjectivity of the Trinity through prolonged mutual presence and growing identification with the life of Christ.

Suggestions for Prayer

- Allow enough time so that you do not rush the process; you are not likely to listen to God when you are in a hurry.
- Avoid the rut of reducing this period of prayer to a technique or a routine.
- In *lectio divina*, there is a temptation to substitute reading for prayer. It is helpful to view your reading and meditation on the text as preparation for a personal prayerful response.
- Do not seek to control the content or outcome of your prayer.
- Remember that *oratio* is a time for heart response as you move from the mind to the will. Prayer embraces the practical consequences of the truth you have seen and endeavors to direct your life in accordance with it.
- Depending on your reading and meditation, your response can take a number of different forms, including adoration, confession, renewal, petition, intercession, affirmation, and thanksgiving. All of these are different ways of calling upon the Lord, but at one time a prayer of adoration may be appropriate, while at another time the Spirit may lead you in a prayer of confession or petition.
- When the Lord speaks to you in the text by way of exhortation or encouragement, it is good to pray it through, that is, to take the time to internalize the message.
- See this time as an opportunity to a move away from your false self (the flesh) toward your true self in Christ.
- Scripture is God-breathed and "profitable for teaching, for reproof, for correction, for training in righteousness" (2 Timothy 3:16). Invite the Spirit to search, teach, encourage, comfort, and correct you. Let him reveal and dispel your illusions, pride, self-centeredness, stubbornness, ungodly attitudes and habits, stinginess, lack of gratitude, manipulation and control, and so forth.
- Prayer can occur at any time during the *lectio* process, and you may find yourself alternating between reading, meditation, and prayer. *Lectio divina* is not a lockstep 1–2–3–4 movement.
- When you are distracted, return to the text to refocus your attention. Teresa of Avila used an image of prayer as a small fire that occasionally needs to be fed by adding a twig or two. A twig is a few words from Scripture, but too many words become branches that could extinguish the fire.
- Bear in mind that in *lectio divina*, prayer is part of the path that leads to contemplation.

CONTEMPLATION (*CONTEMPLATIO*)

Some who use the term *lectio divina* limit it primarily to slow, careful, and prayerful reading of a biblical passage, book, or other spiritual text rather than the whole movement from reading to meditation to prayer to contemplation. As I see it, however, the process of *lectio divina* should begin with reading and culminate in contemplation. Contemplation is often confused with meditation, but as we will see, they are not synonymous.

Meditation and the prayer that flows out of it bring us into communication with the living and transcendent Lord, and as such, they prepare us for contemplation. Meditative prayer should be more than an intellectual exercise; when it is accompanied by affective intention it leads to the love and communion of contemplative prayer. Because of its nature, it is notoriously difficult to communicate the characteristics of contemplative prayer. It is a mysterious territory in which the language is silence and the action is receptivity. True contemplation is a theological grace that cannot be reduced to logical, psychological, or aesthetic categories. Perhaps some general contrasts between meditative and contemplative prayer will help (table 15.1).

MEDITATIVE PRAYER	CONTEMPLATIVE PRAYER
Speech	Silence
Activity	Receptivity
Discursive thought	Loss of mental images and concepts
Vocal and mental prayer	Wordless prayer and interior stillness
Natural faculties of reason and imagination	Mysterious darkening of the natural faculties
Affective feelings	Loss of feelings
Reading and reflection	Inability to meditate
Doing	Being
Seeking	Receiving
Talking to Jesus	Entering into the prayer of Jesus

Table 15.1

When he witnessed the miracle of the transfiguration of Jesus on the holy mountain, the awe-struck Peter inappropriately broke into speech and was silenced by the voice from the cloud that said, "This is My beloved Son, with whom I am well-pleased; listen to Him!" (Matthew 17:4–5). When we enter into the numinous territory of contemplation, it is best for us to stop talking and "listen to Him" in simple and loving attentiveness. In this strange and holy land we must remove the sandals of our ideas, constructs, and inclinations and quietly listen for the voice of God. Periods of contemplation can be little dark nights of faith. During these times, God may seem absent and silent, but his presence and speech is on a deeper level than what we can feel or understand. By preparing a peaceful place in the soul we learn to "rest in the LORD and wait patiently for Him" (Psalm 37:7).

A number of people have been exposed to aspects of contemplative prayer through "centering prayer," a practice that was recently revived and updated by three Cistercian monks, Thomas Keating, William Meninger, and Basil Pennington. This method of prayer is based on the fourteenth-century classic of mystical theology, *The Cloud of Unknowing*. Another approach to contemplative prayer is the "prayer of the heart" that is described in the *Philokalia*, an anthology of quotations from Eastern monastic fathers from the third century to the Middle Ages. In this tradition, invoking the name of the Lord Jesus creates a state of receptivity and interior recollection of the presence of God.

Suggestions for Contemplation

- Take enough time to present yourself before God in silence and yieldedness. Contemplative prayer involves the development of a deeper and more intuitive form of receptivity to the supernatural.
- As with meditation and prayer, do not be concerned with results, feelings, or experiences during contemplation. The important thing is to appear before God in a quiet and receptive mode of being.
- It is helpful to think of a word or an image that encapsulates what I call "the spirit of the passage" that you have been processing in your reading, meditation, and prayer. When your mind wanders during your time for contemplation, center yourself by returning once again to the spirit of the passage.
- Contemplation is a gift very few believers have attempted to develop. Expect that growth in this new terrain will involve time, discipline, and the frustration of apparent failure. Don't allow distractions or lack of initial benefits to dissuade you from this time-tested discipline. True contemplation may require years of fidelity, but any consistency in this practice will greatly reward you.
- Contemplation is especially difficult for more extraverted and sensory temperaments. This is a discipline of silence, of loss of control, of abandoning the attempt to analyze and intellectualize, and of developing the intuitive faculties.
- Remember that you cannot engage in contemplative prayer by your own effort; it is God's work, and it requires a "receptive passivity." In contemplation it is best to abandon self-consciousness and to allow yourself to be drawn into the inexpressible depths of God's love.

- Since *lectio divina* is not a rigid movement through four steps, you may find yourself going back to reading, meditation, or prayer and returning again to the interior silence of contemplation. The amount of time you spend in each of these four elements is up to you, and you should experiment with this. However, I recommend that you practice all four; each has a unique benefit.
- Nourish your interior life by reducing your exposure to radio, television, and other forms of distraction and commotion.

My colleague George Grove uses a set of analogies to integrate the four components of sacred reading (table 15.2).

LECTIO	MEDITATIO	ORATIO	CONTEMPLATIO
Read	Meditate	Pray	Abide
Lips	Mind	Heart	Spirit
Seek	Find	Knock	Open
Food	Chew	Savor	Fill

TABLE 15.2

Lectio divina engages the whole person from the physical to the psychological to the inward spiritual center of our being. It promotes a harmonious unity through an organic process that uses a variety of means. Fidelity and consistency in this long-term activity will gradually enhance and enrich your life.

Suggestions for Sacred Reading as a Whole

- Do not reduce sacred reading to a technique, system, or program. It has been called a "methodless method" that contributes to the development of a mode of being toward God. It is a personal process that cultivates a spiritual outlook of trust, receptivity, expectation, worship, and intimacy with God.
- Always see yourself as a beginner in the sense that you never master this process. There is always more than we think. Remember that discipline and devotion reinforce each other.
- Feel free to adapt this spiritual formation approach to your temperament. More extraverted people, for example, will be comfortable only with short sessions, while more introverted people will tend to take more time in this process.
- Perhaps the most important suggestion is for you to write out the verse or verses you have used for sacred reading on a given day and carry this card with you through your activities. By doing this, you are making that day's

passage your theme for twenty-four hours and using it as a tool to practice the presence of Christ. These cards can also assist you in memorization by moving the texts from short-term to longer-term memory.

- It is possible for some personality types to develop a false supernaturalism by becoming immersed in an artificial interiority. Thinking they are communing with God, they are lost in themselves. This problem of self-delusion and misguided zeal can be corrected by a willingness to accept sound advice through spiritual mentors or directors (we will look briefly at spiritual mentoring and direction in the section on corporate spirituality).

- To aspire to contemplation without cultivating compassion for others is to miss the point and purpose of contemplative prayer. The by-product of devotional spirituality should always be an increased capacity to love and serve others. By the same token, a growing realization of our union with others in Christ will enhance our capacity to know God.

A BLEND OF CONTEMPLATION AND ACTION

The polarity between the contemplative life and the active life has been a source of tension for many centuries. St. Gregory advocated a more contemplative approach to prayer as rest from exterior action in the quest for communion with God. St. Basil promoted a more active approach to prayer in association with work. Carried too far, the contemplative extreme could divorce our primary calling to know God from our secondary calling to express this knowledge in the world. The active extreme tends to elevate our secondary calling of work to the point of replacing our primary calling. A more balanced approach integrates and honors both callings and unites the contemplative and active vocations. St. Benedict encouraged this blended rhythm of rest and action, interior aspiration and exterior obedience, devotion and discipline, prayer and labor, desire for God and service of neighbor, the spring of living water and the stream that flows out of it. By uniting the strengths of both Mary and Martha, we can learn to be contemplatives in action. In this way, devotional spirituality is organically related to holistic and corporate spirituality.

QUESTIONS FOR PERSONAL APPLICATION

- Have you ever practiced a form of *lectio divina* without knowing it?
- What is your understanding of reading *(lectio)* as it is described in this chapter?
- What experience have you had in the past with meditation *(meditatio)*? Do you desire to incorporate more meditation in your encounters with Scripture?

- What forms of prayer *(oratio)* have you practiced in the past? How can prayer become more of a dialogue?
- Have you ever engaged in the practice of contemplation *(contemplatio)* as it is described in this chapter? What might prevent you from pursuing this ancient practice?
- Is it possible for you to become a contemplative in action?

16

DEVOTIONAL SPIRITUALITY
Falling in Love with God

CHAPTER OVERVIEW

As we grow in our understanding that God is our highest good, we become increasingly willing to renounce the aspirations of the world so that we can pursue God's pleasure. This chapter discusses the abiding relationship with Jesus and cultivating a passion for him; it concludes with two psalms of aspiration.

CHAPTER OBJECTIVES

- A keener sense that God alone is our highest good
- A readiness to renounce anything that competes with the Lord for our greatest affection
- An increased appreciation for the implications of the Incarnation
- A desire to abide in Jesus by drawing our life from his
- A clearer sense of what it means to cultivate a passion for Jesus

---

GOD IS OUR HIGHEST GOOD

The section on paradigm spirituality developed the theme that since we cannot serve two masters, the focus of our heart will be either the temporal or the eternal. If it is the temporal, we cannot love God completely. When Christ is a component instead of the center of life, the worries of the world, the deceitfulness of wealth, and the desires for other things choke the word of truth in our lives, and we do not bear lasting fruit (Mark 4:19). If the focus of our heart is the eternal, we will love Christ above his created goods and pleasures and begin to fulfill the enduring purpose for which we were created.

The School of Renunciation

Our problem is that the world is too much with us—it is visible, tangible, intrusive, compelling, and clamorous. But as long as we are in love with the world, we cannot fall in love with God. It takes no effort to walk by sight, but to walk by faith ("the assurance of things hoped for, the conviction of things not seen" [Hebrews 11:1]) requires the painful choice of renunciation. Without renunciation, the gifts of God will take the place of God, and our relationship with him will consist more of wanting things from him rather than wanting him alone. This is more of a mercenary arrangement than a true friendship; if we treated our friends this way, they would soon avoid us. But in his amazing grace, God does not abandon us. Instead, he patiently draws us to himself, and though it may take decades, he brings those who seek him for his goods to the realization that these goods are empty and unsatisfying without him. Thus he gradually peels back the fingers that clutch alternative objects of affection so that he can replace them with himself.

This is no easy process; it involves a series of trials and subsequent deaths to our aspirations and ambitions. Furthermore, no renunciation is complete—when we think we have surrendered everything to Jesus, a new awareness of earthly entanglements seems to surface. The tyranny of tangible goods and the craving to possess them is so deeply rooted in us that the divine extraction process can be agonizing and terrifying. (Read the gripping story of the killing of the red lizard of lust in C. S. Lewis's *The Great Divorce*.) A. W. Tozer's honest and challenging prayer of renunciation in *The Pursuit of God* is on the mark:

> Father, I want to know Thee, but my coward heart fears to give up its toys. I cannot part with them without inward bleeding, and I do not try to hide from Thee the terror of the parting. I come trembling, but I do come. Please root from my heart all those things which I have cherished so long and which have become a very part of my living self, so that Thou mayest enter and dwell there without a rival. Then shalt Thou make the place of Thy feet glorious. Then shall my heart have no need of the sun to shine in it, for Thyself wilt be the light of it, and there shall be no night there. In Jesus' Name, Amen.

Renunciation is an attitude of the heart; it is a matter of apprehending our spiritual poverty rather than a commitment to material poverty. Nevertheless, it does involve abnegating our right to possess anything as well as a looser grip on the things we possess in order that they do not possess us. This includes not only property but also position, friendships, and reputation. Listen to a portion of another prayer by Tozer: "Make me ambitious to please Thee even if as a result I must sink into obscurity and my name be forgotten as a dream."

The more our joy is detached from the things the world teaches us to love, the simpler our approach to God will be. Or to put it the other way around, as we grow in our attachment to Jesus, we progressively distance ourselves from the allurements of the world. When we sacrifice the many for the One, we find that our souls are not restricted but expanded and freed. In fact, when we have Christ, we have everything; all things belong to us in Christ, and we belong to him, and he belongs to God (1 Corinthians 3:21–23). Thus, instead of loving things in themselves, we can learn to love God in all things, as St. Augustine teaches in his *Expositions on the Psalms*:

> Learn in the creature to love the Creator; and in the work Him who made it. Let not that which has been made by Him detain thine affections, so that thou shouldest lose Him by whom thou thyself wert made also.... But why dost thou love those things, except because they are beautiful? Can they be as beautiful as He by whom they were made? Thou admirest these things because thou seest not Him: but through those things which thou admirest, love Him whom thou seest not.

Pursuing God's Pleasure

The Greek mathematician Archimedes demonstrated that he could lift the world with a long enough lever supported on a fulcrum that is placed at the right point outside the earth. Just as this Archimedean point cannot be on the earth, so we cannot transcend the world unless the fulcrum of our affection is the I AM, the unchanging One who spoke the world into being. He is the "one thing [that] is necessary" (Luke 10:42), the "treasure hidden in the field" (Matthew 13:44), the "one pearl of great value" (Matthew 13:46) whose kingdom and righteousness must be sought first (Matthew 6:33) with an undivided heart that chooses him alone as the soul's highest good. The more we want to want him, the more we desire to desire him, the more we will be satisfied. And as John Piper observed in *Desiring God*, God is most glorified when we are most satisfied in him. The only path to lasting pleasure is to risk everything on seeking God's pleasure and approval above our own. Only the things we relinquish to him will be ours in the end. If we believe that God is our highest good, we can offer this prayer in sincerity and truth: "Lord, take away any illusions I may have of becoming great and famous, since you are all those things, and you alone."

THE IMPLICATIONS OF THE INCARNATION

The incarnation of the second person of the Trinity was the most decisive means by which God revealed his glory, goodness, grace, love, holiness, justice, and truth to the world (Hebrews 1:1–3). Through the incarnation, life, death, resurrection, and ascension of Jesus, the Father has become most fully real and accessible to us.

A Gospel of God's Grace, Not Our Goodness

The life of Christ is the unchanging standard by which all other lives must be measured, since his perfect character fully demonstrated the righteousness of God. All other lives—including those of Moses, Buddha, Confucius, Socrates, Muhammad, and Gandhi—fall abysmally short of Jesus' goodness, holiness, beauty, brilliance, and compassion. In the incarnation of Jesus, God revealed the folly of any religion of merit and human attainment. The works systems of other religions are based on a deficient vision of the holiness of God and the depravity of humanity. Immanuel, God with us, offered a "new and living way which He inaugurated for us through the veil, that is, His flesh" by which we can draw near to God "with a sincere heart in full assurance of faith" (Hebrews 10:20, 22). The Incarnation reveals the lie behind any form of spiritual self-reliance.

If God gave us justice by dealing with our sins as they deserve, there would be no hope. "All have sinned and fall short of the glory of God," and "the wages of sin is death" (Romans 3:23; 6:23). But in his Son, God gave us mercy (not getting what we deserve) and grace (getting better than what we deserve). Thus we are not saved by creed, conduct, or church but by the limitless love and grace of Christ (read and reflect on Titus 2:11–14; 3:4–7). This has serious implications for the life of discipleship and devotion. One of these implications is that since Jesus is our King, we must hand over the control of our lives to him. This is never easy or immediate, because we have been conditioned by nature and experience to be self-reliant and self-protective. But we will not grow in the kingdom of God unless we acknowledge Jesus' lordship and right to rule our lives. Even when we do this, we are typically selective in the territory we yield to him. Growing abandonment and transparency is a gradual process for most of Jesus' followers, but there can be decisive crisis moments (the Greek word *krisis* means "judgment") that lead to transformation. Naturally, no one wants to die to self, but losing our lives for Jesus' sake is the currency of kingdom living. This was done decisively at the moment of our conversion (Galatians 5:24; Romans 6:16–17), but it is also an ongoing process (Romans 12:1–2).

Abiding in Jesus by Drawing Our Life from His

The grace of God in Christ initiates us into the joy of fellowship in a family that has full access to the Father and the Son through the indwelling Spirit (1 John 1:1–4). God wants us to enjoy and appropriate our position, possessions, and privileges in Christ, but too often we try to draw from our own accounts rather than rely on his resources. We ask him for his help and strength so that we can live better lives and serve him more effectively. This may sound good at first, but on closer analysis it reveals a misguided strategy to live the spiritual life in our own strength, supplemented by a measure of divine assistance. It was never God's intention to give us a hand in living the Christian life. It is impossible for people to live on a level of Christlike perfection. Christ lives his life in us when we walk by the Spirit. Jesus is not our helper; he is our very life. Instead of making us stronger, God brings us to the point of weakness so that Christ can be strong in us ("power is perfected in weakness" [2 Corinthians 12:9–10]).

"Simplicity and purity of devotion to Christ" (2 Corinthians 11:3) is the essence of devotional spirituality and the key to renewing and sustaining the passion of our first love (Revelation 2:4). We all experience a natural inertia, a downward pull, an entropy of relational energy that deteriorates our communion with God and with others. Unless we are vigilant, the flame of our initial love for Christ can quietly diminish, and even the embers can grow cold. But if we are faithful to the practice of meditating on the glory of God and the beauty of Jesus, we will love him by beholding him. If we spend time with him, practice his presence, follow him, and learn from him, we will love him and become like him.

In our Lord's Upper Room Discourse, he completed the preparation for his departure by teaching his disciples the fundamental spiritual themes that would later be developed in the Epistles. Although it is not a rigid sequence, a series of connections can be drawn from John 15. In verse 8, Jesus said that a key to *glorifying* God is fruit bearing: "My Father is glorified by this, that you bear much fruit, and so prove to be My disciples." In verse 4, Jesus said that a key to *fruit bearing* is abiding in him: "Abide in Me, and I in you. As the branch cannot bear fruit of itself unless it abides in the vine, so neither can you unless you abide in Me." In verse 10, Jesus said that a key to *abiding* is obedience: "If you keep My commandments, you will abide in My love; just as I have kept My Father's commandments and abide in His love." In the same verse, Jesus said that a key to *obedience* is loving him. And in verse 15, Jesus said that a key to *loving* him is *knowing* him: "No longer do I call you slaves, for the slave does not know what his master is doing; but I have called you friends, for all things that I have heard from My Father I have made known to you." There is a mutual relation between fruit bearing, abiding, obedience, love, and personal knowledge of Jesus, and all of these elements reinforce each other. But the heart of devotional spirituality is abiding in Jesus by being in his presence and communing with him in ever-increasing ways. The more we seek him, experience him, and immerse ourselves in him, the more we are transfigured into his image and likeness.

CULTIVATING A PASSION FOR CHRIST

Devotional spirituality is like a delicate grapevine that flourishes only when it is planted in the right soil and carefully cultivated in a good climate. Unless it is nurtured, it will wither through neglect and fail to bear fruit. The fruit of spiritual passion can be threatened by natural enemies.

Enemies of Spiritual Passion

Unresolved areas of disobedience. Resisting the prodding of God in an area of your life may seem subtle, but it can be a more serious grievance to the heart of God than we suppose. It is good to invite the Holy Spirit to reveal any barriers in our relationship with God or people that have been erected by sinful attitudes and actions. When these become evident, deal with them quickly and trust in the power of God's forgiveness through the blood of Christ.

Complacency. Without holy desire we will succumb to the sin of spiritual *acedia*, or indifference, apathy, and boredom. People who lose the sharp edge of intention and calling can slip into a morass of listlessness and feelings of failure. We must often ask God for the grace of acute desire so that we will hunger and thirst for him.

Erosion in spiritual disciplines. Complacency can cause or be caused by a failure to train and remain disciplined in the spiritual life. Several biblical figures, including King Asa (2 Chronicles 14–16), illustrate the problem of starting well in the first half of life and finishing poorly in the last half. When spiritual disciplines begin to erode, spiritual passion declines as well.

External obedience. Many people are more concerned about conformity to rules, moral behavior, and duty than they are about loving Jesus. External obedience without inward affection falls short of the biblical vision of obeying God from the heart (Jeremiah 31:33; Romans 6:17; Ephesians 6:6).

Loving truth more than Christ. Some students of the Word have come to love the content of truth in the Bible more than the Source of that truth. Biblical theology and systematic theology are worthy pursuits, but not when they become substitutes for the pursuit of knowing and becoming like Jesus.

Elevating service and ministry above Christ. It is easier to define ourselves by what we accomplish than by our new identity in Christ. For some people, the Christian life consists more of fellowship, service to those in need, witnessing, and worship than of becoming intimate with Jesus. This leads to the problem of ministry without the manifest presence of God.

Greater commitment to institutions than to Christ. It is easy for churches, denominations, or other organizations to occupy more of our time and attention than does devotion to Jesus. There is a constant danger of getting more passionate about causes than about Christ.

A merely functional relationship. Many people are more interested in what Jesus can do for them than in who he is. We may initially come to him hoping that he will help us with our career, marriage, children, or health, but if we do not grow beyond this gifts-above-the-Giver mentality, we will never develop spiritual passion.

Our love for God can be threatened by these enemies, but other attitudes and actions can stimulate or renew a sense of devotion and intimacy.

Sources of Spiritual Passion

Growing awareness of God as a person. God is an intensely personal and relational Being, and it is an insult for us to treat him as though he were a power or a principle. Some of us find it easier to be comfortable with abstract principles and ideas than with people and intimacy. As we have seen, good things like the Bible, theology, ministry, and church can become substitutes for loving him. As a countermeasure, it is good to ask God for the grace of increased passion for his Son so that, by the power of the Spirit, we will come to love him as the Father loves him.

Sitting at Jesus' feet. When we make consistent time for reading, meditation, prayer, and contemplation, we place ourselves at the feet of Jesus and enjoy his presence. By making ourselves available and receptive to him, we learn the wisdom of spending more time being a friend of Jesus than a friend of others.

Imitating the Master. Our identification with Jesus in his death, burial, resurrection, and ascension has made us new creatures before God (2 Corinthians 5:17). This divinely wrought identification makes it possible for us to imitate Jesus and "follow in His steps" (1 Peter 2:21). If we love the Master, we will want to be like him in his character, humility, compassion, love, joy, peace, and dependence on the Father's will.

Cultivating spiritual affections. Regardless of our natural temperaments, it is important for us to develop true affections (desire, longing, zeal, craving, hunger) for God. The rich emotional life of the psalmists (see Psalm 27:4; 42:1–3; 63:1–8; 145:1–21) reveals a desire for God above all else and a willingness to cling to him during times of aridity. Like them, we must aspire to a love that is beyond us (Ephesians 3:17–19).

Increasing appreciation for the goodness of God. The distractions of the world make it difficult for us to develop a growing appreciation for our relationship with God. We forget that we can enjoy communion with Someone who is infinitely better than the objects of our most powerful natural desires. We must pray for the grace of gratitude and amazement at the unqualified goodness of God's "kindness toward us in Christ Jesus" (Ephesians 2:7).

Focused intention. What do you want (or want to want) more than anything else? God is pleased when we pursue him with a heart that is intent on knowing and loving him. He "begins His influence by working in us that we may have the will, and He completes it by working with us when we have the will," wrote Augustine in *On Grace and Free Will.* As our wills become more simplified and centered on becoming like Jesus, our love for him will grow.

Willingness to let God break our outward self. "Unless a grain of wheat falls into the earth and dies, it remains alone; but if it dies, it bears much fruit. He who loves his life loses it, and he who hates his life in this world will keep it to life eternal" (John 12:24–25). The alabaster vial of the self-life must be broken (Mark 14:3) to release the perfume of the new self in Christ. If we wish to manifest the fragrance of Christ, we must allow God to bring us, in his time and way, to the painful place of brokenness on the cross of self-abandonment to him. This theme resonates in spiritual literature, and one of the clearest expressions is in Watchman Nee's *The Release of the Spirit.*

Desiring to please God more than impress people. If we want to be like Christ, we must embrace his governing goal to be pleasing to the Father (John 8:29; Hebrews 10:7). The enemy of this glorious goal is the competing quest for human approval (John 5:41, 44;

12:43; Galatians 1:10). We cannot have it both ways; we will either play to an Audience of one or to an audience of many. But in the end, only God's opinion will matter.

Treasuring God. Dallas Willard observes in *The Divine Conspiracy* that God "treasures those whom he has created, planned for, longed for, sorrowed over, redeemed, and befriended." Just as God has treasured us, so he wants us to respond by treasuring him above all else. "We love, because He first loved us" (1 John 4:19). The more we realize how God loved and valued us, the greater our capacity to love and value him. In *Beginning to Pray*, Anthony Bloom suggests that one way to treasure God is to find a personal name or expression for God that flows out of our relationship with him, like David's "You, my Joy!"

Maturing in trust. As believers, we trust Christ for our eternal destiny, but most of us find it difficult to trust him in our daily practice. As long as we pursue sinful strategies of seeking satisfaction on our own terms, our confidence will be misplaced. We must learn to trust Jesus enough to place our confidence in his power, not our performance.

TWO PSALMS OF ASPIRATION

Psalm 16: The Lord Is Our Supreme Good and Our Inheritance

"Preserve me, O God, for I take refuge in You" (16:1). David evidently wrote Psalm 16 when he was a refugee driven from the land of Israel and pursued by Saul and his men like a flea on a dog's back. They sought to deprive him of his inheritance from the Lord, saying, "Go, serve other gods" (1 Samuel 26:19). In this psalm, David affirms his single-minded commitment to the Lord and his rejection of anything opposed to God.

We who have committed our lives to Christ are also refugees, for we have turned to the Lord for refuge in a world that would deprive us of enjoying our spiritual inheritance by luring us to serve the gods of money, sex, and power. Like David, we must cultivate the single-minded attitude of looking to God alone for our security, significance, and satisfaction. We must rest in the Lord and regard him as our highest good. "I said to the LORD, 'You are my Lord; I have no good besides You'" (16:2; cf. 73:25).

David cherishes fellowship with people of character and holiness (16:3) and contrasts "the sorrows of those who have bartered for another god" (v. 4) with the blessings of those whose sole hope of inheritance rests in the Lord. "The LORD is the portion of my inheritance and my cup; You support my lot. The lines have fallen to me in pleasant places; indeed, my heritage is beautiful to me" (vv. 5–6). When the Promised Land was distributed among the tribes of Israel, the Levitical priests were given no tract of land. The Lord told them, "You shall have no inheritance in their land, nor own any portion among them; I am your portion and your inheritance among the sons of Israel" (Numbers 18:20).

As believers in Christ, our abundance and security rest in him and not in our earthly possessions. We must not make the mistake of putting our hope in savings, investments, and material goods. "For wealth certainly makes itself wings like an eagle that flies toward the heavens" (Proverbs 23:5). When we recognize that God alone is our portion and our inheritance, we will look beyond our earthly means of provision to him as our true source of provision. And when we discover that the world's treasures and plaudits are as nothing compared to knowing Christ (Philippians 3:7–11), we will be content with God's level of material provision because of the beauty and richness of our spiritual heritage.

David portrays this spiritual heritage in terms of two present benefits and two future prospects.

Two Present Benefits

First, God guides and counsels us. "I will bless the LORD who has counseled me; indeed, my mind instructs me in the night" (16:7). The Spirit of God uses the Word of God to guide, reprove, and teach the child of God. Life is too complex and uncertain to discern the best paths on our own. One of the great benefits of regular time in the Scriptures is the matchless counsel we can discover in its precepts and principles.

Second, God gives us an assurance that transcends our circumstances. "I have set the LORD continually before me; because He is at my right hand, I will not be shaken. Therefore my heart is glad and my glory rejoices; my flesh also will dwell securely" (vv. 8–9). The more we practice his presence in the many situations we encounter, the more personal and real he becomes in our lives. We discover that we can do all things through him who strengthens us (Philippians 4:13) and that we are never alone in any circumstance we face.

Two Future Prospects

First, the security we have in Christ extends not only throughout our earthly sojourn but also beyond this life. "For You will not abandon my soul to Sheol; neither will You allow Your Holy One to undergo decay" (16:10). Peter and Paul both quoted this passage as a messianic prophecy. David "looked ahead and spoke of the resurrection of the Christ" (Acts 2:27–31; 13:35–37) whose body, unlike David's, did not undergo decay. Our sure confidence is that death will be swallowed up in the victory of our resurrection (1 Corinthians 15:51–58).

Second, we will have complete satisfaction and endless joys in the loving presence of the living God. "You will make known to me the path of life; in Your presence is fullness of joy; in Your right hand there are pleasures forever" (16:11). Our inheritance in Christ is beyond all imagination (1 Corinthians 2:9), and the greatest pleasure we have known on this planet is but a faint shadow of the kindnesses he will bestow forever on those who have put their hope in him. "In the perfect happiness of heaven nothing more will remain to be desired; in the full enjoyment of God man will obtain whatever he has desired in other things" (Thomas Aquinas).

Psalm 103: "Bless the Lord, O My Soul"

*O God, I know that if I do not love Thee with all my heart, with all my mind,
with all my soul and with all my strength, I shall love something else with all my
heart and mind and soul and strength. Grant that putting Thee first in all my
lovings I may be liberated from all lesser loves and loyalties, and have Thee as
my first love, my chiefest good and my final joy.*

GEORGE APPLETON, *OXFORD BOOK OF PRAYER*

Any good that takes first place in our hearts is an idol if it is not the Supreme Good,
the living God. We were created to have a relationship with him, and no other person,
possession, or position will satisfy our deepest longings. The Psalter frequently underscores this truth, and Psalm 103, the first of a group of psalms of praise (Psalms 103–
107), reminds us with skill and beauty that God's lovingkindness is the source of our
greatest satisfaction.

A Personal Hymn of Thanksgiving

In the first stanza, David recounts several reasons to praise the Lord from his experience of walking with God: "Bless the LORD, O my soul; and all that is within me, bless
His holy name. Bless the LORD, O my soul, and forget none of His benefits; who par-
dons all your iniquities; who heals all your diseases; who redeems your life from the
pit, who crowns you with lovingkindness and compassion; who satisfies your years
with good things, so that your youth is renewed like the eagle" (vv. 1–5).

Over and over again, the Scriptures exhort us to approach God with praise and
gratitude for the many benefits he has bestowed upon us. But our natural tendency is
to forget what he has done in our lives and to focus instead on our problems, pains,
and disappointments. When this happens, we view God in terms of our circumstances
instead of viewing our circumstances in terms of his character. We become proud and
autonomous (see Deuteronomy 8:12–14, 17–18; 2 Chronicles 32:25) or angry and
embittered because we have forgotten that we lay hold of our hope through faith and
patience (see Romans 15:4; Hebrews 6:10–11, 18–19; 10:35–36). "Bless the LORD, O
my soul, and forget none of His benefits."

A Communal Hymn of Praise

The psalm shifts in the second stanza from an individual thanksgiving to a communal hymn of praise around the theme of God's loyal love (103:6–18). Recalling the
Exodus and the wilderness experience, David writes, "The LORD performs righteous
deeds and judgments for all who are oppressed. He made known His ways to Moses,
His acts to the sons of Israel" (vv. 6–7). The Israelites knew God's works, but Moses
was intimately acquainted with God's ways. Many of us know God through his works,
but few have engaged in the disciplines necessary to draw us into an intimate knowl-

edge of his ways. Moses dared ask to see God's glory, and when the Lord passed by in front of him, God manifested the glory of his presence and character, using words similar to those in the next verses of this psalm. "The LORD is compassionate and gracious, slow to anger and abounding in lovingkindness. He will not always strive with us, nor will He keep His anger forever. He has not dealt with us according to our sins, nor rewarded us according to our iniquities" (vv. 8–10; cf. Exodus 34:6–7).

In contrast to humans, who nurse grievances and are quick to quarrel but slow to forgive, "God, infinitely wronged, not only tempers wrath but tempers justice—though at what cost to Himself, only the New Testament would reveal" (Derek Kidner). The loyal love of the Lord and the forgiveness he offers knows no limits. "For as high as the heavens are above the earth, so great is His lovingkindness toward those who fear Him. As far as the east is from the west, so far has He removed our transgressions from us" (103:11–12). The "breadth and length and height and depth" of the love of Christ surpasses knowledge (Ephesians 3:18–19). Turning from spatial to relational imagery, the psalmist adds: "Just as a father has compassion on his children, so the LORD has compassion on those who fear Him" (v. 13; cf. Isaiah 49:15). The best moments of warmth, affection, and security of unconditional belonging that are ever experienced in earthly families are imperfect and shadowy images of the loyal love of God toward those who know him.

In language reminiscent of Moses' words in Psalm 90:1–6, David contrasts the brevity of human life with the timelessness of God. "For He Himself knows our frame; He is mindful that we are but dust. As for man, his days are like grass; as a flower of the field, so he flourishes. When the wind has passed over it, it is no more, and its place acknowledges it no longer" (103: 14–16). But God's covenant love and grace give us a hope and a purpose that will never fade away, because "the lovingkindness of the LORD is from everlasting to everlasting on those who fear Him" (v. 17).

Notice that this is the third time the expression "those who fear Him" appears in this psalm. Our response to God's great love and mercy should be that of respectful awe, ongoing gratitude, and willing obedience. He extends "His righteousness to children's children, to those who keep His covenant and remember His precepts to do them" (103:17–18). Our Father wants us to prove ourselves doers of the word, not merely hearers who delude ourselves (James 1:22).

The third stanza of the psalm transports us from the individual (103:1–5), to the community of God's people (vv. 6–18), to the entire created order (vv. 19–22). "The LORD has established His throne in the heavens, and His sovereignty rules over all. Bless the LORD, you His angels, mighty in strength, who perform His word, obeying the voice of His word! Bless the LORD, all you His hosts, you who serve Him, doing His will. Bless the LORD, all you works of His, in all places of His dominion; bless the LORD, O my soul!" (see 1 Chronicles 29:10–13). The meditation moves from God's grace to

God's greatness as the psalmist invokes the myriad angelic and heavenly hosts to bless the holy name. Just as these glorious beings and works serve the Lord in perfect obedience, so we whose lives have been redeemed from the pit and crowned with lovingkindness and compassion should order our steps before the Lord in humility, awe, love, and obedience. The wisest investment of time you will ever make is the time you spend in getting to know him better, because to know him is to love him, and to love him is to enter into the joy and pleasure of his service.

REFLECTION

O my soul, above all things and in all things always rest in the Lord, for He is the eternal rest of the saints.

Grant me most sweet and loving Jesus, to rest in You above every other creature, above all health and beauty, above all glory and honor, above all power and dignity, above all knowledge and precise thought, above all wealth and talent, above all joy and exultation, above all fame and praise, above all sweetness and consolation, above all hope and promise, above all merit and desire, above all gifts and favors You give and shower upon me, above all happiness and joy that the mind can understand and feel, and finally, above all angels and archangels, above all the hosts of heaven, above all things visible and invisible, and above all that is not You, my God.

Thomas à Kempis, *The Imitation of Christ*

Therefore the LORD longs to be gracious to you,
And therefore He waits on high to have compassion on you.
For the LORD is a God of justice;
How blessed are all those who long for Him.

Isaiah 30:18

QUESTIONS FOR PERSONAL APPLICATION

- What is the school of renunciation? What deaths have you experienced to your own aspirations and ambitions, and what effect have these had in your walk with God?
- What does it mean to pursue God's pleasure?
- What are the implications of the Incarnation in your thinking and practice?
- How do you relate to the metaphor of abiding in Jesus?
- Which of the eight enemies of spiritual passion have been the greatest challenges to you?
- Which of the ten sources of spiritual passion are the most meaningful to you?

FACET 7

HOLISTIC SPIRITUALITY

Every Component of Life under the Lordship of Christ

There is a general tendency to treat Christianity as a component of life along with other components such as family, work, and finances. This compartmentalization fosters a dichotomy between the secular and the spiritual. The biblical alternative is to understand the implications of Christ's lordship over every aspect of life in such a way that even the most mundane components of life can become expressions of the life of Christ in us.

17

HOLISTIC SPIRITUALITY
The Centrality of Christ

CHAPTER OVERVIEW

Holistic spirituality stresses the centrality of Christ and his relevance to every component of our lives. This biblical alternative to a compartmentalization mentality focuses on the implications of Christ's lordship in such a way that even the most mundane components of life can become expressions of the life of Christ in us. This chapter stresses the cultivation of a heart of wisdom, which is the skill in the art of living life with each area under the dominion of God.

CHAPTER OBJECTIVES

- A desire for personal transformation in the context of everyday life
- An appreciation for the wisdom of seeking Christ in all things
- An increased sense of our need to cultivate a heart of wisdom

---

A DIVINE ORIENTATION

Holistic spirituality may sound like a good candidate for a New Age book title, but as long as we define our terms, words like meditation, contemplation, spirituality, and holistic are useful and meaningful tools. Some people use the word *holistic* in a somewhat pantheistic sense to describe the unity of all things, but the more standard philosophical meaning of holism is that nature synthesizes entities into organized wholes that are greater than the sum of their parts. For example, human beings are more than highly organized collections of atoms, molecules, cells, tissues, organs, and systems. None of these fully account for our minds, affections, and wills, let alone our capacity to relate to the timeless spiritual Being who created us.

There is more to us than we know, and in us, God combines the material and the immaterial into a prodigious unity of activity. Since this is so, the perennial human quest to seek meaning in material goods and achievements always leads to disappointment and dissatisfaction. We were meant for more than created goods; we were meant to find our meaning and purpose in the uncreated Creator of all things. Something in all of us—even when we try to suppress it—points beyond the created order because it longs for more than the world can ever offer.

Those who do not know God are bound to integrate themselves downward by seeking their identity in the elementary principles of this world (Colossians 2:8, 20). Those who "have come to know God, or rather to be known by God" (Galatians 4:9a; 1 Corinthians 8:3), have begun to integrate themselves upward though they are still tempted to "turn back again to the weak and worthless elemental things" that formerly enslaved them (Galatians 4:9b). If we were created to please God by knowing and enjoying him, we will never be whole and complete unless we orient our lives around him and define ourselves in terms of our relationship with him.

Movement toward divine orientation is a process that is never completed in this world but contributes to our preparation for the life of heaven. As followers of the Way, we should grow in our realization that we are pilgrims and wayfarers in this world and that our true citizenship is in the heavenly realm (Philippians 3:20). The more serious we are about our heavenly calling, the more we become aware of the tension caused by the allurements and entanglements of our earthly condition. Many believers have inadvertently resolved this tension by compartmentalizing their lives. They do this by treating their relationship with Christ as a component of their lives along with other components such as family, work, and finances. This **compartmentalization** fosters a dichotomy between the secular and the spiritual, so that the spiritual becomes something we do on certain occasions such as church, Bible studies, and devotional times. The assumption is that the more of these things we do, the more spiritual we are.

By contrast, holistic spirituality stresses the centrality of Christ and his relevance to every component of our lives. This biblical alternative to a compartmentalization mentality focuses on the implications of Christ's lordship over every aspect of life in such a way that even the most mundane components of life can become expressions of the life of Christ in us. In this way, the various secular arenas of life become spiritual to the extent that we surrender them to the lordship of Christ. In this holistic approach, the whole is greater than the sum of the parts, and the parts are increasingly related to the whole. There is no component of life that should remain untouched by the dominion of Jesus.

The heavens are not too high,
His praise may thither fly;
The earth is not too low,
His praises there may grow.

Let all the world in every corner sing,
My God and King!

George Herbert

FALSE PURSUITS OF HAPPINESS

This Christ-centered goal of personal transformation in the context of everyday life is often obscured by attempts to find meaning through false pursuits of happiness.

The seventeenth-century mathematician and philosopher Blaise Pascal observed in his *Pensées* that "all men seek happiness. This is without exception. Whatever different means they employ, they all tend to this end. The cause of some going to war, and of others avoiding it, is the same desire in both, attended with different views. The will never takes the least step but to this object. This is the motive of every action of every man, even of those who hang themselves."

The problem is that people turn to the wrong things in their quest for happiness, thinking that their felicity can be found in possessions, popularity, position, or power. This is why they believe advertising that sells products by means of association rather than true worth. Thus manufacturers of expensive automobiles create ads like "Pursue happiness in a car that can catch it!" as if the human heart could be satisfied by bells and whistles. The truth is that even the most sophisticated toys and treasures are not enough to fulfill the profound craving for meaning in life. As George Gilder observed in *Men and Marriage,* "Men lust, but they know not what for; they wander, and lose track of the goal; they fight and compete, but they forget the prize; they spread seed, but spurn the seasons of growth; they chase power and glory, but miss the meaning of life."

Short-Term Reasons Are Not Enough

The tragedy of life without an ultimate source of meaning is captured in a scene from *Don Quixote.* When Quixote tells Sancho Panza about the look he saw in the eyes of the soldiers who lay dying in his arms, he said their eyes seemed to be asking a question. Sancho asks, "Was it the question 'Why am I dying?'" Quixote replies, "No, it was the question 'Why was I living?'" If we do not have a lasting and satisfying answer to this question, we may deceive ourselves into thinking we are in control or that we know where we are going, but in reality we are lost in the cosmos.

Perhaps the most ruthless appraisal of this condition is Macbeth's despairing soliloquy:

Tomorrow, and tomorrow, and tomorrow,
Creeps in this petty pace from day to day
To the last syllable of recorded time;
And all our yesterdays have lighted fools
The way to dusty death. Out, out, brief candle!

Life's but a walking shadow, a poor player
That struts and frets his hour upon the stage
And then is heard no more. It is a tale
Told by an idiot, full of sound and fury,
Signifying nothing.

This is a logically consistent view of human life without transcendent meaning and hope, but few people arrive at it. Why? One reason is that most people without Christ live unexamined lives and avoid ultimate questions by focusing all their attention on their hour upon the stage. Another reason is that humans have an almost unlimited capacity for avoidance, diversion, entertainment, and escape. In many cases, the only time they confront these questions is when they are faced with tragedy and loss, and even then the window of vulnerability is open for a brief duration.

The Restless Heart

The noted philosopher Mortimer Adler was given the monumental task of co-editing a fifty-five-volume series for Encyclopedia Britannica entitled *The Great Books of the Western World*. Selections from the writings of the finest thinkers in the history of Western civilization are compiled in these books, and the ideas contained in them are arranged in a massive index. When Adler was asked why this index contains more entries under the topic of God than any other topic, his answer was definitive: "It is because more consequences for life follow from that one issue than from any other." If ultimate reality is an infinite and personal Being who created the cosmos and offers us the matchless privilege of an endless relationship with him, then any other good on which we could set our hearts is unworthy of comparison.

In the same *pensée* that was quoted above, Pascal adds, "There once was in man a true happiness of which now remains to him only the dark and empty trace, which he in vain tries to fill from all his surroundings, seeking from things absent the help he does not obtain in things present. But these are all inadequate, because the infinite abyss can only be filled by an infinite and immutable object, that is to say, only by God Himself." This is what Augustine affirmed in book 1 of his *Confessions* when he wrote, "You have made us for Yourself, O Lord, and our hearts are restless until they rest in You."

When Jesus said to the Twelve, "You do not want to go away also, do you?" Simon Peter answered Him, "Lord, to whom shall we go? You have words of eternal life" (John 6:67–68). Peter understood that without Christ, there are no other options; there is nowhere else to turn. This is the truth every believer must come to admit—in times when we are tempted to despair and to abandon our walk with God, there is in fact no where else to turn but to him. To look to anything else for solace is to lean on a broken reed. But to know Christ is to lay hold of the root and the offspring of David, the bright morning star, the Alpha and the Omega, the first and the last, the beginning and the end, the firstborn from the dead, the King of kings and Lord of lords, the Creator and Sustainer of all things, the ultimate and transcendent Source of true meaning and significance.

THE WISDOM OF SEEKING CHRIST IN ALL THINGS

"The fear of the LORD is the beginning of wisdom, and the knowledge of the Holy One is understanding" (Proverbs 9:10). The pursuit of wisdom is directly related to the difference between living in such a way that Christ is the unifying center of our lives rather than a mere component.

A Skillful Life

According to Proverbs, wisdom is a gem with many facets: insight, counsel, prudence, understanding, discernment, discipline, competence, discretion, instruction, guidance, knowledge, and righteousness. But the fundamental concept that embraces all these facets is found in the meaning of the Hebrew word that is most frequently used for wisdom—*chokmah*. This word, along with its variants, appears more than three hundred times in the Old Testament, and it means "skill." Wisdom is skill in the art of living life with each area under the dominion of God. It is the ability to use the best means at the best time to accomplish the best ends.

Wisdom, like life, ultimately belongs to God alone. "With Him are wisdom and might; to Him belong counsel and understanding" (Job 12:13). As Daniel acknowledged,

Let the name of God be blessed forever and ever,
For wisdom and power belong to Him.
It is He who changes the times and the epochs;
He removes kings and establishes kings;
He gives wisdom to wise men
And knowledge to men of understanding.
It is He who reveals the profound and hidden things;
He knows what is in the darkness,
And the light dwells with Him.

Daniel 2:20–22

Wisdom is the Lord's plan by which he transforms a lifeless chaos into a living cosmos (Proverbs 8:22–31). Similarly, wisdom is the Lord's plan by which he can transmute the moral and spiritual chaos of a human life into an incarnation of God's sublime attributes of justice, equity, truth, and faithfulness.

The Wisdom from Above and Below

According to James, "the wisdom from above is first pure, then peaceable, gentle, reasonable, full of mercy and good fruits, unwavering, without hypocrisy" (James 3:17).

Without a relationship with the Source of wisdom, we are limited to human shrewdness and craft: "This wisdom is not that which comes down from above, but is earthly, natural, demonic. For where jealousy and selfish ambition exist, there is disorder and every evil thing" (James 3:15–16).

The Scriptures draw a sharp contrast—earthly wisdom leads to disorder, evil, ugliness, and disappointment; divine wisdom bears the fruit of order, goodness, beauty, and fulfillment. The tragedy is that so many people pursue earthly wisdom hoping to attain the fruit that can be produced only by the wisdom that comes from above.

Divine wisdom is "a tree of life to those who take hold of her, and happy are all who hold her fast" (Proverbs 3:18).

> *How blessed is the man who finds wisdom*
> *And the man who gains understanding.*
> *For her profit is better than the profit of silver*
> *And her gain better than fine gold.*
> *She is more precious than jewels;*
> *And nothing you desire compares with her.*

Proverbs 3:13–15

What do we want out of life? We may crave wealth, prestige, power, and popularity, but these are the longings of the outer, not the inner, self. As believers in Christ, we "joyfully concur with the law of God in the inner man" (Romans 7:22), and our deepest longings for significance, purpose, and fulfillment can be met only in the knowledge of the Author of life.

Wisdom is the skill that forges beauty out of the raw material of our lives. Because it is a skill, no one naturally possesses wisdom; it must be cultivated and developed. This is why there are so many parental exhortations in the first nine chapters of Proverbs to pursue this most priceless and practical of all skills:

> *My son, if you will receive my words*
> *And treasure my commandments within you,*
> *Make your ear attentive to wisdom,*
> *Incline your heart to understanding;*
> *For if you cry for discernment,*
> *Lift your voice for understanding;*
> *If you seek her as silver*
> *And search for her as for hidden treasures;*
> *Then you will discern the fear of the LORD*
> *And discover the knowledge of God.*

Proverbs 2:1–5

But how do we pursue wisdom? The answer is found in the next verse: "For the LORD gives wisdom; from His mouth come knowledge and understanding" (Proverbs 2:6). This wisdom comes from above (James 3:17), and we can never hope to attain it on our own.

The Fear of the Lord

The treasure of wisdom rests in the hands of God, but we need to be more specific. What are the conditions for attaining it? Proverbs 9:10 gives us the answer: "The fear of the LORD is the beginning of wisdom, and the knowledge of the Holy One is understanding." According to the wisdom literature of the Bible, true skill in the art of living life can be achieved only by cultivating the fear of the Lord.

This leads us to yet another question. What is the fear of the Lord? Now we are on the brink of one of the central yet often overlooked concepts of Scripture.

"Behold, the fear of the Lord, that is wisdom;
And to depart from evil is understanding."

Job 28:28

Teach me Your way, O LORD;
I will walk in Your truth;
Unite my heart to fear Your name.

Psalm 86:11

The fear of the LORD is the beginning of wisdom;
A good understanding have all those who do His commandments;
His praise endures forever.

Psalm 111:10

The fear of the LORD is the beginning of knowledge;
Fools despise wisdom and instruction.

Proverbs 1:7

The New Testament, like the Old, exhorts us to live in the fear of God (see Matthew 10:28; Acts 10:35; 2 Corinthians 5:10–11; 7:1; Ephesians 5:21; Colossians 3:22; 1 Peter 1:17). Yet the apostle John tells us that "God is love" and that "there is no fear in love; but perfect love casts out fear, because fear involves punishment, and the one who fears is not perfected in love" (1 John 4:8, 18). "See how great a love the Father has bestowed upon us, that we should be called children of God; and such we are" (1 John 3:1).

When we placed our trust in Christ, God gave us the right to become members of his family (John 1:12). Now nothing can separate us from our loving Father because we are his children (Romans 8:38–39). As believers in Christ, we need not be afraid of God as a punitive power. Instead, the fear of God refers to a particular attitude that we should develop.

Awe and Humility

Part of this attitude is a reverence and an *awe* of God. We should daily remind ourselves of who he is: the Creator of the hundreds of billions of galaxies; the sovereign God who inhabits the future as well as the present and the past; the Almighty One who dwells in all places and from whom no thought is hidden. Clothed in power, glory, and dominion, he reigns over the cosmos in the beauty of holiness. This dimension of holy awe expands to holy terror when God's servants, among them Isaiah, Ezekiel, Daniel, Peter, and John, encounter his manifest presence. Their visions of the living God filled them with overwhelming dread and made them simultaneously aware of the heights of divine holiness and the depths of human sin.

Another part of this attitude is *humility* before our King. "The fear of the LORD is the instruction for wisdom, and before honor comes humility" (Proverbs 15:33). Wisdom is the conscious recognition that all we have and are come from God and that every aspect of our lives needs to be under his dominion. The fool arrogantly vaunts an attitude of independence and autonomy, but the wise person lives in dependence and radical trust in the Author and Giver of life. "I am the vine, you are the branches; he who abides in Me and I in him, he bears much fruit, for apart from Me you can do nothing" (John 15:5). We will grow in wisdom as we daily cultivate the attitude of awe and humility in our walk with God.

> *He has told you, O man, what is good;*
> *And what does the LORD require of you*
> *But to do justice, to love kindness,*
> *And to walk humbly with your God?*
>
> *Micah 6:8*

An amplified paraphrase of Proverbs 9:10a, "The fear of the LORD is the beginning of wisdom," summarizes this attitude: "The cultivation of a reverential attitude of awe for the eternal, holy, and almighty Ruler of all creation and a humble attitude of radical trust and dependence upon him in every facet of life is the foundation upon which true skill in the art of living is built."

The Temporal versus the Eternal

When we ask why so few people seem to nurture this attitude of both awe and humility before God, we arrive at a fundamental struggle that unfolds and is illustrated in most of the pages of Scripture. It is the clash between two different value systems: the temporal versus the eternal. At first blush, the temporal appears to be so much more real and alluring, while the eternal seems remote and sacrificial. But as we saw in the discussion of paradigm spirituality, a closer analysis of the temporal value system shows that it never delivers what it promises. Instead, it leads those who pursue it to emptiness, delusion, and foolishness. Only by embracing the eternal value system will we find the fulfillment, reality, and wisdom we seek as spiritual beings made in the image of God. "And though you have not seen Him, you love Him, and though you do not see Him now, but believe in Him, you greatly rejoice with joy inexpressible and full of glory, obtaining as the outcome of your faith the salvation of your souls" (1 Peter 1:8–9). In contrasting the temporal and the eternal, I am not suggesting a dualism between the two that would render the temporal world in which we live irrelevant. Instead, I am saying that an eternal value system urges us to utilize and leverage the temporal with eternity in view. In this way, we do not put our hope in the temporal but learn in this world how to make the things that will last the growing locus of our hope and desire.

This principle is beautifully illustrated in the oldest of the psalms. The superscription of Psalm 90 (which is the first verse in the Hebrew) tells us that it is "A Prayer of Moses, the man of God." It was evidently written at the end of Moses' life, about thirty-four hundred years ago, as a prayer for the new generation that would cross the Jordan to conquer the Promised Land. Moses struck a timeless chord that resonates in our lives as he cried out in the end, "And confirm for us the work of our hands; yes, confirm the work of our hands" (Psalm 90:17).

The word translated "confirm" means "establish" or "give permanence to." This prayer is the yearning of a mortal for something he can do that will not fade away and be forgotten but will last forever. It is the plea of the worker for the perpetuity of his work in a fleeting world.

Moses was advanced in years by the time he offered this prayer and was painfully aware of the brevity of life. The psalm begins with a meditation on the eternality of God ("even from everlasting to everlasting, You are God" [Psalm 90:2]) and sharply contrasts this with four images of the transitory nature of humanity in verses 3–6. A thousand of our years in God's sight is like twenty-four hours, or even like "a watch in the night" (three hours). Our time on this planet is like a sand castle that is suddenly swept away by a wave of water. It is like a delicate flower that opens in the morning and withers in the evening.

This problem was compounded by the tragedy of the wilderness experience. Speaking of the generation of the Exodus, Moses said, "We have been consumed by Your anger and by Your wrath we have been dismayed" (Psalm 90:7). Because the people believed the spies who said the Israelites could not conquer the land and refused to believe God's promise, that generation forever lost its God-given opportunity. God's judgment sapped them of their most precious resource: time. They were consigned to kill time by wandering in the wilderness for thirty-eight years. It has been estimated that an average of almost ninety people a day perished during these years until only Moses, Joshua, and Caleb remained to represent the generation that left Egypt.

A Heart of Wisdom

It is little wonder that Moses would write, "We have finished our years like a sigh" (Psalm 90:9) and "we fly away" (v. 10). We experience the same dilemma, wandering in the wilderness of routine and crowded schedules as the years race by. But there is a solution to this plight, and it is found in the pivotal verse in the psalm: "So teach us to number our days, that we may present to You a heart of wisdom" (v. 12). If we want to have wisdom, skill in the art of living life with each area under the dominion of God, we must regularly remind ourselves that our days upon this earth are numbered. If we blind ourselves to this reality, our value systems will automatically be distorted and we will serve the wrong master.

If, like Moses, we want the work of our hands to have permanency (Psalm 90:17), we should daily remind ourselves that we are "aliens and strangers" (1 Peter 2:11) on this earth and that our true citizenship is in heaven (Philippians 3:20). Our own works quickly evaporate. But God is eternal (vv. 1–2), and his work abides. Therefore we must invest in that eternal work; his works done through us last forever.

Only two things on earth will go into eternity—God's Word and people. God has placed us here to grow in Christ and to reproduce the life of Christ in others. Each of us has specific opportunities to do this in our own spheres of influence, and as we abide in Christ and let his words abide in us, we will bear lasting fruit (John 15:7–8), and the living God will confirm the work of our hands.

The great saints through the ages learned the wisdom of having only two days on their calendars: today and that day (the day they would be with the Lord). If we want a heart of wisdom, we should learn to live each day in light of that day. When we daily remind ourselves of the purpose for our sojourn on earth, we will cultivate an eternal perspective that influences all our work and all our relationships. In 2 Corinthians 4:16–18, Paul summarized the vision that determined the course of his life: "Therefore we do not lose heart, but though our outer man is decaying, yet our inner man is being renewed day by day. For momentary, light affliction is producing for us an eternal weight of glory far beyond all comparison, while we look not at the things which are seen, but at the things which are not seen; for the things which are seen are temporal, but the things which are not seen are eternal."

Eight Questions

Our exploration of the crucial biblical theme of wisdom has led us through a series of questions.

> *What is wisdom?* Wisdom is skill in the art of living life with every area under the dominion of God. It is the ability to use the best means at the best time to accomplish the best ends. Wisdom is the key to a life of beauty, fulfillment, and purpose.

How do we pursue wisdom? The treasure of wisdom rests in the hands of God. Since it comes from above (James 3:17), we cannot attain it apart from him.

What are the conditions for attaining wisdom? True wisdom can be gained only by cultivating the fear of the Lord (Proverbs 9:10).

What is the fear of the Lord? To fear God is to have an attitude of awe and humility before him. It is to recognize our creaturehood and our need for complete dependence upon him in every activity of our lives.

Why have so few people developed this twin attitude of awe and humility? The temporal value system of this world is based on what is seen, while the eternal value system of Scripture is based on what is unseen. The former exerts a powerful influence upon us, and it is not surprising that so many Christians struggle with giving up the seen for the unseen.

What can enable us to reject the temporal value system and choose the eternal value system? An eternal perspective can be cultivated only by faith, that is, believing God in spite of appearances and circumstances.

How do we grow in faith? Our ability to trust God is directly proportional to our knowledge of God. The better we know him, the more we can trust him.

How can we increase in our knowledge of God? As we will see, the answer rests in the fact that God is a person.

Think about your closest relationships. What conditions had to be met before you could get to know these people in this way? Each of these conditions will tell us something about what is involved in growing in our knowledge of God.

The first condition is that both people are willing to get to know each other. You can know someone only to the extent that he or she is willing to be known. One-sided relationships are always dead ends. Scripture tells us that God, the most significant person in the universe, wants us to know him. He is the initiator, and he waits for our response. When we accept Christ's gift of new life by trusting in him, the relationship begins.

A second condition for a personal relationship is that both people gain knowledge of each other, not merely about each other. We can know a great deal about another person and yet hardly know the person. Similarly, we can be well acquainted with sound theology and have no acquaintance with the living God. Only as we get to know God as a person will we grow in our love for him.

A third condition for a growing relationship is openness, acceptance, and forgiveness. People are often afraid that if others know them as they are, they will be rejected. God tells us that in Christ we have been given the gift of acceptance and forgiveness of sins. He knows us completely, and we do not need to be afraid of being open with him in our thoughts and feelings.

A fourth condition is time spent in communication. No relationship can become intimate without regular expenditure of time in talking, listening, and caring. In the same way, we cannot become intimate with God unless we talk with him and listen to his voice in Scripture on a consistent basis.

Fifth, a quality relationship is developed in action; it is nourished through a series of responses to the needs and desires of one another. To know God is to love him, and to love him is to want to respond to his desires for our lives. Faith in God is trusting him as a person, and trust is manifested in action.

Who is wise? Let him give heed to these things,
and consider the lovingkindnesses of the LORD.

Psalm 107:43

QUESTIONS FOR PERSONAL APPLICATION

- What does holistic spirituality mean to you?
- To what degree is Christ the center of your life? In what areas of your life do you sometimes relegate him to the periphery?
- How have you found yourself enticed by false pursuits of happiness?
- How would you describe a skillful life? How do you define wisdom?

18

HOLISTIC SPIRITUALITY
An Integrated Life

CHAPTER OVERVIEW

An integrated life requires a connection between faith and living, between claiming to follow Christ and becoming like him, between belief and character, between profession and practice. When the focus of the heart is on the eternal, secular activities become spiritual and the ordinary takes on a new dimension. Our relationship with Christ was never meant to be a component of our lives but to be the central hub to which every spoke is connected.

CHAPTER OBJECTIVES

- Prizing a focused heart that sees Christ in all things
- An ambition to pursue the purposes of God instead of our idea of what is best for us
- An aspiration for a single-minded pursuit that centers around Christ in all activities

We sojourn in an increasingly fragmented world that has a way of eroding our commitments and blurring our focus. Our culture has been stricken by such an intensification of choices and changes that our identities, values, and perspectives are being engulfed. Os Guinness in *The Call* uses the word *pluralization* to describe this process of proliferating options that "affects the private sphere of modern society at all levels, from consumer goods to relationships to worldviews and faiths." Guinness argues that the modern idolatry of choice reduces obligations to options and diminishes commitment and continuity. The biblical solution to this menacing dilemma is a growing awareness of our identity as people who have a calling to be followers and servants of Christ.

TWO SETS OF RULES

When we fail to nurture this consciousness of calling to radical commitment to Jesus, we lose our way in this deceptive and alluring world. On an individual and a corporate level, we begin to play by two sets of rules and try to have it both ways—the world's and God's. This becomes possible when we compartmentalize our faith and divorce it from other facets of life such as work, finances, friendships, marriage, and parenting. This divorce between the spiritual and the secular leads to substantial disparities between belief and behavior and an amazing ability to overlook these inconsistencies. As St. Ambrose put it, "You are a sort of imposter when your profession and practice disagree." We become comfortable imposters who claim to know Christ but whose character is not noticeably different from that of the ambient culture. Comparative surveys of people who claim to have made a commitment to Christ reveal that far from being salt and light, they sometimes cannot be distinguished from anyone else when it comes to such things as unethical behavior, problems in the home, financial misconduct, addictions, and mental distress. These people have not made a connection between faith and living, between claiming to follow Christ and becoming like him, between belief and character, between profession and practice. People who participate in corporate worship rarely relate the experiences of church life to the experiences of everyday life. The disparity between 11:00 on Sunday morning and 11:00 on Monday morning can be enormous.

THE FOCUS OF THE HEART

By contrast, a holistic approach to spirituality stresses the relevance of faith in Christ to the routines of daily living. The spiritual life is not limited to personal devotions, spiritual exercises, church activities, and Bible studies. It is nourished by these, but it should be lived and expressed in the ordinary and in the everyday. We must not view our life in Christ as merely an add-on to our life in this world; instead, we must learn to see it as the wellspring of our being and the meaning of our existence. As we develop this biblical perspective we will come to see the falsehood of the sacred-secular dichotomy. How we spend our money or put together a business deal is as much a matter of the spiritual life as how we say our prayers. Everything depends on the focus of our heart. As Walt Henrichsen puts it, the secular becomes spiritual when the focus of one's heart is the eternal. What appears to be a secular job, whether it is in a factory or in a law firm, becomes a spiritual pursuit if the focus of the worker's heart is on God's kingdom and righteousness (Matthew 6:33). By contrast, the spiritual becomes secular when the focus of one's heart is the temporal. People in apparently spiritual vocations, whether ministers or missionaries, can become more ambitious about building the biggest church in the denomination or becoming president of the missionary organization than about seeking the kingdom and righteousness of God. Thus it is not the nature of the work but the focus of the heart that matters in the economy of God.

It is liberating to see that all things can be done to the glory of God regardless of whether they appear to be elevated or ordinary, spiritual or secular, higher or lower, contemplative or active. "Whether, then, you eat or drink or whatever you do, do all to the glory of God" (1 Corinthians 10:31). This means that living in the marketplace is not necessarily less spiritual than living in the monastery; everything depends on the focus of your heart.

SPLENDOR IN THE ORDINARY

It would be an illuminating exercise to read through the commands in the New Testament to see how many of them relate to the mundane and the ordinary. Consider Ephesians 4:25–29, for example:

> Therefore, laying aside falsehood, speak truth each one of you with his neighbor, for we are members of one another. Be angry, and yet do not sin; do not let the sun go down on your anger, and do not give the devil an opportunity. He who steals must steal no longer; but rather he must labor, performing with his own hands what is good, so that he will have something to share with one who has need. Let no unwholesome word proceed from your mouth, but only such a word as is good for edification according to the need of the moment, so that it will give grace to those who hear.

Truthfulness, anger, work, sharing, speech—these are threads that constitute the fabric of daily living. The bulk of our time is spent in commonplace routines: rearing children, commuting, paperwork, phone calls, washing dishes, paying bills, pulling weeds, relating to family and friends. The reality of our faith is demonstrated more in the way we walk with Jesus in the mundane than in the number of religious meetings we attend. If we wish to serve and glorify God, the most authentic expression of this desire will be in the ordinary activities of life. This means that we must learn to depend and look to Jesus as much in our hour-to-hour responsibilities as we should when we are teaching a Bible study or sharing our faith. Regardless of the activity, it is always true that apart from Jesus, we can do nothing of eternal value and bear no lasting fruit (John 15:5). But when we abide in him and he in us, we can discover splendor in the ordinary.

If we want to live as Jesus did, we will seek to develop a spiritual awareness in all things. A quick survey of the gospel of John reveals the human tendency to miss the spiritual by limiting our thinking to the physical. Four examples come to mind. Nicodemus confused spiritual birth with a second physical birth (John 3). The woman at the well confused living water with literal water (John 4). The crowd confused the bread of life with physical bread (John 6); and they confused Jesus' statement about not being found after he goes to the Father with going into hiding (John 7). In Scripture and in nature, the physical points beyond itself to spiritual realities for those who have the eyes to see. We would do well to adapt Elisha's prayer on behalf of his servant: "O LORD, I pray, open his eyes that he may see" (2 Kings 6:17). When we see our lives from a biblical perspective, we will realize that we are on a journey through the fields of the Lord. The everyday experiences we encounter in this journey can be seen and approached as vehicles through which we can manifest kingdom living.

Just as liturgy in corporate worship utilizes the material to express the spiritual, so an incarnational approach to living can transmute the ordinary into the extraordinary. We live more of our lives in the realm of details and drudgery than in the territory of the impressive and inspirational. The life of discipleship to Jesus consists predominantly in obedience and faithfulness to him in the mundane and thankless routines of daily experience. He is our audience, whether people notice or not.

Our vocation in Christ is beyond what we can achieve in our human resources, so we must depend upon and invoke the power of the Spirit of Christ who indwells us (Romans 8:9). If we reflect on how Jesus would live his life if he were we, we will see that the answer relates to an ongoing sense of dependence upon the Father in everything we do. He said, "I do nothing on my own initiative," and "I always do the things that are pleasing to [the Father]" (John 8:28–29). But "those who are in the flesh cannot please God" (Romans 8:8); we can do the things that are pleasing to him only when we walk by the Spirit (Romans 8:9–13; Galatians 5:16, 25) in the details of daily life. Thus all followers of Christ are called to full-time Christian service—we were never meant to be compartmentalized, part-time disciples. We are empowered to serve our Lord and others when we remember to invoke his manifest presence in each area of life. We should learn to invite God's grace into more and more aspects of our lives; no detail is too small to be done without grace. Listen to this observation by Martin Thornton in *Christian Proficiency*: "Because Christ is God and Christ is man, penitence and joy, fear and love, faith and doubt, devotion and works, universal and particular, humanity and men; all combine into Adoration which eliminates none yet is greater than all. The world of commerce, art, education, politics, family, sorrow, pleasure, science and sociology; all is insignificant compared with the infinitely rich reality of God, yet all things are significant . . . because of the Incarnation."

Begin to cultivate the skill of praying in every situation, and you will discover that prayer spiritualizes all aspects of your life. It sanctifies work and makes the ordinary a receptacle of the divine. Prayer also sanctifies relationships and makes us less selfish than we would ordinarily be as we interact with family, co-workers, friends, and neighbors.

The life of the kingdom is sacramental in that it unifies the secular and the sacred, the natural and the spiritual, into a seamless whole. When an action is done in service to the King, it becomes an external expression of an inward grace. To the extent that we do this, we minister as priests (1 Peter 2:5, 9), and our world, whether the marketplace or the home, becomes a sanctuary.

TEMPTATIONS TO LOSE OUR FOCUS

A life that is rooted and grounded in the love of Christ (Ephesians 3:17) reveals the relevance of the indwelling Lord to every relationship and circumstance. But there are many ways in which we can lose our focus and slip back into a compartmentalized, rather than integrated, lifestyle. When this happens, we revert to the sacred-secular dichotomy and learn to tolerate significant discrepancies between the two.

The allure of materialism commonly tempts us to abandon an integrated focus. Just as the sleeping Gulliver was fastened to the ground by scores of threads in *Gulliver's Travels*, the quest for scores of material goods as symbols of success can root us to the world. By itself, no one of them would hold us down, but a multiplicity of materialistic tentacles exerts power over us and demands our time and energy. Part of the subtlety of materialism is that it is a moving target, and few people, even those who are quite wealthy, ever suppose they have enough, let alone more than enough. The quest for wealth lures us away from time with God and with important relationships. Instead of using wealth and serving people, we are increasingly tempted to serve wealth and use people.

Another temptation is the false belief that we have a better understanding and desire for what is best for us than God does. When we entertain this lie, we commit ourselves to various attempts to find happiness apart from God and his purposes. But Scripture teaches us that God can never grant us true joy and peace apart from himself, because he alone is the Source of these gifts.

Some people fail to integrate their lives around Christ because they lack spiritual passion and are unconvinced that obedience to him in all things is worthwhile. Like the people to whom Malachi addressed his prophetic oracle, they suffer from spiritual sloth and indifference. If we fail to hone a sense of divine calling in this world, we can slip into spiritual lethargy, boredom, despondency, and burnout.

Yet another way of losing our focus on Jesus is the desire for honor in the sight of others. If we are more concerned with the opinions of people than with pleasing God, it will be impossible for us to center our lives around the lordship of Christ. People often spend money they don't have on things they don't need to impress people they don't even like. When we are in bondage to the opinions of others, we will seek to manipulate them, and our whole approach to living in this world will become distorted. We slip into artificiality and pretense when we seek the esteem of the world, and we forget God's estimate of who we are and why we are here. The audience to whom we play will eventually shape the content of our belief: "How can you believe, when you receive glory from one another and you do not seek the glory that is from the one and only God?" (John 5:44). We can be freed from the burden of pride and pretense only when we become childlike once again and accept ourselves for who God says we are in Christ.

Biblical wisdom encourages us to inculcate complete and unflinching trust in the infinite and personal God who created us, redeemed us, cares for us, and gives us a purpose, a future, and a hope. One of the underlying issues in Scripture is whether we will pursue our own plans or God's plans; whether we will attempt to control our lives and welfare or look to our heavenly Father for every good thing; whether we will trust our labor or trust our Lord. Trusting the Lord is active, not passive; it means that we do our work with diligence and excellence as for him rather than for people (Colossians 3:23–24) and leave the results in his hands. Only when we let go of ownership of results will we be walking by faith and not by sight.

SEEING LIFE FROM GOD'S SIDE

We can journey through life and end up missing the point. The story is told about three men who were stranded on a small island in the Pacific Ocean. After some weeks, a bottle washed up on shore. When one of the men picked it up and pulled out the cork, out popped a genie who offered each man one wish apiece. The man holding the bottle said, "I want to get off this island and be back with my friends." He disappeared, and the bottle fell into the sand. The second man picked it up, made the same wish, and also disappeared. The third man, not known for his keen intellect, picked up the bottle and said, "I'm lonely—I want my friends back!" If we fail to see life from God's side, our perspective will be distorted and we will miss the point of our earthly existence. Only when we realize that all things become spiritual when they are centered around Christ do we become capable of living an integrated life that is oriented toward the eternal. The meaning of every event is determined by its context; if we learn to contextualize everything around the invisible and the eternal, we begin to see things as they are before God. As Dallas Willard puts it in *The Divine Conspiracy*, "To become a disciple of Jesus is to accept now that inversion of human distinctions that will sooner or later be forced upon everyone by the irresistible reality of his kingdom."

True discipleship requires a new orientation around the kingdom dominion of Christ and a realization that a life centered on him will cost us everything. "If anyone comes to Me, and does not hate his own father and mother and wife and children and brothers and sisters, yes, and even his own life, he cannot be My disciple. Whoever does not carry his own cross and come after Me cannot be My disciple. . . . None of you can be My disciple who does not give up all his own possessions" (Luke 14:26–27, 33). Everything—family, friends, career, self—must be given over to him without reservation. Whatever we hold back will become a rival to Jesus as a substitute source of our allegiance.

THE HIGHEST AMBITION

The way of discipleship and sanctification is not based upon a list of things we don't do. That is the way of control, measurement, comparison, criticism, and arrogance. Instead, the way of discipleship is a single-minded pursuit of the Holy One so that we are set apart for his service and surrendered to his purposes in every facet of life. It is allowing ourselves to be possessed by God in such a way that his indwelling Holy Spirit is free to reorient our hearts, values, and behaviors in each sphere of engagement. Having entered into a relationship with the personal Creator of the universe, our highest calling is to know him in a deeper and richer way. This was the apostle Paul's ambition: "that I may know Him and the power of His resurrection and the fellowship of His sufferings, being conformed to His death" (Philippians 3:10). The kind of knowledge Paul had in mind was experiential knowledge of Christ as a person. There is a subtle tendency among many students of the Word to be more interested in an intellectual knowledge about God than in a personal knowledge of God. The former is important, but God wants us to love him with our hearts and our souls as well as our minds (Matthew 22:37). Above everything else, Paul made it his purpose to know Christ with his whole being.

What is the purpose of your life on this planet? Do you have an unchanging reason for being, a purpose that transcends the seasons and circumstances of life? I propose that if the most significant component of your purpose is not a growing knowledge of the person and character of God, your answer to the question Why am I here? will be at variance with a biblical view of life.

Philippians 3 affirms that true spirituality is not concerned with rules, regulations, and rituals but with the person of Christ Jesus. The focus of Scripture is not on religion but on a relationship. A growing knowledge of Christ involves not only an increased grasp of "the power of His resurrection" but also a greater understanding of "the fellowship of His sufferings, being conformed to His death." The believer's conformity to his death is vividly described in the familiar words of Galatians 2:20: "I have been crucified with Christ; and it is no longer I who live, but Christ lives in me; and the life which I now live in the flesh I live by faith in the Son of God, who loved me and gave Himself up for me." Paul adds that "if we have become united with Him in the likeness of His death, certainly we shall also be in the likeness of His resurrection. . . . If we have died with Christ, we believe that we shall also live with Him" (Romans 6:5, 8).

Our identification with Christ in his death, burial, and resurrection is the basis for our experiencing the power of his resurrection and the fellowship of his sufferings. His divine power gives us everything we need for life and godliness (2 Peter 1:3) when we surrender to the control of the Holy Spirit. This includes the power to endure suffering for Christ's sake, which the Scriptures assure us will occur in the lives of those who want to be more like him. But we are also assured that the sufferings of this present time are not worthy to be compared with the glory that is to be revealed to us (Romans 8:18).

A SINGLE-MINDED PURSUIT

Throughout the centuries of recorded history, the essential quality shared in common by the diversity of men and women who attained greatness has been single-mindedness. Right or wrong, each had a sense of purpose, each knew the direction in which it lay, and each was willing to pay the price necessary to achieve it.

If anything characterized Paul, the apostle to the Gentiles, it was this quality of single-mindedness. For him, Christ was not a component but the whole of his life, and everything he did in word or deed directly or indirectly reflected this ownership. He could summarize both his direction and his destiny in one concise sentence: "For to me, to live is Christ and to die is gain" (Philippians 1:21).

"In order that I may attain to the resurrection from the dead" (Philippians 3:11)—Paul was single-minded in his longing for growth in the experiential knowledge of the person and the power of the resurrected Lord. He realized that through faith in the Son of God he had become a new creature, united with Christ in his death, burial, and resurrection (2 Corinthians 5:17; Romans 6:3–11). And yet he anticipated the time when he would be conformed to the likeness of Christ not only in spirit but also in soul and body. Knowing that he was a pilgrim on earth and a citizen of heaven, he looked forward to the day when he would be given an imperishable resurrected body (1 Corinthians 15:20–58). Paul was not speaking of the resurrection *of* the dead but *from* the dead, that is, the resurrection of the righteous (cf. Luke 20:35). (The word he uses can be translated "out-resurrection," and this is its only appearance in the New Testament.) The expression "in order that I may attain" can also be rendered "if by any means"; Paul is not doubting his participation in the resurrection of believers but communicating his determination to continue on in faithfulness toward that end. The only uncertainty was whether he would be on earth or in the presence of the Lord when that event takes place.

In Philippians 3:12 Paul goes on to say, "Not that I have already obtained it or have already become perfect, but I press on in order that I may lay hold of that for which also I was laid hold of by Christ Jesus." Paul makes it clear that he has not attained the perfect conformity to the person of Christ to which all believers have been called but that he strives to stay in the process. Scripture affirms that no one will achieve perfection in this life. This is in contrast to the legalistic mentality the apostle sought to refute in the earlier portion of Philippians 3. The legalist strives in the efforts of the flesh to attain a human standard of righteousness. Legalism seeks to quantify spirituality into a measurable product. In this way, it produces the complacency of procedures and practices rather than the ever-challenging dynamic of pursuing the person of Christ.

Paul never allowed himself to be satisfied with the status quo in his walk with God, although he would have been tempted to do so if he put his eyes on people rather than the Lord. Instead, he learned the life-changing secret of not comparing himself with others but only with Christ.

He knew the course that was set before him—to "lay hold of that for which also I was laid hold of by Christ Jesus." The overwhelming passion of his life was to know and be like Jesus, and to this end he strove in the power of the Holy Spirit, not in the efforts of the flesh. Our heart's desire should be for the same single-mindedness that drew Paul to press on to the higher calling of the Lord.

> Blessed are those who hunger and thirst for righteousness, for they shall be satisfied.
>
> *Matthew 5:6*

> *O God, You are my God; I shall seek You earnestly;*
> *My soul thirsts for You, my flesh yearns for You,*
> *In a dry and weary land where there is no water.*
>
> *Psalm 63:1*

> *As a deer pants for the water brooks,*
> *So my soul pants for You, O God.*
> *My soul thirsts for God, for the living God;*
> *When shall I come and appear before God?*
>
> *Psalm 42:1–2*

CHRIST: A COMPONENT OF LIFE OR THE CENTER OF LIFE?

It is impossible to progress far in our walk with Christ without a radical shift from an earthbound to a biblical perspective on life. Yet a surprisingly small minority of believers renew their minds on a consistent basis with the Scriptures, and this means that the majority are more likely to be influenced by their culture than by their Creator. As we have seen, the phenomenon of compartmentalization compounds the problem, because many people view Christianity as another compartment of their lives. It is something they practice on Sunday mornings and occasionally at other designated times, but it has little impact on the rest of their week.

For many believers, Christ is *present* in their lives, but his lordship is often resisted or rejected. For others, he is *prominent* in their lives, but there are still areas, such as work and finances, in which they hold onto the driver's wheel. This is usually because they think they are in control or because they are afraid to trust him in these facets of their lives. But there are also believers for whom Christ is *preeminent* as the focus of their being and pursuits. These people acknowledge his sufficiency and supremacy by relegating all areas to his rule and authority. For them, Christ is the hub who orders and integrates every spoke of life. If the claims of Scripture are true, this is the only realistic option for a follower of Christ to follow; the other options are based on the illusion that we are autonomous agents of our destiny. The faulty assumption is that we have both the wisdom and control to accomplish what is best in our lives without complete dependence on the Lord.

As we have seen, it is typical for believers to see Christ as one of several components of life. The circle on left (figure 18.1) consists of a number of larger and smaller circles that represent these components.

A COMPARTMENTALIZED LIFE   A CENTERED LIFE

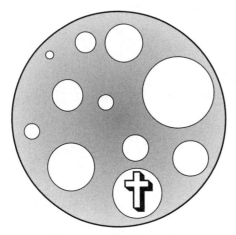 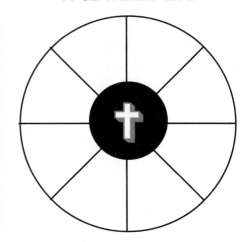

FIGURE 18.1

In this approach, the spiritual compartment has little to do with the other areas of life. As one grows in the Lord, this compartment may become larger, but it is still not well related to the others. As a result, this area is spiritual, and the others are secular. By contrast, in the circle on the right, every facet of life is centered around Christ as the unifying point of integration and coherence. When the heart is focused on him, he becomes relevant to every part of life and empowers us to live before God in our work, our family, and our other activities. In the centered life, there is no distinction between the spiritual and the secular; all things are done for him and through him (Romans 11:36; Philippians 4:13).

My friend Myles Lorenzen created a diagram that well illustrates the various facets of a life that is integrated and centered around Christ (figure 18.2).

The top quadrant represents our relationship with God. Our image of God (center facet) is developed through the Word of God and prayer. The bottom quadrant depicts our relationship with ourselves. Our image of self (center facet) is affected by our inner life and our outer life. The left quadrant represents our relationship with the world and includes the people of the world who do not know Christ (center facet) as well as the things of the world and the systems of the world. The right quadrant portrays our relationship with the body of Christ and includes church life (center facet), family life, and ministry life.

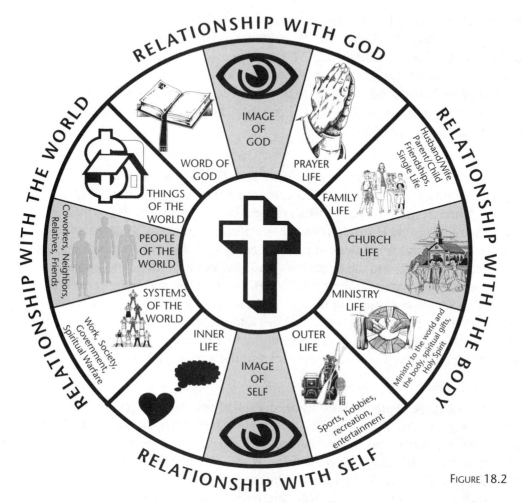

RELATIONSHIP WITH GOD

RELATIONSHIP WITH THE WORLD

RELATIONSHIP WITH THE BODY

RELATIONSHIP WITH SELF

IMAGE OF GOD

WORD OF GOD

PRAYER LIFE

THINGS OF THE WORLD

PEOPLE OF THE WORLD

SYSTEMS OF THE WORLD

INNER LIFE

OUTER LIFE

IMAGE OF SELF

FAMILY LIFE

CHURCH LIFE

MINISTRY LIFE

Husband/Wife, Parent/Child, Friendships, Single Life

Coworkers, Neighbors, Relatives, Friends

Work, Society, Government, Spiritual Warfare

Sports, hobbies, recreation, entertainment

Ministry to the world and the body, spiritual gifts, Holy Spirit

FIGURE 18.2

In this model, the top and bottom quadrants symbolize our vertical relationship with God and the left and right quadrants represent our horizontal relationships with others. The center point of the vertical and the horizontal is the person and work of Christ and our identification with him in his death, burial, and resurrection life. In Christ, our vertical relationship with God makes it possible for us to manifest a new quality of life in our horizontal relationships with people—those who know Jesus and those who do not.

Top Quadrant: Our Relationship with God

Image of God

Our image of the person, powers, and perfections of God is the most determinative thing in our life. As we saw in the section on relational spirituality, loving God completely (with our heart, mind, soul, and strength) is the key to loving self correctly (seeing ourselves as God sees us) and to loving others compassionately (serving others out of the overflow of Christ's life in us). Our image of God must center on his Son because no one knows "the Father except the Son, and anyone to whom the Son wills to reveal Him" (Matthew 11:27). "He who has seen [Jesus] has seen the Father" (John 14:9). The better we know, love, and obey Jesus, the better we will know, love, and obey the Father.

Word of God

The Word of God is the primary vehicle of God's revelation of himself, his plan, and his purposes. The written Word centers on the living and incarnate Word, Jesus Christ. "Then beginning with Moses and with all the prophets, He explained to them the things concerning Himself in all the Scriptures" (Luke 24:27; cf. 24:44). God's personal revelation in his Son was the climax of his self-disclosure to us, for Jesus is "the radiance of His glory and the exact representation of His nature, and upholds all things by the word of His power" (Hebrews 1:1–3). (As an exercise, meditate on the prologue to John's gospel concerning the incarnate Word or Logos of God [John 1:1–18] and on the relationship between the written Word and the living Word in Hebrews 4:12–13.) Christ is called the Word of God (Revelation 19:13), and as we read, study, and meditate on Scripture, we come to know him and the Father more clearly.

Prayer Life

The discipline of prayer, both in devotional times and in practicing God's presence in everyday life, should be centered on Christ. "Until now you have asked for nothing in My name; ask and you will receive, so that your joy may be made full" (John 16:24). "If you abide in Me, and My words abide in you, ask whatever you wish, and it will be done for you" (John 15:7). Jesus is our intercessor and our advocate before the throne of God (Romans 8:34; 1 John 2:1–2), and because he is our faithful and merciful high priest, he opens the way of access to the Father so that we can "draw near with confidence to the throne of grace" (Hebrews 4:16).

Bottom Quadrant: Our Relationship with Self

Image of Self

We cannot truly know ourselves unless we know our God. The only secure, stable, significant, and satisfying basis for self-identity is the reality of our new identification with Christ. Life-changing passages like Romans 6–8, Galatians 2:20, Ephesians 1:3–23; 3:11–21, and Colossians 1:9–23, 27; 3:1–17 redefine all who have come to know Jesus. In him we have a new *derivation,* having been transferred out of the line of Adam and grafted into the line of Christ. In him we also have a new *destiny,* no longer as condemned criminals who are bound to face the wrath of a holy God but as chosen children who are destined to share in Christ's inheritance and to enjoy "the surpassing riches of His grace in kindness toward us in Christ Jesus" (Ephesians 2:7). And in Christ we also have a new *dignity* and purpose in this world as his agents and ambassadors in this passing world (2 Corinthians 5:17–21).

Inner Life

Our complex and subtle inner life can become a morass of contradictory thoughts and urges unless it is centered on Christ. Our hearts, our consciences, our minds, our emotions, and our wills become wayward and troublesome if they are not submitted to the rule and authority of Jesus. Only in him can we discover inner harmony and peace. "The steadfast of mind You will keep in perfect peace, because he trusts in You" (Isaiah 26:3). When we trust in Jesus, delight ourselves in him, commit our way to him, rest in him, and wait patiently for him (Psalm 37:3–7), we discover a peace and joy that eludes us in the world (John 14:27; Philippians 4:6–7). Those who take his yoke upon them and learn from him find rest for their souls (Matthew 11:29). Thus we must cultivate the inner garden of our hearts and minds by centering them on Christ (Romans 8:5–10; Philippians 4:8; Colossians 3:2–4). "Give me your heart, my son, and let your eyes delight in My ways" (Proverbs 23:26).

Outer Life

Our outer life begins with our bodies, the instrument of our agency and expression in the world we know through our five senses. Warning the Corinthians against immorality, the apostle Paul wrote, "Or do you not know that your body is a temple of the Holy Spirit who is in you, whom you have from God, and that you are not your own? For you have been bought with a price: therefore glorify God in your body" (1 Corinthians 6:19–20). We must present our members as instruments of righteousness to God (Romans 6:13) and our bodies as a living and holy sacrifice to God (Romans 12:1). The outer life not only consists in our physical "earthsuits" but also includes activities such as hobbies, sports, entertainment, and other forms of recreation. Each of these activities can be centered on Christ in such a way that his presence is evident in something as apparently mundane as golf, tennis, hiking, or driving.

Left Quadrant: Our Relationship with the World

People of the World

The people of the world are neighbors, co-workers, friends, relatives, and others in our country and around the globe who have not come to know Christ. We must no longer see these people merely as neighbors or co-workers but as people who need to be rescued from the domain of darkness and transferred to the kingdom of God's beloved Son (Colossians 1:13). "Therefore from now on we recognize no one according to the flesh"; thus we should seek to be God's ambassadors of reconciliation (2 Corinthians 5:16–20). We do this by building intentional relationships with unbelievers (1 Corinthians 9:19–23), by being salt and light (Matthew 5:13–16), and by living in such a way that it requires an explanation so that people will ask us to give an account for the hope that is in us (1 Peter 3:15).

Things of the World

Jesus taught that "not even when one has an abundance does his life consist of his possessions" (Luke 12:15). Unless we center our view of possessions on Christ, we will be tempted to give our souls in exchange for things that are destined to disappoint and disappear (Mark 8:36–37). Only when we allow Christ to determine the content of our lives will we learn the secret of contentment. The "worries of the world, and the deceitfulness of riches, and the desires for other things" can be enticements that choke our spiritual vitality and render us unfruitful (Mark 4:19). Instead, we must view the things God gives us in this world as a stewardship he has entrusted to us and for which he will hold us accountable. If we seek his kingdom and righteousness above earthly goods (Matthew 6:33), we will be rich toward God (Luke 12:21) and take hold of that which is life indeed (1 Timothy 6:17–19). The things of the world also include our stewardship over the environment God has entrusted to us.

Systems of the World

We are embedded in a culture that consists of interlocking structures and systems that shape our existence. The spheres of work, society, and government impinge upon our lives and can define and consume us if our lives are not centered on Christ. When we see the lordship of Jesus over all things, these systems become arenas in which we are called to represent the King. Since the world with its various lusts (1 John 2:15–17) is in opposition to the person and purposes of God, those who follow Christ are engaged in a spiritual warfare. As we submit to him and seek to do his will in this world, we become his agents and "appear as lights in the world" (Philippians 2:15).

Right Quadrant: Our Relationship with the Body
Church Life

The Christian life is meant to be lived not in isolation but in community. As the body of Christ, the church is an organism that consists of interdependent parts that make unique contributions to the whole. Christ is the head of the body, and his intention is that each member grows into spiritual maturity and increasing likeness to him. When believers assemble for mutual edification and worship, they are renewed, equipped, and encouraged to love, serve, and build up one another and to be God's people in this world (Ephesians 4:11–16). The body gathered (edification) empowers the body scattered (evangelism).

Family Life

God designed the family to be the foundation of society as the context in which lives are formed and values are inculcated. The husband-wife relationship is to be modeled on the loving relationship between Christ and his bride, the church (Ephesians 5:22–33), and the parent-child relationship is a divinely ordained milieu for nurture, instruction, provision, protection, and character formation (Deuteronomy 6:5–9; Joshua 24:15). These relationships cannot achieve their purpose unless we learn to depend on Christ and let him determine the outcomes. When our lives are centered on him, he gives us the strength to serve our spouse and children in unselfish ways. Broadly considered, family life also includes friendships and the single life, and these too must find their vitality by being oriented around Christ.

Ministry Life

All believers have been entrusted with spiritual gifts for the purpose of ministering to believers and unbelievers in their circles of influence. "As each one has received a special gift, employ it in serving one another as good stewards of the manifold grace of God" (1 Peter 4:10). Only when we are surrendered to Christ are we able to serve people in the power of the Spirit (Matthew 20:25–28). In this way we are inviting Jesus to love and serve people through us. Ministry giftings and callings are manifold (e.g., teaching, evangelism, service to the poor and needy, discipleship, encouragement, hospitality, missions), but they must always be centered on Christ rather than ends in themselves.

The Four Quadrants and the Twelve Facets of Spirituality

The following table (18.1) relates the twelve facets of Christian spirituality to the four quadrants we have just discussed.

RELATIONAL SPIRITUALITY	Center facets of the four quadrants
PARADIGM SPIRITUALITY	Things of the world, inner life
DISCIPLINED SPIRITUALITY	Aspects of all four quadrants
EXCHANGED LIFE SPIRITUALITY	Image of God and of self
MOTIVATED SPIRITUALITY	Image of God and of self, inner life
DEVOTIONAL SPIRITUALITY	Top quadrant
HOLISTIC SPIRITUALITY	Integration of all four quadrants
PROCESS SPIRITUALITY	Inner life as it relates to the other areas
SPIRIT-FILLED SPIRITUALITY	Inner life, ministry life
WARFARE SPIRITUALITY	Systems of the world
NURTURING SPIRITUALITY	People of the world and right quadrant
CORPORATE SPIRITUALITY	Church life, family life, ministry life

TABLE 18.1

All twelve of these facets affect and spill over into the others. The central contribution of holistic spirituality is its emphasis on the relevance of our life in Christ to every aspect of our existence.

QUESTIONS FOR PERSONAL APPLICATION

- How often do you find yourself trying to play by two sets of rules? To what degree is there a tension between your profession and your practice?
- What is the focus of your heart in your work, and how does this affect your perception of the secular and the sacred?
- In what ways do you seek to find transcendence in the ordinary?
- Which of the "Temptations to Lose our Focus" spoke most clearly to your condition?
- How can you move further in the direction of a Philippians 3:10 ambition?
- What does it mean to have a single-minded pursuit?
- As you look at the chart with its four quadrants and twelve facets, to what degree in your life does Jesus occupy the center position in each one of the twelve facets?

19

HOLISTIC SPIRITUALITY
Relationships, Work, and Society

CHAPTER OVERVIEW

This chapter offers a distilled list of principles concerning the integration of faith and practice in three critical relationships (husband-wife, parent-child, and friendships) as well as the two critical arenas of work and society.

CHAPTER OBJECTIVES

- An enhanced appreciation for the biblical design for the marital relationship
- A clear understanding of biblical principles for the parent-child relationship
- A better grasp of the cost and value of quality friendships
- A more scriptural approach to the workplace
- A biblically informed orientation to society

In this chapter I have selected five areas within the facets of family life and systems of the world for additional development. It is important for us to see how our closest relationships play crucial roles in our spiritual formation. The first three of these areas are the critical relationships of husband-wife, parent-child, and friendships, and the last two are work and society. A growing literature seeks to integrate faith and practice in all these areas, but it may be helpful to have a distilled list of principles.

THREE RELATIONSHIPS

The Husband-Wife Relationship

- First Corinthians 7 defends the legitimacy of marriage but also acknowledges the place of the celibate life. Paul relates celibacy to the gift of self-control (vv. 7, 9) and states that there are certain advantages to remaining single if one has this gift. The single person is more free to minister, especially in troubled times, and has fewer distractions to a life of devotion to

God (vv. 29–35). It would be wrong to pressure a person with the gift of celibacy to get married; marriage is a may but not a must.

- Marriage was divinely designed not only to be the basic building block of society but also to provide an earthly analogy of spiritual truth. Marriage is a lifetime covenant of mutual commitment between a man and a woman that leads to oneness on every level: spirit, soul, and body.

- This communion and intimacy between marriage partners is designed to reflect the image of God and provide the context for a lasting relationship of love and respect. This is a high calling, and it is unattainable apart from conscious dependence upon the grace and power of God.

- Genesis 1:26–27 states that male and female together constitute the image of God. "And God created man in His own image, in the image of God He created him; male and female He created them" (Genesis 1:27). The Lord created the masculine and the feminine and endowed them with different characteristics so that each expresses something different about God. In a healthy marriage, these personality differences must be acknowledged and accepted by both partners as complementary rather than competitive.

- The concept of "a helper suitable for him" (Genesis 2:18, 20) speaks of a supportive relationship between allies and in no way implies that one is inferior to another. Loneliness was replaced by companionship and completion, and this is central to God's design for marriage.

- Genesis 2:23–25 teaches that marriage was designed to be a permanent covenant relationship of mutual commitment, support, and esteem.

- When marital problems prevail, they inevitably arise from a failure to leave, a failure to cleave, or a failure to establish a one-flesh relationship (Genesis 2:24). "They shall become one flesh" is the mystery of marriage. This phrase includes the sexual relationship, but it goes beyond this, saying that a man and wife become one, and this is a process. The two complete one another physically, psychologically, and spiritually, and in the New Testament this completeness is used to portray the even deeper mystery of Christ and his bride, the church (Ephesians 5:31–32).

- Growing marriages do not happen by default; they are cultivated by years of mutual effort (discipline) and reliance on the grace of God (dependence).

- The best marriages infuse divine love into the various human loves:

  Epithumia. In a negative sense, this word is translated "lust," but it can also be used in a positive way to speak of legitimate desire. Physical desire should be a part of each marriage; an absence or minimizing of the sexual relationship is symptomatic of problem areas that need to be corrected, such as painful experiences in the past or tension and poor communication in the present. Marriage was divinely designed to create oneness between a man and a woman on every level, and shared sexual pleasure is an important form of love that enriches the other forms of love in a marriage union.

Eros. This word was commonly used in Greek literature, although it does not appear in the New Testament. It is the root of our word *erotic* but is not limited to the sensual dimension of love; it goes beyond this to romantic preoccupation with the beloved. *Eros* can be present with or without *epithumia,* or sexual desire. It can lead to such a powerful identification that it overcomes the distinction between giving and receiving. Because it is such an emotional love, *eros* cannot be summoned at will or sustained without help.

Storgê. Like *eros*, this word is not used in the New Testament. *Storgê* is the love of affection and belonging, and it is born out of familiarity. It is a love shared by members of a family who know they belong together and are comfortable in one another's presence. This kind of love provides a sense of security and an emotional refuge from the outside world.

Phileo. This is the love of friendship, companionship, and openness. It is the product of shared interests, time, insights, vision, and experiences. In *eros*, the lover is occupied with the beloved; in *phileo*, two or more companions are occupied with common interests and activities. Without this dimension of friendship, a marriage will slip into the rut of mediocrity.

Agapê. This is the highest of the loves because it is characterized by unselfishness and giving, even to the point of sacrifice. *Agapê* is not a conditional love that judges others on performance. Nor is it a love that results from mutual attraction or friendship. *Agapê* is a love that sets no conditions and stands firm in spite of circumstances. It is prompted by a willed choice to put another's interest before one's own and to serve another person regardless of his or her response. It relates more to the will than to the emotions. *Agapê* is not theoretical but practical, because it is expressed in actions.

Agapê is not natural. It is a divine love, and our choice to love others in this way requires us to be willing vessels of God's love. It is not something we can manufacture in the power of the flesh. *Agapê* is the only love that can provide a true foundation for a successful Christian marriage, since it is an unconditional covenant commitment to an imperfect person. The other loves are important, and each should be a facet of the marital relationship. But they are like flowers in a garden that must be cultivated, nourished, and weeded by *agapê*. Without it, the other loves can degenerate and become ends in themselves.

- There are various ways to express these loves, and Gary Chapman argues in *The Five Love Languages* that we should seek to discern the predominant languages that best communicate love to our spouse. He distinguishes quality time, words of affirmation, gifts, acts of service, and physical touch.

Knowing this can make us more effective in ministering to the needs of a husband or wife.

- In the marital relationship, it is proper for the husband to concern himself with pleasing and serving his wife and for the wife to desire to please and serve her husband (1 Corinthians 7:3–5, 33–34). The greatest enemy to marriage is the selfish attitude that is concerned with the other person's character and one's own needs. Other-centered love focuses on our own character and the other person's needs.

- If we look to our marriage partners to have our personal worth needs met, we will be exploiting the relationship to get something the other person can never deliver. But if we look to Christ and daily renew our minds with the truth that our needs are fully met in him, we will liberate our partners from unrealistic demands and find fulfillment rather than frustration. When we trust God's love for us and believe his promise that our deepest longings are satisfied in him, we are then free to give to the other person without expecting or demanding anything in return. Even if we are rejected in our efforts to serve, we can continue to give in spite of the pain as we acknowledge our feelings to God and reaffirm our true and unchanging position in Christ. We can do this knowing that we are secure in the love of Christ; our true significance is not threatened when we are hurt and rejected by others.

- It is natural to desire that our partners reciprocate in this process, but this desire must not become our goal, because it depends on the other person for its fulfillment. We must continue to pursue the goal of ministry and leave our desires in God's hands.

- The best thing you can do for your partner is to love Jesus more. If you love Jesus more than you love your spouse, you will love your spouse more than if you loved your spouse more than Jesus.

- Our mates should be our best friends. Too often, however, couples get so wrapped up with their children that they hardly know each other. Then when the children leave, they discover that they are like strangers who have been living for years under the same roof. This does not need to happen, but effort is required to avoid it. Friendships are cultivated by shared thoughts, feelings, and experiences.

- Couples need to develop a spiritual oneness by taking a little time in the morning or evening to study the Bible and pray together. Consistency is crucial.

- Oneness on the level of spirit and soul provides the basis for physical oneness in marriage. From a biblical standpoint, sex should not be regarded as making love but as expressing love. Sexual intimacy was designed to be an expression of spiritual and psychological (mental, emotional, and volitional) intimacy. As

Larry Crabb notes, the two bodies that come together should house two persons who are already together. The sexual relationship was never intended to lead to a good marriage but to be the product of a good marriage.

The Parent-Child Relationship

- The Christian home has been called "a laboratory for the application of biblical truth in a relational setting." It is a training ground for imparting values, for learning how to give and receive love, and for the development of relationships.

- According to Psalm 127:3–5, children are a gift from the Lord. They are God's possession, not ours. He has temporarily placed them under our care—in effect, our children are on loan from God for the eighteen or so years they are under our roof. We have been given the task of rearing them from a state of complete dependence to a state of complete independence so that we can release them to God by the time they reach maturity.

- Many parents make the mistake of building their lives and marriages around their children. They may seek to fulfill their own ambitions and dreams by identifying themselves with their children and living their lives through them. This vicarious attempt to find fulfillment always leads to frustration and disappointment because the children rarely meet such expectations and leave home so soon. It also places them under an intolerable demand of performance standards that they are physically, emotionally, or mentally incapable of attaining.

- Perhaps the most difficult biblical principle to apply as a parent is the need to accept your children as they are. Your true source of identity is in Christ, not your children. Your children may not be as physically or mentally capable as you would like, but if you realize that they are God's possession and not yours, you can accept them for who they are. The practice of this truth can liberate your children from the fear of rejection and failure.

- Parents are responsible to provide for their children's material needs, but they have also been entrusted with the responsibility of shaping their children's character and guiding their spiritual, psychological, intellectual, emotional, and physical growth. This is not to be left by default to outside institutions. The primary spiritual and moral training of children should be in the home, not in the church or school.

- When Christlike attitudes prevail in parents, each member of the household feels that he or she is an important part of the family. Husbands and wives are to model before their children the qualities of mutual respect and concern for one another in the Lord. As this atmosphere extends to their relationship with their children, they will sincerely respect the worth and uniqueness of each child. This recognition of the individuality and dignity of each family member is manifested in a positive and encouraging attitude.

- Since it takes about five positive comments to overcome one negative remark, it is important for parents to be on their children's team, not on their backs. They should avoid favoritism and comparisons of one child with another. It is especially important for parents to admit their mistakes openly and ask forgiveness from their children when they embarrass or insult them, break a promise, or mistreat them. In this way, honesty and esteem for each individual becomes ingrained in the thinking of the children.

- As parents, we cannot impart to our children what we ourselves do not possess. Unless we have a growing relationship with God in Christ, we cannot expect our children to desire the same. The first prerequisite to being a godly parent is to love God with our minds, emotions, and wills, and this requires an ongoing relationship of trust, dependence, and communion with the Lord (Deuteronomy 6:4–5). Only as we respond to God's love can we walk in it; spiritual vitality must be in our hearts before it can be in our homes.

- We must respond not only to God's love but also to his Word (Deuteronomy 6:6). Scripture speaks to every dimension of life, and our effectiveness in any area depends on the degree to which we know and apply relevant biblical principles. If we try to rear children by doing what comes naturally, we will be ineffective.

- We are living models for our children. What we are communicates far more than what we say—spirituality is more caught than taught. The intimacies of home life soon expose an artificial front, so there is little point in teaching what we do not practice. We must demonstrate with our lives the reality of our faith. The greater the correspondence between what we are and what we say, the more completely our children will identify with our standards.

- Young children's view of God is profoundly shaped by their view of their fathers. If a father ignores his child, is unkind to his wife, or is unfair, his child will have a problem with a distorted image of God. Modeling is the most effective method of teaching, whether for good or ill. A healthy view of God is best communicated by parents who have allowed the Holy Spirit to make them authentic, loving, Christlike people. This requires a growing dependence upon the Lord.

- We must live our convictions, but we must also explain them (Genesis 18:19; Deuteronomy 6:7; Isaiah 38:19). There is a danger in some homes of religious activities becoming so church-oriented that they become a substitute for Christian teaching in the home. The Scriptures, however, commission parents to inculcate the Christian world view in children. It is their responsibility to teach their sons and daughters to know and pursue the ways of God.

- "You shall bind them as a sign on your hand and they shall be as frontals on your forehead. You shall write them on the doorposts of your house and on your gates" (Deuteronomy 6:8–9). Spiritual truth must be bound up in our actions ("hand") and attitudes ("head"), and it must be inscribed in our private ("doorposts") and public ("gates") lives. In short, it must move from our hearts into our homes and from our homes into our habits.

- Part of our God-given responsibility as parents is to evangelize and disciple our children. We need to pray for them and ask for insight into their character so that we can rear them in the most appropriate and individual way. Each child should learn to cultivate his or her walk with the Lord. Our real goal must be to teach them that their relationship to Jesus Christ is more important than their relationship to us.

- Because each child has a unique personality, the most effective training is suited to differences in age, abilities, and temperament. Children need to be treated as unique people. In effect, then, Proverbs 22:6 tells us to dedicate our children to the Lord and create a taste within them to know him in ways that are appropriate to their ages and personalities. When they mature, their spiritual heritage will remain a part of them.

- It has been said that children spell love T-I-M-E. The quality of the time we spend with them is essential, but we deceive ourselves if we make this a substitute for quantity. There is a dangerous tendency in our culture to use material possessions as a surrogate for building intimate relationships with children. They are not so easily bought off. Overindulgence by presents will not make up for a failure to express love by spending time with them.

- Like adults, children respond differently to various expressions of love. Gary Chapman argues in *The Five Love Languages of Children* that we should seek to discern the predominant languages that best communicate love to our children, whether this is quality time, words of affirmation, gifts, acts of service, or physical touch.

Friendships

- Relatively few of us experience true friendship. There is a spectrum of intimacy that ranges from acquaintanceship to companionship to untested friendship to the intimacy of established friendship (tested by time and fire). What many people call friends are more likely to be acquaintances or companions.

- It requires an intentional investment of valuable time and energy to cultivate and maintain special friendships.
- As friendship develops, it is natural to begin on the level of facts, to move to the level of opinions, and then to reach the level of feelings.
- C. S. Lewis in *The Four Loves* observes that friendship is the least natural of human loves, since it is not driven by instinct, necessity, or survival value. In addition, true friendship is the least jealous of the loves, and it is essentially free from the need to be needed.
- It is important that we learn to love people without being controlled or consumed by them. When dealing with people, it is wise to hope but not to expect. Never center your whole faith on any human being; only God can sustain that burden.
- Quality friendships are characterized by trust, openness, mutual respect, honesty, and self-disclosure. There is no need for pretense in a real friendship; you can dare to be yourself. A friend accepts and understands you, and this includes your faults as well as your strengths.
- Friendship is founded on sharing a basic consensus of beliefs; it is built on caring about the same truth.
- True friendship is revealed in times of crisis. Times of adversity and distress test the reality of friendship (Proverbs 27:10). "A friend loves at all times, and a brother is born for adversity" (Proverbs 17:17).
- A real friend is empathetic; he or she rejoices with you and weeps with you (Romans 12:15). A false friend resents or is envious at another's good fortune and can secretly gloat at another's misfortune.
- The highest level of friendship includes the dynamic of covenant and commitment. In this covenant relationship, two people agree to walk together for life in trust and loyalty (Proverbs 18:24; Ecclesiastes 4:9–12).
- Friends share "the treasure of common memories, of trials endured together, of quarrels and reconciliations and generous emotions" (Antoine de Saint-Exupéry). They build mutual histories of joys and pains.
- Spiritual friends believe in each other, build into one another's lives, and encourage each other to grow in their relationship with God. They are faithful, and they are willing to ask tough questions to keep one another honest. They sharpen (Proverbs 27:17), counsel (Proverbs 27:9), and encourage one another (Hebrews 3:13).
- A real friend rebukes when necessary and is candid and truthful (Proverbs 17:10; 18:24; 27:6).
- Lasting friendships keep confidences (Proverbs 17:9), listen attentively and empathetically (Proverbs 18:13), and do not seek to control or manipulate.

WORK

- Work is not a result of the Fall. It is a part of God's created order for humanity (Genesis 2:5, 15), and it is patterned after God (Exodus 20:11). Nevertheless, the Fall affected the character of work in such a way that it became associated more with toil than with joy (Genesis 3:17–19). Work becomes idolatrous when it becomes an end in itself (Ecclesiastes 2:4–11, 18–23; Luke 12:16–22), and it can become a means of exploitation and oppression (Exodus 1:11–14; 2:23; James 5:4).

- However, Scripture rebukes idleness and sloth and affirms that work has genuine value (Ecclesiastes 2:24; 3:12–13; 5:18).

- When work is done in and for the Lord, it benefits others and honors God. In creative activity we externalize our identities as people made in the image of God.

- However, our identity transcends our work, and if we do not derive our identity from our relationship with the Lord, our work will tend to shape and define us. Our vocation, or calling, includes our occupations and careers but also transcends them.

- All honest professions are honorable, and there is dignity in manual as well as mental work, as is evident from the occupations of the characters in the Bible. True importance is not found in position or prestige but in the manner in which our work is done and the Audience for whom we do it. Significance is not determined by wisdom, power, or wealth (Jeremiah 9:23–24; Philippians 3:8) but by our relationship with God. Because of this, it is always a mistake to compare ourselves with others.

- Work hard, but do not overwork. The sluggard is reproached in the Old and New Testaments (Proverbs 6:6–11; 12:27; 13:4; 20:4; 21:25–26; 22:13; 24:30–34; 26:13–16; Matthew 25:24–30; Ephesians 4:28; 1 Thessalonians 4:10–12; 2 Thessalonians 3:6–12; 1 Timothy 5:8, 13). But when work becomes the source of our significance and security, we swing to the opposite extreme and become consumed by our work.

- We are called to do our work as unto the Lord instead of seeking to impress and please people (Ephesians 6:5–8; Colossians 3:23–24). Employers should see themselves as accountable to Christ for the way they treat their employees (Ephesians 6:9; Colossians 4:1).

- When we seek to glorify God in whatever we do (1 Corinthians 10:31), we will pursue excellence in our work, whether others notice or not. Consider the superb craftsmanship of Bezalel and Oholiab, the men who constructed the tabernacle in the wilderness (Exodus 35–40). Also imagine the quality and workmanship of the wooden articles that Jesus crafted during his years as a carpenter.

- Remember that God gives us our ability (Romans 12:6), our intelligence (Daniel 2:21), our wealth (Deuteronomy 8:18), and our promotions (Psalm 75:6–7).
- We do not work to provide for our needs. Our culture associates work with the quest for success, significance, provision, esteem, and purpose. By contrast, Scripture teaches us that it is God, not our work, to whom we should look for these things (1 Corinthians 4:7; Philippians 4:19). Believers must come to see that God is their source of provision, and their work is a means he uses to supply their needs.
- If we look to our customers and clients rather than the Lord as our source of provision, we will be far more inclined to manipulate and use them than to minister to them.
- Work embeds us in a temporal environment in which we can exhibit kingdom values and hope. It provides a context in which we can represent Jesus Christ by building relationships; by demonstrating character, conviction, and integrity; and by doing our work with care and quality.
- There should be no secular/spiritual duality regarding work. God has promised that the product of our work will ultimately perish (2 Peter 3:10). It is not the fruit of our labors but the focus of our heart that gives value to our work in the sight of God. Thus secular work becomes spiritual when it is done to please God, and religious work becomes secular when it is done to please and impress people.
- God is not impressed by or dependent upon our abilities or accomplishments. But if we do our work for his sake, it pleases him in the same way that the drawings children make for their parents decorate the refrigerator. These drawings are valued not because they qualify to hang in an art gallery but because of the parent's relationship with the children who made them.
- We cannot contribute to the work of God (Esther 4:13–14; Psalm 115:3; 127:1–2; Ecclesiastes 3:14; Isaiah 46:9–10; 2 Corinthians 3:5), but we can participate in it (John 4:34; 1 Corinthians 3:6–9). If we think that we can add to the work of God, our work becomes so inflated in importance that it can overwhelm relational commitments. We take ourselves too seriously when we think God needs what we have to offer. When leaders attempt to build ministry empires by using people to serve their visions, they make the mistakes of trying to measure the ministry and of basing their significance upon their accomplishments.
- Working harder does not necessarily lead to greater prosperity. There is a correlation but not a fixed causality. In many occupations (e.g., farming, real estate, technology), the ratio of productivity to time invested can vary

dramatically. We may suppose that we can outearn our needs by working harder, but income is only one of several components that can affect our standard of living. If we miss these truths, we will be inclined to sacrifice other priorities (our relationships with God and others) when business is less productive.

- There should be a rhythm between work and leisure in our lives so that we can enjoy periods of refreshment, renewal, restoration, and relationships. Work and rest are equally legitimate in God's economy, but most of us have a tendency to overvalue work. Leisure can be a mode of worship (Leviticus 16:29–31; Deuteronomy 14:22–26) and an expression of contentment with the will of God in our lives. From a biblical standpoint, rest is not so much the absence of activity as it is the presence of God (Exodus 33:14; Nehemiah 8:10–12; Matthew 11:28–30; Mark 6:31; Romans 15:32; Hebrews 3:11–4:11).

SOCIETY

- Truth-centered expressions of Christianity tend to stress evangelism and edification, while deed-centered expressions of Christianity tend to stress social justice. The former focus on the personal and the inward, while the latter are more concerned with the social and the outward. It is more balanced to see this as more of a both-and than an either-or; the two sides can learn from each other, since they both address legitimate concerns.
- The spiritual should have a bearing on the temporal, and prayer can be directly associated with social involvement. There need be no conflict between charity and justice, since these were integrated in the life of our Lord.
- The New Testament teaches that the spiritual and invisible is more fundamental than the physical and visible; followers of the Way must realize that they are sojourners in the world and citizens of heaven. Thus the Great Commission is concerned with evangelism and discipleship. If we forget this priority, the visible will overcome the invisible, and the gospel will be reduced to social action as an end in itself.
- Feeding, clothing, and housing people without sharing the gospel makes them more comfortable in this fleeting world but ignores their eternal destiny. Ministry to physical and social needs must be done in the name of Jesus and with the intention of ministering to spiritual needs as well.
- We express our love for God in loving actions toward people (James 2:15–17; 1 John 3:17–18; 4:20–21).

- As Richard J. Foster observes in *Streams of Living Water*, the social justice tradition is founded on three great themes in the Old Testament: justice and righteousness in relationships (*mishpat*), lovingkindness and compassion (*hesed*), and peace and harmony (*shalom*).
- The Law and the Prophets were concerned with the issues of justice in society and integrated the spiritual and the social. Faith is not merely an inward affair of the heart, but it is to be expressed outwardly.
- A spirituality of justice and peace is illustrated in a wide variety of biblical passages such as Leviticus 19:15; Deuteronomy 10:17–18; Psalm 103:6; 140:12; 146:9; Proverbs 14:31; 19:17; 22:9; Isaiah 1:17; 11:1–5; 58:6–10; Jeremiah 9:23–24; Amos 2–8; Micah 6:8; Luke 4:18–19; 7:21–23; James 1:27.
- In the early history of the church, Christians practiced seven traditional works of mercy: feeding the hungry, giving drink to the thirsty, clothing the naked, harboring the stranger, visiting the sick, ministering to prisoners, and burying the dead.
- Because of dramatic differences in temperament and environment, some believers will be more passionate about social action than others. Appendix A relates the combination of intuition and understanding to a concern for justice, peace, and social relevance. Cultural context is also critical, and it is not uncommon for Christians in third-world countries to view spirituality largely in terms of a commitment to making radical structural changes in society.
- There is always a danger of enslaving theology to current ideology. Without a strong view of biblical authority it is easy to spiritualize the prevailing cultural agenda. "Christian realism . . . is motivated not by a theology which seeks to baptize a current social order but by a theology of dissatisfaction with *all* current social orders, a theology of the God-inspired future which draws future vision into present reality," Kenneth Leech reminds us in *Experiencing God*. The church best influences the world by being distinct from it, not by being diffused in it.
- Our focus of ministry should be shaped by the calling and burden God gives us. We must beware of the common mistake of universalizing our ministry passion. Otherwise we will take on a moralistic attitude and assume that our calling should be obligatory for others.
- Still, it would be unbiblical to avoid any spirituality of social involvement (consider the description of "pure and undefiled religion" in James 1:27). Personal and social holiness go together; personal holiness should spill over into our dealings with people and the social order, and social holiness should be embedded in and empowered by personal holiness.

- We should avoid the error of a privatized and individualistic approach to the spiritual life and the opposite error of reducing theology to a servant of the social system. We need a creative tension between unworldly and worldly components that promotes private passion and social relevance.
- It is effective in many contexts to combine evangelism with social reform as long as the latter does not eventually occlude the former. Some people who sought to integrate the spiritual and the social were John Woolman, William Wilberforce, Lord Shaftesbury, George Müller, General William Booth (The Salvation Army), Dag Hammarskjöld, Martin Luther King Jr., and Mother Teresa.
- Corporate spirituality and a spirituality of social justice should go together and reinforce each other. The community of faith can have a prophetic witness in the context of social concerns and structural institutions.
- However, the New Testament does not teach that the mission of the church is to bring society into conformity with the expectations of God. Its focus is on the inside-out process of personal and corporate transformation and of being salt and light "in the midst of a crooked and perverse generation" (Philippians 2:15).
- A realistic optimism is better than a naïve idealism or a fatalistic pessimism. As an incarnational faith, Christianity has wider implications than does individualistic theology. We should be aware not only of personal sin but also of social and structural sin. But this should be tempered by the realization that only with the coming of the King will his kingdom be established on earth.
- Many evangelicals would profit from a larger view and a heightened awareness of social concerns. For those of us who are not inclined in this direction or who have not been exposed to a spirituality of social engagement, some exposure would be a stretching discipline. Our prayers and actions can be enhanced by a broader vision of the social and political world.
- Prayerfully consider some personal connection with a person or a group in need. Serving widows, visiting prisoners, ministering to the elderly, doing volunteer work in your profession, or participating in a ministry that assists the poor with food, clothing, and housing are all ways of loving and serving people in the name of Jesus (Matthew 25:34–40).
- Combine Spirit-led action with intercessory prayer for the poor and hungry, the oppressed and persecuted, those in authority, and peace among nations. Prayer can have far-reaching effects (Revelation 8:3–5).
- In *The Screwtape Letters*, C. S. Lewis makes a perceptive comment about Christianity and social justice through senior devil Screwtape's counsel to

junior devil Wormwood: "About the general connection between Christianity and politics, our position is more delicate. Certainly we do not want men to allow their Christianity to flow over into their political life, for the establishment of anything like a really just society would be a major disaster. On the other hand, we do want, and want very much, to make men treat Christianity as a means; preferably, of course, as a means to their own advancement, but, failing that, as a means to anything—even to social justice. The thing to do is to get a man at first to value social justice as a thing which the Enemy demands, and then work him on to the stage at which he values Christianity because it may produce social justice."

QUESTIONS FOR PERSONAL APPLICATION

- If you are married, how would you evaluate your practice of *epithumia*, *eros*, *storgê*, *phileo*, and *agapê* in your marital relationship? Which of the husband-wife principles need the most attention?
- If you are a parent, which of the parent-child principles need the most attention in your parenting relationship?
- On the spectrum of intimacy in friendship, how many established friendships do you think you have? Is there anyone with whom you have agreed to walk together for life in trust and loyalty?
- As you review the biblical principles related to work, which of them speak most clearly to you, and which will require more focus?
- Where would you place yourself on the scale that ranges from the personal and the inward to the social and the outward? To what degree are you concerned about social justice?

20

HOLISTIC
SPIRITUALITY
Stewardship and Purpose

CHAPTER OVERVIEW

After looking at the biblical concept of stewardship, this chapter touches on five areas of stewardship: time, talent, treasure, truth, and relationships. Concerning the issue of purpose, holistic spirituality distinguishes our primary calling to know and love God from our secondary calling to express this relationship in everything we do and with everyone we encounter.

CHAPTER OBJECTIVES

- A broader sense of the multiple dimensions of stewardship
- An increased desire to embrace God's purpose for our lives

We have seen that holistic spirituality involves a growing responsiveness to the lordship of Christ in every internal and external facet of our lives. It is not a question of developing a list of theoretical priorities (e.g., God first, family second, work and ministry third) but a matter of allowing the centrality of Christ to determine and empower what we should do in each day. Seen this way, Christ is our Life and Lord in all our activities, and whatever we are doing at the moment becomes our priority focus. When the grace of Christ rules in our lives, we will better discern how to allocate the resources God has entrusted to us.

STEWARDSHIP

As followers of Christ, we must embrace a **stewardship** mindset: we own nothing, and we are not here on our business. As stewards, we manage the possessions of Another; as ambassadors, we manage the affairs of Another. The King owns everything, and we are on his business to serve and represent him in the world.

Stewardship is usually described in terms of time, talent, and treasure, with the primary emphasis on the third. I like to add two other categories of stewardship: truth and relationships. Only these two things—the Word of God and people—will survive the destruction of the present heavens and earth and go on into the new heavens and new earth. If this is so, we are entrusted with the temporal goods of time, talent, and treasure in order to reproduce truth in our relationships. Let me offer a brief word about the biblical concept of stewardship and about each of these five components of stewardship.

The Biblical Concept of Stewardship

The New Testament word for stewardship is *oikonomia*, from which we derive the word *economy*. This word means "management of a household," and it refers to the responsibility that is entrusted to a manager. A steward acts as an administrator of the affairs and possessions of another. Stewards are fully accountable to their masters and may act justly, as did Joseph, who became Potiphar's steward (Genesis 39:4–6), or unjustly, as in Christ's parable of the steward who squandered his master's possessions (Luke 16:1–13). As Christians, we have been entrusted with a stewardship; the things we call our own are not ours but God's. We have no possessions, and we do not even own ourselves: "Or do you not know that your body is a temple of the Holy Spirit who is in you, whom you have from God, and that you are not your own? For you have been bought with a price: therefore glorify God in your body" (1 Corinthians 6:19–20; cf. 3:23). Since we belong to Christ, we no longer have the right to self-determination.

God is our Master, and we are responsible to manage his possessions and affairs. Because we are his servants, all that we have is his. This explodes the popular misconception that we give God his percentage and the rest is ours. According to Scripture, we are accountable to God for everything. Whether we have much or little, our key responsibility as his stewards remains the same: faithfulness. "Let a man regard us in this manner, as servants of Christ and stewards of the mysteries of God. In this case, moreover, it is required of stewards that one be found trustworthy" (1 Corinthians 4:1–2).

In the parable of the talents (Matthew 25:14–30), the amounts differed, but each slave was entrusted with something. The rewards were not based on how much they were given but on what they did with what they were given. Significantly, the first two slaves were equally praised, although the first was given five talents and the second was given two. We must resist the temptation to compare ourselves with others, because comparison is the basis of all dissatisfaction. What matters is not how much we have received but faithfulness to what God has given us and called us to do (Luke 12:42).

When the topic of stewardship comes up, most people think of only one area—money. But from a biblical point of view, stewardship is all-inclusive. It touches every area of life, including our time and talent as well as our treasure. Stewardship is faithfulness in using whatever God gives us (opportunities, interests, skills, employment, family, talents, spiritual gifts, land, money) for his glory. The theme of stewardship ranges from Genesis 1–2, when God made the man and woman stewards of this planet, to Revelation 21–22, when God will make his children stewards of the new creation.

If biblical stewardship involves every facet of life, it requires a basic commitment on our part: we must present ourselves to God as his servants, with no conditions attached. The real issue of stewardship is whether we are administrating our affairs and possessions as though they are ours or as though they are God's. The pattern of our lives is shaped by the decisions we make, and the greatest of these decisions is this: Am I the lord of my life, or is Christ the Lord of my life? We will either seek to rule our own lives (the tragedy of the first Adam) or submit to the rule of God (the triumph of the second Adam). This is the difference between the great *I will* (Isaiah 14:13–14) and the great *thy will* (Matthew 6:10; Mark 14:36). Whether we realize it or not, we face this decision many times in the course of each day. Our answer to this question will determine how we manage the time, abilities, money, truth, and relationships God has placed under our care.

Stewardship of Time

Each of us has been given enough time to accomplish God's purposes for us on this planet. The Scriptures exhort us to invest our time wisely, reminding us that God determines the length of our stay on earth. "Therefore be careful how you walk, not as unwise men but as wise, making the most of your time, because the days are evil" (Ephesians 5:15–16). Toward the end of his life, Moses prayed, "So teach us to number our days, that we may present to You a heart of wisdom" (Psalm 90:12).

"The great dividing line between success and failure can be expressed in five words: I did not have time" (Franklin Field). Time is our most valuable asset, but without a proper perspective, we will spend it foolishly. A biblical perspective on time involves several things. Life is brief, and we cannot be presumptuous about the future (James 4:14). The eternal gives meaning to the temporal (Romans 13:11; 2 Corinthians 4:18). Like other assets, our time is owned by God (Psalm 31:15). We must be sensitive to opportunities so that we can make the most of them (Ecclesiastes 8:5; Colossians 4:5). Our use of time will reflect our priorities (Matthew 6:19–21, 34).

Just as it is wise to budget our financial resources, it is also wise to budget our use of time. Most time is wasted not in hours but in minutes. If we do not regularly assess the way we spend our 168 hours per week, our schedules will be cluttered with activities that may be good but not the best. How much quality time do we spend with the Lord, with our spouse, with our children, and with our non-Christian friends? God wants us to be faithful stewards, not squanderers, of the time he has given us.

Stewardship of Talent

We have seen that in the Scriptures stewardship always relates to the management of something that belongs to someone else. Even our talents and special abilities belong to God. We own nothing that was not first given to us: "What do you have that you did not receive? And if you did receive it, why do you boast as if you had not received it?" (1 Corinthians 4:7). God has entrusted us with aptitudes and abilities, and as good stewards, we must use them for his glory and not our own. This is true not only of musical, artistic, athletic, academic, business, and persuasive talents but also of the spiritual gifts we have received. "Since we have gifts that differ according to the grace given to us, each of us is to exercise them accordingly" (Romans 12:6). Peter specifically relates spiritual gifts to the concept of stewardship: "As each one has received a special gift, employ it in serving one another as good stewards of the manifold grace of God" (1 Peter 4:10). Faithful stewardship of natural talents and spiritual gifts requires that we use them to glorify God and edify others. Our purpose is not to please ourselves but to serve others. "Each of us is to please his neighbor for his good, to his edification. For even Christ did not please Himself" (Romans 15:2–3).

Stewardship of Treasure

We have been entrusted with a multifaceted stewardship, but Scripture particularly stresses the treasure of our financial resources. While the Bible has about five hundred verses on prayer and fewer than five hundred verses on faith, more than twenty-three hundred biblical verses deal with money and possessions. Without apology, our Lord said more about money than he did any other subject, except for the temporal versus the eternal. More than 10 percent of the New Testament relates directly to financial matters.

When it comes to governing our financial affairs, we must choose between two radically different approaches: the values of our society or the values of the Bible. The first alternative tells us to find happiness and peace through money; the second tells us to find the desire of our hearts in the Lord and to be content with what he gives us. Money is a good servant but a bad master. If we follow the world's wisdom, money will dominate us, but if we submit to "the wisdom from above" (James 3:17), money will serve us as we use it to serve God and others.

Why is there such an emphasis? One reason is that God knew we would have trouble managing our money and that we would spend a great amount of time earning, spending, and investing it. A second reason is that money has a profound effect on interpersonal relationships. Many people spend more than half their time thinking about money, and financial difficulties are a major cause of marital conflict and divorce. A third reason is that the way we use our money is a real measure of our commitment to Christ. Scripture relates money to the love of God: "But whoever has the world's goods, and sees his brother in need and closes his heart against him, how does the love of God abide in him?" (1 John 3:17). We can assume an appearance of spirituality in prayer, Christian service, and Bible knowledge, but we cannot fake the way we use our money and possessions. Our checkbooks reveal more about our character and walk with the Lord than we may think.

Scripture exhorts us to maintain two crucial attitudes concerning the stewardship of treasure: ownership and contentment. We will look at the secret of contentment at the end of the section on process spirituality, but here is a brief word on ownership.

God is the owner of all things. "The earth is the LORD's, and all it contains, the world, and those who dwell in it" (Psalm 24:1). We come into the world with nothing and leave it with nothing (Job 1:21; 1 Timothy 6:7), but God says, "Every beast of the forest is Mine, the cattle on a thousand hills. I know every bird of the mountains, and everything that moves in the field is Mine" (Psalm 50:10–11). Everything we have, therefore, comes from him (John 3:27; James 1:17). As we saw in 1 Corinthians 4:7, there is no such thing as a self-made person.

We may believe this truth in theory but deny it in practice. When this happens, we slip into the rebellious attitude that "my power and the strength of my hand made me this wealth" (Deuteronomy 8:17). Instead, we must come to grips with the fact that everything we have in this world belongs to God and is only on loan to us. This includes not only our money and possessions but also our families, careers, and plans for the future. If we can get straight on the principle of 100 percent ownership, we will be ready for the principle of 100 percent stewardship.

Stewardship of Truth

"From everyone who has been given much, much will be required" (Luke 12:48). We rarely think of truth as a matter of stewardship, but all of us will be held accountable for the amount of light we have received. Our Lord prayed for his disciples, "Sanctify them in the truth; Your word is truth" (John 17:17). He told those who had believed him, "If you continue in My word, then you are truly disciples of Mine; and you will know the truth, and the truth will make you free" (John 8:31–32).

The Word of God is the sword of the Spirit that judges the thoughts and intentions of the heart (Ephesians 6:17; Hebrews 4:12–13). God brought us forth by the word of truth, and he calls us to humbly receive and apply this implanted word (James 1:18–25). The Scriptures teach, reprove, correct, and train us in righteousness so that we "may be adequate, equipped for every good work" (2 Timothy 3:16–17). Since we are stewards of truth, it is our responsibility to remain students of the Word through consistent exposure to Scripture with a heart to apply what God teaches.

Stewardship of Relationships

In *The Effective Father*, Gordon McDonald relates a story about James Boswell, the famous biographer of Samuel Johnson. Boswell often referred to a childhood memory of a day he spent fishing with his father. On that special day, his father taught him many insights that Boswell treasured for life. Many years later, someone looked up this day in the journal that Boswell's father kept. The entry had only one sentence: "Gone fishing today with my son; a day wasted."

It is ironic that this man regarded what may have been his most significant investment as a waste of time. Scripture teaches that people are eternal beings who are appointed to a resurrection of life or a resurrection of judgment (John 5:28–29; Daniel 12:2). Since this is so, the time we invest in cultivating relationships by loving and serving people is never wasted.

The resources of time, talent, and treasure the Lord has entrusted to us are never ends in themselves. The wise steward learns to leverage these temporal resources into eternal good, and this is accomplished by learning and living the Word of God and by investing our lives in people.

Other Areas of Stewardship

God owns all things, and we are accountable to him for everything we have and use. This includes our bodies (Romans 12:1; 1 Corinthians 6:19–20), our minds (Romans 12:2; 1 Peter 1:13), our opportunities (Colossians 4:5), and our environment (Genesis 1:28–30). We are stewards in relationship to God, to ourselves, to our neighbor, and to creation. In all of these areas we are called to manage the resources of Another with integrity, and in an increasingly technological society, this will pose difficult ethical questions as well as an increasing struggle with the lures of materialism. There is extensive literature on the various facets of stewardship, and three particularly helpful tools are Randy Alcorn, *Money, Possessions and Eternity* and *The Treasure Principle*; R. Scott Rodin, *Stewards in the Kingdom*; and Tom Sine, *Wild Hope*.

PURPOSE

Holistic spirituality distinguishes our **primary calling** to know and love God from our **secondary calling** to express this relationship in everything we do and with everyone we encounter. If the secondary is not related to the primary, we dichotomize the spiritual and the secular when they should be integrated. When this happens, our relationship with the Lord is disconnected from the activities of our lives.

The opposite error occurs when secondary calling replaces primary calling. When this occurs, work turns into our principal vocation (from the Latin word for "calling"). In this way, the visible and horizontal swallow up the invisible and vertical. Or, to use Francis Schaeffer's expression, "nature eats up grace." When we keep our primary calling first and seek to express it in and through our secondary calling, we become more holistic in our thinking and practice.

Although you cannot fully know or express the fullness of God's calling on your life, it is still wise to ask the Lord for a clearer vision of his unique purpose for your earthly existence. Prayerful development of a personal purpose statement can give you focus and passion, particularly when you review and rethink it from time to time.

In *Chariots of Fire*, Eric Liddell takes his sister Jennie for a walk in the hills of Scotland to explain his commitment to training for the 1924 Olympic Games in Paris. He tells her, "I've decided—I'm going back to China. The missionary service accepted me." Jennie rejoices to hear this, because she fears her brother's calling to be a missionary is threatened by his interest in running.

However, Eric goes on, "But I've got a lot of running to do first. Jennie—Jennie, you've got to understand. I believe that God made me for a purpose—for China. But he also made me *fast*! And when I run, I feel his pleasure. To give it up would be to hold him in contempt. You were right. It's not just fun. To win is to honor him."

Liddell was a man of focus and passion because he pursued a growing sense of God's purpose for his life. *When I run, I feel his pleasure*—what do you do that makes you feel God's pleasure? Frederick Buechner put it this way in *Wishful Thinking: A Theological ABC*: "The place God calls you to is the place where your deep gladness and the world's deep hunger meet." As you become a person of calling and purpose, you come to realize that God's good pleasure is also your good pleasure. Seek satisfaction apart from him, and you will never find it; seek to please him first, and you discover that satisfaction is a by-product of the pursuit of God.

A developing awareness of your divinely ordained purpose should impinge on every facet of your life and spiritualize the whole of your existence. Your calling and purpose are expressed and reinforced in an intentional rule of life. To embrace a rule of living is to seek positive guidelines of behavior that will assist you in fulfilling God's purposes. This is training, not legalism; it is discipline, not drudgery. A holistic rule of life assists you in integrating the various components of daily experience—from devotions to work—under the lordship of Christ. Rule is never an end in itself but a means to the end of expressing your primary and secondary callings. Therefore it is prudent to revisit and revise the ways in which you order your time and resources.

My friend Gayle Jackson has been a great help to me in the area of discerning and expressing biblical purpose, and I have adapted his approach to formulating global and role purposes, goals, and objectives. To illustrate this process, here is an outline of the purposes that relate to my personal purpose statement.

Global and Role Purposes

My life purpose is to be a lover and servant of God and others.
Three global purposes emerge from this personal mission statement:

- Global Purpose 1 (loving God completely): To know God and his character and grow into conformity with his Son in faith, hope, and love.
- Global Purpose 2 (loving self correctly): To see myself in the light of God's character and grow in humility and obedience.

- Global Purpose 3 (loving others compassionately): To see others in the light of God's character and grow in love and service.

Seven role purposes emerge from global purpose 3:

- Role Purpose 1 (husband): To love and serve my wife in such a way that she is free to live up to her full potential as a woman of God.
- Role Purpose 2 (father): To love and serve my daughter and son-in-law in such a way that they know that Dad and Mom know and love God.
- Role Purpose 3 (son): To love and serve my mother and father in such a way that they know that they are honored and cherished.
- Role Purpose 4 (friend): To love and serve my friends in a way that nurtures commitment, transparency, and vulnerability in relationships of mutual acceptance and esteem.
- Role Purpose 5 (neighbor): To love and serve my neighbors in such a way that they want to know Christ (seekers) or grow in him (believers).
- Role Purpose 6 (minister): To love and serve unbelievers and believers in such a way that seekers are evangelized and Christians are edified.
- Role Purpose 7 (writer and publisher): To love and serve readers in a way that helps them manifest eternal values in a temporal arena by drawing them to intimacy with God and a better understanding of the culture in which they live.

Prayerfully reflect on your own global and role purposes. Then consider what specific goals and objectives would assist you in fulfilling these purposes for your life.

As an appendix to this section on holistic spirituality, here is a list of forty personal principles and values that I have collected and review from time to time. It is convicting for me to go through these, since they are all beyond my experience. This list may be of use to you as you seek to integrate your life in Christ with your life in the world.

1. Faith: a radical trust in the sovereignty and goodness of God. God is in control and has my best interests at heart.
2. Hope: anchored in the promises of God.
3. Love: a deepening love for God (mind, emotions, will, actions) based on growing intimacy with him.
4. The temporal versus the eternal—I must treat the temporal as temporal and the eternal as eternal by esteeming the invisible over the visible.
5. More than anything else, a passion to know God.
6. Compassion for the lost.
7. Since I cannot live on yesterday's faith, I must be willing to take greater risks based on God's character and promises.

8. A growing awareness of my profound need for grace in all things.
9. A clearer understanding of the truth that my deepest needs are met in Christ, so that I am secure enough to serve others without manipulating relationships to get my needs met.
10. Developing a spirit of humility, complete dependence, and teachability.
11. A willingness to forgive others as Christ has forgiven me.
12. Treating people with grace, dignity, and possibility.
13. A stewardship mentality—increased awareness of God's ownership of all things and an attitude of contentment in all things.
14. Commitment to ongoing exercise and renewal of spirit, soul, and body.
15. Personal integrity—a congruence between the inside and the outside.
16. Openness and honesty in relationships.
17. Radical commitment to the Great Commandment.
18. Radical commitment to the Great Commission.
19. Standing firm in the spiritual warfare by submitting to God and resisting the lures of the world, the flesh, and the devil.
20. Practicing Christ's presence in all things and doing everything to his glory.
21. Accountability to godly people and a willingness to respond with humility to exhortation and rebuke so that I will not be enmeshed in self-deception.
22. Maintaining an ongoing sense of childlike wonder and awe.
23. Focusing on the process and not the product; genuine ministry flows out of being as an extension of who I am in Christ.
24. Walking in the power of the Spirit and putting no confidence in the flesh.
25. Being fully alive to the present and not living in the past or the future.
26. Living each day as though it were my last, and treating relationships in the same way. Cultivating the mentality of a sojourner, pilgrim, stranger, and alien as I wait expectantly for my true home.
27. Growing responsiveness and sensitivity to God's loving initiatives.
28. An ongoing attitude of thanksgiving and joy that transcends my circumstances. A willingness to cling to God's character in the midst of life's pains and pleasures.
29. Manifesting the fruit of the Spirit by abiding in Christ.
30. A commitment to ongoing renewal of the mind so that I can grow in intimacy with God and not be seduced by the culture.
31. An increased willingness to live out the truth that everything God asks me to do is for my ultimate good, and that everything he asks me to avoid is detrimental to my soul.
32. An awareness that good and evil both increase at compound interest, and a corresponding desire to live in the light of Luke 16:10.

33. A desire to give my life in exchange for the things God declares to be important; a willingness to define success by the standard of the Word (relational) and not by the standard of the world (functional).

34. The pursuit of godly mentors who are further along in the spiritual journey.

35. An understanding that habits of holiness are sustained by discipline and dependence; unholy habits are sustained by default.

36. I must be faithful to the process and let go of ownership of the results.

37. A firm belief that since the ministry cannot be measured, I must be content with what God has given me and not compare my ministry with others.

38. Asking God for the three faithful wounds of contrition, compassion, and longing after God.

39. Continued and responsible cultivation of giftedness while at the same time depending less on knowledge and skills and more on the power of the Holy Spirit.

40. Commitment to the centrality of Christ in all I am and do.

QUESTIONS FOR PERSONAL APPLICATION

- How do you define biblical stewardship? What are the requirements of a steward?
- How would you rank yourself in your stewardship of your time? Your talents? Your treasure? Your knowledge of truth? Your relationships? Your body? Your environment?
- What is your understanding of your primary and secondary callings? Have you created a purpose statement for your life and for your roles?

FACET 8

PROCESS SPIRITUALITY

Process versus Product,
Being versus Doing,

In our culture, we increasingly tend to be human doings rather than human beings. The world tells us that what we achieve and accomplish determines who we are, but the Scriptures teach that who we are in Christ should be the basis for what we do. The dynamics of growth are inside out rather than outside in. This section talks about becoming faithful to the process of life rather than living from one product to the next. It also focuses on what it means to abide in Christ and to practice his presence.

21

PROCESS SPIRITUALITY
Process versus Product

CHAPTER OVERVIEW

Process spirituality is concerned with faithfulness during the ongoing journey rather than living from one product to the next. Instead of living in the future, we are encouraged to be alive to the present in light of our future hope. This involves a daily process of growing in grace and living in faith, hope, and love.

CHAPTER OBJECTIVES

- A renewed appreciation for the value of living in the present
- An understanding that growth is a step-by-step process that requires an ongoing series of responses to the Lord's initiatives
- A fresh vision for the way biblical faith, hope, and love can free us to be alive to what God is doing in the present

In our society, we increasingly tend to be human doings rather than human beings. The world tells us that what we achieve and accomplish determines who we are, but the Scriptures teach that who we are in Christ should be the basis for what we do. The dynamics of growth are inside out rather than outside in. Process spirituality is concerned with faithfulness during the ongoing journey rather than living from one product to the next. It also focuses on what it means to abide in Christ and to practice his presence.

Recall from the introduction that I created the twelve categories in this book to reflect the various dimensions of biblical truth as they relate to practical experience on a personal and corporate level. Some of them, including disciplined and devotional spirituality, are rooted in historical traditions, but others portray hands-on applications of Christian principles. This is especially true of paradigm, holistic, and **process spirituality**. Process spirituality is concerned with being alive to the present moment and with the step-by-step process of responding to God's loving initiatives in our lives.

LIVING IN THE FUTURE

For many people, life has become so filled with the if-onlys of the future that today becomes an inconvenient obstacle in the path of reaching tomorrow. As Walker Percy observed in his novel *Lancelot*, "To live in the past and future is easy. To live in the present is like threading a needle." During most of our lives, we have a natural tendency to invest our energies in goals and accomplishments we hope to achieve in the days ahead. The problem is that even when we are able to attain these ends, we are already thinking of the next one. Thus, by moving from product to product, we are rarely alive to the realities of the present. We are fully capable of doing this for decades, but there eventually comes a point where the days ahead are few and the memories behind are abundant. At this point, many people make an unconscious switch to living in the past instead of the future.

I am not saying that being alive to the ongoing process implies the elimination of planning and goal setting. Without a clear vision of the results we desire, we will not move in the direction of creating them, whether in business or in acquiring a skill. In *The Path of Least Resistance*, Robert Fritz distinguishes primary, secondary, and fundamental choices. Primary choices are choices about major results, and secondary choices help you take a step toward your primary result. A fundamental choice is a choice in which you commit yourself to a basic life orientation or a basic state of being. Fritz argues that it is easy for people to move through life by default without a clear idea of what they really want:

> "What do you want?" I asked a man during a workshop.
> "I want to get in touch with myself," he said.
> "What will you have once you are in touch with yourself?" I asked, trying to help him focus on the result he wanted.
> "Then I can see what holds me back," he replied.
> "What will happen once you can see what holds you back?"
> "Then I can overcome the way I sabotage myself."
> "Once you know that," I asked again, "then what?"
> "Then I can stop doing it."
> "What will happen when you stop doing it?"
> "Well, I don't know," was the reply.

This exchange illustrates two things: first, many people don't know where their process is taking them, and second, it is better to choose what we want to create than to focus on avoiding what we don't want.

From a biblical perspective, our fundamental choice should be to know and become like the Lord Jesus, and this in turn should shape our primary and secondary choices in life. This fundamental choice is compatible with living in the present, the only point at which time intersects eternity. This aspiration animates our present, makes us alive to the process of daily experience, and informs our planning.

By contrast, an unbiblical fundamental choice, whether by default or by design, will never satisfy us because it will not address our deepest need as people created to know and enjoy their Creator. In this situation, our lack of contentment in the present will delude us into thinking that it will be found in the future—hence, product-to-product living.

A STEP-BY-STEP JOURNEY

The best metaphor for life as a whole and for the spiritual life in particular is that of a journey. Literature abounds with this imagery (e.g., John Bunyan's *Pilgrim's Progress*). As followers of the Way (Acts 9:2; 19:9, 23; 22:4; 24:14, 22), we are travelers on a quest, a voyage, an odyssey, a pilgrimage. If we are following Christ, we are headed for home, but there are stages along the way and lessons to be learned. This is why it is a mistake to view the spiritual life as a static condition or a state of being that can be attained by a combination of technique and information. To follow Christ is to move into territory that is unknown to us and to count on his purposeful guidance, his grace when we go off the path, and his presence when we feel alone. It is to learn to respond to God's providential care in deepening ways and to accept the pilgrim character of earthly existence with its uncertainties, setbacks, disappointments, surprises, and joys. It is to remember that we are in a process of gradual conformity to the image of Christ so that we can love and serve others along the way.

Seen in this light, the primary point of this earthly existence is preparation for our eternal citizenship in heaven (see DeVern F. Fromke, *The Ultimate Intention*, and Paul E. Billheimer, *Destined for the Throne*). In this life we stumble in many ways (James 3:2) because we are still in process. Our sanctification is not yet complete. Sanctification is both an event (we were sanctified when we gave ourselves to Christ [1 Corinthians 6:11]) and a process (we are being sanctified [Romans 12:2; Philippians 2–3; 1 John 2:28]). Spiritual formation is the lifelong process of becoming in our character and actions the new creations we already are in Christ (2 Corinthians 5:17); it is the working out of what God has already worked in us (Philippians 2:12–13).

The Christian life is not conformity to prevailing standards of holiness but a step-by-step process. This process of genuine response to what God is doing in our lives is more critical than the visible product. I remember a new believer who in his enthusiasm for having found Christ sometimes swore when he prayed. Laundry-list legalism with its inventory of don'ts (the filthy five, the nasty nine, the dirty dozen) and do's would measure such a person as carnal and disobedient. But I submit that this new convert, who knew little but applied what little he knew, was more pleasing to the heart of God with his ungainly prayers than a person who is eloquent in public prayer but is harboring unconfessed sin. In this case, the former gives the appearance of disobedience when he is obedient to where he is in his journey; the latter gives the appearance of obedience when he is disobedient to what he knows. External appearances are often deceptive, and this is why God looks at the heart.

Rahab the harlot had little knowledge about the God of Israel but applied the knowledge she had (Hebrews 11:31; James 2:25); the Pharisees knew the Scriptures but rejected God's purposes. The spiritual life is not a matter of external conformity, and it cannot be measured. Instead of comparing ourselves with others (2 Corinthians 10:12), it is better to seek fidelity in our own journey. Holiness relates to where we are now, not where we need to be later.

We are called to be apprentices of Jesus in kingdom living, and this requires time, development, and patience. As the Gospels illustrate, knowing and believing in Christ is a dynamic process (consider the disciples in John 1, 2:11, and 16:30–31; the woman at the well in John 4; the man born blind in John 9; and Nicodemus in John 3, 7, and 19). Spiritual formation is gradual, and we become more substantial and real as we cooperate with the process by years of small choices in favor of God's purposes. Each choice, whether to obey or resist, makes the next one possible.

GROWING IN GRACE

Growth in Christlike virtues such as obedience, patience, courage, wisdom, service, humility, gentleness, and love is never automatic or easy. To use Teresa of Avila's metaphor, the soul is an interior castle that we must invite God to occupy room by room. This requires a lengthy series of deaths along the way: "If anyone wishes to come after Me, he must deny himself, and take up his cross and follow Me. For whoever wishes to save his life will lose it, but whoever loses his life for My sake and the gospel's will save it" (Mark 8:34–35). Progress in following the Way necessitates an intentional, ongoing commitment to a protracted course of spiritual formation.

Our task is to place ourselves under the conditions favorable to growth and look to God for our spiritual formation. He uses different paces and methods with each person. Since the inner life matures and becomes fruitful by the principle of growth (1 Peter 2:2; 2 Peter 3:18), time is a significant part of the process. As nature teaches us, growth is not uniform—like a vine or a tree, there may be more growth in a single month than in all the rest of the year. If we fail to accept this uneven developmental process, we will be impatient with God and with ourselves as we wait for the next growth spurt or special infusion of grace.

In a culture that promotes instant gratification, it can be wearisome for us to wait patiently for God's timing. Many of us are tempted to bypass grace and take matters into our own hands as we seek some method, technique, seminar, or experience that will give us the results we want when we want them. But we are as incapable of changing ourselves through our own efforts as we are of manipulating God to transform us more quickly.

In his grace, the Lord invites us to cooperate with the formative work of his Holy Spirit in our lives by engaging in the disciplines of faith, repentance, and obedience and by trusting in his ways and in his timing. Inevitably, God's timing will seem painfully slow to us, but as we grow in wisdom, we learn to be more patient with the divine process, knowing that he alone knows what we need and when we need it. Thus spiritual formation is nourished by years of disciplined fidelity to the sovereign call of God. Indeed, we will fail and disobey and do many foolish and grievous things throughout the process, but fidelity means that we get up and return to Jesus each time we fall. "Each day has enough trouble of its own" (Matthew 6:34). May we allow the ordinary demands of everyday living to drive us to the grace of Jesus, to the love of the Father, and to the fellowship of the Spirit (2 Corinthians 13:14).

FAITH, HOPE, AND LOVE

"But now faith, hope, love, abide these three; but the greatest of these is love" (1 Corinthians 13:13). The great theological virtues of faith, hope, and love encapsulate the dynamic of the spiritual life in Christ. Although all three relate to God's creative purposes from eternity to eternity, faith particularly focuses on Christ's redemptive work for us in the past, hope looks to the ultimate completion of this work in the future, and love manifests the life of Christ through us in the present.

Faith

Biblical faith is intrinsically bound up with hope because it is grounded in a Person we have not yet seen (see Romans 8:24–25; 1 Peter 1:7–9). "Now faith is the assurance of things hoped for, the conviction of things not seen. . . . And without faith it is impossible to please Him, for he who comes to God must believe that He is and that He is a rewarder of those who seek Him" (Hebrews 11:1, 6). Faith is pleasing to God because it is the measure of the risk we place in his character and promises. Those who trust in Christ are hoping that what he has promised, he is able also to perform (Romans 4:21).

The essence of walking in faith is acting on the conviction that God alone knows what is best for us and that he alone is able to accomplish it. The problem with faith is that it goes against the grain of human inclination and culture because it is based on the invisible and uncontrollable. We may give lip service to the proposition that God alone knows what is best for us, but in practice we are inclined to follow our viewpoints, especially when times are tough.

The risks of faith are pleasing to God since they honor his testimony in spite of appearances to the contrary. A. W. Tozer put it this way in *The Root of the Righteous:*

> A real Christian is an odd number, anyway. He feels supreme love for One whom he has never seen; talks familiarly every day to Someone he cannot see; expects to go to heaven on the virtue of Another; empties himself in order to be full; admits he is wrong so he can be declared right; goes down in order to get up; is strongest when he is weakest; richest when he is poorest and happiest when he feels the worst. He dies so he can live; forsakes in order to have; gives away so he can keep; sees the invisible; hears the inaudible; and knows that which passeth knowledge.

This faith that pleases God involves three components: knowledge, trust, and action.

Component 1: Knowledge

Unless we know the truth, the truth cannot set us free. Faith in the biblical sense is not based on our feelings and opinions or on those of others but on the authority of divine revelation. Since the heart cannot rejoice in what the mind rejects, it is important to understand that biblical faith is not a leap into the dark but a step into the light. It is a faith founded on fact, and there are credible answers to the intellectual barriers that are often erected against Christianity. For example, *I'm Glad You Asked*, a book I co-authored with Larry Moody, outlines the answers to twelve basic objections to Christianity. The component of knowledge in our faith will be enriched when we renew our minds with God's truth, and this requires the discipline of regular personal time in the Scriptures.

Component 2: Trust

Faith is only as good as the object in which it is placed. If the object is worthy of our faith, it will sustain us even when our faith is weak. When I was in seminary, one of my professors told the story of his grandfather, who wanted to cross the icy Susquehanna River. He was unsure of the thickness of the ice, so he began to cross gingerly on his hands and knees. When he was about halfway across, he heard a great rumbling sound. Looking over his shoulder, he was embarrassed to see a large wagon drawn by four horses storming past him on the ice! His faith had been weak, but its object was worthy. There is no more trustworthy foundation for our faith than Christ, the Rock and Anchor of our soul. When we place our trust in him, we can be sure that he will carry us safely to the other side.

Component 3: Action

Knowledge and trust are best displayed in action. Regardless of what we say, what we do will reveal what our hearts truly believe and trust. Faith in Christ has the property of growing through acts of obedience, and an obedient faith results in a greater knowledge of God. So there is a reciprocal relationship between the faith components of knowledge and action; the better we know him, the more we want to obey him, and the more we obey him, the better we will know him. Everything hinges on what we trust. If we trust our own wisdom, our hands are too full of ourselves to receive the gifts of God. When we empty our hands of self-reliance, self-righteousness, self-pity, and other self sins, they will be empty enough to receive the life of Christ in us and display his life to others.

Hope

A few years ago, I attended the funeral of one of the most extraordinary people I have ever known. Several months after giving her life to Christ, Emily Meredith was diagnosed with a brain tumor. During the next five years, the courage, love, hope, and peace she displayed could be explained only by the power of the Holy Spirit in her life. In spite of her ordeal, she was never known to complain. The Christlike quality of her life made an indelible impact on hundreds of people, and by the age of twenty-one she had accomplished the purpose for which she was sent and was ready for her heavenly homecoming. While her family grieves her passing, their sorrow is tempered by an unflinching hope in the promises and character of God (1 Thessalonians 4:13–18).

Hope is a powerful biblical motivator because it is related to the promise of long-term gain. We just observed that faith and hope are linked; faith takes the risk of commitment before knowledge, and hope gives us the reason for the risks of faith. Each of the men and women of faith listed in Hebrews 11 understood that God rewards those who seek him and risked the temporal in order to gain the eternal. Moses, for example, chose to endure ill-treatment with the people of God instead of enjoying the passing pleasures of sin, because he considered the reproach of Christ greater riches than the treasures of Egypt; for he was looking to the reward (Hebrews 11:25–26).

Worldly hope tells us to pursue passing pleasures, but biblical hope warns us not to sell ourselves so cheaply. God calls us to give ourselves to the things that will last and will not disappoint us in the end. If we focus our hearts on the eternal, we will enjoy the temporal as well; but if our primary pursuit is the temporal, we will lose not only the eternal but also the temporal.

In *A Layman's Guide to Applying the Bible*, Walt Henrichsen and Gayle Jackson describe four kinds of people: those with no hope, those who have a misplaced hope, those who have an ill-defined hope, and those who have a proper hope.

Those with no hope. Few people can live for long without some sense of hope. The venerable Bede portrayed human existence without the resurrection as a bird that flies out of darkness into a window of a brilliantly lighted banqueting hall, only to dart briefly across the hall and fly out another window into the blackness of night. If this earth is all there is, life is a fleeting episode; it mocks our deepest aspirations and longings for more than this planet seems to offer. Some existentialists counsel us to accept the idea that life is meaningless and to live with courage in spite of the absurdity of existence. But no one can live consistently with such a hopeless philosophy.

Those who have a misplaced hope. Almost everyone we meet lives with some kind of hope, some reason for getting up each morning and going on with life. But it would not take much probing to reveal the shallowness and inadequacy of the things in which most people put their faith and hope. When men put their hope in money, power, and position for their sense of self-worth and fulfillment, they will discover, as countless others have before, that these things will let them down. When women hope first in their family, their possessions, or their social status to satisfy their longing for security and significance, they too will be disillusioned.

Those who know Jesus are not immune to the problem of misplaced hope. I believe the reason so many people can swallow the camel of eternity and strain at the gnats of the temporal is that this earth seems real to them while heaven seems vague and distant. With this mindset, it takes less faith to trust Christ for the afterlife than it does for this life.

Those who have an ill-defined hope. Bob Hope once told a story about being in a plane that was struck by lightning. "Do something religious!" shrieked a little old lady across the aisle. "So I did," he wisecracked. "I took up a collection." People tend to do something religious in life-threatening situations. I heard the testimony of an Atlanta businessman who described an experience he had before putting his faith in Christ. He was staying at the Hilton in Las Vegas when a fire broke out in the hotel. Thinking he was going to die, he cried out to God to deliver him. As he later reflected on this terrifying experience, he observed, "I didn't pray to the gods of work, money, golf, or family." During times of tribulation and adversity, we clarify the nature of our hope (see Romans 5:3–5). Hope developed in good circumstances tends to be unreliable because it is untested. But God uses times of adversity and few alternatives to bring us into contact with a hope that will not let us down.

Those who have a proper hope. The only firm foundation for our hope is the unchanging character of the living God. When we find our refuge in Christ, we lay hold of a hope that is an anchor of the soul, a hope that will not disappoint because it is both sure and steadfast (Hebrews 6:18–19; 1 Peter 2:6). This biblical hope provides us with stability and direction because it draws us toward the promises of God. Since these promises are an extension of the Lord's character, a proper hope is founded on a willingness to trust in him. The apostle Paul lived out the truth that "the things which are seen are temporal, but the things which are not seen are eternal" (2 Corinthians 4:18). In the same way, the heroes of faith listed in Hebrews 11 welcomed the promises of God from a distance and longed for a reward that was unseen by earthly eyes.

Their faith was the assurance of the things for which they hoped and the conviction of things not seen (Hebrews 11:1).

Paul revealed his longing for completeness in his relationship to Christ when he wrote to the saints in Philippi: "Brethren, I do not regard myself as having laid hold of it yet; but one thing I do: forgetting what lies behind and reaching forward to what lies ahead, I press on toward the goal for the prize of the upward call of God in Christ Jesus" (Philippians 3:13–14). The apostle avoided the morass of complacency and self-satisfaction through his understanding of the spiritual life as a process that leads ever higher and deeper in the personal knowledge of Jesus Christ, the Creator and Sustainer of all things in the heavens and on earth, visible and invisible (Colossians 1:16–17). In his single-mindedness ("one thing I do"), he concentrated on the goal of growing conformity to Christ.

The world's agenda burdens us with a multiplicity of worries and "desires for other things" (Mark 4:19) that can never satisfy the spiritual hunger of the human heart. But our Lord wants us to lay aside every encumbrance and the sin that so easily entangles us, so that we can run with endurance the race that is set before us as we fix our eyes on Jesus, the Author and Perfecter of faith (Hebrews 12:1–2).

Paul lets us in on a discipline that can revolutionize our lives: "one thing I do: forgetting what lies behind and reaching forward to what lies ahead." A. W. Tozer wrote that "we must face today as children of tomorrow. We must meet the uncertainties of this world with the certainty of the world to come."

Too many of us allow the present to be dominated by the regrets and the successes of the past. Paul refused to allow the past to control the present. If he had dwelled on his successes in Judaism, he would have been inclined to put his confidence in the efforts of the flesh rather than the grace of Christ. If he kept reviewing his failures and short-comings, he would have been paralyzed by a sense of inadequacy and discouragement.

All of us have said and done things we wish we could undo or redo. In varying degrees, we have also experienced the pains of mistreatment and rejection. Though we cannot change the past, we can change our understanding of the past as we embrace the unconditional love of Christ who blesses us with forgiveness, healing, and restoration. The Scriptures exhort us to overcome the bondage of the past by living in the light of the future to which we have been called. The past is inalterable, but our lives in the present have a direct bearing on the quality of eternity. When we learn to see our past in light of our future, we see that our past has relevance but our future reforms our past and determines who we are. In this way, we avoid the common pitfalls of camping permanently in denial or of camping permanently in sorrow.

This is why Paul added, "Reaching forward to what lies ahead, I press on toward the goal for the prize of the upward call of God in Christ Jesus." This is a metaphor of a runner who strains his body in his determination to win the race. The apostle's life was compelled by a singleness of purpose that shaped all of his activities. Like an athlete in a race, he had a clearly defined goal, and he disciplined himself to attain it. But the prize he had in mind was not a fading laurel wreath; it was the reward of the upward call of God in Christ Jesus. Elsewhere he wrote that "everyone who competes in the games exercises self-control in all things. They then do it to receive a perishable wreath, but we an imperishable. Therefore I run in such a way, as not without aim" (1 Corinthians 9:25–26; see Acts 20:24; 2 Timothy 4:7–8).

If we applied the same zeal in our walk with the Lord that we use in our sports and hobbies, many of us would be further along the course. It takes time and discipline to "run with endurance the race that is set before us," but this discipline must be set in a context of a transcendent hope and dependence upon the Spirit of Christ who indwells us and enables us to run in his victory.

Thus the meaning of the present is largely shaped by our understanding of our destiny. Two telling lines in *The Iliad* of Homer seem to encapsulate the world view of Greek mythology: "Such is the way the gods spun life for unfortunate mortals, that we live in unhappiness, but the gods themselves have no sorrows." We live in unhappiness and death ends all—with such a perspective, it is not surprising that many Greek thinkers sought refuge from absurdity in variations of Stoicism and Epicureanism. But for the believer in Christ, the ultimate context of meaning and purpose is our participation in the everlasting kingdom of God. Each today in Christ can be animated by an eschatological spirituality of hope. As new creatures, we are no longer defined by our brief past, but by our unbounded future.

Love

The gospel decisively deals with the twin problems of guilt over the past and anxiety about the future. In Christ, we enjoy forgiveness of sins (past) and anticipation of heaven (future). This is where we often stop, but the gospel is more than forgiveness and eternal life; it is also the power to manifest kingdom living in the present. As I heard Darrell Bock put it, the gospel is the offer of God's ability to make us into the people we were meant to be all along. In Christ, we have been freed from the bondage of the past and apprehension about the future so that we can enjoy the liberty of being alive to the opportunities of the present. The gospel is not a negative matter of keeping sin at bay but a positive manner of walking with Christ and of loving and serving people through him.

The blood of Christ paid the penalty of sin, the cross of Christ overcomes the power of sin, and our resurrection in Christ will remove the presence of sin. We live between the cross and the resurrection, but even now Christ's resurrection life empowers us to live and love. We have been engrafted into the life of the ascended Lord, and as "partakers of the divine nature" (2 Peter 1:4), our life is "hidden with Christ in God"

(Colossians 3:3). This makes it possible for us to have an intimate connection between faith and practice, between being and doing, so that what God has already done in our inner life will become increasingly visible through his transforming work in our outer life. In this way, the hope of our glorious future can be incorporated by faith into our present relationships and circumstances.

Life *in* Christ is the life *of* Christ in us—appropriated in the past, active in the present, and anticipating the future. "But now faith, hope, love, abide these three; but the greatest of these is love" (1 Corinthians 13:13). Love is the greatest virtue because it is the application of faith and hope to our relationships in the present (see table 21.1).

Because eternal life is a new and ongoing quality of life in us that will last forever, the journey of spiritual transformation with its pains and joys and its failures and advances is a process of rendering this new creation increasingly visible.

FAITH	← LOVE →	HOPE
Appropriated in the PAST	**Active in the PRESENT**	**Anticipating the FUTURE**
Forgiveness and grace (Gospels)	Love and community (Acts)	Purpose and hope (Epistles)
Salvation	Sanctification	Glorification
Positional (deliverance from the penalty of sin)	Progressive (deliverance from the power of sin)	Ultimate (deliverance from the presence of sin)
Significance	Satisfaction	Security
Hindsight	Insight	Foresight
History	Our story	His story
Humility	Obedience	Trust
Knowing	Doing	Being
Mind	Will	Emotions
Seeing	Acting	Expecting
Life	Love	Light

TABLE 21.1

QUESTIONS FOR PERSONAL APPLICATION

- To what extent do you find yourself living in the future or in the past?
- What is the practical difference between conformity to prevailing standards of holiness and a step-by-step process?

- What does it mean to grow in grace? What conditions are favorable to your spiritual growth? What has God used to form you along the way?
- How do you define biblical faith?
- Do you sometimes struggle with a misplaced or ill-defined hope?
- How can a biblical vision of faith, hope, and love free you to be more alive in the present?

22

PROCESS SPIRITUALITY

Being versus Doing

CHAPTER OVERVIEW

The modern dilemma of busyness tempts us to elevate doing over being, and this chapter offers several suggestions that can enhance the daily endeavor of living before the Lord. Another temptation is to focus more on causes than on Christ and thus to emphasize activity for the Lord more than intimacy with him. The chapter concludes with some suggestions for practicing the presence of Jesus.

CHAPTER OBJECTIVES

- A clearer sense of how to deal with the problem of busyness in our lives
- A realization that our natural temptation will be to substitute service and activity for devotion and intimacy with God
- Greater skill in practicing the presence of Jesus

Perhaps the greatest threat to applying these truths about process spirituality is the busyness that stems from the way we define ourselves in terms of achievements and accomplishments. We live in a future-oriented culture that relates time largely to efficiency and productivity. We are more inclined than ever to use time to accomplish results than to enhance relationships.

THE PROBLEM OF BUSYNESS

The civil religion of America worships the god of progress and inspires us to compete, achieve, and win for the sake of competing, achieving, and winning. Life for many people in the business world has been colorfully described as a matter of "blowing and going," "plotting and planning," "ducking and diving," "running and gunning," "slamming and jamming," "moving and shaking," "juking and jiving."

Longshoreman philosopher Eric Hoffer wrote, "We are warned not to waste time, but we are brought up to waste our lives." This is evident in the tragedy of many people who in the first half of their lives spend their health looking for wealth and in the last half spend their wealth looking for health.

My associate Len Sykes relates the problem of busyness to five areas.

In our home. We miss relational opportunities when we are dominated by excessive activities. Consider taking an inventory of activities like television, children's lessons and sports, meetings, or time spent on the computer and see how some of these can and should be pared. Deuteronomy 6:5–9 exhorts parents to know and love God and to teach their children about him "when you sit in your house and when you walk by the way and when you lie down and when you rise up." God intended the home to be a sanctuary for spiritual and personal development in a relational setting of love and acceptance. This requires an ongoing process involving both formal and spontaneous times together.

In our work. The mistake of looking to work rather than God for security and significance coupled with the pressured quest for more of this world's goods drive us to the idolatry of materialism and busyness. If we don't have enough time to cultivate a quality relationship with God, our spouse, and our children, we are working too long and too hard. As Gordon Dahl put it, "Most middle-class Americans tend to worship their work, to work at their play, and to play at their worship."

In our recreation. Hard-charging approaches to recreation and vacations can devitalize us and keep us from enjoying personal and relational renewal. The Sabbath principle of restoration through being-time provides a balanced rhythm of work and rest.

In our church work or ministry. This can become another arena of busyness and frustration, especially when we take on activities and responsibilities in order to please people and meet their expectations. Not every need and request is a calling from God.

In our walk with God. Excessive activity draws us away from the time it takes to cultivate intimacy with God. We are often inclined to define our relationship with God in terms of doing things for him rather than spending time with him.

A few suggestions will enhance the daily process of living before the Lord.

- Like Jesus, you must develop a clear sense of your mission so that you can invest your time with God's calling in mind. You should also develop an understanding of your limits so that you will budget time with the Father for restoring your inner resources. There are many good things you could do, but the good can become the enemy of the best.
- Free yourself from bondage to the opinions, agendas, and expectations of others. Learn to say no to invitations and requests that may flatter you but could drain your time and energy.

- Seek a balance between rest and work, recharging and discharging, depth and breadth, inward and outward, reflection and practice, thinking and application, contentment and accomplishment.
- Ask yourself how much is enough. Unbridled wants kill contentment and drive us to greater busyness.
- Resist the temptation to allow work to invade rest.
- Look for ways to reduce your commitments so that you will not do a shoddy job on numerous tasks instead of an excellent job on a few. There is a tension between the desires to please God and to pursue success, and we will be tempted to resolve this tension by putting a spiritual veneer over the quest for success. It is better to pursue excellence in what we do for the glory of God (1 Corinthians 10:31) rather than success to receive honor from people.
- Realize that rest requires faith, because it seems nonproductive from the world's point of view. Since you cannot measure the product of time spent in developing your relationships with God and people, it is a risk to invest a significant amount of time in these ways.
- Budget time in advance for the important things that could get swept away in the daily grind. If you do not learn to make the urgent things flow around the important, the important will be overwhelmed by the urgent.
- Be aware of the human tendency to avoid an honest examination of ourselves in the presence of God. Many people seek diversions, distractions, and busyness to elude this encounter.
- Try to live from moment to moment and hold a looser grip on your long-term plans. "Our great business in life is not to see what lies dimly at a distance, but to do what lies clearly at hand" (Thomas Carlyle).
- Be aware of the distinction between *chronos* (chronological, everyday events) and *kairos* (special opportunities and occurrences). Seek to be available to make the most of the opportunities or *kairos* moments God providentially gives you (Ephesians 5:16; Colossians 4:5), since the most significant thing you do in the course of a day may not be in your daily calendar. "Be ready in season and out of season" (2 Timothy 4:2) to redeem the special moments God sends your way. Seek to manage time loosely enough to enhance relationships rather than tightly to accomplish results.
- "Wherever you are, be all there. Live to the hilt any situation you believe to be the will of God" (Jim Elliott).

CAUSES VERSUS CHRIST

All of us have a built-in hunger for security, significance, and satisfaction, but our world teaches us to pursue these things in the wrong places. It should come as no surprise, then, that the dreams and goals promoted by our culture have also infected our whole approach to the spiritual life. There are Christian books, seminars, and churches that have baptized the media agenda of self-orientation, success, and ambition with a spiritual veneer. Many believers are encouraged to set their heart on goals that actually distance them from Christ. By contrast, Scripture teaches that our meaning is not found in a quest for self but in a calling to know God.

Intimacy versus Activity

Any dead fish can float downstream, but to swim against the current of our times, we must be spiritually alive. As the New Testament portrays it, real life in Christ is countercultural. The world defines who we are by what we do, but the Word centers on who we are in Christ and tells us to express that new identity in what we do. Being and doing are interrelated, but the biblical order is critical: what we do should flow out of who we are, not the other way around. Otherwise our worth and identity are determined by achievements and accomplishments, and when we stop performing, we cease to be valuable. When people answer the question Who are you? by what they do, the world has a way of responding, "So what have you done lately?"

In Christ we have a secure and stable basis for worth and dignity, because these are founded on what God has done for us and in us. When we have been re-created and incorporated into the glorified life of the ascended Christ, God has penetrated to the roots of our being and given us a new nature. Thus being should have priority over doing, but being should be expressed in doing. This balanced interplay would be lost if we disconnected the two. My friend Skip Kazmarek warns against this disjunction and illustrates this concern with a cartoon that shows a man lying on a couch, with a Gangster Psychologist (according to the diploma on the wall) sitting next to him. The psychologist says, "Well, just because you rob, murder, and rape doesn't mean you're a bad *person*." We are not disjointed, disconnected, severed entities. Mind, body, and spirit exist in an integrated whole. How we act affects how we think, and how we think affects our relationship with God. Sometimes we think of ourselves as being one way while we continue to do the opposite, but this is a dangerous construct.

External action should derive from internal reality, and this requires a rhythm of solitude and engagement, restoration and application, intimacy with Christ and activity in the world. The life of Jesus illustrates this pattern of seeking significant time to be alone with the Father (Luke 5:16; Mark 1:35; 6:31) so that he would have the inner power and poise to deal with the outward pressures imposed upon him by his friends and enemies. People who work and minister without adequate restoration through prayer and meditation do not have the interior resources to manifest the fruit of the Spirit in a stress-filled world. During the quiet times of the devotional life, we gain the perspective and power we need to live with character and composure in the context of daily demands (see table 22.1). "In repentance and rest you will be saved, in quietness and trust is your strength" (Isaiah 30:15).

BEING	DOING
Intimacy with Christ	Activity in the world
Solitude	Engagement
Abiding	Serving
Interior	Exterior
Relational calling	Dominion calling
Calling	Character
Invisible	Visible
Real life	Reflected life
Restoration of spiritual energy	Application of spiritual energy
Perspective	Practice
Rest	Work

TABLE 22.1

In table 22.1, the real life (the left column) should energize the reflected life (the right column). The problem is that people typically approach the spiritual life in terms of the right column, supposing that their actions and service will lead to intimacy in their relationship with God. While the greatest commandment exhorts us to love the Lord our God with all our heart, soul, mind, and strength (Mark 12:30), we tend to reverse the order, thinking we can go from the outside in rather than the inside out. Instead of ministry flowing out of our relationship with God, many people suppose that ministry will determine their relationship with God.

The perennial problems of perfectionism and legalism stem from this vision of the spiritual life as a series of duties and tasks to be accomplished. Legalism is a spiritual disease that has afflicted the church since its inception. I cannot recall having met a legalistic Christian who is characterized by deep joy. This is because legalists attempt to achieve, through their own efforts, an externally imposed standard of performance in the hope that this will earn them merit in the sight of God and others. This produces insecurity, frustration, denial, and failure for several reasons:

- The Scriptures tell us that we can do nothing to earn favor before God, since all of our own efforts fall short of his character and righteousness (Romans 3:23; Titus 3:5–7).

- Just as none of our actions will make God love us more, it is equally true that nothing we can think, say, or do will make God love us less than he does (Romans 5:6–10).
- Spiritual growth is accomplished by Christ's life in us, not by our own attempts to create life. Our responsibility is to walk in the power of the Spirit and not in dependence on the flesh (Galatians 2:20; 5:16–25).
- The focus of the Christian life should not be deeds and actions but a relationship; it is centered not on a product but on a Person. It is a matter of abiding in Christ Jesus (John 15:1–10) rather than fulfilling a set of religious formulae.

The New Testament teaches that allegiance to Christ has displaced devotion to a code (Romans 7:3–4), but there is a human tendency to avoid God through religious substitutes. Many people miss the point that while intimacy with Christ leads to holiness, attempts to be holy do not necessarily lead to intimacy. Sanctification is generated not by moral behavior but by the grace of a relationship with Christ. If we miss this, we will be driven to causes rather than called to Christ, and activity will take precedence over intimacy. People who are driven eventually burn out. "If I am devoted to the cause of humanity only, I will soon be exhausted and come to the place where my love will falter; but if I love Jesus Christ personally and passionately, I can serve humanity though men treat me as a door-mat" (Oswald Chambers).

Joshua and Joash

The lives of Joshua and Joash poignantly illustrate the contrast between being called and being driven. Four scenes from Joshua's life capture the heart of this faithful man. In the first scene, Joshua is present with Moses at the tent of meeting. When Moses entered this tent, the pillar of cloud would descend and stand at the entrance to the tent, and the Lord would speak with Moses (Exodus 33:7–10). The key to the life of Joshua is revealed in Exodus 33:11: "Thus the LORD used to speak to Moses face to face, just as a man speaks to his friend. When Moses returned to the camp, his servant Joshua, the son of Nun, a young man, would not depart from the tent." Joshua remained in the tent of meeting because he had a passion to know and be with God. This personal knowledge of God served him well in the second scene, when he and Caleb were two of the twelve spies who were sent from Kadesh to view the land of Canaan (Numbers 13–14). Although all twelve spies saw the same things, ten of them interpreted what they saw from a human perspective and were overwhelmed by the size and number of the people. Only Joshua and Caleb saw the opposition through a divine perspective, and they encouraged the people to trust in the Lord: "Only do not rebel against the LORD; and do not fear the people of the land, for they will be our prey.

Their protection has been removed from them, and the LORD is with us; do not fear them" (Numbers 14:9). Tragically, the people believed the fearful conclusions of the majority of the spies, and the Israelites were consigned to wander in the wilderness, literally killing time for thirty-eight years until the generation of the Exodus perished in the wilderness.

In the third scene, the Lord prepares Joshua to lead the generation of the conquest into the land of Canaan. In Joshua 1:1–9, the Lord encourages him to be a courageous and obedient man of the Word who meditates on it day and night. Because he knew and loved God and renewed his mind with the book of God's law, Joshua finished well. In the fourth scene, Joshua is nearing the end of his earthly sojourn when he gathers and exhorts the people of Israel to serve the Lord only and to put away all forms of idolatry. He concludes his exhortation with this famous stance: "As for me and my house, we will serve the LORD" (Joshua 24:15). As Bob Warren puts it in his "Thoughts from the Hill" letter, "Because [Joshua] spent more time being a friend to God than a friend to others he avoided the pitfall of becoming enslaved to unproductive activity. But because he understood the necessity of intimacy over activity, his activity was energized beyond anything he could have imagined."

By contrast, King Joash (2 Chronicles 22:10–24:27) appeared to start well but finished poorly. He was the only royal offspring of the house of Judah who escaped Athaliah's murderous plot to take the throne. After Joash was protected and reared in the temple by Jehoiada the priest, Athaliah was put to death and the seven-year-old Joash became Judah's king. "Joash did what was right in the sight of the LORD all the days of Jehoiada the priest" (24:2), and he championed the project of restoring the temple in Jerusalem. But when Jehoiada died, Joash listened to foolish counsel, abandoned the house of the Lord, and gave himself over to idolatry. He even murdered Jehoiada's son when he rebuked Joash for forsaking the Lord.

Joash was involved with religious activities (the temple restoration project), but he never developed a relationship with the God of Jehoiada. He was driven by causes but avoided the more fundamental calling to know the Lord. Because the godly activity of his younger years was never energized by intimacy with the Lord, he failed miserably in the end.

It is easy to become more concerned with good causes than with knowing Christ. As Oswald Chambers notes in *My Utmost for His Highest*, "Beware of anything that competes with loyalty to Jesus Christ. . . . The greatest competitor of devotion to Jesus is service for Him. . . . We count as service what we do in the way of Christian work; Jesus Christ calls service what we are to Him, not what we do for Him. . . . The one aim of the call of God is the satisfaction of God, not a call to do something for Him." Our primary purpose is not to do something for Christ but to know him; our activities and abilities are useless for the kingdom unless he energizes them, and this will not happen if they take precedence over intimacy with him. We become weary when we attempt more public ministry than we can cover in private growth.

Even worthy causes—rearing godly children, building a company for Christ, knowing the Scriptures, leading people to the Lord, discipleship ministry—will not sustain us if we are not cultivating a personal relationship with Jesus. Many believers fall into the trap of striving for goals that are inferior to their purpose of knowing and enjoying God. When this happens, we attempt to do God's work in our own power and get on the treadmill of outward activities without an interior life.

It is crucial for us to form the habit of holy leisure, of quiet places and times alone with the Lord, so that we will restore our passion and intimacy with Christ. In this way, service will flow out of our life with him, and our activities and abilities will be animated by dependence upon his indwelling power. Restoration and renewal are especially important after periods of intense activity. When we seek and treasure God's intentions and calling, our personal knowledge of him (knowing) shapes our character (being) and conduct (doing). Although we are more inclined to follow Jesus into service than into solitude, the time we spend in "secluded places" with him (Mark 1:35; 6:31) will energize our service.

PRACTICING HIS PRESENCE

Our times of solitude with Jesus should not be limited to secluded places; we can choose to enjoy solitude with him even in the activities of everyday living. Private prayer consists of mental prayer (meditation and contemplation, discussed in devotional spirituality), colloquy (conversational prayer with God, discussed in disciplined spirituality), and the prayer of recollection (practicing the presence of God). This recollection of God can be habitual or actual. *Habitual recollection* is analogous to a man's or a woman's love for a spouse or children and does not require an ongoing consciousness. Just as we can form a habitual identity as being a husband, a wife, or a parent, so we can ask for the grace to form a habitual state of mind as a follower of Jesus Christ. *Actual recollection* involves turning to God at regular times throughout the day. This is more along the lines of what Brother Lawrence, Frank Laubach, and Thomas Kelly pursued in their quest for a more conscious awareness of God in the routines of everyday life.

Note the process imagery in Scripture that stresses an ongoing awareness of the presence of Christ: abide in Jesus and let his words abide in you (John 15:4–7); set your mind on the things of the Spirit (Romans 8:5–6); walk by the Spirit (Galatians 5:16, 25); keep seeking the things above where Christ is (Colossians 3:1–2); rejoice always, pray without ceasing, in everything give thanks (1 Thessalonians 5:16–18); run with endurance the race that is set before us, fixing our eyes on Jesus (Hebrews 12:1–2). The spiritual life is not a measurable product but a dynamic process.

We can practice the presence of Jesus in these ways:

- Send up "flash prayers" at various times during the day. These are brief prayers or mental notes that acknowledge God's presence or lift up others. They can be offered when waking, sitting down for a meal, walking, driving, waiting, listening, and so forth.

- Try using the same short prayer throughout the course of a day, such as the Jesus Prayer ("Lord Jesus Christ, Son of God, have mercy on me, a sinner") or another brief prayer (e.g., "I love you, Lord"; "I thank you in all things"; "By your grace, Lord"; "Thank you, Jesus").

- Pray and work (*ora et labora*). Do your work with an ear that is cocked to the voice of God. When you combine prayer and action, even trivial tasks can be spiritualized through a divine orientation. Invite the Lord to animate your work so that the ordinary is translated into the eternal.

- Play to an Audience of one; live *coram deo* (before the heart of God). Seek obscurity and anonymity rather than public accolades so that you will desire to please God rather than impress people.

- Ask Jesus to energize your activities and cultivate an attitude of dependence on him, even in areas where you have knowledge and skill.

- Monitor your temptations as they arise (the lust of the flesh, the lust of the eye, the pride of life) and turn these moments into opportunities to turn your eyes to Jesus. We do not overcome sin by trying to avoid it but by focusing on Jesus.

- Experiment with prayer. For instance, try praying for strangers you see while you are walking or waiting or driving. Ask the Lord to direct your prayers and listen for his promptings and impressions. Reach beyond your own concerns and become a channel of God's grace and mercy to others.

- Develop an eye that looks for God's beauty and handiwork in nature when you are walking and driving: plants, flowers, birds, trees, the wind, clouds, the color of the sky, and so forth. Learn to savor the wonders of the created order, since they point beyond themselves to the presence and awesome mind of the Creator.

- Turn the other pleasures of this life (times with close friends, enjoyment of great music and food) into sources of adoration for the One who made these things possible. Cultivate a sense of gratitude for the goodness of life and the tender mercies of God that are often overlooked.

- Ask for the grace to see every person you meet and every circumstance you face today as a gift of God. Whether these experiences are bitter or sweet, acknowledge them as coming from his hand for a purpose. Look for the sacred in all things, and notice the unlovely and those who are usually overlooked. Remember that the EGRs (extra grace required) in our lives are there for a purpose.

- Because we tend to live ahead of ourselves by dwelling in the future, try occasional time-stopping exercises by standing in and relishing the present moment. Realize that Jesus is with you and in you at this moment and thank him for never leaving or forsaking you even in the smallest of things (Deuteronomy 31:6; Hebrews 13:5).

Intimacy and activity, solitude and engagement, interior and exterior, calling and character, rest and work—both sides of each of these spectra are important. A balanced life of being and doing will nourish restoration and application.

QUESTIONS FOR PERSONAL APPLICATION

- What practical measures can you take to reduce the problem of busyness in your life?
- Why are people more naturally attracted to causes in the name of Christ rather than Christ himself? In what ways have you struggled with this issue?
- How can you move in the direction of treasuring intimacy with Jesus? Why do we typically substitute or confuse activity for the Lord with knowing him?
- What can you do to enrich your practice of Christ's presence?

23

PROCESS SPIRITUALITY
Trust, Gratitude, and Contentment

CHAPTER OVERVIEW

Process spirituality stresses a progressive spiritual formation that moves from the inside to the outside rather than outside in. Letting loose of control and results and cultivating a heart of gratitude (for God's deliverance in the past, benefits in the present, and promises for the future) are also relevant to living in the present. The chapter concludes with the secret of contentment, which relates to the issue of whether it is Christ or self who determines the content (e.g., money, position, family, circumstances) of our lives.

CHAPTER OBJECTIVES

- An understanding that holiness is a new quality of life that progressively flows from the inside to the outside
- Increased willingness to trust God by letting loose of control and results
- More skill in cultivating a heart of gratitude
- A better grasp of the issues that relate to contentment

Our culture teaches us that people are basically good and that their internal problems are the result of external circumstances. But Jesus taught that no outside-in program will rectify the human condition, since our fundamental problems stem from within (Mark 7:20–23). Holiness is never achieved by acting ourselves into a new way of being. Instead, it is a gift that God graciously implants within the core of those who have trusted in Christ. All holiness is the holiness of God within us—the indwelling life of Christ. Thus the process of sanctification is the gradual diffusion of this life from the inside (being) to the outside (doing), so that we become in action what we are in essence. Our efforts faithfully reveal what is within us, so that when we are dominated by the flesh we will do the deeds of the flesh, and when we walk by the Spirit we will bear the fruit of the Spirit (Galatians 5:16–26).

A PROCESS FROM THE INSIDE TO THE OUTSIDE

Holiness is a new quality of life that progressively flows from the inside to the outside. As J. I. Packer outlines it in *Keep in Step with the Spirit*, the nature of holiness is transformation through consecration; the context of holiness is justification through Jesus Christ; the root of holiness is co-crucifixion and co-resurrection with Jesus Christ; the agent of holiness is the Holy Spirit; the experience of holiness is one of conflict; the rule of holiness is God's revealed law; and the heart of holiness is the spirit of love. When we come to know Jesus we are destined for heaven because he has already implanted his heavenly life within us. The inside-out process of the spiritual life is the gradual outworking of this kingdom righteousness. This involves a divine-human synergism of dependence and discipline so that the power of the Spirit is manifested through the formation of holy habits. As Augustine put it, "Without God we cannot; without us, he will not." Disciplined grace and graceful discipline go together in such a way that God-given holiness is expressed through the actions of obedience. Spiritual formation is not a matter of total passivity or of unaided moral endeavor but of increasing responsiveness to God's gracious initiatives. The holy habits of immersion in Scripture, acknowledging God in all things, and learned obedience make us more receptive to the influx of grace and purify our aspirations and actions.

"Beloved, if our heart does not condemn us, we have confidence before God" (1 John 3:21). It is wise to form the habit of inviting God to search your heart and reveal "any hurtful way" (Psalm 139:23–24) within you. Sustained attention to the heart, the wellspring of action, is essential to the formative process. By inviting Jesus to examine our intentions and priorities, we open ourselves to his good but often painful work of exposing our manipulative and self-seeking strategies, our hardness of heart (often concealed in religious activities), our competitively driven resentments, and our pride. "A humble understanding of yourself is a surer way to God than a profound searching after knowledge," advises Thomas à Kempis in *The Imitation of Christ*. Self-examining prayer or journaling in the presence of God will enable us to descend below the surface of our emotions and actions and to discern sinful patterns that require repentance and renewal. Since spiritual formation is a process, it is a good practice to compare yourself now with where you have been. Are you progressing in Christlike qualities such as love, patience, kindness, forgiveness, compassion, understanding, servanthood, and hope? To assist you, here is a prayer sequence for examination and encouragement that incorporates the Ten Commandments, the Lord's Prayer, the Beatitudes, the seven deadly sins, the four cardinal and three theological virtues, and the fruit of the Spirit. This can serve as a kind of spiritual diagnostic tool.

Search me, O God, and know my heart;
Try me and know my anxious thoughts;

And see if there be any hurtful way in me,
And lead me in the everlasting way.

Psalm 139:23–24

Watch over your heart with all diligence,
For from it flow the springs of life.

Proverbs 4:23

The Ten Commandments
You shall have no other gods before me.
You shall not make for yourself an idol.
You shall not take the name of the Lord your God in vain.
Remember the Sabbath day, to keep it holy.
Honor your father and your mother.
You shall not murder.
You shall not commit adultery.
You shall not steal.
You shall not bear false witness against your neighbor.
You shall not covet.

The Lord's Prayer
Our Father who is in heaven,
Hallowed be your name.
Your kingdom come,
Your will be done,
On earth as it is in heaven.
Give us this day our daily bread.
And forgive us our debts, as we also have forgiven our debtors.
And do not lead us into temptation,
But deliver us from evil.
For yours is the kingdom and the power and the glory forever.

The Beatitudes
Poverty of spirit (nothing apart from God's grace)
Mourning (contrition)
Gentleness (meekness, humility)
Hunger and thirst for righteousness
Mercy to others
Purity of heart (desiring Christ above all else)
Peacemaking
Bearing persecution for the sake of righteousness

The Seven Deadly Sins
Pride
Avarice
Envy
Wrath
Sloth
Lust
Gluttony

The Four Cardinal and Three Theological Virtues
Prudence (wisdom, discernment, clear thinking, common sense)
Temperance (moderation, self-control)
Justice (fairness, honesty, truthfulness, integrity)
Fortitude (courage, conviction)
Faith (belief and trust in God's character and work)
Hope (anticipating God's promises)
Love (willing the highest good for others, compassion)

The Fruit of the Spirit
Love
Joy
Peace
Patience
Kindness
Goodness
Faithfulness
Gentleness
Self-control

LETTING LOOSE OF CONTROL AND RESULTS

One of the great enemies of process spirituality is the craving to control our environment and the desire to determine the results of our endeavors. Many of us have a natural inclination to be manipulators, grabbers, owners, and controllers. The more we seek to rule our world, the more we will resist the rule of Christ; those who grasp are afraid of being grasped by God. But until we relinquish ownership of our lives, we will not experience the holy relief of surrender to God's good and loving purposes. Thomas Merton put it this way in *New Seeds of Contemplation*:

This is one of the chief contradictions that sin has brought into our souls: we have to do violence to ourselves to keep from laboring uselessly for what is bitter and without joy, and we have to compel ourselves to take what is easy and full of happiness as though it were against our interests, because for us the line of least resistance leads in the way of greatest hardship and sometimes for us to do what is, in itself, most easy, can be the hardest thing in the world.

Our resistance to God's rule extends to our prayerful attempts to persuade the Lord to bless our plans and to meet our needs in the ways we deem best. Instead of seeking God's will in prayer, we hope to induce him to accomplish our will. Thus even in our prayers we can adopt the mentality of a consumer rather than a servant.

Perhaps the most painful lesson for believers to learn is the wisdom of being faithful to the process and letting loose of the results (see table 23.1).

OPPORTUNITY	OBEDIENCE	OUTCOME
Divine sovereignty	Human responsibility	Divine sovereignty

TABLE 23.1

We have little control over opportunities we encounter and the outcomes of our efforts, but we can be obedient to the process.

Distorted dreams and selfish ambitions must die before we can know the way of resurrection. We cannot be responsive to God's purposes until we abandon our strategies to control and acknowledge his exclusive ownership of our lives. This surrender to the life of Christ in us appears to be the way of renunciation, but we discover that it is the way of affirmation. "For whoever wishes to save his life will lose it, but whoever loses his life for My sake, he is the one who will save it" (Luke 9:24). The better we apprehend our spiritual poverty and weakness, the more we will be willing to invite Jesus to increase so that we may decrease (John 3:30).

Another key to staying in the process is learning to receive each day and whatever it brings as from the hand of God. Because God's character is unchanging and good, whatever circumstances he allows in the life of his children are for their good, even though they may not seem so at the time. His will for us is "good and acceptable and perfect" (Romans 12:2), so the trials, disappointments, setbacks, tasks, and adversities we encounter are, from an eternal vantage point, the place of God's kingdom and blessing. This perspective (Romans 8:28–39) can change the way we pray. Instead of asking the Lord to change our circumstances to suit us, we can ask him to use our circumstances to change us. Realizing that "the sufferings of this present time are not worthy to be compared with the glory that is to be revealed to us" (Romans 8:18), we can experience "the fellowship of [Christ's] sufferings" through "the power of His resurrection" (Philippians 3:10). Thus Blaise Pascal prayed in his *Pensées:*

With perfect consistency of mind, help me to receive all manner of events. For we know not what to ask, and we cannot ask for one event rather than another without presumption. We cannot desire a specific action without presuming to be a judge, and assuming responsibility for what in Your wisdom You may hide from me. O Lord, I know only one thing, and that is that it is good to follow You and wicked to offend You. Beyond this, I do not know what is good for me, whether health or sickness, riches or poverty, or anything else in this world. This knowledge surpasses both the wisdom of men and of angels. It lies hidden in the secrets of Your providence, which I adore, and will not dare to pry open.

We are essentially spiritual beings, and each today that is received with gratitude from God's hand contributes to our preparation for our glorious and eternal destiny in his presence. In "the sacrament of the present moment," as Jean-Pierre de Caussade described it in *Abandonment to Divine Providence*, "it is only right that if we are discontented with what God offers us every moment, we should be punished by finding nothing else that will content us." When we learn to love God's will, we can embrace the present as a source of spiritual formation.

As we grow in dependence on Christ's life and diminish in dependence on our own, the fulfillment of receiving his life gradually replaces the frustration of trying to create our own. In this place of conscious dependence God shapes us into the image of his Son. Here we must trust him for the outcome, because we cannot measure or quantify the spiritual life. We know that we are in a formative process and that God is not finished with us yet, but we must also remember that we cannot control or create the product. Furthermore, we cannot measure our ministry or impact on others in this life. If we forget this, we will be in a hurry to accomplish significant things by the world's standard of reckoning. François Fénelon noted in *Christian Perfection* that "the soul, by the neglect of little things, becomes accustomed to unfaithfulness." Faithfulness in the little, daily things leads to faithfulness in much (Luke 16:10). Henri Nouwen used to ask God to get rid of his interruptions so he could get on with his ministry. "Then I realized that interruptions *are* my ministry." As servants and ambassadors of the King, we must be obedient in the daily process even when we cannot see what difference our obedience makes.

CULTIVATING A HEART OF GRATITUDE

A young man with a bandaged hand approached the clerk at the post office. "Sir, could you please address this post card for me?" The clerk did so gladly and then agreed to write a message on the card.

He then asked, "Is there anything else I can do for you?" The young man looked at the card for a moment and then said, "Yes, add a P.S.: 'Please excuse the handwriting.'"

We are an ungrateful people. Writing of humanity in *Notes from the Underground*, Dostoevsky says, "If he is not stupid, he is monstrously ungrateful! Phenomenally ungrateful. In fact, I believe that the best definition of man is the ungrateful biped." Luke's account of the cleansing of the ten lepers underscores the human tendency to expect grace as our due and to forget to thank God for his benefits. "Were there not ten cleansed? But the nine—where are they? Was no one found who turned back to give glory to God, except this foreigner?" (Luke 17:17–18).

Remember: God's Deliverance in the Past

Our calendar allocates one day to give thanks to God for his many benefits, and even that day is more consumed with gorging than with gratitude. Ancient Israel's calendar included several annual festivals to remind the people of God's acts of deliverance and provision so that they would renew their sense of gratitude and reliance upon the Lord.

In spite of this, they forgot: "They became disobedient and rebelled against You.... They did not remember Your abundant kindnesses.... They quickly forgot His works" (Nehemiah 9:26; Psalm 106:7, 13). The prophet Hosea captured the essence of this decline into ingratitude: "As they had their pasture, they became satisfied, and being satisfied, their heart became proud; therefore they forgot Me" (13:6). When we are doing well, we tend to think that our prosperity was self-made. This delusion leads us into the folly of pride, and pride makes us forget God and prompts us to rely on ourselves in place of our Creator. This forgetfulness always leads to ingratitude.

Centuries earlier, Moses warned the children of Israel that they would be tempted to forget the Lord once they began to enjoy the blessings of the Promised Land. "Then your heart will become proud and you will forget the LORD your God who brought you out from the land of Egypt, out of the house of slavery.... Otherwise, you may say in your heart, 'My power and the strength of my hand made me this wealth'" (Deuteronomy 8:14, 17). The antidote to this spiritual poison is found in the next verse: "But you shall remember the LORD your God, for it is He who is giving you power to make wealth" (8:18).

Our propensity to forget is a mark of our fallenness. Because of this, we should view remembering and gratitude as a discipline, a daily and intentional act, a conscious choice. If it is limited to spontaneous moments of emotional gratitude, it will gradually erode, and we will forget all that God has done for us and take his grace for granted.

Remember: God's Benefits in the Present

"Rebellion against God does not begin with the clenched fist of atheism but with the self-satisfied heart of the one for whom 'thank you' is redundant," Os Guinness writes in *In Two Minds*. The apostle Paul exposes the error of this thinking when he asks, "What do you have that you did not receive? And if you did receive it, why do you boast as if you had not received it?" (1 Corinthians 4:7). Even as believers in Christ, it is natural to overlook the truth that all that we have and are—our health, our intelligence, our abilities, our lives—are gifts from the hand of God, and not our own creation. We understand this, but few of us actively acknowledge our utter reliance upon the Lord throughout the course of the week. We rarely review the many benefits we enjoy in the present. And so we forget.

We tend toward two extremes when we forget to remember God's benefits in our lives. The first extreme is presumption, and this is the error we have been discussing. When things are going our way, we may forget God or acknowledge him in a shallow or mechanical manner. The other extreme is resentment and bitterness due to difficult circumstances. When we suffer setbacks or losses, we wonder why we are not doing as well as others and develop a mindset of murmuring and complaining. We may attribute it to bad luck or misfortune or not getting the breaks, but it boils down to dissatisfaction with God's provision and care. This lack of contentment and gratitude stems in part from our efforts to control the content of our lives in spite of what Christ may or may not desire for us to have. It also stems from our tendency to focus on what we do not possess rather than all the wonderful things we have already received.

"Rejoice always; pray without ceasing; in everything give thanks; for this is God's will for you in Christ Jesus" (1 Thessalonians 5:16–18). We cannot give thanks and complain at the same time. To give thanks is to remember the spiritual and material blessings we have received and to be content with what our loving Lord provides, even when it does not correspond to what we had in mind. Gratitude is a choice, not merely a feeling, and it requires effort especially in difficult times. But the more we choose to live in the discipline of conscious thanksgiving, the more natural it becomes, and the more our eyes are opened to the little things throughout the course of the day that we previously overlooked. G. K. Chesterton had a way of acknowledging these many little benefits: "You say grace before meals. All right. But I say grace before the concert and the opera, and grace before the play and pantomime, and grace before I open a book, and grace before sketching, painting, swimming, fencing, boxing, walking, playing, dancing and grace before I dip the pen in the ink." Henri Nouwen observed that "every gift I acknowledge reveals another and another until, finally, even the most normal, obvious, and seemingly mundane event or encounter proves to be filled with grace."

Remember: God's Promises for the Future

If we are not grateful for God's deliverance in the past and his benefits in the present, we will not be grateful for his promises for the future. Scripture exhorts us to lay hold of our hope in Christ and to renew it frequently so that we will maintain God's perspective on our present journey. His plans for his children exceed our imagination, and his intention is to make all things new, to wipe away every tear, and to "show the surpassing riches of His grace in kindness toward us in Christ Jesus" in the ages to come (Ephesians 2:7).

Make it a daily exercise, either at the beginning or the end of the day, to review God's benefits in your past, present, and future. This discipline will be pleasing to God, because it will cultivate a heart of gratitude and ongoing thanksgiving.

THE SECRET OF CONTENTMENT

"We want a whole race perpetually in pursuit of the rainbow's end, never honest, nor kind, nor happy *now*, but always using as mere fuel wherewith to heap the altar of the future every real gift which is offered them in the Present." Uncle Screwtape's diabolical counsel to his nephew Wormwood in C. S. Lewis's *The Screwtape Letters* is a reminder that most of us live more in the future than in the present. We think that the days ahead will make up for what we perceive to be our present lack. We think, "When I get this or when that happens, then I'll be happy," but this exercise in self-deception overlooks the fact that even when we get what we want, it never delivers what it promised.

Most of us don't know precisely what we want, but we are certain we don't have it. Driven by dissatisfaction, we pursue the treasure at the end of the rainbow and rarely drink deeply at the well of the present moment, which is all we ever have. The truth is that if we are not satisfied with what we have, we will never be satisfied with what we want.

The real issue of contentment is whether it is Christ or ourselves who determine the content (e.g., money, position, family, circumstances) of our lives. When we seek to control the content, we inevitably turn to the criterion of comparison to measure what it should look like. The problem is that comparison is the enemy of contentment—there will always be people who possess a greater quality or quantity of what we think we should have. Because of this, comparison leads to covetousness. Instead of loving our neighbors, we find ourselves loving what they possess.

Covetousness in turn leads to a competitive spirit. We find ourselves competing with others for the limited resources to which we think we are entitled. Competition often becomes a vehicle through which we seek to authenticate our identity or prove our capability. This kind of competition tempts us to compromise our character. When we want something enough, we may be willing to steamroll our convictions in order to attain it. We find ourselves cutting corners, misrepresenting the truth, cheating, or using people as objects to accomplish our self-driven purposes.

Only when we allow Christ to determine the content of our lives can we discover the secret of contentment. Instead of comparing ourselves with others, we must realize that the Lord alone knows what is best for us and loves us enough to use our present circumstances to accomplish eternal good. We can be content when we put our hope in his character rather than our own concept of how our lives should appear.

Writing from prison to the believers in Philippi, Paul affirmed that "I have learned to be content in whatever circumstances I am. I know how to get along with humble means, and I also know how to live in prosperity; in any and every circumstance I have learned the secret of being filled and going hungry, both of having abundance and suffering need" (Philippians 4:11–12). Contentment is not found in having everything but in being satisfied with everything we have. As the apostle told Timothy, "We have brought nothing into the world, so we cannot take anything out of it either. If we have food and covering, with these we shall be content" (1 Timothy 6:7–8). Paul acknowledged God's right to determine his circumstances, even if it meant taking him down to nothing. His contentment was grounded not in how much he had but in the One who had him. Job understood this when he said, "Naked I came from my mother's womb, and naked I shall return there. The LORD gave and the LORD has taken away. Blessed be the name of the LORD" (Job 1:21). The more we release temporal possessions, the more we can grasp eternal treasures. There are times when God may take away our toys to force us to transfer our affections to Christ and his character.

A biblical understanding of contentment leads to a sense of our competency in Christ. "I can do all things through Him who strengthens me" (Philippians 4:13). As Peter put it, "His divine power has granted to us everything pertaining to life and godliness" (2 Peter 1:3). "Not that we are adequate in ourselves to consider anything as coming from ourselves, but our adequacy is from God" (2 Corinthians 3:5). Contentment is not the fulfillment of what we want but the realization of how much we already possess in Christ.

WHO DETERMINES THE CONTENT OF YOUR LIFE?	
SELF	**CHRIST**
Comparison ⇩ Covetousness ⇩ Competition ⇩ Compromise	Contentment ⇩ Competency ⇩ Compassion ⇩ Character

TABLE 23.2

A vision of our competency in Christ enables us to respond to others with compassion rather than competition, because we understand that our fundamental needs are fulfilled in the security and significance we have found in him. Because we are complete in Christ, we are free to serve others instead of using them in the quest to meet our needs. Thus we are liberated to pursue character rather than comfort and convictions rather than compromise.

Notice the contrast between the four horizontal pairs in table 23.2.

As we learn the secret of contentment, we will be less impressed by numbers, less driven to achieve, less hurried, and more alive to the grace of the present moment.

Questions for Personal Application

- What is your experience with self-examining prayer and with journaling? Experiment with the prayer sequence for examination and encouragement to enhance your understanding of where you are in the formative process.
- How is it possible to let loose of control and results? What areas of your life do you resist surrendering to God?
- What steps can you take to enhance your sense of gratitude to God for the past, present, and future?
- Who determines the content of your life? What can you do to move from the left column to the right column (table 23.2)?

S P I R I T - F I L L E D
S P I R I T U A L I T Y

Walking in the Power of the Spirit

Although there are divergent views of spiritual gifts, Spirit-centered believers and Word-centered believers are agreed that until recently the role of the Holy Spirit has been somewhat neglected as a central dynamic of the spiritual life. This section considers how to appropriate the love, wisdom, and power of the Spirit and stresses the biblical implications of the Holy Spirit as a personal presence rather than a mere force.

SPIRIT-FILLED SPIRITUALITY
Walking in the Power of the Spirit

CHAPTER OVERVIEW

Beginning with an overview of the person and work of the Holy Spirit, this chapter goes on to discuss walking in the power of the Spirit and the need for a balanced Spirit-filled spirituality that seeks to unite the mind and the heart instead of setting them in opposition. The chapter continues with a synopsis of three Spirit-centered movements and looks at the related issues of Spirit baptism and filling.

CHAPTER OBJECTIVES

- Greater appreciation for the person and ministries of the Holy Spirit
- A better sense of what it is to walk in the power of the Spirit
- Clearer perspective on the three Spirit-centered movements of the twentieth century
- Increased understanding of the baptism and fullness of the Holy Spirit

"The Holy Spirit has long been the Cinderella of the Trinity. The other two sisters may have gone to the theological ball; the Holy Spirit got left behind every time." Until recently, this observation by Alister E. McGrath in *Christian Theology: An Introduction* characterized the experience of most people in the church. The majority of believers have been content to acknowledge the existence of the Holy Spirit, but on the level of personal encounter, their relationship has been largely limited to the Father and the Son. But the winds of change have been blowing, and an unparalleled movement in the twentieth century has created a new awareness of the person and ministry of the Holy Spirit. The past few decades have seen an explosion of worldwide church growth, and the fastest-growing churches are those that have centered on the fullness of the Spirit. At the same time that a number of mainline denominations have experienced significant membership loss, the Pentecostal and charismatic renewal movements have reached tens and now hundreds of millions of people around the world.

Spirit-filled spirituality, although underemphasized by mainstream Christianity until the twentieth century, has been an essential part of spiritual formation since the days of the early church in the book of Acts. But it has been plagued by people's tendency to move toward the polar opposites of rejection or obsession. The extreme of rejection is marked by fear of experiential excess or loss of control and by theological rigidity. The extreme of obsession is stamped by emotionalism, sensationalism, and vulnerability to manipulation and false teaching. A more balanced perspective combines openness to the surprising work of the Spirit with discernment that tests experience in light of the Scriptures and the fruit that it produces.

THE PERSON AND WORK OF THE HOLY SPIRIT

The role of the Holy Spirit as a central dynamic of Christian spirituality is an expression of the trinitarian life of God. The Father sent the Son into the world and empowered him by anointing him with the Spirit. When the Son ascended to the Father after completing his earthly mission of redemption and reconciliation, he sent the Spirit to continue his work through those who have been made alive to him in the world. The triune God is a relational Being whose cosmic work of creation, redemption, and reconciliation integrally involves all three persons of the Godhead. In the Old Testament, the Spirit of God participated in the creation of the heavens and the earth, revealed God's word and will by inspiring prophetic messengers, and endowed specific people with skill, leadership, and strength. But while the Spirit's indwelling in Israel was selective and temporary, as in the cases of Samson and Saul, after the Day of Pentecost in Acts 2, it was universal to all believers, and permanent.

The ministry of the Holy Spirit is multifaceted, but three essential aspects are bearing witness to Jesus Christ, applying Christ's redemptive work in human hearts, and working personally and progressively to form Christlikeness in the lives of believers. He empowers us to live a new quality of life, he purifies and purges us as we submit to his authority and control, and he equips us with **spiritual gifts** and opportunities to build up others in the faith. But as J. I. Packer observes in *Keep in Step with the Spirit*, there are limitations to seeing the doctrine of the Spirit as essentially about power, purity, or performance. Although all of these are vital components of the Spirit's work, it is best to see the Spirit as an active, personal presence in our lives. The Holy Spirit glorifies Jesus Christ by mediating Christ's presence to us. The Spirit assures us of the Father's love and care, brings us into personal fellowship with Jesus, and transforms our character so that we become more like him.

It is wrong to speak of the Holy Spirit as an it—he is a living and loving person, not a force to be utilized. Jesus called him the Paraclete, a name that means "one called alongside" to help (John 14:16, 26; 15:26; 16:7). *Paracletos* is variously translated Helper, Comforter, Counselor, Advocate, Intercessor, Supporter, and Strengthener, and each of these terms carries a different nuance of the Spirit's ministry to us. The Paraclete guides us into the truth (John 16:13) and makes Christ's provision for our sin and his personal presence real in our lives. He makes it possible for the people of God to be progressively conformed and transformed into the image of Christ (2 Corinthians 3:17–18).

The Scriptures use a variety of images to convey the manifold riches of the Holy Spirit's work, and part of that work includes these twelve ministries.

1. *Convicting.* The Spirit convicts unbelievers of sin, righteousness, and judgment (John 16:8–11). Apart from this ministry, people would never realize their sinful condition and desperate need for the saving grace of God.

2. *Regenerating.* The Spirit imparts eternal life through the new birth, and this in turn implants the divine nature in the child of God (Titus 3:5; 2 Peter 1:4). We who were formerly dead (Ephesians 2:1–3) have become new creatures who are alive to God (2 Corinthians 5:17; Romans 6:3–11; Ephesians 2:4–6).

3. *Baptizing.* By the Spirit, all believers in Christ have been "baptized into one body" (1 Corinthians 12:13), and in this way we have been adopted by the Holy Spirit into the family of God (Romans 8:9, 15; Ephesians 1:5). There are differing views of Spirit baptism, and we will return to this later.

4. *Sealing.* The Holy Spirit of promise is the pledge of our inheritance, and he seals all who trust in Christ for the day of redemption (Ephesians 1:13–14; 4:30; 2 Corinthians 1:22). The Father gives us the Spirit as a pledge or a down payment that guarantees the fulfillment of his promises.

5. *Indwelling.* The Spirit of God permanently indwells all believers in Christ (John 14:16–17; Romans 8:9), so that our bodies are temples of the Holy Spirit who is in us (1 Corinthians 6:19).

6. *Filling.* When we are filled by the Holy Spirit, we are under his control (Ephesians 5:18). The filling of the Spirit produces the fruit of Christian character and maturity (Acts 6:3, 5; Galatians 5:22–23).

7. *Empowering.* This is another aspect of the filling of the Spirit, and it relates to his sovereign and surprising power for ministry in word and deed (Acts 4:8, 31; 13:9–10).

8. *Assuring.* The Spirit testifies to the truth of our life in Christ and bears witness with our spirits that we are children of God (Romans 8:16; 1 John 3:24; 5:7–8).

9. *Illuminating.* The Spirit of God who inspired the Scriptures (2 Peter 1:21) also illuminates the Scriptures "so that we may know the things freely given to us by God" (1 Corinthians 2:10–16). Because the things of the Spirit are spiritually discerned, the Spirit gives believers insight into the meaning and application of God's Word.

10. *Teaching.* Jesus promised his disciples that the Spirit of truth would "guide you into all the truth" and "disclose to you what is to come" (John 16:13). The divine anointing teaches us (1 John 2:27), and the Spirit glorifies the Son by making Jesus' words known to us (John 16:14).

11. *Praying.* Because we do not know how to pray as we should, "the Spirit Himself intercedes for us with groanings too deep for words" (Romans 8:26). The Holy Spirit searches our hearts and speaks to the Father through us (Romans 8:27). When we pray in the Spirit (Ephesians 6:18), we have access through Christ to the Father (Ephesians 2:18).

12. *Gifting.* As we will see, the manifold gifts of the Holy Spirit are given to the community of faith for the mutual edification of all the members of the body. These gifts are energized and directed by the Spirit as they are exercised in others-centered love (1 Corinthians 13).

WALKING IN THE POWER OF THE SPIRIT

The Christian life is the life of Christ in us; without a moment-by-moment reliance on the Holy Spirit, this level of living is impossible. Sanctification is both a state and a process; when we come to Jesus, we are set apart to God by the Spirit's application of the work of Christ in our lives. We are called to realize this state of sanctification (God's inworking [Philippians 2:13]) in a progressive way by obedient conformity to the character of the indwelling Christ (our outworking [Philippians 2:12]). This is accomplished as we keep in step with the Spirit; "if we live by the Spirit, let us also walk by the Spirit" (Galatians 5:25). To be sanctified is to be possessed by God's Spirit, to respond to his transforming purposes in obedient faith, to bear the fruit of the Spirit by abiding in Christ (Galatians 5:22–23), and to pursue the process of maturation in holiness in our relationships with God, his people, and the people of the world.

Spiritual maturity is directly proportional to Christ-centeredness. To be more preoccupied with the subjective benefits of the faith than with the person and pleasure of Christ is a mark of immaturity. The Spirit bears witness to and glorifies Jesus Christ; spiritual experiences, whether personal or corporate, should center on Christ and not ourselves. The tendency of some people and movements to glorify the gifts of the Giver more than the Giver of the gifts is incompatible with the biblical portrait of the ministry of the Holy Spirit.

However, many believers attempt to live the Christian life in their own power instead of the power of the Spirit. As A. W. Tozer remarked in *Paths to Power*, "the average professed Christian lives a life so worldly and careless that it is difficult to distinguish him from the unconverted man." But even among diligent students of the Word there is a temptation to depend more on human initiative and effort than on the power of the indwelling Spirit of God. It is easy and comforting to reduce God to a set of biblical propositions and theological inferences rather than a living person who cannot be boxed in, controlled, or manipulated by our agendas. There are common forms of Bible deism that assume (ironically, without biblical warrant) that God no longer communicates to his people or personally guides them apart from the words of Scripture. When we make assumptions that are closed to the surprising work of the Holy Spirit, they have a way of determining and limiting our experience of the power of God.

Personal attempts to live the spiritual life in human power are written large in corporate attempts to worship and serve in human power. Although the church began and moved in the power of the Spirit, many in the church today are conditioned to think in terms of their experiences rather than the experiences of God's people in Scripture. This leads to a desupernaturalized corporate expectation that in some ways is more informed by a naturalistic, closed-universe world view than by a biblical world view that is open to the unpredictable sovereign acts of God. The church is not primarily a socioeconomic institution but a spiritual organism that must depend on personal and collective visitations of the Holy Spirit for its continued vitality. In *Fresh Wind, Fresh Fire*, Jim Cymbala argues that unless congregations persistently call upon the Lord, their store of spiritual power will dissipate with time. Without the Spirit's unction, the divine Presence will not be evident in our worship and service.

SPIRIT AND TRUTH

We need both the fire of the Spirit and the light of the Word, but many believers and churches have made this an either-or rather than a both-and by tending to be either Spirit-centered or Word-centered. Power without sound teaching is vulnerable to shallowness and lack of discernment; doctrine without power is vulnerable to dryness and spiritual torpor. But when power and truth, deed and word, experience and explanation, manifestation and maturity, are combined in our personal and corporate lives, the Spirit is welcomed and Christ is glorified.

A balanced Spirit-filled spirituality seeks to unite the mind and the heart instead of setting them in opposition. When we love God with our minds and with our hearts, faith and feeling unite and reinforce each other (see 1 Peter 1:8–9). The coldness and brutality of truth without love and the sentimentality and sloppiness of love without truth both fall short of Paul's vision in Ephesians 4:15: "But speaking the truth in love, we are to grow up in all aspects into Him who is the head, even Christ." An adequate theology of grace encompasses cultivation of the mind and formation of the heart; it affirms not only the intellect and the will but also the dimension of intuitive and experiential apprehension. The body of Christ consists of believers who encounter the Holy Spirit in differing ways due to their unique temperaments and experiences. All of us profit when we welcome the balance that this diversity offers.

THREE SPIRIT-CENTERED MOVEMENTS

The twentieth century saw three distinct Spirit-centered phenomena: the Pentecostal movement, the charismatic renewal movement (Protestant and Catholic), and the Third Wave movement.

The Pentecostal Movement

Pentecostalism had its roots in the nineteenth-century Holiness movement with its emphasis on a second work of the Holy Spirit after conversion to foster sanctification. In 1901, Charles Parham led a revival in which most of his student body at Bethel Bible College in Topeka, Kansas, experienced the gift of tongues. He associated speaking in tongues with the events on the day of Pentecost (Acts 2) and saw it as the initial evidence of the baptism with the Holy Spirit. In 1906, William J. Seymour, a black Holiness minister who was influenced by Parham's teachings, went to Los Angeles and preached on the baptism with the Spirit and speaking in tongues. A revival took place at his faith mission on Azusa Street, and this led to a major movement that rapidly spread throughout North America and eventually took hold in Asia, Latin America, and Africa. This Pentecostal movement was rejected by mainstream Christendom and spawned its own denominations, including the Assemblies of God, the Churches of God, and the Holiness Pentecostal Church. The Full Gospel Business Men's Fellowship International has also promoted Pentecostal doctrine and practice.

The Charismatic Renewal Movement

Surprising those on both sides of the Pentecostal fence, a sudden neo-Pentecostal movement within mainline Protestant churches simultaneously erupted in various parts of North America in the early 1960s. This movement stressed the baptism and gifts of the Spirit as the means of spiritual renewal within institutional churches, and its leaders included Dennis Bennett and Rita Bennett, John L. Sherrill, and Agnes Sanford (Episcopalians); Larry Christenson (Lutheran); Tommy Tyson (Methodist); Don Basham (Disciples of Christ); and Rodman Williams (Presbyterian). Books like the Bennetts' *Nine O'Clock in the Morning* and *The Holy Spirit and You*, Sherrill's *They Speak with Other Tongues*, and Williams's *The Gift of the Spirit Today* have influenced many in what came to be called the charismatic renewal movement. Unlike Pentecostals, the majority of charismatic Christians chose to remain within the mainline denominations and to adapt their experience to a wide range of ecclesiastical patterns.

Charismatic renewal reached the Roman Catholic Church in 1966 when members of the faculty of Duquesne University sought the power of the Holy Spirit described by David Wilkerson in *The Cross and the Switchblade*. This led to a significant experience of renewal among students (the Duquesne Weekend) that influenced other Catholic communities at Notre Dame and Michigan State. This movement spread through conferences, Life in the Spirit seminars, the Cursillo movement, the Word of God Community, and numerous publications. Catholic writers like Ralph Martin (*New Covenant* magazine), Kilian McDonnell *(The Holy Spirit and Power)*, and Léon Joseph Cardinal Suenens *(A New Pentecost?)* sought to relate the vitality of the spiritual gifts to biblical theology and historic spirituality and stressed the corporate use of the gifts in the Christian community.

The Third Wave Movement

Since the 1970s a growing number of churches and ministries that are independent of both Pentecostal and mainline denominations have sought the power and gifts of the Spirit. Many of these evangelicals avoid the terms *Pentecostal* and *charismatic*, and to distinguish this third Spirit-centered phenomenon, C. Peter Wagner coined the term "the Third Wave" in *The Third Wave of the Holy Spirit*. The most notable expression of this movement has been the growth of the Vineyard Fellowship, founded by the late John Wimber, who stressed the importance of openness to signs and wonders in *Power Evangelism* and *Power Healing*.

Not surprisingly, all three of these movements have generated substantial controversy concerning the nature and extent of spiritual gifts, the meaning of Spirit baptism, and the problem of discerning the validity of a wide range of personal and corporate experiences. There has been a tendency to turn descriptions into prescriptions and to emphasize experience over explanation. Many in the first two movements have made the unfortunate assumption that people have not been baptized with the Holy Spirit if they have not spoken in tongues. This has led to an overemphasis on this gift that has polarized many in the body of Christ. In recent years, however, a body of literature that deals with the manifestations of the Spirit from a more scholarly and biblically based perspective has appeared. Writers like Michael Green *(I Believe in the Holy Spirit)*, Charles E. Hummel *(Fire in the Fireplace)*, Gordon D. Fee *(God's Empowering Presence* and his commentary on *The First Epistle to the Corinthians)*, Wayne A. Grudem *(The Gift of Prophecy* and *Systematic Theology)*, Jack Deere *(Surprised by the Power of the Spirit* and *Surprised by the Voice of God)*, Zeb Bradford Long and Douglas McMurry *(Receiving the Power)*, and Doug Banister *(The Word and Power Church)* have developed a more articulate and responsible charismatic-evangelical theology.

All three of these Spirit-centered movements continue to flourish, and although there is some overlap among them, they retain their distinctive character (the weakness of the "three waves" metaphor is that it could imply that the previous waves have receded). In spite of differences, the Pentecostal, charismatic, and Third Wave movements are all centered on the ministry and manifestations of the Spirit. Because of this I will refer to all who are involved in these three movements as Spirit-centered believers (SCBs) and distinguish them from Word-centered believers (WCBs), who are noncharismatic in doctrine and practice. As we will see, there are strengths and weaknesses on both sides, and a balanced Spirit-filled spirituality should seek the strengths of both.

SPIRIT BAPTISM

There has been a wide range of interpretations, even among SCBs, of the meaning of Spirit baptism. In the late nineteenth century, the Wesleyan-Holiness movement associated it with a "second blessing" after conversion that produces the holiness of "entire sanctification." Evangelical leaders like Dwight L. Moody and Reuben A. Torrey also viewed Spirit baptism as a postconversion experience but related it to a divine bestowal of power for ministry. It was not until the Pentecostal movement that Spirit baptism was associated with an experience of tongues. Many in the charismatic movement adopted a neo-Pentecostal view of tongues as the initial sign of Spirit baptism, but an increasing number of charismatic Christians have concluded that tongues is one of many possible charisms that could accompany Spirit baptism. Others in charismatic renewal have turned to a sacramental model of Spirit baptism as a "release" of the Spirit, since the grace of the Spirit was already received in Christian initiation. Third Wave Christians speak more in terms of filling with the Spirit or of openness to the power and gifts of the Spirit, and this may involve "breakthrough" experiences of personal and corporate spiritual renewal.

There are seven New Testament references to Spirit baptism (Matthew 3:11; Mark 1:8; Luke 3:16; John 1:33; Acts 1:5; 11:16; 1 Corinthians 12:13), and the first six were fulfilled on the day of Pentecost. Some distinguish the passage in 1 Corinthians from the others by translating it as baptism "by" the Spirit (into the body of Christ) as opposed to baptism "in" the Spirit (into the power of the Spirit). But all of these verses use the same Greek preposition (en), which can be translated "with," "in," or "by." There is no biblical basis for distinguishing two kinds of Spirit baptism. The experiences of the disciples at Pentecost (Acts 2:1–4), the Samaritans (Acts 8:14–17), the Gentile household of Cornelius (Acts 10:44–47), and the Ephesian disciples of John the Baptist (Acts 19:1–7) all relate to the initial arrival of the Holy Spirit into a person's life that Paul later associates with becoming a member of the body of Christ (1 Corinthians 12:13). It is therefore better not to equate postconversion experiences of the Spirit's filling, empowering, or manifestations with the word baptism but with God's wonderful works of renewal through the power of the indwelling Spirit.

Since the time of Pentecost, the Spirit's new covenant ministry of baptizing, indwelling, and sealing is given to every believer at the time of regeneration. But subsequent experiences of the Spirit's filling, outpouring, and clothing with power are given to many believers in accordance with the sovereign purposes of God. There is no single prescription or pattern to postconversion experiences of renewal, and it would be a mistake to make one person's experience normative for others.

INWARD AND OUTWARD FILLINGS

The manifestations of the Spirit are manifold, but the New Testament distinguishes two primary ways in which believers can be filled with the Spirit. *The inward work of the Spirit* produces Christlike character and spiritual maturity. The Greek verb *plêroô* and its cognate *plêrês* refer to filling as a growing state of being. These words are used of spiritually mature believers like Stephen and Barnabas who are controlled by the Spirit (see Luke 4:1–2; Acts 6:3, 5; 7:55; 11:24; 13:52; Ephesians 5:18–19). *The outward work of the Spirit* concerns divine empowerment for ministry and service. The Greek verb *pimplêmi* refers to filling as a temporary experience of the sovereign power of God that is evident in action. This word is used of specific manifestations of the Holy Spirit in the lives of people like Elizabeth, Peter, and Saul (see Luke 1:41–42, 67; Acts 2:4; 4:8, 31; 9:17–20; 13:9–10; see also table 24.1).

THE INWARD WORK OF THE SPIRIT	THE OUTWARD WORK OF THE SPIRIT
Filling: *plêroô* and *plêrês*	Filling: *pimplêmi*
A growing state of being	A temporary experience
Produces character and wisdom	Empowers for ministry and service
The fruit of the Spirit	The gifts of the Spirit
The Spirit within	The Spirit upon
Purity	Power
Maturity	Manifestations
Becoming	Acting

TABLE 24.1

A healthy Spirit-filled spirituality requires both kinds of filling, but there is an unfortunate tendency among WCBs to stress the inward work of the Spirit and neglect the outward work of the Spirit, and among SCBs to reverse that focus. When this happens, a WCB can be strong in knowledge and/or character and shallow in power and deed. Churches and individuals who quench the outward work of the Spirit become ineffective in transformational ministry. Their explanation exceeds their experience.

On the other hand, an SCB can be strong in power and deed and shallow in knowledge and/or character. When experience runs ahead of biblical explanation, a person is vulnerable to deception and emotional manipulation. And when experience surpasses character, the Spirit is grieved and power is eventually lost. Power without character becomes more of a curse than a blessing and leads to the error of confusing spiritual manifestations with spiritual maturity.

Character and gifting are both important; we need the fruit of the Spirit (the inward work) as well as the power of the Spirit (the outward work). Purity and power work best together and reinforce each other. It is also important that we relate Spirit-filled spirituality to the ordinary affairs and challenges of life and not limit the work of the Spirit to extraordinary phenomena.

A full-orbed spirituality involves grounding in biblical truth and sound doctrine (knowing), growing character and personal experience with God (being), and developing gifts and skills in the service of others (doing), as figure 24.1 illustrates.

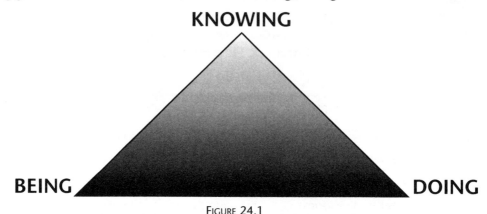

FIGURE 24.1

When a person or a group neglects any one of these three areas, distortions are inevitable. Because of our backgrounds and temperaments, some of us will naturally be attracted to knowing, some to being, and others to doing. It is wise to discern our personal tendencies and to seek balance in our thinking, affections, and choices through exposure to people in the body of Christ who will stretch and exhort us.

QUESTIONS FOR PERSONAL APPLICATION

- As you consider the twelve ministries of the Holy Spirit that were outlined in this chapter, which of them are the most meaningful to you, and which seem more remote?
- Why do you think the three Spirit-centered movements occurred when they did, and what experience have you had with any of them?
- Where do you find yourself on the WCB/SCB spectrum?
- Are you drawn more to the inward work of the Spirit or the outward work of the Spirit?

25

SPIRIT-FILLED SPIRITUALITY
The Gifts of the Spirit

CHAPTER OVERVIEW

This chapter considers diversity and unity in the body of Christ and the nature and purposes of spiritual gifts as significant expressions of Spirit-centered spirituality. It presents the benefits of the gifts and the controversy over some of the gifts, and after a brief description of the gifts, there is a word about discovering and developing these endowments by the Holy Spirit of special abilities to every member of the body of Christ for the edification of others.

CHAPTER OBJECTIVES

- Enhanced clarity concerning the nature and purposes of the gifts of the Spirit
- An appreciation for the benefits of the spiritual gifts
- An improved grasp on discovering and developing our gifts
- Knowledge of how the gifts can be used and abused

God has given each believer a combination of opportunities and gifts that is perfectly suited to his or her situation in life. Every Christian is a minister with a unique contribution to make to the body of Christ. The central thrust of our ministries depends on the spiritual gifts we have received. As we will see, the exercise of these gifts in a context of community contributes to the nurture and edification of the body. Thus the gifts of the Spirit are an integral part of our spiritual formation.

DIVERSITY AND UNITY IN THE BODY OF CHRIST

When the Holy Spirit descended on the day of Pentecost in Acts 2, a new organism was created. This organism consists of all those who have received the gift of eternal life in Christ Jesus. In Romans 8:14–17, Galatians 4:4–7, and Ephesians 2:19, it is described as a spiritual household or *family*. By virtue of both adoption and new birth, we have become sons and daughters of God. This organism is also called a holy *temple* in Ephesians 2:20–22 and 1 Peter 2:4–5, and believers are its living stones. But the most frequently used metaphor for this new creation is the *body* of Christ (see Romans 12:4–5; 1 Corinthians 12:12–27; Ephesians 1:22–23; 3:6; 4:4–16; 5:23–30; Colossians 1:18; 2:19).

The three major New Testament lists of the gifts are all introduced by a description of the unity and diversity in this spiritual body. Paul's metaphor for the church could not be more appropriate, because both the universal church (all believers) and the local church (geographically localized groups of believers) are unities that are built out of diverse elements. Christ is the head and ruler of the body (Ephesians 1:22; 4:15; Colossians 1:18), and believers are the individual members or components. In this analogy, each Christian has been given a special function to perform and the ability to fulfill it in a way that will benefit the other members. There is quantitative and qualitative growth when believers discover and actively use their spiritual gifts. Each part of the body depends on the rest for its well-being, and there are no useless organs. This is why edification through teaching and fellowship is so necessary in the local church. The biblical concept of *koinonia* or fellowship communicates the fact that isolation leads to atrophy. Just as no organ can function independently of the others, so no believer can enjoy spiritual vitality in a relational vacuum. The Spirit has sovereignly distributed spiritual gifts to every member of the body, and no single member possesses all the gifts. Thus growth does not take place apart from mutual ministry and dependence.

The body of Christ is an organism, not a dictatorship or a democracy. As such, the local church is best structured around the distribution and function of the spiritual gifts found in its members.

As an exercise, consider how Paul outlines the role of God-given gifts in the edification of the body in Ephesians 4:4–16. What are the seven points of unity found in verses 4–6? According to 4:7–10, what is the basis for the giving of gifts to the church? Verse 12 speaks of quantitative (corporate) growth, while verse 13 speaks of qualitative (individual) growth. How does 4:11–13 relate to 4:14–16?

THE NATURE AND PURPOSE OF SPIRITUAL GIFTS

The Greek word most frequently used for spiritual gifts is *charismata*, a word that relates to the grace *(charis)* of God. Concerning these gifts, Paul writes, "to each one of us grace was given according to the measure of Christ's gift" (Ephesians 4:7). Another word, *pneumatikos*, means "spiritualities" or "spiritual things." Because the work of God can be accomplished only by the power of God, a spiritual gift is the endowment by the Holy Spirit of a special ability to every member of the body of Christ for the edification of others.

Twelve principles relate to God's design for spiritual gifts.

1. *Every Christian has one or more spiritual gifts.* "But to each one is given the manifestation of the Spirit for the common good. . . . But one and the same Spirit works all these things, distributing to each one individually just as He wills" (1 Corinthians 12:7, 11). "But to each one of us grace was given according to the measure of Christ's gift" (Ephesians 4:7). "As each one has received a special gift, employ it in serving one another as good stewards of the manifold grace of God" (1 Peter 4:10).

2. *Many believers have received more than one spiritual gift.* Because there is such a variety of gifts, the number of possible combinations is immense. Each multigifted Christian has received a combination of spiritual abilities that is perfectly suited to his or her God-given ministry. There are differences of opinion as to whether these gifts are vested, or resident in individual believers, or situational, that is, Spirit-gifted for particular situations and needs. Some also regard the gifts listed in Romans 12 and Ephesians 4 as motivational gifts that are permanently resident and distinguish these from the more situational gifts listed in 1 Corinthians 12. Although this view seems somewhat forced, there is a sense of expectancy and spontaneity in 1 Corinthians 12 and 14 (see 14:26) that can allow for the dynamic empowering of believers in unforeseen ways as well as ways that are consistent with past gifting. In my view, a believer may have both resident and situational gifts.

3. *Spiritual gifts may be given at the moment of regeneration, but they may lie undiscovered and dormant for a long period of time.* Multigifted Christians often discover their combination of gifts through a gradual process.

4. *Spiritual gifts can be abused and neglected, but if they are received at regeneration, it would appear that they cannot be lost.* The Corinthian church illustrates that believers can be highly gifted but spiritually immature.

5. *Spiritual gifts are not the same as the gift of the Spirit.* The gift of the Spirit has been bestowed on all believers (John 14:16; Acts 2:38), and every member of the body should walk in the power of this divine Person. The gifts of the Spirit, on the other hand, are distributed "to each one individually just as He wills" (1 Corinthians 12:11).

6. *Spiritual gifts are not the same as the fruit of the Spirit.* Spiritual fruit is produced from within; spiritual gifts are imparted from without. Fruit relates to Christlike character; gifts relate to Christian service. The fruit of the Spirit, especially love, should be the context for the operation of the gifts of the Spirit. Paul made it clear in 1 Corinthians 13 that spiritual gifts without spiritual fruit are worthless.

Fruit is eternal, but gifts are temporal (1 Corinthians 13:8); the former is a true measure of spirituality, but the latter is not.

7. *Spiritual gifts are not the same as natural talents.* Unlike the natural abilities that everyone has from birth, spiritual gifts belong exclusively to believers in Christ. In some cases, the gifts of the Spirit coincide with natural endowments, but they transcend these natural abilities by adding a divinely infused quality. Both are given by God (James 1:17) and should be developed and used according to their purpose for the glory of God (1 Corinthians 10:31).

8. *All Christians are called to a ministry, but not all are called to an office.* Ministry is determined by divinely given gifts and opportunities (Ephesians 3:7). Offices (evangelist, teacher, deacon, elder) are humanly recognized and appointed spheres of ministry within the body.

9. *Some spiritual gifts are more useful in local churches than others because they result in greater edification of the body.* Paul exhorted the Corinthian church to "earnestly desire the greater gifts" (1 Corinthians 12:31; cf. 14:5).

10. Charismata *literally means "grace gifts."* These gifts are sovereignly and undeservedly given by the Holy Spirit. There is no basis for boasting or envy. Every member of the body has a special place and purpose. Whether more or less prominent in the eyes of others, the same standard applies to all: it is required of stewards that one be found faithful (1 Corinthians 4:2). Work with what God has given to you (2 Timothy 1:6), and seek to please him rather than people (Galatians 1:10; 1 Thessalonians 2:4).

11. *Gifts are God's spiritual equipment for effective service and edification of the body.* They are not bestowed for self-aggrandizement or as an evidence of a special enduing of the Spirit but for the profit and edification of the body of Christ. The possessor is only the instrument and not the receiver of the glory. Gifts were given "so that in all things God may be glorified through Jesus Christ" (1 Peter 4:11).

12. *High mobilization of spiritual gifts was the key to the rapid multiplication of the church in the New Testament (Romans 1:11).* In *Christ Loved the Church*, William MacDonald illustrates this principle of multiplication with two diagrams. The first (figure 25.1) portrays the purpose of gifts as stated in Ephesians 4:12 ("for the equipping of the saints for the work of service, to the building up of the body of Christ"). The second diagram (figure 25.2) depicts the dynamic in 2 Timothy 2:2 that results when many believers actively use their gifts.

THE BENEFITS OF GOD'S GIFTS

It is important that you discover and develop the spiritual gifts that God has bestowed on you. These gifts are desirable for three basic reasons.

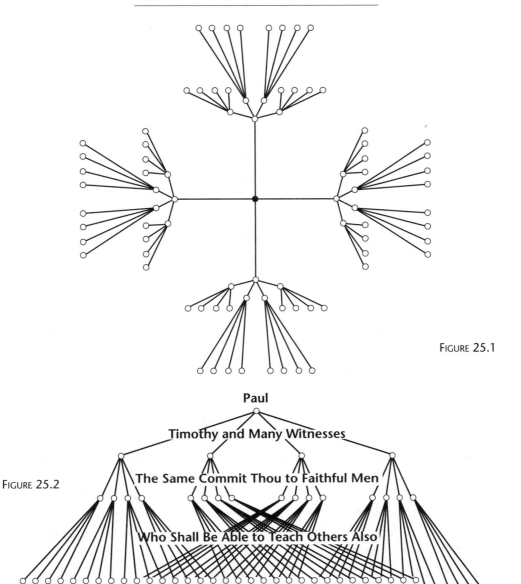

FIGURE 25.1

Paul

Timothy and Many Witnesses

FIGURE 25.2

The Same Commit Thou to Faithful Men

Who Shall Be Able to Teach Others Also

Diagrams from William MacDonald, *Christ Loved the Church,* © 1966, used by permission of Walterick Publishers.

You will be satisfied. Knowing and using your gifts will give you an understanding of the unique and indispensable ministry you have been called to accomplish in the body of Christ. You will discover a significant part of your purpose for being on this planet and realize that God has made you competent to produce something that will last for eternity. You will have a sense of fulfillment and joy in the service of others as you become an available instrument through whom the Holy Spirit can work.

In addition, knowledge of your spiritual gifts will greatly assist you in discerning and affirming the will of God at various points in your life. God will not call you to accomplish anything without giving you the power and enabling to do it. You will be able to make more intelligent decisions about possible involvement in specific opportunities and training in light of your God-given function in the body (Romans 12:4). You will also use your time more effectively by focusing on the things you have been equipped to do well rather than expending your energy in areas of minimum potential.

Others will be edified. Remember that the primary purpose of spiritual gifts is ecclesiastical—they are given to build up and purify the church as the body and bride of Christ. As you exercise your spiritual gifts, you will play a substantial role in serving other people and leading them into maturity (Ephesians 4:12–16). If you fail to develop your gifts or let them decline through disuse, your brothers and sisters in Christ will be hurt because they will be deprived of the unique ministry that only you could perform in their lives.

God will be glorified. According to 1 Peter 4:10–11, your spiritual gifts are ultimately designed to bring glory to God. This is your highest calling, and it relates to all three persons of the Godhead. As you use your spiritual gifts in conjunction with the power and fruit (especially love) of the Holy Spirit and in the name and lordship of Jesus Christ, the Father receives the glory.

DEBATE OVER THE GIFTS

All believers are charismatic in the sense that they believe in the exercise of spiritual gifts (*charismata*). But in another sense, not all believers are charismatic; a primary distinction between Spirit-centered believers (SCBs) and Word-centered believers (WCBs) lies in their view of controversial gifts such as prophecy, healing, and tongues. SCBs believe that all the gifts are still given, but many WCBs believe that the controversial gifts have ceased. **Cessationists** generally make a distinction between sign gifts and edification gifts. Sign gifts, they say, served their purpose in the first century by attesting to the authority of the apostles and their divinely inspired message. Once the New Testament canon was complete, miraculous gifts were no longer necessary, and they gradually disappeared from the church. WCBs use Hebrews 2:3–4, for example, to imply that signs and wonders had ceased by the time of the second generation of Christians. Some also build a case for the cessation of sign gifts from 1 Corinthians 13:8–10.

I was formerly a cessationist, but I have come to view these biblical and historical arguments as inconclusive and unconvincing. For example, concerning the time of the cessation of the gifts, a better case can be made that Paul's phrase "when the perfect comes" (1 Corinthians 13:10) refers to the second advent of Christ rather than the completion of the canon of Scripture. In addition, a closer look at church history shows a decline but not a loss of extraordinary gifts (see Jack Deere, *Surprised by the Voice of*

God), and this decline was related to the replacement of ministry as charism by an institutional model of ministry as office. The teaching that miracles and words of knowledge are not valid for today derives from theological axioms that cannot be demonstrated from the Scriptures. Our beliefs about these matters are shaped more by our environment, traditions, and teachers than we might suppose, and it is easy to conclude that certain gifts are inoperative if we have not seen them or if we hear only of how they are misused.

A BRIEF DESCRIPTION OF THE GIFTS

Because the exercise of spiritual gifts is central to Spirit-filled spirituality, we will take a concise look at the nature of the gifts and offer a word about discovering, developing, and using them.

"As each one has received a special gift, employ it in serving one another as good stewards of the manifold grace of God. Whoever speaks, is to do so as one who is speaking the utterances of God; whoever serves is to do so as one who is serving by the strength which God supplies; so that in all things God may be glorified through Jesus Christ, to whom belongs the glory and dominion forever and ever. Amen" (1 Peter 4:10–11). These verses imply a twofold classification: speaking gifts, or ministry of the Word, and serving gifts, or ministry of practical service. The following are the gifts as listed in Romans 12, 1 Corinthians 12, and Ephesians 4.

Prophecy (Romans 12:6; 1 Corinthians 12:10, 28–29; 14:1–40; Ephesians 4:11)—the ability to receive and proclaim a message from God. This could involve foretelling future events, although its primary purpose as seen in 1 Corinthians 14:3 is forthtelling: "one who prophesies speaks to men for edification and exhortation and consolation." In this sense, this gift is exhibited when preaching is accompanied with authority and Spirit-led power to encourage and admonish. Many SCBs affirm that prophecy can also involve a revelation from God (1 Corinthians 14:26), whether through a dream, vision, or message. This should not be confused with the normative Word of God to all believers, or canonical prophecy. Congregational prophecy, unlike the canonical prophecy of Scripture, is a message from God for a specific people, place, and time, and it should be tested by leaders in the church (1 Corinthians 14:29). Is it spoken in love? Does it edify the congregation? Is it consistent with Scripture? Does it honor God?

Service (Romans 12:7)—the ability to identify and care for the physical needs of people through a variety of means. The Greek word for this gift is the same as that for "ministry" or "deacon," but the gift should not be confused with the office.

Teaching (Romans 12:7; 1 Corinthians 12:28–29; Ephesians 4:11)—the ability to explain clearly and to apply the truths of God's Word so that others will learn. This requires the capacity to interpret Scripture accurately, engage in necessary research, and organize the results in ways that effectively communicate to others.

Exhortation (Romans 12:8)—the ability to motivate people to respond to the truth by providing timely words of counsel, encouragement, and consolation. When this gift is exercised, others are challenged to stimulate their faith by putting God's truth to the test in their lives.

Giving (Romans 12:8)—the ability to contribute material resources with generosity and cheerfulness for the benefit of others and the glory of God. Christians with this spiritual gift need not be wealthy.

Leadership (Romans 12:8)—the ability to discern God's purpose for a group, to set and communicate appropriate goals, and to motivate others to work together to fulfill them in the service of God. A person with this gift is effective at delegating tasks to followers without manipulation or coercion.

Mercy (Romans 12:8)—the ability to deeply empathize and engage in compassionate acts on behalf of people who are suffering physical, mental, or emotional distress. Those with this gift manifest concern and kindness to people who are often overlooked.

Wisdom (1 Corinthians 12:8)—the ability to apply the principles of the Word of God in a practical way to specific situations and to recommend the best course of action at the best time. The exercise of this gift skillfully distills insight and discernment into excellent advice.

Knowledge (1 Corinthians 12:8)—the ability to discover, analyze, and systematize truth for the benefit of others. With this gift, one speaks with understanding and penetration. But "the word of knowledge" can also involve supernatural perception and discernment for the purpose of ministering to others.

Faith (1 Corinthians 12:9)—the ability to have a vision for what God wants to be done and to believe confidently that it will be accomplished in spite of circumstances and appearances to the contrary. The gift of faith transforms vision into reality.

Healing (1 Corinthians 12:9, 28, 30)—the ability to serve as a human instrument through whom God cures illnesses and restores health. The possessor of this gift is not the source of power but a vessel who can heal only those diseases the Lord chooses to heal. This spiritual gift should not be confused with the signs and wonders performed by Jesus and the apostles, and it should not be discredited because of the abuses of grandstanding faith healers. Like other *charismata* such as teaching and evangelism, the gift of healing involves varying degrees of development and effectiveness. Healing prayer is not limited to physical disease but can also extend to emotional, relational, and spiritual concerns. Thus inner healing, or healing of memories, concerns emotional wounds such as repressed fears, anger, humiliation, and rejection.

Miracles (1 Corinthians 12:10, 28, 29)—the ability to serve as an instrument through whom God accomplishes acts that manifest supernatural power. Miracles bear witness to the presence of God and the truth of his proclaimed Word and appear to occur most frequently in association with missionary activity. The gospel message carries its own authority, but God sometimes graciously uses miracles to authenticate and open doors for the proclamation of forgiveness and life in Christ.

Distinguishing of spirits (1 Corinthians 12:10)—the ability to discern the spirit of truth and the spirit of error (cf. 1 John 4:6). With this gift, one may distinguish reality versus counterfeits, the divine versus the demonic, true versus false teaching, and in some cases, spiritual versus carnal motives.

Tongues (1 Corinthians 12:10, 28, 30; 14:1–40)—the ability to receive and impart a spiritual message in a language the recipient never learned. For other members of the body to be edified, this message must be interpreted either by the recipient (1 Corinthians 14:13) or by another person with the gift of interpretation (1 Corinthians 14:26–28).

The controversial nature of this gift merits several observations. First, Paul qualified the public use of this gift, stating that in a meeting of the church, two or at the most three could speak in a tongue, it must be done in turn, and a person with the gift of interpretation must be present so that the body would be edified (1 Corinthians 14:26–28). Second, there are a number of differences between the manifestation of tongues at Pentecost (Acts 2:1–13) and its use in Corinth (1 Corinthians 14), and these differences suggest that the two are not identical. It has been argued that the latter are not messages to the congregation but praises spoken to God (1 Corinthians 14:2) that edify the congregation as such when they are interpreted. If this is so, they are devotional rather than prophetic. However, Paul did refer to various "kinds of tongues" in his discussion of spiritual gifts in 1 Corinthians 12:10 and 12:28, and Paul's statement that tongues are a sign to unbelievers (1 Corinthians 14:22) suggests that they were known languages that required interpretation. Third, Paul's allowance for different kinds of tongues, coupled with his statements in 1 Corinthians 14:2, 4, 14–15, 28, has led many to distinguish a private use of tongues, often called a prayer language (14:14–15), from the public use of tongues which must be interpreted. Paul wrote that "if there is no interpreter, he must keep silent in the church; and let him speak to himself and to God" (14:28). People use this prayer language to facilitate adoration and intercession, but the primary use of the gift of tongues is for mutual edification. Fourth, the gift of tongues is easily counterfeited and often abused. It can be a source of spiritual pride, excessive preoccupation, and divisiveness, and this is why the gifts of discernment and interpretation are important to the body. Fifth, the gift of tongues has been tainted because it was assumed to be the passport to power or the key sign of the Holy Spirit. But a growing number of SCBs have come to see that tongues are not the only sign of the filling of the Spirit and that not all believers are to manifest this gift (1 Corinthians 12:17–19, 30).

Interpretation of tongues (1 Corinthians 12:10, 30; 14:5, 13, 26–28)—the ability to translate into the vernacular a message publicly uttered in a tongue. This gift may be combined with the gift of tongues (1 Corinthians 14:13), or it can operate separately (1 Corinthians 14:26–28).

Apostleship (1 Corinthians 12:28, 29; Ephesians 4:11)—in the New Testament, the apostles were not limited to the Twelve but included Paul, Barnabas, Andronicus, Junias, and others as well (Acts 14:14; Romans 16:7; 1 Corinthians 15:5, 7; 1 Thessalonians 2:6). If the requirement for the office of apostle includes having seen the resurrected Jesus (Acts 1:22; 1 Corinthians 9:1), this office ceased to exist by the second century. However, many believe that the gift of apostleship continues to be given. As a spiritual gift, this is the ability to begin and/or to oversee new churches and Christian ministries with a spontaneously recognized authority.

Helps (1 Corinthians 12:28)—the ability to enhance the effectiveness of the ministry of other members of the body. This is the only use of this word in the New Testament, and it appears to be distinct from the gift of service. Some writers suggest that while the gift of service is more group-oriented, the gift of helps is more person-oriented.

Administration (1 Corinthians 12:28)—this word, like helps, appears only once in the New Testament, and it is used outside of Scripture of a helmsman who steers a ship to its destination. This suggests that the spiritual gift of administration is the ability to steer a church or Christian organization toward the fulfillment of its goals by managing its affairs and implementing necessary plans. A person may have the gift of leadership without the gift of administration.

Evangelism (Ephesians 4:11)—the ability to be an unusually effective instrument in leading unbelievers to a saving knowledge of Christ. Some with this gift are most effective in personal evangelism, while others may be used by God in group evangelism or cross-cultural evangelism.

Shepherding or pastoring (Ephesians 4:11)—Peter was commissioned by Christ to shepherd his sheep (John 21:16), and Peter exhorted the elders in the churches of Asia Minor to do the same (1 Peter 5:2; cf. Acts 20:28). A person with this spiritual gift has the ability to lead, nourish, protect, and personally care for the needs of a "flock" of believers. Not all people with the office of pastor (elder, overseer) have or need the gift of pastoring or shepherding, and many with this gift do not have or need the office.

OTHER GIFTS

None of the lists in Romans 12, 1 Corinthians 12, and Ephesians 4 are complete, and it is evident that there are other spiritual gifts apart from those listed above. C. Peter Wagner in *Your Spiritual Gifts* suggests seven others: celibacy (the ability to enjoy being single and maintain sexual self-control [1 Corinthians 7:7–9]); voluntary poverty (the ability to renounce material comfort and adopt a lifestyle of relative poverty [1 Corinthians 13:3]); martyrdom (the ability to display an attitude of joy while suffering or even dying for the faith [1 Corinthians 13:3]); hospitality (the ability to welcome and provide for those in need of food and lodging [Romans 12:13; 1 Peter 4:9]); missionary (the ability to minister effectively in a second culture); intercession (the ability to pray for a long period of time on a regular basis for the ministries and needs of others); and exorcism (the ability to discern and cast out demons with authority). Other spiritual gifts (e.g., music, craftsmanship) are also given to members of the body of Christ for mutual edification.

COMBINATIONS AND VARIATIONS OF GIFTS

Many if not all believers have combinations of two or more spiritual gifts. Some combinations are unusual, while others are commonly combined. Gifts that work together include shepherd (pastor)-teaching, leadership-administration, evangelism-teaching, tongues-interpretation, and discernment-exorcism. In addition, Paul distinguishes three parameters in 1 Corinthians 12:4–6: "gifts" *(charismaton)*, "ministries" *(diakonion)*, and "effects" *(energematon)*. In *Body Life*, Ray Stedman links gifts to the Spirit, saying that a gift is a specific capacity or function; he links ministries to Jesus, saying that a ministry is the sphere in which a gift is performed; and he links effects or energizings to the Father, saying that an energizing is "the degree of power by which a gift is manifested or ministered on a specific occasion." There are variations not only in the gifts and gift combinations but also in the spheres and manifestations of gifts. For example, there are many variations in the spiritual gift of teaching. Some are more effective with small groups, others with large groups; some can effectively communicate with youth, while others are best at teaching adults.

DISCOVERING YOUR SPIRITUAL GIFTS

Three Prerequisites

As you seek to discover your spiritual gift or gifts, ask yourself these questions: Have I received the gift of salvation in Christ? Unlike natural talents, spiritual gifts are bestowed only on believers. Am I walking in fellowship with the Lord? To be effective, spiritual gifts must be manifested in the context of the fruit of the Holy Spirit. This fruit is impeded by unconfessed sin and a failure to abide in Christ (John 15:4). Do I want to develop my gifts? This will not happen by accident.

Six Suggestions

1. *Asking.* Begin to ask God to show you your gifts (see Philippians 4:6–7; James 1:5). God wants you to discover and implement the gifts he has given you, and this is a request you can make with confidence and expectation.
2. *Awareness.* Be aware of the biblical teaching on spiritual gifts by studying Romans 12, 1 Corinthians 12–14, and Ephesians 4. Look at one or more of the helpful books on spiritual gifts that are now available. Seek out other Christians who clearly know and use their spiritual gifts. Ask them about their gifts and how they discovered them.

3. *Aspiration*. God is committed to your joy, not your misery. "Delight yourself in the LORD; and He will give you the desires of your heart" (Psalm 37:4). As you pray and learn about the various gifts, ask yourself what you would most want to do. "For it is God who is at work in you, both to will and to work for His good pleasure" (Philippians 2:13). Your feelings should not be the only test, but they may indicate the direction for you to take. For example, Paul told Timothy, "If any man aspires to the office of overseer, it is a fine work he desires to do" (1 Timothy 3:1).

4. *Activity*. Just as we discover our natural talents by trying numerous things, in the same way we can discover our spiritual gifts by experimenting with several of the available gifts. If we don't try, we will never know. This requires availability and a willingness to learn our weaknesses as well as strengths.

5. *Ability*. Activity eventually points to ability. Don't be premature in your personal evaluation, because ability increases with practice. Be sensitive to areas of improvement. Look for opportunities within the community of believers of which you are a part, and seek the evaluation of mature believers who are familiar with your activities. Because of the danger of self-deception, spiritual gifts are best recognized by other members of the body.

6. *Affirmation*. The final affirmation of a spiritual gift is the blessing that should result from its exercise. As you use your gift or gift combination in the power of the Spirit, God will confirm and establish you in your ministry, and there will continue to be positive feedback from those to whom you minister. It has been said that "desire may indicate it, ability will confirm it, and blessing will accompany it."

DEVELOPING YOUR SPIRITUAL GIFTS

Having discovered your gift or combination of gifts, you are accountable to yourself, others, and God to develop and cultivate that which the Spirit has implanted within you. In *The Dynamics of Spiritual Gifts*, William McRae suggests that the gifts of the Spirit are developed in three ways.

By exercise. Like natural talents, spiritual gifts are developed by practice, not just by desire. Without regular exercise, they will atrophy. Pursue opportunities and persevere in the use of your gifts. Small home groups may be the best laboratory for practicing and experiencing spiritual gifts, and you should consider joining or starting such a group in your church.

By evaluation. Be open to the evaluation and counsel of other believers. Periodically ask godly people to evaluate your ministry in terms of strengths, weaknesses, and ways to improve.

By education. More educational and developmental materials are available today than ever before. Take advantage of any books, classes, or tapes that can help you improve your God-given abilities.

DANGERS OF ABUSE

The exercise of spiritual gifts is critical to the qualitative and quantitative growth of the body of Christ. For this reason, we must be careful to avoid the many pitfalls associated with this crucial subject. Here are ten:

1. *Spiritual gifts are not merely for personal use.* They are designed for the edification of others. Others should benefit primarily; the user should benefit secondarily.
2. *Spiritual gifts are not gained by merit or by begging.* The term *charismata* tells us that they are given solely by the grace of God (see Ephesians 4:7). The Holy Spirit distributes them "to each one individually just as He wills" (1 Corinthians 12:11).
3. *Spiritual gifts can be abused by being exercised in the power of the flesh.* If they are not being used in the power of the Spirit and through the love of Christ, they are of no value (1 Corinthians 13:1–3).
4. *The discovery and use of spiritual gifts is not a game or an option.* Your gifts will shape your ministry, and your ministry can have eternal consequences. God has called us to be committed and faithful to him, and this is reflected in part by our stewardship of the abilities and opportunities he has given to us.
5. *Spiritual gifts should not be a cause of discouragement.* As a rule, they develop gradually, and this requires time and work. Don't be in a hurry, and don't become jealous of the gifts bestowed on others. As we have seen, gifts vary in nature, combination, extent, and intensity. God is sovereign in his distribution, and he has given you the gifts that perfectly suit your personality and circumstances. There is no reason to envy another person's ministry. God has called us to faithfulness, not results.
6. *Spiritual gifts should not be a cause of pride.* Since they are sovereignly distributed according to the grace of God, they ought to be regarded as divinely entrusted responsibilities, not status symbols, achievements, or trophies. Christian character and maturity are measured by the fruit of the Spirit (Galatians 5:22–23), not spiritual gifts.
7. *Spiritual gifts should not be sought as ends in themselves.* In some circles, there is a tendency to exalt the gifts above the Giver.
8. *Avoid extreme positions on the gifts that are not warranted by Scripture.* Examples of such teachings are that we should not seek to discover spiritual gifts or that a Spirit-filled Christian can have all the gifts.

9. *The gifts of the Spirit can be counterfeited not only by the flesh but also by satanic and demonic forces.* Scripture counsels us to be sensitive to this problem. See Matthew 7:22–23; 24:24; 2 Corinthians 11:13–15; 1 Timothy 4:1; 2 Peter 2:1.

10. *Avoid the temptation of projecting your gifts onto others.* Our thinking is naturally colored by the gifts we have been given, and if we are not careful, we will take the prescription that works for us and turn it into the norm for everyone. This can lead to a judgmental perspective on our part and a sense of guilt on the part of others who are not gifted in the same way.

DIRECTIONS FOR USE

Four principles should govern our use of spiritual gifts.

1. *Remember that the Holy Spirit is the true dynamic behind the gifts.* They must be exercised in dependence upon his power.

2. *Spiritual gifts function best in the sphere of love, the "more excellent way" of 1 Corinthians 12:31.* Paul placed his great description of love (1 Corinthians 13) in the middle of the most extensive biblical passage on spiritual gifts (1 Corinthians 12–14). It is no accident that the two other major lists of spiritual gifts (Romans 12 and Ephesians 4) also include exhortations to love (see Romans 12:9–10; Ephesians 4:15–16).

3. *In your ministry, concentrate your energy in productive areas.* It is wise to maximize time in gift-related activities and minimize time in activities for which you are not suited.

4. *Scripture commands all believers to perform certain ministries regardless of individual gifts.* Ministry roles such as intercession, faith, service, helps, mercy, and giving are the responsibility of all believers, not just those who are specifically gifted in these areas. For example, some have the spiritual gift of evangelism, but all believers have a role of evangelism that corresponds to the opportunities they have been given.

QUESTIONS FOR PERSONAL APPLICATION

- Which of the twelve principles that relate to God's design for spiritual gifts resonate most with you?
- Where do you find yourself in the debate over the gifts? Have you been exposed to both sides of the debate?

- What combination of spiritual gifts do you think you have been given? If this is not clear to you, prayerfully apply the six suggestions for discovering your spiritual gifts and seek to develop them by exercise, evaluation, and education.
- Which of the ten dangers of abuse concern you the most?
- Which of the four directions for use is the most important to you?

26

SPIRIT-FILLED SPIRITUALITY
Openness and Discernment: A Balance

CHAPTER OVERVIEW

This chapter examines the strengths and weaknesses of the Spirit-centered movement and focuses on the balance both of truth and power and of word and Spirit. It also considers the issues of background and temperament, the way true Spirit manifestations glorify Christ, and ways of appropriating the power of the Spirit.

CHAPTER OBJECTIVES

- An appreciation for a balanced combination of openness and discernment concerning the work of the Spirit
- A desire to embrace the strengths of the Word-centered (truth) and Spirit-centered (power) approaches
- A better understanding of how to appropriate the power of the Spirit

---

A Spirit-filled spirituality must avoid the extremes of a naïve, unquestioning receptivity to any new experience on the one hand and a close-minded, hypercritical rigidity on the other. Instead, we should seek a balance between openness to the surprising works of the Spirit and biblical discernment of the spirit of truth versus the spirit of error (1 John 4:6). There are real abuses and excesses among Spirit-centered believers (SCBs), such as inaccurate, manipulative, and condemning prophetic words; emotionalism; undue emphasis on demonism; or the use of external manifestations as badges of spirituality. But Word-centered believers (WCBs) have a way of throwing out the baby with the bathwater. Such distortions do not invalidate the gifts any more than the ever-present danger of legalism, pharisaism, and hypocrisy invalidate the gospel. Instead of criticism by caricature and focusing on bizarre behavior, it is better to practice spiritual discernment while welcoming the work of the Spirit. It is healthy not only to keep the windows open but also to keep the screens on.

An excellent example of this balance can be found in Jonathan Edwards's *Religious Affections*. In this insightful work, Edwards affirms a cautionary, not cynical, attitude toward claims based on extraordinary experiences, since outward manifestations are ambivalent. External phenomena can be caused by natural works or spiritual power. Thus true supernatural operations must be distinguished not by the experiences alone but by the larger context of Christ-centeredness and permanent character ("gracious affections").

The balanced combination of openness and discernment is evident in Paul's exhortation in 1 Corinthians 14:39–40: "Therefore, my brethren, desire earnestly to prophesy, and do not forbid to speak in tongues. But all things must be done properly and in an orderly manner." An "orderly manner" does not exclude physical manifestations, since these often appear in Scripture, and it would be a mistake to delimit Paul's words in so strict a way that we quench the fire of the Spirit. However, manifestations are secondary to fruit, since the kingdom of God is "righteousness and peace and joy in the Holy Spirit" (Romans 14:17).

STRENGTHS AND WEAKNESSES OF BOTH SIDES

As we have seen, there is a continuum (fig. 26.1) from the polar opposites of Spirit without Word (A) and Word without Spirit (E). No believer is devoid of Word or Spirit, but we have described SCBs as being on the left of C (somewhere around point B) and WCBs as being on the right of C (somewhere around point D). The center point C represents a balanced affirmation of Spirit and Word that seeks to embrace the strengths of both sides.

Spirit				**Word**
A	**B**	**C**	**D**	**E**

FIGURE 26.1

The strengths of the WCB side include emphasis on biblical doctrine, depth of preaching and teaching, and concern with growth in character and Christlike behavior. But the WCB side can be prone to the following weaknesses (these potential problems are generalizations and are not true of all WCBs): an antisupernatural and rationalistic bias that has been influenced by a post-Enlightenment world view, a controlling mentality that is afraid of disruption of the way things "ought" to be done, a judgmental attitude toward other expressions of worship and practice, an arrogant and condescending spirit, and a penchant to love doctrine more than God or people.

Since Spirit-filled spirituality is concerned with the work of the Holy Spirit in the people of God, we will offer a more detailed outline of the strengths and weaknesses of the SCB side. Please remember that these nine positives and negatives are generalizations that are not true of all SCBs.

SCB Strengths

- trinitarian emphasis and affirmation of the reality of the Holy Spirit
- universality of gifts and every-member ministry
- stress on mutual edification within the body of Christ
- dependence on the power of God; Spirit-empowered living
- recognition of the legitimate need for expressing emotion and enthusiasm
- joyfulness in worship and life; new dimensions of worship
- love of Scripture
- boldness in sharing Christ; enthusiasm for evangelism
- commitment to small-group ministry

SCB Weaknesses

- gifts without graces; *charismata* can be stressed over character; emphasis on the outward can lead to neglect of the inward
- unhealthy pursuit of dramatic experiences; some become conference junkies who quest after spiritual highs; spirituality built on unusual or exciting experiences; demand for immediate results
- pride and elitism regarding spiritual experiences
- an exaggerated discontinuity of the supernatural with the natural; underplaying less dramatic gifts
- excessive emotionalism and exhibitionism
- shallowness in biblical doctrine and teaching; anti-intellectual tendency
- vulnerable to manipulation, deception, and authoritarianism
- can be susceptible to the prosperity gospel and word-faith teaching with its simplistic and unbiblical view of blessing and suffering
- excessive fixation on demonic activity

TRUTH AND POWER, WORD AND SPIRIT, INWARD AND OUTWARD

All too often, the SCB/WCB debate takes place between practitioners and theologians. Each side brings a limited perspective that needs to be balanced by the other. We should seek to combine practical experience with doctrinal depth, repeated filling with the Holy Spirit with responsible biblical exegesis, empowered witness and service with understanding of Scripture in context, fervent prayer for God's power with fervid love for God's truth. We should listen to God's authoritative voice in Scripture without being closed to other ways in which God may communicate through the gifts of the Spirit. SCBs should not focus so much on power, signs, and wonders that they depersonalize the Holy Spirit. This was the sin of Simon the magician, who sought to manipulate supernatural power (Acts 8:9–24). WCBs should seek to advance God's kingdom not in word only but also in the power and authority of the Spirit, who changes people and sets them free. All of us need the inward journey in which we are increasingly rooted and grounded in the soil of God's truth and love and the outward journey in which we express this truth and love in divinely energized action.

EXPERIENCE AND EXPECTATION, BACKGROUND AND TEMPERAMENT

Our expectations regarding the nature and extent of God's activity today are shaped by our assumptions and world view. These expectations have a great deal to do with our experience. WCBs accuse SCBs of having expectation-shaped experiences that are contoured by a miraculous-oriented subculture. But this argument cuts both ways, since a nonmiraculous conditioning can make people impervious to the surprising work of the Spirit. If we do not desire, pray, and expect God to stretch out his hand to do extraordinary things (see Acts 4:29–31), it is unlikely that we will see the manifestations of God's power. But these extraordinary things can occur in ordinary ways, and we would do well not to draw too sharp a distinction between the natural and the supernatural, lest we remove the latter from daily life and fail to see the hand of God in all ministry and spiritual gifts, whether healing or teaching. On the Word-centered side, the teaching and preaching of Scripture should have content, depth, and relevance, but on the Spirit-centered side, it should also be energized and anointed by the Spirit.

Like the other approaches to the spiritual life (e.g., disciplined spirituality and devotional spirituality), Spirit-filled spirituality is strongly affected by the personal factors of background and temperament. Because of these differences, some people will be drawn toward a Word-centered emphasis on truth and spiritual fruit, while others will be spontaneously attracted to a Spirit-centered emphasis on experience and spiritual gifts. In light of this, the body of Christ needs the kind of cross-pollination that avoids the faults of the other side while welcoming its strengths.

RENEWAL AND REVIVAL

In many cases, Spirit-centered renewal movements have brought new life and vitality on a corporate and personal level. But as beneficial as this joy and exuberance can be, this form of renewal is often not the same as revival. The latter involves the Spirit's gracious and outpouring work of revealing the holiness of God and the consequent need for godly sorrow, radical repentance, and personal humility. In revival, God confronts people through his anointed messengers of his purity and Word, and this leads to the serious business of repentance, return, and restoration. Renewal therefore needs to be deepened by a growing realization of the holiness of God and the sinfulness of sin.

THE SPIRIT POINTS TO CHRIST

Any movement that begins with the Spirit ought to end in Christ. Speaking of the Holy Spirit, Jesus said, "He will glorify Me, for He will take of Mine and will disclose it to you" (John 16:14). The Spirit empowers the gifts, not as ends in themselves but as means of maturing the body into the image of Christ so that he will be lifted up and honored. Notice that Paul's prayers for the churches at Ephesus, Philippi, and Colossae have nothing to do with reveling in performance and experiences; instead, these prayers concern their growing realization of the in-Christ relationship. He prays that they would know Christ, manifest his character, and increase in their knowledge and assurance of God's love and inward power (see Ephesians 1:17–19; 3:16–19; Philippians 1:9–11; Colossians 1:9–12).

APPROPRIATING THE POWER OF THE SPIRIT

The power of the Holy Spirit was central in the life of Christ Jesus. He was conceived by the power of the Spirit; the Spirit descended upon him at his baptism; he was led about by the Spirit in the wilderness; he returned to Galilee in the power of the Spirit; he was anointed by the Spirit to preach the gospel, to heal, and to deliver people from demonic bondage; he spoke of the need to be born of the Spirit; he rejoiced greatly in the Holy Spirit; he promised the gift of the Spirit of truth to his disciples; and he breathed on them after his resurrection saying, "Receive the Holy Spirit." Christ was engulfed in the Spirit of God and did all things through dependence on the Spirit's power. This same power indwells all of Jesus' followers, both Jew and Gentile, and energizes kingdom living. The kingdom of God is already and not yet; the future presence and power of God now indwells his people (1 Corinthians 4:20). In one sense, we suffer and groan as we await the consummation of God's kingdom (Romans 8:23), but in another sense, we rejoice in our suffering as overcomers through the already present kingdom life and power of Christ (Romans 5:3–5; Philippians 4:4–5; 1 Peter 4:13).

It is impossible for us to live the Christian life in our own power; access to the new life of God's kingdom is through Christ himself, and he has promised to live it in us as we walk in the power of the indwelling Spirit. We are filled with the Spirit when we turn from our own resources and allow him to control us (Ephesians 5:18). Recall that we need both the inward filling of the Spirit for character and wisdom and the outward filling of the Spirit for ministry and service.

How do we seek the visitation of the Spirit? While Scripture offers no step-by-step formula, the experience of the saints as well as biblical principles point to certain requisites that prepare the way.

Admitting our weakness. When we call on God out of a spirit of humility, contrition, and brokenness, we are acknowledging our desperate need for him. God's power is perfected in our weakness (2 Corinthians 12:9–10).

Surrendering our will. If a farmer is to cultivate a field, that field must be plowed and harrowed before it can receive the seed that matures and bears fruit. This is a painful and upsetting process, but God uses times of crisis to bring us to the point of surrendering our will to his. When we become weary of our own resources and efforts, our growing sense of frustrated inadequacy drives us to God. As we realize our powerlessness, our increasing dependence makes the Spirit of God more real to us. Instead of working for God, we learn to invite him to work in and through us.

Confessing our disobedience. Purity leads to power. We grieve and quench the Spirit when we tolerate unconfessed sins, questionable behavior, impure thoughts, lack of integrity, dishonesty, selfishness, immorality, and other forms of disobedience. Scripture calls us to present ourselves to God as those alive from the dead and our members as instruments of righteousness to God (Romans 6:13). Instead of focusing on having the Holy Spirit, we should be more concerned with the Holy Spirit having us. "The one who keeps His commandments abides in Him, and He in him. We know by this that He abides in us, by the Spirit whom He has given us" (1 John 3:24).

Sanctifying our desires. Those who consciously long for the cleansing, empowering, and quickening of the Spirit will cry out to God in holy desire. This is the theme of Jean-Pierre de Caussade's spiritual classic, *Abandonment to Divine Providence*; a pure and contrite heart and a fundamental abandonment to God's loving purposes bring us the treasures of his grace. Prayer and communion with Christ lead to spiritual power.

Trusting in God's promise to fill us. Scripture commands us to be filled with the Spirit (Ephesians 5:18) and exhorts us to walk by the Spirit (Galatians 5:16, 25), to be led by the Spirit (Romans 8:14–16; Galatians 5:18), to live by the Spirit (Romans 8:11–13; Galatians 5:25), and to set our minds on the Spirit (Romans 8:5–9). Thus we can be assured that God's desire is for his children to be Spirit-filled. When we trust in and appropriate his promise to fill us, we can be confident that this is a request our Father will be pleased to grant.

QUESTIONS FOR PERSONAL APPLICATION

- Do you find yourself leaning more toward the side of openness or toward the side of discernment? What can you do to sustain a balance in this area?
- What is your own assessment of SCB strengths and weaknesses?
- What role has your combination of experience and expectations had in your understanding of Spirit-filled spirituality?
- How would you assess yourself in the five requisites of admitting your weakness, surrendering your will, confessing your disobedience, sanctifying your desires, and trusting in God's promise to fill you?

FACET 10

WARFARE SPIRITUALITY

The World, the Flesh, and the Devil

The spiritual warfare is not optional for believers in Christ. Scripture teaches and illustrates the dynamics of this warfare on the three fronts of the world, the flesh, and the devil. The worldly and demonic systems are external to the believer, but they entice and provide opportunities for the flesh, which is the capacity for sin within the believer. This section outlines a biblical strategy for dealing with each of these barriers to spiritual growth.

27

WARFARE
SPIRITUALITY
Warfare with the Flesh and the World

CHAPTER OVERVIEW

Warfare spirituality centers on the dynamics of the spiritual conflict on the three fronts of the world, the flesh, and the devil. Our perception of this warfare is shaped by our world view, but the Old and New Testaments reveal the existence of a highly ordered spiritual world that exists between God and us. This chapter considers spiritual warfare on the two fronts of the flesh and the world.

CHAPTER OBJECTIVES

- A realization that our understanding of spiritual warfare relates to our world view
- A perspective on spiritual conflict that is informed by both the Old and New Testaments
- A better understanding of the nature of the warfare with the flesh and of resources for dealing with temptations
- A clearer strategy for our warfare with the world

As followers of Christ, we are engaged in a cosmic conflict, whether we know it or not. Scripture teaches and illustrates the dynamics of this warfare on the three fronts of the world, the flesh, and the devil. The worldly and demonic systems are external to believers, but they entice and provide opportunities for the flesh, which is the capacity for sin within us. This overview of warfare spirituality will outline a biblical strategy for dealing with each of these barriers to spiritual growth.

WORLD VIEWS AND WARFARE

Our world view consists of our basic assumptions about reality. Almost all primordial cultures recognize a reality that has been overlooked by those whose thinking has been shaped by the modern Western world view. This world view developed a logical and coherent way of approaching aspects of reality, but it rules out spiritual aspects as imaginary or unscientific. As a result, Western Christians often accept a two-tiered view of reality in which there is an excluded middle realm between those of religion and science. They answer ultimate questions in theistic terms and relate to the world in empirical and naturalistic terms, but they typically exclude the middle territory between these two realms that consists of angelic and demonic spiritual powers. By contrast, many people in the two-thirds world cultures (Africans, Asians, Latin Americans, and the inhabitants of Oceania) know intuitively the reality of the spirit world but have not contextualized this reality within a theistic framework. The extremes of animism and spiritism on one pole and rationalism and materialism on the opposite pole both overlook aspects of reality that are affirmed by the world view of Scripture.

More often than we think, our unconscious presuppositions and unquestioned axioms influence our theology. Each of us has a set of theological, cultural, and emotional filters that affect our perception and interpretation of the things we see and experience. We seem to be caught in a vicious circle: our experience influences our theology, and our theology influences our experience. Furthermore, our theology affects the way we interpret the Bible, and the way we interpret the Bible affects our theology. Because of this, it is necessary to reassess both our experience and theology on an ongoing basis; if we fail to do this, we get locked into a system that is impervious to new insights. Those who use Scripture to defend rather than challenge their cultural presuppositions may ignore or resist the biblical affirmation of the reality of the spirit world.

THE REALITY OF THE WARFARE

From the beginning of the Old Testament to the end of the New Testament, the Bible reveals the existence of a vast, highly ordered, and complex spiritual world that exists between God and us. Instead of a rigid dichotomy between the natural and the supernatural, the Scriptures disclose the direct involvement of the supernatural in the natural realm. A careful analysis of the Bible reveals a pervasive "supranatural" warfare dimension that involves a present cosmic-earthly conflict. Those who ignore or reject this reality are ill equipped to deal with spiritual powers of evil in the world.

Spiritual Conflict in the Old Testament

- The Old Testament affirms the existence of invisible spirit beings who were corrupted into malevolent agents and became enemies of the person and purposes of God. The serpent (Genesis 3; Psalm 74:14; Isaiah 27:1), evil spirits (1 Samuel 16:14–23; 18:10; 19:9), deceiving spirits (1 Kings 22:21–23), demons (Leviticus 17:7; Deuteronomy 32:17; Psalm 106:37), and powerful territorial beings who are opposed to God's angels (Daniel 10:13, 20–21) are all spiritual forces of evil.

- The account of the temptation and Fall (Genesis 3) reveals that human rebellion against the rule of God was prompted by a powerful evil being who had previously turned against God. As a result, cosmic rebellion extended to the earth, and the tragedy of the curse can be overcome only by God's redemption of nature (Romans 8:19–23). Using the tactics of doubt and deception, the serpent (later identified in Revelation 12:9 as the dragon, the devil, and Satan) instigated the downfall of the human race.

- The fall of those who had been created in the image and likeness of God led to an ongoing enmity between humanity and Satan along with the prophecy that the seed of the woman would crush the serpent (Genesis 3:15). This is fulfilled in the redemptive work of Christ and his defeat of the Evil One on our behalf.

- The warfare between the two seeds is illustrated in the story of Cain and Abel (Genesis 4) and in the account of the increase in human wickedness (Genesis 6). The sin of Babel (Genesis 11) illustrates a recurring pattern of human autonomy and defiance of God. The nations devise idolatrous religions that serve their own interests rather than the true Creator, and this is evident in the story of the plagues and the Exodus of Israel from Egypt. In the ten plagues, God demonstrated his person and power in refutation of all the gods of Egypt (Exodus 7:4–5; 9:14–16; 12:12; 15:11).

- Near the end of his life, Joshua had to exhort the people to fear the Lord and put away the foreign gods of Mesopotamia, Egypt, and Canaan (Joshua 24:14–24). The people of Israel often succumbed to the idolatrous practices of the surrounding nations during the years of the judges and kings. These pagan rituals included child sacrifice to demons (2 Kings 3:27; 16:3; Psalm 106:37–38; Ezekiel 16:20–21; 23:37).

- The stories of Saul's progressive demonization (1 Samuel 16:14–23; 18:10–11; 19:9–10; 20:33; 28:7–19), Ahab's worship of Baal (1 Kings 16:30–33), and Elijah's challenge to the prophets of Baal (1 Kings 18:20–40) illustrate an ongoing spiritual conflict.

- This conflict is also evident in the denouncements of idolatry, pagan ceremonies on high places, images of Baal and Astarte, and cult prostitution in the prophetic oracles of Isaiah (e.g., 57), Ezekiel (e.g., 8; 14), Hosea (e.g., 2:13; 4:12–14), and other prophets to Israel and Judah.

Spiritual Conflict in the New Testament

- The New Testament paints a far clearer picture of the spiritual warfare that exists in heaven and on earth. Jesus identifies Satan as the origin of evil (John 8:44) and directly confronts him during the forty days of temptation in the wilderness (Luke 4:1–13).

- Jesus' ministry was opposed by demonic spirits (Mark 1:23–27), and he demonstrated his authority over them by casting them out on numerous occasions (Mark 1:34, 39). When Jesus cast out demons by the Spirit of God, he liberated people who were in spiritual bondage and displayed the power of God's kingdom (Matthew 12:22–29; Luke 13:10–16).
- The story of Jesus' deliverance of the Gerasene demoniac (Mark 5:1–20) graphically portrays the reality and potential extent of demonic control. A quick survey of the Gospels reveals that a significant part of Jesus' recorded ministry consisted of freeing people from evil spirits. It is easy to overlook this aspect of our Lord's ministry through "text management," but the Gospels frequently attribute human misery to demonic activity.
- When Jesus appointed the Twelve, they were given authority to cast out demons (Mark 3:14–15; 6:7, 13; Matthew 10:7–8), and when he commissioned the seventy, they also received authority to engage in a deliverance ministry (Luke 10:17–20).
- Some writers claim that after the Lord's resurrection and ascension, his disciples gave less attention to the spirit world. Indeed, Christ's ministry was the decisive invasion of the kingdom of darkness by the kingdom of God, and it is not surprising that Jesus' confrontation with demonic opposition was so intense. In addition, he defeated Satan and his demons, and while the warfare has continued, Jesus' followers engage a vanquished foe. But it is significant that there are more references to the spirit world in Acts, the Epistles, and Revelation (about 178) than in the four Gospels (about 150). There are also more references to evil spirits in the New Testament (208) than there are to Satan (120).
- Acts records a number of demonic encounters in the ministry of the disciples (Acts 5; 8; 16; 19). Spiritual warfare is also a repeated theme in the Epistles and Revelation (e.g., Romans 16:17–20; 1 Corinthians 5:5; 7:5; 2 Corinthians 2:11; 10:3–5; 11:13–15; 12:7–10; Ephesians 2:2; 6:10–20; 1 Thessalonians 2:18; 3:5; 2 Thessalonians 2:1–12; 1 Timothy 1:18–20; 4:1; 5:15; 2 Timothy 2:26; 2 Peter 2:4; 1 John 4:1–6; 5:19; Jude 6; Revelation 2:9, 13, 24; 9:11, 20; 12–13; 16:13–14; 20:1–3, 7–10).
- Just as God has his holy angels, the devil has his own hierarchy of evil rulers and authorities (Ephesians 3:10; Revelation 12:3–4, 7–9), but Satan and his angels are destined for eternal fire (Matthew 25:41).
- The New Testament portrays unregenerate humanity as being in bondage to the world system, to the desires of the flesh, and to Satan, "the prince of the power of the air" (Ephesians 2:1–3). Without Christ, people are spiritually

dead, blinded by "the god of this world" to the truth of the gospel (2 Corinthians 4:3–4), and held captive by the devil to do his will (2 Timothy 2:26).

- The unredeemed are called "the sons of the evil one" (Matthew 13:37–39) and "the children of the devil" (1 John 3:8–10; John 8:44). They are under the dominion of Satan (Acts 26:18) and subject to the domain of darkness (Colossians 1:13). The "whole world lies in the power of the evil one" (1 John 5:19), whom Jesus called "the ruler of this world" (John 12:31; 14:30; 16:11).

WARFARE ON THREE FRONTS

"The seventy returned with joy, saying, 'Lord, even the demons are subject to us in Your name.' And He said to them, 'I was watching Satan fall from heaven like lightning'" (Luke 10:17–18). "The Son of God appeared for this purpose, to destroy the works of the devil" (1 John 3:8b).

Christ has already won the victory, but until he returns, the battle still rages on three fronts: the world, the flesh, and the devil (Ephesians 2:2–3).

The world. "In the world you have tribulation, but take courage; I have overcome the world" (John 16:33b). "For whatever is born of God overcomes the world; and this is the victory that has overcome the world—our faith" (1 John 5:4).

The flesh. "But I say, walk by the Spirit, and you will not carry out the desire of the flesh. For the flesh sets its desire against the Spirit, and the Spirit against the flesh; for these are in opposition to one another, so that you may not do the things that you please" (Galatians 5:16–17).

The devil. "The ruler of this world has been judged" (John 16:11b). "The word of God abides in you, and you have overcome the evil one.... Greater is He who is in you than he who is in the world" (1 John 2:14b; 4:4b).

The Scriptures abound with military images of conflict, warfare, and adversaries in the believer's life. It is not a question of whether we are engaged in a spiritual warfare; the question is how effectively we are fighting. The moment we put our trust in Jesus Christ we were enlisted as soldiers in his army. This is why Paul tells Timothy, "Suffer hardship with me, as a good soldier of Christ Jesus. No soldier in active service entangles himself in the affairs of everyday life, so that he may please the one who enlisted him as a soldier" (2 Timothy 2:3–4). As new creatures in Jesus Christ (2 Corinthians 5:17), we face a daily battle against the opposing forces of the world system, fleshly desires, and "spiritual forces of wickedness" (Ephesians 6:12b). For us to be overcomers, we need discipline, resistance, the skillful use of spiritual weapons, and dependence upon the power of God.

It is important that we maintain a biblical balance as we consider the warfare. "There are two equal and opposite errors into which our race can fall about the devils. One is to disbelieve in their existence. The other is to believe, and to feel an excessive and unhealthy interest in them. They themselves are equally pleased by both errors" (C. S. Lewis, preface to *The Screwtape Letters*). Those who ignore the biblical teaching about the reality of the enemy and the weapons of the warfare put themselves in a dangerous position of vulnerability.

The other extreme of excessive preoccupation with demonic forces is just as hazardous. It is easy to look for demons behind every compulsion, craving, and curse. The fact is that the flesh is fully capable of these activities; no one needs to be forced into selfishness, pride, gluttony, self-pity, lust, or a bad temper. "The devil made me do it" can become an excuse that keeps us from accepting responsibility for our attitudes and actions. There is a problem when a Christian becomes more conscious of the satanic kingdom than of the person and work of the Lord Jesus Christ.

WARFARE WITH THE FLESH

Warfare with the flesh is directly related to the section on exchanged life spirituality, so the following thoughts concerning this front will be brief.

The word *flesh* is used in more than one way in Scripture. Sometimes it refers to the physical body, as in Galatians 2:20 and Colossians 2:24. In other passages it refers to what Paul calls "the law of sin which is in my members." "For I joyfully concur with the law of God in the inner man, but I see a different law in the members of my body, waging war against the law of my mind and making me a prisoner of the law of sin which is in my members" (Romans 7:22–23).

In Victor Hugo's story "Ninety-Three," the crew members of a ship tossed in a violent storm are more terrified by a crashing sound below than by the storm itself. They know that it is the sound of a cannon that has torn loose and that it is crashing into the sides of the ship with each brutal wave. Two of the men risk their lives to go below and fasten the cannon before it breaks through and sends the ship to the bottom of the sea.

We are like that ship: our souls are more imperiled by the inward power of sin than by the outer storms of the world and the devil. Because of the biblical stress on personal accountability, this indwelling "law of sin" is the primary locus of the spiritual warfare.

On our deepest spiritual level, we are new creatures who are alive to God because of our salvation in Christ. But on our soulish and physical levels, we still await the fullness of our redemption (Romans 8:23). Until that time, the old appetites, attitudes, memories, and habits can surface at any time and wage war against the life of Christ in us. The conflict is inward versus outward (Romans 7:22–23), that is, between the Holy Spirit, who indwells our spirit, and our flesh. This conflict does not diminish with conversion but becomes more intense as we pursue the Spirit-directed and Spirit-empowered life.

Paul contrasts the deeds of the flesh with the fruit of the Spirit in Galatians 5:19–23. The flesh manifests itself in "immorality, impurity, sensuality, idolatry, sorcery, enmities, strife, jealousy, outbursts of anger, disputes, dissensions, factions, envying, drunkenness, carousing, and things like these." This list begins with moral sins (immorality, impurity, sensuality), moves to religious sins (idolatry, sorcery), and concludes with social sins (enmities, strife, jealousy, outbursts of anger, disputes, dissensions, factions, envying) and sins of intemperance (drunkenness, carousing). By contrast, the fruit of the Spirit is "love, joy, peace, patience, kindness, goodness, faithfulness, gentleness, self-control," and none of these are born by the flesh. Instead of love, the flesh produces unforgiveness, hate, rejection, and hostility. Instead of joy, the flesh produces bitterness, resentment, despair, depression, insecurity, and worry. Instead of peace, the flesh produces fear, discord, strife, jealousy, and nervousness. Instead of patience, the flesh produces intolerance, impatience, and restlessness. Instead of kindness, the flesh produces cruelty, harshness, and aggression. Instead of goodness, the flesh produces malice, wickedness, and depravity. Instead of faithfulness, the flesh produces disloyalty, infidelity, and dishonesty. Instead of gentleness, the flesh produces stubbornness, pride, and cursing. Instead of self-control, the flesh produces rebellion, lust, and gluttony.

No two people have an identical combination of fleshly dispositions. Some have more of a problem with temper or envy, while others may have greater difficulties with unforgiveness or lust. Before we can effectively deal with the flesh, we must be honest enough with ourselves to determine our particular form of carnality.

As an exercise, go through the lists of fleshly manifestations given above and in 1 Corinthians 6:9–10, Galatians 5:19–21, Ephesians 4:25–31, and Colossians 3:5, 8–9. Use these to spot the areas in which you frequently find yourself tempted. As you make this diagnosis, ask the Holy Spirit to convict you of any unconfessed sins in your life. Unless we repent of our sins, we will not enjoy intimacy with God.

The warfare with the flesh, like the conflict with the world and the forces of darkness, will continue throughout the time of our stay on earth. The flesh can never be reformed or improved; it can only be put to death. "Now those who belong to Christ Jesus have crucified the flesh with its passions and desires" (Galatians 5:24).

When we trusted in Christ, we were transferred from the domain of darkness to the kingdom of God (Colossians 1:13). God removed us from the line of Adam and placed us in Christ. Our new identity is in him: we died with him, we were buried with him, we were raised with him, and we are seated in the heavenly realms with him (Romans 6:3–11; Ephesians 2:5–6). The old self died and the new self came alive. "Knowing this, that our old self was crucified with Him, in order that our body of sin might be done away with, so that we would no longer be slaves to sin; for he who has died is freed from sin.... Even so consider yourselves to be dead to sin, but alive to God in Christ Jesus" (Romans 6:6–7, 11).

Because of our union with Christ in his death and resurrection, we can approach the spiritual warfare from a position of victory. It is true, as Romans 7 tells us, that the flesh or power of sin is still with us, but it need no longer have dominion over our lives. Romans 6–8 tells us two things we can do to overcome the force of the flesh. The first is to reckon or consider ourselves to be dead to sin but alive to God. We must believe what God has said is true of us, regardless of how we feel. This belief should lead to action: "Therefore do not let sin reign in your mortal body so that you should obey its lusts, and do not go on presenting the members of your body to sin as instruments of unrighteousness; but present yourselves to God as those alive from the dead, and your members as instruments of righteousness to God" (Romans 6:12–13). We must obediently present ourselves to God as people who are no longer slaves to sin but slaves of righteousness (Romans 6:19).

The second thing we can do is found in Romans 8:12–13: "So then, brethren, we are under obligation, not to the flesh, to live according to the flesh—for if you are living according to the flesh, you must die; but if by the Spirit you are putting to death the deeds of the body, you will live."

Paul adds in Galatians 5:16, 25, "Walk by the Spirit, and you will not carry out the desire of the flesh.... If we live by the Spirit, let us also walk by the Spirit." By the power of the Spirit, the flesh has been crucified with its passions and desires. The flesh is overcome not by resolutions or self-effort but by walking in submission to the rule of the Holy Spirit.

If we fail to appropriate these resources, we will be under the dominion of the flesh. This in turn makes us vulnerable to the other two forces in the spiritual warfare, the world and the devil. The world and its lusts appeal to the flesh and add fuel to the fire. Demonic forces also use the flesh as the means of invasion into the believer's life. Thus willful indulgence in fleshly sins can lead to other forms of bondage. Sin begins in the thoughts (these can be prompted by the flesh, the world, or by demonic suggestions) and if unchecked moves along a downward continuum to choice, to habit, to loss of control, to bondage, and finally to almost total control. As Ed Murphy notes in *The Handbook for Spiritual Warfare*, the last two stages involve evil supernaturalism.

Personal Affirmations for Handling Temptations

This set of affirmations is one you can use, by the grace of God, as preventive medicine for four major areas of temptation. I developed these affirmations because I sensed the need for a specific way of thinking in areas of habitual temptation and struggle. This is particularly helpful in that split second between temptation and response that mysteriously illuminates the whole dynamic of choosing to walk in the power of the Spirit or in the power of the flesh. It can be helpful to use spiritual exercises and tools that draw us to a biblical pattern of thought in times when the warfare becomes more intense. Just as judo leverages the force of an opponent to one's advantage, so these affirmations can convert the force of temptation into a positive spiritual reminder.

Remember that these are not automatic formulas. They must be part of a divine-human process that involves dependence on God's grace in your life.

Temptation to Anger

1. This is sin. "The anger of man does not achieve the righteousness of God" (James 1:20). (This is not dealing with anger against sin [cf. Ezekiel 7:3; Mark 3:5] but with sinful anger [Galatians 5:20].)
2. I do not want to sin. Sin is beneath the dignity of the person I have become in Christ Jesus (Ephesians 2:4–7).
3. I do not have to sin. I am no longer under the power of sin, but I am alive to God in Christ Jesus (Romans 6:11; 8:12–14).
4. Then why am I tempted to get angry? Because I have embraced wrong thinking. I have committed myself to unrealistic plans. (I am using "unrealistic plans" in the sense of plans that, for whatever reason, did not come to fruition. For example, I may be committed to the short-term plan of catching a particular flight so that I can get to a meeting on time. If a flat tire blocks this plan, it was unrealistic—it was not realized. The problem was not in desiring to get to the meeting on time but in making my sense of well-being dependent on it. Insofar as depression is anger turned inward, these affirmations are relevant for depression as well.)
5. The correct way to think is to remember that God is in control and has my best interests at heart (Romans 8:28).
6. My response to this truth is first to trust in the Lord and not lean on my own understanding (Proverbs 3:5–6). Since point 5 is true, God must have intentions in this situation that I cannot presently grasp.
7. Second, I will walk by the Spirit and not carry out the desire of the flesh (Galatians 5:16). The fruit of the Spirit is love, joy, peace, patience, kindness, goodness, faithfulness, gentleness, self-control (Galatians 5:22–23).

Temptation to Seek Revenge

1. This is sin. "Never pay back evil for evil to anyone. . . . If possible, so far as it depends on you, be at peace with all men. Never take your own revenge" (Romans 12:17–19).
2. I do not want to sin. Sin is beneath the dignity of the person I have become in Christ Jesus (Ephesians 2:4–7).

3. I do not have to sin. I am no longer under the power of sin, but I am alive to God in Christ Jesus (Romans 6:11; 8:12–14).

4. Then why am I tempted to seek revenge? Because I want justice. (This may be as trivial as someone cutting me off in traffic or as deep-seated as harboring a resentment against another person for years.)

5. But God did not give me justice (what I deserve); he treated me with mercy (not giving me what I deserve) and grace (giving me better than I deserve).

6. Because I have been forgiven, I will forgive others and treat them with mercy and grace (Colossians 3:12–15). (The better I understand God's mercy and grace in my life, the more I will be willing and ready to forgive others when they sin against me.)

7. I will walk by the Spirit and not carry out the desire of the flesh (Galatians 5:16). The fruit of the Spirit is love, joy, peace, patience, kindness, goodness, faithfulness, gentleness, self-control (Galatians 5:22–23).

Sexual Temptation

1. There is no future in this. It would damage my relationship with God and could destroy my relationship with my spouse and children, as well as damage my reputation and discredit my ministry (1 Corinthians 6:18).

2. I will not degrade this person but will treat her or him with dignity and honor. I will treat her or him as a subject, not an object; she or he has been created in the image of God.

3. I will let the attractiveness direct me to praise for the greatness of her or his Creator. (This is a kind of "spiritual judo" in which you use quick movement and leverage to throw your opponent; in this case, you redirect the incoming force from temptation to praise.)

4. I am no longer under the power of sin, but I am alive to God in Christ Jesus (Romans 6:11). I am not a skin-wrapped package of glands but a new creation in Christ (2 Corinthians 5:17).

5. I will walk by the Spirit and not carry out the desire of the flesh (Galatians 5:16; 2 Timothy 2:22).

6. I will fix my eyes on Jesus, the Author and Perfecter of faith (Hebrews 12:2).

Temptation to Covet

1. This is sin. "You shall not covet" (Exodus 20:17).

2. I do not want to sin. Sin is beneath the dignity of the person I have become in Christ Jesus (Ephesians 2:4–7).

3. I do not have to sin. I am no longer under the power of sin, but I am alive to God in Christ Jesus (Romans 6:11; 8:12–14).

4. Then why am I tempted to covet? Because I am not content with what I have.

5. My lack of contentment stems from comparison with other people. (There will always be people who have better possessions, positions, marriages, children, or ministries than I have. The more I focus on this, the more I can be consumed by jealousy, envy, and resentment.)

6. I will take my eyes off other people's possessions and fix my eyes on Jesus, the Author and Perfecter of faith (Hebrews 12:2).

7. God is in control and has my best interests at heart (Romans 8:28). Therefore I will be content and thankful with what he gives me.

Because each person has a unique "flesh signature" (people are tempted in differing ways and degrees), you can adapt these affirmation structures to other areas of temptation. It is wise to name honestly and specifically any besetting sins you regularly encounter so that you are better prepared to respond to temptations in these areas. The time-honored list of the seven deadly sins can be a useful diagnostic tool: pride, envy, anger, sloth, greed, gluttony, and lust. Pride, with its self-inflation, debasement of others, personal ambition, presumption, and vanity is the cardinal sin from which the other sins proceed. Thus the prayerful pursuit of humility is critical to spiritual progress and victory in the warfare with the flesh. Biblically speaking, humility relates to a growing awareness before God that apart from him, we are nothing and can accomplish nothing of lasting value; all things are "from Him and through Him and to Him" (Romans 11:36). Proverbs 3:5–7 is apropos here, particularly the exhortation in verse 7, "Do not be wise in your own eyes; fear the LORD and turn away from evil."

WARFARE WITH THE WORLD

The section on paradigm spirituality relates to the warfare with the world, so the following material on this aspect of spiritual warfare will be brief.

There are three New Testament words for "world," and each is used in different ways. Notice how the major word, *kosmos*, is used in these three verses.

For God so loved the world, that He gave His only begotten Son, that whoever believes in Him shall not perish, but have eternal life.

John 3:16

If you were of the world, the world would love its own; but because you are not of the world, but I chose you out of the world, because of this the world hates you.

John 15:19

Do not love the world nor the things in the world. If anyone loves the world, the love of the Father is not in him.

1 John 2:15

In the first of these verses, "world" refers to people, the objects of God's love. But in the other two verses, the world is our enemy. In these contexts, it is the organized system of temporal values that are opposed to the life of Christ in the believer. In *The Adversary*, Mark Bubeck defines the world as "a composite expression of the depravity of man and the intrigues of Satan's rule, combining in opposition to the sovereign rule of God." As such, the world promotes an attitude of independence from God.

Ephesians 2:1–3 reveals the interrelationship of the three fronts of the world, the flesh, and the devil: "And you were dead in your trespasses and sins, in which you formerly walked according to the course of this world, according to the prince of the power of the air, of the spirit that is now working in the sons of disobedience. Among them we too all formerly lived in the lusts of our flesh, indulging the desires of the flesh and of the mind, and were by nature children of wrath, even as the rest."

The world system aggravates the battle with the flesh by promoting and providing opportunities for indulging the deeds of the flesh (Galatians 5:19–21). The world in turn is shaped by the manifestations of the flesh and by the satanic warfare against the plans of God. "For all that is in the world, the lust of the flesh and the lust of the eyes and the boastful pride of life, is not from the Father, but is from the world" (1 John 2:16). Moreover, the "prince of the power of the air" (Ephesians 2:2) is the "ruler of this world" (John 12:31), and "the whole world lies in the power of the evil one" (1 John 5:19).

Of the three forces, the world may be the most neglected. Yet it is a powerful force that has programmed much of our thinking from the moment of birth. The world is an enticing magnet that constantly lures us to conform to its standards. It tempts us to seek the approval and plaudits of people rather than God. It pulls us into greater involvement with the temporal value system with its quest for wealth, power, prestige, position, and popularity and draws us away from the eternal value system revealed in Scripture. Worldliness is not merely a matter of questionable activities. It is also a heart attitude. When Christians are in bondage to "the elementary principles of the world" (Colossians 2:8), they cannot enjoy the freedom and victory that is in Christ.

As citizens of heaven and pilgrims on this planet, we experience a constant tension between the temporal and the eternal arenas. We are called to be in the world but not of it; we must walk in the world without being molded by it. The key to overcoming the values of the world is renewing the mind with the truths of Scripture. "And do not be conformed to this world, but be transformed by the renewing of your mind, so that you may prove what the will of God is, that which is good and acceptable and perfect" (Romans 12:2). We need to internalize biblical values through a daily program of reading, memorizing, meditating on and personalizing Scripture. This has a price: it takes time and discipline. But it is more than worth the cost, because nothing is more life changing. There is no greater step we can take in becoming overcomers in the spiritual warfare ("I have written to you, young men, because you are strong, and the word of God abides in you, and you have overcome the evil one" [1 John 2:14b]). Only in this way will the Word become the basis for our thinking. The mind is a battlefield on which two opposing world views, the material versus the spiritual, contend for our allegiance. John tells us that faith is "the victory that has overcome the world" (1 John 5:4), and our faith is proportionate to the degree to which we have assimilated God's truth. We must renew our minds with the reality of our union with Christ (Galatians 2:20; 6:14). Jesus has overcome the world (John 16:33) and its ruler (John 16:11; Colossians 2:15). His life secures our victory, and he is able to deliver us out of this present evil age (Galatians 1:4; Hebrews 2:14–15; 1 John 4:4).

Not all aspects of human cultures are opposed to the gospel; some are compatible (e.g., marital fidelity, love and care of children), some are neutral (e.g., food, dress, housing), and others are incompatible (e.g., religion and spiritualism). The gospel transcends temporal and cultural boundaries, so only the incompatible components of a culture need to be rejected and replaced. The problem is that many believers in different cultures have failed to make a clean break with cultural practices that are opposed to the lordship of Christ. The lure of syncretism causes believers in some parts of the world to hold on to their pre-Christian fear and obedience to the spirits ("those which by nature are no gods" [Galatians 4:8]). In the West, there is a growing movement among cultural Christians who have a low view of biblical authority to combine the gospel with beliefs from traditional religions or spirit magic. The powerful forces of cultural relativism, pluralism, secularization, pragmatism, naturalism, pantheism, and New Age syncretism are utterly incompatible with the biblical vision of truth and life in Christ. In addition, materialism is a growing entry point of demonic influence in the West.

It requires discipline and discernment to resist the temptation to conform to what others think and do (Romans 12:1–2). The pervasive influence of education, media, and entertainment seduces us to trivialize and condone many cultural expressions of sin. In the past, Christians had a way of externalizing worldliness by avoiding certain places, things, and activities. More recently, the tendency has been to go too far in the opposite direction because of a profound loss of discernment that embraces a mentality of consumerism and accumulation.

Since worldliness is both external and internal, we must cultivate a greater sense of detachment. We would do well to return to the ancient practice of meditating on the vanity of the world, the brevity of life, and the eternality of the life to come. It can be a painful process of surrender and renewal for us to wrench our hope and identity from that which is passing away and to transfer our hope and identity to the enduring promises of God. If we do not serve the Lord with a whole heart, we will serve the gods of this world; "choose for yourselves today whom you will serve" (Joshua 24:14–23). Scripture reminds us that the world with its threefold lust of the flesh, lust of the eyes, and pride of life is passing away (1 John 2:15–17; 1 Corinthians 7:29–31) and that friendship with the world is hostility toward God (James 4:4). There is no middle ground, no neutral territory. We must choose our master (Luke 16:13), and if it is the Lord Christ, it will require the great cost of denying ourselves, taking up our crosses, and following our Master wherever he commands us to go (Matthew 16:24–26). Part of this cost is that the world will hate Christ's close followers just as it hated him (John 15:18–21; 16:20; 17:14; 1 John 3:13). As we "keep seeking the things above, where Christ is" (Colossians 3:1), we will be able to use the world without being used by it.

As an exercise, meditate on the following passages to see how they relate to our conflict with the world system: Luke 9:23–25; John 15:18–19; 17:14–17; 2 Corinthians 4:17–18; 5:7; 10:3–5; Philippians 4:8; Colossians 2:8; 3:1–4.

QUESTIONS FOR PERSONAL APPLICATION

- How has your culture and world view influenced your understanding of the middle realm of angelic and demonic spiritual powers?
- What is your understanding of the present cosmic-earthly conflict?
- How would you describe your own warfare on the three fronts of the world, the flesh, and the devil?
- What resources do you use in the warfare with the flesh? Can you identify your unique flesh signature? Try adapting the affirmation structures that were presented in this chapter to your own areas of temptation.
- What resources do you use in the warfare with the world? In what ways have your mind, emotions, and will been influenced by the lures of wealth, power, prestige, position, popularity, and pleasure?

28

WARFARE SPIRITUALITY
Warfare with the Devil and His Angels

CHAPTER OVERVIEW

This chapter develops the third front of the spiritual warfare with Satan and his demonic hosts. It outlines the nature and work of Satan and of demons, looks at degrees, symptoms, and causes of demonic activity, and discusses deliverance from demonic activity.

CHAPTER OBJECTIVES

- A more biblical grasp of the nature and work of our spiritual adversaries
- A more practical understanding of demonic activity and of resources for deliverance

"Finally, be strong in the Lord and in the strength of His might. Put on the full armor of God, so that you will be able to stand firm against the schemes of the devil. For our struggle is not against flesh and blood, but against the rulers, against the powers, against the world forces of this darkness, against the spiritual forces of wickedness in the heavenly places. Therefore, take up the full armor of God, so that you will be able to resist in the evil day, and having done everything, to stand firm" (Ephesians 6:10–13).

Recent years have seen the appearance of a wealth of literature that stresses this theme. A few representative works are Merrill F. Unger, *Biblical Demonology, Demons in the World Today,* and *What Demons Can Do to Saints*; Kurt Koch, *Occult Bondage and Deliverance*; Jessie Penn-Lewis with Evan Roberts, *War on the Saints*; Mark I. Bubeck, *The Adversary* and *Overcoming the Adversary*; C. Fred Dickason, *Angels, Elect and Evil*; Neil T. Anderson, *The Bondage Breaker* and *Victory Over the Darkness*; Michael Green, *Exposing the Prince of Darkness*; C. Peter Wagner, *Engaging the Enemy* and *Warfare Prayer*; Victor M. Matthews, *Spiritual Warfare*; George Otis Jr., *The Twilight Labyrinth*; Charles H. Kraft, *Christianity with Power, Defeating Dark Angels,* and *Behind Enemy Lines*; Thomas B. White, *The Believer's Guide to Spiritual Warfare,* and David

Powlison, *Power Encounters*. Three of the most helpful books on warfare spirituality are Gregory A. Boyd, *God at War*; Ed Murphy, *The Handbook for Spiritual Warfare*; and Clinton E. Arnold, *Three Crucial Questions about Spiritual Warfare*.

As members of the body of Christ, we play a crucial role in a universal conflict with "spiritual forces of wickedness in the heavenly places." The "schemes of the devil" involve a highly organized structure that is constantly waging war on believers. Satan's invisible army consists of vast numbers of spiritual beings in a hierarchy of rulers, powers, world rulers, and spirit forces. Unlike David, we may have few human enemies, but his experiences in the Psalms are relevant to us because our spiritual enemies abound.

The New Testament exhorts us to realize that a war is going on, to recognize the strategies of the enemy, and to know how to fight. Of late there has been a renewed awareness of the need to be aggressive in the spiritual warfare, and this is particularly true of many who are active in Spirit-filled spirituality. But there is still a widespread problem of passivity. Too many believers are either skeptical or naïve regarding the reality of satanic and demonic activity in the lives of believers.

The two extremes of morbid fascination and fear are even worse. Some people become obsessed with the subject, studying and thinking more about demons than about Christ. Others become fearful, convincing themselves that they are defeated. Instead of claiming the truths of Scripture, they have been misled by experiences of failure into feeling or thinking that Satan is invincible and that they can do nothing to be overcomers. Fear is the opposite of faith, and it leads to defeat. Satan's primary target of attack is the mind (2 Corinthians 4:4; 10:3–6; 11:3). As children of God, we have been given authority, power, and victory in Christ. But it is our responsibility to claim aggressively the truth of Scripture regardless of our feelings and to stand firm in the fact that we are dead to the dominion of sin and Satan in our lives (Romans 6:12–14). We cannot hope to face spiritual powers in our own strength. Christ alone is invincible, and "we overwhelmingly conquer through Him who loved us" (Romans 8:37). He is able to preserve us complete until his coming, to equip us in every good thing to do his will, and to keep us from stumbling (1 Thessalonians 5:23–24; Hebrews 13:20–21; Jude 24). "Submit therefore to God. Resist the devil and he will flee from you" (James 4:7).

THE NATURE AND WORK OF SATAN

Both the Old and New Testaments repeatedly acknowledge the existence of Satan. Scripture teaches that he is a personal being who possesses intellect, emotion, and will (Zechariah 3:1–2; Luke 4:1–13; 2 Corinthians 11:3; Revelation 20:7–8). He was created by God as an angel (Isaiah 14:12–13; Matthew 25:41; Revelation 12:9), and as "the anointed cherub," he was originally perfect in beauty and blameless in his ways until his rebellion against God (Ezekiel 28:12–15). He is evidently the most powerful creature God ever made (Jude 9). His heart was lifted up because of his beauty; his splendor corrupted his wisdom, and he raised himself up against God in an act of titanic self-assertion (Ezekiel 28:16–17; Isaiah 14:12–15; these prophetic passages refer to historical characters, but it appears that the poetry also uses these figures to allude to a cosmic dimension of spiritual evil).

Because of his rebellion, Satan's character was distorted, and he became a powerful force of evil in the universe. He has dominion over a vast army of fallen angels and rules over the world system. His titles and names reveal his position, power, and practices.

Names That Reveal His Position and Power

- The ruler of this world (John 12:31; 16:11)—he is the prince of the world system.
- The prince of the power of the air (Ephesians 2:2)—his forces surround the earth.
- The god of this age (2 Corinthians 4:4)—he influences the changing philosophies and politics of this planet.
- The ruler of the demons (Matthew 12:24; Luke 11:15)—he leads a host of demonic forces.
- Lucifer (Isaiah 14:12; cf. 2 Corinthians 11:14)—he was a light bearer in his original state, and since his fall, he disguises himself as an angel of light.
- The serpent of old (Revelation 12:9)—he has been at work since the beginning of human history.
- The great dragon (Revelation 12:3–4, 7, 9)—he is a fierce and destructive enemy.

Names That Reveal His Practices

- Satan, or adversary (Zechariah 3:1; Luke 22:3; 1 Peter 5:8)—he is a relentless opponent of believers.
- Devil, or slanderer (Luke 4:2; 1 Peter 5:8; Revelation 12:9)—he works to defame God and his children.
- The evil one (John 17:15; 1 John 5:18)—he is completely corrupt.
- The destroyer (Revelation 9:11)—he seeks to destroy physical and spiritual life.
- The tempter (Matthew 4:3; 1 Thessalonians 3:5)—he entices people to do evil.
- The accuser (Revelation 12:10)—he accuses us before God and works to make us condemn ourselves.
- The deceiver (Revelation 12:9; 20:3)—he promotes false philosophies and spiritual counterfeits.
- A murderer (John 8:44)—he seeks the death of his victims.
- A liar, and the father of lies (John 8:44)—his promises and enticements are false.

No believer can afford to ignore the activities of so powerful an adversary. The devil's work is strategic and far-reaching. His schemes and methods (2 Corinthians 2:11; Ephesians 6:11) are subtle and shrewd. One of the crucial warfare strategies of the devil and his demonic forces is camouflage, concealment, illusion, deception, and delusion.

His Program Against All Humanity

- He opposes the person and program of God. It is his desire to make himself "like the Most High" (Isaiah 14:14). Thus he seeks the worship and service that God alone deserves.
- He conceals his identity by disguising himself as an angel of light and counterfeiting the truth (2 Corinthians 11:13–15). He offers good things but through the wrong means and for the wrong reasons (Matthew 4:3–10).
- He deceives the nations (Revelation 20:3) and influences governments to hinder the spread of the gospel.
- He works against the unsaved by taking away the word from their hearts (Luke 8:12) and blinding their minds to the gospel (2 Corinthians 4:3–4).
- He inspires spiritual counterfeits—false religions and false prophets (1 John 2:18, 22; 4:3).
- He promotes the pursuit of the occult for hidden knowledge and power (Deuteronomy 18:9–13).
- He implants wicked thoughts and plans into people's minds (John 13:2; Acts 5:3).
- He can inflict disease and death (Job 2:1–7; Acts 10:38; Hebrews 2:14).

His Program Against Believers

- He seeks to destroy the reputations and ministries of believers (Luke 22:31; 1 Timothy 3:7). If he cannot directly defeat a Christian's ministry, he may seek to do it indirectly by attacking a loved one.
- He incites the persecution of the saints (Revelation 2:10).
- He hinders the plans of believers (1 Thessalonians 2:18).
- He attempts to make Christians doubt God's love; he seeks to slander God and cause people to question God's goodness (Genesis 3:1–5).
- He accuses believers before God (Revelation 12:10).
- He heaps guilt and self-condemnation upon Christians because of their sins and makes them believe the lie that they must pay for them.
- He promotes a neglect of confession of sin (Ephesians 4:26–27) and defeats Christians by making them feel that God would not forgive them because they have committed the same sin so many times before.
- He encourages believers to rely on their own strength by making plans and acting independently of God (2 Chronicles 16:7–10).

- He tempts Christians on several fronts: lying (Acts 5:3), sexual sins (1 Corinthians 7:5), unforgiveness (2 Corinthians 2:10–11), pride and self-exaltation (1 Timothy 3:6), discouragement (1 Peter 5:6–10), and worldly preoccupation (1 John 2:15–17; 5:19).

THE NATURE AND WORK OF DEMONS

The Bible amply supports the existence of demons. They are mentioned in the Old Testament (Leviticus 17:7; Deuteronomy 32:17; Psalm 106:37) and in the teaching of Christ and the apostles (Mark 1:23–27; 1 Timothy 4:1; 2 Peter 2:4). In the Gospels, demons are called "unclean spirits" (Mark 7:25–26) and "evil spirits" (Luke 8:2) as well as the angels of the devil (Matthew 25:41). The word for "demon" (*daimonion*) does not mean "devil." That word comes from *diabolos*, or "slanderer," a name for Satan. Evidently, demons are the angelic beings who joined with Satan in his rebellion against God (Matthew 25:41; Jude 6; Revelation 12:4). Satan is the "ruler of the demons" (Matthew 12:24), and they are organized to accomplish his plan of overthrowing the kingdom of God (Ephesians 6:11–12; Revelation 12:7).

Like Satan, demons are personal beings; they are not superstitions, impersonal forces, or psychological states. They have intelligence (Mark 1:23–24; Luke 8:27–33), emotion (Luke 8:28; James 2:19), and volition (Matthew 12:44; Luke 8:32). They differ in rank and power (Ephesians 6:12) and also in degree of wickedness (Matthew 12:45). Some demons appear to produce foolishness and nonsense; others seek to degrade and destroy.

Properties of Demons

- They are depraved in their persons and work. In their fallen state, demons are twisted and perverse. They are creatures of darkness, bitterly opposed to the holy character of God.
- They are spirit beings (Matthew 8:16; Luke 10:17, 20). They are not limited by normal physical barriers (e.g., a legion of demons in one man [Luke 8:30]). Demons are incorporeal, but as creatures, they are finite and limited (Matthew 12:43).
- They are invisible but capable of manifesting themselves (Revelation 9:7–10; 16:13–14).
- They have the power of speech through the people they inhabit (Mark 1:24).
- They possess superhuman intelligence. They knew the true identity of Christ (Mark 1:24, 34; 5:7) and enabled a girl to predict future events (Acts 16:16).
- They have supernatural power. Demons can physically overpower and afflict humans (Matthew 8:28; Acts 19:13–16). They can also afflict the mind and emotions.

Program of Demons

- They obey Satan (Matthew 12:24; Revelation 12:7) and greatly extend his power and influence on people, nations, and the world system (Daniel 10:13, 20; John 12:31; Ephesians 2:2; 1 John 5:19).
- They induce physical and mental ailments (Matthew 12:22; Mark 9:17–29; Luke 8:27–33; 2 Corinthians 12:7). For example, Jesus cast out a spirit of infirmity, a deaf spirit, a blind spirit, and a mute spirit.
- They promote idolatry (Leviticus 17:7; Deuteronomy 32:17; Psalm 96:5).
- They seek to enslave people to the occult. This includes spiritism, foretelling the future, physical and psychic phenomena, magic, and witchcraft (Leviticus 19:31; Deuteronomy 18:9–12; Acts 13:6–11).
- They support temporal value systems and philosophies (2 Corinthians 10:3–5).
- They encourage lawlessness, immorality, and rebellion among people (2 Thessalonians 2:3–4, 7). Like their master, demons try to steal, kill, and destroy.
- They pervert the gospel of grace (1 Timothy 4:1–3; Colossians 2:18).
- They inspire false teachers and spiritual counterfeits (2 Corinthians 11:13–15; 2 Peter 2:1–2; 1 John 4:1–4). They are part of the dynamic behind pagan religions and pseudo-Christian cults.
- They oppose believers and seek to defeat their spiritual life (Ephesians 6:10–11). Demons are active in promoting strife, jealousy, selfish ambition, and divisions in the church (1 Timothy 4:1–3; 2 Timothy 3:1–8; James 3:14–16). The devil and his demons seek to hold us captive to do their will (2 Timothy 2:26).

Degrees of Demonic Activity

To deny the existence and influence of demons would be to ignore or mythologize the many gospel accounts of Christ's ministry of delivering people from demonic bondage. These were more than psychological delusions or hallucinations. From the first-century church in the book of Acts to the present there have been clear evidences of demonic oppression and control.

The Bible does not use the term "demon possession." The usual expression is that a person "has" a demon or an unclean spirit. The Greek word *daimonizomenoi* means "to be demonized." This term allows for different degrees of demonization, ranging from influence to oppression to control.

Influence. All Christians are targets for the forces of Satan. They can assault us on the physical and psychological levels, working to corrupt our lives and defeat our ministries. Demons seek to plant thoughts into our minds, influence our emotions, and weaken our wills. They inject deceptive, accusing, and condemning thoughts and attitudes that are opposed to the truth of Scripture (2 Corinthians 10:3–6; 11:3). Satanic powers are constantly active in tempting and enticing believers (1 Corinthians 7:5; 12:2–3; 1 Timothy 5:14–15). They may throw obstacles in our path to thwart our growth and the progress of the gospel (1 Thessalonians 2:18; Romans 15:22). Demonic activity on this level can lead to apostasy and doctrinal corruption (1 Timothy 4:1–3).

Jesus' rebuke of Peter in Matthew 16:22–23 illustrates at least the first degree of influence by satanic forces in the life of a believer. On this level, the attack is from the outside, but it can be intense. Nevertheless, demons cannot defeat any part of a believer's life that is yielded to the Holy Spirit. If one has not allowed the powers of darkness to build a stronghold in his or her life, the attacks can go no further.

Oppression. Just as there are different degrees to which a Christian can be yielded to God and empowered by the Spirit, so there are varying degrees of bondage to demonic powers. Christians as well as non-Christians may be harassed, oppressed, depressed, and tormented by unclean spirits. When believers give in to demonic suggestions and temptations, this can lead to levels of attack that are more intense than influence.

Demonic oppression is characterized by obsessive thoughts and behavior. During times of intense attack, the whole personality may be distorted and enslaved to irrational impulses, black moods, uncontrollable anger, and compulsive lying.

Demonization moves from the external to the internal when the body and personality are invaded by one or more wicked spirits. The story of Ananias and Sapphira illustrates this internal influence by satanic forces. "But Peter said, 'Ananias, why has Satan filled your heart to lie to the Holy Spirit and to keep back some of the price of the land?'" (Acts 5:3). Unrighteous anger and rage can be another entry point: "Be angry, and yet do not sin; do not let the sun go down on your anger, and do not give the devil an opportunity" (Ephesians 4:26–27).

Control. The most severe degree of demonic activity is the domination of the mind, speech, and behavior. In this condition, the victim is subject to episodes of control by the inhabiting demon(s) who change the personality and use the body as a vehicle. When they speak through someone, they refer to him or her in the third person.

Demonic control can be willing (e.g., seances, channeling, witchcraft) or unwilling (e.g., transference through bloodlines). Demonization may contribute to mental illness, but the two should be distinguished. Mental distress can be due to a variety of causes, including brain chemistry, emotional trauma, depressive illness, persistent guilt, obsession with evil, and conscious disobedience to the Word. This is why it is wise to practice discernment before engaging in ministry, particularly in the case of deliverance ministry.

Can a Christian be demonically controlled? This is a debated issue. Some writers argue that the personal indwelling of the Holy Spirit (John 14:17; Romans 8:9; 1 Corinthians 6:19–20) prohibits the invasion of demons in a believer's body. But the indwelling

Spirit does not exclude the presence of evil within the saint, because the flesh, or power of sin in our members, is very real (Romans 7:15–24; Galatians 5:16–17). The Bible does not teach that Christians are immune to demonic entry, and it is clear from the experience of many missionaries and counselors that believers can be internally oppressed. However, this is not the same as what is popularly called possession, in which a person is fully controlled or owned by demonic forces.

The Holy Spirit indwells the Christian on a deeper level than any wicked spirit can reach. However, the practice of habitual sin could give demons ground for invading a believer's body and psyche (mind, emotions, and will). A demon may try to get others to move in to increase their dominion over aspects of the personality. As they influence one's thinking, feeling, and choosing, it may be difficult to distinguish one's own thoughts and impulses from theirs. But demons are temporary intruders whose domination can be overcome when their ground for staying is removed.

Symptoms of Demonic Activity

How can we discern whether a problem is caused by the flesh, the world, or the devil? A host of physical and psychological disorders can be organically caused (e.g., severe allergies and hypoglycemia), and it is wise to consider this possibility first. A physical examination may reveal a condition that can be treated by diet or medication.

Most problems are caused by walking in the flesh (recall the list of fleshly sins in the last chapter). It is foolish to suppose we are pawns in the warfare when we are responsible for the choice to sin or obey God. Many things we blame on the world and Satan are the results of fleshly indulgence. But by giving in to the power of sin in our members and to the temptations of the world, we can open the door to demonic bondage. If we gain no victory after actively seeking to appropriate our resources in Christ, confessing our sins, and renewing our minds, we should ask for spiritual discernment and consider the possibility of demonic influence.

Remember the importance of avoiding the first extreme of ignoring the biblical teaching about the reality of demonization and the second extreme of attributing every problem and temptation to demons. The common symptoms in the following list are only indicators of *possible* demonic activity. Do not look at them in isolation, for they could also be caused by physical, psychological, or spiritual problems. But the evidence of demonization may be more significant if several are present at once.

- Self-destructive, suicidal, or murderous thoughts
- Uncontrollable anger or fits of rage and violence
- Compulsive cursing and blasphemy
- Strong aversion to the name of Jesus, Bible reading, or prayer
- Profound depression, gloom, or despair

- Intense and irrational bitterness and hatred
- Obsessive temptations or excessive cravings
- Overwhelming feelings of guilt and self-reproach
- Inability to renounce a dominating sin
- Sudden and unaccountable physical symptoms (e.g., pressure, choking, seizures, spells of unconsciousness)
- Uncontrollable fear or dread
- Recurring nightmares
- Supernatural knowledge; clairvoyant or mediumistic powers
- Rapid changes and distortions of facial expressions or voice
- Multiple personality disorders
- Unnatural physical strength
- Poltergeist phenomena and apparitions

This is not a complete list. By themselves, none of these symptoms indicate demonic activity. We must avoid the "when in doubt cast it out" mentality of the self-appointed demon inspector.

Causes of Demonic Activity

Because we live in an increasingly immoral and godless society, the pressures and opportunities to conform are greater than ever. Television, radio, magazines, newspapers, films, and thousands of Internet sites are always ready to expose us to values, attitudes, and belief systems that distort our thinking and weaken our resolve. The flesh is the port of entry for the influences of the world and the devil. In most cases, demonization in the life of a Christian results from the repeated practice of sins in the mind or body (e.g., those listed in Mark 7:21–22 and Galatians 5:19–21).

When believers do not respond to the warnings of conscience and Scripture and to the conviction of the Holy Spirit, they are in bondage to the flesh. There is such an affinity between the deeds of the flesh and the powers of darkness that indulgence in the former can lead to enslavement by the latter. The Scriptures take a more serious view of sin than we usually think, since we actually forsake the Lord in the action of disobedience (2 Chronicles 24:20). It is dangerous to harbor unconfessed sin (see Psalm 32:1–6), since Christians who do not repent and renounce their sins cannot walk in victory. Instead, they are increasingly vulnerable to temptation; sinful thoughts and actions become obsessive and overpowering as their wills are gradually weakened. In this state, they continue to give up territory to the enemy and become more susceptible to demonic subjection. The forces of wickedness take the ground that is yielded to them by sin in the life of the believer. They will not retreat until their ground is renounced.

Becoming a Christian does not automatically overcome all the strongholds of the past. For example, the practice of occultism in any of its many forms often leads to a residual problem of demonization that must be confronted. Occultism is an abomination in the sight of God (Leviticus 20:6), and indulgence in such things as magic, astrology, Ouija boards, tarot cards, palmistry, spiritualism (spiritism), psychic phenomena, New Age techniques, and non-Christian religious practices is perilous.

Not all demonic strongholds are caused by sin in the life of the victim; some can be induced through childhood trauma such as sexual, physical, psychological, and religious abuse. In other cases demonization occurs as a result of spiritual heredity. Sins such as occultism, curses, and witchcraft in the lives of parents or grandparents can affect subsequent generations (this may have been the reason why the boy in Mark 9:17–29 was demonized since childhood). After prohibiting idolatry, the Lord declared, "I, the LORD your God, am a jealous God, visiting the iniquity of the fathers on the children, on the third and the fourth generations of those who hate Me" (Exodus 20:5).

Deliverance from Demonic Activity

It is foolish to ignore the methods and power of the enemy. This makes our families and us vulnerable while Satan and his forces work unnoticed and unchallenged. Many overlook the fact that about 25 percent of Jesus' ministry as recorded in the Gospels involved deliverance from demonic affliction. The forces of evil did not disappear when Jesus left the earth.

Believers need to learn how to pull down strongholds (2 Corinthians 10:4), wrestle against principalities and powers (Ephesians 6:12), and resist the devil (James 4:7). Merrill F. Unger noted in *What Demons Can Do to Saints* that the Christian's armor is for external, not internal, foes. "But if the Christian fails to use his armor, will the foe stop short of invading the believer's citadel? If he does invade, this is precisely why the believer may become enslaved and need to call on Christian warriors to come to his rescue in prayer battle if he ever is to be delivered from Satan's snare into which he has been 'taken captive by him at his will' (2 Timothy 2:26)."

We must recognize that we have been given authority and victory in the spiritual warfare (Matthew 10:1; Luke 9:1; 10:19). As C. Fred Dickason observes in *Angels, Elect and Evil,* "The apostles and their followers cast out demons in their day (Acts 5:16; 16:16–18), and Paul states that Christians have all they need to wage warfare against Satan (Ephesians 6:10–18). Though we have no resources of our own, we have all we need in Christ by virtue of our union with Him (Colossians 2:9–15)." Because of the cross, Satan is a defeated foe (John 12:31). Christ has "disarmed the rulers and authorities" (Colossians 2:15) and is exalted "far above all rule and authority and power and dominion" (Ephesians 1:21; Philippians 2:9–11; 1 Peter 3:22). Furthermore, as believers in Christ, we have been raised with him and seated with him in the heavenly places (Ephesians 2:6). The Lord "rescued us from the domain of darkness, and transferred us to the kingdom of His beloved Son" (Colossians 1:13). In our new position, we have authority in Christ and power in the Spirit.

The problem is that many believers do not exercise their authority, and this is what the forces of darkness count on. We must not only know that we have been liberated from the authority of the devil through the blood of Jesus Christ; we must also act upon this fact.

If symptoms of demonic activity continue after using the biblical resources for dealing with the flesh, a direct confrontation with the forces of darkness may be necessary. Again, demonic influence is only one of several possible causes of physical and mental illness, and we should be careful not to overemphasize it or jump too quickly to conclusions.

There are certain conditions for deliverance from demonic influence or oppression.

Salvation. Without Christ, there is no hope of victory over the powers of evil. Only through the Son of God can you be set free from the bondage of sin and Satan (John 8:36). You must affirm your faith in Jesus Christ.

Willingness. You must desire to be set free. If symptoms continue after dealing with the flesh, you must be willing to admit the possibility of demonic activity.

Confession. Believers who fail to acknowledge their sins cut themselves off from fellowship with God and become vulnerable to satanic attack. Restoration of fellowship requires repentance, because sin is rebellion against the holy God (Matthew 3:8; James 4:8–9). You must honestly examine yourself and confess any known sins of thought, word, or deed (Psalm 32:5; 139:23–24; 1 Corinthians 11:31; 1 John 1:9). In this way, you reclaim ground that you have yielded to the adversary (Ephesians 4:27). Confession should be as specific as possible, especially when it relates to sins of involvement with the occult. Ask the Lord to bring such sins in your past to light.

Renunciation. You must renounce Satan and make a clean break from his works (2 Corinthians 4:2). Verbally break any curses or connections with the sins of previous generations in your family, particularly in the area of the occult and false religions (Exodus 20:3–5). Renounce any contacts with mediums and destroy any occult paraphernalia (horoscopes, Ouija boards, magic books, tarot cards; see Acts 19:18–19).

Forgiveness. You must be willing to forgive all who have wronged you (Matthew 6:14–15; 18:21–35). Ask the Lord to show you any areas of unforgiveness, and ask for his grace and enabling to forgive yourself and others. Only in this way will you be free from the root of bitterness with its hatred, resentment, and anger that can become territory for demonic strongholds. It may be necessary to reconcile the past by inviting God to expose hidden areas of pain, injustice, rejection, and abuse in light of his presence and truth. As Leanne Payne observes in *The Healing Presence* and *Restoring the Christian Soul*, this need for inner healing, or healing of the emotions, can be directly related to spiritual warfare. Inner healing is best accomplished in the presence of believers who are skilled in this area of ministry.

Submission to God. You must humble yourself before God and acknowledge your complete dependence upon him. "But He gives a greater grace. Therefore it says, 'God is opposed to the proud, but gives grace to the humble.' Submit therefore to God. Resist the devil and he will flee from you" (James 4:6–7). You cannot have victory over Satan without first submitting yourself to the person and will of God (Romans 12:1–2).

Resistance. When the conditions of salvation, confession, renunciation, forgiveness, and submission to God are met, the devil and his demons have no legal right to harass you. Use the authority you have been given in Christ and stand firm against the powers of evil. Persistence in calling upon the Lord will break through spiritual strongholds. "Be of sober spirit, be on the alert. Your adversary, the devil, prowls about like a roaring lion, seeking someone to devour. But resist him, firm in your faith" (1 Peter 5:8–9a).

If spirits of wickedness have gained a beachhead in your life, you may need to confront them directly. In the name of Jesus (Mark 16:17; Luke 10:17; Acts 16:18; Philippians 2:9–10) and in dependence upon the power of the Holy Spirit (Matthew 12:28), command them to leave. In cases of severe oppression, the assistance of other believers who are skilled in this area of ministry may be necessary to combat the forces of darkness.

QUESTIONS FOR PERSONAL APPLICATION

- In your experience regarding negative spiritual forces, have you leaned more toward the direction of skepticism/indifference or toward the direction of fascination/fear? What can you do to sustain a biblical balance?
- What is your level of awareness of the work of Satan and of demons? To what degree does this affect your journey in spiritual formation?
- Have you encountered evident demonization in your life or in other people?
- The seven conditions of salvation, willingness, confession, renunciation, forgiveness, submission to God, and resistance are beneficial even when demonic activity is not evident. Try going through these seven elements in your next time of prayer.

29

WARFARE SPIRITUALITY
The Weapons of Our Warfare

CHAPTER OVERVIEW

This chapter completes the section on warfare spirituality with a positive look at the resources God has provided for us to prevail in the triple warfare with the world, the flesh, and the devil. In addition to the armor of God, twelve other resources are listed, and the chapter concludes with the need for balance and discernment in the warfare, the work of God's elect angels, and the future of the warfare on the three fronts.

CHAPTER OBJECTIVES

- A renewed appreciation for the armor of truth, righteousness, peace, faith, salvation, the Word, and prayer
- An awareness of resources that are at our disposal for waging spiritual warfare against the world, the flesh, and the devil

For though we walk in the flesh, we do not war according to the flesh,
for the weapons of our warfare are not of the flesh,
but divinely powerful for the destruction of fortresses.
2 CORINTHIANS 10:3–4

The spiritual warfare is an ongoing process; though they vary in intensity, battles take place every day. The experience of the conflict often increases when believers get serious about walking with the Lord. This is why it is important for us to grow and mature in areas in which we have experienced healing and deliverance. Because our adversary is relentless, Scripture exhorts us to "be strong in the Lord, and in the strength of His might" (Ephesians 6:10). We need to be prepared for sudden skirmishes by wielding the weapons God has provided for our victory.

This requires discipline and dependence; the spiritual life is both a three-front battle and a faith rest in God's promises. On the side of *discipline,* Jesus tells us to deny ourselves, take up his cross daily, and follow him (Luke 9:23). We are no longer under the dominion of the flesh; through Christ we can crucify the flesh with its passions and desires (Galatians 5:24). Yielding to fleshly appetites and becoming comfortable with things God detests (Galatians 5:19–21) leads to spiritual vulnerability.

On the side of *dependence*, God wants us to walk not in our own strength but in the power of his Spirit. "If we live by the Spirit, let us also walk by the Spirit" (Galatians 5:25). Too many believers regard the Spirit-filled life as an option. The fullness of the Spirit is essential for genuine victory and ministry (Ephesians 5:18). Unconfessed sin grieves and quenches the Spirit (Ephesians 4:30; 1 Thessalonians 5:19). We must acknowledge our sins of relying on our own effort and yield all areas of our lives to God (Romans 6:13, 19). As we depend upon the Spirit for guidance and empowering, Christ is glorified in our lives.

THE ARMOR OF GOD

Paul exhorts us to "put on the full armor of God" so that we can "stand firm against the schemes of the devil" (Ephesians 6:11). This metaphor makes it clear that the spiritual warfare is proactive; we must be prepared, ready to resist, and empowered to advance into enemy territory. Christ is the Victor who calls us to stand on the ground he has won through his blood. As long as we are prepared for battle, we need not retreat before any intruder. It is wise to pray on the armor of God each morning, because without it we are open to attack. The prayers in Mark Bubeck's *The Adversary* and *Overcoming the Adversary* are excellent for this purpose. This is particularly important for people who have introspective and passive personalities, since they can be more susceptible in the warfare if they do not develop the discipline of the active stance upon the truth of Christ's authority.

As we have seen, the key to warfare with the flesh is reckoning; the key to warfare with the world is renewing; and the key to warfare with the devil is resisting. The spiritual armor in Ephesians 6:14–18 relates to our victory over all three of these forces.

The Belt of Truth

The Roman soldier's belt was used to hold his tunic and sword scabbard in place. Satan and his forces are deceivers, and the belt of biblical truth will defend us against their lies. The more we understand about the person of Christ and our invincible position in him, the more we will be able to stand firm in Christ's authority against the forces of evil. We should not fear the adversary, because we are more than conquerors in Christ. The Lord Jesus defeated Satan at Calvary, and we are united with him in his crucifixion, burial, resurrection, ascension, and reign. He has given us his life, and we are secure in him. As we focus on our in-Christ relationship and ask God to make it not merely a theology but a reality in our thinking and behavior, the Word of God will abide in us, and we will overcome the Evil One (1 John 2:14).

The Breastplate of Righteousness

A soldier's breastplate protected the vital organs that would otherwise be vulnerable. In the same way, we are vulnerable unless we are clothed with the righteousness of Christ. This righteousness was imputed to us, or placed on our account, the moment we trusted in Christ.

The Lord wants us to be righteous not only in our position but also in our practice. Paul tells us to "put on the breastplate of faith and love" (1 Thessalonians 5:8), and this is the outworking of righteousness in Christian conduct. We must be careful to walk in dependence on Christ's righteousness and not in our own goodness. When we fail, we need to deal promptly with sin in our lives and be quick to forgive those who sin against us so that we will not be victimized by unforgiveness, hate, bitterness, and resentment.

The Sandals of Peace

The soldier's sandals protected his feet and enabled him to hold his ground or move quickly because the soles were studded with hobnails. The "preparation of the gospel of peace" speaks of a readiness to enter the fray and share the only message that leads to peace with God (Romans 5:1). This peace with God (reconciliation) is the basis for the peace of God (Philippians 4:7) in the believer's experience. When we walk in fellowship with God by humbling ourselves and casting our anxieties upon him (1 Peter 5:6–7), we enjoy inner peace even in adversity (Romans 16:20).

We have fellowship with God by submitting to his purposes for our lives. Similarly, we have fellowship and peace with other believers when we are "subject to one another in the fear of Christ" (Ephesians 5:21). We need the strength that comes from the body of Christ; the sheep that wanders from the flock is the most assailable. Hebrews encourages us to "consider how to stimulate one another to love and good deeds, not forsaking our own assembling together" (Hebrews 10:24–25). This also involves submission to spiritual authority (Hebrews 13:17).

The Shield of Faith

The large oblong shields used by Roman soldiers interlocked and protected them from spears and flaming arrows. The Lord is our shield and protector in all circumstances; our faith should be in him, not our circumstances or efforts. As we trust in him, he becomes the source of our confidence and hope. Adopting a faith stance reveals Satan as a defeated foe and enables us to walk in the victory Christ has won for us. It is important that we be preoccupied with our Lord and keep our eyes on him, not the enemy. He calls us to submit to his sovereign purposes even when we are unable to understand our trials and afflictions. When we affirm his will and cling to Christ in times of adversity, the fruit of the Spirit comes forth. Total commitment means that God is the center of our existence, not our families, careers, or aspirations (Matthew 22:37; John 12:26).

The Helmet of Salvation

A wise soldier would not think of going into battle without headgear. As Christians, we should regularly cover and protect our minds by being conscious of our new position in Christ. This includes monitoring our thought lives by rejecting those things that are not of God (e.g., gossip, criticism, immoral thoughts, self-condemnation, fear), and dwelling on what is true, honorable, right, pure, lovely, of good repute, excellent, and worthy of praise (Philippians 4:8). This also means avoiding environments, television shows, films, Internet sites, and books that would distort our thinking or solicit us to evil.

In 1 Thessalonians 5:8, Paul describes the helmet as "the hope of salvation." When difficult times come, we should not focus on our feelings but stand by faith on the truth of God's goodness and love. We have a sure hope in Christ, and in him we can overcome the negative thoughts of hopelessness and despair that come from the enemy.

The Sword of the Spirit

This double-edged sword is the offensive weapon in the believer's armory. Wielding the weapon of Scripture, believers are to be aggressive combatants, not passive spectators. But a sword will do us little good if we are unskilled in its use. To be effective, we must gain facility in handling the Word so that we can apply it with wisdom to all circumstances. This requires the discipline of a daily investment of time in prayerful and expectant Bible reading. Our minds are renewed as we regularly memorize and meditate on the Word. In this way, we put on the mind of Christ.

During his temptation, Jesus used the Scriptures to combat the adversary (Luke 4:1–13). How can we expect to overcome temptations and obstacles if we fail to do the same? God's Word is a lamp (Psalm 119:105), a purifying agent (Psalm 119:11; Ephesians 5:26), a source of spiritual food (Matthew 4:4; 1 Peter 2:2), and a mirror for the soul (James 1:23–25). When we know and understand it, we will be able to use God's words to pierce through the lies and traps set by the enemy. We will also be able to discern "the spirit of truth and the spirit of error" (1 John 4:6).

Prayer and Petition

Like the Word, prayer is an offensive weapon that is available to every believer. Nothing accomplishes as much as prayer; it is the means by which we lay hold of our strength in the Lord. Through prayer we put on the armor of God and walk in the power of the Holy Spirit. Through praise and thanksgiving we silence the enemy and enter into God's presence (Psalm 100). This is the opposite of the grumbling and complaining that stems from an absence of faith.

We must persevere in prayer. The quality of our prayer life will determine the degree of our spiritual vitality. "Rejoice always; pray without ceasing; in everything give thanks; for this is God's will for you in Christ Jesus" (1 Thessalonians 5:16–18). Like Bible reading and study, endurance in prayer requires discipline: continuing to trust, laying hold of our position and God's promises, refusing to doubt or to be overcome by setbacks.

Paul tells us not only to pray for ourselves but also to intercede as prayer warriors on behalf of others as the Spirit directs (Ephesians 6:18–19).

OTHER RESOURCES

• It is easy to neglect the corporate dimension of the spiritual warfare, and this includes the fact that Paul portrays the armor of God in Ephesians 6 in collective terms. This spiritual equipment is designed for an army, not a group of isolated individuals. Thus the body of Christ works as a community of believers who use their spiritual gifts to worship, serve, witness, and fight together against a common enemy.

• Spiritual warfare is more than an encounter between truth and error; it involves both the proclamation of the truth and the demonstration of the power of the Holy Spirit (Luke 24:49; Acts 1:8; 1 Corinthians 2:4).

• Deliverance from spiritual strongholds can take place on a personal level, with the assistance of a brother or sister, on a pastoral level, or through those who have been called to a special ministry of discernment and deliverance.

• The ultimate source of victory over spiritual forces of wickedness in the heavenly places is the reality that Christ has already defeated Satan and his demons on the cross (Luke 10:18; John 12:31–32; 16:11).

• The Lord entrusts us with the resources of delegated authority and team ministry to equip us to overcome the opposition of the kingdom of darkness to the work of winning people to Christ and bringing them into the kingdom of God.

• Since the unredeemed are spiritually lost and under the rule of Satan, God has given us the powerful resource of intercession for the lost through the authority of the mighty name of the Lord Jesus.

• The renewed mind and the committed will are critical resources in the warfare. C. S. Lewis creatively illustrates the battle of the mind in *The Screwtape Letters*, and this perceptive work reminds us of the importance of the thought life. We would do well to monitor our thoughts in a specific and honest way, and one way to do this is to write a list of negative thoughts that regularly occur to us. I see no biblical evidence that the devil and demons can read our thoughts, but it does appear that they can enflame our minds with vain and false ideas. It is possible to be overscrupulous by failing to distinguish temptation from sin. But it is equally possible to overlook the distinction between involuntary and obsessive thoughts. The best way to overcome wrong and negative thinking is by practicing the skill of setting your mind on the Spirit (Romans 8:5–9) and on the truth (Philippians 4:8; Colossians 3:2).

• Concerning the will, the sequence in James 4:7 is significant: "Submit therefore to God. Resist the devil and he will flee from you." You cannot successfully resist Satan unless you have first submitted your will to God's plan and purpose for your life. When you choose to "draw near to God," he will "draw near to you" (James 4:8).

• Disciplined spirituality has a direct bearing on warfare spirituality. The spiritual disciplines of prayer, study (Scripture reading and memorization), meditation, fasting, confession, fellowship, and worship can be significant resources in the warfare against the flesh, the world, and the devil. Remember how Jesus used the Scriptures he had memorized to resist the temptations of the devil (Luke 4:2–13).

• Many people have found that the Daily Affirmation of Faith and the Warfare Prayer (composed by Victor M. Matthews in *Spiritual Warfare* and adapted by Mark Bubeck in *The Adversary* and Ed Murphy in *The Handbook for Spiritual Warfare*) to be potent resources for strength and renewal.

• St. Patrick's Breastplate is a time-tested prayer that has encouraged millions of believers through the centuries. Patrick, the great fifth-century missionary to Ireland, was inspired by the triune Godhead and the incarnation of Christ when he composed this prayer for spiritual protection:

> *I bind unto myself today the strong name of the Trinity,*
> > *By invocation of the same, the Three in One, and One in Three.*
> *I bind this day to me for ever, by power of faith,*
> > *Christ's Incarnation; His baptism in the Jordan river;*
>
> *His death on the cross for my salvation.*
> > *His bursting from the spiced tomb; His riding up the heav'nly way;*
> *His coming at the day of doom;*
> > *I bind unto myself today.*
>
> *I bind unto myself today the power of God to hold and lead,*
> > *His eye to watch, His might to stay, His ear hearken to my need;*
> *The wisdom of my God to teach, His hand to guide, His shield to ward,*
> > *The Word of God to give me speech, His heav'nly host to be my guard.*
>
> *Against all Satan's spells and wiles, against false words of heresy,*
> > *Against the knowledge that defiles, against the heart's idolatry,*
> *Against the wizard's evil craft, against the death-wound and the burning,*
> > *The choking wave, the poison'd shaft, protect me Christ, till Thy returning.*
>
> *Christ be with me, Christ within me, Christ behind me, Christ before me,*
> > *Christ beside me, Christ to win me, Christ to comfort and restore me,*

Christ beneath me, Christ above me, Christ in quiet, Christ in danger,
  Christ in hearts of all that love me, Christ in mouth of friend and stranger.

I bind unto myself the name, the strong name of the Trinity,
  By invocation of the same, the Three in One, and One in Three,
Of whom all nature hath creation, Eternal Father, Spirit, Word.
  Praise to the Lord of my salvation; salvation is of Christ my Lord.

• I created Morning Affirmations to help people renew their minds at the beginning of the day. These affirmations guide you through a biblical perspective on the fundamental issues of life: Who am I? Where did I come from? Why am I here? Where am I going? In this way, you review God's perspective on your faith, your identity, your purpose, and your hope. These affirmations can serve as a useful tool in the threefold spiritual warfare.

Morning Affirmations
1. Submitting to God
- Because of all you have done for me, I present my body to you as a living sacrifice for this day. I want to be transformed by the renewing of my mind, affirming that your will for me is good and acceptable and perfect (Romans 12:1–2).

2. Adoration and Thanksgiving
- Offer a brief word of praise to God for one or more of his *attributes* (e.g., love and compassion, grace, mercy, holiness, goodness, omnipotence, omnipresence, omniscience, truthfulness, unchanging character, eternality) and/or *works* (e.g., creation, care, redemption, loving purposes, second coming).
- Thank him for the good things in your life.

3. Examination
- Ask the Spirit to search your heart and reveal any areas of unconfessed sin. Acknowledge these to the Lord and thank him for his forgiveness (Psalm 139:23–24).

4. My Identity in Christ

- "I have been crucified with Christ; and it is no longer I who live, but Christ lives in me; and the life which I now live in the flesh I live by faith in the Son of God, who loved me, and delivered Himself up for me" (Galatians 2:20).
- I have *forgiveness* from the penalty of sin because Christ died for me (Romans 5:8; 1 Corinthians 15:3).
- I have *freedom* from the power of sin because I died with Christ (Colossians 2:11; 1 Peter 2:24).

- I have *fulfillment* for this day because Christ lives in me (Philippians 1:20–21).
- By *faith,* I will allow Christ to manifest his life through me (2 Corinthians 2:14).

5. Filling of the Spirit

- Ask the Spirit to control and fill you for this day.
- I want to be filled with the Spirit (Ephesians 5:18). When I walk by the Spirit, I will not carry out the desire of the flesh (Galatians 5:16). If I live by the Spirit, I will also walk by the Spirit (Galatians 5:25).

6. Fruit of the Spirit

- Pray on the fruit of the Spirit: love, joy, peace, patience, kindness, goodness, faithfulness, gentleness, self-control (Galatians 5:22–23).
- "Love is patient, love is kind, and is not jealous; love does not brag and is not arrogant, does not act unbecomingly; it does not seek its own, is not provoked, does not take into account a wrong suffered, does not rejoice in unrighteousness, but rejoices with the truth; bears all things, believes all things, hopes all things, endures all things" (1 Corinthians 13:4–7).

7. Purpose of My Life

- I want to love the Lord my God with all my heart, and with all my soul, and with all my mind, and I want to love my neighbor as myself (Matthew 22:37, 39). My purpose is to love God completely, love self correctly, and love others compassionately.
- I will seek first your kingdom and your righteousness (Matthew 6:33).
- I have been called to follow Christ and to be a fisher of men (Matthew 4:19).
- I will be a witness to those who do not know him and participate in the Great Commission to go and make disciples (Matthew 28:19–20; Acts 1:8).
- I want to glorify the Father by bearing much fruit, and so prove to be Christ's disciple (John 15:8).

8. Circumstances of the Day

- I will trust in the Lord with all my heart and not lean on my own understanding. In all my ways I will acknowledge him, and he will make my paths straight (Proverbs 3:5–6).
- "God causes all things to work together for good to those who love God, to those who are called according to His purpose" (Romans 8:28; also see 8:29).
- I acknowledge that you are in control of all things in my life and that you have my best interests at heart. Because of this I will trust and obey you today.
- Review and commit the events of this day into the hands of God.

9. Protection in the Warfare

Against the World: Renew

- I will set my mind on the things of the Spirit (Romans 8:5).
- Since I have been raised up with Christ, I will keep seeking the things above, where Christ is, seated at the right hand of God. I will set my mind on the things above, not on the things that are on earth (Colossians 3:1–2; also see 3:3–4; Hebrews 12:1–2).
- I will be anxious for nothing, but in everything by prayer and supplication with thanksgiving I will let my requests be made known to God. And the peace of God, which surpasses all comprehension, shall guard my heart and my mind in Christ Jesus. Whatever is true, whatever is honorable, whatever is right, whatever is pure, whatever is lovely, whatever is of good repute, if there is any excellence and if anything worthy of praise, I will let my mind dwell on these things (Philippians 4:6–8; also see 4:9).

Against the Flesh: Reckon

- I know that my old self was crucified with Christ, so that I am no longer a slave to sin, for he who has died is freed from sin. I will reckon myself as dead to sin but alive to God in Christ Jesus. I will not present the members of my body to sin as instruments of unrighteousness, but I will present myself to God as one alive from the dead, and my members as instruments of righteousness to God (Romans 6:6–7, 11, 13).

Against the Devil: Resist

- As I submit myself to God and resist the devil, he will flee from me (James 4:7).
- I will be of sober spirit and on the alert. My adversary, the devil, prowls about like a roaring lion, seeking someone to devour. But I will resist him, firm in my faith (1 Peter 5:8–9).
- I will take up the full armor of God that I may be able to resist and stand firm. I put on the belt of *truth* and the breastplate of *righteousness;* I put on my feet the preparation of the gospel of *peace;* and I take up the shield of *faith* with which I will be able to extinguish all the flaming missiles of the evil one. I take the helmet of *salvation* and the sword of the Spirit, which is the *Word* of God. With all *prayer* and petition I will pray at all times in the Spirit and be on the alert with all perseverance and petition for all the saints (Ephesians 6:13–18).

10. The Coming of Christ and My Future with Him

- Your kingdom come, your will be done (Matthew 6:10).
- You have said, "I am coming quickly." Amen. Come, Lord Jesus (Revelation 22:20).

- I consider that the sufferings of this present time are not worthy to be compared with the glory that is to be revealed to me (Romans 8:18).
- I will not lose heart, but though my outer man is decaying, yet my inner man is being renewed day by day. For momentary, light affliction is producing for me an eternal weight of glory far beyond all comparison, while I look not at the things which are seen, but at the things which are not seen; for the things which are seen are temporal, but the things which are not seen are eternal (2 Corinthians 4:16–18).
- My citizenship is in heaven, from which also I eagerly wait for a Savior, the Lord Jesus Christ (Philippians 3:20).
- (Also consider 2 Timothy 4:8; Hebrews 11:1, 6; 2 Peter 3:11–12; 1 John 2:28; 3:2–3.)

BALANCE AND DISCERNMENT

A balanced view of spiritual warfare does not limit it to evil spirits or to the flesh or to the world system but acknowledges the reality of all three in varying combinations. There has been a tendency in different parts of the church for some to focus on internal personal evil (the flesh), others on external structural evil (the world), and still others on spiritual evil. Any one of these can be overemphasized or underplayed, and this has been particularly true of spiritual evil. Scripture affirms that the war with evil is multidimensional; instead of compartmentalizing it, we should take into account the physical, the personal, the cultural, and the spiritual influences that impinge upon us. A given problem can have organic, psychological, and spiritual components, and it would be a mistake to rule out any of these from the outset.

The two basic approaches concerning the spiritual forces of darkness have tended to be neglect and denial on the one hand and paranoia and sensationalism on the other. Those in the first camp need to reexamine their theology in light of the ongoing experience of a growing number of Christian workers both here and abroad, and those in the second camp need to evaluate and interpret their experience in light of biblical truth. A better approach to this issue affirms the reality of Satan and unclean spirits, applies the weapons of the warfare, and balances this with the other facets of spirituality. While the church is an army, it is also a family, a hospital, a school, a mission center, and an organism.

Another issue that requires balance and discernment is the relatively new practice of confronting territorial spirits, that is, demonic forces that have authority over geopolitical areas (e.g., cities, regions, and nations). This practice is based on such accounts as the spiritual conflict between the archangel Michael and the powerful princes of Persia and Greece (Daniel 10:12–21; 12:1), Old Testament references to "high places" and regional deities (Deuteronomy 12:2; 1 Kings 18:18–19), and the worship of the goddess Artemis throughout the province of Asia (Acts 19:24–37). Spiritual mapping, as it is sometimes called, involves research on spiritual obstacles to revival (the sins of people groups—e.g., racism, pornography, terrorism, or drug abuse) as well as intercessory warfare prayer for strategic kingdom advancement in cities and countries. This growing movement has been criticized for centering its energy on an approach that is not warranted by Scripture and for an excessive emphasis on the demonic. Clinton E. Arnold provides a better perspective in *Three Crucial Questions about Spiritual Warfare* by distinguishing between prayers against demons afflicting individuals and prayers against territorial spirits. In the former case, believers can pray to God and command evil spirits to leave the afflicted person; in the latter case, they can ask God to hinder and thwart territorial spirits, but believers do not have the authority to command territorial spirits to leave a geographical area. In both cases, the primary emphasis is on practicing the presence of God, not the presence of demons.

THE WORK OF ANGELS

God's elect (unfallen) angels also play an important role in the spiritual warfare that includes and transcends the human race. The Lord uses his angels to minister to us in a variety of ways (e.g., protection, provision, and answers to prayer).

The existence and work of angels is not a matter of speculation. The word for "angel" appears more than 270 times in Scripture, and angels are mentioned in seventeen Old Testament and seventeen New Testament books. They play a role in so many biblical stories that they cannot be dismissed without seriously distorting the historical narratives as well as the teachings of Christ and the apostles.

Before the earth existed, angels were created by God as perfect spirit beings (Job 38:7). Since they do not procreate (Matthew 22:28–30), all angels were simultaneously put to the same test: rebel with Satan or remain loyal to God. Those who fell made a deliberate decision and cannot be redeemed. They are confirmed in their depravity and destined for "the eternal fire which has been prepared for the devil and his angels" (Matthew 25:41). Those who acknowledged the Lord's rule are confirmed in their holiness and will serve him forever as his messengers and ministers.

The elect angels are an innumerable host (Hebrews 12:22; Revelation 5:11) that is highly organized to reflect the wisdom and power of God (e.g., the ranks of thrones, dominions, rulers, and authorities [Colossians 1:16]). They are personal beings with intelligence (Matthew 28:5), emotion (Job 38:7; Isaiah 6:3), and volition (Hebrews 1:6). As creatures, they are localized (Hebrews 1:14) and limited in power and knowledge (1 Peter 1:12). Angels are immortal (Luke 20:36) and accountable to God. They appear in the Bible in the form of men (Genesis 18:1–8; Luke 24:4) and in unusual forms characterized by majesty and dignity (Ezekiel 1:5–21; 10; Daniel 10:5–6; Revelation 4:6–8). In our mortal frailty, we are lower than the angels (Psalm 8:4–6), but in our position in Christ we are above them, as will be evident when we receive our glorified resurrection bodies (1 Corinthians 6:3; Philippians 3:21).

The Hebrew and Greek words for "angel," *malak* and *angelos*, both mean "messenger." Other names for angels are sons of the mighty, sons of God, *elohim*, holy ones, stars, ministers, and host. Scripture alludes to three classifications of angels: cherubim (Ezekiel 1:5–8; 10:18–22), seraphim (Isaiah 6:2, 6), and living creatures (Revelation 4:6–9), and mentions two angels by name, Gabriel and the archangel Michael.

Angels worship God and serve him by carrying out his will (Psalm 103:20–21). During Christ's earthly life, they predicted and announced his birth, protected him as an infant, and strengthened him after his temptation and after his ordeal at Gethsemane. In similar ways, angels serve, protect, strengthen, and encourage those who trust in the Lord. God used angels in Scripture to mediate his word and will to his people, to direct his people, to provide for his people, and to deliver them from physical and spiritual dangers. They are "ministering spirits, sent out to render service for the sake of those who will inherit salvation" (Hebrews 1:14). Few of us realize the significant work angels do on our behalf.

THE FUTURE OF THE WARFARE

The Father has given all judgment to the Son (John 5:22). Some demons have already been judged and bound (2 Peter 2:4; Jude 6). Others will be loosed during the period of tribulation (Revelation 9:1–11; 16:13–14). Through the cross, Christ defeated Satan's kingdom (John 12:31; Luke 10:18). He "disarmed the rulers and authorities" and "triumphed over them" (Colossians 2:15; 1 Peter 3:22). "The Son of God appeared for this purpose, to destroy the works of the devil" (1 John 3:8b). "The ruler of this world has been judged" (John 16:11), and the sentence will be carried out when the Lord returns. Before the end, the warfare will become even more intense when the restraining ministry of the Holy Spirit is removed and Satan empowers the man of lawlessness (2 Thessalonians 2:6–12). Through the Antichrist and false prophet, Satan will persecute believers (Revelation 13:4–8). Michael and his angels will wage war with Satan and his angels and cast them out of heaven (Daniel 12:1; Revelation 12:7–9). With the return of Christ, Satan will be bound (Isaiah 14:15; Revelation 20:1–3). After this time, there will be a final conflict, and Satan and his forces will be permanently cast into the lake of fire (Matthew 25:41; Revelation 20:7–10).

The warfare with the *flesh* will be ended when we are resurrected and glorified (Romans 8:18–25; 1 Corinthians 15:50–58; 1 Thessalonians 4:17). The coming of the Lord Jesus will also end the warfare with the *world*, since he will overthrow the present world system with its atrocities, cruelties, and injustice and establish his reign in righteousness (Matthew 25:31–34). The warfare with the *devil* and his angels will also cease when Christ returns. Our hope is eschatological—we await the certain coming of our Lord and the new heaven and new earth where God will dwell among his people and "wipe away every tear from their eyes; and there will no longer be any death; there will no longer be any mourning, or crying, or pain" (Revelation 21:3–4).

"Therefore, my beloved brethren, be steadfast, immovable, always abounding in the work of the Lord, knowing that your toil is not in vain in the Lord" (1 Corinthians 15:58; cf. 2 Corinthians 4:16–18; Titus 2:13; Revelation 22:20).

QUESTIONS FOR PERSONAL APPLICATION

- How often do you pray on the seven elements of the armor of God?
- Which three of the twelve other resources do you think can be of most help to you?
- Pray through St. Patrick's Breastplate. Which part is most meaningful to you?
- Try incorporating the Morning Affirmations each day during the next week.
- How often do you think of the manifold work of angels?
- How does your understanding of the future of the warfare affect your present practice?

N U R T U R I N G   S P I R I T U A L I T Y

A Lifestyle of Evangelism and Discipleship

The believer's highest call in ministry is to reproduce the life of Christ in others. Reproduction takes the form of evangelism for those who do not know Christ and edification for those who do. This section develops a philosophy of discipleship and evangelism and looks at edification and evangelism as a way of life; lifestyle discipleship and evangelism are the most effective and realistic approaches to unbelievers and believers within our sphere of influence.

30

NURTURING SPIRITUALITY
A Philosophy of Discipleship

CHAPTER OVERVIEW

Nurturing spirituality involves a lifestyle of discipleship and evangelism, and these two processes reinforce each other. Discipleship is concerned with the postconversion half of the spectrum of spirituality. The chapter outlines eleven biblically based principles that can guide and enrich the practice of discipleship.

CHAPTER OBJECTIVES

- A greater willingness to grow by nurturing others through edification and evangelism
- A more full-orbed philosophy of discipleship as a way of life

---

In the first birth we receive the gift of *bios*, biological life; in the second birth we receive the greater gift of *zoê*, spiritual life. Just as we mature and reproduce on the biological level, God wants us to "be fruitful and multiply, and fill the earth" (Genesis 1:28; 9:1) on the spiritual level. This divinely ordained process of growth and reproduction after our kind is a significant facet of the spiritual life, because it is directly related to God's purpose for us to become like his Son and to reproduce the life of Jesus in others. He calls us to nurture people spiritually by building into them, feeding them, protecting them, encouraging them, training them, and assisting in their maturation so that they can learn to do the same with others.

A LIFESTYLE OF NURTURING OTHERS

Nurturing spirituality relates to a lifestyle of evangelism and discipleship. When we are part of the process of introducing people to Jesus and encouraging them to grow after they have come to know him, we discover that our own passion and spiritual vitality is enhanced. Few joys compare with the experience of seeing a friend come to new life in Christ. And one of life's deepest satisfactions is witnessing the gradual miracle of personal transformation in converts who are serious about becoming disciples. By contrast, the mediocrity of nondiscipleship cuts off the fruit of the Spirit and leads to a lack of love, joy, and peace. Dallas Willard puts it this way in *The Spirit of the Disciplines*:

> Nondiscipleship costs abiding peace, a life penetrated throughout by love, faith that sees everything in the light of God's overriding governance for good, hopefulness that stands firm in the most discouraging of circumstances, power to do what is right and withstand the forces of evil. In short, it costs exactly that abundance of life Jesus said he came to bring (John 10:10).

Evangelism and discipleship are concrete expressions of love and purpose. Since the God-infused love of *agapê* relates to the steady intention of one's will toward another's highest good, it chooses to seek the supreme good for both unbelievers and believers. Clearly, the greatest good for those who do not know Christ is to be delivered from the domain of darkness, death, and condemnation and to be transferred to the kingdom of the light, life, and love of God (Colossians 1:13–14). And the highest good for those who do know Christ is to mature into his likeness through growing conformity to his image (Romans 8:29). Thus nurturing spirituality personally expresses the *agapê* of God through evangelism (unbelievers) and edification (believers). The Great Commandment relates to the vertical dimension of loving God with all our heart, soul, mind, and strength, and to the horizontal dimension of loving our neighbors as ourselves (Mark 12:30–31). This Great Commandment is like a bow that gives impetus to the focused arrow of the Great Commission to make disciples of all the nations (Matthew 28:18–20). Our love for God gives us the power to love others as he would have us love them, and this others-centered love is expressed in evangelism and edification. Thus we are divinely commissioned to display and reproduce the life of Christ in the lives of the people in our spheres of influence. We are charged to be ambassadors of the King (2 Corinthians 5:14–21), and when we take this commission seriously, we find that our souls are enlarged by embracing a clear sense of destiny and purpose. When we are on the King's business as agents of reconciliation, we develop a kingdom mentality and order our lives in accordance with our Lord's purposes.

All of us give our lives in exchange for something, whether this is temporal or eternal. "For what will it profit a man if he gains the whole world and forfeits his soul? Or what will a man give in exchange for his soul?" (Matthew 16:26). If we are wise, we will follow Jesus by giving our lives in exchange for people. The apostle Paul knew this was the most significant way to live: "Having so fond an affection for you, we were well-pleased to impart to you not only the gospel of God but also our own lives, because you had become very dear to us" (1 Thessalonians 2:8). As Dag Hammarskjöld noted, "It is more noble to give yourself completely to one individual than to labor diligently for the salvation of the masses."

A SPECTRUM OF SPIRITUALITY

A whole spectrum of spiritual formation ranges from unwillingness even to consider the claims of Christ to the spiritual maturity of a reproducing disciple (see figure 30.1).

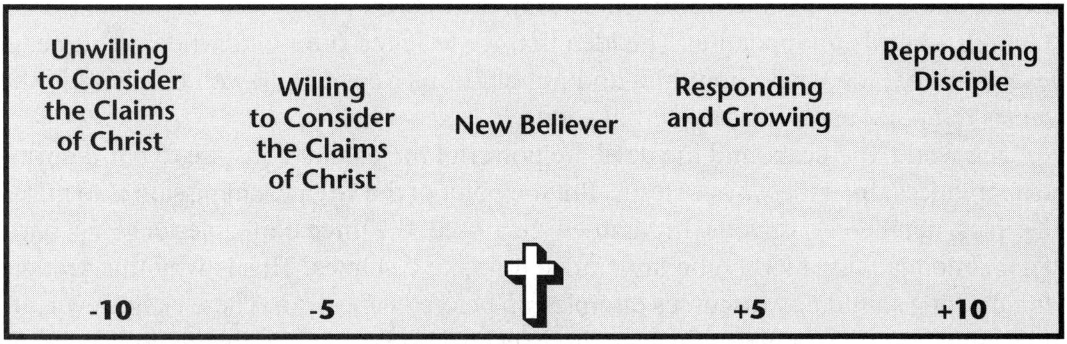

FIGURE 30.1

Evangelism is concerned with the left half of the spectrum, and edification relates to the right half. On this scale, no one ever arrives at a +10 in this life; the formative process is never complete during our earthly sojourn. The problem is that many who come to Christ fail to make more than a modicum of progress in spiritual maturity. Like planets around the sun, some believers orbit in closer proximity than others. Those who are like Mercury, Venus, and Earth remain in close fellowship with the Son, while others, like Uranus, Neptune, and Pluto, have a way of defining the limits of the solar system. Some professing Christians are like remote comets that come in to fly by every several years. Or to use another analogy, in the Middle East flocks of sheep follow behind their shepherds. Some sheep follow hard on the heels of the shepherd, while others move only because the sheep in front of them have moved. Still others are on the periphery of the flock. Like these distant sheep, the majority of believers live on the level of secondhand rather than firsthand experience of the Shepherd.

On the side of sovereign grace, it is mysterious why some believers progress in spiritual formation and others do not. But on the side of human responsibility, a variety of stumbling blocks impede advancement in the Way. Some people come to Jesus as a solution to their relational, physical, emotional, or financial problems. When he doesn't rectify their difficulties in the way they had hoped, their unrealized expectations can paralyze further growth. We cannot follow Jesus when we are asking him to follow us. We limit our spiritual development when we fail to make the transition from seeing Jesus as a problem solver to seeing him as our life.

Other people slip into religious activities as ends in themselves or develop spectator or consumer mentalities in the church. Devotion to duty or to safety and comfort dissipates passion for the person of Christ.

Many people back off when they encounter their first taste of the cost of discipleship. When they come to suspect that the cost of living in Christ is dying to self (John 12:24–26), they may reach for their rights rather than embrace the Cross. In a culture that feeds our natural fleshly aspirations through the promotion of self-realization, self-actualization, self-fulfillment, and self-esteem, the biblical principle of self-denial (Mark 8:34–38) sounds unappealing. The idea that we forfeited our rights when we came to Jesus and that life is all about him and not about us does not sit well in a world that values temporal assets above eternal goods.

The world, the flesh, and the devil are powerful forces that conspire to bar the way to apprenticeship in the ways of Jesus. But the point of the Great Commission is to make disciples, not merely converts. In Matthew 28:19–20, the three participles of going, baptizing, and teaching modify the imperative to make disciples. This is why this section on nurturing spirituality discusses discipleship before evangelism. There is, however, an integral relationship between the two: discipleship should result in the multiplication of converts, and evangelism should be coupled with an intention to make disciples.

I am part of a ministry team called Reflections Ministries whose purpose statement is "to provide safe places for people to consider the claims of Christ and to help them mature and bear fruit in their relationship with him." It is our intention not only to see people come to Christ but also to help them move from spiritual infancy to the maturity of Christlike character and spiritual reproduction. The Father is glorified when believers become like Jesus ("conformed to the image of His Son" [Romans 8:29]) and bear much fruit (John 15:8), and the Father's glory is the ultimate purpose of discipleship.

On the right half of the spectrum of spirituality, LeRoy Eims distinguishes four phases in the movement from conversion to maturity in *The Lost Art of Disciple Making*: converts, disciples, workers, and leaders. These four levels can be associated with the activities of evangelizing, establishing, equipping, and empowering (see table 30.1).

Before we discuss this discipleship process, we should view it in the context of a biblical philosophy of discipleship.

EVANGELIZING	ESTABLISHING	EQUIPPING	EMPOWERING
Converts	Disciples	Workers	Leaders

TABLE 30.1

A BIBLICAL PHILOSOPHY OF DISCIPLESHIP

If we do not start with a philosophy of discipleship, the process or product of discipleship will drive our philosophy by default. Since our perspective should shape our practice, we will begin with a brief look at a few biblically based principles that can guide and enrich the practice of discipleship.

We Must Be Disciples to Make Disciples

We teach what we believe, but we reproduce what we are. Although God in his grace may often use us in spite of ourselves, we normally cannot impart what we do not possess. Discipleship does not happen by accident; it is a process that is animated by an ongoing intention of the heart. No one suddenly stumbles into spirituality, and if we do not decide to apprentice ourselves to Jesus' authority, we will not become his disciples. Similarly, if we do not consciously intend to reproduce the life of Christ in others, we will miss our calling to make disciples.

The more we know Christ, the better we can make him known. When Paul told the Corinthians "I determined to know nothing among you except Jesus Christ, and Him crucified" (1 Corinthians 2:2), he saw himself as a messenger who was sent to introduce the people of Corinth to a Person with whom he had an intimate relationship. He wanted them to be more impressed with Jesus than they were with him, but this required a personal introduction to Jesus, not a list of his attributes. We must know Christ as a person before we can guide others to this level of spiritual intimacy.

Personal revival flows from fresh commitments to radical obedience and expresses itself in the focused presence of the life of Christ in us and through us. Like farmers (2 Timothy 2:6), we reap what we sow; spiritual nurture cannot be separated from our own spiritual formation, since we reproduce after our own kind.

Discipleship Is a Dependent Process

Discipleship is not an event but an ongoing process that requires conscious dependence on the presence and power of the Holy Spirit (John 16:8–14). "Now we have received, not the spirit of the world, but the Spirit who is from God, so that we may know the things freely given to us by God, which things we also speak, not in words taught by human wisdom, but in those taught by the Spirit, combining spiritual thoughts with spiritual words" (1 Corinthians 2:12–13). Apart from the work of the Spirit, we are powerless to accomplish anything of lasting good. God is the one who causes spiritual growth, not us (1 Corinthians 3:6). Discipleship is sanctification—the growing experiential knowledge of the person of Christ.

Our natural tendency is to depend more on skill, knowledge, programs, and written materials than on the ministry of the Spirit of God. We must learn the secret of ministering out of weakness, brokenness, and humility so that the power of Christ may dwell in us (2 Corinthians 12:9–10). As with the other areas of our lives, we are not in control, though we usually entertain the illusion that we are. "The mind of man plans his way, but the LORD directs his steps. . . . Commit your works to the LORD, and your plans will be established" (Proverbs 16:9, 3). The humility of fervent dependence on divine rather than human resources should permeate the discipleship process.

Concentration Is Crucial to Multiplication

While Jesus ministered to the masses, he focused his time and training on a small number of disciples. He was closer to the Twelve than to the seventy, and closer to the three (Peter, James, and John) than to the rest of the Twelve. Instead of dissipating the bulk of his energy on the curious multitudes, our Lord concentrated on a handful of people who were teachable and committed. By building his life into these men, he was equipping them to reach an ever-widening circle of people through multiplication rather than addition. As Robert E. Coleman put it in *The Master Plan of Evangelism*, "Better to give a year or so to one or two people who learn what it means to conquer for Christ than to spend a lifetime with a congregation just keeping the program going." We would do well to invite God to raise up and send us the people he wants us to nurture instead of recruiting people on our own. Prayerful and patient discernment on the front end will make us far more effective in the long term. True discipleship requires a significant investment of time and energy, and we want our limited resources to bear as much fruit as possible.

People Are Not Our Disciples

Those who are active in discipleship ministries face the ever-present danger of supposing that the people they nurture are their disciples. When this happens, several negative consequences can follow. Disciplers may attempt to control the product, they may derive their identity more from their product than from their relationship to Christ, and they may tend to make their disciples overly dependent upon their ministry and gift mix. This possessive mentality can prevent them from freely exposing their disciples to other valuable resources. These inherent errors are minimized when we grasp the concept that all ministry is part of a larger matrix. True discipleship flows out of a multiplicity of influences, some smaller and some greater. When we realize that the people we love, serve, and nurture are Jesus' disciples and not ours, we can minister to them with an open hand. As part of a larger matrix of ministries, we are invited to participate in a slice of what the Spirit of God is doing in their lives, but we never have the whole pie. The Lord may call you to nurture some people for a brief moment or for a long season, but they never were and never will be yours. They are always his. A willingness to expose people to other gifts and resources is a mark of the humility of authentic security in Christ. Wherever we are involved in the nurturing process, the goal is ever for us to decrease and for Jesus to increase.

Looking at discipleship through the lens of spiritual parenting, there is a developmental process (cf. 1 John 2:12–14) in which the needs of the disciple and the required role of the discipler gradually change. I have adapted table 30.2 from insights shared by my friend Bruce Witt.

No single discipler can effectively fill all these roles in the life of a disciple. But wherever we are in this process with various believers, we should remember that we should nurture them in a relational context of love, care, patience, and encouragement.

DEVELOPMENTAL LEVEL	DEVELOPMENTAL		ROLE OF DISCIPLER	DEVELOPING SPIRITUAL FOCUS
	Needs	Goals		
Babies (new converts)	Love, protection, nourishment	Health, growth	Mother	New life
Children (disciples)	Boundaries, obedience	Training, learning	Father	Life in Christ
Young adults (workers)	Growing independence and activity	Contribution, maturity	Coach	Christ's life in us
Adults (leaders)	Relationships	Multiplication	Peer	Christ's life through us

TABLE 30.2

Reproduction Is a Mark of Discipleship

"The things which you have heard from me in the presence of many witnesses, entrust these to faithful men who will be able to teach others also" (2 Timothy 2:2). Just as Timothy and "many witnesses" were recipients of the apostle's teaching and training, Paul exhorts them to transmit these things to a third generation of "faithful men." But the process of reception and transmission is still not complete until these faithful men learn how to teach yet a fourth generation of "others." Biblical discipleship equips people to dig their own wells and to develop the skills to minister to others. We become generational links when we show disciples how to train people who will in turn reach others.

There Is No Maturity without Ministry

For the follower of Christ, ministry is never optional—it is a calling for all believers, not merely a subset of professionals. Laypeople bypass abundant ministry opportunities when they stumble over the assumption that if they cannot teach or preach, they are limited to vicarious ministry through their financial support of those who can. This spectator mentality causes people to overlook the God-given circumstances and abilities with which they have been entrusted. All believers can be involved in some aspect of discipleship, even if this is limited to their families. No arena is insignificant, since reward is based on faithfulness to opportunity rather than the size of our ministry. We stunt our growth when we fail to serve others with eternal values at heart.

We Cannot Measure Our Ministries

Although people often try, the real essence of nurturing ministry cannot be appraised in this life. Human attempts to count converts and quantify discipleship miss the point that the bulk of our impact in this world is hidden and that only God knows the true nature of our ministries. Many who appear to make a big splash in this world may be far less effective from heaven's viewpoint than many obscure but faithful saints. We can participate in the work of God, but we cannot measure or control what he is doing in us and through us. Thus it is always unwise to determine effectiveness by comparing one person with another or one ministry with another.

From a human vantage point, evangelism and discipleship ministries are less visible and quantifiable than social service ministries and therefore harder to fund. But even with nurturing ministries, people often make the unbiblical assumption that bigger is better. This is why people are more impressed by ministries that adapt models from the business world than by ministries that are more relationally oriented. This is not to say that one is better than another, since the Lord can use both models. But on this side of eternity, we cannot measure the ultimate impact of a person or ministry. Instead, we are called to live with an ambiguity that drives us to walk by faith and not by sight. Every so often, God in his kindness may give us a glimpse that we are moving in the right direction through a word of encouragement or an expression of gratitude, but if we get too much feedback, we will be in danger of living for the results and using our impact on people to justify our existence. When we redefine our view of success in light of what will count for eternity, we are more motivated by what is pleasing to the heart of God than by what is impressive in the eyes of people.

Discipleship Is More Than a Program

Programmatic and curriculum-based approaches to discipleship have their place, but a biblical vision of nurturing ministry involves the whole person. Discipleship is more than a cognitive dump; teaching and training are important components, but they should be imparted in a context of personal association and community. What we are often speaks louder than what we say. Thus there is no substitute for the relational dimension of inviting people to be with us (Mark 3:14) in a variety of settings so that nurturing becomes incarnational and multidimensional. This requires a greater commitment of time and effort, but spiritual reproduction through personal transformation is the most effective and full-orbed way.

Alluding to his relational ministry of discipleship, Paul used the metaphor of formative growth: "My children, with whom I am again in labor until Christ is formed in you" (Galatians 4:19). Biblical discipleship cannot be reduced to a program or even to a process; it is also the growing presence of a Person.

Discipleship Requires a Servant Attitude

"He who has the bride is the bridegroom; but the friend of the bridegroom, who stands and hears him, rejoices greatly because of the bridegroom's voice. So this joy of mine has been made full. He must increase, but I must decrease" (John 3:29–30). When disciplers slip into an authoritarian role or see themselves as spiritual gurus, they miss the spirit of being a friend of the bridegroom. John the Baptist did not call attention to himself but to Jesus, the bridegroom. Because John stood and heard Jesus and rejoiced in his voice, John could delight in being Jesus' attendant and in his calling as a servant of those who were invited to the wedding. Jesus told his disciples, "when you do all the things which are commanded you, say, 'We are unworthy slaves; we have done only that which we ought to have done'" (Luke 17:10). When we cultivate the attitude of a servant, we discern that Jesus attributes our sacrificial service for the benefit of others as service to him ("to the extent that you did it to one of these brothers of Mine, even the least of them, you did it to Me" [Matthew 25:40]).

Spiritual Friendship Is a Component of Discipleship

Just as Paul and Silas imparted their own lives to the people they served in Thessalonica (Acts 17:1–9; 1 Thessalonians 2:7–12), we must make ourselves personally available and transparent to the people we disciple. Spiritual friendship is founded on a mutuality that exists for the purpose of helping each other grow in grace and character. (This is not the same as spiritual direction or mentoring; we will look at these in the section on corporate spirituality.) While our Lord commands us to love all, we can befriend only a few. This dimension of holy friendship makes discipleship a two-way street where the discipler and the disciple both give and receive. Spiritual friendship moves beyond the level of personal gratification to the cultivation of Christlike virtue (2 Peter 1:5–9) and requires a deliberate intention to be open to one another and to God's formative purposes. Praying for one another and with one another is an essential part of this mutual relationship.

Effective Discipleship Requires More Than One Method

When it comes to spiritual nurturing, one size does not fit all. There is a tendency in discipleship ministries to turn models and methods into masters. The assumption is that if a method works well for some, it must be appropriate for all. As a result, people whose temperaments do not resonate with the proffered method may conclude that there is something deficient in their spiritual commitment.

This misguided tendency toward homogeneity can reduce discipleship to a cloning process: "When you've completed our program, you'll look like this." When the rich diversity of personal temperaments and cultural factors is not taken into account (see appendix A, "The Need for Diversity"), discipleship becomes program-driven rather than person-specific. A teaching or training method that inspires one person may be unrealistic and inappropriate for another. Disciplers who fail to grasp this can create expectations that inevitably lead some people to a sense of inadequacy and frustration. A variety of tools are needed, and this is why there is a multiplicity of discipleship ministries and approaches. Some are more programmatic, and others are more relational; some stress the cognitive, and others stress the affective or the volitional. Just as God created the cosmos as a unity out of profound diversity, so the body of Christ is a unity in diversity.

QUESTIONS FOR PERSONAL APPLICATION

- In your pilgrimage, in what ways has nurturing others assisted you in your spiritual formation?
- How do evangelism and discipleship relate to love and purpose?
- Recalling the metaphor of a flock of sheep, where would you place yourself as a follower of the Shepherd?
- Which of the eleven discipleship principles spoke most directly to you?

31

NURTURING SPIRITUALITY
The Process, Product, and Context of Discipleship

CHAPTER OVERVIEW

The process of discipleship should incorporate three primary dynamics of exposing, equipping, and encouraging/exhorting. These relate not only to knowing (teaching) and doing (training) but also to being (character). The chapter concludes with a discussion of both the product of discipleship and the contexts in which discipleship can take place.

CHAPTER OBJECTIVES

- A practical grasp of the discipleship process of exposing, equipping, encouraging, and exhorting
- An understanding of the goals of discipleship and the contexts in which discipleship can take place

---

THE PROCESS OF DISCIPLESHIP

There are three primary dynamics in the discipleship process: exposing, equipping, and encouraging/exhorting. The first centers on the example and character of the discipler, the second centers on the nature of the teaching and training, and the third centers on the accountability and character of the disciple (table 31.1).

It is important to note that these dynamics are not chronological but concurrent.

The left and right columns are incarnational and focus on the heart of the discipler and the disciple. While knowing, being, and doing (Ezra 7:10) are all important, the being-character-heart component is the one that is most often overlooked in the discipleship process.

EXPOSING	EQUIPPING		ENCOURAGING AND EXHORTING
Example (modeling)	Teaching	Training	Obedience and accountability
	Thinking	Habits	
	Theory	Technique	
	Truth	Skills	
	Principles	Practice	
Being (discipler)	Knowing	Doing	Being (disciple)
Character	Convictions	Conduct	Character
Heart	Head	Hands	Heart

TABLE 31.1

Exposing

As we have seen, we must be disciples to make disciples. When disciplers grow in the way they incarnate the grace and truth of life in Christ, they also grow in authenticity and personal authority. Their holy aspiration and personal passion become contagious as they make discipleship attractive. Their words are empowered by their example, and their vision of kingdom living galvanizes others to lay hold of the same vision and passion. But when disciplers descend from growth to maintenance or to regression in their walk with the Lord, they minister out of the borrowed capital of their former vitality and depend on their knowledge and skill rather than the fullness of the Spirit. Their authenticity and spiritual charisma erode, and they can no longer encourage others to do those things they hear and see in them (Philippians 4:9).

Exposure to people who exhibit a radiant walk with God is a powerful impetus in the life of a disciple, because this provides a tangible demonstration of the relevance of biblical truth to daily endeavor. Such people inspire by imparting words and works, lips and life, attitudes and actions. They give their experience of Christ away to others as they teach through both precept and example. This combination of tutoring and imitation fleshes out and adorns the nurturing process.

Equipping

Equipping is the second primary dynamic in the discipleship process and should involve both teaching and training. Unfortunately, most discipleship programs seem to be limited to this dimension, and many of these emphasize either imparting knowledge (teaching) or developing skills (training).

The purpose of equipping is to show people how to learn *and* apply the Word in such a way that the truth is understood and integrated in the context of everyday life. In this way, disciples progress in principles and in practice, in theory and in technique, in convictions and in conduct.

Teaching

The living Word of God, Jesus Christ, is made known through the written Word of God, and the written Word of God is disclosed through the proclaimed Word of God in preaching and in teaching. Solid teaching helps renew the mind and enables believers to adjust their thinking in light of the world view revealed in Scripture. Our thinking molds our lives, and progress in true spirituality requires the development of a biblical filter system. As we conform our thinking to the Word rather than the world, we become increasingly confident in God's sovereign and loving purposes, and this growing level of trust spills over into our priorities and the decisions that flow from them. There is no permanent change without a change in perspective, since our perspective shapes our priorities, and our priorities shape our practice.

A wealth of teaching tools is available, and a few of these will be mentioned below. Basic teaching programs usually provide an overview of core issues such as salvation, elements of spiritual growth, Bible reading, prayer, marriage and parenting, evangelism, and stewardship. Intermediate and advanced teaching programs often include apologetics, Bible book studies, Old Testament and New Testament surveys, biblical and systematic theology, and church history.

However, some crucial areas are frequently overlooked in discipleship programs, and this is unfortunate, since a number of these have far-reaching practical implications. These areas include

- a clear view of the authority and truth of Scripture
- a biblical value system
- a biblical view of hope
- a biblical view of purpose
- a biblical view of motivation
- a biblical view of contentment and gratitude
- the development of personal convictions
- the role of tribulation in our lives
- a biblical view of work and leisure
- the challenges of our culture to the application of biblical truth
- the nature of the spiritual warfare and of our spiritual resources
- the process of spiritual formation

When laypeople are taught to think through these issues, they are better equipped to relate timeless truths to the concerns of daily experience.

Training

Discipleship programs that are limited to imparting knowledge run the risk of orthodoxy without orthopraxy, correct thinking without appropriate application. Teaching equips disciples with truth, but training equips them with skills. Training programs center on the formation of holy habits and practical skills so that disciples will acquire ingrained responses to the opportunities, challenges, and temptations they encounter every day. Teaching without training can lead to a growing disparity between what people claim to believe and what they believe as evidenced in their actions. When people experience increasing tension between their beliefs and their behavior, they will usually opt to modify their beliefs rather than their behavior. Since this process is often unconscious, people are capable of living with a prodigious gap between their profession and their practice. Thus it is just as important to focus on practice as it is on principles.

Training in positive habit formation and life skills relates to the disciplines of the spiritual life. These in turn are modeled after the disciplines Jesus practiced (e.g., solitude, silence, study, meditation, prayer, and fasting). In this way, disciples are shown how to become apprentices of the Master in their habits of thinking, feeling, and action. These developing skills and habits equip them to respond spontaneously in biblically appropriate ways to people and circumstances.

Discipleship training programs stress different skills and techniques, but the most common training objectives include Bible study skills (e.g., reading, inductive study methods, memorization, meditation), cultivation of a daily quiet (devotional) time, methods of prayer, how to share one's faith with others, discerning God's will, identification and use of spiritual gifts, laying hold of spiritual resources, dealing with temptation, and leadership development.

Since there is a reciprocal relationship between thinking and habits, attitudes and actions, belief and behavior, it is important to avoid the two extremes of all theory or all technique. The equipping dynamic in the discipleship process should strive for a balanced combination of teaching and training.

While there are basic things all believers need to know and practice, it is helpful to be familiar with more than one of the many teaching and training resources that are available. If we limit ourselves to a single approach, we will be less capable of effectively adapting the discipleship process to the disposition of an individual or a group.

A sample of some teaching and/or training resources and books includes

Bible Study Fellowship
CBMC Operation Timothy series
Christian Leadership Concepts' two-year equipping program
Navigators 2:7 series
Precept Ministries

Search Ministries' *Foundations*, *Questions*, and *Connexions* workbooks

Vision Foundation's Ministry in the Marketplace series

Dietrich Bonhoeffer, *The Cost of Discipleship*

J. Robert Clinton, *The Making of a Leader*

Robert E. Coleman, *The Master Plan of Evangelism*

LeRoy Eims, *The Lost Art of Discipleship*

Os Guinness, *The Call*

Howard Hendricks and William Hendricks, *As Iron Sharpens Iron*

Walter A. Henrichsen, *Disciples Are Made—Not Born*

Walter A. Henrichsen and William N. Garrison, *Layman, Look Up! God Has a Place for You*

John Musselman, *The Disciplemaker: A Reference for Mentors*

Henri J. M. Nouwen, *In the Name of Jesus*

Jim Petersen, *Lifestyle Discipleship*

Eugene H. Peterson, *A Long Obedience in the Same Direction*

J. Oswald Sanders, *Spiritual Leadership*

Paul D. Stanley and J. Robert Clinton, *Connecting: The Mentoring Relationships You Need to Succeed in Life*

David Watson, *Called and Committed: World-Changing Discipleship*

Michael J. Wilkins, *Following the Master: Discipleship in the Steps of Jesus*

Dallas Willard, *The Divine Conspiracy*

Avery T. Willis Jr., *MasterLife I and II*

Carl Wilson, *With Christ in the School of Disciple Building*

Encouraging and Exhorting

The third primary dynamic in the discipleship process concerns the character and heart of the disciple. Progress in spiritual growth requires a growing apprentice to be receptive and responsive. Without the humility of a teachable spirit and a willingness to respond to teaching, reproof, correction, and training in righteousness (2 Timothy 3:16), a person will not go far in the way of discipleship. And since effective nurturing addresses the whole person, the discipling relationship requires sincerity, authenticity, and candor. As some groups put it, both the discipler and the disciple need to be FAT (faithful, available, teachable) and HOT (honest, open, transparent).

For many people, formation in these qualities will not come easily, since they are foreign to a culture that touts autonomy and individualism. This is where progressive obedience to the Word and personal accountability come in. The discipler should create an atmosphere in which obedience and submission to the lordship of Christ is the expected norm. Teaching and training should never be seen as ends in themselves but as servants of the central impetus of discipleship: radical commitment to the person of Jesus. This level of commitment comes with the pricetag of personal dedication, self-denial, and the obedience of the Cross. Without accountability, these biblical norms and the rest of Scripture become negotiable.

It is always wise to give specific assignments to spiritual apprentices so they will have tangible opportunities to implement and internalize the things they are learning. These assignments can keep them from sliding into complacency, and they provide a concrete context for encouragement, exhortation, supervision, review, and evaluation. In this way, disciplers can assist them in their thinking and vision, encourage them in times of defeat and discouragement, and exhort them to press on in the formation of character and conviction.

THE PRODUCT OF DISCIPLESHIP

Earlier we observed that the essence of nurturing ministry cannot be appraised in this life. We cannot measure the being-character-heart dimension of discipleship, since this internal dynamic is not quantifiable by human observation (see 1 Corinthians 4:3–5). Only God can "bring to light the things hidden in the darkness and disclose the motives of men's hearts; and then each man's praise will come to him from God" (1 Corinthians 4:5).

We can, however, appraise the equipping dimension (teaching and training), and because of this, there is a natural tendency to measure the outcome of discipleship in terms of specific levels of knowledge and/or skill. The human disposition to count, control, measure, and manipulate makes us more comfortable with reducing discipleship to a program that creates a quantifiable product. If we overlook this tendency, we will be inclined to define discipleship in terms of outward conformity rather than inward transformation. To do this is to miss the essence of spiritual formation—becoming like the Master by moving from faith *in* Christ to the faith *of* Christ.

Having said this, there are a number of attributes and virtues that Scripture exhorts us to emulate and incarnate. A few of those attributes are love (John 13:35; 1 John 3:23), purity of heart (1 Timothy 1:5; 2 Timothy 2:22), self-denial (Matthew 16:24–26; Mark 8:34–37), obedience (John 14:21; 15:10), willingness to suffer for the sake of righteousness (2 Timothy 3:12; 1 Peter 4:1–2, 12–16), commitment to an eternal perspective (Luke 14:25–35; 2 Corinthians 4:16–18), accountability (Luke 12:42–48), compassion, kindness, humility, gentleness, and patience (Colossians 3:12; James 5:7–11).

A brief look at our Lord's high-priestly prayer in John 17 reveals several additional marks of discipleship: desire to glorify God (vv. 1, 4–5), seeking to fulfill the Father's purpose (v. 4), manifesting God's name to others (vv. 6, 26), imparting God's words to others (v. 8); intercessory prayer (vv. 9, 20), active involvement in the world (vv. 11, 15, 18), unity with other believers (vv. 11, 21–23), desire to nurture others (v. 12), being set apart from the world (vv. 14, 16), being sanctified through the Word (vv. 17, 19), passion for God's presence and glory (v. 24), and yearning to know the Father (v. 25).

Sid Buzzell, Bill Perkins, and I structured *The Leadership Bible* around forty-three leadership qualities that relate to personal development, skills, and relationships. Because discipleship involves the modeling and development of leadership, it is appropriate to list these qualities with a central biblical passage for each:

Personal Development
character (Proverbs 2:1–11)
commitment (Romans 12:1–2)
courage/risk-taking (Joshua 1:1–9)
dependence on God (Matthew 6:25–34)
humility (Philippians 2:1–11)
integrity (1 Samuel 12:1–4)
leader qualifications (1 Timothy 3:1–12)
obedience to God (1 Samuel 15)
priorities (Luke 12:16–21)
purpose/passion (Philippians 3:7–9)
self-discipline (1 Corinthians 9:24–27)
values (Psalm 15)
vision (2 Corinthians 12:1–6)
wisdom (Proverbs 8)

Skills
accountability (2 Samuel 11:1–5, 27)
change/innovation (Mark 2:18–22)
communicating vision (1 Chronicles 28)
communication skills (Proverbs 18:13)
conflict management (Matthew 5:23–24; 18:15–17)
decision making (Nehemiah 1)
double-loop learning (learning that addresses the root causes of problems
    [John 21:15–19])
empowerment (Acts 1:8)
justice (Amos 5:24)
leadership development (Luke 10:1–24)
the learning organization (Judges 2:1–11)
long-range planning (Genesis 3:15)
management of human resources/human resource development
    (Ephesians 4:11–16)
problem solving (Nehemiah 6:1–14)

quality/excellence (Colossians 3:23–24)
rewards (Hebrews 11)
situational leadership (Luke 6:12–16)
stewardship (Matthew 25:14–30)
stress management (1 Samuel 18:6–11)
structure/organization (Exodus 18)
systems thinking (1 Corinthians 12:12–29)
team building (2 Samuel 23:8–17)
time management (Psalm 90:12)

Relationships
encouragement (Acts 9:27)
exhortation (2 Timothy 2:14–21)
healthy alliances (1 Samuel 22:1–5)
interpersonal relationships (Hosea 2)
power and influence (Psalm 82)
servant leadership (John 13:1–17)

In *The Lost Art of Disciple Making,* LeRoy Eims has developed specific profiles of a convert, a disciple, a worker, and a leader. Profiles like these can be helpful in evaluating the product of discipleship as long as we remember that we cannot measure the being-character-heart dimension of nurturing ministry.

THE CONTEXT OF DISCIPLESHIP
Marriage, Parenting, Friendships, Work, and Society

When we encounter people who are engaged in discipleship ministries, we usually hear about programs and methods that are used in specific group or individual settings. While small-group and one-on-one approaches to discipleship are strategic aspects of spiritual nurturing, they are often mistaken for the whole. It is possible to be active in a ministry of discipleship and to overlook the most obvious opportunities. For instance, it is an occupational hazard of youth workers to disciple other people's children and to overlook their own.

In the earlier discussion of holistic spirituality, we took a brief look at marriage, parenting, friendships, work, and society. If we can make the mental shift of relating nurturing spirituality to holistic spirituality, we will begin to see that the most obvious discipleship settings have been placed in front of us. Those who are married, for example, would do well to see their marriage as a mutual discipling relationship. It should not be surprising that among couples who pray and read the Scriptures together on a consistent basis, the divorce rate is minimal. When husbands take the initiative in spiritually nurturing their wives in a gentle and supportive way, they foster an environment in which spiritual oneness grows and enhances psychological and physical oneness.

Similarly, we should view the parent-child relationship as another primary context of discipleship. When parents model what it is to love and walk with Jesus, they develop an authenticity that gives them authority and credibility when they teach and train their children. Spiritual nurture of children should not be left to spontaneous moments; it is better to see this as an intentional process that is energized by a desire that our children come to love Jesus even more than they love us.

When we keep an eye open for discipleship opportunities, we will discover these not only in our marriage and parenting relationships but also in our friendships and our relationships at work. We must avoid the common error of separating our vocation and our ministry. Our work provides us with a sphere of influence and interaction, and the cultivation of a godly, wise, and winsome character can open doors of personal ministry as ambassadors of Christ. Similarly, our friendships take on a new dimension when we perceive them as a context in which we love and serve people with eternal purposes at heart.

Society is also a potential arena for nurturing spirituality when we recognize a specific burden to be active in the world as a calling to express the love and mercy of Christ to those who are in need. Responsive action in the present moment requires a willingness to be sensitive and open to daily opportunities we might otherwise pass over.

Small-Group and One-on-One Discipleship

A personal commitment to meeting regularly with a small group and/or with individuals for the purpose of spiritual development is always worth the investment of time and effort. Both one-on-one and small-group discipleship can be done on a basic or more advanced level, but in every case, the relational component should be as central as the content. We should never minimize the incarnational dynamic of nurturing spirituality. The equipping dynamic of teaching and training can include everything from apologetics to leadership training, but the discipleship process works best when exposing, equipping, and encouraging/exhorting all function in synchrony.

In *The Disciplemaker: A Reference for Mentors*, John Musselman advocates five elements of group life:

1. accountability questions (personal life, family life, and corporate life)
2. spiritual disciplines (worship, quiet time, prayer life, Bible study, Scripture memory, and witnessing)
3. Bible study/discussion
4. sharing together (good news/victories, temptations/defeats, prayer requests, and general information)
5. prayer

Notice that the equipping component of discipleship (Bible study/discussion) is flanked by the being/character/heart component of discipleship. Normally more time is devoted to Bible study and discussion than to any of the other elements, but all of them contribute to the optimal effectiveness of the group.

In small-group and one-on-one discipleship, our vision should be to bring apprentices to the point where they are willing and able to do the same thing in the lives of others.

Team Ministry

One way to offset our cultural tendency toward individualism is to be part of a team ministry, whether this is associated with a church or with a ministry organization. The Gospels tell us about the team Jesus built around him, and Acts and the Epistles show that the apostles followed his example by ministering in tandem with others.

A team ministry provides fellowship, interdependence, encouragement, division of labor, cooperation, synergism, and a broad gift mix. Members of a ministry team commit to a common cause by covenanting together to fulfill a vision and mission. They also commit to a community (each other), and this partnership creates an environment of grace and mutual bonding as they purpose to walk together in peace and trust.

In any team ministry, it is normal to encounter a creative tension between the individual and the community. But the diversity of many projects can be brought into the unity of a larger vision that contextualizes these projects and is too big for one person to achieve.

It is wise to count the cost of being a team player, and this includes the conscious choice to focus on others' positive attributes in light of a commitment to an ongoing relationship. A team requires the interpersonal chemistry of like-minded, sympathetic collegiality and mutual respect. When the members meet together, they encourage each other and "stimulate one another to love and good deeds" (Hebrews 10:24–25). Team ministry relates to the need for corporate spirituality, and we will consider this facet of the gem of spirituality in the next section of this book.

QUESTIONS FOR PERSONAL APPLICATION

- Have you encountered a discipleship ministry that is strong in all three dynamics of exposing, equipping, and encouraging/exhorting? Why is this so rare, and which element is most often neglected?
- Do you find yourself more naturally drawn to knowing, to being, or to doing?

- Return to the attributes and virtues that Scripture exhorts us to emulate and incarnate. How would you evaluate yourself in each of these qualities?
- In what context(s) have you engaged in discipleship? What areas have you overlooked?

32

NURTURING SPIRITUALITY
A Philosophy of Evangelism

CHAPTER OVERVIEW

Beginning with the significance of evangelism, this chapter then outlines a philosophy of evangelism by discussing eight biblically based principles: evangelism is a process; the results belong to God; cultivating requires more time than reaping; evangelism largely relates to the church scattered; evangelism is an eternal investment; we can evangelize for the wrong reasons; evangelism involves a combination of words and deeds; and evangelism and discipleship should be integrated.

CHAPTER OBJECTIVES

- Increased passion to be engaged in a lifestyle of relational evangelism
- A more full-orbed philosophy of evangelism as a way of life

---

Near the end of his life, Aldous Huxley, author of *Brave New World*, arrived at this conclusion: "It is a bit embarrassing to have been concerned with the human problem all one's life and find at the end that one has no more to offer by way of advice than 'Try to be a little kinder.'" Without God, humanistic answers to the questions of earthly existence ultimately reduce to naïve bromides and platitudes.

THE SIGNIFICANCE OF EVANGELISM

Perspective

The Scriptures paint a sobering and realistic portrait of the human condition. People delude themselves with short-term aspirations and pleasures, but a brutally honest analysis of life on this side of the grave without hope on the other side would lead to despair. If death ends all, human life is a mere incident in an indifferent universe, a meaningless blip in cosmic time.

In "My Speech to the Graduates," Woody Allen confronted this dilemma with ironic humor: "More than any other time in history, mankind faces a crossroads. One path leads to despair and utter hopelessness. The other, to total extinction. Let us pray we have the wisdom to choose correctly. I speak, by the way, not with any sense of futility but with a panicky conviction of the absolute meaninglessness of human existence which could easily be misinterpreted as pessimism." This ironic statement is simultaneously humorous and tragic, depicting as it does the corporate and individual human condition without a transcendent and timeless foundation for meaning.

Ecclesiastes 3:11 tells us that God has set eternity in our hearts. Since this is so, people have deeply embedded desires for meaning and fulfillment that no natural happiness will satisfy. In *The Weight of Glory*, C. S. Lewis observes that "almost our whole education has been directed to silencing this shy, persistent, inner voice; almost all our modern philosophies have been devised to convince us that the good of man is to be found on this earth." Someone noted that while people in our culture are reading the *Times*, we should be reading the eternities. The more we develop a biblical perspective, the clearer we see the true emptiness and hopelessness of people without Christ.

Purpose

Those who have been found by Jesus know that life does have a purpose. But even believers tend to forget the important because of the clamor of the urgent. Like the Israelites who disbelieved God at Kadesh Barnea and wandered in the wilderness as the years raced by, our lives can become a wilderness of routine and of crowded schedules. While the urgent tasks call for immediate attention, we can overlook the important things, since they can always be deferred. We rationalize our postponement of the important by letting the good become the enemy of the best.

We need a heart of wisdom (Psalm 90:12); if we blind ourselves to reality, our whole value system will be distorted ("As if you could kill time without injuring eternity"—Thoreau). The eternal gives meaning to the temporal. When we live in the light of our true destiny, we see our calling and purpose from a biblical perspective. Instead of asking, "What will I leave behind me?" it is better to ask, "What am I going to send ahead?" As ambassadors of Christ, we have been entrusted with a ministry of reconciliation (2 Corinthians 5:16–21) in a lost and dying world.

The Lord Jesus summarized the purpose of his earthly life in these impassioned statements: "For the Son of Man has come to seek and to save that which was lost.... For even the Son of Man did not come to be served, but to serve, and to give His life a ransom for many" (Luke 19:10; Mark 10:45). When we resonate with our Lord's purpose, we lay hold of an enduring legacy.

In the discussion of discipleship we saw that the purpose of our earthly sojourn as "aliens and strangers" (1 Peter 2:11) is spiritual growth and reproduction. We are called to growing conformity with Christ, and the trials and obstacles of this life are designed to produce Christlike character as we learn to depend more and more on him. We are also called to the sublime privilege of reproducing the life of Christ in others. God has seen fit to use ordinary people like us to accomplish his extraordinary work of creating eternal life where formerly there was darkness and death. It would have been easy for him to communicate the word of life directly to those whom he foreknew, but instead he entrusted us with the priceless message of the Good News. What greater calling can we have than to be used by the living God as spiritual obstetricians and pediatricians?

Priority

Human works quickly erode or evaporate, but the works we invite the eternal God to do in and through us abide forever. Scripture urges us to invest in eternity by making God's purposes our highest priority. In his parting words to his disciples, Jesus stressed the priority of spiritual multiplication (Matthew 28:19–20; Acts 1:8). Seeking the lost was central to our Lord's teaching and ministry (Luke 15), and he wanted this to be central in the lives of his followers.

This desire to reach the lost was also the heartbeat of the teaching and example of the apostle Paul (see 1 Corinthians 9:19–27; 2 Corinthians 5:16–21). At the end of his life he told Timothy that he had fought the good fight and finished the course (2 Timothy 4:7–8). Like Jesus, he set about his Father's business by making a priority of seeing others enter the kingdom. He even went so far as to say that he could be willing to be accursed if it would mean the salvation of his Jewish kinsmen (Romans 9:1–3). Many believers are not willing to go across the street for their unsaved friends. Unless evangelism is a priority in our lives, it is unlikely that it will even be a part of our lives.

A BIBLICAL PHILOSOPHY OF EVANGELISM

Evangelism Is a Process

With the permission of Search Ministries, I have adapted many of the following concepts from two of their lifestyle evangelism seminars. I want to acknowledge my indebtedness to Larry Moody, Dave Krueger, Bill Kraftson, Ed Diaz, Bob Shelley, and to the other members of the Search Ministries team.

Most people associate evangelism with an event (conversion), but from a scriptural perspective, it is more of a process. In fact, the Bible uses agricultural imagery to portray the dynamic process of evangelism (e.g., John 4:35–39; 1 Corinthians 3:6–9). Crops do not happen—reaping a harvest is the outcome of a lengthy series of events that cannot be bypassed or overlooked.

The first phase in this series is the preparation of the soil. Unless the ground is cleared and plowed, it will not be ready to receive the seed. After the soil is harrowed and furrowed, the second phase, sowing the seed, takes place. Cultivation, the third phase, is the lengthiest part of the agricultural process; it involves irrigation, fertilization, and weed control. Only when the crop is mature is it ready to undergo the brief fourth phase of reaping.

When we substitute "soul" for "soil," the spiritual analogy of these four phases to the process of evangelism becomes obvious (see figure 32.1).

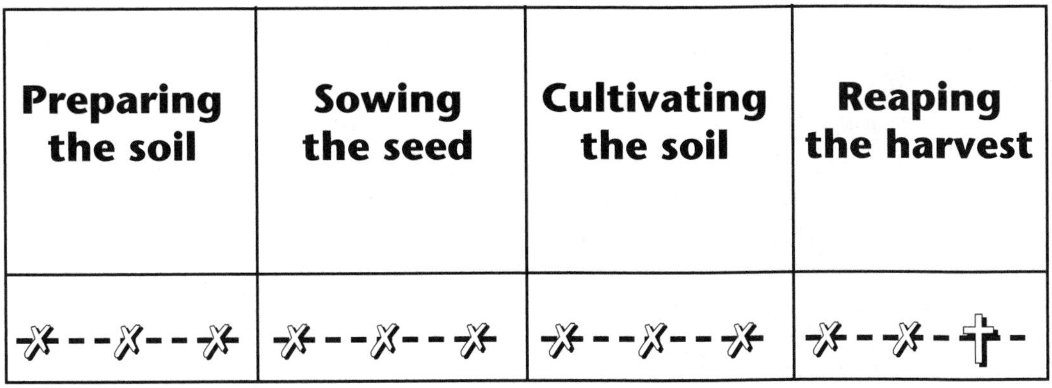

Preparing the soil	Sowing the seed	Cultivating the soil	Reaping the harvest
✗ - - ✗ - - ✗	✗ - - ✗ - - ✗	✗ - - ✗ - - ✗	✗ - - ✗ - ✝ -

FIGURE 32.1

Before people are ready to receive the seed of the Word, their souls must be prepared, and there are many ways in which this can happen. Often God uses adversities and setbacks to pull people away from their illusions of autonomy so they can begin to see their true condition of spiritual need. The sowing of the seed is exposure to the truths of the Word of God, and the process of cultivation is the gradual realization that these truths speak to their deep needs. The Lord uses his servants in each of these phases as they pray for people without Christ, develop relationships with them in areas of common ground, and share their own journeys when appropriate.

Jesus prepared the soil when he asked the Samaritan woman for a drink of well water (John 4:7–10). In speaking to her, Jesus overcame three barriers: first, the racial barrier (Jews had no dealings with Samaritans), second, the gender barrier (Jewish rabbis would not address women), and third, the social barrier (this woman had a poor reputation among her own people). Jesus knew everything she had done, and yet he gently and lovingly offered her the living water of eternal life.

The parable of the soils in Matthew 13:3–9 and Mark 4:1–20 illustrates the phase of seed sowing and underscores the need for receptivity to the Word of life. The seed does not take permanent root when the soil is unprepared.

The cultivation phase is illustrated in the fact that Jesus was called "a friend of tax collectors and sinners" (Matthew 11:19) and in Paul's desire to find areas of common ground in order to win Jews and Gentiles to Christ (1 Corinthians 9:19–23).

The final phase of reaping the harvest is depicted in the metaphor Jesus used of the Samaritans as a field that is white for harvest (John 4:35–38). This image is immediately followed by an account of the Samaritans' coming to faith in Jesus (John 4:39–42).

The key concept to be gleaned from this process principle is the liberating truth that if we are involved in any one of these four phases, we are doing evangelism. Believers who prepare the soil, sow the seed, or cultivate the planted soil are as much a part of the evangelistic process as those who are given the privilege of reaping the harvest. In addition, when we are sensitive and responsive to the opportunities God places in our path, we will find ourselves participating in different phases of the process, depending on the individual and the purposes of God. With one person we may be given an opportunity to participate in the seed-planting phase by sharing truths from Scripture. In another case, we may have an opportunity to water or fertilize the spiritual truth that has already been sown. While our desire is to see our friends come to Christ (the harvest), we can be assured that whether we are involved in preparing, sowing, watering, or reaping, we are part of the same process.

The Results Belong to God

In any area of life and ministry, we should understand that we *contribute* nothing to the purposes of God. He has no lack or deficiency, and for us to make a contribution would mean that we bring something to the table that he does not already possess. However, God does invite us to *participate* in his purposes by being a part of what his Spirit is accomplishing in the lives of people. This means that in evangelism, as in other areas of life, we are called to be faithful to the process and to leave the results to God. When we abandon our attempts to control the outcome and seek to be obedient to the prompting of the Spirit, we can rest in the fact that God will use us as he sees fit in the lives of the outsiders that we encounter and pray for. The image of "outsiders" and "those who are outside" is used in Scripture to depict people who have not come to faith in Jesus (see Mark 4:11; Colossians 4:5). Our desire in the evangelistic process is for outsiders to become insiders in the family of God.

We are incapable of changing others, although we often make the mistake of trying. When we adopt the goal of changing people, we are committing ourselves to manipulating and coercing them. But when we realize that the whole process of evangelism begins and ends with God, we can take comfort in the fact that he is in control and that we are given the privilege of participation.

"I planted, Apollos watered, but God was causing the growth. So then neither the one who plants nor the one who waters is anything, but God who causes the growth. Now he who plants and he who waters are one; but each will receive his own reward according to his own labor. For we are God's fellow workers; you are God's field, God's building" (1 Corinthians 3:6–9). God causes the growth, not us; we can no more lead a person to conviction and the new birth than we can cause a plant to grow by pulling it out of the ground. Even so, the Lord chooses to use his children in the process of evangelism. Divine sovereignty and human responsibility mysteriously mesh together in the evangelistic enterprise just as they do in other areas such as prayer. Just as a godly farmer patiently and diligently creates the right conditions through preparation, planting, and cultivation while looking to God for the growth of the crop, so we must see evangelism as a divine-human process.

If we overlook these truths, we can easily slip into one of two opposite errors. The first error is to think we have failed if a person we are working with does not come to faith in Christ. We may also take it as a personal rejection when people dismiss or ignore our message to them about the Good News. An understanding that evangelism is a process and that the results belong to God will help us avoid this wrong thinking.

The second error is to take the credit when we experience the joy of leading someone to Jesus. It typically takes multiple encounters and exposures to the gospel before people are ready to respond, and the believer who reaps the harvest is only one of several influences. When we hear about someone coming to Christ, we can reasonably assume that there was a history of intercession and exposure before the person came to faith. Moreover, God gives us opportunities to proclaim the gospel, but our proclamation is impotent apart from the power of the Holy Spirit. When we realize that our task is to love, serve, and pray for outsiders and to share the Good News when the opportunity arises, we can relax in the sovereignty of God and leave the outcome in his hands.

Cultivating Requires More Time Than Reaping

Most models of evangelism center on the reaping side of the agricultural spectrum, and this is understandable, since the harvest is the desired result of the whole process. The problem, however, is that this tends to promote a more confrontational style than most people would prefer, and it could also foster a superficial "hit and run" technique that leads to questionable conversions and a general lack of follow-up (see figure 32.2). The unstable configuration on the left portrays the problem of attempting to reap with minimal cultivation. There are exceptions, but we should expect the cultivation phase of evangelism to take more time than the reaping phase. Otherwise we may be inclined to bruise the fruit by attempting to pick it too soon. The stable triangle on the right illustrates the importance of planting the seed of the gospel in well-prepared soil in such a way that reaping is the by-product of faithful and patient cultivation.

This series of contrasts adapted from Tim Down's *Finding Common Ground* is instructive (table 32.3):

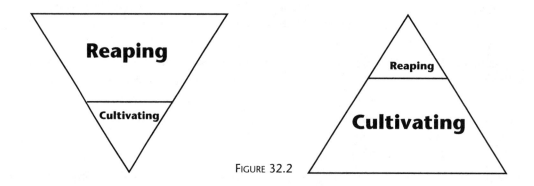

FIGURE 32.2

THE HARVESTER FOCUSES ON	WHILE THE SOWER FOCUSES ON
The end result	Preparing the way
Proclamation	Persuasion
Immediate results	Gradual change
Individual effort	Team impact
Points of disagreement	Common ground
Answers	Questions
Justice	Love
Courage	Wisdom

TABLE 32.3

Evangelism Largely Relates to the Church Scattered

The primary focus of the church gathered is edification. This is the purpose of spiritual gifts and the ministry of the Word as believers assemble to build one another in a context of compassion, kindness, humility, gentleness, patience, and love (Colossians 3:12–14). Evangelism takes place in churches, but the bulk of evangelism should take place in the context of the church scattered (this includes such activities as home groups in which Christ-centered community touches outsiders in neighborhoods through the witness of believers who love one another). As believers grow in their faith, it should be natural for them to desire to represent Christ in their community, their workplaces, their neighborhoods, and their friendships. In some settings, however, the assumption is made that outsiders should be brought into the church so that the pastor can lead them to Christ. When this happens, the church becomes a "stained-glass aquarium" in which the minister does the fishing while the laity plays a passive role. By contrast, it is important for churches and ministries to equip laypeople to be effective ambassadors of Christ in the natural settings in which they exert an influence. Edification (the body gathered) builds up believers so that they will be better equipped to evangelize (the body scattered).

Evangelism Is an Eternal Investment

The parables of the lost sheep, the lost coin, and the lost son in Luke 15 are one parable in three movements. In each case something of value was lost, an effort was made to find it, and when it was found, the result was joy and celebration. The application of these stories is that "there is joy in heaven in the presence of the angels of God over one sinner who repents" (v. 10). Each person is of great value to God, and when we participate in the process of helping people come into the Father's household, we share in the Father's joy. In the parable of the unrighteous steward that follows in Luke 16, Jesus teaches that we can leverage the temporal assets of time, talent, treasure, and truth into eternal gain. "And I say to you, make friends for yourselves by means of the wealth of unrighteousness, so that when it fails, they will receive you into the eternal dwellings" (v. 9). This is what the apostle Paul anticipated when he told the Thessalonians, "For who is our hope or joy or crown of exultation? Is it not even you, in the presence of our Lord Jesus at His coming? For you are our glory and joy" (1 Thessalonians 2:19–20). When we invest our lives and resources in the spiritual service of others in our walk and in our words, we are investing in eternal relationships. In effect, we are building a portfolio in heaven and sending our assets ahead of us. We are also pursuing what pleases the Father and participating in his purposes.

There are a variety of things we will be able to do better in heaven than we can possibly do on earth. These include music, prayer, fellowship, worship, and the study of general and special revelation. But we tend to overlook the one thing we will not be able to do in heaven that we can do on earth—serve those who are in desperate need. When we leave this planet we will never again have the privilege of sharing the gospel and serving the lost.

Those who want to be rich toward God will give their lives in exchange for the things he declared to be important. Jesus said in Luke 16:15, "That which is highly esteemed among men is detestable in the sight of God." Those who seek the Father's heart will respond to his Son's call: "Follow Me, and I will make you fishers of men" (Matthew 4:19).

We Can Evangelize for the Wrong Reasons

In his letter to the Philippians, Paul told them that some people were "preaching Christ even from envy and strife, but some also from good will" (1:15). The former were doing it out of selfish ambition, while the latter were doing it out of love (1:16–17). But Paul's wise response was, "Only that in every way, whether in pretense or in truth,

Christ is proclaimed; and in this I rejoice" (1:18). Regardless of our intentions, if the gospel is proclaimed, God's Word will accomplish his purpose, even if it is in spite of the messenger's motives (Isaiah 55:10–11). Still, as ambassadors of Christ, we do well to examine our reasons for sharing our faith, so that we will align our hearts with what delights our Father.

Two unseemly motivations for proclaiming the gospel are guilt and pride. Many believers have been taught to feel guilty when they fail to share their faith with outsiders. When this happens, the burden can grow so great that they may suddenly buttonhole an unsuspecting victim and blurt out the gospel before running back into hiding until the guilt builds up again. This kind of "gospel grenade" experience is painfully embarrassing for all involved.

Others have slipped into the error of pride by sharing their faith to hang more scalps on their spiritual belt or carve more notches on their Bible. Those who take pride in numbers and in comparing results with others have a way of trying to force the decision, like a salesman who won't remove his foot from the door until the person signs on the dotted line.

By contrast, in 2 Corinthians 5 Paul mentions three biblical motivations for proclaiming the Good News. First, he does so because he seeks to be pleasing to the Father. "Therefore we also have as our ambition, whether at home or absent, to be pleasing to Him" (v. 9). It pleases the Father when we speak well of his Son to others. Second, he wishes to receive the Lord's reward at the judgment seat of Christ for faithfulness to the opportunities he has been given (v. 10). "Therefore, knowing the fear of the Lord, we persuade men" (v. 11). It is a rich reward to have friends who will spend eternity with us because we were privileged to participate in God's purposes for their lives. Third, he is compelled by Christ's love and his love for Christ to be Christ's ambassador in this world (vv. 14–20). The secret to loving the unlovable is to be controlled by Christ's love for them.

Evangelism Involves Words and Deeds

In recent years, the concept of lifestyle, relational, or friendship evangelism has been taught in a growing number of churches and ministries. This relational approach to evangelism as a way of life has the advantages of stressing the cultivation process and of being less threatening to most believers than methods that are more confrontational. But it is important to avoid the two extremes of all friendship without evangelism and all evangelism without friendship. By being dependent on the Spirit and sensitive to the opportunities he provides, we can seek the right balance between incarnation and proclamation (table 32.4).

Biblical evangelism is a lifestyle to be lived, not a lesson to be learned; it is a process more than a program.

FRIENDSHIP	EVANGELISM
Love	Truth
Actions	Reasons
Walk	Talk
Life	Lips
Incarnation	Proclamation
Intention	Information

TABLE 32.4

Evangelism and Discipleship Should Be Integrated

Just as discipleship should lead to evangelism, evangelism in turn should lead to discipleship. Evangelism is the beginning of the journey of knowing Jesus, not the end. Our Lord commissioned us to make disciples, not decisions (Matthew 28:18–20). The joy of the journey commences with conversion and increases with maturity. As a spiritual father, Paul wanted his converts in Thessalonica to grow into the fullness of formation in the image of Christ. "You are witnesses, and so is God, how devoutly and uprightly and blamelessly we behaved toward you believers; just as you know how we were exhorting and encouraging and imploring each one of you as a father would his own children, so that you would walk in a manner worthy of the God who calls you into His own kingdom and glory" (1 Thessalonians 2:10–12).

Spiritual obstetrics should naturally and smoothly transition into spiritual pediatrics. This follow-up process requires love, patience, and acceptance, since growth is gradual and young children tend to make messes.

QUESTIONS FOR PERSONAL APPLICATION

- How motivated are you to be involved in a lifestyle of evangelism?
- Which of the eight evangelism principles spoke most directly to you?
- How do you respond to the principles that evangelism is a process and that the results belong to God? In what way is this freeing to you?
- Why is it typical for many who engage in evangelism to focus more on reaping than on cultivating?
- Have you ever tried to evangelize for the wrong reasons? How did this affect your attitude toward evangelism?

33

NURTURING
SPIRITUALITY
Overcoming the Barriers to Evangelism

CHAPTER OVERVIEW

There are barriers on both sides of the door of evangelism. Barriers for believers include hard-sell methods, fear, inadequacy, indifference, limited time, and isolation from unbelievers. The three barriers for unbelievers are emotional, intellectual, and volitional. These can be overcome through building trust relationships, graciously answering objections, and prayer. This chapter concludes with a look at the contexts in which evangelism can take place.

CHAPTER OBJECTIVES

- Deeper insight on the barriers that prevent most believers from sharing their faith
- An awareness of the emotional, intellectual, and volitional barriers that keep people away from a relationship with Christ
- Encouragement that we have been given natural settings in which we can cultivate winsome relationships with unbelievers

---

In practice, both believers and unbelievers are uncomfortable with evangelism. James Stuart, professor of New Testament at the University of Edinburgh, puts it this way: "The threat to Christianity is not atheism, materialism, or communism. The greatest threat to Christianity is Christians who are trying to sneak into heaven incognito without ever having shared their faith."

BARRIERS FOR BELIEVERS

Jesus told his disciples, "The harvest is plentiful, but the workers are few. Therefore beseech the Lord of the harvest to send out workers into His harvest" (Matthew 9:37–38). Several barriers prevent workers from going into the field.

The Barrier of Method

I came across a cartoon that depicts three people in a church office discussing evangelism. One of them says, "When I was a kid I would go up to someone's porch, ring the doorbell, and run like the dickens. I still do it, except now our church calls it 'outreach training.'" In another cartoon, an evangelist is holding forth in the pulpit and the whole audience is standing at the front of the sanctuary—everyone except one terrified person hiding in a pew with a hymnal covering his head. The evangelist says, "As we sing the 314th verse of 'Just as I Am,' isn't there ONE MORE who will come?" Yet another cartoon pictures a barber sharpening his straight razor on a leather strap as he asks the customer in his chair, "Are you ready to die?"

Many people associate evangelism with hard-sell methods and scare tactics. There are a number of unbiblical stereotypes that have kept people away from the real thing.

The scalp hunter. This is the person who tries to save souls to add to his collection of spiritual trophies.

The shoehorn approach. No matter how inappropriate, this person will use any opening he can to slip in the gospel.

The con-man approach. In this approach, the gospel is introduced under false pretenses.

The 2 x 4 approach. The evangelist puts undue pressure on the unbeliever as he seeks to blast him with a blessing and clobber him into the kingdom.

There is enough offense to the gospel (1 Corinthians 1:18–24) without adding our own offense to it. Paul urged his readers, "Give no offense either to Jews or to Greeks or to the church of God; just as I also please all men in all things, not seeking my own profit but the profit of the many, so that they may be saved" (1 Corinthians 10:32–33).

Scripture illustrates different methods of evangelism, and three of these are proclamational, confrontational, and relational. The apostle Peter used a *proclamational* approach in his sermon on the day of Pentecost (Acts 2). About three thousand souls were added to the family of God that day (v. 41). This method of public proclamation requires a special gifting and anointing, and only a small percentage of believers can do it well.

Philip the deacon illustrates a *confrontational* approach in his one-time encounter with the Ethiopian eunuch (Acts 8:26–39). All of us are called to represent Christ, but a few believers are given a particular gift of personal evangelism that enables them to be effective in sharing the gospel without first developing a relational history with outsiders.

The *relational* approach is portrayed in the apostle Paul's description of his intimate personal engagement with people in Thessalonica (1 Thessalonians 2:1–12). "Having so fond an affection for you, we were well-pleased to impart to you not only the gospel of God but also our own lives, because you had become very dear to us" (v. 8). Unlike the first two approaches, the relational approach is accessible to anyone who is willing to cultivate personal relationships with outsiders. For most of us, evangelism is best accomplished when it flows out of relationships in an unforced, conversational way.

In *Becoming a Contagious Christian,* Mark Mittelberg and Bill Hybels suggest that at least six styles of evangelism are illustrated in the New Testament and that people today feel most comfortable using primarily one of those styles. The styles are interpersonal, testimonial, intellectual, invitational, confrontational, and service. Mittelberg relates these styles to the church in *Building a Contagious Church.*

The Barrier of Fear

Although we have been called to shake the salt and shine the light, most of us dilute the salt and cover the light. Two primary reasons why most believers do not share their faith are fear of rejection and fear of failure. No one wants to be disliked, alienated, labeled, and avoided. Many Christians are afraid to tell others about Christ because they think they are being personally rejected if their audience does not respond positively. This fear stems from an inadequate view of God. As believers in Christ, we must recognize that our security and identity are found in him, not in our vacillating relationships with others. We must also realize that when people reject our message, this need not mean that they are rejecting us. Rather, they are saying no to God's offer of life in Christ.

While the fear of rejection is often the result of an inadequate view of God, the fear of failure generally results from an inadequate view of evangelism. As we have seen, the typical evangelistic model is confrontational rather than conversational. Few people feel comfortable with an approach that lays all the stress on closing the sale or reaping the harvest. The relational model offers an alternative approach that views evangelism as a process that can take days, weeks, or years. When we participate in the process at any point and leave the results in God's hands, we can relax in the relationship and depend on God's power. "God has not given us a spirit of timidity, but of power and love and discipline" (2 Timothy 1:7; see Psalm 56:3–4; Nehemiah 4:14). When we remember that we are God's children and that he has promised his presence and power as we communicate the Good News (Matthew 28:20), we can rest in him.

The Barrier of Inadequacy

The problem of people who feel fearful or guilty regarding evangelism is compounded by the barrier of inadequacy. Many who would otherwise wish to share their faith feel unprepared to do so. We can overcome this barrier if we remember two things. First, our adequacy comes from Jesus, not from ourselves. Apart from him, we are incapable of changing other people, let alone leading them to Christ. "Such confidence we have through Christ toward God. Not that we are adequate in ourselves to consider anything as coming from ourselves, but our adequacy is from God, who also made us adequate as servants of a new covenant" (2 Corinthians 3:4–6a). When we engage in the process of evangelism, we are committing ourselves to something that cannot occur unless God does it through us.

Second, if we are unprepared to share the gospel or to answer the objections people may have, the solution is to "be diligent to present yourself approved to God as a workman who does not need to be ashamed, accurately handling the word of truth" (2 Timothy 2:15). Most believers do not know how to make a simple gospel presentation with an unmarked Bible, but this is not difficult to learn. Similarly, most do not know how to answer the common questions that are likely to surface when we seek to plant the seed of the Word. However, this need not prevent us from going into the field, since good answers are readily available, as we will see. As Howard Hendricks put it, if you fail to prepare, you prepare to fail.

The Barrier of Indifference

The story is told that when William Jennings Bryan was asked to speak in front of a little congregation in West Virginia, he began by saying, "I have three points today. First, millions are dying and going to hell. Second, you people don't give a damn. Third, some of you are more concerned that I said 'damn' than that millions are dying and going to hell." We serve a God who sent his Son to seek and to save the lost, but it is easier for us to be more concerned with side issues than with what is close to the Father's heart.

It is remarkable that within two years of conversion to Christianity, most believers have few if any non-Christian friends. Surveys taken in churches indicate that the longer a person is a believer, the fewer unbelieving friends he or she has. Often the only people who are trying to share their faith are the new converts, the babes in Christ. The more mature and better-equipped Christians are not reaching out in the way they could and should.

I like to tell the tale of the airplane that carried four people and only three parachutes. There was the pilot, a genius, a minister, and a Boy Scout. When the engine caught fire and the plane began to go down, the pilot ran out of the cockpit, grabbed one of the parachutes, and bailed out. The genius stood up and said, "I am the world's smartest man! The world needs what I have to offer." He grabbed one and jumped out, leaving the minister and the scout. The minister told the boy, "Your whole life is before you—take the last parachute." The scout answered, "Don't sweat it, mister—the world's smartest man just bailed out with my backpack!" In a real sense, the world is going down in flames, and people are putting their hope in the backpacks of works, merit, possessions, position, and power. But the gospel tells us that the only true parachute is Jesus Christ.

We need to remember what is at stake. "He who has the Son has the life; he who does not have the Son of God does not have the life" (1 John 5:12). The stakes associated with the message we share are high, for they involve nothing less than people's eternal destiny.

The Barrier of Time

Even when we do want to get involved, we find ourselves busier than ever. This is when we need to recall that our perspective shapes our priorities and that our priorities shape our practice. If we wish to store up treasures in heaven, we must "seek first His kingdom and His righteousness" (Matthew 6:33) and trust God to energize our activities. The Bible frequently reminds us of the brevity of our time on earth and of our need to invest this resource in the best possible way. "Therefore be careful how you walk, not as unwise men but as wise, making the most of your time, because the days are evil" (Ephesians 5:15–16; also see Psalm 90:12; Ecclesiastes 8:5; Colossians 4:5; James 4:14–17).

Jesus was never in a hurry to do the will of his Father, and yet he had time to complete the task for which he had come. "I glorified You on the earth, having accomplished the work which You have given Me to do" (John 17:4). We also have been given enough time to accomplish God's purposes for our lives.

If we examined the way we invest the 168 hours we have been allotted each week by charting our activities in 15-minute blocks, we would probably pinpoint a significant amount of wasted time, cluttered agendas, and excessive commitments. We need to revisit our schedules in light of biblical priorities to see how well they reflect the important things like time with family and with Christian and non-Christian friends. If we are not cultivating an eternal perspective, our priorities and practice will inevitably be distorted.

The Barrier of Isolation

There is no impact without contact, but some believers have espoused the mentality that they must stay aloof from relationships with outsiders. Fearing that their thinking and behavior would be polluted by such contacts, these people have confused the biblical teaching about separation with an unbiblical practice of isolation. Distinctiveness is not the same as dissociation, and Scripture does not teach us to isolate ourselves from outsiders. Instead, it tells us to dissociate from Christians who are bringing reproach on the testimony of Christ by their immoral behavior. "I wrote you in my letter not to associate with immoral people; I did not at all mean with the immoral people of this world, or with the covetous and swindlers, or with idolaters, for then you would have to go out of the world. But actually, I wrote to you not to associate with any so-called brother if he is an immoral person" (1 Corinthians 5:9–11).

Indeed, we should not participate with anyone in the practice of evil or impurity (2 Corinthians 6:14–18), but it is possible to have extensive areas of common ground without compromise in our relationships with unbelievers (1 Corinthians 9:19–23). We are not to be friends with the world system (James 4:4; 1 John 2:15–17), but we should follow Jesus in being friends with the people of the world (Matthew 11:19). Like our Lord, we should love sinners but hate sin; too often people love sin and hate sinners. Our mission is not to get people to clean up their acts but to lead them to the One who can change them from the inside out.

Another cause of isolation is the "holy huddle" or the sit, soak, and sour syndrome. The Sea of Galilee teems with life because water flows in and out of it. The Dead Sea, by contrast, is aptly named, since the water flowing into it has no outlet. Edification and *koinonia* are important to the spiritual health and nurture of believers, but the inflow of teaching and fellowship (Acts 2:42) should be balanced by the outflow of outreach into the community (Acts 2:47). Knowing Christ (edification) should always be coupled with making him known (evangelism).

BARRIERS FOR UNBELIEVERS

The Emotional Barrier

Many unbelievers have a negative attitude toward organized religion or Christians because of painful experiences they have had. Those who have been reared in oppressive or legalistic homes or whose only association with Christianity is hypocrisy and exploitation will naturally develop an emotional barrier to the gospel. The only effective way to overcome this barrier is to build relational bridges by loving and serving outsiders in areas of common interest. Walls are easier to build than bridges, but people will never believe we want them in heaven when we don't want them in our living rooms. Distrust and negative stereotypes are gradually overcome by being a safe, nonmanipulative, loving, and trustworthy friend. It has been said that people don't care how much you know until they know how much you care. As we pray for our non-Christian friends and cultivate relationships based on common-ground activities, they begin to see a quality of life and a hope in us that requires an explanation.

We cannot effectively introduce ideological tension (the message of Jesus Christ to an unbeliever) when there is relational tension. Only through our love and concern will we earn the right to be heard. Friendship expressed through common-ground activities with unbelievers is a bridge that enables us to go into their world to bring them into ours. Cultivating friendships takes time and effort, but this is by far the most effective vehicle for the communication of the message of life in Jesus.

Many believers fear that if they spend any time with outsiders, it will cause them to compromise their convictions. But Paul wrote that "I have become all things to all men, so that I may by all means save some" (1 Corinthians 9:22; see vv. 19–27). Regardless of what people were like or where they were in their spiritual pilgrimage, Paul sought to identify with them as much as possible. His primary procedure in helping them come to Christ was to establish common ground without compromise. He consistently applied the principle of communication without contamination.

If we always talk in general terms about reaching the world for Christ, we may miss out on reaching the world in which we live. Our task is to be faithful in concentrating our attention on the people God has placed in our spheres of influence. The parable of the lost sheep in Luke 15:3–7 illustrates the need for individual attention and concerted effort to seek that which is lost (cf. Luke 19:10). It is easy to spend our time keeping the ninety-nine comfortable and to forget about the one that is lost. The shepherd left the flock to graze in the pasture and diligently pursued the missing sheep until it was found. He focused his attention on the one because each individual is of great value. This is why heaven rejoices over one sinner who repents (Luke 15:7, 10, 32).

The Intellectual Barrier

Socrates observed that the unexamined life is not worth living; it is also true that the unexamined faith is not worth believing. John Stott wisely stated that while we cannot pander to intellectual arrogance, we must cater to intellectual integrity. There are different intentions behind the questions people ask, but if someone is genuinely seeking an answer, we are responsible to provide it for him or her. If a professor tells a class all the questions that will be on an upcoming examination, the students are without excuse if they don't know the answers. Part of our preparation for effective evangelism is to have an answer for the questions we know we are likely to encounter. If a new question comes up and we don't know the answer, we should honestly admit it. This will give us an opportunity to find the answer and get back with our friend. But if we get caught again by the same question and have failed to do our homework, we are responsible.

Many believers think they could never learn to defend their faith intelligently, because there must be thousands of objections that would have to be answered. But in practice, the vast majority of the objections to Christianity are variations and combinations of only twelve basic questions. In *I'm Glad You Asked*, Larry Moody and I outline the answers to these common objections:

1. Does God really exist?
2. Why believe in miracles?
3. Isn't Christianity just a psychological crutch?

4. Is the Bible trustworthy?
5. If God is good, why do evil and suffering exist?
6. How can Christ be the only way to God?
7. Will God judge those who never heard about Christ?
8. If Christianity is true, why are there so many hypocrites?
9. Isn't a good moral life enough to get into heaven?
10. Isn't just believing in Christ too easy?
11. What does it mean to believe?
12. Can people be sure of their salvation?

When we learn how to deal with these issues, each of these objections becomes an opportunity to clarify the message about Christ. If people ask specific subquestions for which we don't have good answers, there is no reason to become threatened. Simply affirm that they have raised a good question and that you will get back with them when you have found the answer. In this way, you will gain skill and knowledge by being involved in the process. Here are a few of the many resources for good answers:

Kenneth Boa and Larry Moody, *I'm Glad You Asked*

Kenneth Boa and Robert M. Bowman Jr., *An Unchanging Faith in a Changing World*, *Faith Has Its Reasons*, and *Twenty Compelling Evidences That God Exists*

Paul Copan, *True for You, but Not for Me* and *That's Just Your Interpretation*

William Lane Craig, *Reasonable Faith* and *No Easy Answers*

David DeWitt, *Answering the Tough Ones*

Norman Geisler, *Christian Apologetics*

Norman Geisler and Ron Brooks, *When Skeptics Ask*

R. Douglas Geivett and Gary R. Habermas, eds., *In Defense of Miracles*

Gary R. Habermas, *Ancient Evidence for the Life of Jesus* and *The Resurrection of Jesus*

Peter Kreeft, *Making Sense out of Suffering* and *Fundamentals of the Faith*

C. S. Lewis, *The Problem of Pain* and *Miracles*

Josh McDowell, *Evidence That Demands a Verdict*

Alister McGrath, *Intellectuals Don't Need God and Other Modern Myths* and *A Passion for Truth*

J. P. Moreland, *Scaling the Secular City*

Timothy R. Phillips and Dennis L. Okholm, eds., *Christian Apologetics in the Postmodern World*

Ravi Zacharias, *Can Man Live without God?*

Gregory Boyd, *Letters from a Skeptic*

Paul Chamberlain, *Can We Be Good without God?*

Peter Kreeft, *Christianity for Modern Pagans*, *Yes or No: Straight Answers to Tough Questions about Christianity*, *Between Heaven and Hell*, and *Socrates Meets Jesus*

C. S. Lewis, *Mere Christianity*

Josh McDowell, *More Than a Carpenter*

John R. W. Stott, *Basic Christianity*

Lee Strobel, *The Case for Christ* and *The Case for Faith*

The heart cannot rejoice in what the mind rejects. Since many of the intellectual barriers result from distorted information, we are seeking to help our friends make a well-informed response to the claims of Christ. But it is also important for us to do this in a gentle and loving way, since "the Lord's bond-servant must not be quarrelsome, but be kind to all, able to teach, patient when wronged, with gentleness correcting those who are in opposition, if perhaps God may grant them repentance leading to the knowledge of the truth" (2 Timothy 2:24–25).

Peter also gives us clear insight into dealing with the intellectual barrier: "Sanctify Christ as Lord in your hearts, always being ready to make a defense to everyone who asks you to give an account for the hope that is in you, yet with gentleness and reverence" (1 Peter 3:15). This verse presupposes that the quality of our lives will cause people to ask us to explain why we are different. This requires spiritual preparation ("sanctify Christ as Lord in your hearts") as well as intellectual preparation ("always being ready to make a defense") and relational preparation ("with gentleness and reverence"). We need both knowledge (what to say) and skill (how to say it).

Peter tells us to make a defense without being defensive. Similarly, the book of Jude tells us to take the offense without being offensive: "Beloved, while I was making every effort to write you about our common salvation, I felt the necessity to write to you appealing that you contend earnestly for the faith which was once for all handed down to the saints" (Jude 3).

When the opportunity arises, it is important to be able to make a simple and clear presentation of the message of salvation in Scripture. A number of helpful tools can help you do this, and one of the most effective is the material in "The Search," a booklet published by Search Ministries. This booklet looks at God's position, our condition, God's provision, and our decision. Other helpful tools are available from Evangelism Explosion and the Billy Graham Evangelistic Association.

We learn to listen with love (Proverbs 18:2, 13; James 1:19) by asking helpful questions and actively listening for expressions of felt needs and concerns as well as emotional and intellectual barriers. By giving our friends the others-centered gift of focused attention and by taking a genuine interest in them, we create an atmosphere of love and acceptance in which the seed of the gospel can be planted.

The Volitional Barrier

We saw that the emotional barrier is erected because of negative experiences and associations with religion in general and Christianity in particular and that the key to overcoming this barrier of feelings is the bridge of friendship. Second, the intellectual barrier is erected because of misconceptions and a conceptual bias against a biblical worldview, and this barrier of thinking is overcome by turning objections into opportunities to share the truth about Jesus. Third, the volitional barrier is erected because of a sinful nature that is at enmity with God, and this barrier of the will can be overcome only by prayer and the convicting ministry of the Holy Spirit (John 16:8–11).

Evangelism will not be effective because of method or skills but because of the solid foundation of prayer. The whole process of cultivating quality relationships for Christ must begin with prayer, be sustained by prayer, and end with prayer as God produces the fruit. The true battle is waged on the field of prayer. Thus when prayer is reduced to an afterthought in evangelism, the proverbial cart is placed before the horse.

The apostle Paul recognized the critical relationship between prayer and the spread of the gospel and spelled this out in Ephesians and Colossians:

> With all prayer and petition pray at all times in the Spirit, and with this in view, be on the alert with all perseverance and petition for all the saints, and pray on my behalf, that utterance may be given to me in the opening of my mouth, to make known with boldness the mystery of the gospel, for which I am an ambassador in chains; that in proclaiming it I may speak boldly, as I ought to speak.
> *Ephesians 6:18–20*

> Devote yourselves to prayer, keeping alert in it with an attitude of thanksgiving; praying at the same time for us as well, that God will open up to us a door for the word, so that we may speak forth the mystery of Christ, for which I have also been imprisoned; that I may make it clear in the way I ought to speak.
> *Colossians 4:2–4*

Combining these two passages, we can find the answer to three questions about prayer in relation to effective evangelism: how to pray, what to pray, and for whom to pray.

How to Pray

First, we are to devote ourselves to prayer (Colossians 4:2). We should persevere and not lose heart as we pray for others. Second, we should "pray at all times in the Spirit" (Ephesians 6:18). We must be sure that there is no hindrance of unconfessed sin or improper motives in our hearts. Third, Paul tells us in both passages to keep alert in our prayers. Where prayer prevails, power falls. Fourth, we are to pray "with an attitude of thanksgiving" (Colossians 4:2). This is an expectant attitude that believes God is at work in our lives and in the lives of those for whom we are praying.

What to Pray

First, we should pray for an open door for the word, that is, the right opportunities to share the gospel. Second, we should pray for an open mouth (Ephesians 6:19) so that we will make use of Spirit-prepared opportunities. Third, we should pray for clarity in our presentation (Colossians 4:4). Fourth, we should pray for boldness in proclaiming the mystery of the gospel (Ephesians 6:19–20). This is not the same as brazenness or brashness; rather, it means to speak freely, openly, and without embarrassment when the opportunity arises.

For Whom to Pray

In Colossians 4:3, Paul says, "praying at the same time for us as well." Believers involved in the front-line activity of relational evangelism need to pray for one another. And we also need to pray specifically for the outsiders God has brought into our lives.

Prayer is the prelude to all effective evangelism. The process of cultivation begins on our knees, and as D. L. Moody reminded us, we must talk to God about people before we talk to people about God.

Some Christians have developed an us-versus-them mentality, thinking that unbelievers are the enemy. But unbelievers are not the enemy; they are victims of the enemy.

> And even if our gospel is veiled, it is veiled to those who are perishing, in whose case the god of this world has blinded the minds of the unbelieving so that they might not see the light of the gospel of the glory of Christ, who is the image of God.
>
> *2 Corinthians 4:3–4*

> And you were dead in your trespasses and sins.
>
> *Ephesians 2:1*

> With gentleness correcting those who are in opposition, if perhaps God may grant them repentance leading to the knowledge of the truth, and they may come to their senses and escape the snare of the devil, having been held captive by him to do his will.
>
> *2 Timothy 2:25–26*

According to these texts, people without Christ are spiritually blinded, spiritually dead, and held captive by Satan. We must avoid the wrong reactions of treating them with contempt, avoiding them like vermin, and judging them. We tend to judge the world and talk to ourselves when we should be judging ourselves and talking to the world.

It is important for us to realize that unbelievers will have difficulty in understanding and responding to the gospel. The fruit comes from the root, and we should not expect regenerate behavior from unregenerate people. Finally, we should remember their spiritual condition and recall that we were once in the same plight.

THE CONTEXT OF EVANGELISM

The visual and verbal media may be effective, but nothing can match the power of the personal touch. Christ, the visible expression of the invisible God, came to disclose the heart, the essence, and the being of the eternal God in the clearest way of all—personal revelation. And he has called the church to personally manifest his life to the world. We are letters of Christ, "known and read by all men" (2 Corinthians 3:2–3). We are to be communicators of a message the world desperately needs to hear, and this communication must take place not only with our lips but also with our lives. Our words must be authenticated by the quality of our character, by the genuineness of our love and service of people, and by the corporate love within the Christian community.

Our friends without Jesus need to know that they are important to us for who they are and not because they are warm bodies we want to persuade. This will be reflected in our words, attitudes, and actions. When there is a discrepancy between our talk and our walk, what we are will speak so loudly that others will not hear what we say. People are looking for reality, not role plays.

Colossians 4:5–6 nicely balances the two issues of our words and our works (table 33.1).

WALK WISELY	TALK GRACIOUSLY
Colossians 4:5	Colossians 4:6
Conduct yourselves with wisdom toward outsiders, making the most of the opportunity.	Let your speech always be with grace, as though seasoned with salt, so that you will know how you should respond to each person.
Relational	Evangelism

TABLE 33.1

Like the two wings on an airplane, talk and walk must be balanced and symmetrical. We must avoid the two extremes of all talk and no walk and all walk and no talk. The first is evangelism without friendship; the second is friendship without evangelism.

Both Colossians 4:5 and Ephesians 5:15–16 tell us to walk in wisdom by making the most of the *kairon* (times, opportunities) the Lord puts in our paths. We are called to a life of constant alertness to opportunities for bearing witness to the hope that is in us. We need eyes to see these moments and a will that is trained to act. It is a matter of our inner time controlling our external time, and not vice versa.

Most of us have far more ministry opportunities than we realize. God has sovereignly given us relational networks in four areas:

1. Family—our biological network
2. Friends—our social network
3. Co-workers—our vocational network
4. Neighbors—our geographical network

Within each of these spheres, we experience differing degrees of closeness, ranging from casual contacts to intimate friendships. It is a helpful exercise to think about the people in each of your four networks and to pray for God's direction as to which of these relationships he would have you cultivate for his purposes. As you identify the people the Lord would have you love and serve in this way, creatively consider what interests you share in common with each of these people (e.g., sports, children, picnics, recreation, the arts, clubs, food, travel). Then begin to schedule these common-ground activities with the unbelievers for whom you are praying.

Remember that people are not projects. It is good to desire and pray for their salvation, but this outcome must never become a personal goal. If it degenerates into a goal, you will seek to manipulate the relationship to bring it about, and this will have negative consequences. Your part is to love and serve them unconditionally and to leave the results to God.

When you have natural opportunities to transition from small talk to spiritual things, seek to avoid clichés and theological jargon and be sensitive enough not to be pushy or argumentative. Treat outsiders with "gentleness and reverence" (1 Peter 3:15) and use responses that stimulate rather than stifle open discussion.

Recalling the spectrum of spirituality we discussed earlier, there is a variety of methods that are appropriate to people at different points on the left side of the spectrum (–10 to–1). These include one-on-one cultivation, open forums (discussion parties in homes), small-group evangelism, exploratory Bible studies with individuals or groups, and special outreach events. Of the many resources that can equip and encourage you to be more effective in your God-given arena of influence, these are especially helpful.

Search Ministries' *Beginnings, Foundations, Questions, Connexions,* and *The Search Open Forum* workbooks, and *Heart for the Harvest* seminar
Joseph Aldrich, *Life-Style Evangelism* and *Gentle Persuasion*
George Barna, *Evangelism That Works*
Michael Cocoris, *Evangelism: A Biblical Approach*
Lyman Coleman, Peter Menconi, and Richard Peace, *Support Group Series*

Robert E. Coleman, *The Master's Way of Personal Evangelism*

Tim Downs, *Finding Common Ground*

Leighton Ford, *The Power of Story*

Michael Green, *Evangelism Now and Then*

Joel D. Heck, ed., *The Art of Sharing Your Faith*

Howard G. Hendricks, *Say It with Love*

Roberta Hestenes, *Using the Bible in Groups*

Bill Hybels and Mark Mittelberg, *Becoming a Contagious Christian*

Bob Jacks and Betty Jacks with Ron Wormser Sr., *Your Home a Lighthouse*

James Kennedy, *Evangelism Explosion*

Paul Little, *How to Give Away Your Faith*

Mark McCloskey, *Tell It Often—Tell It Well*

Arthur G. McPhee, *Friendship Evangelism*

J. I. Packer, *Evangelism and the Sovereignty of God*

Archie Parish and John Parish, *Best Friends*

Richard Peace, *Small Group Evangelism*

Jim Peterson, *Living Proof* and *Evangelism as a Lifestyle*

Rebecca Manley Pippert, *Out of the Salt Shaker and into the World*

Matthew Prince, *Winning through Caring*

Ron Rand, *Won by One*

Lee Strobel, *Inside the Mind of Unchurched Harry and Mary*

Dawson Trotman, *Born to Reproduce*

Jerry Wiles, *How to Win Others to Christ*

Our Lord teaches us that the need is urgent and the rewards are eternal.

Do you not say, "There are yet four months, and then comes the harvest"? Behold, I say to you, lift up your eyes and look on the fields, that they are white for harvest. Already he who reaps is receiving wages and is gathering fruit for life eternal; so that he who sows and he who reaps may rejoice together.

John 4:35–36

Then He said to His disciples, "The harvest is plentiful, but the workers are few. Therefore beseech the Lord of the harvest to send out workers into His harvest."

Matthew 9:37–38

Jesus bookended his earthly ministry with evangelism. He began by calling his disciples to be fishers of men (Matthew 4:19) and ended by commissioning them to be his witnesses in the world (Acts 1:8).

As we develop an eternal perspective, become involved in the process, depend upon God's power, and trust God for the outcome, we will have the joy of being a part of the eternal purposes of the living God.

QUESTIONS FOR PERSONAL APPLICATION

- Which of the barriers for believers have been most debilitating in your life? What can you do to overcome them?
- What experiences have you had with proclamational, confrontational, and relational evangelism?
- How comfortable are you with building nonmanipulative relationships with unbelievers?
- How would you rate your ability to answer the twelve basic objections? If you are weak on some of them, you would do well to consult some of the resources that have been listed in this chapter.
- How specific and consistent are you in your intercessory prayers for unbelievers in your spheres of influence?

FACET 12

CORPORATE SPIRITUALITY
Encouragement, Accountability, and Worship

We come to faith as individuals, but we grow in community. This section discusses the need for community, challenges and creators of community, the nature and purpose of the church, soul care, servant leadership, accountability, and renewal.

34

CORPORATE SPIRITUALITY
The Need for Community

CHAPTER OVERVIEW

Corporate spirituality focuses on the dynamics of life together in the Spirit as an essential source of spiritual health and maturity. Spiritual formation involves both personal and corporate dimensions, and the Scriptures provide strong foundations for community. Ministry should flow out of both solitude and community, but there are a number of challenges to community in our culture.

CHAPTER OBJECTIVES

- An enhanced appreciation of the corporate dimension of spiritual formation
- A better realization of the interplay between solitude, community, and ministry in our spiritual walk
- An understanding of the threats to community in our culture and ways of building the corporate dimension of the spiritual life

Because God has created us in his image, we are relational beings who thrive best in community. Corporate spirituality focuses on the dynamics of life together in the Spirit as an essential source of spiritual health and maturity, but it also recognizes the fragility of this process and the many ways in which it can be undermined.

Community has been deteriorating in the Western world, and it is being challenged on several fronts. We have witnessed a growing pursuit of autonomy and self-determination. Our culture has been marked by a quest for independence, self-preservation, control, privatization, avoidance of accountability, superficial relationships, and alienation. It appears that people are busier than ever and lonelier than ever (this is illustrated in *The Saturated Self* by Kenneth J. Gergen and *Bowling Alone* by Robert Putnam). Technology, mobility, media, entertainment, distractions, travel, information overload, and transience all contribute to the growing plight of social instability and interpersonal tension. Time-saving inventions have only made our lives more hyperactive and stress-filled, and our addictions to urgency and performance make us externally driven rather than internally called. This cultural overemphasis on individualism has been aggravated by an increasing distrust of institutions, traditions, and authority.

We cannot return to the past, but we can learn how to treasure relationships as ends rather than means, and we can recapture a transcending biblical vision of commitment and community that will make us more human and less controlled by our culture.

PERSONAL AND CORPORATE

We come to faith as individuals, but we grow in community. Life in Jesus is not meant to be solitary and individualistic but shared and collective. Indeed, when we stand before Christ, we will be judged individually according to our works (2 Corinthians 5:10; Romans 14:12), but the nurture of the community of faith is designed to prepare us for our everlasting life with the Lord and with one another.

Evangelicals have a way of stressing the individual side of the spectrum, while liberals tend to emphasize the corporate side of the spectrum. On the theological right, the focus of attention is on justification before God and on the hope of the afterlife. On the theological left, the accent is on social justice and relevance in the current milieu. The danger of the right is that the gospel can become privatized and socially irrelevant; the danger of the left is that the gospel can be reduced to social ethics, inclusivism, and pluralism.

The full counsel of Scripture offers a better way that balances the personal and the corporate. It does so by affirming the good news of kingdom living in the present tense. Forgiveness of sins and the hope of heaven free us to walk with Jesus today and to draw our life from him in the context of our daily endeavors and encounters. This present relationship with Jesus makes us alive to the opportunities, requirements, and challenges of our unfolding lives. The spiritual life is both personal and social; it is both dependent upon God (transcendent) and active in the world (immanent). It weds personal holiness with social holiness and melds devotion to Jesus with service to others.

BIBLICAL FOUNDATIONS FOR COMMUNITY

In the wider cosmic story of Scripture, salvation is not an end but the necessary means to overcome the relational alienation with God, ourselves, others, and nature that was caused by the tragic introduction of sin. God is a relational being whose costly gift of salvation made it possible for our sinful condition of estrangement to be overcome so that we could enjoy a relationship with him as beloved children rather than condemned outsiders. Earlier in this book we observed that the mystery we call God is a community of being: the Lover, the Beloved, and the Love that flows among them. This trinitarian vision of the One and the Many, the Unity in diversity, the Three in

One, is found only in the Bible. In the progress of revelation, the Old Testament lays the foundation for the fuller expression of the three-personed God of the New Testament. It has been said that "the Old is in the New revealed; the New is in the Old concealed." The plural pronouns ("Let Us make man in Our image, according to Our likeness" [Genesis 1:26]; "Come, let Us go down and there confuse their language" [Genesis 11:7]), as well as a variety of other passages that distinguish the persons of God (e.g., Yahweh and Adonai in Psalm 110:1; the Ancient of Days and the Son of Man in Daniel 7:9–14), point to the New Testament mystery of God as one essence who subsists as three eternal and co-equal persons.

Since God made us in his image and likeness, we have been created for community with him and with one another. The Bible is unique in its portrayal of God as a covenant maker and keeper. As we enter into the benefits of the new covenant through the blood of Christ (Jeremiah 31:31–33; Luke 22:20), we become members of a new community that is called to reflect the glory of the Godhead in its corporate unity (John 17:22–26). The two greatest commandments are to love God and our neighbor (Mark 12:30–31), and the clearest expression of our love for God is our love for others (1 John 4:7, 11, 20–21). In effect, our Lord tells us, "If you love me, you will love the people I love."

The devastating consequence of the Fall (Genesis 3) was the fourfold alienation from God, ourselves, others, and nature. For those in Christ, a significant healing has begun on each of these levels, but it will not be complete until the redemption of our body and the redemption of the created order (Romans 8:19–23). In this both-and tension between the now and the not yet, we who have been renewed in Christ have already become new creatures (2 Corinthians 5:17). God's redemptive plan is to restore relationships on every level—with God, self, others, and creation—so that we will experience and express the *shalom* (peace, love, unity, harmony) of the Trinity. As John D. Zizioulas puts it in *Being as Communion*, we have been transferred from a hypostasis (substance or essence) of biological existence to a hypostasis of ecclesial existence. In the new birth, we are no longer identified with natural necessity but with the freedom of the life of Christ in communion with God and with the community of faith.

ACCEPTING THE POLARITIES

Comparatively speaking, the Old Testament lays more stress on corporate life while the New Testament more fully develops the personal dimension in addition to the social dimension of life in community. But both Testaments affirm the personal and the corporate as well as the inextricable relationship between the two. The personal inside-out transformation that is realized through the presence and action of Jesus is meant to reconcile and renew our relationships with others. Since spirituality does not flourish in isolation, the corporate process of discipleship should inform and supplement personal discipleship. Unfortunately, there is a natural tendency to be pulled toward the extremes of individualism or institutionalism. The individualistic extreme minimizes the value of life in community, while the institutional extreme causes the person to be lost in the service of the institution.

It is best to avoid the two horns of this dilemma by embracing the both-and tension between solitude and community. Dietrich Bonhoeffer put it well in *Life Together*:

> *Let him who cannot be alone beware of community.* He will only do harm to himself and to the community. Alone you stood before God when he called you; alone you had to answer that call; alone you had to struggle and pray; and alone you will die and give an account to God. You cannot escape from yourself; for God has singled you out. If you refuse to be alone you are rejecting Christ's call to you, and you can have no part in the community of those who are called. . . . *Let him who is not in community beware of being alone.* Into the community you were called, the call was not meant for you alone; in the community of the called you bear your cross, you struggle, you pray. You are not alone, even in death, and on the Last Day you will be only one member of the great congregation of Jesus Christ. If you scorn the fellowship of the brethren, you reject the call of Jesus Christ, and thus your solitude can only be hurtful to you.

When we accept the polarities of solitude and community, we discover that our personal walk with God is nourished in communion with others and that this life of unity in diversity and oneness in plurality is a reflection of trinitarian life.

SOLITUDE, COMMUNITY, AND MINISTRY

In a series on "Moving from Solitude to Community to Ministry," Henri Nouwen uses Luke 6:12–19 to illustrate the combination of these three disciplines in the life of our Lord. Jesus spent the night in solitude with God, and in the morning he formed community by gathering his disciples around him. Then in the afternoon Jesus ministered with his disciples to the physical and spiritual needs of the people who came to hear him. In the same way, we should imitate this inside-out order that flows from devotion to Christ (solitude), to devotion to the community, to devotion to the gospel (ministry). Community is the bridge that connects solitude (intimacy with God) with ministry to believers and unbelievers.

Commitment to Christ and to the Cross (Solitude)

As we saw in the discussion of holistic spirituality, when our lives are centered on Christ, each of the components (e.g., family, work, finances, and friends) finds its proper place. When we discussed exchanged life spirituality, we saw that our identity as being beloved by the Father and participants in the life of his Son makes us secure and significant. In the section on devotional spirituality we noted that inward intimacy with Christ energizes our outward activities. Disciplined spirituality focuses on the ways in which we can cultivate this intimacy with the Lord, and process spirituality emphasizes the need to be alive to the precious present by letting doing flow out of being. Relational spirituality stresses the order of loving God completely as the key to loving self correctly and loving others compassionately. Spirit-filled spirituality and warfare spirituality reminds us that we wage warfare against the world, the flesh, and the devil by means of the weapons of the Spirit and that the Holy Spirit empowers us to live lives that require an explanation. Nurturing spirituality expresses the inner life of Christ in the outer ministry of evangelism and edification. Motivated spirituality encourages us to be prompted by the things God declares to be important, and paradigm spirituality tells us to leverage the temporal for eternal gain.

Each of these facets of spirituality centers on Christ and our personal walk with him. As we come to know him and embrace his cross by losing our lives to find his, we learn to treasure the Godhead. Through personal encounter, through growing trust, wonder, and awe, and through realization of God's love and acceptance of us in Christ, we learn to let God love himself in us through his indwelling Spirit.

Commitment to Community

As believers grow in the solitude of intimacy with the Lord, their capacity for life in community increases as well. True community in Christ is not a collection of lonely or isolated individuals but a dynamic interaction of people who know they are accepted and beloved in Christ. God does not call us to be Christians at large or a colony of hermits but a vital organism of others-centered people of which Christ is the head. True solitude and community enrich each other through the creative interplay of the vertical and horizontal dimensions of our love for God and our love for his people.

The corporate life of the body of Christ is not optional. Although community is never easy, we are impoverished without it, and the benefits far exceed the drawbacks. Among other things, community provides a context for

- relational enrichment and commitment
- trust, love, and acceptance
- mutual submission out of reverence for Christ
- encouragement and accountability
- forgiveness and reciprocal confession under the cross
- physical, psychological, and spiritual healing
- nourishment in the life of Scripture, meditation, and prayer
- participation in a corporate calling and purpose
- love for neighbor as an essential expression of the spiritual life
- ministry and service

- expression of unity in diversity
- guidance and sustenance in spiritual disciplines
- support for those in physical, emotional, and financial need
- an environment of growth and transformation
- celebration of one another's gifts
- existence for others

Our personal life together with Christ should both support and be fed by our corporate life together in Christ. Each of us needs a rhythm of solitude and community, of withdrawal and engagement, of intimacy and activity, of being served by and serving others, and of personal and corporate growth.

Commitment to Ministry

We are not called to be prominent in ministry but to be devoted to Christ. But this intimacy with him (solitude) is expressed and enriched in the communion of the saints as believers gather together to serve and support one another (community). Ministry to the body of believers (edification) and to outsiders (evangelism) should flow out of the combination of being connected to God (solitude) and connected to each other (community). Commitment to the person of God (Romans 12:1–2) displays itself in commitment to the purposes of God (Romans 12:3–8) and in commitment to the people of God (Romans 12:9–21). Outward ministry does not determine personal and corporate intimacy but should find its source in this intimacy with God and his people. Because we have experienced God's acceptance, forgiveness, and love, we can mediate these graces to people who are suffering. Brokenness, contrition, and surrender to Jesus as well as the nurture of the community of faith prepare us to bear fruit in our ministry to believers and unbelievers.

CHALLENGES TO COMMUNITY

The church has never been without its manipulators, controllers, dissenters, and faction builders. Those who create confusion in the body of Christ display fleshly patterns that all of us are capable of practicing. To make matters worse, few of these people ever realize the corporate damage they inflict, because it is easy to justify manipulative behavior by giving it a spiritual veneer of concern for the best interests of the group.

The church at Corinth had members who were killing community through their divisiveness, pride, comparison, carnality, competition, envy, criticism, immorality, lawsuits, idolatry, complaining, selfishness, and doctrinal error. When we try to count, control, compare, and compete we are striving to justify ourselves and our interests rather than seeking the interests of Christ and others. In his appeal to the Philippians to pursue a unity of mind, love, spirit, and purpose, the apostle Paul exhorted them to "do nothing from selfishness or empty conceit, but with humility of mind regard one another as more important than yourselves; do not merely look out for your own personal interests, but also for the interests of others" (Philippians 2:3–4). This is possible only when we walk in the Spirit and derive our identity from Christ rather than the vacillating opinions of others. We noted earlier in this book that when we are liberated from bondage to the expectations and opinions of people, the ironic result is that we become capable of serving them far better. The desire to be pleasing to Christ empowers us to serve his people.

While churchmen focus on building the institution, Christ-centered people focus on loving Christ and on building the body of believers. As a friend of mine puts it, a churchman can become chairman of the church board if he does four things: gives a lot, attends a lot, supports the leadership of the church wherever it wants to go, and keeps his personal sin profile low enough so as not to cause embarrassment. When he is blocked or disgruntled, he casts the ultimate vote by no longer attending or giving.

Just as the fundamental threat to community is self-centeredness, the vital builder of community is others-centeredness. Hell is self-centered and isolational; heaven is others-centered and relational. Corporate spirituality carries a high price because it requires us to go against the grain of our fallen instinct for privatization and control. But Scripture teaches us that it is more than worth the cost, since the greatest experiences of joy take place when they are shared with others. Joy quickly atrophies when it is hoarded. The spiritual life is not simply a matter between an individual and God; it was never meant to be privatized or individualistic but to be shared in community with the people of God. Our personal relationship with Jesus Christ is revealed and expressed in the ways we relate to the people around us.

My friend Bill Smith has developed a helpful comparison between a modern individualistic world view and a more biblical communal world view (table 34.1).

These contrasts also illustrate the orientations and strategies of the old heart versus those of the new heart. I have adapted the charts in table 34.2 from two diagrams in Larry Crabb's *Connecting*.

At any point, a believer can walk in the power and pursuits of the flesh or in the power and purposes of the Spirit. This is a matter not only of knowledge but also of the will. Only as we yield to the Spirit's control (Ephesians 5:18) do we walk in the power to consider the needs of others above our own. When this happens, we contribute to the health and well-being of the body of believers.

CREATORS OF COMMUNITY

The psychologist Alfred Adler noted that "it will appear in the end that we have no problems in our lives but social problems; and those problems can be solved only if we are interested in others." William James similarly exhorted his readers to give them-

	MODERN WORLD VIEW (individualistic)	BIBLICAL WORLD VIEW (communal)
BASIS	Contractual	Covenental
VIEW OF SELF	Autonomous (self-reflective)	Interdependent (social, relational)
VIEW OF RELATIONSHIPS	Exchange (contractual)	Communal (covenantal)
SOURCE OF MORAL AUTHORITY	Relativistic (self-constructed)	Transcendent (established by God)
REASON FOR CHURCH INVOLVEMENT	Needs-related	Relational give and take
HIGHEST VIRTUE	Self-esteem	Love
APPROACH TO CONFLICT RESOLUTION	Communication (negotiation)	Moral approach (reintegration or reconciliation)
LIFE PURPOSE	Self-fulfillment	Self-transcendence (love)
FOUNDATION OF FORGIVENESS	Generating self-forgiveness	Receiving forgiveness
PRIMARY MOTIVATION TO FORGIVE	Personal health (functional coping)	Glory to God and communal harmony

TABLE 34.1

selves to "the higher vision of the inner significance of people." Scripture, however, teaches us that we cannot fully do these things without a new heart in Christ. Perhaps Thomas Merton most succinctly summarized the human condition: "We are not at peace with each other because we are not at peace with ourselves. And we are not at peace with ourselves because we are not at peace with God." But "having been justified by faith, we have peace with God through our Lord Jesus Christ" (Romans 5:1), and this new condition makes it possible for us to be at peace with ourselves and with each other. The solace of sweet surrender and self-denial in Christ is the key to bibli-

THE OLD HEART OR THE FLESH Where Bad Urges Come From		
Personal Problems		
Disconnection from others	Basic life strategy: Do what works for self; avoid what doesn't.	My final value is me!
Disconnection from others	Self-preserving Dynamics as we encounter life	Am I enough? Will you cooperate?
Disconnection from self	Denied longings	Justified selfishness	I'll get what I can!
Disconnection from God	Unbelief: He can't be *that* good!	Independence from God/dependence on self

THE NEW HEART OR THE SPIRIT Where Good Urges Come From		
Faithfulness through Trials		
Connection with others	Basic life strategy: Yield to the good; resist the bad.	My final value is God! He's the Point.
Connection with others	Spiritual (Self-denying) Dynamics as we meet life	My adequacy is in Christ. I'm here to give.
Connection with self	Embraced longings	Godly conscience	I want to live for him.
Connection with God	Belief: He is *that* good!	Dependent on God for life

TABLE 34.2

cal community. As we make our dwelling place in Jesus, we discover the truth of Augustine's words: "Lord, your best servants are those who wish to shape their life on your answers rather than shape your answers on their wishes." When we lose our lives in Christ, we are gradually transformed from being self-absorbed to being "ex-centrics" who reach out to others. As this happens, we realize that the statement "this church doesn't feed me" is not necessarily a good reason for leaving. It may be that we have been called into such a community to feed others.

True community in Christ is not created by attempts to make it happen; instead, it is a by-product of others-centeredness, and this in turn is a by-product of finding our lives by losing them for Jesus' sake (Matthew 16:25). If the leading enemy of corporate spirituality is selfishness, the leading contributor to community is the servanthood that issues out of self-denial. While the world values celebrities, the Word values servants. When Jesus became a servant to his disciples by kneeling down with a towel and a basin (John 13:3–17), he showed that greatness in the kingdom of God does not look like greatness in the eyes of the world. To be like God, we must become conformed to his Son. "God is Christlike, and in him there is no unChristlikeness at all" (Michael Ramsey's adaptation of 1 John 1:5).

After we are converted to Christ, we must be converted to his cross. The conversion to the cross is an ongoing process that involves a series of deaths: death to experiencing life on our own terms, death to our quest for comfort and happiness, death to our own dreams, and death to autonomy and independence. Death is the only way to resurrection, and none of these deaths is bigger than God. In the New Testament, a cruciform view of the spiritual life is neither extraneous nor optional. There it is normative for the disciple to take the Calvary road (see François Fénelon, *Christian Perfection*, Roy Hession, *The Calvary Road*, and John White, *The Cost of Commitment*).

Conversion to Christ and to the cross should lead in turn to conversion to community. Kingdom living is about loving and serving God and others, and it is most clearly embodied in the eight Beatitudes that introduce our Lord's Sermon on the Mount (Matthew 5:1–12):

1. "Blessed are the poor in spirit, for theirs is the kingdom of heaven." Poverty of spirit is the realization of our bankruptcy before God and our consequent need of his grace.
2. "Blessed are those who mourn, for they shall be comforted." Growing awareness of the depth of our sin leads to contrition and repentance.
3. "Blessed are the gentle, for they shall inherit the earth." Those who understand their true condition before God have nothing to boast about; instead, they walk in the humility of radical dependence upon God for all things.
4. "Blessed are those who hunger and thirst for righteousness, for they shall be satisfied." People who cultivate passion for God and his character discover that satisfaction is the by-product of seeking God's approval above that of people.
5. "Blessed are the merciful, for they shall receive mercy." The more we realize how mercifully God has treated us in the past and present, the greater our capacity to show mercy and grace to those who injure us.

6. "Blessed are the pure in heart, for they shall see God." Those who are pure in heart will one thing above all else. Because of this, they are single-minded, not double-minded, and they walk in simplicity, not duplicity.

7. "Blessed are the peacemakers, for they shall be called sons of God." People who enjoy peace with God and with themselves become peacemakers in their relationships with others.

8. "Blessed are those who have been persecuted for the sake of righteousness, for theirs is the kingdom of heaven." Those who are serious about serving the best interests of believers and outsiders run the risk of rejection, misunderstanding, and betrayal. But they press on through the pain when their eyes are focused on Jesus.

Notice the corporate implications of the Beatitudes—when our character is centered on Christ, our conduct with others is marked by humility, compassion, gentleness, sincerity, mercy, truthfulness, reconciliation, and security.

The body of Christ is the New Testament context for relational unity in diversity and oneness in plurality. We will look at the nature and purpose of the living organism of the church in the next chapter.

Questions for Personal Application

- Are you drawn to or away from community? Where would you place yourself in the spectrum from the personal to the corporate? Do you need more balance?

- What are the biblical foundations for community?

- How are you presently integrating the three dimensions of solitude, community, and ministry? Which is the strongest in your life? The weakest?

- What challenges to community have you encountered in your own experiences with the body of Christ?

- What can you do to move further away from an individualistic mentality in your spiritual formation?

35

CORPORATE SPIRITUALITY

The Nature and Purpose of the Church

CHAPTER OVERVIEW

This chapter outlines a biblical approach to the nature of the church and looks at seven purposes of the church: corporate love and compassion; corporate identity and purpose; corporate nurture and service; corporate discernment; corporate forgiveness and reconciliation; corporate authority and submission; and corporate worship and prayer.

CHAPTER OBJECTIVES

- A deeper sense of the nature and role of the body of Christ in spiritual formation
- A stronger grasp of the biblical purposes for community

The spiritual life was never meant to be lived alone but in a context of community with like-minded believers. Without the encouragement, support, teaching, love, exhortation, and prayers of other members of the body of Christ, we would be unable to grow in the faith and embrace values that are diametrically opposed to those of our culture. As the epistle of James (1:26–27) teaches us, "pure and undefiled religion in the sight of our God and Father" is not a compartmentalized, private matter. Instead, a growing vertical relationship with Christ is meant to spill over into every facet of our lives and have an effect on each one of our horizontal relationships. Christian maturity does not spring out of isolation but is nourished through involvement.

Nevertheless, to use Luke Timothy Johnson's phrase, the church is "a messy grace." It is riddled with the full range of human qualities from the delightful to the dreadful. People who seem perfectly normal in a Bible study or fellowship group can suddenly change as soon as you call it a church. Expectations inflate, controllers rise to the surface, personal "crit-o-meters" register unusually high readings, and a few people become downright weird. Still, with all its faults and corporate idiosyncrasies, participation in the life of a church is a necessary discipline and grace, particularly in a culture that is driven by independence and individualism.

THE NATURE OF THE CHURCH

New Testament metaphors for the church include the body of Christ (1 Corinthians 12:27; Ephesians 5:29–30; Colossians 1:18), the bride of Christ (2 Corinthians 11:2; Ephesians 5:23–32; Revelation 19:7), the temple of the Holy Spirit (1 Corinthians 3:16–17; Ephesians 2:19–22; 1 Peter 2:5), members of God's family (Ephesians 2:19), and a people for God's own possession (1 Peter 2:9). These images show that the church is more like a living organism than an organization. The necessary institutional dimensions of this organism should serve the communal and relational dimensions, but it usually works the other way around. This is largely because the organization is more tangible, measurable, and controllable than the organism.

The New Testament speaks of the church as an *ekklesia,* an assembly, congregation, or community. As Stanley J. Grenz observes in *Created for Community,* this word speaks of a people in relationship rather than an edifice or an organization. Acts and the Epistles teach that there is one church in many places and that believers who meet together for edification in various places are part of a single body whose head is Christ. The church is a spiritual family of brothers and sisters whose personal and corporate identity is rooted and grounded in the love of Christ (Ephesians 3:17). When the church meets together as a family, the members minister to one another through teaching, *koinonia* (fellowship), sharing, prayer (Acts 2:42), mutual service and encouragement (Hebrews 10:23–25), exercise of spiritual gifts (Romans 12; 1 Corinthians 12–14; Ephesians 4), the Lord's Supper (1 Corinthians 11:17–30), and giving of thanks and worship (Ephesians 5:19–21; Colossians 3:16).

The organic image in Ephesians 4:16 of a body that is "being fitted and held together by what every joint supplies, according to the proper working of each individual part" shows that the church is a corporate reality rather than a collection of separate individuals. For the church to thrive, the cells must work together to create tissues, the tissues must function together to form organs, the organs must function together to create systems, and the systems must operate in synchrony through the directives of the brain. Just as the cells serve the body, so the body through its vascular capillary system nourishes and sustains the cells. The church is a dynamic and synergistic community in which the total is greater than the sum of its parts.

To use another image, the church is a colony of resident aliens who constitute an alternative society as citizens of an unearthly *polis* (city; Hebrews 11:10, 16; Revelation 21:2, 10). It is a family of people whose real citizenship is in heaven (Philippians 3:20) and whose earthly sojourn as pilgrims, strangers, and exiles (Hebrews 11:13; 1 Peter 2:11) should be marked by longing for home, a nostalgia for heaven, since "the end of all things is near" (1 Peter 4:7). This familial community is called to be salt and light in the world at large. It is a community of people who are connected through their solitude with Christ and who are also connected through their suffering and through their celebration of the triune Godhead.

THE PURPOSE OF THE CHURCH

Six Distortions

This biblical vision of the body of Christ as a communal organism has been distorted through the centuries by the human agendas of grasping for power, control, and wealth. In addition, the disease of institutionalism has ossified the organism to the degree that the church has become identified with the carapace of buildings rather than a living body of believers. A third source of distortion in recent years is the proliferation of pastors whose churches are extensions of their identities and whose "edifice complexes" are driven by a quest for significance. All three of these distortions lead to the organism serving the organization rather than the organization serving the organism. When community is reduced to places, programs, and performances, corporate vitality becomes a thin veneer. This is not to speak against large churches per se; many large churches center around Christ and corporate life. Furthermore, small churches can be guilty in miniature of the same errors.

A fourth distortion of the biblical vision for the body of Christ has been the rise of post-Enlightenment liberalism and, in more recent years, the rise of postmodernism in various denominations and local churches. When religious leaders repackage cultural agendas in spiritual language, parishioners no longer receive the milk and meat of the Word but become spiritually and morally emaciated on the husks of the world.

A fifth distortion of the New Testament purpose of body life is associated with the rapid growth of suburbia. The proliferation of automobiles changed the rules—the parish model no longer applies to suburbanites. This has led to a greater fluidity of options. People are more influenced by subjective factors and less influenced by distance, denominations, and theology in their choice of churches. Greater mobility in nonparish contexts has also increased the problem of excessive social, economic, and racial homogeneity. Mobility has led not only to diminished diversity but also to a decreased level of commitment. For some people, churches are like restaurants; if they tire of one cuisine, there is always another.

A sixth distortion of true community is caused by the current tendency to impose marketing, management, psychological, and entertainment models on church growth, leadership, soul care, and programs. An uncritical use of these techniques leads to manipulation rather than ministry. The church should be situated in God's narrative rather than personality or local culture.

Seven Purposes

We have seen that the New Testament vision of the church as the body of Christ, the bride of Christ, the temple of the Holy Spirit, members of God's family, and a people for God's own possession is organic and cannot be defined in terms of independence or self-reliance. The interdependence of shared community with God and with one another is expressed in a multiplicity of noble and mundane tasks that combine together to develop personal and corporate maturity in Christ.

The community of faith should minister to the whole person: intellect (reasonable knowledge), emotion (spiritual experience), and will (obedient action). This trilogy of knowing, being, and doing is developed by fostering reliable beliefs, godly affections, and Christlike character in relationship.

Seven purposes emerge from the New Testament vision of the church as an organic community of believers.

Corporate Love and Compassion

It is easier to talk about the importance of loving people than it is to get along with those we see on a daily basis. Someone put it this way: "To live above with the saints we love—oh, that will be glory. But to live below with the saints we know—well, that's another story." Nevertheless, God has called us to a unity in diversity by exhibiting the only kind of love that makes this possible.

> So, as those who have been chosen of God, holy and beloved, put on a heart of compassion, kindness, humility, gentleness and patience; bearing with one another, and forgiving each other, whoever has a complaint against anyone; just as the Lord forgave you, so also should you. Beyond all these things put on love, which is the perfect bond of unity.
>
> *Colossians 3:12–14*

Biblical love is a God-empowered volitional commitment to the best interests of others. The love of Christ as expressed through us is selfless (1 Corinthians 13:4–7), servant hearted (Galatians 5:13–14; Philippians 2:3–4), and covers a multitude of sins (James 5:20). This love fosters an atmosphere of acceptance, trust, and willingness to disclose our real needs to other members of the body. It treasures the rainbow of personalities that constitute the people of God and reciprocally mediates God's care, compassion, and grace.

Corporate Identity and Purpose

We do not discover our identities in isolation; we are connected through a common story. In a context of relationships, first with God and then with others, our purpose and identity are defined. This communal identity flows from the realization that we are alive not for ourselves but for the Lord and one another. We have become "a people for God's own possession" so that we may proclaim the excellencies of him who has called us out of darkness into his marvelous light (1 Peter 2:9) on two axes: to the ends of the earth and to the end of this age.

The more we give ourselves to Jesus, the greater our capacity to seek the interests of others above our own (Philippians 2:4). Our faith, hope, and love become a corporate possession when they are expressed and nurtured in the life of the believing body (1 Corinthians 13:13). Notice how these three cardinal virtues are embedded in a communal context:

> Let us draw near with a sincere heart in full assurance of *faith*, having our hearts sprinkled clean from an evil conscience and our bodies washed with pure water. Let us hold fast the confession of our *hope* without wavering, for He who promised is faithful; and let us consider how to stimulate one another to *love* and good deeds, not forsaking our own assembling together, as is the habit of some, but encouraging one another; and all the more as you see the day drawing near.
>
> *Hebrews 10:22–25 (emphasis added)*

The sacraments of baptism and communion are expressions of our corporate identity, the former being the seal and the latter being the ongoing reaffirmation of our identity as members of the community of faith. Baptism is a demonstration of identification with the gospel story, and communion is a retelling of this story.

Just as each of us should develop a personal purpose statement, every local church and ministry should prayerfully formulate a corporate purpose statement so that the members can embrace a common vision for their place and time in history. In this way, they can make deeper commitments to a purpose that transcends any one of them. "Therefore if there is any encouragement in Christ, if there is any consolation of love, if there is any fellowship of the Spirit, if any affection and compassion, make my joy complete by being of the same mind, maintaining the same love, united in spirit, intent on one purpose" (Philippians 2:1–2; cf. 1:27).

The New Testament frequently underscores the importance of unity among brothers and sisters in Christ. The church is to be a community of unity within diversity in which the walls of racism, sexism, nationalism, and elitism are to be broken down (Galatians 3:28). Our Lord said that the unity of God's children would demonstrate to the world that the Savior had come. In his high-priestly prayer on behalf of his disciples and those who would believe in him through their word, Jesus prayed "that they may all be one; even as You, Father, are in Me and I in You, that they also may be in Us, so that the world may believe that You sent Me" (John 17:21).

Corporate Nurture and Service

One of the primary purposes for believers to assemble together is to create a meaningful context in which they can mutually encourage and edify one another through the exercise of the spiritual gifts that have been given to the body. In *Spirit-filled spirituality*, we discussed the purpose and dynamics of the gifts of the Spirit and saw that they are others-centered graces "for the equipping of the saints for the work of service, to the building up of the body of Christ" (Ephesians 4:12). The rich diversity of gifts and temperament types in the body promotes maturity and wholeness when that diversity is empowered by the Spirit.

The more we realize that we are allies on the journey rather than independent agents, the more clearly we will see that personal spiritual growth does not take place in a relational vacuum. In this world, we are part of a community of pilgrims who are traveling toward God, and we are meant to assist, nurture, and encourage one another along the way. Commitment to a local community of faith enhances personal growth by providing a corporate context for identity, involvement, and ministry. This commitment to mutual nurture and service is most clearly expressed in the New Testament reciprocal "one another" commands:

Positive Exhortations
- wash one another's feet (John 13:14)
- love one another (John 13:34)
- be devoted to one another in brotherly love (Romans 12:10a)
- give preference to one another in honor (Romans 12:10b)
- be of the same mind toward one another (Romans 12:16; 15:5)
- build up one another (Romans 14:19)
- accept one another (Romans 15:7)
- admonish one another (Romans 15:14)
- greet one another (Romans 16:16; 1 Corinthians 16:20)
- wait for one another (1 Corinthians 11:33)
- have the same care for one another (1 Corinthians 12:25)
- through love serve one another (Galatians 5:13)
- bear one another's burdens (Galatians 6:2)
- show tolerance for one another (Ephesians 4:2)
- be kind to one another (Ephesians 4:32a)
- forgive one another (Ephesians 4:32b)
- speak to one another in psalms and hymns and spiritual songs (Ephesians 5:19)
- be subject to one another (Ephesians 5:21)
- regard one another as more important than yourselves (Philippians 2:3)

- teach and admonish one another (Colossians 3:16)
- comfort one another (1 Thessalonians 4:18)
- encourage one another (1 Thessalonians 5:11a; Hebrews 3:13)
- build up one another (1 Thessalonians 5:11b)
- live in peace with one another (1 Thessalonians 5:13)
- seek after that which is good for one another (1 Thessalonians 5:15)
- stimulate one another to love and good deeds (Hebrews 10:24)
- confess your sins to one another (James 5:16a)
- pray for one another (James 5:16b)
- keep fervent in your love for one another (1 Peter 4:8)
- be hospitable to one another (1 Peter 4:9)
- use your gifts to serve one another (1 Peter 4:10)
- clothe yourselves with humility toward one another (1 Peter 5:5)

Negative Exhortations
- do not judge one another (Romans 14:13)
- do not bite and devour one another (Galatians 5:15)
- do not become boastful, challenging one another (Galatians 5:26a)
- do not envy one another (Galatians 5:26b)
- do not lie to one another (Colossians 3:9)
- do not speak against one another (James 4:11)
- do not complain against one another (James 5:9)

Biblical servanthood can be expressed in a variety of ways. It is seen in a concern for other people as individuals, such as praying for them by name. It is communicated in helping with another's physical or emotional needs. It is visible in a real concern for the spiritual condition of others. It is manifested in words that convey love and encouragement. And it is demonstrated in a gracious and gentle correcting of those who are in error.

We have seen that in Christ, all our deepest needs are fully satisfied. This is a liberating truth, and the more we embrace it, the more we escape the natural bondage to selfish pursuits. Believers who grow in this understanding become less inclined to milk and manipulate relationships in order to authenticate their security and significance. They do not need to compare, dominate, and compete with others because their worth is based on a timeless and unwavering relationship with the living God. Instead of grabbing, they can unconditionally give to others. Just as Christ never lived for himself but emptied and humbled himself for others (Philippians 2:5–8), so we who are significant and secure in him can follow Paul's injunction to focus on the interests of others (Philippians 2:3–4). Jesus summarized his earthly mission in Mark 10:45: "Even the Son of Man did not come to be served, but to serve, and to give His life a ransom for many." As his life is displayed in us, we become true servants of God and others.

Fellowship with God should produce fellowship with like-minded followers of Jesus. Holiness does not thrive in isolation—we need the environment of a body of believers bounded by love and mutual servanthood. When unconfessed sin creates barriers in our fellowship with God, it distorts our relationships with others. Sin leads to pretense, a lack of transparency, and a desire to be served rather than serve. Walking in God's light leads to humility, openness, and a desire to give rather than grab.

Corporate Discernment

Discerning God's will does not take place in isolation but in community. The authenticity, encouragement, affirmation, and support of other members of the body of Christ can be rich sources of spiritual insight for brothers and sisters who desire to make good choices. However, we should be mindful of a number of built-in obstacles to discernment in community. In *Listening to God in Times of Choice*, Gordon T. Smith observes several of these hindrances: communal expectations, people who try to control and coerce, people who use emotional blackmail, and those who flatter or are otherwise dishonest. When we are aware of the manipulative downside of community, we can focus on the positive resources of community.

Healthy community can create an environment of authenticity in which we are encouraged to be honest with God, with one another, and with ourselves. Such an environment enhances self-knowledge by spurring us to become honest about our desires and our feelings. Community can also create an environment of mutual encouragement and hope, since we cannot discern well in times of discouragement and depression. The gifts of empathic listening as well as words of blessing and affirmation are priceless resources in our quest for godly discernment.

Corporate Forgiveness and Reconciliation

Our Lord's exhortation to be merciful, just as our Father is merciful (Luke 6:36) applies not only to personal forgiveness but also to corporate forgiveness in the body of Christ. Paul exhorted the Corinthians to forgive and comfort a brother who repented after being disciplined by the church (1 Corinthians 2:6–11). The biblical basis for personal and communal forgiveness and reconciliation is the gracious work of Christ on our behalf: "Be kind to one another, tender-hearted, forgiving each other, just as God in Christ also has forgiven you" (Ephesians 4:32).

In our earlier discussion of relational spirituality, we noted that forgiveness is not forgetting or pretending that the wrong done to us does not matter. Instead, forgiveness is a choice; it is a willful decision to treat another with mercy and grace. It is costly to acknowledge the hurt and to live with the consequences of other people's sins, but personal and corporate forgiveness is the necessary path to healing and reconciliation. Without this choice, we will bear a burden of bitterness and diminish our experience of God's love and forgiveness.

"If possible, so far as it depends on you, be at peace with all men" (Romans 12:18). Because of the wealth of human diversity, some forms of interpersonal conflict are natural and beneficial; we can grow through diversity, and this is why unity is not the same as uniformity (Ephesians 4:1–13). In the economy of God, people's rough edges can be unintentional sources of our sanctification.

Other forms of conflict stem from sinful motives and actions (Mark 7:20–23; James 4:1–2). Even here, conflict can give us an opportunity to love and serve others and to be more conformed to the image of Christ. When a situation merits attention, it is healthy to seek reconciliation by having the courage and integrity to approach the other person instead of talking to others about that person (Matthew 18:15). If we make this approach in gentleness, humility, concern, compassion, and a genuine desire to understand the other person's perspective, resolution is far more likely. We may even discover that repentance and confession are needed on our part.

In serious situations when resolution is not achieved through personal confrontation, it may be necessary to go on to the second or third stages outlined in Matthew 18:16–17 by involving other members of the community. The biblical intention behind corporate discipline should never be punishment but reconciliation.

Corporate Authority and Submission

God has ordained different spheres of authority in the home, the workplace, the church, and the state. For our own well-being and protection, it is important for all of us to be under some form of authority (Matthew 8:5–10). When authority and equality are modeled on the divine Trinity, it is possible to avoid two extremes, that of authoritarianism, which minimizes equality, and egalitarianism, which minimizes authority. Since the role of elders and deacons in the local church (1 Timothy 3:1–13; Titus 1:5–9) is to serve the members of the body through guidance, teaching, and pastoral care, submission to this godly influence should be a source of liberty and security. As we submit to the strengths of those who are appointed to leadership in the community of faith, they protect us from our weaknesses.

Corporate Worship and Prayer

The New Testament says surprisingly little about worship in the church. In fact, the book of Revelation speaks more about the worship of God than do Acts and the Epistles combined. The most explicit passages in the Epistles about corporate worship are Ephesians 5:19–20 and Colossians 3:15–16:

Speaking to one another in psalms and hymns and spiritual songs, singing and making melody with your heart to the Lord; always giving thanks for all things in the name of our Lord Jesus Christ to God, even the Father.

Let the peace of Christ rule in your hearts, to which indeed you were called in one body; and be thankful. Let the word of Christ richly dwell within you, with all wisdom teaching and admonishing one another with psalms and hymns and spiritual songs, singing with thankfulness in your hearts to God.

Even in these passages, part of the purpose of the "psalms and hymns and spiritual songs" is to teach and admonish one another. The worship dimension is most clearly connected with corporate thanksgiving to God.

Nevertheless, worship has always been a central component of corporate spirituality, and the early church quickly assimilated and adapted elements of synagogue liturgy. By the second century, the liturgy of the Eucharist (derived from *eucharisteô*, "give thanks") or Holy Communion became the central vehicle of corporate worship, and parts of this ancient liturgy are still in use.

Many Christians in the twentieth century have erroneously equated worship with music and generally with a particular kind of music, whether traditional or contemporary. Music is a meaningful component of worship, but other elements, such as corporate prayer, the ministry of the Word, and communion, have always been important components of worship, and it is a mistake to reduce the whole to one of its parts.

In recent years, a growing number of evangelicals have discovered the value and power of liturgical worship. Liturgy embeds us in historical tradition and practice, and it can foster a sense of awe, wonder, mystery, and majesty. It involves more active participation of the congregants (sit to learn, stand to worship, kneel to pray) and can invite a richer sensory involvement as well (e.g., taste [the bread and wine], touch [the sharing of the peace], smell [flowers or incense], sound [psalmody, music, chant], and sight [decorative artwork]). Liturgy also encourages a corporate awareness and celebration of the annual seasons of Advent, Christmas, Epiphany, Lent, Easter, and Pentecost.

Corporate worship and prayer also involves the creative mixture of the various temperaments (see appendix A). For example, the feeling function is expressed in the experience of community in celebration; the thinking function appreciates the reception of the Word, the sensing function enjoys the commemoration of Christ's work in the past, and the intuitive function stresses the dimension of anticipation of Christ's return. (*Prayer and Temperament* by Chester P. Michael and Marie C. Norrisey, *How We Belong, Fight, and Pray* by Lloyd Edwards, and *Who We Are Is How We Pray* by Charles J. Keating are resources that relate personality to congregational dynamics.)

"When we don't feel like worshiping, the community should carry us along in its worship. When we can't seem to pray, community prayer should enfold us. When the Scripture seems closed for us, the community should keep on reading, affirming and incarnating it around us" (M. Robert Mulholland Jr., *Invitation to a Journey*).

We have seen that the New Testament vision of the body of Christ involves corporate love, compassion, identity, purpose, nurture, service, discernment, forgiveness, reconciliation, authority, submission, worship, and prayer. In the next chapter we will look at the corporate concerns of soul care, leadership, accountability, and renewal.

QUESTIONS FOR PERSONAL APPLICATION

- Why has the church as an organization taken precedence over the church as an organism? How does this differ from the New Testament imagery of the church?
- Which of the six distortions of the biblical vision of the body of Christ have you observed?
- Of the seven purposes of the church, which are the most meaningful to you? Which of them do you think are least commonly realized in churches today?

36

CORPORATE
SPIRITUALITY
Soul Care, Leadership,
Accountability, and Renewal

CHAPTER OVERVIEW

This chapter looks at the soul-care spectrum from spiritual friendship to spiritual guidance to spiritual mentoring to spiritual direction and considers the relationship among clinical counseling, pastoral counseling, and soul-care ministries. It also has a word on inner healing, servant leadership, accountability, renewal, and the future of community.

CHAPTER OBJECTIVES

- An appreciation for the soul-care ministries of spiritual friendship, guidance, mentoring, and direction
- A clearer perspective on the role of counseling, inner healing, servant leadership, accountability, and corporate renewal

Corporate spirituality affirms that growth involves the whole person and that it is enhanced in relation rather than isolation. Growth in spiritual maturity is a gradual process of formation into the image and character of Jesus Christ that is fostered by the power of the Spirit, by spiritual disciplines, and by the loving support of a genuine community. We develop in our thinking, our character, and our application when we are connected to authentic people who share the journey with us, particularly when some of them have progressed further down the road than we have. In this way we learn how to respond biblically to the requirements and demands of reality.

There has been a growing realization, however, that going to church is not necessarily the same as experiencing the dynamics of living in community (see *The Connecting Church: Moving Beyond Small Groups to Authentic Community* by Randy Frazee). More often than not, people relate to the church more as an organization (buildings, programs, budgets, administration) than as an organism. A healing community, by contrast, centers on connecting with God, with others, and with ourselves, and such communities can exist both inside and outside local church structures. Small and large prayer groups, study groups, fellowship groups, and worship (prayer and praise) groups offer community dynamics to their participants. Many of these groups have no association with specific churches or denominations, while others are organized by local churches.

SOUL CARE AND COUNSELING

As pastors and church leaders have become increasingly aware of the need for true community, many have sought to implement new congregational structures to meet this need. Some churches have developed a model that is built around four components: celebration, congregations, cells, and cores (e.g., Bill Hull, *The Disciple-Making Pastor* and *The Disciple-Making Church*). In the celebration the church gathers as a whole for worship, preaching, and prayer; in the congregations, the church gathers in moderate-sized groups for fellowship and learning. The cells are small groups for support, instruction, prayer, and accountability. The core groups constitute the individual family units within the church. Not all of these groups successfully provide the dynamics of community to their participants, particularly when they are designed to meet objectives other than providing an environment of grace for the expression of body life.

In addition to large- and small-group experiences, another important dimension of life together in Christ is one-on-one ministry. Person-to-person interaction can be a by-product of group life, or it can take place outside of group structures. As Bruce Demarest notes in *Satisfy Your Soul*, there is a spectrum of personal soul-care ministries that ranges from informal, unstructured, and reciprocal ministry to formal, structured, and one-directional ministry (table 36.1).

There are no rigid boundaries between these ministries, and they can overlap in varying degrees. But it is helpful to distinguish these four degrees of personal ministry, since they have always existed among the people of God.

INFORMAL UNSTRUCTURED RECIPROCAL			FORMAL STRUCTURED ONE-DIRECTIONAL
→	→	→	→
Spiritual friendship	Spiritual guidance	Spiritual mentoring	Spiritual direction

TABLE 36.1

Spiritual Friendship

This is the most natural and spontaneous form of personal soul care, and it involves the give and take of unstructured interaction between friends who walk together in peace and trust. These people have discovered that our needs for healing and spiritual growth are not met by looking for one new group or relationship after another but through the cultivation of deeper relationships with certain people God has sovereignly placed in our lives. Caring engagement and personal service among spiritual friends is brought to the most profound level through their shared experience with Jesus. This kind of spiritual alliance should also be a central component of every marriage.

Spiritual Guidance

The next form of soul care involves informal interaction between people who may differ in spiritual maturity though not necessarily in spiritual authority. Guidance can take place through correspondence, through recommended reading, and through offering spiritual counsel as necessary. People who serve others as spiritual guides are able to provide help and healing through words of encouragement, exhortation, and advice.

Spiritual Mentoring

This more formal and structured dimension of soul care entails the ministry of shepherding by people who use their spiritual knowledge and experience to equip others. Mentors are often disciplers who expose, equip, encourage, and exhort others in their walk with Christ (see the first two chapters in the section on nurturing spirituality). Many of them teach and train responsive people with the intention of bringing them to the point of doing the same with others. Mentors take pleasure in seeing potential in others and enjoy the process of equipping them to attain it.

As Paul D. Stanley and J. Robert Clinton observe in their mentoring book *Connecting* (also see Keith R. Anderson and Randy D. Reese, *Spiritual Mentoring* and Howard and William Hendricks, *As Iron Sharpens Iron*), there are various forms and degrees of mentoring that range in involvement from intensive to occasional to passive. Mentors can function as disciplers, spiritual guides, coaches, counselors, teachers, sponsors, or peers. In addition, there are historical mentors whose writings still speak to us and guide us even though these people are now with the Lord.

People who are serious about spiritual growth and ministry need to be part of a relational network that includes vertical (mentors) and horizontal (peers or co-mentors) relationships. Mentoring relationships are most effective when there is compatibility, clear purpose, regularity, accountability, open communication, confidentiality, a definite life cycle, periodic evaluation and revision of expectations, and closure.

Spiritual Direction

Until recently, Protestants have thought little about the ancient art of spiritual direction, the most formal and one-directional of the four levels of personal soul-care ministries. More people are becoming aware of the benefits of this form of pastoral care that focuses on the cultivation of prayer, discernment, and practical implementation of spiritual truth.

In the early centuries of the church, spiritual direction was associated with desert monasticism and continued to develop within monastic contexts as a means of providing intensive personal guidance. As "physicians of the soul" who help people understand the workings of God in their lives, spiritual directors must be people of wisdom, depth, skill, and prayer. To be effective in this form of soul care, they must be marked by a combination of *knowledge* (Scripture, spiritual classics and spiritual theology, psychology, the nature and machinations of the psyche), *discernment* (the ability to perceive the nature of souls, sensitivity to the difference between the work of the Spirit and the work of the flesh and/or false spirits), and *character* (vitality in faith and prayer, holiness of life, humility and brokenness through personal suffering, loving concern, openness to the ministry of the Spirit).

Spiritual directors help people discern the workings of grace in their lives and offer them guidance and assistance as they seek to progress in prayer and obedience. Their relationship with those who seek their ministry is not authoritarian or that of a professional service (e.g., the counselor-client model) but as companions on the spiritual journey who enhance inner desire and clarify the movement of the Spirit. They care for the soul through cleansing, discernment, clarification, alignment, and implementation.

Such directors must be sought out, but it is not easy to find them. When we do, we should not expect them to flatter us or cater to our illusions. Instead, we must approach them in a spirit of humility and let them know what we think, feel, and desire. Good directors will ask appropriate questions, listen skillfully, reveal barriers to growth, assist in confession and repentance, show how to listen to God and how to implement spiritual disciplines, rebuke and encourage as necessary, and offer their presence and compassion. Spiritual directors have skill in distinguishing between spiritual and psychological problems (e.g., spiritual aridity versus psychosomatic illness or infantile moodiness).

A few of the many helpful books that discuss spiritual direction are Thomas Merton, *Spiritual Direction and Meditation*; Martin Thornton, *Christian Proficiency*; Kenneth Leech, *Soul Friend*; Simon Chan, *Spiritual Theology*; Eugene Peterson, *The Contemplative Pastor*; and David G. Benner, *Sacred Companions*.

God uses fellow believers as instruments of growth, and this is true of spiritual friendship, guidance, mentoring, and direction. We are too close to ourselves to see things as they are, and at times our self-deception and insensitivity makes us vulnerable to becoming "hardened by the deceitfulness of sin" (Hebrews 3:13). All of us need the insight, hope, affirmation, and tenderhearted engagement that soul friends can offer.

The Role of Counseling

The development of the various schools within psychology, psychopathology, and psychotherapy in the twentieth century has influenced the church in a number of ways. Personality theory has changed our view of the human psyche, and the clinical-therapeutic approach to treatment has centered on a medical model for the cure of psychological disorders in patients. These "talking cures" have been adapted by professional counselors who meet with clients in clinics or offices and, with increasing frequency, in churches.

Of late, a number of observers (e.g., Larry Crabb, *Connecting*) have challenged the assumptions behind this therapeutic approach. First, the counseling movement is largely disassociated from a context of community and continuous involvement with people. It promotes a clinical model built around professional therapists who treat individuals rather than an organic model built around the resources of the community of faith (Romans 15:1; Galatians 6:1–2). Second, it focuses primarily on the cure of sickness rather than the care of the soul. It emphasizes the treatment of psychological disorders over a period of time instead of the healing of soul wounds with a view to spiritual nurture and health. Third, it assumes that the power to provide healing for deep problems is derived more from technical training and clinical expertise than from relational resources (caring engagement, empathetic listening, conscientious concern) and spiritual resources (the indwelling life of Christ, the sanctifying work of the Spirit, affirmation of goodness and hope in Jesus).

It would be irresponsible to suggest that there is no place for professional counselors. Wisdom urges us to steer a course between two extremes. The first extreme denigrates all psychology as deluded or demonic; the opposite extreme reduces the soul and the spirit to current psychological categories. On the one hand, qualified professionals are best equipped to deal with problems that are related to organic factors such as brain chemistry; cognitive, behavioral, and anxiety disorders; and difficulties that can be alleviated through empirically based communicational and relational techniques. Psychology as a discipline can teach us much about motivational and behavioral forces such as temperaments, defense mechanisms, the implications of emotional wounds and of false images of God, addictive behaviors, the causes of perfectionism and other compulsive behaviors, and the dynamics of false guilt.

On the other hand, the best environment for healing a wide variety of problems and disorders is the more natural and relational context of caring community. A multitude of mature believers can be equipped in churches and other corporate contexts to become effective caregivers who combine counseling and spiritual resources.

Clinical counseling, pastoral counseling, and soul-care ministries (e.g., spiritual direction) have distinctive and overlapping areas, and each has its strengths and limitations. Since we are holistic and integrated beings, the community of believers should avail itself of the strengths of the first two and more actively develop the third.

There is an extensive literature on the relationship between psychology and spiritual formation, and a handful of helpful titles includes Gordon W. Allport, *The Individual and His Religion*; Ernest Becker, *The Denial of Death*; Don S. Browning, *Religious Thought and the Modern Psychologies*; Thomas J. Burke, ed., *Man and Mind: A Christian Theory of Personality*; Lawrence J. Crabb Jr., *Basic Principles of Biblical Counseling* and *Effective Biblical Counseling*; C. Stephen Evans, *Preserving the Person*; Peter Homans, ed., *The Dialogue Between Psychology and Theology*; Malcolm A. Jeeves, ed., *Behavioural Sciences: A Christian Perspective* and *Human Nature at the Millennium*; Stanton L. Jones and Richard E. Butman, *Modern Psycho-Therapies*; William Kirk Kilpatrick, *Psychological Seduction* and *The Emperor's New Clothes*; David Myers and Malcolm A. Jeeves, *Psychology through the Eyes of Faith*; Robert C. Roberts and Mark R. Talbot, eds., *Limning the Psyche*; Mary Stewart Van Leeuwen, *The Person in Psychology* and *The Sorcerer's Apprentice: A Christian Looks at the Changing Face of Psychology*; and Paul C. Vitz, *Psychology as Religion*.

Inner Healing

The ministry of inner healing, also called healing of memories, involves the prayerful application of Christ's power and presence to heal the causes of damaged emotions. Those who are gifted and skilled in this area explore root memories through the guidance of the Holy Spirit and offer healing prayer and biblical images that contribute to the restoration of the wounded soul.

The reality of sin has made us both victims and agents, and the soul wounds we sustain are inflicted not only by others (e.g., physical, sexual, verbal, or emotional abuse; legalism, perfectionism, rejection, betrayal, performance-based acceptance) but also by self (e.g., denial, rationalization, projection, bitterness, unforgiveness, hatred, prejudice). Soul healing is based on Jesus' identification on the cross with our undeserved suffering as well as our deserved punishment.

The healing ministry of Jesus, which makes up about a fifth of the gospel texts, makes it clear that we serve a God who is concerned about the whole person and that in addition to the spiritual implications of the Atonement, there are also physical and psychological implications (Isaiah 53:4–5; Matthew 4:24; Mark 1:34; Luke 4:18). The Lord mediates his healing grace and power through his people (Luke 9:1; 10:9; Acts 3:1–10; 4:7–10; 5:14–16; 8:6–7; 9:32–41; 14:8–10; 19:11–12; 28:8–9; 1 Corinthians 12:9, 28; James 5:14–16), and he can transform those who have been wounded into healed caregivers.

Some influential books that discuss inner healing include Francis MacNutt, *Healing*; Leanne Payne, *The Healing Presence* and *Restoring the Christian Soul*; Mark Pearson, *Christian Healing*; John and Paula Sandford, *The Transformation of the Inner Man*; Agnes Sanford, *The Healing Gifts of the Spirit*; David A. Seamands, *Healing for Damaged Emotions* and *The Healing of Memories*; and John Wimber, *Power Healing*.

SERVANT LEADERSHIP

As Walter A. Henrichsen and William N. Garrison observe in *Layman, Look Up! God Has a Place for You*, there is no New Testament basis for the clergy/laity ministry dichotomy that relegates laypeople to a secondary role in ministry. Just as the Reformation put the Scriptures in the hands of the laity, there is now a realization that we need to put the ministry into the hands of the laity. The fact that all believers in Christ share in a holy and royal priesthood (1 Peter 2:5, 9) means that all of us have the same access into the Holy of Holies (Hebrews 10:19–22) to offer sacrifices of praise, thanksgiving, and service (Hebrews 13:15–16; Romans 12:1; 1 Peter 4:10–11). The biblical doctrine of the priesthood of believers teaches us that we are all called to full-time ministry in our spheres of influence. As we cultivate our personal walk with God and nurture others through discipleship and witness, we engage in the enduring work of God.

At the same time, God has appointed certain people for places of shepherding and leadership in churches and ministries. These are people whose gifting and character demonstrate a level of maturity that makes them models for others to follow (1 Corinthians 11:1; 1 Timothy 3:1–13; Titus 1:5–9; 1 Peter 5:1–5; Hebrews 13:17). Such leadership in the body is learned through training and experience, earned through service, and discerned by the community. "Remember those who led you, who spoke the word of God to you; and considering the result of their conduct, imitate their faith" (Hebrews 13:7). These servant leaders develop a vision for what God is doing in the lives of others and enjoy helping them mature and reach their potential. They are more interested in discipling people than in directing programs. As these leaders model, teach, train, and develop new leaders, they serve people by helping them move from a self-centered to an others-centered and Christ-centered orientation. In this way, they are involved in healing the wounded, maturing the healing, and releasing the maturing.

Through painful experience, Henri J. M. Nouwen encountered and warned about three temptations that can keep leaders from being servants. His insightful *In the Name of Jesus* should be read by every person who aspires to leadership in the body of Christ. The first temptation is to be relevant, that is, to make significant contributions to the contemporary world. The discipline here is to move from relevance to prayer by listening to God's voice and loving Jesus more than what we do or accomplish. The second temptation is to be spectacular, that is, to gain the plaudits and commendations of people. The discipline here is to move from popularity to ministry by becoming embedded in a confessing and caring community. The third temptation is to be powerful, that is, to be in control and to use the power of this world in the name of serving God. The discipline here is to move from leading to being led by choosing love over power and seeking the downward mobility of surrender to the leadership of Jesus so that he increases and we decrease.

Some additional titles that address servant leadership are J. Robert Clinton, *The Making of a Leader*; Robert K. Greenleaf, *Servant Leadership*; Henri J. M. Nouwen, *The Wounded Healer*; and J. Oswald Sanders, *Spiritual Leadership*.

ACCOUNTABILITY AND RULE

Accountability

The issue of one-on-one and group accountability has been widely discussed in the last few years, and like so many other areas, an unbalanced approach can lead to one of two extremes. The first extreme is lack of accountability before other people. Sometimes this is couched in the pious-sounding statement, "I am accountable only to God." The opposite extreme is a harsh, authoritarian approach in which accountability is used to pressure people into someone's definition of obedience. In this situation, exhortation eclipses affirmation in the same way that law often overrides grace.

A balanced approach to accountability esteems the value of being in relationship with people who love us enough to take the risks of honesty and candor when necessary.

Biblical accountability is not a matter of external imposition but of voluntary submission. "Obey your leaders and submit to them, for they keep watch over your souls as those who will give an account. Let them do this with joy and not with grief, for this would be unprofitable for you" (Hebrews 13:17). There are few churches in which the elders genuinely "keep watch over [the] souls" of the flock, and yet we need such a ministry in our lives.

Accountability can relate to overt sin (1 Samuel 13:13), to doctrinal impurity (Galatians 2:14), to the impressions we create before others (Romans 14:15–16), and to decision making (1 Kings 22:6–8). The purpose of accountability is to protect us from the sins of presumption, self-deception, and rationalization. In addition, accountability communicates that "I also am a man under authority" (Matthew 8:9). If we are wise, we will not put our confidence in ourselves but in Christ (Philippians 3:3; 2 Corinthians 3:5). True accountability is inversely proportional to confidence in the flesh. Thus we need a mental shift from seeing accountability as optional to viewing it as a necessary nutrient for spiritual health. Adapting the story of Nathan's rebuke of David for his adultery and murder (2 Samuel 12), we should find a Nathan with whom we can share our struggles before a Nathan finds us to confront us with our sin.

The problem is that it is easy to convey the appearance of accountability without the reality. When Christian leaders, for example, are "accountable" to people who will back them in whatever they say or do, image defeats substance. Another way of feigning accountability is withholding information. This is why it is necessary to maintain honesty and transparency as well as regular interaction with those to whom we are accountable.

Accountability should be invited rather than imposed, and it need not be reciprocal. When we seek the benefits of personal and group accountability, we should prayerfully look for people who have a vital walk with God, who are marked by integrity, honesty, and character, and who can be objective about the decisions we need to make. In this way, the support of community upholds us in our disciplines and encourages us to stay on the path of discipleship.

Rule

Another time-tested approach to accountability is *Rule*, a word derived from the Latin word *regula*, meaning "rule, pattern, model, example." A Regular Christian is one who embraces some form of Rule in the spiritual life. Rule has to do with a pattern of disciplines that is practiced by a community (e.g., the *Rule* of St. Benedict), though it can also be embraced by an individual or a small group. Rule relates to order in a life of prayer, study, silence, solitude, and other disciplines, and its intention should be one of true freedom and skill rather than rigidity or legalism. Personal Rule can be made in consultation with a spiritual director, and common Rule can be established among friends who wish to be united in a common bond of spiritual love and support. When groups are committed to corporate Rule and prayer, they can become remnants within the visible church and agents of renewal.

RENEWAL

As we have seen, personal spiritual formation is enhanced in the context of community with like-minded believers. There is also a mutual dynamic between personal renewal and corporate renewal, and this is evident in the patterns of awakenings in the history of the church. Various renewal and reform movements preceded the Reformation (see appendix B, "The Richness of Our Heritage"). Subsequent to the Reformation, English Puritans and German Pietists stressed the need to go beyond nominal churchmanship to repentance and saving faith. Both groups realized the futility of reforming doctrines and institutions in the church without personal revitalization. They desired to see *ecclesia reformata semper reformanda*, a reformed church always reforming.

The early eighteenth century saw the remarkable appearance of three concurrent renewal movements: the First Great Awakening in America (e.g., Jonathan Edwards), the Evangelical Revival in England (e.g., John Wesley, George Whitefield), and Continental Pietism (e.g., Count Ludwig von Zinzendorf). In spite of their diversity (Puritan Calvinism, Wesleyan Arminianism, and Pietistic Lutheranism), these movements all sought the experiential application of biblical truth through encounter with both Word and Spirit.

The Second Great Awakening in the late eighteenth and early nineteenth century was led by Lyman Beecher and other evangelists in America and by the evangelicals William Wilberforce and Charles Simeon in England. Later evangelical renewal movements in the nineteenth and twentieth centuries were primarily fostered by lay evangelists without formal theological training (e.g., Charles Finney, D. L. Moody, Billy Sunday). During this time, revivals became associated with new methods of mass evangelism. But there was also a stress on the outpouring of the Holy Spirit, as in the Prayer Revival of 1857–1859 (a spontaneous, lay-directed movement of daily prayer meetings) and the Welsh revival of 1904–1905.

The Deeper Life movement and the Pentecostal movement at the beginning of the twentieth century stressed different aspects of experiential encounter with the Spirit of God. In recent years, the parachurch evangelism and discipleship movement in the second half of the twentieth century, the Jesus movement in the 1960s and 1970s, the charismatic movement from the 1960s to 1980s, and the subsequent Third Wave movement all illustrate the diversity of corporate renewal.

The terms *awakening*, *renewal*, and *revival* are based on biblical metaphors for the infusion of the Holy Spirit in Christian experience (e.g., Romans 6:4; 8:2–11; Ephesians 1:17–23; 3:14–19; 5:14). Generally they are used synonymously for corporate spiritual revitalization.

J. Edwin Orr sought to find a unifying pattern in these diverse movements by using the sequence of Acts 1 and 2. The corporate prayer of dependence on the Holy Spirit in Acts 1 was followed in Acts 2 by the animation and growth of the church through the Spirit-empowered ministry of preaching, teaching, evangelism, and healing. An alternate pattern of revival is based on the return to God's Word under kings Josiah and Hezekiah. In addition, Richard F. Lovelace distinguishes cyclical and continuous models of renewal.

Renewal spirituality centers on repentance and personal conversion as well as prayerful preparation and waiting for the sovereign and sudden movement of the Holy Spirit. Renewal is God's sovereign work, and it does not depend on the implementation of a particular set of principles or on human efforts to make it happen. It is initiated in sovereign and surprising ways by the Spirit of God as he moves his people to a continuous watch of concerted corporate prayer. In *Dynamics of Spiritual Life* and *Renewal as a Way of Life*, Richard F. Lovelace outlines the preconditions, primary elements, and secondary elements of renewal. I have adapted table 36.2 from Lovelace's outline.

I. PRECONDITIONS OF RENEWAL: PREPARATION FOR THE GOSPEL	
A. Awareness of the holiness of God	• His justice • His love
B. Awareness of the depth of sin	• In your own life • In your community
II. PRIMARY ELEMENTS OF RENEWAL: DEPTH PRESENTATION OF THE GOSPEL	
A. Justification: You are accepted	
B. Sanctification: You are free from bondage to sin	• In Christ
C. The indwelling Spirit: You are not alone	
D. Authority in spiritual conflict: You have authority	
III. SECONDARY ELEMENTS OF RENEWAL: OUTWORKING OF THE GOSPEL IN THE CHURCH'S LIFE	
A. Mission: Following Christ into the world, presenting his gospel	• In proclamation • In social demonstration
B. Prayer: Expressing dependence on the power of His Spirit	• Individually • Corporately
C. Community: Being in union with his body	• In microcommunities • In macrocommunities
D. Theological integration: Having the mind of Christ	• Toward revealed truth • Toward your culture

TABLE 36.2

True renewal begins with the Spirit's conviction of the holiness of God and the depth of sin (John 16:8). It properly leads to the fourfold personal realization of acceptance in Christ (justification, Romans 5:1–11), freedom from bondage to sin (sanctification, Romans 6:1–18), the power of God (the indwelling Holy Spirit, Romans 8:1–27), and the authority of the believer (standing firm in the spiritual warfare, Ephesians 6:10–18; James 4:7). These primary elements of personal renewal should move believers beyond the individual level to the corporate level. This is expressed in the secondary elements of corporate renewal: involvement in mission (Acts 1:8), waiting on God in corporate prayer (Acts 1:13–14), participation in community (Acts 2:42–47), and theological renewal of the mind to reflect the mind of Christ (1 Corinthians 2:1–16). Thus both personal spiritual formation and corporate renewal are centrifugal movements (directed outward from the center).

In practice, renewal movements are really variations of this idealized scheme; often some of the primary and secondary elements are either underplayed or overstressed. In addition, revivals can take aberrant forms through the corrupting forces of the world, the flesh, and the devil. Faulty theology is another source of distortion in revival movements; however, good theology does not always produce corporate renewal, and poor theology does not always prevent corporate renewal. Some of these movements seem to stop as suddenly as they started, while others have long-term ripple effects.

A growing number of churches and ministries have been coming to the realization that the truth of the Scriptures and the presence of the Spirit must both be fully released within the believing community. Two examples are described in *Fresh Wind, Fresh Fire* by Jim Cymbala and *The Word and Power Church* by Doug Banister. These churches, however, do not report identical patterns of experience, and it would be a mistake to try to turn what God does in one church into a prescription or a recipe for all churches.

True renewal is not a matter of institutional reorganization or public appeal; rather, it centers on the power of the Spirit (fire), the authority of the Word (fuel), and unity in prayer (fellowship) within the remnant of committed believers in the body of Christ. When prayer becomes pervasive, when passion becomes contagious, and when the power of God becomes evident, the community of faith grows both in quality (discipleship) and in quantity (evangelism).

THE FUTURE OF COMMUNITY

The Bible is a grand narrative about the creation of a perfect cosmic order, the Fall and its distortions of that order, God's redemptive program to create a whole new order through the work of his Son, and the full realization of the kingdom of God in which there will be complete harmony, security, and joy in the community of all who have found freedom in the will of the divine Lover of their souls. As Tom Sine describes this coming community in *Wild Hope*, God's intentions are

- to create a new peoplehood in which persons from every tongue and tribe and nation are reconciled to the living God
- to establish a new community of righteousness in which there is no more sin, personal or structural
- to fashion a new order of justice in which there is no more oppression of the poor

- to build a new international community of peace in which the instruments of warfare are transformed into the implements of peace
- to establish a new society of wholeness in which the blind see, the deaf hear, and the possessed are set free
- to host a huge festival of celebration in which peoples from all ethnic and cultural backgrounds joyously celebrate the reign of God in our midst
- to usher in a new future in which we are reconciled not only to our God and to one another but also to the entire created order

QUESTIONS FOR PERSONAL APPLICATION

- What experience have you had with spiritual friendship? With spiritual guidance? With spiritual mentoring? With spiritual direction? Which of these would be most beneficial to you at this point in your spiritual journey?
- Why do you think few Protestants have encountered spiritual direction?
- What experience have you had with inner healing?
- Although servant leadership is sometimes discussed, why do you think the real thing is so rarely practiced in Christian churches and organizations?
- Do you have genuine accountability in your life? Why is it so easy to have the appearance of accountability without the reality?
- What is the nature of your personal Rule in your spiritual formation?
- Have you encountered some of the elements of corporate renewal?

CONTINUING ON THE JOURNEY
What It Takes to Finish Well

CHAPTER OVERVIEW

What does it take to stay in the race? This concluding chapter considers a variety of issues related to finishing well, including intimacy with Christ, fidelity in the spiritual disciplines, a biblical perspective on the circumstances of life, teachability, personal purpose, healthy relationships, and ongoing ministry.

The actor Lee Marvin, who died of a heart attack in 1987 at the age of sixty-three, once made this despondent statement: "They put your name on a star on Hollywood Boulevard and you find a pile of dog manure on it. That's the whole story, baby." If we are citizens of this world only, Marvin was right; the achievements of fame, position, possessions, and power will not endure and will not satisfy. Our monuments and accomplishments will crumble around us and offer little comfort at the end of our brief sojourn on this earth.

By contrast, consider Peter Kreeft's words in *Three Philosophies of Life*:

The world's purest gold is only dung without Christ. But with Christ, the basest metal is transformed into the purest gold. The hopes of alchemy can come true, but on a spiritual level, not a chemical one. There is a "philosopher's stone" that transmutes all things into gold. Its name is Christ. With him, poverty is riches, weakness is power, suffering is joy, to be despised is glory. Without him, riches are poverty, power is impotence, happiness is misery, glory is despised.

Once we have committed our lives to Christ, there should be no turning back—indeed, if we think about it, there is nothing of real and lasting substance to which we can turn apart from him. In spite of this truth, there is an epidemic of believers who drop out of the race during their middle years. Many begin well but finish poorly. It can be gradual erosion through a series of small compromises or a more sudden point of departure, but any number of things can divert us from the course on which we are called to run.

What does it take to finish well? How can we run in such a way that we can say with Paul, "I have fought the good fight, I have finished the course, I have kept the faith" (2 Timothy 4:7; Acts 20:24; 1 Corinthians 9:24–27)? A number of observers have considered the characteristics of people who "run with endurance the race that is set before [them]" (Hebrews 12:1). I have arrived at a set of seven such characteristics:

1. *Intimacy* with Christ
2. Fidelity in the spiritual *disciplines*
3. A biblical *perspective* on the circumstances of life
4. A *teachable*, responsive, humble, and obedient spirit
5. A clear sense of personal *purpose* and calling
6. Healthy *relationships* with resourceful people
7. Ongoing *ministry* investment in the lives of others

The seven key words are intimacy, disciplines, perspective, teachable, purpose, relationships, and ministry, and it is important to note that these characteristics move from the inside to the outside. The first two concern our vertical relationship with God (being), the next three concern our personal thinking and orientation (knowing), and the last two concern our horizontal relationships with others (doing). Here is a brief word about each of these seven crucial characteristics.

INTIMACY WITH CHRIST

The exhortation, "Let us run with endurance the race that is set before us" in Hebrews 12:1 is immediately followed by these words in 12:2: "fixing our eyes on Jesus, the author and perfecter of faith." If we wish to run with endurance and finish our race well, we must continue to look at Jesus rather than the circumstances or the other runners. Remember Jesus' strong words in Luke 14:26: "If anyone comes to Me, and does not hate his own father and mother and wife and children and brothers and sisters, yes, and even his own life, he cannot be My disciple." The Scriptures call us to love and serve these people, but our Lord tells us that he must be preeminent in our affections. Our love and pursuit of him must make all other relationships seem like hatred in comparison.

Telescopic photographs of the sun often reveal massive areas on the solar photosphere called sunspots. These are temporary cool regions that appear dark by contrast against the hotter photosphere that surrounds them. But if we could see a sunspot by itself, it would be brilliant. In the same way, our love for others should shine except when compared with our love for the Lord Christ. Although we have not yet seen Jesus, we can love him and hope in him who first loved us and delivered himself up for us (1 Peter 1:8; Ephesians 5:2).

Our highest calling is to grow in our knowledge of Christ and to make him known to others. If any person, possession, or position is elevated above the Lord Jesus in our minds and affections, we will be unable to fulfill this great calling. Instead, we will sell ourselves cheaply for the empty promises of a fleeting world.

We would be wise to ask this question from time to time to examine our hearts and our direction in life: Does my desire to know Christ exceed all other aspirations? If not, whatever is taking his place in the center of our affections must yield to him if we are to know the joy of bearing spiritual fruit as his disciples.

A key secret of those who finish well is to focus more on loving Jesus than on avoiding sin. The more we love Jesus, the more we will learn to put our confidence in him alone. To quote Kreeft again (*Christianity for Modern Pagans*),

> the great divide, the eternal divide, is not between theists and atheists, or between happiness and unhappiness, but between seekers (lovers) and non-seekers (nonlovers) of the Truth (for God is Truth). . . . We can seek health, happiness or holiness; physical health, mental health or spiritual health as our *summum bonum*, our greatest good. . . . Christ's first question in John's Gospel is the crucial one: "What do you seek?" (1:38). This question determines what we will find, determines our eternal destiny, determines everything.

FIDELITY IN THE SPIRITUAL DISCIPLINES

In the section on disciplined spirituality, we saw that the disciplines are not ends in themselves but means to the end of intimacy with Christ and spiritual formation. The problem is that anything, when left to itself, tends to decline and decay. The second law of thermodynamics, which says that the quantity of useful energy in any closed system gradually diminishes, can be broadly applied to other systems, from information theory to relationships. Without an infusion of ordered energy, entropy (a measure of randomness and disorder) increases. In the case of objects and relationships, an infusion of directed intentionality and effort is necessary to sustain order and growth.

The twenty disciplines we touched upon earlier (solitude, silence, prayer, journaling, study, meditation, fasting, chastity, secrecy, confession, fellowship, submission, guidance, simplicity, stewardship, sacrifice, worship, celebration, service, and witness) can enhance our character, our thinking, and our practice. No one consistently practices all of these disciplines, and some are less meaningful for some people than for others, but fidelity to the disciplines we most need in our spiritual journeys will keep us on the path and bring repeated times of personal renewal.

A BIBLICAL PERSPECTIVE ON THE CIRCUMSTANCES OF LIFE

Without a growing sense of desperation, we will not maintain our focus on God. The Lord lovingly uses trials and adversities in a variety of creative ways in our lives, and part of the purpose of our suffering is to drive us to dependence on him alone. This is part of the point of the midlife process, as we face the combination of diminishing capacity and increasing responsibility. We usually come to grips with our mortality in an experiential way in our late thirties to mid-forties, though some see it sooner and others manage to defer it for a few more years.

As God's children, our pain causes us to ask, to seek, and to knock (Matthew 7:7–8), and in his time, God responds by revealing more of himself to us. This personal knowledge increases our faith and our capacity to trust his character and his promises. Only as we experientially realize that we cannot survive without God will we willingly submit to his purposes in the midst of affliction. A growing faith involves trusting God through the times we do not understand his purposes and his ways.

Tribulation plays a significant role in clarifying hope (see Romans 5:3–5), because it can force us to see the bigger picture. As we saw in the section on paradigm spirituality, we must cultivate an eternal perspective in this temporal arena in order to understand that "the sufferings of this present time are not worthy to be compared with the glory that is to be revealed to us" (Romans 8:18). When we view our circumstances in light of God's character instead of God's character in light of our circumstances, we come to see that God is never indifferent to us and that he uses suffering for our good so that we will be more fully united to Christ (Hebrews 12:10–11; 1 Peter 4:12–17). In addition, he comforts us in our afflictions (2 Corinthians 1:3–5) and reminds us that they will not endure forever (2 Corinthians 4:16–18).

In *The Problem of Pain*, C. S. Lewis argues that God allows pain in our lives not because he loves us less but because he loves us *more* than we would wish:

Over a sketch made idly to amuse a child, an artist may not take much trouble: he may be content to let it go even though it is not exactly as he meant it to be. But over the great picture of his life—the work which he loves, though in a different fashion, as intensely as a man loves a woman or a mother a child—he will take endless trouble—and would, doubtless, thereby *give* endless trouble to the picture if it were sentient. One can imagine a sentient picture, after being rubbed and scraped and re-commenced for the tenth time, wishing that it were only a thumb-nail sketch whose making was over in a minute.

As we renew our minds with a growing biblical perspective on the experiences and circumstances of life, we come to see that this life is a time of sowing the seeds of eternity rather than multiplying ephemeral treasures on earth. Such a perspective reduces our anxieties (Matthew 6:25–34), increases our contentment (Philippians 4:11–13; 1 Timothy 6:6–8), and strengthens our trust and hope (Hebrews 6:13–20). With the shrinking of space and the acceleration of time in a postmodern age, we need rhythm and pacing or we will be in danger of spiraling downward and fading out in the end. It is always wise to review and adapt our pace to the larger story.

A TEACHABLE, RESPONSIVE, HUMBLE, AND OBEDIENT SPIRIT

Those who finish well maintain an ongoing learning posture through the seasons of their lives. A smug, self-satisfied attitude causes people to plateau or decline on the learning curve, and this is inimical to spiritual vitality. In our youth, we have a problem with foolishness and lack of focus; in our middle years, we struggle with double-mindedness and entanglement; when we reach our later years, our great challenge is teachability. Those who maintain a childlike sense of wonder, surprise, and awe do not succumb to rigidity and hardening of the categories. Such people who continue to grow in grace "will flourish in the courts of our God. They will still yield fruit in old age; they shall be full of sap and very green" (Psalm 92:13–14).

Humility and responsive obedience is the key to maintaining a teachable spirit. Humility is the disposition in which the soul realizes that all of life is about trust in God, and that "from Him and through Him and to Him are all things" (Romans 11:36). The mystery of the grace of God humbles us more than our sinfulness, because grace teaches us to be preoccupied with God, and not with ourselves. When we surrender to this grace and invite God to be our all in all, we displace the self through the enthronement of Christ. We would do well to make the following prayer, adapted from the end of Andrew Murray's book on *Humility*, a part of our devotional lives:

> Lord God, I ask that out of Your great goodness You would make known to me, and take from my heart, *every kind and form and degree of pride*, whether it be from evil spirits, or my own corrupt nature; and that You would awaken in me the *deepest depth and truth of that humility* which can make me capable of Your light and Holy Spirit.

Like our Lord in the days of his flesh, we must learn obedience through the things that we suffer (Hebrews 5:7–8). As Thomas Merton put it in *Spiritual Direction and Meditation*, "We must be ready to cooperate not only with graces that console, but with graces that humiliate us. Not only with lights that exalt us, but with lights that blast our self-complacency."

Obedience requires risk taking, because it is the application of biblical faith in that which is not seen and that which is not yet (Hebrews 11:1). As we mature in Christ, we learn to live with ambiguity in this world by trusting God's character and promises in spite of appearances to the contrary.

A CLEAR SENSE OF PERSONAL PURPOSE AND CALLING

Life without a transcendent source of purpose would be an exercise in futility. As Malcolm Muggeridge puts it,

It has never been possible for me to persuade myself that the universe could have been created, and we, *homo sapiens*, so-called, have, generation after generation, somehow made our appearance to sojourn briefly on our tiny earth, solely in order to mount the interminable soap opera, with the same characters and situations endlessly recurring, that we call history. It would be like building a great stadium for a display of tiddly-winks, or a vast opera house for a mouth-organ recital. There must, in other words, be another reason for our existence and that of the universe than just getting through the days of our life as best we may; some other destiny than merely using up such physical, intellectual and spiritual creativity as has been vouchsafed us.

Although we realize that we never arrive in this life, God has called each of us to a purposeful journey that involves risks along the way and is sustained by faithfulness and growing hope. This calling or vocation transcends our occupations and endures beyond the end of our careers. As we seek the Lord's guidance in developing a personal vision and clarity of mission, we move beyond the level of tasks and accomplishments to the level of the purpose for which we "live and move and exist" (Acts 17:28). We are first called to a Person, and then we are called to express this defining relationship in the things we undertake, realizing that the final outcome of our lives is in the hands of God. We have a sense of destiny, but our ignorance of the invisible geography of the new creation means that we must trust God for what he is calling us to become. Reinhold Niebuhr put it well:

Nothing that is worth doing can be achieved in our lifetime; therefore we must be saved by hope. Nothing which is true or beautiful or good makes complete sense in any immediate context of history; therefore we must be saved by faith. Nothing we do, however virtuous, can be accomplished alone; therefore we are saved by love.

There is always a chasm between our aspirations and our accomplishments, between our capacities and our contributions. This discrepancy turns from an occasion for despair to an opportunity for hope when we see it as our nostalgia for our true home.

This hope is the realization that our purpose is not measurable and that our earthly calling is but the preface to the endless creative activity and community of heaven.

HEALTHY RELATIONSHIPS WITH RESOURCEFUL PEOPLE

In the section on corporate spirituality, we looked at the spectrum of supportive soul-care relationships that moves from spiritual friendship to spiritual guidance to spiritual mentoring to spiritual direction. We also considered the important dimensions of servant leadership as well as personal and group accountability. Each of these relationships is a valuable resource that can encourage, equip, and exhort us to stay on the course we have been called to run. People who finish well do not do so without the caring support of other growing members of the body of Christ. These relationships help us to increase in intimacy with Christ, to maintain the needed disciplines, to clarify our long-term perspective, to sustain a teachable attitude, and to develop our purpose and calling.

ONGOING MINISTRY INVESTMENT IN THE LIVES OF OTHERS

We saw in the exchanged life spirituality section that Jesus Christ gave his life for us (salvation), so that he could give his life to us (sanctification), so that he could live his life through us (service). Spirit-filled spirituality stressed the importance of discovering and developing the spiritual gifts we have received and of exercising them in the power of the Spirit for the edification of others. Nurturing spirituality centered on cultivating a lifestyle of evangelism and discipleship so that we are part of the process of introducing people to Jesus and assisting them in their spiritual growth after they have come to know him. The life God implants within us is meant not only to permeate our beings but also to penetrate and multiply in the lives of others. Believers who finish well are marked by ongoing outreach and sacrificial ministry for the good of other people. Those who squander the resources, gifts, experiences, and hard-learned insights God has given them by no longer investing them in the lives of others soon wither and withdraw.

BARRIERS TO FINISHING WELL

It is obvious that when we reverse these seven characteristics of people who finish well, we arrive at a corresponding list of barriers to running the course. Instead of doing this, let me observe that a failure to sustain the first characteristic (intimacy with Christ) is the key obstruction to progress in the other six. Indeed, the others contribute to our intimacy with Christ, but regression in our relationship with Jesus will soon erode fidelity in the others. The real question then is, What causes us to drift away from abiding in Jesus? In some way or another, the spiritual sin of pride and autonomy usually heads the list. This can take many forms, such as ego-driven ambition (often inspired by insecurity), unwillingness to learn from others, comparison and envy, refusal to submit to authority, strategies designed to avoid pain and vulnerability, and bitterness with God for allowing personal affliction and loss.

The more visible sins of moral or ethical compromise and failure are generally the by-products of inner spiritual disintegration—the loss of the clear eye (Matthew 6:22–23) and the pure heart (Matthew 5:8; 1 Timothy 1:5; 2 Timothy 2:22). Declining passion for Christ eventually subverts calling and character.

MORE THOUGHTS ON PERSPECTIVE, RESPONSIVENESS, AND PURPOSE

A Perspective on Problems

Have you ever seen another person grow in character and depth in times of apparent success? It would be so much simpler if having things go our way was also beneficial to us in the long run, but because of self-centeredness and shortsightedness, this is rarely the case. Until the Lord returns, we will continue to learn and grow more through setbacks and failures than through success as the world defines it. Listen to the observations of a man who had enjoyed an eminently successful career in the eyes of his peers:

> Contrary to what might be expected, I look back on experiences that at the time seemed especially desolating and painful with particular satisfaction. Indeed, I can say with complete truthfulness that everything I have learned in my seventy-five years in this world, everything that has truly enhanced and enlightened my existence, has been through affliction and not through happiness, whether pursued or attained.
>
> *Malcolm Muggeridge*

If any of us could be transported to heaven for even a five-minute visit, we would never be the same after our return to earth. For the first time, we would have a true perspective on the frailty and brevity of life on earth and the absurdity of giving our hearts to things that will not last.

John White observed that "it is want of faith that makes us opt for earthly rather than heavenly treasure. If we really believed in celestial treasures, who among us would be so stupid as to buy gold? We just do not believe. Heaven is a dream, a religious fantasy which we affirm because we are orthodox. If people believed in heaven, they would spend their time preparing for permanent residence there. But nobody does."

Our perspective on life, whether temporal or eternal, will determine the set of rules by which we play, the standards and character we pursue, the source of our hope, and the difference between obedience and disobedience to God's precepts and principles.

In his "Meditation in a Toolshed," C. S. Lewis depicted the difference between looking *at* a beam of light and looking *along* the beam. As he entered a dark toolshed, he could see nothing but a sunbeam that came from a crack at the top of the door. At first, he looked at the shaft of light with thousands of specks of dust floating in it, but then he did something most of us have done at one time or another. He moved until the beam fell on his eyes, and at that moment, the toolshed and the sunbeam vanished. Looking along the beam, he saw green leaves moving on the branches of a tree outside, and beyond that, the sun itself. Perspective makes all the difference.

Imagine a world where people's problems cease at the moment they put their faith in Christ. They suddenly become immune to bodily ailments, they enjoy complete harmony in their personal and professional relationships, and success and affluence are theirs for the asking. This trouble-free state of affairs is not far from the scenario touted by the peddlers of the prosperity gospel.

It may sound good at first, but consider a few of the implications. They may trust Christ for their salvation, but it would be extremely difficult for them not to look to the world for everything else. Because there are no obstacles, they would soon take God for granted and presume upon his grace; their prayers would become more like conjuring tricks than acknowledgments of love and dependence on the Lord. And since everything goes their way, it would be almost impossible for them to cultivate true Christian character. They would never develop qualities like endurance (James 1:3), steadfastness (1 Corinthians 15:58), thanksgiving (1 Thessalonians 5:18), diligence, moral excellence, self-control, perseverance, godliness (2 Peter 1:5–6), compassion, humility, gentleness, patience (Colossians 3:12), and faithfulness (Galatians 5:22), since these are related to hoping in God in a context of adversity.

Far from promising a life of ease and prosperity, the New Testament affirms that those who follow Christ will face a new dimension of obstacles and struggles that they did not know before they committed their lives to him. In fact, the intensity of the spiritual warfare is proportional to the seriousness of a believer's response to the terms of discipleship. "Indeed, all who desire to live godly in Christ Jesus will be persecuted" (2 Timothy 3:12). This is why Paul encouraged the disciples in Asia Minor to continue in the faith, saying, "Through many tribulations we must enter the kingdom of God" (Acts 14:22). At the end of his last discourse to his disciples, Jesus assured them, "These things I have spoken to you, so that in Me you may have peace. In the world you have tribulation, but take courage; I have overcome the world" (John 16:33).

Our responses to the trials we encounter expose our level of trust in the sovereignty and goodness of the Lord. At a special exhibition of Rembrandt paintings, a custodian overheard some of the museum patrons making critical remarks about the work of the great artist. He quietly remarked, "It is not the artist but the viewers who are on trial."

I confess that when I move through times of conflict and adversity, it is all too easy for me to develop a wrong attitude toward God, and it is not so easy to thank him for what he can accomplish through the problem. But I can also acknowledge with thanksgiving that whenever I stopped rebelling against him and started trusting in his sovereignty, love, goodness, and wisdom, he never let me down. If you think back, I think you will be able to say the same.

Responding to God's Initiatives

"You did not choose Me but I chose you, and appointed you that you would go and bear fruit, and that your fruit would remain" (John 15:16).

God's grace is always previous to our response; whenever we pursue him it is because he has already pursued us. Whenever we love him, it is because he has first loved us (1 John 4:8–21). Whenever we offer up prayers, it is because he has already invited us to do so.

Our Responses Determine Our Direction

Nevertheless, God holds us accountable for our responses to his initiatives. Indeed, the quality of our relationship with him and the entire direction of our lives are determined by the nature of our responses to his loving impulses in our lives. We have been given a response-ability, an ability to respond to or neglect these divine initiatives, and from a human standpoint, our relationship with God is determined by our willingness to reciprocate. Without an ongoing response of our personality to God's personality, our relationship with him will be shallow or nonexistent.

The most significant response we will ever make is related to the gospel, the good news about Christ's gift of forgiveness and newness of life. This gift is not ours unless we respond to it by coming to Christ on his terms, which include not merely intellectual assent but personal reception. Coming to Christ is a volitional commitment in which we turn away from our former trust in our own efforts to achieve or merit God's favor and turn instead to an exclusive trust in Christ and his righteousness on our behalf. This faith response is an affront to our natural pride because it involves the admission of our desperate need and hopeless condition without Jesus.

In 1938, a German merchant vessel was in the midst of a storm in the North Atlantic. The pressure of the sea was so great that the plates in the hull began to buckle, and within moments the ship sank. Almost miraculously, one sailor stayed afloat by holding onto a cot mattress that had somehow not soaked through and was somewhat buoyant. Then from the south came a British cutter. The German sailor was spotted along with the wreckage of the sunken ship. The British ship "hove to," even though this was a very dangerous thing to do in a storm. The German sailor rose and fell on the billowing waves. A seaman on deck threw out a lifesaver. The big doughnut landed next to the German sailor, but the sailor looked up and saw the British flag and the British faces. He knew that these people represented the traditional enemy of Germany. He turned his back on the lifesaver, and slowly the mattress that buoyed him up sank under the waves. The sailor was lost.

When I read this account, I saw it as a parable of God's offer of salvation. Jesus' gift of deliverance from spiritual death is the lifesaver, and part of us instinctively resists taking hold of it because, without Christ, we are enemies of God (Romans 5:10). Like the German sailor, we can stubbornly refuse God's offer, but if we do, we can never blame him for our demise. The judgment is not a matter of degree. As Kreeft observes, "There are only two kinds of people in the world; and they are not the good and the bad, but the living and the dead, the twice-born and the once-born, the children of God and the children of Adam, the pregnant and the barren. That is the difference between heaven and hell" (*Love Is Stronger Than Death*).

The most important response of our lives is to say yes to the gospel. As Brennan Manning notes in *The Lion and the Lamb*, "There are two elements which are central in the Christian experience. First, a man hears God say, 'Thou art the man.' Secondly, he replies, 'Thou art my God.'" The former is the point of conviction (see 2 Samuel 12:7), and the latter is the point of turning from self to Christ.

An Ongoing Series of Responses

Once having come to Christ in this way, the spiritual life becomes a continuous series of daily responses to the Lord's promptings in our lives. In each case we will choose to walk by sight or by faith, by law or by grace, by the flesh or by the Spirit, by our will or God's will, by submission or resistance, by dependence or by autonomy, by worldly wisdom or by divine wisdom, by betting everything on God's promises and character or by trying to control our world on our own terms, by the temporal or by the eternal, by trying to find our lives or by losing them for Christ's sake. Until we see Christ, we will always be engaged in this warfare in which we are tempted on a daily basis to drop out of the process of the obedience of faith.

One of the things that helps me gain a sense of perspective during times of temptation or discouragement is to review the fact that since I came to Christ in June 1967, I have never regretted an act of obedience, but I have always come to regret acts of disobedience. Yet obedience is still difficult because it is sometimes counterintuitive and usually countercultural. As G. K. Chesterton put it, "The problem with Christianity is not that it has been tried and found wanting, but that it has been found difficult, and left untried."

A clenched fist cannot receive the gift of the one thing most needful. Sin quenches the Holy Spirit and removes our joy, certainty, and peace. This is why it is wise to stop and ask God to reveal to you whatever is in your life that is blocking the Spirit of God. Name it for what it is and give it to God so that the blockage will be removed.

As Romans 12:1–2 makes clear, God does not ask us to do anything for him until he has informed us about what he has done for us. But overexposure and underresponse lead to a bad heart. God is more pleased with our response than with how much we know. The reason that Rahab the harlot is found in Hebrews 11 as an illustration of faith is that although she knew little, she applied what little she knew. The

Pharisees, by contrast, knew a great deal but did not respond in their hearts to what they knew. The Magi had little knowledge about the Messiah but engaged in a long and tedious journey to find him, while the scribes in Jerusalem, knowing Messiah would be born in Bethlehem, didn't even bother to accompany the Magi on the six-mile journey from Jerusalem to Bethlehem.

May God grant us the grace to respond in faith and obedience to the things he calls us to trust and apply.

Developing a Biblical Purpose

We mentioned the importance of purpose in the discussions of motivated and holistic spirituality, and the following thoughts are supplementary.

Missing the Plane of Life

How did it happen that now for the first time in his life he could see everything so clearly? Something had given him leave to live in the present. Not once in his entire life had he allowed himself to come to rest in the quiet center of himself but had forever cast himself forward from some dark past he could not remember to a future which did not exist. Not once had he been present for his life. So his life had passed like a dream.

Is it possible for people to miss their lives in the same way one misses a plane?

The answer to this question raised in Walker Percy's novel *The Second Coming* is an unqualified affirmative. Someone once said, "Fear not that your life will come to an end but rather that it will never have had a beginning."

In the film *Awakenings*, a number of patients who had been in a catatonic state for some thirty years were temporarily brought to full consciousness through a new medication. While some were elated, others were embittered that so much of their lives was spent in oblivion. But they all seized the preciousness of each day, especially when they learned that their awakenings would only be temporary.

There is a sense in which many people live without being truly awake, without thinking and questioning, without a sense of wonder and awe. It is easy, even for believers in Christ, to lurch through life, never developing a clear picture of the unique purpose for which God placed them on this planet.

People without a Purpose

In the words of Václav Havel, "The tragedy of modern man is not that he knows less and less about the meaning of his own life, but that it bothers him less and less." I find it astounding that the bulk of people on our planet seem to journey through years and even decades without seriously wrestling with the fundamental question of why they are here and what they want their lives to add up to in the end. Many business and professional people get on a fast track in pursuit of an elusive vision of success without questioning whether they are selling themselves too cheaply by investing their precious years of life in something that, even if attained, will never satisfy. It is like the two-edged story of the airline pilot who announced the good news that due to a strong tail wind, the plane was making great time, but the bad news that due to an equipment failure, they were hopelessly lost. Many people appear to be making great time on a journey to futility. They may experience the thrill of the bungee jump without realizing the cord is not attached to their ankles or waists but to their necks.

In a conversation from *Alice in Wonderland*, Alice asks the Cheshire Cat, "Would you tell me, please, which way I ought to go from here?" "That depends a good deal on where you want to get to," said the Cat. "I don't much care where," said Alice. "Then it doesn't matter which way you go," said the Cat. If we have not decided where we are going, one road will do as well or as poorly as another. The problem is that the outcome of the unexamined life is rarely satisfactory. If we fail to pursue God's purpose for our lives, we are likely to suffer from destination sickness, the discovery that when we reach our destination, it's not all it was cracked up to be (cf. Ecclesiastes 2:17). This sickness is captured in John Steinbeck's summation of a character in *East of Eden* who gave his life for that which let him down in the end: "He took no rest, no recreation, and he became rich without pleasure and respected without friends."

Letting the Destiny Determine the Journey

It is much wiser to follow Kierkegaard's advice to define life backwards and live it forwards—start from the destiny and define the journey in light of it. Few of us would think of taking a two-week vacation without any plans as to where we will go or what we will do. But what many wouldn't dream of doing on this scale, they do on the greatest scale of all: their entire earthly existence. To avoid this fatal error we should ask ourselves, "What do I want my life to add up to, and why?" "At the end of my sojourn, what will I want to see when I look back?" From a biblical perspective, the real question is not what we will leave behind (the answer to this is always the same—we will leave everything behind) but what will we send on ahead (cf. Matthew 6:20).

Many people define themselves in terms of their activities and accomplishments. But those who have experienced the grace, forgiveness, and newness of life in Christ are recipients of a new source of identity that redefines their mission and purpose on earth. Instead of seeking purpose by comparing themselves with others, they can discover God's purpose for their lives in the pages of his revealed Word.

God's Ultimate Purpose

It has been observed that there are three dimensions of purpose in Scripture (see the helpful Vision Foundation booklet "Establishing Your Purpose"). The first is God's ultimate purpose in creating all things. Prior to creating time, space, energy, and matter, God alone existed, complete and perfect in himself. As a triune, loving community of being, he had no needs, and it was not out of loneliness or boredom that he created the realms of angels and humans. We know from Scripture that part of God's ultimate purpose in creation is the manifestation of his glory to intelligent moral agents who bear his image and who can respond in praise and wonder to his awesome person, powers, and perfections. But in our present state, we can hardly scratch the surface of the unfathomable wisdom of God's ultimate purpose for the created order.

God's Universal Purpose

The second dimension of biblical purpose is God's universal purpose, the intention he has for all people who acknowledge the lordship of Jesus. This level of purpose is shared by all believers and is communicated to us in a number of passages. There are various ways of expressing it, but they can be reduced to two essential areas: knowing God experientially (spiritual growth) and making God known to others (spiritual reproduction).

In his high-priestly prayer after the Upper Room Discourse, Jesus said, "This is eternal life, that they may know You, the only true God, and Jesus Christ whom You have sent" (John 17:3). This knowledge is not merely propositional and theological but also personal and devotional. Eternal life is the experiential knowledge of God, and it involves a growth process that is inaugurated when a person trusts Christ and receives his gift of forgiveness and new life. The greatest treasure a person can own is increasing intimacy with the living Lord of all creation. Although this should be our highest · ambition, many believers give their hearts to the quest for lesser goods and boast and delight in things that are destined to perish. This is why we should frequently heed the powerful words of Jeremiah 9:23–24: "Thus says the LORD, 'Let not a wise man boast of his wisdom, and let not the mighty man boast of his might, let not a rich man boast of his riches; but let him who boasts boast of this, that he understands and knows Me, that I am the Lord who exercises lovingkindness, justice and righteousness on earth; for I delight in these things,' declares the LORD."

The Scriptures expressly communicate the purpose for which we have been created: "For those whom He foreknew, He also predestined to become conformed to the image of His Son, so that He would be the firstborn among many brethren" (Romans 8:29). God's purpose for us is nothing less than Christlikeness! Here are four observations on this high and holy purpose. (1) It is impossible for us to attain. Only when we recognize our weakness and inability to be conformed to the image of Christ will we be ready to allow him to live his life through us, for this is the genius of the spiritual life. (2) On the human side of the coin, we will be as spiritually mature as we chose to be. If we do not engage in the disciplines of discipleship, such as habitual time in the Word of God and prayer, we will not become more intimate with God. (3) Growing intimacy with God is crucial to Christlike character. The personal, experiential knowledge of God transforms the heart and expresses itself in sacrificial acts of love and service toward others. (4) If God's purpose for us is not the focus of our lives, something else will be, and whatever it is will not be worthy of our ultimate allegiance. Therefore ask God for the grace to make it your highest ambition to be pleasing to him (2 Corinthians 5:9).

We summarized God's universal purpose for all who know Christ as knowing God experientially (spiritual growth) and making him known to others (spiritual reproduction). The first part relates to the question Who do you want me to be, Lord? The second relates to the question What do you want me to do? It is prudent to consider the first question before launching into the second, because biblically speaking, being precedes doing; who we are in Christ is foundational to what we do. Typically, however, we put activities and objectives before purpose and define ourselves more by measurable accomplishments than by godly character. The result is that our activities determine our purposes. But purposes developed in this way are shaped by comparison with peers and role models and never lead to the universal and unique purposes for which God created us. Instead, we should embrace a biblical perspective on purpose and let this determine our objectives and activities.

Developing a Vision of Your Unique Purpose

If God's universal purpose for us is to grow in the knowledge of Christ (edification) and to make him known (evangelism), how do we develop a vision of the unique ways he would have us apply this purpose in our lives? The answer is that we must launch a prayerful process of discovery that involves a thoughtful assessment of what God has gifted, called, and equipped us to do. Every believer has a unique combination of experiences, gifts, and relational networks that form a sphere of ministry opportunities. We can be assured that the Lord will not call us to a task for which he has not equipped us (1 Thessalonians 5:24), but we can also be certain that the development of our life message and purpose does not happen suddenly.

The most critical component in the process of discerning our unique purpose is prayer. We would do well to persist in asking God to clarify the vision of our calling, since we will never be able to discover it on our own. This is a divine-human process of preparation and illumination in which each of our positive and negative experiences can be sovereignly used by God in such a way that we can, through his power, make a lasting impact in the lives of others. But commitment must precede knowledge (John 7:17); we must trust God enough to commit ourselves in advance to whatever he calls us to be and to do.

Another essential component in this process is our time in the Scriptures. God uses his Word to train and equip us for ministry, and our effectiveness is related to the depth of our Bible reading, study, and memorization. The price is time and discipline, but the benefits are always disproportionate to the expenditures. If we are shallow in the Word, we will be superficial in our knowledge of God and less effective in our relationships with others.

Other components that relate to your unique purpose are your personal experiences, skills, education, temperament, and roles as well as your spiritual gifts. Each of these elements is relevant to your vision of the specific outworking of God's universal purpose in your life.

Begin to ask God to clarify your personal vision of purpose. This will not happen by doubling up on activities but through prayer, exposure to Scripture, and times of reflection. This process may take months or years, but it should lead to a brief written statement of purpose that can be used to determine and evaluate your objectives and activities. In this way, your activities will be determined more by the Word than by the external pressures of the world.

A biblical purpose is always an unchanging reason for being. It holds true for you regardless of your circumstances or season of life. When a Christ-centered purpose becomes the focus of your life, it harmonizes all the other areas, such as family, work, finances, and ministry.

A FINAL WORD ON THE TWELVE FACETS

Recall the point we made in the introduction that the twelve facets of spiritual formation are all part of the same gem and thus are inextricably bound together. For example, Spirit-filled spirituality informs all the others because it is only in the power of the Holy Spirit that we can be formed into the image of Christ. Relational spirituality affects all the others, because loving God and others is the central expression of our faith. And so it is with the remaining ten.

But we also observed that because of our widely differing temperaments, each of us has a unique personal pattern that involves differing degrees of attraction and resistance to the various facets. It is good to understand that we are naturally drawn to some more than others, but it is also beneficial to stretch ourselves through deliberate exposure to the ones we tend to resist.

It is my prayer that you benefit from this diversity of approaches that have been used to cultivate spiritual growth and that you explore some of the facets that may have been less familiar to you.

The LORD bless you, and keep you;
The LORD make His face shine on you,
And be gracious to you;
The LORD lift up His countenance on you,
And give you peace.

Numbers 6:24–26

QUESTIONS FOR PERSONAL APPLICATION

- How would you rate yourself in the seven characteristics of people who finish well? Which ones need more attention?
- Why is the first characteristic (intimacy with Christ) the key to the other six?
- What is your perspective on problems?
- How responsive have you been to God's initiatives in your life? Have you discerned a pattern in the way and timing of your responses?
- Why is the issue of developing a biblical sense of purpose and mission so critical to perseverance?
- What is your vision of your unique purpose?

APPENDIX A

THE NEED
FOR DIVERSITY

CHAPTER OVERVIEW

There are a variety of approaches to the spiritual life, but these are facets of a larger gem that is greater than the sum of its parts. *Conformed to His Image* takes a broader, more synthetic approach by looking at all of these facets and seeing how each of them can contribute to the larger whole. Some people are attracted to different facets, and this relates in part to our personality profile (the Myers-Briggs Type Indicator is a valuable tool for this purpose). Readers are asked to identify the ones they are most and least attracted to and are encouraged to stretch themselves by trying one they would normally not pursue.

The facets of spirituality discussed in *Conformed to His Image* point to the centrality of the Lord Jesus Christ, and each of them adds a unique dimension to the gem of the spiritual life. Thus it would be a mistake to reduce our understanding of the sanctification process to any one of these approaches, and yet this is commonly done. For instance, a number of writers who stress the truths of the exchanged life ignore the need for the disciplines of the faith or the corporate aspects of spiritual growth. Others are so concerned about the reality of the spiritual warfare that they overlook the process of integrating our relationship with Christ in our daily routines.

When we are excited about the power of the Holy Spirit, or about corporate worship, or about the spiritual disciplines, or about sharing our faith with others in a relational way, it is easy to focus so intently on the insights we have gained in one of these areas that we come to view this single approach as the panacea for spiritual development. This leads to a one-sidedness that leaves us vulnerable to the latent weaknesses of any approach when it is carried too far. For instance, devotional spirituality can lead to an individualistic sentimentality, while disciplined spirituality can lead to an overemphasis on willpower and self-effort. But when these approaches are fit together into a more comprehensive whole, they inform and balance one another. When we view them as complementary components, we are less inclined to think of them as formulas or recipes. Instead, each facet is a symbiotic, divine-human dynamic that requires both dependence and discipline. When we reduce these approaches to techniques, we miss the Augustinian truth that we come to God by love and not by navigation. It is essential to acknowledge the primacy of God's grace over determined self-actualization, or we will deceive ourselves into thinking that our efforts and methods are the means of spiritual growth. As soon as we succumb to this illusion, we will try to control God by our formulas and routines.

Even when we acknowledge that there are several legitimate and complementary approaches to growth in the spiritual life, there is a natural tendency to limit ourselves to the one that best fits our personality and to assume that if it works for us, it should work for others. And because of this tendency, many new believers are exposed to only one or two approaches, neither of which may be particularly helpful in view of their temperaments and predispositions. In recent years, these concerns have been addressed by writers who have sought to identify various types of Christian spirituality and to relate these types to differing mental and emotional character traits. For example, Allan H. Sager in *Gospel-Centered Spirituality* adapted a phenomenology of spirituality developed by Urban T. Holmes in *A History of Christian Spirituality*. This typology involves both a horizontal and a vertical continuum. The vertical scale concerns a person's relational orientation to God, and this can range from purely cognitive and speculative illumination of the mind at one end of the spectrum to purely affective and emotional illumination of the heart at the opposite end of the spectrum. The horizontal scale concerns a person's preferred means of pursuing the spiritual life, and this can range from a purely **kataphatic** orientation to a purely **apophatic** orientation. The term *kataphatic* is derived from a Greek word that means "affirmative," and this refers to the tradition known as the *via affirmativa*, the way of affirmation. This tradition, more characteristic of the West, stresses the knowledge of God through general and special revelation. The term *apophatic* is derived from a Greek word that means "negative," and this speaks of the tradition known as the *via negativa*, the way of negation. This tradition, more characteristic of the East, stresses God's transcendence and mystery. Thus a kataphatic style of spirituality uses symbols, images, and metaphors while an apophatic style emphasizes God's hiddenness.

In reality, no one is purely cerebral with no emotion or solely heart without mind (the vertical scale). Similarly, no believer behaves as if God is utterly hidden or completely knowable (the horizontal scale). Instead, as the Types of Christian Spirituality table (A.1) shows, there is a wide range for diversity that incorporates elements from each of the types in manifold ways.

TYPES OF CHRISTIAN SPIRITUALITY

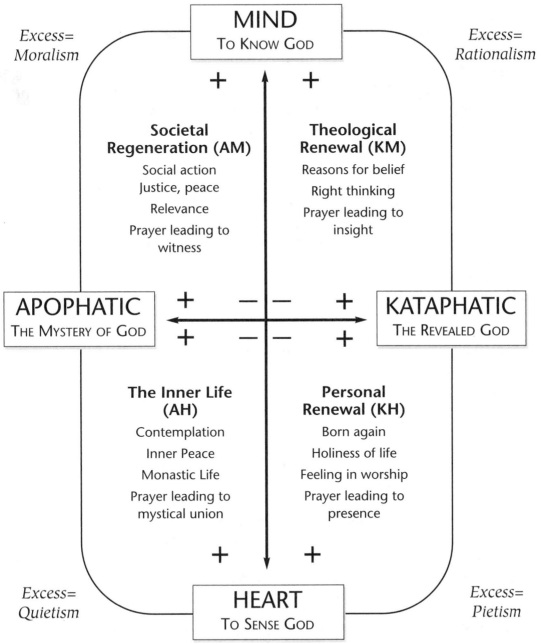

MIND
To Know God

Excess=
Moralism

Excess=
Rationalism

+   +

Societal Regeneration (AM)

Social action
Justice, peace
Relevance
Prayer leading to witness

Theological Renewal (KM)

Reasons for belief
Right thinking
Prayer leading to insight

APOPHATIC
The Mystery of God

KATAPHATIC
The Revealed God

+ — — +
+ — — +

The Inner Life (AH)

Contemplation
Inner Peace
Monastic Life
Prayer leading to mystical union

Personal Renewal (KH)

Born again
Holiness of life
Feeling in worship
Prayer leading to presence

+   +

HEART
To Sense God

Excess=
Quietism

Excess=
Pietism

Based on "A Circle of Sensibility" from *A History of Christian Spirituality* © 1980 by Urban Holmes III. Used by permission.

TABLE A.1

A K+/M+ (high kataphatic/high mind) is very different in orientation and style from an A+/H+ (high apophatic/high heart). There are also differences within each quadrant; for example, within the K/H quadrant, there are nine combinations that range from a K-/H- to a K+/H+.

Apophatic/Heart (A/H) spirituality involves both intuition and feelings, and this combination encourages a diligent pursuit of an inward consciousness of God that stresses prayer and solitude. Theologians of the inner life include Bernard of Clairvaux, Thomas à Kempis, and Cistercian monastics such as Thomas Merton. Taken too far, this form of spirituality can lead to quietism—a neglect of the world and an excessive introspection.

Kataphatic/Mind (K/M) spirituality involves both revelation and understanding, and this combination encourages rational engagement with spiritual truth. Advocates of theological renewal include Thomas Aquinas, Ignatius of Loyola, Martin Luther, John Calvin, and Karl Barth. Taken too far, this form of spirituality can lead to rationalism—an overly dogmatic emphasis that stresses logic to the exclusion of mystery and propositional truth over against personal response.

Kataphatic/Heart (K/H) spirituality involves both revelation and feelings, and this combination encourages outward expression of inner change and transformation of society one life at a time. Proponents of personal renewal include St. Benedict, several Puritan writers, Charles Wesley, and many modern evangelicals. Taken too far, this form of spirituality can lead to pietism—an excessive emotionalism, experientialism, and anti-intellectualism.

Apophatic/Mind (A/M) spirituality involves both intuition and understanding, and this combination encourages bold action and a concern for social justice. Champions of societal regeneration include the prophet Amos, Francis of Assisi, Albert Schweitzer, and Martin Luther King Jr. Taken too far, this form of spirituality can lead to moralism—a mindset of cultural condemnation and an excessive emphasis on action over being.

Using the twelve facets of spirituality that are presented in this book, we can draw a *very general* correlation between these facets and the four types of spirituality we have just discussed (table A.2).

These generalizations admit many exceptions, since aspects of each of the twelve facets relate to each of the four quadrants above. But it is helpful to note, for example, that people with a K/H bent are far more likely to be drawn to exchanged life or Spirit-filled spirituality than they will be to corporate spirituality or an emphasis on social justice that is more characteristic of those with an A/M orientation.

A different but equally helpful typology of spiritual orientations can be derived from the Myers-Briggs Type Indicator (MBTI). This preference indicator was adapted by Katharine Briggs and Isabel Myers from Carl G. Jung's personality classifications in *Psychological Types*. In recent years, Jung has become popular in Christian as well as

APOPHATIC/MIND	KATAPHATIC/MIND
• Corporate spirituality • Holistic spirituality • Warfare spirituality	• Paradigm spirituality • Motivated spirituality • Nurturing spirituality
APOPHATIC/HEART	**KATAPHATIC/HEART**
• Devotional spirituality • Disciplined spirituality • Process spirituality	• Relational spirituality • Exchanged life spirituality • Spirit-filled spirituality

TABLE A.2

New Age circles, and the use of his ideas by Christian writers and counselors requires more discernment than is often practiced. Jung's preoccupation with the movement toward wholeness and individuation and his fascination with mandalas, Eastern mysticism, alchemy, and occultism led to the development of a speculative, complex, and esoteric psychological theory with unavoidably metaphysical overtones. Unlike most personality theorists, Jung explicitly recognized the importance of spiritual concerns, but his attempt to resurrect spiritual symbolism that is devoid of creedal content led him to an amalgam of psychology and spirituality that approximates a rival religion that replaces dogma with the contents of the unconscious. Jung spurned the idea of God as an objective transcendent reality and turned instead to primal symbols stripped of their transcendent referents. Thus the use of Jung's typology in this appendix is not an endorsement of his system of thought.

The MBTI uses four pairs of preferences, and each of these pairs forms a continuum.

1. The extraversion/introversion (E/I) scale concerns a person's relative preference for being energized by the outer world of people and things versus the inner world of ideas. Extraverts are active, outgoing, participative, open, and verbal thinkers. Introverts are reflective, inwardly directed, reserved, and mental thinkers.

2. The sensing/intuition (S/N) scale concerns one's relative preference for perceiving and processing information through known facts versus possibilities and relationships. Sensors are oriented toward tangible sensory data, details, and present reality. Intuitives are oriented toward abstract idealistic associations, future possibilities, and theoretical patterns.

3. The thinking/feeling (T/F) preference concerns the way people arrive at conclusions. Thinkers base their judgments more on impersonal, objective analysis and

are concerned with justice, truth, and logic. Feelers base their judgments more on personal, subjective values and are concerned with harmony, tact, and humane treatment.

4. The judging/perceiving (J/P) scale concerns people's preferential orientation to outer life. Judgers are more inclined toward a systematic, organized, and planned lifestyle that involves goals, deadlines, and controlled procedures. Perceivers are more inclined toward a flexible and spontaneous lifestyle that welcomes change, surprise, and open-ended approaches.

When these four preferential pairs are combined, they result in sixteen basic personality types ranging from ESTJ to INFP. But there are many nuances within each of these personality types, since each pair constitutes a continuum that can range, for example, from a strong E to a borderline E or I to a strong I. Thus this typology allows for the uniqueness of each individual while offering insights into the way people can be grouped according to preferential patterns. It should be noted that there is no hint of superiority or inferiority in these patterns, since they are based on personal preferences. Additional factors such as intelligence, abilities, skills, drive, and maturity add an enormous number of personality nuances.

Those who follow Christ tend to gravitate toward the spiritual activities that nurture their preferential patterns. Up to a point, this is healthy, because it provides great diversity within the unity of the body of Christ. But as M. Robert Mulholland Jr. observes in *Invitation to a Journey*, each of the four preferential pairs, when carried to either extreme (e.g., all T and no F or all F and no T) can lead to a spiritually unhealthy one-sidedness. For instance, when extraversion is carried too far, it can result in such an emphasis on the social dynamics of the spiritual life that there is no room for the depth that solitude and reflection can provide. Strong introverts, by contrast, can avoid community and practice spiritual isolation. Similarly, strong thinkers can be too prone to a highly analytical and systematic approach to the spiritual life, while strong feelers can be vulnerable to sentimentality, emotionalism, and the quest for repeated experiential authentication.

Earle C. Page, in connection with the Center for Applications of Psychological Type, has developed two helpful charts that illustrate several connections between the MBTI preferences and one's spiritual orientation. The first of these, "Finding Your Spiritual Path," is a useful diagnostic tool (table A.3).

The second chart, "Following Your Spiritual Path," points to the positive and negative spiritual expressions that are associated with the four preference pairs (table A.4).

Several authors relate these personality styles to the practice of spirituality and distinctive approaches to prayer. I have summarized the prayer typology developed by Charles J. Keating in *Who We Are Is How We Pray* (table A.5).

If we combine Keating's work with other sources, we can create a distillation of the sixteen personality types in terms of spiritual orientation and prayer (table A.6).

Finding Your Spiritual Path

Note: These words are meant to suggest, not to define or to limit understanding.

Preferred Attitude, Function, or Lifestyle	EXTRAVERSION E	INTROVERSION I	SENSING S	INTUITION N	THINKING T	FEELING F	JUDGMENT J	PERCEPTION P
Primary Arena	World/Other	Ideas/Self	Body	Spirit	Mind	Heart	Will	Awareness
Preference for	Action	Reflection	Sensory reality Details Status quo	Possibilities Patterns Change	Objective values	Subjective values	Initiative	Response
Significant Aspects of Reality	Exterior	Interior	Immediacy Concreteness	Anticipation Vision	Theory Principles	Feeling, Memory, Ideal	Product Categorical	Process Conditional
Windows through which God's Revelation is Received	People Events Scripture Natural world	Individual Experience Inspiration Inner world	Society Institutions "The Seen"	Insight Imagination "The Unseen"	Reason Speculation	Relationships Emotions	Order "Ought"	Serendipity "Is"
Significant Aspects of God	Immanence Creator Imago Dei	Transcendence Identity of God and inner self	Incarnation	Mystery Holy Spirit	The Absolute Principle First Cause	Relational Familial (e.g. Father)	Judge Ruler	Redeemer Healer
Approach to Bible, Religious Experience	Social	Solitary	Practical Literal	Symbolic Metaphorical	Analytical Abstract	Personal Immediate	Systematic	Of-the-Moment
Avoids (Hell)	Exclusion Loneliness	Intrusions Confusion	Ambiguity	Restriction Repetition	Inconsistency Ignorance	Conflict Estrangement	Helplessness Disorder	Regimentation Deadlines
Seeks (Heaven)	Participation Reunion	Incorporation Fulfillment	Physical harmony Faithfulness Obedience	Aesthetic harmony Mystical union	Conceptual harmony Enlightenment Justice, Truth	Personal harmony Communion Appreciation	Closure Productivity Work ethic	Openness Receptivity Play ethic
Prayer	Corporate	Private	Sensuous (eyes, ears, nose, hands, mouth)	Intuitive	Cognitive	Affective	Planned	Unplanned
Natural Spiritual Path	Action	Refection	Service	Awareness	Knowledge	Devotion	Discipline	Spontaneity
Needed for Wholeness	Reflection	Action or Participation	Awareness or Understanding	Service or Embodiment	Devotion	Knowledge	Spontaneity	Discipline

By Earle C. Page. Copyright © 1982 Center for Applications of Psychological Type, Gainesville, Florida. Used by permission.

TABLE A.3

473

Following Your Spiritual Path

Note: Our aim is a balanced, centered spirituality. These words are meant to facilitate understanding, not to stifle individuality.

SPIRITUAL PATH	ACTION E	REFLECTION I	SERVICE S	AWARENESS N	KNOWLEDGE T	DEVOTION F	DISCIPLINE J	SPONTANEITY P
Some Positive Expressions	Assertiveness Building community	Independence Deepening community	Love Pleasure	Ecstasy Anticipation	Equanimity Objectivity	Compassion Rapport, Trust	Discrimination Competence	Acceptance Serenity
Some Negative Expressions	Anger Attack	Fear Withdrawal	Attachment	Elation Depression	Apathy Criticalness	Sentimentality Overprotectiveness	Inappropriate control Judging others	Failure to take responsibility
Underdevelopment May Lead to	Isolation Lack of circumspection	Emptiness Dependence	Abstraction Overlooking	Flatness	Confusion	Coldness Distrust	Loss of purpose Indecision	Premature closure Baseless conclusions
Overdevelopment May Lead to	Impatience Shallowness	Withholding Idiosyncrasy Inappropriate intensity	Idolatry Frivolity Inappropriate conformity	Illusion Impracticality Stubbornness Fickleness	Reductionism Cynicism Dogmatism Rumination	Credulity Personalizing Blaming	Rigidity Perfectionism	Passivity Impulsiveness Procrastination
Special Temptations and Vulnerabilities	Distraction Suggestibility	Inaction Inclusion by others	Superstition Suspicion Fear of change	Primitive sensuality Psychogenic illness	Emotional explosion, exploitation, indulgence Contaminated thinking	Idealizing authority Pseudo-objectivity Hurt feelings	Self-righteousness Scrupulosity	Rebelliousness Carelessness
Needed for Wholeness	Reflection	Action or Participation	Awareness	Service or Embodiment	Devotion	Knowledge	Spontaneity	Discipline

By Earle C. Page. Copyright © 1982 Center for Applications of Psychological Type, Gainsville, Fl. Used by permission.

TABLE A.4

THE INTROVERTED PERSONALITY	Prayer within ourselves—complex, nonconforming, personal
THE EXTRAVERTED PERSONALITY	Open prayer—outward orientation, communal
THE INTUITIVE PERSONALITY	Prayer of hope—possibilities, spiritual communion, reflection
THE SENSING PERSONALITY	Practical prayer—contact with environment, present orientation
THE FEELING PERSONALITY	Feeling prayer—emotional dynamics, personal integration
THE THINKING PERSONALITY	Prayer of reason—rationally ordered and logical approach, truth orientation
THE JUDGING PERSONALITY	Orderly prayer—little ambiguity, structural orientation
THE PERCEIVING PERSONALITY	Lived prayer—accepts ambiguity, several approaches, enthusiastic

TABLE A.5

ISTJ INTROVERTED SENSING WITH THINKING	ISFJ INTROVERTED SENSING WITH FEELING
• Serious, quiet, thorough, orderly, logical, private • Sense of responsibility • Private spirituality • Enjoys scheduled and consistent prayer • Conscience orientation; will of God	• Dependable, conservative, strong sense of duty, often taken for granted • Desires to please God • Attracted to orderly spiritual regimen • Silent, private prayer • Community orientation; present expression of spirituality
ISTP INTROVERTED THINKING WITH SENSING	**ISFP** INTROVERTED FEELING WITH SENSING
• Practical, precise, reserved, objective • Action over prayer; practice of the presence of God • Individual approach to prayer and spiritual growth • Needs time for private meditation • Thinking and concentration, but needs practical application	• Free spirit, impulsive, intense feelings, artistic, appreciation for life • Open to social dimensions of personal spirituality • Flexible prayer forms; needs the discipline of private reflection • Present-tense, experiential orientation

ESTP	ESFP
EXTRAVERTED SENSING WITH THINKING	**EXTRAVERTED SENSING WITH FEELING**
• Action-oriented; pragmatic, realistic; unpredictable and flexible • Experiences of community, praise, singing • Requires minimal spiritual structure • Spontaneous prayers • Communal theological orientation	• Charismatic, attractive personalities • Lives primarily for the moment • People-oriented spirituality • Attracted to religious externals • Generous servants, accepting of others • Community orientation
ESTJ	**ESFJ**
EXTRAVERTED THINKING WITH SENSING	**EXTRAVERTED FEELING WITH SENSING**
• Responsible, orderly, administrative skills, realistic, conservative • Organized approach to spiritual growth, consistent • Institutional spirituality • Practical theological orientation	• Highly sociable, friendly, sympathetic, sentimental, caring • Attracted to prayer groups • Intercessory prayers • Practical application of spirituality • Attracted to experiential mysticism
INFJ	**INTJ**
INTROVERTED INTUITION WITH FEELING	**INTROVERTED INTUITION WITH THINKING**
• Gentle, compassionate, accepting, inspirational; can be stubborn • Not attracted to formal or repetitive prayer • Need for silence; contemplative and conversational prayer • Spiritually reflective on daily events • Mystical orientation	• Self-confident, decisive, pragmatic, single-minded, independent • High achiever; controlling, determined; logically oriented • Attracted to new insights, ideas, inspirations, improvements • Introspective prayer life • Needs time for spiritual reflection
INFP	**INTP**
INTROVERTED FEELING WITH INTUITION	**INTROVERTED THINKING WITH INTUITION**
• Idealistic, subjective interpretation; noble service for the benefit of others • Solitary and silent prayer • Personal, spontaneous response to God • Spiritual reflection on daily activities • Desires human support of spiritual development	• Good memory, intelligent, power of concentration, problem solver • Prefers to pray alone; logical, coherent prayer form • Needs space for concentration and evaluation of spiritual insights • Attracted to theological concepts; appraiser of new spiritual insights

ENFP	ENTP
EXTRAVERTED INTUITION WITH FEELING	EXTRAVERTED INTUITION WITH THINKING
• Optimistic, enthusiastic, imaginative, highly intuitive, skilled with people • Needs significant time for prayerful reflection • Spontaneous, unstructured prayer • Not institutionally motivated • People-oriented spirituality; able to deal with different people and events	• Ingenious, open to new possibilities, resourceful, enthusiastic, innovative • Enjoys novelty, originality, and new forms of prayer • Spontaneous, improvised prayers • Not inclined to a spiritual regimen • Attracted to spiritual conversations with others
ENFJ	**ENTJ**
EXTRAVERTED FEELING WITH INTUITION	EXTRAVERTED THINKING WITH INTUITION
• Motivates people, persuasive, natural leader • Comfortable with many types of prayer; needs time for reflection • Dislikes repetition and routine • People-centered spiritual orientation	• Effective leader, seeks power and competency, outgoing organizer • Theological spirituality • Need experiences of community • Attracted to structured, logical, consistent prayer forms

TABLE A.6

Books like *Type Talk* (Otto Kroeger and Janet M. Thuesen), *Please Understand Me* (David Kiersey and Marilyn Bates), and *Life Types* (Sandra Hirsh and Jean Kummerow) are profitable resources for discerning and understanding your personality type. With this information, you can see why you may be attracted to a particular approach to the spiritual life, while a spouse or a friend may be uninterested in this approach but drawn to another. The first two of these books take the sixteen types and divide them into four basic temperaments (table A.7).

THE SJ TEMPERAMENT	THE SP TEMPERAMENT
ESTJ, ISTJ, ESFJ, ISFJ	ESFP, ISFP, ESTP, ISTP
THE NF TEMPERAMENT	**THE NT TEMPERAMENT**
ENFJ, INFJ, ENFP, INFP	ENTJ, INTJ, ENTP, INTP

TABLE A.7

THE SJ TEMPERAMENT	THE SP TEMPERAMENT
• James	• Peter
• Duty	• Action
• Gospel of Matthew	• Gospel of Mark
• Ignatian spirituality	• Franciscan spirituality
• God as one	• God as love
• Prayer style: structured; use of sensible imagination	• Prayer style: informal, spontaneous, brief, practical
• About 38 percent of the U.S. population	• About 38 percent of the U.S. population
• *Epimethean* (practical, conservative, obligation, work ethic, history)	• *Dionysian* (free spirit, impulsive, initiative, active, *carpe diem*)
• Traditional (past orientation)	• Adventurous (present orientation)
• Economic/commerce	• Aesthetic/artistry
• D (dominance)	• I (influencing)
• Motivated by results	• Motivated by recognition
• Under pressure: autocratic	• Under pressure: antagonistic
• Task-initiator	• Relational-initiator
• Choleric	• Sanguine
THE NF TEMPERAMENT	THE NT TEMPERAMENT
• John	• Paul
• Vision	• Ideas
• Gospel of John	• Gospel of Luke
• Augustinian spirituality	• Thomistic spirituality
• God as good	• God as true
• Prayer style: meditative; use of creative imagination	• Prayer style: discursive reflection, directed change
• About 12 percent of the U.S. population	• About 12 percent of the U.S. population
• *Apollonian* (personal authentication, verbal creativity, literary skill)	• *Promethean* (intelligence, power, competence, understanding)
• Idealistic (future orientation)	• Inventive (possibility orientation)
• Religiosity/ethics	• Theoretical/science
• S (steadiness)	• C (compliance)
• Motivated by relationships	• Motivated by being right
• Under pressure: agreeable	• Under pressure: avoidance
• Relational-responder	• Task-responder
• Phlegmatic	• Melancholic

TABLE A.8

These four temperaments are broader generalizations than the sixteen types, but they are valuable tools for distinguishing fundamental styles of spirituality, as Chester P. Michael and Marie C. Norrisey demonstrate in *Prayer and Temperament*. Michael and Norrisey associate four key spiritual leaders in the history of the church with these four temperaments: Ignatius of Loyola (SJ), Francis of Assisi (SP), Thomas Aquinas (NT), and Augustine of Hippo (NF). (The brief history of Christian spirituality in appendix B contextualizes these and other figures.) In table A.8 I have attempted to illuminate the characteristics of the four temperaments and relate them to the spiritual dimension.

Although there seems to be a broad correspondence between these four temperaments and the Performax Personal Profile System (DISC), I must stress that because each individual is unique, there are many exceptions. For instance, a person with an NT temperament can be a high D (dominance) instead of a high C (compliance). It is also important to remember that no person is all one temperament, since each of us displays unique combinations and degrees of these personality qualities. But ideally the personal and spiritual maturation process should move us in the direction of becoming a blended synthesis of all four temperaments, so that we can adapt to people and situations in increasingly flexible and appropriate ways.

As before, using the twelve facets of spirituality in this book, we can draw a *very general* correlation between the twelve facets and these four temperaments (table A.9).

THE SJ TEMPERAMENT	THE SP TEMPERAMENT
• Disciplined spirituality • Motivated spirituality • Holistic spirituality	• Corporate spirituality • Spirit-filled spirituality • Warfare Spirituality
THE NF TEMPERAMENT	**THE NT TEMPERAMENT**
• Relational spirituality • Devotional spirituality • Exchanged life spirituality	• Paradigm spirituality • Process spirituality • Nurturing spirituality

TABLE A.9

It is important to appreciate and affirm your temperamental predisposition regarding spirituality and prayer so that you avoid the discouragement of thinking you must be unspiritual if you don't follow a prescription that works well for someone else. For instance, it can be liberating for SPs to realize that as spontaneous and informal people, they will not be naturally attracted to the more structured SJ approaches to prayer and spiritual growth. Similarly, as conceptually oriented people, NTs are less inclined to corporate spirituality and Spirit-filled spirituality than are SPs.

At the same time, it is wise and spiritually healthy to identify your opposite preference, type, and temperament and to engage in the discipline of stretching yourself by trying an approach you would normally not pursue. Deliberate participation in a style or facet of spirituality that you are ordinarily inclined to avoid can be a significant source of spiritual growth and greater balance. Using the four preference pairs, for example, it is easy to see that if we are left to ourselves, we would gravitate away from the "shadow" side of our preference pattern. Thus extraverts would tend to avoid contemplation and solitude, while introverts would tend to avoid social engagement in the spiritual community. Intuitives would tend to avoid the balance and realism of sensory input, while sensors would tend to avoid the value of contemplative and reflective aspects of spirituality. Thinkers would tend to avoid the affective and emotional side of the spiritual life, while feelers would tend to avoid the conceptual and rational aspects of the faith. Judgers would tend to avoid a spontaneous openness to the work of the Spirit, while perceivers would tend to avoid the benefits of the planned and structured side of spirituality.

As an exercise, consider where you think you best fit in regard to the four preference pairs, the sixteen types, and the four temperaments. Then select an approach to spirituality or prayer that would draw you to a greater depth and balance by forcing you to stretch yourself in new and unfamiliar territory. The more you accept the need for this dynamic tension between affirming your natural dispositions and engaging in less preferred ways of being and doing, the more full-orbed and Christlike you will become in your spiritual journey. The Lord Jesus enjoyed the richness of a mystical union with his heavenly Father but coupled this profound personal experience with social passion and engagement.

In *Rediscovering Holiness*, J. I. Packer addresses the problem of "rhapsody without realism" and "rule-keeping without relating," and argues that all of us, regardless of temperament and natural aptitude, need a healthy balance of doctrine, experience, and practice. We should ask God for the grace to give us the desire and power to choose this biblical combination of knowing, being, and doing.

Appendix B

THE RICHNESS
OF OUR HERITAGE

CHAPTER OVERVIEW

This appendix outlines a brief history of spirituality by tracing prominent approaches to the spiritual life through the ancient, medieval, and modern churches. This provides a broader perspective and a sense of continuity with others who have pursued intimacy with God before us. Twelve recurring issues and extremes emerge from this overview, and this appendix concludes with a word about the variety of approaches that can illuminate our own journey.

A BROADER PERSPECTIVE

Most Protestants approach church history and spiritual formation as though nothing of significance occurred between the closing of the New Testament canon in the first century and the Protestant Reformation in the sixteenth century. And even then, there are typically only a few brief pauses along the way to acknowledge Luther, Calvin, Wesley, Edwards, Whitefield, Spurgeon, and Moody before racing into our own time. Moreover, only a small percentage of contemporary Christians are serious readers (I'm happy you are one of them), and of these, only a meager fraction (I hope you are one of them) expose themselves to the great spiritual writers of previous centuries. As a result, most believers are impoverished by a parochial perspective and are unable to glean from the rich legacy that has been left to us by the followers of the Way since the church's birth.

This appendix attempts to summarize some of the key people and movements that have contributed to our spiritual heritage so that you will have a broader perspective and a sense of continuity with others who have pursued intimacy with God in previous centuries. This appendix will highlight the impressive variety of approaches to Christian discipleship over time and geography and will touch on the strengths and weaknesses of some of these styles of spirituality. This process can stretch our awareness, challenge some of our assumptions, and encourage us to explore other facets of the spiritual life.

As heirs of the extraordinary array of Christian spirituality produced by twenty centuries of development, we have a greater wealth of resources at our disposal than did any previous generation. In view of this, it is ironic that there seems to be an unprecedented shallowness and attachment to the current cultural agenda in many of our churches. The emphasis on management models, techniques from pop psychology, and programmatic relevance has led to more interest in buildings, budgets, and body counts than in relational discipleship and spiritual formation. But there are hopeful signs of disenchantment with the status quo as increasing numbers of believers are looking for greater depth and rootedness in true spirituality.

It was only in the last two centuries that Roman Catholic theologians distinguished mystical theology or spirituality from doctrine as a specialized field. As we will see, however, there is an integral relationship between theology and application; unbiblical and unbalanced doctrines lead to practical distortions. Still, there is prodigious room within the boundaries of theological orthodoxy for a surprising variety of spiritual expressions.

ANCIENT, MEDIEVAL, AND MODERN SPIRITUALITY: A PREVIEW

Church historians have long noted that the combination of the ancient, medieval, and modern periods in the history of the church is shaped like an hourglass. The ancient church (Pentecost to c. 600) was characterized by rapid expansion to the continents of Asia, Africa, and Europe. The medieval church (c. 600 to c.1500) was marked by withdrawal as internal divisions and the rise of Islam greatly diminished the Christian influence in Asia and Africa. The modern church (c.1500 to the present) saw a new expansion beyond the boundaries of Europe, and in the past few decades, the churches of the third world have shown the greatest vitality, expansion, and missionary fervor.

The ancient church, after it became the official religion of the Roman Empire, was rapidly transformed from a network of periodically persecuted believers into a politically and financially powerful institution. Local churches were organized under regional bishops, and these bishops convened churchwide councils to debate and clarify doctrinal and practical matters. While some of the church fathers dealt with various heresies such as Montanism, Gnosticism, and Neo-Platonism, others developed increasingly ascetic lifestyles and left the local churches to pursue desert spirituality. These desert hermits and monks developed a mystical approach to spiritual formation that was combined with ascetic practices in the growing monastic communities. The three spiritual stages of purgation, illumination, and union were developed and practiced among members of the monastic orders.

Christianity became a predominantly European phenomenon in the Middle Ages, and the Western and Eastern branches of the church formally separated during this period. The spirituality of the Eastern church became increasingly apophatic and hesychastic (the practice of stillness and mystical prayer). Monasticism flourished in the medieval Western church, and the Benedictine, Carthusian, and Cistercian orders continued to develop a contemplative approach to spirituality. New mendicant orders like the Dominicans and Franciscans were formed, and the rise of scholasticism was paralleled by a rise in a spirituality of service and sacrifice. Mysticism reached its zenith on the European Continent and in England in the latter part of the Middle Ages, and the remarkable writings of these Continental and English mystics explored the inner terrain of the soul's journey toward God.

The section on "Spirituality in the Modern Church" in this appendix begins with the impact of the four branches of the Protestant Reformation and touches on Lutheran, Reformed, Anabaptist, and Anglican spirituality. In the Catholic Church, significant spiritual figures arose in sixteenth-century Spain and in seventeenth- and eighteenth-century France. An outline of the varied spiritualities of a number of post-Reformation Protestant movements (Puritans, Quakers, Pietists, Evangelicals, revivalism, Methodists, holiness groups, and Pentecostals) is followed by several recent spiritual figures. This section concludes with a number of recent developments (Vatican II, the ecumenical movement, the charismatic movement, twelve-step spirituality, psychological approaches, and creation-centered spirituality) and a word on modern Orthodoxy and spiritual developments in Latin America, Africa, and Asia.

As we consider the history of Christian spirituality during the ancient, medieval, and modern periods, I must stress that this is only a highly selective thumbnail sketch in outline form. Many books (such as *The Study of Spirituality*, edited by Cheslyn Jones, Geoffrey Wainwright, and Edward Yarnold, SJ; *Handbook of Christian Spirituality* by Michael Cox; the three-volume *A History of Christian Spirituality* by Louis Bouyer, Jean Leclercq, and François Vandenbroucke; *A History of Christian Spirituality* by Urban T. Holmes; and *Thirsty for God* by Bradley P. Holt) explore this rich subject in far more detail.

SPIRITUALITY IN THE ANCIENT CHURCH

The Biblical Foundation

The entire Bible points to Jesus Christ as the decisive revelation of God in human history. His redemptive work is the basis for overcoming the Fall with its four alienations among people and God, themselves, others, and the created order. A full-orbed biblical spirituality addresses the substantial healing available in Christ in these four areas and anticipates the complete harmony that will come with the new heaven and earth. Jesus' Upper Room Discourse (John 13–17) outlines the essential components of the spiritual life, and the Epistles (e.g., Romans 6–8) further develop the meaning of "you in Me, and I in you" (John 14:20).

The Early and Later Patristics (Church Fathers)

The church quickly changed from a messianic sect within Judaism to a predominantly Gentile movement that experienced frequent persecution until 313, when Constantine declared Christianity to be a legitimate religion in the Roman Empire. As the church fathers debated and clarified the doctrines of the Trinity and the person and work of Christ, the church as a whole was being consolidated into an institution with growing political and financial power.

Early Christian Worship

The earliest churches adapted the elements of prayer, singing of psalms, reading of Scripture, teaching, and preaching that were used in synagogue worship. There was an emphasis on the use of the charisms, or spiritual gifts, in the earliest assemblies, but this declined by the second century.

The Didache

The *Didache*, or *Teaching of the Twelve Apostles*, reveals the rapid development of structure and hierarchical organization in the second-century church.

The Montanists

The followers of Montanus, an influential second-century leader in Asia Minor, stressed the imminence of Christ's *parousia*, or return, and were criticized for charismatic excesses and doctrinal aberrations.

The Martyrs

Because of the persecution of the church in the second and third centuries, the theme of martyrdom was developed as an expression of ultimate commitment to Christ. Ignatius, bishop of Antioch (c. 35–c.107), addressed epistles to several churches on his way to martyrdom in the Colosseum during the reign of the emperor Trajan. Many women were also martyred, among them Perpetua, who died for her faith in Carthage around 200.

Gnosticism

The church was plagued by Gnostic heretics who attributed the creation of the material world to an inferior deity (the Demiurge) and denied that Absolute Spirit could ever be incarnated. This led to the twin extremes of asceticism and antinomianism and an emphasis on attaining salvation through hidden knowledge *(gnosis)*. The second-century patristics Justin Martyr, Irenaeus, and Tertullian refuted the heresy of Gnosticism in their writings.

Asceticism

The spiritual practice of asceticism took two forms in the early church. The unhealthy form denied the goodness of creation and replaced the grace of God with human effort. The healthier form avoided these problems and engaged in self-discipline rather than self-punishment. Tertullian (c.160–c.225), a Latin church father who was gifted in doctrinal theology, was excessively rigorous in his ascetic practice of separation from the world.

Hellenistic Influences

Origen of Alexandria (c.185–284) was steeped in Greek philosophy and profoundly affected the church for centuries to come with his allegorical interpretation of Scripture. He and others after him were influenced by the developing Neo-Platonism of the time (his contemporary Plotinus, the key Neo-Platonist philosopher, taught that the ruling goal of life is union with the Absolute, or One). Origen adapted this philosophy into three spiritual levels of development in the soul's journey to God. The moral level corresponds to Proverbs and relates to behavior; the natural level corresponds to Ecclesiastes and relates to intellectual development; and the contemplative level corresponds to the Song of Songs and relates to spiritual union with God (Origen's allegorical interpretation of the Song of Songs would be used by spiritual writers for centuries to come).

Mysticism

By the fourth century, mysticism became a dominant theme in Christian spirituality. Like the term *asceticism*, the word *mysticism* can refer to both healthy and unbiblical spiritual practices. In its more biblical sense, mysticism refers to a personal apprehension of the transcendent and ultimate Being. This experience of the presence of God transforms and gives meaning to the created order. By contrast, unbiblical forms of mysticism include oneness mysticism, in which the mystic seeks complete absorption and loss of identity in God, and nature mysticism, in which the mystic seeks oneness with all things. The word *union* can relate to either the theistic or pantheistic forms of mysticism, while the word *communion* refers to a loving I/Thou relationship between two persons and affirms the Creator-creation distinction. Discernment is required, since some Christian mystics mean communion when they write of union, while others do not.

Desert Spirituality

Beginning in the third century, a number of men and women entered the deserts of Egypt to live solitary and ascetic lives in the quest for greater intimacy with God. Antony (c. 251–356), described in Athanasius's *Life of Antony*, was the most famous of these early desert hermits, and some of these monks and nuns practiced extreme and bizarre ascetic methods. Anchorites (hermits) also lived in the Syrian desert, and among these were pillar hermits like Simeon the Elder and Daniel Stylites, who lived for decades on small platforms on top of pillars. Ephrem (c. 306–373), another ascetic whose symbolic poetic writings were copied by Syrian monks, influenced Eastern Christianity with his view of the spiritual life as a progression toward *theosis*, or divinization. This concept, based on the imagery of becoming "partakers of the divine nature" (2 Peter 1:4), became a fundamental theme in the spirituality of the Eastern church.

Monastic Spirituality

Pachomius (c. 290–346) organized a number of desert monasteries and convents, and many of the desert fathers and mothers were associated with these monastic communities, while others lived as solitaries. John Cassian (c. 360–435), a pupil of John Chrysostom, went to Egypt to study desert monasticism, and there he was exposed to the teachings of Evagrius of Pontus (c. 345–399). Evagrius was a Christian Platonist who taught that there are three stages in life (the practical, the natural, and the theological). In his *Institutes* and *Conferences*, John Cassian brought the teachings of Evagrius and other desert monastics to the West, where they had an impact on Benedictine monasticism.

Benedict (c. 480–547), founder of the Benedictine order, developed a system of monastic governance through a *Rule* that provided for *ora et labora*, a combination of prayer and physical labor. The Benedictine *Rule* influenced the entire Western monastic system, as did Benedict's prescription of daily *lectio divina*, or sacred reading (*lectio divina* is discussed in the section on devotional spirituality).

In the East, Evagrius knew the Cappadocian fathers Basil of Caesarea (c. 330–379), Basil's brother, Gregory of Nyssa (c. 330–c. 395), and their friend Gregory of Nazianzus (330–389). Basil of Caesarea wrote two monastic rules that stressed obedience as opposed to self-will, thanksgiving for all things, and the spiritual process of restoring the divine image. Gregory of Nyssa developed a mystical doctrine of ascent that involves a progressive movement into the darkness of growing realization of the incomprehensibility of God.

Augustine

Augustine of Hippo (354–430), the greatest of the Latin fathers, sought to reconcile a personal relationship with God with a strong respect for the authority of the church. As a thinker, he blended a keen intelligence with a powerful intuition; as a practitioner, he combined a contemplative way of living with a life that was active in the world. His *Confessions* broke new ground with an autobiographical narrative of his developing spiritual life. Augustine's inward journey was driven by an intense longing for God ("You have made us for yourself, and our heart is restless, until it rests in you") that was increasingly satisfied in his trinitarian reflections and occasional mystical experiences.

Pseudo-Dionysius

A mystical theologian, probably a Syrian monk who flourished about 500, penned four books in Greek under the pseudonym Dionysius the Areopagite (Acts 17:34). The writings of Pseudo-Dionysius, as he has come to be known, are *The Divine Names*, *The Mystical Theology*, *The Celestial Hierarchy*, *The Ecclesiastical Hierarchy*, and a collection of letters. These writings were influenced by Neo-Platonism and in turn exerted a powerful influence on Eastern and Western Christian spirituality, particularly in their description of the three spiritual stages. In the *purgative* stage, the soul is cleansed; in the *illuminative* stage, the soul receives the light of God; and in the *unitive* stage, the soul experiences oneness with God. Pseudo-Dionysius was also influential in the development of apophatic theology. He followed the *via negativa*, or the negative way of stripping away intellectual images and attributions of God, and argued that the kataphatic approach was of utility only for spiritual beginners.

Celtic Spirituality

After Patrick (c. 389–c. 461) evangelized among the Celtic people, he established monasteries for men and women throughout Ireland. The abbots and abbesses (such as Brigid) of these monasteries provided spiritual oversight, and exposure to the writings of the desert fathers prompted strict ascetic practices. The white martyrdom of asceticism often included daily reciting of all 150 psalms; the blue martyrdom spoke of exceptional penance for sin (e.g., lengthy praying in icy water); and the red martyrdom referred to the shedding of blood. The Celtic practice of private confession with specific penances later spread to the rest of the Western church, and the Celtic concept of the *anamchara*, or soul friend, influenced the Catholic practice of spiritual direction. The Celtic tradition is marked by beautiful prayers, such as St. Patrick's Breastplate.

SPIRITUALITY IN THE MEDIEVAL CHURCH

General Trends

The period from about 600 to about 1500 was characterized by the spread and consolidation of the church throughout northern and eastern Europe, and during these centuries the Anglo-Saxon, German, Scandinavian, Ukrainian, and Russian cultures were Christianized. The same period, however, also saw a declining Christian influence in Africa and Asia. In addition, the Latin West, centered in Rome, and the Greek East, centered in Constantinople, became increasingly alienated, and they formally separated in 1054. In the West, the Dark Ages were followed by a period of high scholasticism in the Roman Catholic Church, and theological systemization was generally separated from mysticism. By contrast, the Eastern Orthodox Church never made such a distinction between theology and mysticism; in Orthodoxy, church dogma and personal experience of the divine mysteries were inextricably bound.

The Eastern Church

The trinitarian emphasis of the seven ecumenical councils from 325 to 787, the traditions of the Greek theologians, and the geographical and cultural distance between the Western and Eastern churches led to distinctive beliefs and practices in the Orthodox Church. Orthodox spirituality is largely characterized by apophatic theology, and this is evident in the writings of mystical theologians like John Climacus (c. 570–c. 649), Simeon the New Theologian (949–1022), and Gregory Palamas (1296–1359). In *The Ladder of Divine Ascent*, John Climacus, abbot of the monastery on Mount Sinai before becoming an anchorite (a solitary), described the stages of the mystical ascent of the soul to God. Simeon and Gregory were proponents of hesychasm, which refers to the practice of stillness, silence, and mystical prayer. Gregory distinguished the energies of God that can be known by humans and the essence of God that cannot be known. The vision of God, though imperfect in this life, is possible through a synergy between divine grace and human will.

All of these theologians stressed the grace-given discipline of unceasing prayer, or the prayer of the heart. The most common form of this continual Jesus Prayer is "Lord Jesus Christ, have mercy on me," but there are several variations. The Jesus Prayer is also known as a breath prayer, since it is associated with breathing; it is designed to lead beyond thoughts to a state of *hesuchia,* or stillness, as it unites the mind and the heart. Another attribute of Orthodox spirituality since the Byzantine period of the church is the use of distinctively styled paintings as objects of veneration. These icons function as windows on eternity and are supposed to be used as vehicles through which one venerates the person represented in the image.

Monasticism

In the Western Church during the Middle Ages, the whole monastic system was reformed and expanded. A stable communal life was made possible through the spiritual disciplines of self-denial and voluntary submission that related to the three vows of poverty, chastity, and obedience. The early scholastic thinker Anselm of Canterbury (c.1033–1109), best known for his contributions to systematic and philosophical theology, was also immersed in monastic life. Before he became the archbishop of Canterbury, Anselm served as the abbot of the monastery of Bec in Normandy, where he developed the poetry of intimate, personal devotion in his *Prayers and Meditations*.

The Carthusian Order was a strictly contemplative order of monks founded by Bruno (c. 1032–1101) in 1084. This stringent approach to monastic spirituality demanded perfect renunciation, mortification, silence, and solitude.

Bernard of Clairvaux (1090–1153) was a monastic reformer who administered a vast network of Cistercian monasteries throughout Western Europe. He has been called Doctor Mellifluus because of the sweetness of his teachings in contrast to the harshness and aridity of a number of medieval writers. His book on *The Love of God* distinguishes three stages of the spiritual life (animal, rational, and spiritual) and four degrees of love (loving self for one's own sake, loving God for one's own sake, loving God for God's sake, and loving self for God's sake). Like his contemporaries, he accepted the fourfold method of interpreting Scripture that was inherited from earlier writers like Origen and John Cassian: literally (in the historical context), allegorically (seeing Christ throughout Scripture), tropologically or morally (obedience to moral instruction), and anagogically (the contemplative level). Thus his *Sermons on the Song of Songs* uses the erotic language of the Song of Songs to develop the spiritual theme of the soul's spiritual intimacy with God.

Bernard's close friend William of Saint-Thierry (c.1085–1148) was the abbot of the Benedictine abbey of Saint-Thierry before he resigned that post to become a Cistercian monk. Like Bernard, William wrote on the Song of Songs and portrayed it as the contemplative union between the soul and Christ. In *The Golden Epistle*, William eloquently combines intellectual illumination with ardent spiritual love as he outlines the journey of grace through which one finds, possesses, and enjoys God.

Mendicant Orders

The thirteenth century saw the development of a new approach to monasticism that embodied greater involvement and service in the world. Mendicants, or friars who lived by begging alms, were organized in religious houses under the direction of priors. Dominic Guzman (c. 1170–1221) founded an Order of Preachers known as Dominicans that was devoted to theological study and preaching. Until the fifteenth century, this order practiced individual and corporate poverty, and the Dominican stress on education produced great scholars like Albertus Magnus (c. 1200–1280) and his pupil, Thomas Aquinas (1225–1274), known as Doctor Angelicus, who was the high-water mark of scholasticism. Works like the *Summa Theologica* and the *Summa Contra Gentiles* reveal Aquinas's genius for systematizing theological truths, but his writings were also infused with a living understanding of experiential spiritual knowledge. When he was urged near the end of his life to complete his *Summa*, he replied that everything he had written seemed like straw in comparison with what was revealed to him in his contemplation of God.

The Franciscan Order, another order of mendicants, was founded by Francis of Assisi (c. 1182–1226). Francis' joy, simplicity, love of nature, generosity, faith, and passion for Christ was infectious, and his associates (known as Friars Minor, or little brothers) went on ever-widening missions in service of others. *The Little Flowers of St. Francis*, a collection of legends and traditions about Francis, gives a beautiful portrait of the vitality and spirit of the early Franciscans. Clare of Assisi (1194–1253) founded a second order for women known as the Poor Clares, and a third order known as the Tertiaries, or Brethren of Penitence, was founded for laypeople who sought a dedicated spirituality in the routines of ordinary life. Bonaventure (1221–1274), known as Doctor Seraphicus, was the greatest of the Franciscan theologians. Bonaventure stressed that in comparison with the mystical illumination that God graciously grants to those who pursue him, the most illustrious human wisdom is folly.

Other mendicant orders include the Carmelites (reorganized in the thirteenth century), the Augustinian hermits or friars, and the Capuchins (a later offshoot of the Franciscan Order that stressed poverty, austerity, and preaching).

Continental Mysticism

Highly mystical writings flourished both on the European continent and in England in the twelfth through the fifteenth centuries. These works must be read with careful discernment, since they are alloys that consist of varying proportions of gold and gravel. The gold is made up of authentic spiritual insights and powerful imagery, while the gravel may be composed of unbiblical teaching, psychological hysteria, or various degrees of pantheism.

Hugh of St. Victor (c. 1096–1141) was a mystical theologian who lived at the Augustinian monastery of St. Victor near Paris. Hugh's work was strongly influenced by the Platonic tradition, and he wrote a commentary on *The Celestial Hierarchy* of Pseudo-Dionysius. Another Victorine, Richard of St. Victor (d. 1173), was the first medieval mystic to systematically examine the psychology of mystical experience. He distinguishes the three ascending mental activities of thinking, meditation, and contemplation, and his works on the *Preparation of the Soul* and on *Contemplation* progress from the contemplation of visible things to the contemplation of invisible things, and from there to the final transforming union.

Hildegard of Bingen (1098–1179) was the founder and first abbess of the Benedictine community at Bingen on the Rhine. This remarkable woman composed liturgical music, books on natural science and medicine, the first known morality play (*Play of Virtues*), and visionary literature. In her most important work, *Scivias*, she dictated an extensive account of twenty-six visions she received as a *summa* of Christian doctrine on such matters as the nature of the universe, the kingdom of God, the fall of humanity, sanctification, and the end of the world.

Amalric of Bena (d. c. 1207) was a pantheistic mystic who was a master at the University of Paris. He taught that when the soul rises to God by means of love, it loses its distinctiveness from God and becomes God himself. Although his teaching was declared heretical, it influenced pseudo-mystical groups like the Brethren of the Free Spirit.

Mechthild of Magdeburg (c. 1210–c. 1280), like Hildegard of Bingen, was a German mystic and spiritual writer who experienced vivid pictorial visions. In *The Flowing Light of the Godhead*, Mechthild sometimes used the language of ecstasy and elevated eroticism to describe the divine presence. Her vision of the Sacred Heart contributed to later Roman Catholic devotion.

The German Dominican mystic Meister Eckhart (c. 1260–c. 1327) made significant but flawed contributions to mystical theology in his commentaries on Genesis and John, in his sermons, and in his treatises (e.g., *The Book of Divine Consolation*). Eckhart described himself as "God-intoxicated" and distinguished the God of religious experience, who is revealed in the form of a person, from the Godhead, which is an undifferentiated and unrevealable eternal Unity that transcends all human understanding. Because of his pantheistic tendencies, a number of his statements were condemned as heretical.

The teachings of Hildegard, Mechthild, and Eckhart strongly influenced a fourteenth-century spiritual and mystical movement that came to be known as *Gottesfreunde*, the Friends of God. Those in this company contrasted the externality of the ecclesiastical institutions with the inward and personal transformation made possible by spiritual union with God. The anonymous *Theologica Germanica* crystallized the spirituality of the Friends of God movement, and this significant volume later influenced Martin Luther. The *Theologica* taught that the differentiated temporal world must be transcended before the soul can know the undifferentiated divine Reality.

Johann Tauler (c. 1300–1361), a German Dominican, was an inspirational preacher and teacher in the Friends of God movement. Tauler was strongly influenced by the mystical theology of Meister Eckhart and taught three stages of self-dying: mortification in hope of heaven, spiritual and physical deprivations with no thought of self, and complete harmonization with God's will. His contemporary Henry Suso (Heinrich Seuse; c. 1295–1366) was another Dominican associate of the Friends of God. His autobiographical *Life of the Blessed Henry Suso* describes his ecstatic visions, and his *Book of Eternal Wisdom* bears the pantheistic overtones of his mentor, Meister Eckhart.

Suso's highly unstable spirituality was marked by ferocious mortification and self-inflicted torments.

The Flemish mystic Jan van Ruysbroeck (John Ruusbroec; 1293–1381), a close friend of Tauler and Suso, was influenced by the writings of Augustine, Pseudo-Dionysius, Bernard of Clairvaux, and Meister Eckhart. His treatises (*The Spiritual Espousals*, *The Sparkling Stone*, *A Mirror of Eternal Blessedness*, and *The Little Book of Clarification*) made a profound impression on his time by combining both the intellectual and the affective strands of mysticism. Ruysbroeck insisted that the traditional purgative, illuminative, and unitive stages are cumulative rather than sequential. In *The Sparkling Stone*, he developed a progression from an active life (a good person who serves others), to an interior life (a spiritual person who yearns for God and purges creaturely images from the imagination), and finally to a contemplative life (a contemplative person who experiences loving union with God but can remain active in the world). The third stage is attained by only a few, and then only momentarily.

Gerard Groote (1340–1384), a disciple of Ruysbroeck, was the founder of the Brethren of the Common Life, a lay association that had some connections with the Friends of God movement. The members lived in community and called this movement *Devotio Moderna*, the Modern Devotion. Groote's preaching against the decadence of the church was empowered by his deep personal experience of the Holy Spirit.

Thomas à Kempis (c. 1380–1471), who wrote a biography of Gerard Groote, was the probable author of the enduring spiritual classic *The Imitation of Christ*. The spirituality of the Brethren of the Common Life was based on the life of Christ as the true center of the soul, but it overreacted to the abuses of scholasticism and devalued the intellectual life. This is reflected in *The Imitation of Christ*, which also tends to negate the things of the created order.

Like Thomas à Kempis, who was born the year she died, Catherine of Siena (c. 1347–1380) reacted to the corruption and degeneracy of the medieval church. Although she experienced visions, ecstasies, and demonic struggles, Catherine differed from many mystics by cultivating an altruistic spirituality that addressed social concerns. She practiced strict austerities, but her love for Christ compelled her to serve the sick and the poor.

Nicholas of Cusa (c. 1400–1464), a German cardinal and philosopher, was a gifted thinker whose mystical theology of spirituality (*On Learned Ignorance*, *Dialogue on the Hidden God*, *On Seeking God*, *On the Vision of God*, *On the Summit of Contemplation*) pointed beyond the boundaries of human reason. He argued that the road to truth leads to the *coincidentia oppositorum*, the "coincidence of opposites" in the person of God (e.g., God is infinitely great and infinitely small, the center and the circumference, everywhere and nowhere).

Catherine of Genoa (1447–1510) combined rigorous personal discipline with active philanthropy; she established the first hospital in Genoa. After a decade of an unhappy marriage, she had a profound spiritual experience that transformed her life. Catherine's mysticism was focused more on the infinite God than on the person of Christ, and she felt submerged in the immensity of God's love.

English Mysticism

England in the later Middle Ages produced a number of prominent contemplatives who sought the grace of God to achieve unmediated knowledge of God through transcendent prayer. Richard Rolle (c. 1300–1349) studied at Oxford, later became a hermit, and wrote widely in English as well as Latin. His mystical life included periodic experiences of fiery warmth and the sweetness of heavenly music. His treatises (e.g., *Meditations on the Passion, Ego Dormio, The Form of Living*) center on a passionate devotion to Christ and encourage reading, prayer, and meditation.

The unknown author of the fourteenth-century devotional classic *The Cloud of Unknowing* was familiar with Rolle's writings and was also inspired by Pseudo-Dionysius, Thomistic theology, and Rhineland mystics like Johann Tauler. *The Cloud of Unknowing* develops an apophatic mysticism of darkness that stresses the incomprehensibility of God and instructs the advanced reader in the proper ordering of the contemplative life.

Walter Hilton (d. 1396) was influenced by Richard Rolle and *The Cloud of Unknowing*, and in his principal work, *The Scale of Perfection*, he distinguished two stages of reform in faith and reform in feeling. For him, the highest degree of contemplation was a combination of cognition and affection.

Julian of Norwich (c. 1342–c. 1416) lived as an anchoress (a solitary), and in May 1373 she received sixteen visions, or showings. These *Revelations of Divine Love* are described in a shorter, earlier text and in a longer, later text. Her visions of the passion of Christ and of the Holy Trinity led to a realization that divine love is the answer to all the mysteries of existence, including the problem of evil.

SPIRITUALITY IN THE MODERN CHURCH

The Protestant Reformation

A number of reformers, among them John Wycliffe (c. 1329–1384), the Lollards, John Huss (c. 1369–1415), and William Tyndale (c. 1494–1536), addressed the growing moral, doctrinal, and spiritual corruption of the church. But the actual Protestant withdrawal from Roman authority took place in four movements: the Lutheran and Reformed branches of Protestantism, the Anabaptists, and the Anglicans.

Lutheran Spirituality

After Martin Luther (1483–1546) realized that people are justified by grace alone through faith alone, he eliminated practices that sought to merit rather than receive the grace of God, such as prayers to the saints, indulgences, relics, pilgrimages, and vows of celibacy. He also introduced new elements to corporate spirituality, including the singing of hymns and the use of the vernacular Bible. Although he appreciated the mystical tradition in the *Theologica Germanica*, Luther was opposed to the apophatic mysticism inherited from Meister Eckhart and others. His was a more kataphatic spirituality of the Cross that was based on biblical revelation and personal reception of the grace of God made available through the redemptive work of Christ.

Johann Arndt (1555–1621) was more concerned with communicating Luther's Christian experience than in codifying his theology. His sermons and writings like *True Christianity* promoted spiritual renewal and provided the groundwork for later Lutheran Pietism. By contrast, Jakob Boehme (1575–1624) was an unorthodox Lutheran mystic whose terminology had more in common with alchemy and astrology than with the Scriptures.

Reformed Spirituality

The Swiss reformer Ulrich Zwingli (1484–1531) was more radical than Luther in his rejection of Catholic tradition. Zwingli's spirituality of the Word minimized the liturgical, aesthetic, mystical, and sacramental aspects of corporate worship and eliminated any practices that were not commanded in the New Testament (e.g., vestments, visual art, and musical instruments in church).

John Calvin (1509–1564) took a more moderate position than did Zwingli. After escaping from France to Switzerland, Calvin directed the new religious and political order of Geneva. In his *Institutes of the Christian Religion*, Calvin stressed that every person who has been called by the sovereign grace of God into a faith relationship with Christ possesses a mystical in-Christ union. Calvin understood this union to be a present possession resulting from the gift of sanctification that accompanies justification. This is very different from the usual medieval mystical approach to union with God as the product of a progressive series of spiritual or contemplative stages.

Anabaptist Spirituality

The Anabaptists, or rebaptizers, generally affirmed believers' baptism, and this led to the practice of rebaptizing those who had been baptized as infants. This was the most radical and unstable of the Reformation movements, and most Protestants as well as Catholics were vigorously opposed to these groups. Some held that direct inspiration from God superseded biblical doctrine, and this spiritual anarchy was paralleled by political anarchy. By contrast, Menno Simons (1496–1561), the founder of the

Mennonites, gathered fragments of these groups into a more stable and less emotionally driven movement that encouraged its members to avoid immorality and false teaching. In general, Anabaptist spirituality is characterized by dependence on the inspiration of the Holy Spirit in worship, close community, simplicity in lifestyle, uncompromising morality, separation from worldly culture, and pacifism.

Anglican Spirituality

Thomas Cranmer (1489–1556) was the chief architect of the 1549 *Book of Common Prayer*. His stylistic genius enabled him to synthesize a liturgy that continues, in revised form, to be used throughout the world. The collects, or common prayers, in this book (Cranmer wrote some, but he derived most of them from the medieval Sarum Missal and Breviary) are among the most beautiful prayers in the English language.

Anglican spirituality has been immeasurably enriched by the metaphysical poetry of John Donne (1571/2–1631), George Herbert (1593–1633), and Henry Vaughan (1622–1695). Donne's religious poems and sermons are marked by subtlety and striking imagery, and they are often centered in the passion of Christ, human sinfulness and mortality, and the quest for salvation. Herbert's spiritual poetry, especially his collection of poems entitled *The Temple*, is redolent of an intensely personal relationship with God.

Other notable Anglican writers include Jeremy Taylor (1613–1667), author of *The Rule and Exercise of Holy Living* and *The Rule and Exercise of Holy Dying*; William Law (1686–1761), author of *A Serious Call to a Devout and Holy Life*; and the high churchman and poet John Keble (1792–1866), author of *The Christian Year*.

The Catholic Counter-Reformation

The Catholic Counter-Reformation, centered in the Council of Trent (1545–1563), was a conservative response to the theological challenges of the Protestants and to the need for significant institutional reform.

Spanish Spirituality

Ignatius of Loyola (c. 1491–1556) founded a new religious order in 1540 called the Society of Jesus, or the Jesuits. This order became the spearhead of the Counter-Reformation and the fountainhead of missionary endeavors in America, Africa, and Asia (e.g., Francis Xavier). Loyola wrote a manual for spiritual direction in retreats called *Spiritual Exercises*, and this highly structured Ignatian approach to prayer and spirituality has continued to be used to the present time.

Teresa of Avila (1515–1582) was a reformer of the Carmelite Order and a perceptive interpreter of mystical experience and spiritual development. *The Way of Perfection*, her *Life*, and *The Interior Castle* develop the spirituality of prayer, meditation, and contemplation and describe the soul's journey to God through the purgative, illuminative, and unitive stages. The seven mansions in *The Interior Castle* are self-knowledge; detachment; humility and aridity; affective prayer; beginning union with God; mystical experience and the prayer of quiet; and peaceful union with God.

John of the Cross (1542–1591) was profoundly affected by Teresa, and his spiritual development was forged in a life of pain, conflict, and passion for God. In *The Ascent of Mount Carmel* and *The Dark Night of the Soul* he described the purgation of the soul by the night of the senses. After a period of rest, this night may be followed by a second painful purification, the night of the spirit, in order to prepare the soul for the transforming union of spiritual marriage described in *The Living Flame of Love*.

French Spirituality

Francis de Sales (1567–1622) is best known for his *Introduction to the Devout Life*, a product of his spiritual direction of a number of individuals. In his writings, de Sales stressed that a life of holiness is not limited to the clergy or religious but is also available to those who are active in the world. Salesian spirituality emphasizes a resolute volitional commitment to God regardless of emotional distractions.

Pierre de Bérulle (1575–1629), a friend of de Sales, founded a distinct school of French spirituality that detailed the cultivation of the interior life. Brother Lawrence of the Resurrection (Nicholas Herman; c. 1611–1691) wrote a devotional classic, *The Practice of the Presence of God*, that chronicled his practice of God's presence in the routines of daily activities. The philosopher and mathematician Blaise Pascal (1623–1662) had a transforming spiritual experience in 1654 that led to a spirituality of the heart (outlined in his extraordinary *Pensées*) that was centered on faith in the person of Christ as Savior. Pascal was influenced by Jansenism, a morally rigorous movement with predestinatory overtones that challenged Jesuit theology and practice and was denounced by the Catholic Church.

Another movement, called Quietism, was also denounced by the church. A Spanish priest named Miguel de Molinos (c. 1640–1697) was condemned for his advocacy of the "holy indifference" of spiritual passivity and complete surrender of the will in *The Spiritual Guide*. Madame Jeanne-Marie Guyon (1648–1717) and her spiritual correspondent François Fénelon (1651–1715) were influenced by Molinos and were persecuted for popularizing the passive prayer of Quietism. Guyon's books, *Short and Very Easy Method of Prayer* and *The Spiritual Torrents*, taught that all distinct ideas, including the attributes of God and the mysteries of the life of Christ, should be avoided in mental prayer. Fénelon's *Spiritual Letters* and *Christian Perfection* provide practical guidance to the process of abandonment of the self to God.

John Pierre de Caussade (1675–1751) sought to restore a balanced approach to mysticism in view of the overreaction to Quietism, and his *Abandonment to Divine Providence* stressed the powerful theme of "the sacrament of the present moment."

Charles de Foucauld (1858–1916) and The Little Flower, Thérèse of Lisieux (1873–1897), are two more recent examples of spiritual abandonment and the practice of renunciation in small things.

Protestant Movements

Following the Reformation period, the Lutheran and Reformed movements went through three developmental periods. In the confessional period, leaders attempted to define and defend their doctrinal positions. The Pietist period reacted to this preoccupation with dogmatic orthodoxy and called for a living faith and personal devotion. The rationalist period (which overlapped the Pietist period) reflected the Enlightenment view that autonomous human reason could arrive at final truths and could test revelatory claims. The influence of radical biblical criticism, evolutionary theory, and antisupernaturalism withered the spirituality of many mainline church leaders and often reduced religious practice to the teaching of universal ethical norms.

Puritans

Between 1550 and 1700, the Puritans sought to purify the Anglican Church by bringing it into greater conformity with Reformed theology and practice. Puritan spirituality centered on self-examination and personal faith, and it minimized what were called "popish" trappings, such as church ornamentation, vestments, and organs.

Pastor-theologians like Richard Baxter (1615–1691) and John Owen (1616–1683) sought to integrate Reformed theology, spiritual experience, and effective action. Their many writings (such as Baxter's *The Reformed Pastor; The Saints' Everlasting Rest; Call to the Unconverted; A Christian Directory;* and Owen's *The Death of Death in the Death of Christ; Sin and Temptation; Indwelling Sin;* and *Discourse Concerning the Holy Spirit*) combine spiritual insight and theological precision with pastoral concern and practical exhortation.

The well-known Puritan John Bunyan (1628–1688) suffered imprisonment because of his convictions, and he produced some of his writings in prison. After writing his autobiography, *Grace Abounding to the Chief of Sinners*, he wrote his enduring classic, *Pilgrim's Progress*, an allegory of the Christian life as a struggle between desires that are prompted by the world versus the upward call of God.

Quakers

The Society of Friends, founded by George Fox (1624–1691), renounced many of the practices of external religion and centered on a corporate mysticism that involved waiting for the Holy Spirit to speak through people in their meetings. The life and *Journal* of the American antislavery campaigner John Woolman (1720–1772) illustrate the Quaker spirituality of sacrifice, simplicity, social justice, and humanitarianism.

Pietists

Philipp Jakob Spener (1635–1705) was the founder of German Pietism, a movement that called Lutherans out of their spiritual lethargy to a vital spirituality. His *Pia Desideria* (*Pious Hopes*) advocated such radical things for the time as lay activism, midweek Bible studies, sermons that edify rather than display erudition, and the teaching of pastoral care in seminaries. August Hermann Francke (1663–1727), a teacher who expounded the Bible along devotional lines, extended Pietist reform to a socially sensitive spirituality by founding orphanages, schools, and other institutions.

Pietism, with its emphasis on inward personal conversion and outward practical renewal, later spread to Scandinavian Europe, where it challenged the conventionalism of the state churches. The negative side of this movement was its tendency toward legalism, self-righteousness, and anti-intellectualism.

In a class by himself, Sören Kierkegaard (1813–1855) attacked both Hegelian rationalism and the spiritual lethargy of the Danish church in his profound existential writings. In his *Either/Or* and *Stages on Life's Way*, he developed three stages or spheres of existence that he called aesthetic, ethical, and religious ("religion A" or "religion in the sphere of immanence," and "religion B" or "religion in the sphere of transcendence"). His spirituality of inward passion and subjective appropriation is developed in many of his books, such as *The Sickness Unto Death*, *Fear and Trembling*, and *Christian Discourses*.

Evangelicals

The eighteenth-century Church of England saw a similar pietistic movement in response to the growing religious and moral torpor of the time. This spiritual deadness was caused in part by the influence of Enlightenment rationalism, and it was refreshing for many to hear the fervent preaching of evangelicals like John Newton (1725–1807). Evangelical spirituality (illustrated in the moving *Letters of John Newton*) encouraged lay involvement and family prayer and Bible reading. Newton influenced another evangelical, William Wilberforce (1759–1833), to serve God by staying in Parliament instead of taking holy orders. As a result, Wilberforce promoted social reform and was largely responsible for the abolition of the slave trade. His *Practical View of the Prevailing Religious System of Professed Christians* called believers to personal repentance and Christian responsibility.

Evangelicalism was also associated with growing philanthropy and concern for unreached peoples, and this led to the formation of organizations like the Church Mission Society, the British and Foreign Bible Society, and the Baptist Missionary Society, whose first missionary was William Carey (1761–1834). This missionary-minded spirituality was characterized by a global perspective, intercessory prayer, and a love and concern for unmet people.

Revivalism

The two Great Awakenings in eighteenth-century America brought a revival-oriented spirituality marked by conviction of sin, personal repentance, and what Jonathan Edwards (1703–1758) described as *Religious Affections*. The tradition of revivalistic preachers like George Whitefield (1714–1770) was carried on in the nineteenth century by evangelists such as Charles G. Finney (1792–1875) and Dwight L. Moody (1837–1899). Revival spirituality stresses not only repentance and personal conversion but also prayerful preparation and waiting for the sovereign and sudden movement of the Holy Spirit (e.g., the lay prayer revival of 1857–1859 and the Welsh revival of 1904–1905).

Methodists

John Wesley (1703–1791) and his brother Charles (1707–1788) were influenced by *The Imitation of Christ* and William Law. Their highly disciplined approach to the spiritual life led to the charge of Method-ism, but only after an unsuccessful missionary experience in Georgia did Wesley experience true conversion at a meeting of Moravians on Aldersgate Street in London. Wesley's spirituality of the warm heart and fervent preaching made him unwelcome in Anglican churches, but it was only after his death that Methodism became a separate denomination.

Holiness Groups

The early Methodist emphasis on personal holiness and the possibility of entire sanctification, or Christian perfection, prepared the way for Wesleyan-inspired holiness movements and organizations like The Salvation Army, founded by William Booth (1829–1912). This approach to spirituality focuses on the need for a second work of the Holy Spirit after conversion to empower a life of holiness. The Keswick victorious life conventions in England and America also stress the need for practical holiness, though this movement has more to do with exchanged life spirituality.

Pentecostals

In the 1906 Azusa Street revival in Los Angeles, William Seymour (1870–1922), following Charles Parham, related the second blessing of the holiness movements to the Pentecostal experience of the baptism in the Holy Spirit (Acts 2). Speaking in tongues was the manifestation of this baptism, and this highly experiential approach to spirituality rapidly spread through new denominations like the Assemblies of God and the Church of God. Pentecostalism is now the fastest growing segment of Christianity throughout the world, largely because this approach to spirituality appeals to the emotions and is highly accessible to the poor and the uneducated.

Recent Spiritual Figures

Evelyn Underhill (1875–1941) turned to the study of the mystics in her spiritual struggles, and her books (e.g., *Mysticism, The Life of the Spirit and the Life of To-day*, and *Worship*) have done much to expose her twentieth-century audience to the spiritual wealth of Christian mysticism and the value of spiritual direction.

Frank Laubach (1884–1970) was a modern Brother Lawrence in his practice of abiding in the presence of Christ while engaging in daily life. He described his experience of constant awareness of Christ in his *Letters by a Modern Mystic* and *The Game with Minutes*. Like Laubach, Thomas Kelly (1893–1941) believed that "there is a way of ordering our mental life on more than one level at once." In *A Testament of Devotion*, he argued that it is possible to maintain the deeper level of divine attendance through mental habits of inward orientation.

A. W. Tozer (1897–1963) was an evangelical mystic who possessed both a rich knowledge of the Scriptures and an extraordinary intimacy with God. He was almost alone among his conservative evangelical peers in his familiarity with the writings of earlier spiritual writers, including the Catholic mystics. Two of his works, *The Knowledge of the Holy* and *The Pursuit of God*, are already becoming spiritual classics because of the way they inflame their readers to follow God.

C. S. Lewis (1898–1963), the most important Christian apologist of the twentieth century, displays a remarkably integrated spirituality of both the mind and the heart in books like *Mere Christianity, The Screwtape Letters*, and his autobiography, *Surprised by Joy*.

Dietrich Bonhoeffer (1906–1945) was martyred for his denunciation of Hitler, and in his important works, *The Cost of Discipleship, Life Together*, and *Letters and Papers from Prison*, he expounded a spirituality of Christian community and radical discipleship in a corporate context.

Thomas Merton (1915–1968), a Cistercian monk, has done more than any other person in the modern era to communicate the riches of contemplative spirituality. His captivating autobiography, *The Seven Storey Mountain*, and his many books on spiritual formation (e.g., *Contemplative Prayer* and *New Seeds of Contemplation*) have made the practice of contemplative prayer more appealing and accessible to contemporary readers.

Martin Luther King Jr. (1929–1968) illustrated a spirituality of social justice in his leadership in the civil rights movement, and his writings (*Letter from Birmingham Jail, Strength to Love*) show that his social activism was rooted in his Christian convictions.

Henri Nouwen (1932–1996) was a skillful and perceptive advocate of incorporating spirituality in daily life. His many books (e.g., *Making All Things New, The Genesee Diary, The Wounded Healer, The Way of the Heart*, and *In the Name of Jesus*) make a compelling case for a lifestyle of solitude, silence, and prayer.

Dallas Willard (*The Spirit of the Disciplines, In Search of Guidance, The Divine Conspiracy,* and *Renovation of the Heart*) and Richard J. Foster (*Celebration of Discipline, Freedom of Simplicity, Money, Sex and Power, Prayer: Finding the Heart's True Home,* and *Streams of Living Water*) are two recent advocates of the profound benefits of disciplined spirituality.

Recent Developments

The Second Vatican Council in 1962–1965 (Vatican II) marked a significant difference in Catholic spirituality and in Catholic-Protestant relationships. Tridentine (the Council of Trent, 1545–1563) and Vatican I (1868–1870) Catholicism generally held that only Roman Catholics are true Christians, that the laity has less access to spiritual perfection than the religious (members of religious orders, such as the Benedictines, Cistercians, Dominicans, Franciscans, and Jesuits), and that spirituality consists of progression toward the mystical vision of God. These assumptions have been challenged since Vatican II, and Catholic spirituality has become more accessible to the laity.

The ecumenical movement (e.g., the World Council of Churches, 1948) has sought to engender a spirit of reconciliation and Christian unity, though it has been vulnerable to the problem of reducing the Christian message to a lowest common denominator. Still, there has been increased awareness of a need for a more cross-cultural spirituality in which one culture balances and informs another, as well as efforts to achieve an ecumenical spirituality of worship (e.g., the community of Taize in France, in which Catholics and Protestants worship together).

Catholics and Protestants have also participated in the charismatic movement that has developed since the 1960s and 1970s. Unlike classical Pentecostalism, the charismatic movement has reached people in mainline denominations, and the effect has generally been to move people from a liberal theological stance to a more evangelical and Spirit-led approach to the faith.

Twelve-step spirituality has also grown in recent decades, and this model, derived from the twelve steps of Alcoholics Anonymous, has been adapted by many churches. The recovery movement promotes a spiritually oriented methodology for assisting people who have been enmeshed in addictive behaviors. Books like *The Twelve Steps for Christians* seek to relate these steps to biblical principles.

The growing cultural embeddedness of psychology has generated a variety of self-focused (e.g., self-help, self-fulfillment, self-esteem, and self-actualization) approaches to spirituality that are more anthropocentric than Christocentric. Interest has also swelled in spiritual techniques for inner healing as well as the interpretation of dreams, and while some of these approaches can be helpful, they are susceptible to misuse and unbiblical theology. With ever-greater frequency, the psychology of Carl Jung has been uncritically applied to a spiritualized version of the process of "individuation." These psychological influences on Christian spirituality have produced a mixture of new insights and profound dangers.

The recent "creation centered" spirituality must be approached with even greater caution. The Jesuit theologian Pierre Teilhard de Chardin (1881–1955) had experiences of the numinous in nature and developed a cosmic panentheistic spirituality. In books like *The Phenomenon of Man* and *The Divine Milieu* he argued that the cosmos is evolving into Point Omega, the body of Christ. Along similar lines, the ex-Dominican priest Matthew Fox (*Breakthrough: Meister Eckhart's Creation Spirituality in New Translation* and *The Coming of the Cosmic Christ*) has discarded the fall-redemption theme and replaced it with a divinizing creation spirituality. These writers illustrate the growing tendency to conflate aspects of Christian spirituality with New Age thinking, and this is also evident in the popular books of former Catholic monk Thomas Moore (e.g., *Care of the Soul*; *The Re-Enchantment of Everyday Life*).

Orthodoxy

The practice of spirituality in Eastern Orthodoxy has changed little since the medieval period (see "The Eastern Church" above). Two important developments in the modern period are a newer version of the *Philokalia* and the worldwide popularity of *The Way of a Pilgrim*. The original *Philokalia* ("the love of beauty," referring to love of God as the source of all things beautiful) was a small collection of spiritual writings selected by Basil of Caesarea (c. 330–379). These included passages from Origen of Alexandria as well as some of the desert fathers. In the eighteenth century, Macarius of Corinth (1731–1805) and Nicodemus of the Holy Mountain (1749–1809) edited a vast collection of texts from the fourth to the fifteenth century. They published this larger version of the *Philokalia* in 1782, and it has had a pronounced impact on modern Orthodoxy. The spirituality of this collection stresses the need for spiritual direction, vigilance, attentiveness, stillness, and the continual remembrance of God.

Although the "Jesus Prayer" was developed between the fifth and eighth centuries, only in the twentieth century has it come to be used on a large scale by Orthodox laypeople. This is largely due to a book by an anonymous pilgrim that first appeared in 1884. *The Way of a Pilgrim* is a compelling account of a Russian pilgrim's exposure to the *Philokalia* and his effort to learn the secret of praying without ceasing. *The Way of a Pilgrim* has popularized the use of "the prayer of the heart" throughout the world as a means of achieving a state of stillness and awareness of the Lord's presence.

Latin America, Africa, and Asia

The widespread social injustice in Latin America led to the development of a theology of liberation from oppression, and this liberation theology has been adopted by theologians around the world. In contrast to traditional Catholic spirituality, liberation spirituality appeals to laypeople and focuses on communal action rather than interior mysticism. In many hands, this theology has been reduced to social and economic revolution with a spiritual veneer, but writers like Gustavo Gutiérrez (*We Drink from Our Own Wells: The Spiritual Journey of a People*) and Jon Sobrino (*Spirituality of Liberation: Toward Political Holiness*) have sought to develop a biblical and spiritual foundation for this movement. When this approach is embedded in a personal and communal relationship to God, it challenges the excessive emphasis on individualistic psychology that is characteristic of North American spirituality.

Liberation concepts have also been adapted to spirituality in the African setting, particularly to the issues of foreign manipulation, poverty, oppression, and apartheid (e.g., Bakole Wa Ilunga, *Paths of Liberation: A Third World Spirituality*; John de Gruchy, ed., *Cry Justice! Prayers, Meditations and Readings from South Africa*). There has been a growing effort to contextualize the Christian faith in such a way that it is more compatible with African culture without compromising the message of the gospel.

In recent years, Christianity has seen unprecedented growth in Asia, and its encounter with Asian cultures has led to distinctive approaches to spirituality. The books of Kosuke Koyama (*Waterbuffalo Theology, Three Mile an Hour God, Mount Fuji and Mount Sinai*) and of A. J. Appasamy (*The Gospel and India's Heritage*) illustrate the need for cultural adaptations in spiritual formation.

TWELVE RECURRING ISSUES AND EXTREMES

As I reflected on the spirituality of the ancient, medieval, and modern churches, it became evident that a number of themes and issues recurred during these centuries. There were also several pendulum swings that relate to these issues. These unbalanced extremes are always unbiblical, and they force an either-or on a number of areas that are better viewed as both-and. As we look at twelve of these recurring issues, think of each of them as a continuum or a spectrum from all x and no y to all y and no x. In some cases, the ideal is a balanced affirmation of both x and y, while in other cases, there is room for differing degrees of x and y, as long as either extreme is avoided.

Religious versus Laity

Most of the spiritual figures mentioned in this appendix were unmarried members of monastic communities and/or religious orders. The Catholic and Orthodox churches have tended to separate the religious (referring to members of religious orders) from the laity, and only in recent years have these churches questioned the assumption that the laity has less access to spiritual perfection than the religious. To a lesser degree, this clergy/laity distinction vis-à-vis spirituality has been practiced in

Protestantism as well, and this has resulted in the unbiblical assumption that progression toward the heights of spirituality is something to be left to the professionals.

The time has come for the church to affirm that spiritual growth is God's intention for every believer. Indeed, the majority of the godliest characters in the Bible, such as Abraham, David, Daniel, and Nehemiah, were laypeople, not priests. However, it would be prudent to avoid the opposite extreme, which is to see no value in the lifestyle of chastity, poverty, and obedience that is pursued by those in religious orders. While Paul affirmed the value of marriage, he also made it clear that those who remain in a single state for the Lord's sake enjoy the advantage of "undistracted devotion to the Lord" (1 Corinthians 7:32–35).

Human Responsibility versus Divine Sovereignty

The church has seen frequent pendulum swings from an overemphasis on human responsibility that overlooks divine sovereignty to such a stress on the sovereignty of God that the human side is eliminated. (The former is associated with the extremes of Arminianism, while the latter is associated with the extremes of Calvinism.) Some of the spiritual figures in church history have placed so much importance on human works in their theology and spirituality that they have overlooked the grace of God in salvation and spiritual growth. This tendency appears far more frequently than its opposite, since the human heart is more naturally inclined to a works orientation than to a grace orientation (this is evident in the non-Christian religions of the world). However, it is possible to stress the role of sovereign grace in spiritual growth in such a way that it underplays the value of works born out of obedience.

Legalism versus License

This continuum is similar to the one just discussed, but it focuses more on the practical outworking of the spiritual life. In the section on exchanged life spirituality we defined legalism as striving in the effort of the flesh to achieve a human standard of righteousness, and we defined license (or libertinism) as an attitude that takes the grace of God for granted and minimizes the consequences of sin. In the history of spirituality, the former extreme surfaces more frequently, and it is associated with an overemphasis on rules and regulations. The effort to quantify and measure spirituality generally reduces it to conformity with human expectations and standards. However, there are instances of the opposite extreme, such as the medieval mystical sects known as the Brethren of the Free Spirit.

Corporate versus Personal

It is healthy to pursue a balance of both corporate spirituality and personal spirituality. In the modern West, an excessive individualism and interest in the psychology of the self has often separated believers from the spiritual benefits of life in community. But it is also possible to focus so much on the institutional side of the church that the personal and inward aspects of Christian living are overlooked. Many great figures in the history of spirituality have achieved a balance between mutual servanthood in corporate life and a personal quest for spiritual depth. The extremes of social action without personal spiritual consciousness and spiritual individualism without social relevance are both unbiblical. The former is the trap of liberal Christianity, and the latter is the snare of conservative Christianity.

Creation-Denying versus Creation-Affirming

Most approaches to Christian spirituality in the history of the church have tended to minimize the wonder, glory, and splendor of the created order. The creation-denying influence of Gnosticism and Neo-Platonism profoundly shaped ancient and medieval spirituality, and this dualistic philosophy (nature and the body as evil and spirit as good) continues to emaciate many in the body of Christ. An incarnational theology that affirms the beauty and goodness of God's work in the created order is a needed corrective. In recent decades, however, there has been a growth in creation-centered spiritualities that are moving toward the opposite extreme of panentheism or full-blown pantheism.

Self-Denying versus Self-Affirming

Some of the figures discussed in this appendix (e.g., Henry Suso) carried asceticism to a fine art and practiced gruesome forms of self-abnegation. This practice of physical mortification and rigorous asceticism often went far beyond the biblical associations of repentance with fasting and sackcloth and led to a morbid correlation between self-inflicted pain and spiritual progress. Scripture teaches that God uses trials and adversities in our lives to draw us closer to him, but this is very different from the self-mortifying practices of many in the history of the church. More recently, the opposite extreme of self-affirmation, self-realization, and self-actualization has been taking hold, and increasing numbers of people are on a quest for a shallow feel-good, self-help spirituality. It is easy to miss the biblical balance of finding abundant life through growing surrender to the lordship of Christ. True self-denial comes through the renunciation of self-centered strategies and through a spiritual and moral paradigm shift from an egocentric to a theocentric universe.

Technique Orientation versus Spontaneous Orientation

Many have sought to reproduce the spiritual vitality of others through the development of knowledge, skills, and techniques. For example, a misguided approach to the *Spiritual Exercises* of Ignatius of Loyola can lead to a formula-driven methodology of prayer and meditation. The opposite of a skill-based spirituality is a spirituality that eschews all disciplines and structures. A more biblical balance is a relational spirituality that combines both form (structure) and freedom (spontaneity) in the pursuit of spiritual maturity.

Christocentric Contemplation versus Theocentric Contemplation

Christocentric contemplation refers to the pursuit of union with the triune God through contemplation of the person and work of Christ as revealed in the New Testament Gospels and Epistles. This Christ-centered approach is illustrated in the writings of Bernard of Clairvaux and Thomas à Kempis. By contrast, the way of **theocentric contemplation** involves the movement from contemplation of the reflection of God's attributes in the created order to direct contemplation of the heavenly Archetype. The danger of an exclusively Christocentric spirituality is the practical minimization of the soul's attention to the Father and the Holy Spirit. The danger of an exclusively theocentric spirituality that centers on the co-inherence of the Creator and the created is the blurring of the distinction between God and the cosmos. Both Pseudo-Dionysius and Meister Eckhart had a problem in this area; in their writings, pantheistic images of absorption were more ultimate than an I/Thou relationship.

Doing versus Being

The pendulum swing between the realization of spiritual identity through outward action versus inward reflection has not lost momentum over the centuries of church history. In our time, it is easier for most of us to relate to the former more than the latter, but other times and cultures stress being over doing. From a biblical perspective, who we are in Christ should determine what we do, but both are crucial, since concrete doing should flow out of abstract being.

Active versus Passive

This spectrum is similar to the second and ninth spectra, but it is more concerned with the dynamics of actively seeking God versus passively responding to God's initiatives. The activist extreme overlooks the fact that God's grace is always previous to our reception. The passivist extreme minimizes the reality of human responsibility in the spiritual journey. The length of this continuum can be illustrated by the distance between the social activism of doing things for God and the spiritual passivity of the Quietist teaching of "holy indifference" to the will of God. A better balance is an ongoing series of choices (active) to allow Christ to love and serve people through us (passive).

Kataphatic versus Apophatic

The history of spirituality well illustrates both the *via positiva* and the *via negativa* concerning the knowledge of God. As we saw in appendix A, kataphatic spirituality affirms the positive knowledge of God through his general revelation in nature and his special revelation in the written and incarnate Word or *logos*. By contrast, apophatic spirituality insists that God is unknowable to the human mind and transcends all temporal attributes. Making a distinction between acquired contemplation and infused contemplation, the apophatic way argues that one cannot acquire knowledge of God but that God can choose to infuse transcendent knowledge. Scripture provides a balance between these two extremes by affirming the richness of God's manifold revelation (e.g., Hebrews 1:1–3) while at the same time declaring that the truths of God are "spiritually appraised" by those who have "the mind of Christ" and are inaccessible to the natural man (1 Corinthians 2:14–16).

Objective Truth versus Subjective Experience

The turbulent history of doctrinal development and spiritual formation reveals yet another continuum. This spectrum ranges from a totally objective orientation in revealed truth to a totally subjective orientation in personal experience. Catholic scholasticism and Reformed confessionalism illustrate one side of the spectrum, and medieval mysticism illuminates the other side. When objective truth is carried to an extreme, it can wither into a word-based rationalism divested of personal engagement. When subjective experience is carried to an extreme, it can degenerate into unbridled emotionalism, self-delusion, and hysteria. Thus there are churches that promote truth without love and churches that promote love without truth. Both truth and love are needed for a full-orbed spiritual life, but the history of spirituality reveals something of a division of labor. In *very general terms,* Catholic and Orthodox mystics have a richer depth of spiritual understanding and experience than Protestants because this has been the focus of their attention. Protestants have a more developed understanding of biblical, systematic, and dogmatic theology than Catholics and Orthodox because this has been the focus of their attention. The relative shallowness of both liberal and conservative Protestant spirituality has created a recent interest among a number of Protestants in mining the treasures of Catholic and Orthodox spirituality. If those who do this retain a biblically grounded theology that enables them to discern the spirit of truth and the spirit of error, they will be far richer for the experience.

THE LADDER OF PERFECTION

The three stages of the Ladder of Perfection *(Scala Perfectionis)* were originally presented in the writings of Pseudo-Dionysius and further developed by later mystics like Jan van Ruysbroeck and Teresa of Avila. The three stages, or ways, are preceded by Awakening, which refers to the soul's initial encounters with God. These experiences can be slow and incremental or sudden and intense, but they lead to a growing awareness of the sinfulness of the self and the holiness of God.

The first stage is the Purgative Way, and this involves a process of purifying the soul through renunciation, contrition, and confession of blatant sins and willful disobedience. This process becomes more subtle as sins of omission and unconscious sins are gradually brought to the surface and renounced before God. Purgation involves brokenness, gradual death to the tyrannous dominion of the ego, and sometimes wrenching transfers of trust from self-reliance to reliance on Christ alone for the soul's well-being. The Purgative Way is a painful but needful process of finding Christ's life by losing one's own life (increasing mortification) and thus moving from anxiety to trust.

The second stage is the Illuminative Way, which refers to a growing realization of the presence of God within as one is increasingly consecrated to God. In this stage, prayer is less an activity or an appendage and more a vital reality that flows out of one's being. Life takes on an aura of the mystery of God as one moves toward what Nicolas of Cusa called "learned ignorance," an increased awareness of how little we know. The Illuminative Way is often characterized by growing love and others-centeredness as one expresses love for God through acts of love and service to others.

The third stage is the Unitive Way, also described as contemplation and abandonment to grace. This stage involves a growing experiential understanding of the mystery of "you in Me, and I in you" (John 14:20) and "it is no longer I who live, but Christ lives in me" (Galatians 2:20). In *Spiritual Passages*, Benedict J. Groeschel uses the writings of Teresa of Avila and John of the Cross to develop the general pattern of the Unitive Way (see his chart of the Purgative, Illuminative, and Unitive Ways that follows in table B.1). The first phase of contemplation, or simple union with God, begins with the prayer of quietness in which one is yielded to God through purified desire and simplified will. This may be followed by what John of the Cross called the dark night of the senses, a time of dryness and painful stripping away of the intellectual and emotional assurances of God's presence and care. The second phase of contemplation, or full union with God, involves detachment from self and a certitude of the indwelling presence of God. This phase may be accompanied by an occasional experience of spiritual ecstasy that Teresa called wonder or rapture. John of the Cross described a second night, which he called the dark night of the spirit, that God may use to purge the last vestiges of self-will. The highest level of the spiritual mountain described by the mystics is transforming union, or spiritual marriage. This union of all desire and complete harmony with God involves a transmutation of personal identity in Christ and the realization of the oneness described in John 17:20–23.

This experiential mysticism of ascent with its quest for perfection and communion with God needs to be balanced by the biblical insights that are developed in Reformation theology. The believer in Christ has already received "every spiritual blessing in the

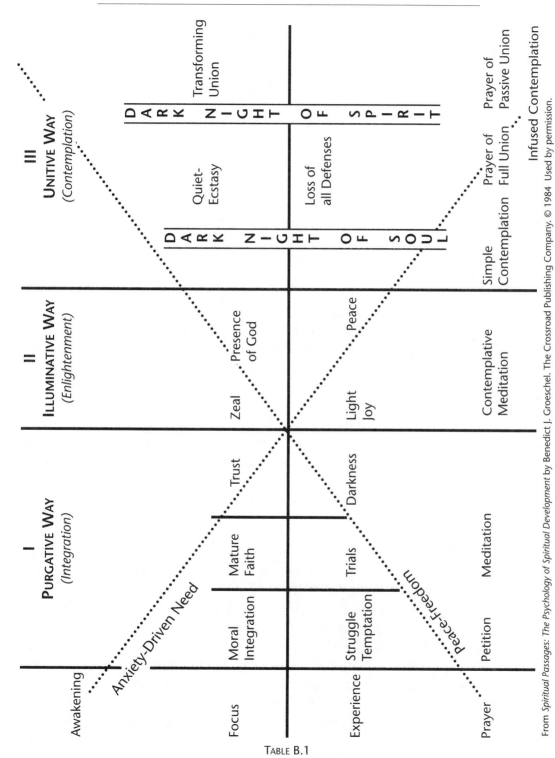

TABLE B.1

From *Spiritual Passages: The Psychology of Spiritual Development* by Benedict J. Groeschel. The Crossroad Publishing Company. © 1984 Used by permission.

heavenly places in Christ" (Ephesians 1:3), and the gift of spiritual union with God is realized in the mystery of "Christ in you, the hope of glory" (Colossians 1:27). By reviewing the twelfth issue discussed above, you will see that the Ladder of Perfection with its Purgative, Illuminative, and Unitive Ways focuses more on subjective experience than on objective (biblical) truth. The danger of this focus is the mistaken assumption that spiritual union with God does not exist until it is realized in experience. This assumption is incompatible with the many biblical truths about the believer's radically new identity in Jesus Christ. Though the best writers avoid this, the Ladder of Perfection can also be misconstrued as a product of human struggle and merit more than the grace of God. From a biblical perspective, God's sovereign grace must infuse the whole process of spiritual formation in such a way that growth in sanctification is by grace through faith. The objective truth of our position in Christ is not determined by our subjective experience but should gradually shape and be realized in our experiential practice.

My friend Bill Fagan describes six stages of spiritual growth that have some points of comparison with the Purgative, Illuminative, and Unitive Ways. The first stage is *spiritual birth*. This involves coming to an understanding of personal sinfulness and being justified in Christ (John 3; Romans 1–3). The second stage is *service*. Out of love and gratitude, the believer uses natural talents in an effort to serve God. Third, this leads to *frustrated inadequacy*, the painful discovery that we cannot live the spiritual life in our own power (Romans 7). The fourth stage is the experiential realization of our *identity with Christ* in his death, burial, and resurrection (Romans 6) and the awareness that Christ lives in us through the power of the Holy Spirit (Romans 8). The fifth stage is an ongoing process of reprogramming or *renewing of the mind* (Romans 12) that involves many cycles of surrender and trust and of emptying and filling as the Holy Spirit replaces the lies we have believed with the truth of our identity in Christ (John 8:32). The sixth stage is *union with Christ* that can be progressively experienced now but is only fully realized in the next life.

A VARIETY OF APPROACHES

The history of Christian spirituality reveals an enormous diversity of approaches and styles. A number of root metaphors dominate the insights and systems developed by individual writers and schools of spirituality through the centuries. In *Thirsty for God*, Bradley P. Holt distinguishes six sets of these fundamental images that appear again and again in different contexts. The first set of metaphors depicts the basis of the Christian life as *rescue, redemption, and justification,* and these are central in the Lutheran and Reformed traditions (by contrast, Orthodoxy rarely uses the image of justification). The second set, *growth, unification, and healing,* focuses on the process of Christian living, and is used metaphorically by Catholic mystics and experientially by

Pentecostals and charismatics. The third set depicts the spiritual life as *walking, journeying, climbing, and homing,* and these images of travel are used by a variety of schools and writers. The most popular example is John Bunyan's *Pilgrim's Progress.* The fourth set of images is *death and resurrection,* and this speaks of the cycle of departure and return, sin and forgiveness, despair and hope. The metaphor of progression toward resurrection in the life of God is characteristic of Orthodoxy. The fifth set of root metaphors is *battle and warfare,* and many Pietist and evangelical writers use these images. The sixth set, *thirst and hunger,* stresses the human need for life and satisfaction in God.

In appendix A, we took a brief look at the great variety of temperamental differences and related this to the diversity of approaches to spirituality. As we have seen in this appendix, it is evident that these differing spiritual styles are also strongly influenced by cultural factors. Someone reared in a context of eighteenth-century German Pietism would approach the spiritual life in a dramatically different way than if he or she were reared at the same time in France or in Russia.

The combination of your nature (temperament) and nurture (culture) will predispose you to particular styles of spirituality, but as we argued before, it is helpful to stretch yourself through the discipline of deliberate exposure to a facet of spirituality you would ordinarily overlook or avoid. For instance, most readers of this book are probably unfamiliar with the practice of contemplative prayer. But in the history of spirituality, a surprising amount of emphasis has been placed on the importance of this form of prayer. Because of this, I recommend that you try developing skill in the practice of *lectio divina,* or sacred reading, that is developed in the section on devotional spirituality.

Many writers through the centuries have distinguished three approaches to Christian living: the active life, the contemplative life, and the mixed life. The first focuses on doing more than being, the second focuses on being more than doing, and the third approach, which I recommend, is a balanced combination of being and doing in which the latter flows out of the former.

GLOSSARY

Apophatic. The term *apophatic* is derived from a Greek word that means "negative," and this speaks of the tradition known as the *via negativa*, the way of negation. This tradition, more characteristic of the East, stresses God's transcendence and mystery. See *kataphatic*.

Beatific vision. The blessed vision of God that will be granted in heaven to those who have known him in this life. It is the ultimate uniting with the true Satisfier of the heart's deepest desires.

Cessationist. One who draws a distinction between sign gifts and edification gifts and believes that the former disappeared from the church after the completion of the New Testament canon.

Christocentric contemplation. The pursuit of union with the triune God through contemplation on the person and work of Christ as revealed in the New Testament Gospels and Epistles. See *theocentric contemplation*.

Compartmentalization. The common practice among believers to see Christ as one of several compartments or components of life along with work, finances, children, marriage, health, sports, and so forth.

Compunction. The sorrowful realization of our preoccupation with selfish interests; in this state we are pierced and stung by the truth of our sinful condition and distance from God.

Contemplation. The prayer of silence and yieldedness in the presence of God. This ancient practice is often associated with the fruit of *lectio divina*, or sacred reading.

Contemplative. The devotional approach of apprehending God not by hearsay but by personal encounter. This is the way of the heart as it pursues its *summum bonum*, the highest good for which it was created.

Detachment. An orientation of the heart *away* from narcissistic enslavement to earthly desires, acquisitions, and ambitions and *toward* an others-centered pursuit of God and love for people. This transformational shifting of our center from the I to the Thou involves a painful and gradual purgation of the desire for perishing things that desensitize us to heavenly desire.

Eternal value system. An orientation of one's priorities around a biblical perspective that treasures God and his promises above the temporal pleasures of this world that are destined to pass away. See *temporal value system*.

Exchanged life. Identification with Christ in his crucifixion and resurrection (Romans 6; Galatians 2:20) means that our old life has been exchanged for the life of Christ. This approach to spirituality moves from a works to a grace orientation and from legalism to liberty because it centers on our acknowledgment that Christ's life is our life.

Fear of the Lord. The fear of the Lord not only means the cultivation of a reverential awe and even terror of God but also relates to the mindset of a subject in a great kingdom. It is the recognition that the King has all power and authority in his hand and that the subject's life, occupation, and future are dependent on the good pleasure of the King. It can also relate to the fear of displeasing God.

The flesh. The power or "law of sin" which is in our members (Romans 7:14–25). This is not the same as the "old self" that was put to death at the cross (Romans 6:6). Although we received a new spirit when we came to Christ, we are still encased in the same body with its physical needs and cravings. Nor was our soul or personality (mind, emotions, and will) instantly transformed.

Formational reading. An in-depth process of reading Scripture that approaches the text with humility, openness, and submission so that we will be mastered by God's truth as it moves from the mind to the heart. See *informational reading*.

Holistic spirituality. An approach to the spiritual life that stresses the centrality of Christ and his relevance to every component of our lives. This biblical alternative to a compartmentalization mentality focuses on the implications of Christ's lordship over every aspect of life in such a way that even the most mundane components of life can become expressions of the life of Christ in us.

Informational reading. A linear process that seeks to analyze and understand the biblical text. See *formational reading*.

Kataphatic. The term *kataphatic* is derived from a Greek word that means "affirmative," and this refers to the tradition known as the *via affirmativa*, the way of affirmation. This tradition, more characteristic of the West, stresses the knowledge of God through general and special revelation. See *apophatic*.

Lectio divina. The practice of sacred reading, usually consisting of the four elements of reading a text, meditating on it, turning it into a personalized prayer, and contemplation.

Legalism. Striving in the effort of the flesh to achieve a human standard of righteousness. Legalism emphasizes an external set of rules and prohibitions rather than the inner life in the Spirit.

Liberty. The freedom in Christ to do as Christ pleases rather than doing what we have to do (legalism) or doing as we please (license).

License. A do-what-you-want-to-do mentality that takes the grace of God for granted and minimizes the consequences of sin.

Meditation. Unlike Eastern meditation, which involves emptying the mind of rational constructs, Christian meditation fills the mind with truth acquired by rumination on a biblical text.

Motivator. An incentive that prompts us to act. Worldly or temporal motivators include fear of loss, guilt, pride, hope of personal gain, reputation, prestige, and pleasure. Biblical motivators include no other options, the fear of the Lord, love and gratitude, rewards, our identity in Christ, purpose and hope, and longing for God.

Mysticism. An intuitive and heart-oriented approach to spiritual formation that explores the inner terrain of the soul's journey toward God.

Naturalism. A world view that denies the transcendent and regards the natural universe as the ultimate reality.

Nurturing spirituality. An approach to the spiritual life that emphasizes a lifestyle of evangelism and discipleship. When we are part of the process of introducing people to Jesus and encouraging them to grow after they have come to know him, we discover that our own passion and spiritual vitality are enhanced.

Paradigm. A way of seeing based on implicit or explicit rules that shape one's perspective. A paradigm shift takes place when the rules or boundaries change, so that we no longer see things from the same perspective; when the rules change, our way of seeing is altered.

Postmodern. A post-Enlightenment approach to the world that relativizes truth, morality, and aesthetics as socially conditioned constructs.

Presupposition. A fundamental assumption about life that is held by faith. All people—from skeptics to theists—embrace presuppositions, whether tacitly or consciously.

Primary and secondary calling. God's primary calling in our lives is to know and love him; our secondary calling is to express this relationship in everything we do and with everyone we encounter. If the secondary is not related to the primary, we slip into the error of dichotomizing the spiritual and the secular when they should be integrated.

The opposite error occurs when secondary calling replaces primary calling. When this occurs, our work becomes an end in itself.

Process spirituality. An approach to the spiritual life that is concerned with being alive to the present moment and with the step-by-step process of responding to God's loving initiatives in our lives.

Rule. A word derived from the Latin word *regula*, meaning "rule, pattern, model, example." A Regular Christian is one who embraces some form of Rule in the spiritual life. Rule has to do with a pattern of disciplines that is practiced by a community (e.g., the *Rule* of St. Benedict), though it can also be embraced by an individual or a small group.

Spirit-filled spirituality. An approach to the spiritual life that ideally combines openness to the surprising work of the Spirit with discernment that tests experience in light of the Scriptures and the fruit that it produces.

Spiritual formation. The grace-driven developmental process in which the soul grows in conformity to the image of Christ.

Spiritual gifts. The endowment by the Holy Spirit of special abilities to every member of the body of Christ for the edification of others.

Spirituality. Authentic, biblically orthodox approaches to the spiritual life.

Stewardship. A steward acts as an administrator of the affairs and possessions of another. Stewards are fully accountable to their masters and may act justly or unjustly. Realms of biblical stewardship include time, talent, treasure, truth, relationships, our bodies, and the created order.

Temporal value system. An orientation of one's priorities around a cultural perspective that pursues the promises of this world above the promises of the Word. See *eternal value system*.

Theocentric contemplation. The movement from contemplation of the reflection of God's attributes in the created order to direct contemplation of the heavenly Archetype. See *Christocentric contemplation*.

Wisdom. The skill in the art of living life with each area under the dominion of God. It is the ability to use the best means at the best time to accomplish the best ends.

The world. The organized system of temporal values that are opposed to the life of Christ in the believer. It has been defined as a composite expression of the depravity of humanity and the intrigues of Satan's rule, combining in opposition to the sovereign rule of God. As such, the world promotes an attitude of independence from God.

World view. One's primary orientation to the world, including one's view of the nature of ultimate reality and of human origin, purpose, and destiny.

WORKS CITED

This is a selected list of a portion of the works cited in this book.

Alcorn, Randy. *Money, Possessions and Eternity*. Wheaton: Tyndale, 1989.

Alexander, Donald L., ed. *Christian Spirituality: Five Views of Sanctification*. Downers Grove, Ill.: InterVarsity, 1988.

Anders, Max. *The Good Life*. Dallas: Word, 1993.

Anderson, Neil T. *The Bondage Breaker*. Eugene, Ore.: Harvest House, 1990.

Anonymous. *The Cloud of Unknowing*. New York: Paulist, 1981.

Anonymous. *The Theologica Germanica*. Translated by Bengst Hoffman. New York: Paulist, 1980.

Anonymous. *The Way of a Pilgrim*. Translated by Olga Savin. Boston: Shambhala, 1996.

Appleton, George, ed. *Oxford Book of Prayer*. New York: Oxford University Press, 1985.

Arnold, Clinton E. *Three Crucial Questions about Spiritual Warfare*. Grand Rapids: Baker, 1997.

Augustine. *Confessions*. New York: Penguin, 1961.

Baxter, William. *The Reformed Pastor*. Portland, Ore.: Multnomah, 1982.

Benner, David G. *Sacred Companions*. Downers Grove, Ill.: InterVarsity, 2002.

Bennett, Dennis and Rita Bennett. *The Holy Spirit and You*. Plainfield, N.J.: Logos International, 1971.

Benson, Bob, Sr. and Michael W. Benson. *Disciplines for the Inner Life*. Nashville: Thomas Nelson, 1989.

Bernard of Clairvaux. *The Love of God*. Portland, Ore.: Multnomah, 1983.

_____. *Selected Works*. Translated by G. R. Evans. New York: Paulist, 1987.

Bloom, Anthony. *Beginning to Pray*. New York: Walker and Company, 1986.

Boa, Kenneth and Robert Bowman. *Faith Has Its Reasons*. Colorado Springs: NavPress, 2001.

Boa, Kenneth and Larry Moody. *I'm Glad You Asked*. Wheaton, Ill.: Victor, 1982.

Bonhoeffer, Dietrich. *The Cost of Discipleship*. New York: Macmillan, 1963.

_____. *Life Together*. San Francisco: Harper and Row, 1954.

Bounds, E. M. *Power through Prayer*. Grand Rapids: Baker, 1963.

Bouyer, Louis. *A History of Christian Spirituality*. 3 vols. New York: Seabury Press, 1963–69.

Boyd, Gregory A. *God at War*. Downers Grove, Ill.: InterVarsity, 1997.

Brand, Paul and Yancey, Philip. *Fearfully and Wonderfully Made*. Grand Rapids: Zondervan, 1980.

_____. *In His Image*. Grand Rapids: Zondervan, 1984.

Brother Lawrence. *The Practice of the Presence of God*. Westwood, N. J.: Revell, 1958.

Bubeck, Mark I. *The Adversary: The Christian versus Demon Activity*. Chicago: Moody, 1975.

Buechner, Frederick. *Wishful Thinking: A Theological ABC*. New York: Harper and Row, 1973.

Bunyan, John. *Grace Abounding to the Chief of Sinners*. London: Penguin, 1987.

_____. *The Pilgrim's Progress*. Grand Rapids: Zondervan, 1966.

Carmody, John. *Holistic Spirituality*. New York: Paulist, 1983.

Casey, Michael. *Sacred Reading: The Ancient Art of Lectio Divina*. Ligouri, Mo.: Triumph Books, 1995.

_____. *Toward God: The Ancient Wisdom of Western Prayer*. Ligouri, Mo.: Triumph Books, 1996.

_____. *The Undivided Heart: The Western Monastic Approach to Contemplation*. Petersham, Mass.: St. Bede's Publications, 1994.

Chambers, Oswald. *My Utmost for His Highest*. New York: Dodd, Mead and Company, 1951.

Chan, Simon. *Spiritual Theology: A Systematic Study of the Christian Life*. Downers Grove, Ill.: InterVarsity, 1998.

Coleman, Robert E. *The Master Plan of Evangelism*. 2d ed. Grand Rapids: Revell, 1994.

Cox, Michael. *Handbook of Christian Spirituality*. San Francisco: Harper and Row, 1983.

Crabb, Larry. *Connecting: Healing for Ourselves and Our Relationships*. Nashville: Word, 1997.

_____. *Inside Out*. Colorado Springs: NavPress, 1988.

Curtis, Brent and John Eldredge. *The Sacred Romance*. Nashville: Thomas Nelson, 1997.

de Caussade, Jean-Pierre. *Abandonment to Divine Providence*. New York: Image, 1973.

Deere, Jack. *Surprised by the Power of the Spirit*. Grand Rapids: Zondervan, 1993.

_____. *Surprised by the Voice of God*. Grand Rapids: Zondervan, 1996.

Demarest, Bruce. *Satisfy Your Soul*. Colorado Springs: NavPress, 1999.

Dieter, Melvin G. et al. *Five Views on Sanctification*. Grand Rapids: Zondervan, 1987.

Downey, Michael. *Understanding Christian Spirituality*. New York: Paulist, 1997.

Downs, Tim. *Finding Common Ground*. Chicago: Moody, 1999.

Dubay, Thomas. *Fire Within*. New York: Ignatius, 1989.

Dupré, Louis and Don E. Saliers, eds. *Christian Spirituality: Post-Reformation and Modern*. New York: Crossroad, 1989.

Edwards, Jonathan. *Religious Affections*. Portland, Ore.: Multnomah, 1984.

Edwards, Lloyd. *How We Belong, Fight, and Pray.* New York: Alban Institute, 1993.

Eldredge, John. *The Journey of Desire.* Nashville: Thomas Nelson, 2000.

Elliott, T. S. *The Waste Land and Other Poems.* New York: Harvest, 1962.

Fadiman, Clifton, ed. *The Little, Brown Book of Anecdotes.* Boston: Little, Brown and Company, 1985.

Fénelon, François. *Christian Perfection.* Minneapolis: Bethany, 1975.

Foster, Richard J. *Celebration of Discipline.* San Francisco: Harper and Row, 1978.

_____. *Prayer: Finding the Heart's True Home.* San Francisco: HarperSanFrancisco, 1992.

_____. *Streams of Living Water.* San Francisco: HarperSanFrancisco, 1998.

Foster, Richard J. and James Bryan Smith, eds. *Devotional Classics.* San Francisco: HarperSanFrancisco, 1993.

Francis de Sales. *Introduction to the Devout Life.* New York: Image, 1972.

Fritz, Robert. *The Path of Least Resistance.* New York: Fawcett Columbine, 1984.

Groeschel, Benedict J. *Spiritual Passages: The Psychology of Spiritual Development.* New York: Crossroad, 1983.

Grudem, Wayne A., ed. *Are Miraculous Gifts for Today?* Grand Rapids: Zondervan, 1996.

_____. *Systematic Theology.* Grand Rapids: Zondervan, 1994.

Guinness, Os. *The Call: Finding and Fulfilling the Central Purpose of Your Life.* Nashville: Word, 1998.

_____. *In Two Minds.* Downers Grove, Ill.: InterVarsity, 1976.

Guyon, Jeanne. *Experiencing the Depths of Jesus Christ.* Goleta, Calif.: Christian Books, 1975.

Hall, Thelma. *Too Deep for Words.* New York: Paulist, 1998.

Hallesby, O. *Prayer.* Minneapolis: Augsburg, 1994.

Hand, Thomas A. *Augustine on Prayer.* New York: Catholic Book Publishing, 1963.

Henrichsen, Walter and Gayle Jackson. *A Layman's Guide to Applying the Bible.* Grand Rapids: Zondervan, 1985.

Herbert, George. *The Complete English Poems.* New York: Penguin, 1991.

Hession, Roy. *The Calvary Road.* Fort Washington, Pa.: Christian Literature Crusade, 1950.

Hildegard of Bingen. *Scivias.* Translated by Columba Hart and Jane Bishop. New York: Paulist, 1990.

Hilton, Walter. *The Scale of Perfection.* Translated by John. P. H. Clark and Rosemary Dorward. New York: Paulist, 1991.

_____. *Toward a Perfect Love.* Translated by David L. Jeffrey. Portland, Ore.: Multnomah, 1985.

Holmes, Urban T. *A History of Christian Spirituality.* San Francisco: Harper and Row, 1980.

Holt, Bradley P. *Thirsty for God: A Brief History of Christian Spirituality.* Minneapolis: Augsburg, 1993.

Hull, Bill. *The Disciple-Making Church.* Grand Rapids: Revell, 1990.

_____. *The Disciple-Making Pastor.* Grand Rapids: Revell, 1988.

Hummel, Charles E. *Fire in the Fireplace: Charismatic Renewal in the Nineties*. Downers Grove, Ill.: InterVarsity, 1993.

Ignatius of Loyola. *The Spiritual Exercises*. Translated by Anthony Mottola. New York: Image, 1964.

Imbach, Jeff. *The River Within*. Colorado Springs: NavPress, 1998.

Issler, Klaus. *Wasting Time with God*. Downers Grove, Ill.: InterVarsity, 2001.

Jones, Cheslyn, Geoffrey Wainright, and Edward Yarnold, eds. *The Study of Spirituality*. New York: Oxford University Press, 1986.

Julian of Norwich. *Revelations of Divine Love*. Translated by Clifton Wolters. Harmondsworth, Middlesex, England: Penguin, 1966.

Keating, Charles J. *Who We Are Is How We Pray: Matching Personality and Spirituality*. Mystic, Conn.: Twenty-Third Publications, 1987.

Keener, Craig S. *Three Crucial Questions about the Holy Spirit*. Grand Rapids, Baker, 1996.

Kelly, Thomas R. *A Testament of Devotion*. San Francisco: HarperSanFrancisco, 1992.

Kreeft, Peter. *Christianity for Modern Pagans*. San Francisco: Ignatius, 1993.

_____. *Three Philosophies of Life*. San Francisco: Ignatius, 1989.

Law, William. *A Serious Call to a Devout and Holy Life*. Grand Rapids: Eerdmans, 1966.

Leclercq, Jean. *The Love of Learning and the Desire for God*. Translated by Catharine Misrahi. New York: Fordham University Press, 1982.

Leech, Kenneth. *Experiencing God: Theology as Spirituality*. San Francisco: Harper and Row, 1985.

_____. *Soul Friend: An Invitation to Spiritual Direction*. San Francisco: HarperSanFrancisco, 1992.

Lewis, C. S. *Mere Christianity*. New York: Macmillan, 1960.

_____. *The Problem of Pain*. New York: Macmillan, 1962.

_____. *The Screwtape Letters*. New York: Macmillan, 1952.

_____. *Surprised by Joy: The Shape of My Early Life*. New York: Harcourt, Brace and World, 1955.

_____. *The Weight of Glory and Other Addresses*. Grand Rapids: Eerdmans, 1965.

Long, Zeb Bradford and Douglas McMurry. *The Collapse of the Brass Heaven*. Grand Rapids: Chosen, 1994.

_____. *Receiving the Power*. Grand Rapids: Chosen, 1996.

Lovelace, Richard F. *Dynamics of Spiritual Life: An Evangelical Theology of Renewal*. Downers Grove, Ill.: InterVarsity, 1979.

MacDonald, Gordon. *Ordering Your Private World*. Nashville: Oliver-Nelson, 1984.

MacDonald, William. *Christ Loved the Church*. Kansas City: Walterick Publishers, 1956.

Manning, Brennan. *Lion and Lamb*. Old Tappan, N.J.: Chosen, 1986.

McGinn, Bernard, John Meyendorff, and Jean Leclercq, eds. *Christian Spirituality: Origins to the Twelfth Century*. New York: Crossroad, 1985.

McGrath, Alister E. *Beyond the Quiet Time*. Grand Rapids: Baker, 1995.

_____. *Christian Spirituality*. Oxford: Blackwell Publishers, 1999.

_____. *Christian Theology: An Introduction*. 2d ed. Oxford: Blackwell Publishers, 1997.

McRae, William. *The Dynamics of Spiritual Gifts*. Grand Rapids: Zondervan, 1976.

Merton, Thomas. *Contemplative Prayer*. New York: Image, 1969.

_____. *New Seeds of Contemplation*. New York: New Directions, 1961.

_____. *Spiritual Direction and Contemplation*. Collegeville, Minn.: Liturgical Press, 1960.

Meyer, F. B. *The Christ Life for Your Life*. Chicago: Moody, n.d.

Michael, Chester P. and Marie C. Norrisey. *Prayer and Temperament: Different Prayer Forms for Different Personality Types*. Charlottesville, Va.: Open Door, 1991.

Mulholland, M. Robert Jr. *Invitation to a Journey*. Downers Grove, Ill.: InterVarsity, 1993.

_____. *Shaped by the Word: The Power of Scripture in Spiritual Formation*. Nashville: Upper Room, 1985.

Murphy, Ed. *The Handbook for Spiritual Warfare*. Nashville: Thomas Nelson, 1996.

Murray, Andrew. *Absolute Surrender*. Chicago: Moody, n.d.

_____. *Humility*. New Kensington, Pa.: Whitaker House, 1982.

Nee, Watchman. *The Normal Christian Life*. Fort Washington, Pa.: Christian Literature Crusade, 1957.

_____. *The Release of the Spirit*. Indianapolis, Ind.: Sure Foundation, 1965.

Needham, David C. *Birthright*. Portland, Ore.: Multnomah, 1979.

Nicholas of Cusa. *Selected Spiritual Writings*. New York: Paulist, 1997.

Nouwen, Henri J. M. *In the Name of Jesus*. New York: Crossroad, 1992.

_____. *Life of the Beloved: Spiritual Living in a Secular World*. New York: Crossroad, 1992.

_____. *The Way of the Heart*. New York: Ballantine, 1981.

Packer, J. I. *Keep in Step with the Spirit*. Old Tappan, N.J.: Revell, 1984.

_____. *Knowing God*. Downers Grove, Ill.: InterVarsity, 1973.

Pascal, Blaise. *The Mind on Fire: An Anthology of the Writings of Blaise Pascal*. Portland, Ore.: Multnomah, 1989.

Payne, Leanne. *The Healing Presence*. Grand Rapids: Baker, 1995.

_____. *Real Presence*. Grand Rapids: Baker, 1995.

_____. *Restoring the Christian Soul through Healing Prayer*. Wheaton, Ill.: Crossway, 1991.

Percy, Walker. *Lancelot*. New York: Farrar, Strauss, Giroux, 1977.

_____. *Second Coming*. New York: Farrar, Strauss, Giroux, 1980.

Petersen, Jim. *Living Proof*. Colorado Springs: NavPress, 1989.

Peterson, Eugene H. *The Contemplative Pastor*. Grand Rapids: Eerdmans, 1989.

_____. *A Long Obedience in the Same Direction*. Downers Grove, Ill.: InterVarsity, 1980.

Piper, John. *Desiring God*. Portland, Ore.: Multnomah, 1986.

_____. *The Pleasures of God*. Portland, Ore.: Multnomah, 1991.

Pseudo-Dionysius. *The Complete Works*. Translated by Colm Luibheid. New York: Paulist, 1987.

Raitt, Jill, ed. *Christian Spirituality: High Middle Ages and Reformation*. New York: Crossroad, 1988.

Rolle, Richard. *The English Writings*. Translated by Rosamund S. Allen. New York: Paulist, 1988.

Ruusbroec, John. *The Spiritual Espousals and Other Works*. Translated by James A. Wiseman. Mahwah, N.J.: Paulist, 1985.

Sager, Allan H. *Gospel-Centered Spirituality*. Minneapolis: Augsburg, 1990.

Sanders, J. Oswald. *Spiritual Leadership*. Chicago: Moody, 1967.

Schaeffer, Francis A. *The God Who Is There*. Chicago: InterVarsity, 1968.

_____. *He Is There and He Is not Silent*. Wheaton: Tyndale, 1972.

_____. *True Spirituality*. Wheaton: Tyndale, 1971.

Scougal, Henry. *The Life of God in the Soul of Man*. Reading, Berkshire, England: Cox and Wyman, 1996.

Sine, Tom. *Wild Hope: Crises Facing the Human Community on the Threshold of the 21st Century*. Dallas: Word, 1991.

St. John of the Cross. *Dark Night of the Soul*. New York: Image, 1959.

Stanley, Paul D. and J. Robert Clinton. *Connecting: The Mentoring Relationships You Need to Succeed in Life*. Colorado Springs: NavPress, 1992.

Stedman, Ray C. *Body Life*. Glendale, Calif.: Regal, 1972.

Stott, John R. W. *Christian Counter-Culture: The Message of the Sermon on the Mount*. Downers Grove, Ill.: InterVarsity, 1978.

Sunshine, Linda, ed. *The Illustrated Woody Allen Reader*. New York: Knopf, 1993.

Swenson, Richard A. *Margin: Restoring Emotional, Physical, Financial, and Time Resources to Overloaded Lives*. Colorado Springs: NavPress, 1992.

_____. *More Than Meets the Eye: Fascinating Glimpses of God's Power and Design*. Colorado Springs: NavPress, 2000.

Tan, Siang-Yang and Douglas H. Gregg. *Disciplines of the Holy Spirit: How to Connect to the Spirit's Power and Presence*. Grand Rapids: Zondervan, 1997.

Teresa of Avila. *Interior Castle*. Translated by E. Allison Peers. New York: Image, 1989.

Thomas, Gary. *Sacred Pathways*. Grand Rapids: Zondervan, 2000.

Thomas, W. Ian. *The Saving Life of Christ*. Grand Rapids: Zondervan, 1961.

Thomas à Kempis. *The Imitation of Christ*. Translated by William C. Creasy. Notre Dame, Ind.: Ave Maria Press, 1989.

Thornton, Martin. *Christian Proficiency*. Cambridge, Mass.: Cowley Publications, 1959.

Tozer, A. W. *Man the Dwelling Place of God*. Harrisburg, Pa.: Christian Publications, 1966.

_____. *The Knowledge of the Holy*. New York: Harper and Row, 1961.

_____. *Paths to Power*. Camp Hill, Pa.: Christian Publications, n.d.

_____. *The Pursuit of God*. Harrisburg, Pa.: Christian Publications, 1948.

_____. *The Root of the Righteous*. Camp Hill, Pa.: Christian Publications, 1955.

Trumbull, Charles G. *Victory in Christ*. Fort Washington, Pa.: Christian Literature Crusade, 1959.

Underhill, Evelyn. *Mysticism*. New York: Image, 1990.

Waddell, Helen. *The Desert Fathers*. Ann Arbor: Ann Arbor Paperbacks, 1957.

Wagner, C. Peter. *Your Spiritual Gifts Can Help Your Church Grow*. Ventura, Calif.: Regal, 1979.

Ware, Kallistos. *The Orthodox Way*. Crestwood, N.J.: St. Vladimir's Seminary Press, 1986.

White, John. *The Fight*. Downers Grove, Ill.: InterVarsity, 1976.

Wilkins, Michael J. *In His Image: Reflecting Christianity in Everyday Life*. Colorado Springs: NavPress, 1997.

Willard, Dallas. *The Divine Conspiracy*. San Francisco: HarperSanFrancisco, 1998.

_____. *Renovation of the Heart*. Colorado Springs: NavPress, 2002.

_____. *The Spirit of the Disciplines*. San Francisco: Harper and Row, 1988.

Williams, Rowan. *Christian Spirituality*. Atlanta: John Knox, 1979.

Zizioulas, John D. *Being as Communion*. Crestwood, N.J.: St. Vladimir's Seminary Press, 1993.

SUBJECT INDEX

SCRIPTURE INDEX

Kenneth Boa is engaged in a ministry of relational evangelism and discipleship, teaching, writing, and speaking. He holds a B.S. from Case Institute of Technology, a Th.M. from Dallas Theological Seminary, a Ph.D. from New York University, and a D.Phil. from the University of Oxford in England.

Dr. Boa is the president of Reflections Ministries, an organization that seeks to provide safe places for people to consider the claims of Christ and to help them mature and bear fruit in their relationship with him. He is also president of Trinity House Publishers, a publishing company that is dedicated to the creation of tools that will help people manifest eternal values in a temporal arena by drawing them to intimacy with God and a better understanding of the culture in which they live.

Recent publications by Dr. Boa include *Faith Has Its Reasons; An Unchanging Faith in a Changing World; Face to Face; Pursuing Wisdom; The Art of Living Well; Wisdom at Work; Living What You Believe;* and *Sacred Readings.* He is a contributing editor to *The Open Bible,* the *Promise Keeper's Men's Study Bible,* and *The Leadership Bible,* is the consulting editor of the *Zondervan NASB Study Bible,* and is the editor-in-chief of *The Life Promises Bible.* He also writes a free monthly teaching letter called *Reflections.* If you would like to be on the mailing list, call 800-DRAW-NEAR (800-372-9632).